T0361958

Strategic Renewal

Strategic Renewal is an original research anthology offering insight into a subject area which, although critical for the sustained success of organizations, has received relatively little attention as distinct from the more general phenomenon of strategic change.

Firstly, by providing a summary of the literature, this research anthology helps graduate students and new researchers grasp the current state of affairs in the field. Secondly, this research anthology will help update the knowledge base of the existing researchers in the field. By bringing together various studies, the research anthology determines the core concepts of the field and elucidates the key gaps and future research areas. Through contributions building on the knowledge bases of other disciplines, this research anthology develops an interdisciplinary research agenda, giving the reader an in-depth understanding of the mediating, moderating, and antecedent variables concerning strategic renewal.

Strategic Renewal aims to provide a state-of-understanding to the subject, as well as a clear picture of the cross-disciplinary landscape that informs the subject. Thus, this research anthology is essential reading for managers, consultants, and other practitioners, as well as students and scholars of business.

Aybars Tuncdogan is a lecturer (Assistant Professor) in Marketing at King's Business School, King's College London. He is a Fellow of the Higher Education Academy, a committee member of the British Academy of Management's marketing group and an editorial review board member of *Industrial Marketing Management.*

Dr Adam Lindgreen is Professor of Marketing at Copenhagen Business School where he heads the Department of Marketing. He also is Extra Ordinary Professor with University of Pretoria's Gordon Institute of Business Science. Dr Lindgreen received his PhD from Cranfield University. He has published in the *California Management Review, Journal of Business Ethics, Journal of Product and Innovation Management, Journal of the Academy of Marketing Science, and Journal of World Business,* among others.

Henk Volberda is Professor of Strategic Management & Business Policy and Director of Knowledge Transfer at Rotterdam School of Management, Erasmus University. Moreover, he is Scientific Director of the Erasmus Centre for Business Innovation.

Frans van den Bosch is Emeritus Professor of management interfaces between organizations and environment at the Department of Strategic Management & Entrepreneurship, Rotterdam School of Management, Erasmus University.

Routledge Studies in Innovation, Organizations and Technology

Social Inclusion and Usability of ICT-Enabled Services
Edited by Jyoti Choudrie, Panayiota Tsatsou and Sherah Kurnia

Strategic Marketing for High Technology Products
An Integrated Approach
Thomas Fotiadis

Responsible Research and Innovation
From Concepts to Practices
Edited by Robert Gianni, John Pearson and Bernard Reber

Technology Offsets in International Defence Procurement
Kogila Balakrishnan

Social Entrepreneurship and Social Innovation
Ecosystems for Inclusion in Europe
*Edited by Mario Biggeri, Enrico Testi, Marco Bellucci, Roel During, and
H. Thomas R. Persson*

Innovation in Brazil
Advancing Development in the 21st Century
Edited by Elisabeth Reynolds, Ben Ross Schneider and Ezequiel Zylberberg

Strategic Renewal
Core Concepts, Antecedents, and Micro Foundations
*Edited by Aybars Tuncdogan, Adam Lindgreen, Henk Volberda, and
Frans van den Bosch*

For more information about the series, please visit www.routledge.com/
Routledge-Studies-in-Innovation-Organizations-and-Technology/book-
series/RIOT

Strategic Renewal

Core Concepts, Antecedents, and Micro Foundations

Edited by Aybars Tuncdogan, Adam Lindgreen, Henk Volberda, and Frans van den Bosch

Routledge
Taylor & Francis Group

LONDON AND NEW YORK

First published 2019 by Routledge

2 Park Square, Milton Park, Abingdon, Oxfordshire OX14 4RN
52 Vanderbilt Avenue, New York, NY 10017

Routledge is an imprint of the Taylor & Francis Group, an informa business

First issued in paperback 2020

British Library Cataloguing-in-Publication Data
A catalogue record for this book is available from the British Library

Library of Congress Cataloging-in-Publication Data
A catalog record has been requested for this book

ISBN: 978-1-4724-8647-9 (hbk)
ISBN: 978-0-367-67137-2 (pbk)

Typeset in Bembo
by Integra Software Services Pvt. Ltd.

For Yonca and Meryem—Aybars
For Rob, a colleague and a friend—Adam
For Anna—Henk
For Trudy—Frans

Contents

Figures

Tables

About the editors

Aybars Tuncdogan

Dr Aybars Tuncdogan is a lecturer (Assistant Professor) in marketing at King's Business School, King's College London. Currently, he lectures on "Digital Marketing" and "Research in Marketing" at the marketing department, and on "Digital Political Marketing" at the war studies department. In the past, he also taught modules such as Advertising and Integrated Marketing Communications, Marketing Decision-Making, MSc Research Clinic, Strategic Business Planning, and Organizational Dynamics at different institutions.

Prior to joining King's College London, he worked as a lecturer in Marketing & Strategy at Cardiff University. He completed his PhD at the Rotterdam School of Management, Erasmus University with his thesis entitled "Decision Making and Behavioral Strategy: The Role of Regulatory Focus in Corporate Innovation Processes". Previously, he finished his MPhil in Business Research (with distinction) also at Erasmus University, and his Bachelor's degree (with college honours) at Earlham College, with a double major in Computer Science and Business Management.

His research employs psychological constructs for the purpose of understanding how we can explain, predict, and shape managers', consumers' and collectives' (e.g., teams, organizations, consumer tribes) strategic decisions. In line with this goal, he has concentrated on traits and trait-like chronic individual differences governing behaviour and their interactions with environmental elements. Likewise, he is interested in the applications of artificial intelligence in marketing decision-making. His papers on individual differences and regulatory focus have been published in *Leadership Quarterly*, his research on management teams' regulatory focus and exploratory innovation has appeared in *Long Range Planning*, and his research on psychological antecedents of food neophilia has appeared in *Personality and Individual Differences*. Dr Tuncdogan is also a member of several professional bodies and serves as a reviewer for numerous academic journals, including *Industrial Marketing Management, Journal of Management Studies, Leadership Quarterly, Organization Studies, Journal of Product Innovation Management* and *IEEE Transactions on Engineering Management* among others. In addition, he is a Fellow of the Higher Education Academy, a committee member of the British Academy of Management's marketing group and an editorial review board member of *Industrial Marketing Management.*

Adam Lindgreen

After studies in chemistry (Copenhagen University), engineering (the Engineering Academy of Denmark), and physics (Copenhagen University), Adam Lindgreen completed an MSc in food science and technology at the Technical University of Denmark. He also finished an MBA at the University of Leicester. Professor Lindgreen received his PhD in marketing from Cranfield University. His first appointments were with the Catholique University of Louvain (2000–2001) and Eindhoven University of Technology (2002–2007). Subsequently, he served as Professor of Marketing at Hull University's Business School (2007–2010); University of Birmingham's Business School (2010), where he also was the research director in the Department of Marketing; and University of Cardiff's Business School (2011–2016). Under his leadership, the Department of Marketing and Strategy at Cardiff Business School ranked first among all marketing departments in Australia, Canada, New Zealand, the United Kingdom, and the United States, based upon the hg indices of senior faculty. Since 2016, he has been Professor of Marketing at Copenhagen Business School, where he also heads the Department of Marketing. Since 2018, he also is Extraordinary professor with University of Pretoria's Gordon Institute of Business Science.

Professor Lindgreen has been a visiting professor with various institutions, including Georgia State University, Groupe HEC in France, and Melbourne University. His publications have appeared in *Business Horizons, California Management Review, Entrepreneurship and Regional Development, Industrial Marketing Management, International Journal of Management Reviews, Journal of Advertising, Journal of Business Ethics, European Journal of Marketing, Journal of Business and Industrial Marketing, Journal of Marketing Management, Journal of the Academy of Marketing Science, Journal of Product Innovation Management, Journal of World Business, Psychology & Marketing,* and *Supply Chain Management: An International Journal,* among others.

Professor Lindgreen's books include *A Stakeholder Approach to Corporate Social Responsibility* (with Kotler, Vanhamme, and Maon), *Managing Market Relationships, Memorable Customer Experiences* (with Vanhamme and Beverland), and *Sustainable Value Chain Management* (with Maon, Vanhamme, and Sen).

The recipient of the "Outstanding Article 2005" award from *Industrial Marketing Management* and the runner-up for the same award in 2016, Professor Lindgreen serves on the board of several scientific journals; he is co-editor-in-chief of *Industrial Marketing Management* and previously was the joint editor of the *Journal of Business Ethics'* section on corporate responsibility. His research interests include business and industrial marketing management, corporate social responsibility, and sustainability. Professor Lindgreen has been awarded the Dean's Award for Excellence in Executive Teaching. Furthermore, he has served as an examiner (for dissertations, modules, and programs) at a wide variety of institutions, including the Australian National University, Unitec, University of Amsterdam, University of Bath's Management School, University of Lethbridge, and University of Mauritius.

Professor Lindgreen is a member of the International Scientific Advisory Panel of the New Zealand Food Safety Science and Research Centre (a partnership between government, industry organizations, and research institutions), as well as of the Chartered Association of Business Schools' Academic Journal Guide (AJG) Scientific Committee in the field of marketing.

Beyond these academic contributions to marketing, Professor Lindgreen has discovered and excavated settlements from the Stone Age in Denmark, including the only major kitchen midden—Sparregård—in the south-east of Denmark; because of its importance, the kitchen midden was later excavated by the National Museum and then protected as a historical monument for future generations. He is also an avid genealogist, having traced his family back to 1390 and published widely in scientific journals (*Personalhistorisk Tidsskrift*, *The Genealogist*, and *Slægt & Data*) related to methodological issues in genealogy, accounts of population development, and particular family lineages.

Henk Volberda

Henk Volberda is Professor of Strategic Management & Business Policy and also Director of Knowledge Transfer at Rotterdam School of Management, Erasmus University. Moreover, he is Scientific Director of the Erasmus Centre for Business Innovation. He has been a visiting scholar at the Wharton School at the University of Pennsylvania and Cass Business School, London and obtained his PhD *cum laude* in Business Administration at the University of Groningen.

His work on strategic flexibility, coevolution, and new organizational forms has led to an extensive number of published articles in academic journals including the *Academy of Management Journal*, *Business History*, *Corporate Governance*, *Decision Support Systems*, *European Management Journal*, *European Management Review*, *Global Strategy Journal*, *Group & Organization Management*, *International Business Review*, *International Journal of Management Research*, *Journal of Business Ethics*, *Journal of Business Research*, *Journal of Business Venturing*, *Journal of Management*, *Journal of Management Studies*, *Journal of International Business*, *Journal of Product Innovation Management*, *Leadership Quarterly*, *Long Range Planning*, *Management and Organization Review*, *Management Science*, *Organization Studies*, *Organization Science*, *R&D Management*, *Strategic Entrepreneurship Journal*, *Sloan Management Review*, *Strategic Management Journal*, and *Technology Analysis & Strategic Management*.

His book *Building the Flexible Firm: How to Remain Competitive* (1998) published by Oxford University Press received wide acclaim and has been translated into many languages. His book *Rethinking Strategy* (Sage, 2001) was awarded with the ERIM Best Book Award. His international textbook *Strategic Management: Competitiveness and Globalization* (Cengage, 2011) is used at many European Business Schools. Professor Volberda has received multiple awards for his research on organizational flexibility and strategic change. Recently his new book *Re-inventing Business Models: How firms cope with disruption* (Oxford University Press, 2018) appeared. He is the recipient of the NCD Award, the ERASM Research Award, the Erasmus University Research Award, the Igor Ansoff Strategic Management Award, Cap Gemini Ernst & Young Strategy Award, the ERIM Impact Award, the ERIM Article Award, the SAP Strategy Award, the European Management Review Best Paper Award, and the European Academy of Management Best paper Award. He is a member of the editorial boards of *Long Range Planning, Journal of Management Studies, Journal of Strategy and Management, Management and Organization Review, Organization Science*, and *Organization Studies*. In 2014, 2015, 2016, 2017 as well as 2018 he is listed in the "*The World's Most Influential Scientific Minds*" and identified as a *Highly Cited Researcher* by Clarivate Analytics. He is also a member of the Chartered Association of Business School's Academic Journal Guide (AJG) Scientific Committee in the field of strategy.

Henk Volberda is also active in executive education and consulting and has worked with many large European corporations, including ABN Amro, Air France KLM, BP, Cap Gemini, Coface, DSM, Ericsson, ING, KPN, NXP, Port Authority Rotterdam, Rabobank, Randstad, Schlumberger, Vopak, and Shell. He is member of the Supervisory Board of NXP Netherlands and advises several European governmental agencies on innovation policy and economic performance.

Frans van den Bosch

Frans A.J. Van Den Bosch is Emeritus Professor of Management Interfaces Between Organizations And Environment at the Department of Strategic Management & Entrepreneurship, Rotterdam School of Management, Erasmus University (RSM).

Professor van den Bosch's major research interests lie in the development of integrative strategy frameworks incorporating both the externally and internally focused view of strategy; the application of these frameworks to general management issues such as management models, non-technological sources of innovations like management innovation; strategic renewal processes, organizational ambidexterity and corporate governance.

He has been appointed as an honorary ERIM fellow and until April 2012 was among others chairman of the Programme Board of the Erasmus Research Institute of Management (ERIM); coordinator of the ERIM Research Programme in Strategy; director of the Erasmus Strategic Renewal Centre (ESRC); and director of the Dutch Partner Institute of the World Economic Forum (WEF).

Since May 2012, he has had a part-time appointment focusing mainly on research, PhD supervision and MSc thesis supervision. On the occasion of his Valedictory Lecture (May 2012) associated with his departure as full-time professor he received a Royal Order ("Officier in de Orde van Oranje-Nassau").

He has published several books and over 175 articles in scientific journals including chapters in books on strategy, international business, general management, economics, and industry studies.

His scientific papers have appeared in, among others, the *Academy of Management Journal, Business and Society, Corporate Governance,* the *Economist,* the *European Management Journal, International Studies of Management and Organization,* the *Journal of Management Studies, Long Range Planning, Management Science, Organization Science, Organization Studies* and *Strategic Management Journal.*

Professor van den Bosch is actively involved in the business community and public sector. His former roles include that of vice-chairman of the Rotterdam Chamber of Commerce, member of the Rotterdam City Council, chairman of the Rotterdam Enterprise Prize Committee, advisor of a Dutch trade union association and chairman of the Board of Non-executive Directors of Dutch companies. At present he is on the Board of Non-executive Directors of a large Dutch Foundation providing care for elderly people.

He is a fellow of the Netherlands Institute for Advanced Study in the Humanities and Social Sciences (NIAS) and a board member of several scientific journals including *Long Range Planning* and *Organization Studies.*

He has supervised 34 PhD theses, has been member of more than 30 PhD committees, and acted as an external examiner at, among others, Antwerp University, City University London, Warwick University, and the Indian Institute of Science.

Earlier in his career, Professor van den Bosch was an Assistant Professor and an Associate Professor of Economics at the Faculty of Economics, Erasmus University Rotterdam. He later joined the Delft Graduate School of Management as an Associate Professor of Economics. He was appointed Professor of Management at RSM in 1988.

He holds a BA in mechanical engineering with distinction from the Polytechnic of Rotterdam and a MSc in economics degree *cum laude* from Erasmus University Rotterdam. He has a PhD in law from Leiden University, the Netherlands.

About the contributors

Petra Andries is Assistant Professor of Entrepreneurship and Strategy at Ghent University (Belgium). She conducts research in the field of entrepreneurship and innovation management. Petra has published in international journals on topics including entrepreneurial opportunities, knowledge management, collaboration, and IP appropriability, and has provided companies and policy makers with advice in these domains.

Bas Bosboom obtained his Master of Science in Strategy from the Rotterdam School of Management, Erasmus University. He has worked as a strategy consultant for various companies and, in 2016, joined Incentro. There, Bas specializes in online (neuro) marketing and holocracy. He is the founding CEO of Final 500 Records, a music record label.

Anna Bos-Nehles is Assistant Professor in the field of Human Resource Management at the University of Twente (The Netherlands). Her main research interest lies in the role of line managers towards HRM implementation effectiveness and their effect on innovative employee behaviour. Her research has been published in peer-reviewed international outlets such as *Human Resource Management, International Journal of HRM, Personnel Review*, and *European Journal of International Management*.

Matej Černe, PhD is Assistant Professor in the Department of Management and Organization at the University of Ljubljana, Faculty of Economics, Slovenia. He's also Head of the Open Innovation Systems Laboratory and Head of the Centre for Innovation Research CERINNO within the Centre of Excellence for Biosensors, Instrumentation, and Process control (CO BIK). His research interests include non-technological innovations, creativity, organizational behavior and psychology, leadership, and multi-level issues in management. His research has been published in top management journals (e.g., *Academy of Management Journal, Human Resource Management*), and he also serves as an editorial board member for *The Leadership Quarterly* and *Economic and Business Review*, and as Editor-in-Chief of the *Dynamic Relationships Management Journal*.

Sophie De Winne is Professor of Human Resource Management at the Faculty of Economics and Business, KU Leuven (Belgium). She focuses in her research on the relationship between HRM and performance (both individual and organizational), the trend towards individualization of the employment relationship, the role of line managers in HRM, and the relationship between employee turnover and firm performance. She has been published in international journals such as *Journal of Management Studies, Human Resource Management Journal, Small Business Economics, Journal of Business Ethics, MIT Sloan Management Review* and the *International Journal of Human Resource Management.*

Yanqing Duan is the Director of Business and Information Systems Research Centre (BISC), in the Business School of the University of Bedfordshire. Professor Duan received her BSc and MSc from China Agricultural University and PhD from Aston University, UK. Her principal research interest is the use and impact of emerging Information and Communication Technologies (ICT) in organizations. Her recent research has focused on how, why, and to what extent big data and analytics is impacting on decision making, innovation, and organizational performance. She has received many research grants from various funding sources, such as: European Commission, UK Department For International Development (DFID), JISC, British Council, etc. She has published over 180 peer-reviewed articles, including papers in *European Journal of Information Systems*, IEEE transaction on Engineering Management, *Information & Management, European Journal of Marketing, Journal of Business Research, The Information Society, Production Planning and Control, Expert Systems with Applications*, and *Information Technology & People.*

Abdelghani Es-Sajjade is Assistant Professor in Management at the College of Business Administration, University of Dammam. He completed an MSc in Strategic Management at the Erasmus University Rotterdam School of Management. His doctoral work (PhD) in management was completed at the University of Leeds. Abdelghani is interested in organizational capabilities, innovation, and entrepreneurship. He was part of the MANETEI (EU FP7) project in which he worked with companies as Sabic, HP, Royal DSM, and Philips to examine the management of emerging technologies. Prior to moving into academia he worked in the fields of business intelligence, corporate ventures, and start-ups for Deutsche Telekom and Vodafone.

Qile He is currently the Associate Head of School for Research of the School of Strategy and Leadership at Coventry University. He is now a member of the Faculty Research Committee and is also an Associate at the Centre for Business in Society. His research interests fall in the area of knowledge transfer in the context of interfirm alliances. He is also interested in sustainable supply chain management, supply chain optimization in agriculture, as well as innovation strategies and processes of organizations.

He has published over 50 papers in refereed journals, books, and leading international conference proceedings. These include prestigious international journals, such as *International Journal of Production Economics, International Journal of Production Research,* and *Supply Chain Management: An International Journal.* He is a Senior Fellow of the Higher Education Academy and a Chartered Member of the Chartered Institute of Logistics and Transport. He is currently the co-chair for the Inter-organizational Collaboration SIG, British Academy of Management.

Tomislav Hernaus, PhD is Assistant Professor of Organizational and Work Design at the Faculty of Economics and Business, University of Zagreb and a Visiting Professor at the Faculty of Economics, University of Ljubljana. He holds a Certificate in Organization Design received from the Center for Effective Organizations, Los Angeles. He is the author or co-author of three books, a dozen book chapters, and a significant number of scientific papers published in refereed journals such as the *Human Resource Management Journal, Journal of Organizational Change Management, Expert Systems with Applications*, and *Business Process Management Journal*. His multi-level research interests include organization design, business process management, HR organization, work design and job interventions, innovative work behavior, and knowledge hiding.

Mariano L.M. "Pitosh" Heyden is Associate Professor of Strategy & International Business at the Monash Business School (Melbourne, Australia). He obtained his PhD from the Rotterdam School of Management, Erasmus University (Rotterdam, The Netherlands) in 2012. Dr. Heyden's research interests are at the intersection of strategic leadership (focusing on decision-makers across the hierarchy), corporate governance (focusing on external governance, boards of directors, and corporate social responsibility), and organizational adaptation (focusing on renewal/change, innovation, and corporate entrepreneurship). His peer-reviewed work appears in international outlets such as *Journal of Management, Organization Studies, Journal of Management Studies, Human Resource Management, Long Range Planning, Global Strategy Journal*, and *Journal of Business Ethics*, as well as several book chapters in edited volumes published by Palgrave Macmillan and Springer. His research-informed perspectives on topical issues can be found in media outlets such as ABC News, Business Insider, The Conversation, and the World Economic Forum's Agenda. He receives funding from the Australian Research Council under the prestigious Discovery Early Career Research Award scheme.

Quy Nguyen Huy is Professor of Strategic Management at INSEAD and Solvay Chaired Professor of Technological Innovation. His research focuses on the social and emotional dimensions of strategic processes including strategic change, innovation, and entrepreneurship. His research has won multiple awards from the Academy of Management and was published in prestigious academic and practitioner journals including the *Administrative Science Quarterly*, the *Academy of Management Review*, the *Academy of Management Journal*, *Academy of Management Annals*, *Journal of Business Ethics*, *Organization Science*, *Strategic Management Journal*, *Strategic Organization*, *Harvard Business Review*, and *MIT Sloan Management Review*.

Dinesh N. Iyer is Assistant Professor of Management at Rutgers University, School of Business-Camden. He received his PhD from Purdue University. His research focuses on behavioral theory and its applications to corporate strategy, firm performance, and organizational learning. His articles have appeared in journals such as the *Academy of Management Journal*, *Journal of Business Research*, and *American Journal of Business*.

Päivi Karhu DSc. (Econ. & Bus. Adm.), is a researcher at Lappeenranta University of Technology (LUT), School of Business and Management. Her research interests lie in organizational ambidexterity, organizational dualities, and managerial cognitive processes. Before joining academia, she worked in the fields of IT sourcing and banking.

Saeed Khanagha is Assistant Professor of Strategy at Radboud University Nijmegen and is visiting research fellow at Rotterdam School of Management and Leeds University Business School. Beside academic engagements, he has been working for several years for Ericsson and, as part of this role, he currently leads a EU-funded Horizon 2020 project entitled Complex and Open Innovation for Networked Society (COINS). His research focuses on the foundations of dynamic capabilities for the adoption of emerging technologies, including organizational forms, management innovation, and affective and cognitive influences on firms' ability to adapt. His research has been published in a number of leading journals such as *Journal of Management Studies* and *Long Range Planning*.

Jan Kietzmann, a Professor of MIS and Innovation and Entrepreneurship at Simon Fraser University in Vancouver, British Columbia, Canada, focuses his research on organizational and social perspectives related to emerging technologies. His current studies include such phenomena as social media, crowdsourcing, user generated content, and sharing economies.

Emile Lancée is Assistant Professor in Digital Marketing Strategy at VU University Amsterdam since 2004. He has written many books in the field of digital marketing, of which *Digital Marketing Strategy* (ISBN 9789082126051) is the most impactful. He is an often-invited keynote speaker for digital marketing topics.

Daniella Laureiro-Martinez works at the Department of Management Technology and Economics at ETH Zurich. She received her PhD from Bocconi University. She studies the cognitive and neuropsychological antecedents of strategy and innovation. Her research combines neurosciences and psychology to understand creativity, decision-making, organizational learning, and problem solving in managers, entrepreneurs, and innovative leaders. Daniella teaches managerial cognition, innovation and creativity, and methods courses at the Masters, Executive and PhD levels. Her publications have appeared in *the Strategic Management Journal, Organization Science, Journal of Business Venturing Insights*, the *Journal of Neuroscience, Psychology and Economics* and in the open-source nature journals *Frontiers in Human Neuroscience* and *Frontiers in Psychology*. She is part of the Editorial Board of the *Strategic Management Journal*. Daniella has been an active contributor to SMS and AoM, most notably through her organization of different workshops and her roles as representative-at-large for the Behavioral Strategy Interest Group of SMS, and for the Managerial and Organizational Cognition and the Technology and Innovation Management Divisions of AoM.

Ian P. McCarthy is a Professor in Technology and Operations Management in the Beedie School of Business at Simon Fraser University. He received his PhD in industrial engineering from the University of Sheffield. His research deals with innovation management, operations management, and industry dynamics.

Olimpia Meglio earned her PhD in Business Administration from the University of Naples Federico II. She is currently Associate Professor of Management at University of Sannio. Her research interests revolve around mergers and acquisitions (and attendant issues of ambidexterity, integration capability, or acquisition performance), process research methods, intergenerational transition in family businesses, and venture capital capabilities. She has authored several book chapters with international publishers and edited a companion about Mergers and Acquisitions for Routledge. Her research has appeared in *Human Resource Management, Scandinavian Journal of Management*, and *Long Range Planning*.

Tom Mom is a Professor of Strategic Growth and Implementation in the department of Strategic Management & Entrepreneurship of RSM Erasmus University Rotterdam. He is also the Academic Director of RSM's Executive MBA, Director of the Erasmus Executive Programme in Strategic Management, and a high-performing member of the Erasmus Research Institute of Management (ERIM). His research interests include fast growing organizations, new business development and corporate growth, ambidexterity, strategic renewal, and strategy execution. His research output appeared in journals such as the *Journal of Management, Journal of Management Studies, Organization Science, Organization Studies, MIT Sloan Management Review, California Management Review, Human Resource Management*, and *Long Range Planning*.

Julia Nieves, PhD in Business Administration, is an Assistant Professor at the University of Las Palmas de Gran Canaria. She has combined her teaching work with her professional activity in the financial and audit sectors. Her research focuses on knowledge strategic management and innovation in services, with particular emphasis on hospitality industry. She has published in journals such as *Tourism Management, International Journal of Hospitality Management,* and *International Journal of Contemporary Hospitality Management.*

Javier Osorio, PhD in Business Administration, is an Associate Professor at the University of Las Palmas de Gran Canaria. He has worked as organizational advisor for private and governmental bodies. His research has focused on information systems management, strategic planning, and innovation in organizations. He has published in journals such *as International Journal of Hospitality Management* and *Knowledge Management Research and Practice.*

Kathleen Marshall Park received her PhD from the MIT Sloan School of Management. She is an Assistant Professor of Administrative Sciences, Strategy and Innovation at Boston University and a Research Fellow in the Leadership Center at the MIT Sloan School of Management. Her research interests include international mergers and acquisitions, innovation, emerging markets, corporate governance, leadership, and executive careers. Her research has been published in journals including the *Journal of Management History, Competition and Change: The Journal of Global Business and Political Economy, Thunderbird International Business Review,* and the *Routledge Companion for Mergers and Acquisitions,* as well as numerous additional chapters with internationally recognized publishers. Her work has been recognized with awards from the Academy of Management, the European Academy of Management, and the Global Business and Technology Association. In her faculty and research affiliations with Boston University in the US, the Gulf University for Science and Technology in Kuwait, as well as with the Massachusetts Institute of Technology, she has formed international research partnerships for studying leadership, innovation, and internationalization in the emerging markets of the Arabian Gulf.

Leyland F. Pitt, MCom, MBA, PhD, PhD, is Professor of Marketing and the Dennis F. Culver EMBA Alumni Chair of Business, Beedie School of Business, Simon Fraser University, Vancouver, Canada, and affiliate Professor of Marketing at the Royal Institute of Technology (KTH), Stockholm, Sweden. The focus of his research is on the interface between marketing and technology, with particular emphasis on technology's role in shaping and creating customers.

Kirk Plangger is an Assistant Professor of Marketing at the King's Business School at King's College London. His research focuses on consumer-led digital marketing strategy and is principally interested in how digital technologies mediate and change the buying process and how organizations should address these technologies.

Paavo Ritala DSc. (Econ. & Bus. Adm.), is a Professor of Strategy and Innovation at the School of Business and Management at Lappeenranta University of Technology (LUT). His main research themes include collaborative innovation, organizational renewal, knowledge sharing and protection, coopetition, platforms, and ecosystems, as well as sustainable value creation. His research has been published in journals such as *Journal of Product Innovation Management, Industrial and Corporate Change, Industrial Marketing Management, British Journal of Management,* and *Technovation.* He is also closely involved with business practice through company-funded research projects, executive and professional education programs, and in speaker and advisory roles. Professor Ritala currently serves as an Associate Editor of *R&D Management.*

Karen Robson's research investigates consumer innovation, including how and why consumers repurpose or use proprietary offerings in ways not intended by the manufacturer and the intellectual property law implications of this practice. She conducts research on "gamification", or the application of game design principles in non-gaming contexts.

Derek Ruth received his doctorate in Strategic Management from Purdue University in 2006. His research focuses on innovation, entrepreneurship, and the boundaries of the firm. Derek has presented his research at national and international conferences in the United States and abroad. His articles have appeared in a variety of journals including the *Journal of Business Research, Journal of Leadership, Organizational Studies,* and the *Journal of Purchasing and Supply Management.*

Christine Scheef is postdoctoral researcher at the University of St. Gallen (Switzerland). She is also the General Manager of the St. Gallen Institute of Management in Asia located in Singapore. She holds a PhD in strategic management from the University of St. Gallen. Her research focus is on behavioural strategy, upper echelons, executive characteristics and experiences, successions, and functional roles in the top management team. She has published in the *Strategic Management Journal* and teaches undergraduate and graduate courses on strategic management and corporate strategy at the University of St. Gallen and Singapore Management University.

Barton M. Sharp, the Mike and Kristina McGrath Professor of Entrepreneurship at Northern Illinois University, earned his PhD in Strategic Management from the Krannert School of Management at Purdue University in 2009. Bart comes to academics by way of a background in aerospace engineering, which has informed his research interests in innovation, organizational learning, and entrepreneurship. His work has appeared in the *Journal of Management,* Academy of Management Learning and Education, *Organizational Research Methods,* and *Strategic Organization,* among others. He has been recognized with a Great Professor Award from the University Honors Program at NIU and has also received an

Undergraduate Outstanding Teaching Award from the Management Department Student Advisory Board.

Jatinder S. Sidhu is Associate Professor of Strategic Management at the Rotterdam School of Management, Erasmus University, where he teaches flagship courses on strategic management and organizational identity. He obtained his PhD degree at the Tinbergen Institute, Erasmus School of Economics, Rotterdam, Netherlands. His current research focuses on issues related to identity, gender, and diversity in organizations, the upper echelons of management, organizational learning, and innovation. His work has appeared in several journals including *European Management Review, International Business Review,* Journal *of Management,* Journal *of Management Studies,* Journal *of Product Innovation Management,* and *Organization Science.*

David Teece is the Tusher Professor in Global Business and the Director of the Tusher Center on Intellectual Capital at the Haas School of Business at the University of California, Berkeley. He has published six books and over 200 articles in which he has analyzed the role of innovation and intellectual property in the competitive performance of the enterprise. He is also Founder and Chairman of Berkeley Research Group, LLC ("BRG"), for which he also consults.

C. Annique Un (PhD, MIT Sloan School of Management, M.B.A., B.B.A., University of Notre Dame Mendoza College of Business) is Associate Professor of International Business and Strategy at the D'Amore-McKim School of Business, Northeastern University. She previously served on the faculty at the University of South Carolina and Cornell University. An expert on innovation in international business, she analyzes the advantage of foreignness in innovation, the use of R&D collaboration to innovate, and differences in R&D investments by foreign and domestic firms. Her research has appeared in leading academic journals such as *Strategic Management Journal, Journal of International Business Studies, Research Policy,* and *Journal of Product Innovation Management* and has received awards from INFORMS and the Academy of International Business.

Patrick A.M. Vermeulen is a full Professor of Strategy and International Management at the Institute for Management Research of Radboud University in the Netherlands. He also received his PhD from Radboud University. His research interests include institutional change and institutional complexity, innovation in developing countries, and organization design. In his work he uses varied methodologies, but with an emphasis on qualitative research. Patrick's research has been published in, among others, the *Academy of Management Journal, Organization Studies, Strategic Organization, Research Policy, Long Range Planning,* and the *International Journal of Research in Marketing.*

Qiang Wu is currently a lecturer in Logistics and Transport in Aston University. His research interests include sustainable supply chain management, and innovation strategies and capabilities for corporate sustainability. His published papers have appeared in *Strategic Change, EuroMed Journal of Business* and *Society and Business Review.*

Preface and acknowledgment

The last two decades of business history have been marked by continuously elevating levels of environmental dynamism and complexity. Likewise, disruptive periods of plummeting munificence such as the recent series of economic crises have been further complicating this situation. To help businesses, corporations, and industries meet external demands and to increase humanity's prosperity, academics have been striving for a better comprehension of successful strategic renewal.

Indeed, the importance of strategic renewal is regularly emphasized in the strategic management literature, and there is a rapidly growing body of knowledge. However, research in the area is fragmented due to there being little communication across different literature streams. Our research anthology will summarize current knowledge regarding the concept of strategic renewal and its surrounding concepts. In doing so, we aim to contribute to the field in three ways. First, by summarizing the field, especially by means of literature reviews and conceptual papers, we hope to increase dialog across different streams of the strategic renewal literature and to decrease the fragmentation in the field. Second, by bringing together various studies, we intend to determine the core concepts of the field and elucidate the key gaps and future research areas. Finally, through contributions building on the knowledge bases of other disciplines (e.g., psychology, marketing, human resources, finance, leadership, etc.) we aim to develop an interdisciplinary research agenda. Doing so is necessary, especially for an in-depth understanding of the mediating, moderating, and antecedent variables concerning strategic renewal.

The practical contributions of this research anthology are also threefold. First, providing a summary of the literature will help graduate students and new researchers grasp the current state of affairs in the field. Indeed, both learning and teaching become substantially easier when the boundaries of a concept are relatively clear and when the most relevant information is summarized in one source. Second, this anthology will help update the knowledge base of existing researchers in the field. Finally, for managers, consultants, and other practitioners, reading select parts of a book on strategic renewal is more feasible than trying to search through various papers to find practically useful fragments of different streams of the academic strategic renewal literature.

A systematic, interdisciplinary examination of strategic renewal therefore is necessary, to establish an essential definition and up-to-date picture of the field. This examination ideally would:

- Outline key concepts within the literature of strategic renewal;
- Examine their emergence at different levels of analysis; and
- Point towards areas of future research.

Hence, this is research anthology focuses on addressing these objectives. More specifically, this anthology examines how organizations achieve successful strategic renewal in 18 chapters reflecting five main topic parts:

- Introduction
- Core concepts
- Psychological antecedents and micro-foundations of strategic renewal
- Strategic renewal beyond organizational and national boundaries
- Interdisciplinary perspectives and future directions

Part 1: introduction

The first Part of the book consists of one chapter, "A brief look at the strategic renewal literature", written by the editors. They discuss the concept of strategic renewal and introduce the different streams of research within the literature on strategic renewal (e.g., dynamic capabilities, exploration–exploitation, ambidexterity). This chapter is intended to introduce strategic renewal vocabulary to the general reader and provide an in-depth introduction to the other chapters in the book.

Part 2: core concepts

The second section consists of five chapters focusing on core strategic renewal concepts such as overall strategic renewal (as an outcome), dynamic capabilities, ambidexterity, and radical/incremental product innovation. The outcomes of these variables (e.g., performance), as well as the factors driving them (e.g., human capital), are also considered in this section. It is beneficial for readers, especially those new to the field of strategic renewal, to understand these concepts before moving on to more specific subjects in the field of strategic renewal, including the micro-foundations of strategic renewal and strategic renewal beyond organizational boundaries.

Part 3: psychological antecedents and micro-foundations of strategic renewal

The third section focuses specifically on emerging research on using a behavioural-strategy perspective to understand strategic renewal. In recent years, there has been substantial interest in the micro-foundations of strategic renewal at lower levels of analysis (e.g., individual and team levels). This interest has resulted in an influx of theories from the fields of social psychology, cognitive psychology, and, most recently, neuropsychology. The four chapters in this section examine strategic renewal through a psychological lens.

Part 4: strategic renewal beyond organizational and national boundaries

Another area of research in the literature on strategic renewal looks beyond organizational or national boundaries. Traditionally, strategic renewal is endogenous to an organization; however, organizations may also be able to renew themselves through carefully selected organizational partnerships such as alliances and mergers. Alternatively, instead of developing new capabilities in-house, organizations may be able to purchase small firms that fit their strategic renewal goals (such as gaining a specific exploitative capability or innovative product). In addition, moving beyond an organization's national boundaries may have certain advantages and disadvantages in terms of innovation and strategic renewal. This section consists of three chapters focusing on these issues.

Part 5: interdisciplinary perspectives and future directions

The concept of strategic renewal can be examined from a variety of perspectives and is relevant in numerous fields. The fifth section consists of five chapters that introduce some of these perspectives (e.g., institutional theory), provides examples of interdisciplinary research within the literature on strategic renewal (e.g., service research), and points towards future research directions (e.g., the effects of new technologies on strategic renewal).

Closing remarks

We extend a special thanks to Routledge and its staff, who have been most helpful throughout this entire process. Equally, we warmly thank all of the authors who submitted their manuscripts for consideration for this book. They have exhibited the desire to share their knowledge and experience with the book's readers—and a willingness to put forward their views for possible challenge by their peers. We also thank the reviewers, who provided excellent, independent, and incisive consideration of the anonymous submissions.

We hope that this compendium of chapters and themes stimulates and contributes to the ongoing debate surrounding strategic renewal. The chapters in this book can help fill some knowledge gaps, while also stimulating further thought and action pertaining to the multiple aspects surrounding strategic renewal.

Aybars Tuncdogan
King's Business School, King's College London, United Kingdom

Adam Lindgreen
Copenhagen Business School, Denmark and University of Pretoria's
Gordon Institute of Business Science, South Africa

Henk Volberda
Rotterdam School of Management, Erasmus University, the Netherlands

Frans van den Bosch
Rotterdam School of Management, Erasmus University, the Netherlands

September 30, 2018

January 31, 2019

Part 1

Introduction

1   A brief look at the strategic renewal literature

In the last three decades, businesses have been facing rapidly increasing levels of dynamism, complexity, and competition in the global business landscape (e.g., Schmitt, Raisch, and Volberda, 2018; Wang, Senaratne, and Rafiq, 2015). In fact, such complaints involving not knowing exactly against whom the organization is competing are rampant among managers. More importantly, the situation is not only very difficult to deal with for business people, but they also predict that it will only worsen. For instance, in a large-scale study conducted by the IBM Corporation with 1541 CEOs from 60 countries and 33 industries, 79% of the participants expected complexity levels to rise even higher, and the creative co-creation of products and services was indicated as the key to survival in this hostile environment (IBM, 2010). Strategy scholars have been trying to invent solutions that will help businesses cope with their difficult environments and prepare management students for survival out in the field. Thus, the concept of strategic renewal has become a key area of dialogue within the strategic management literature (e.g., Albert, Kreutzer, and Lechner, 2015; Friesl, Garreau, and Heracleous, 2018; Kwee, Van den Bosch, and Volberda, 2011; Schmitt et al., 2018; Teece, 2014; Volberda, Baden-Fuller, and Van den Bosch, 2001; Williams, Chen, and Agarwal, 2017).

Strategic renewal is a multidimensional and multilevel concept (Volberda, 2017), and understanding how organizations can successfully achieve strategic renewal requires us to understand several distinct but related mechanisms. Some of the key mechanisms in the main focus of the strategic renewal literature include dynamic capabilities, exploration–exploitation, ambidexterity, and product innovation, although more are being proposed by scholars and practitioners every day. This brief chapter will serve two purposes. First, it will introduce the chapters in this book in a more in-depth manner and, while doing so, also touch upon the key streams of research within the strategic renewal literature.[1] Second, it will provide the novice reader with the strategic renewal vocabulary necessary to understand these chapters. The remainder of this chapter is structured into four sections ("Core concepts", "Psychological antecedents and microfoundations of strategic renewal", "Strategic renewal beyond organizational and national boundaries", and "Interdisciplinary perspectives and future directions"), which is in line with the overall structure of the book.

Core concepts

In this section, we will introduce five core areas of research within the strategic renewal literature. That said, the literature is not limited to these concepts – some of the emerging perspectives will be discussed later in the section entitled "Interdisciplinary perspectives and future directions".

Dynamic capabilities

The resource-based view (RBV) (Barney, 1991, 2001, 2017; Kull, Mena, and Korschun, 2016; Lioukas, Reuer, and Zollo, 2016; Nason and Wiklund, 2018) defines organizations as aggregates of diverse resources and proposes this heterogeneity of resources as a key element of competitive advantage (e.g., Peteraf, 1993). As explained at the beginning of this chapter, however, we are going through a time when the global business landscape is more dynamic, complex, and competitive than ever before (e.g., Schmitt et al., 2018; Wang et al., 2015). In today's markets, it is difficult – if not impossible – to have a distinct static configuration of resources that will provide competitive advantage in the long term. The dynamic-capabilities view (Teece, Pisano, and Shuen, 1997) extends the static perspective by providing an explanation of how organizations can reconfigure their resources to keep up with external demands (e.g., Karim and Capron, 2016; Schilke, 2014; Schilke, Hu, and Helfat, 2018). In other words, the dynamic-capabilities view puts forward the idea that if sustainable competitive advantage is not possible by means of a static configuration, organizations can keep changing their resources to create temporary periods of competitive advantage and can sustain competitive advantage in the long term through a series of competitive advantages. In this sense, the dynamic-capabilities view may almost be considered a highly developed and organized structure for engaging in serial entrepreneurship or, more specifically, serial corporate entrepreneurship. Another distinctive characteristic of the dynamic-capabilities view – one that has been explored to a lesser extent – is that it is also helpful in understanding how organizations can affect and modify their external environments (Helfat and Winter, 2011; Schilke et al., 2018; Teece, 2007).

In the original paper by Teece et al. (1997), the dynamic-capabilities view was proposed, and dynamic capabilities were defined as "the firm's ability to integrate, build, and reconfigure internal and external competences to address rapidly changing environments" (p. 510). Since then, a number of other definitions that build on, complement, and extend this one have been proposed in order to provide more conceptual insight into the nature of this construct. For instance, Barreto (2010) proposed the definition that "a dynamic capability is the firm's potential to systematically solve problems, formed by its propensity to sense opportunities and threats, to make timely and market-oriented decisions, and to change its resource base" (p. 271). Likewise, Helfat and Raubitschek (2018) defined dynamic capabilities as "a subset of capabilities directed towards strategic change, both at the organizational and individual level" (p. 1393). Another well-known definition is from a prominent paper by Zollo and Winter (2002) that explains what dynamic capabilities are and how they work by first defining the term *operating routines*. Specifically, according to Zollo and Winter (2002), operating routines are learning processes "geared towards the operational functioning of the firm (both staff and line activities)", and "a dynamic capability is a learned and stable pattern of collective activity through which the organization systematically generates and modifies its operating routines in pursuit of improved effectiveness" (p. 340). In sum, the dynamic-capabilities view has been employed to explain innovation, strategic renewal, and long-term performance in a range of fields including strategic management (e.g., Girod and Whittington, 2017), innovation management (e.g., Piening and Salge, 2015), marketing (e.g., Wilden and Gudergan, 2015), human-resource management (e.g., Jalali and Rezaie, 2016), microeconomics (e.g., Brusset and Teller, 2017), public management (e.g., Piening, 2013), information systems (e.g., Karimi and Walter, 2015), and tourism management (e.g., Leonidou, Leonidou, Fotiadis, and Aykol, 2015).

The first chapter of this volume is by David Teece, the father of the dynamic-capabilities view. In his chapter, Teece ponders the questions of why strategic change is necessary and how it can be achieved. In particular, he reflects upon diverse perspectives to describe why strategic change is difficult. Next, he differentiates between efficiency and efficacy to explain that certain kinds of change are more difficult than others. Following that, he describes how the dynamic-capabilities view addresses this problem – that is, how successful strategic renewal is possible through the formation and enactment of dynamic capabilities.

In the next chapter, Qiang Wu, Qile He, and Yanqing Duan provide a review of the literature on the dynamic-capabilities view and on corporate strategic change towards sustainability. They delineate a conceptual model depicting the main dimensions of dynamic capabilities for corporate sustainability and competitive advantage, namely: scanning capability, sensing capability, and reconfiguration capability.

Exploration–exploitation

The concepts of exploration and exploitation concern two key types of activity in which an entity (e.g., individual manager, group, organization) engages for performance and survival. According to March's (1991) original definition, exploration activities are the "things captured by terms such as search, variation, risk taking, experimentation, play, flexibility, discovery, innovation" (p. 71). A lack of sufficient exploration is known to cause obsolescence and can eventually lead to the entity being swept away in the long term by changes in the environment (e.g., Alexiev, Jansen, Van den Bosch, and Volberda, 2010; Levinthal and March, 1993; McGrath, 2001). On the other hand, exploitation activities are those that involve "refinement, choice, production, efficiency, selection, implementation, execution" (March, 1991, p. 71). Insufficient exploitation can put the short-term survival of the entity at risk (e.g., Levinthal and

March, 1993; Tuncdogan, Van den Bosch, and Volberda, 2015; Uotila, Maula, Keil, and Zahra, 2009). Therefore, it is necessary for all entities to engage in both exploration and exploitation to survive and perform well in the long term (Jansen, Simsek, and Cao, 2012; O'Reilly and Tushman, 2013). In this book, the chapter by Mom, Tuncdogan, and van den Bosch is on exploration and exploitation, although due to its focus on a psychological antecedent (regulatory focus), we will discuss that later in this text within the part entitled "Psychological antecedents and micro-foundations of strategic renewal".

Ambidexterity

In the previous paragraph, we discussed the fact that both exploration and exploitation are necessary for the survival of an organization. Currently, the ambidexterity literature can be considered as an extension of exploration–exploitation research, as it focuses on the question of what the ideal balance is between these two concepts.

Alluding to the idea of being able to use both hands – or having "two right hands" – the concept of ambidexterity actually dates further back within the organizational literature (See Duncan, 1976) than the concept of exploration and exploitation (i.e., March, 1991). However, over time the two streams of research became intertwined (e.g., Tushman and O'Reilly, 1996), and the concept of ambidexterity was redefined as the pursuit of both exploration and exploitation (e.g., Betz, Zapkau, and Schwens, 2017; Koryak, Lockett, Hayton, Nicolaou, and Mole, 2018). That said, there is no clear consensus regarding how it should be conceptualized and operationalized. One popular view is that exploration and exploitation are mutually exclusive activities as they draw on the same pool of resources, which is also known as the "balance dimension of ambidexterity" (Cao, Gedajlovic, and Zhang, 2009). Following this view, ambidexterity is the "middle point" at which the organization engages in an equal amount of exploration and exploitation (Lavie, Stettner, and Tushman, 2010). In this case, as a variable, ambidexterity is operationalized as the absolute difference between exploration and exploitation (e.g., He and Wong, 2004). In contrast, the alternative view, known as the "combined dimension of ambidexterity" (Cao et al., 2009), takes into account the synergies between exploration and exploitation and considers them as orthogonal concepts, whereby both can be high or low at the same time (e.g., Gupta, Smith, and Shalley, 2006; Jansen, van den Bosch, and Volberda, 2006; Katila and Ahuja, 2002). In this view, ambidexterity is calculated as the product of the two variables (i.e., exploration times exploitation – e.g., He and Wong, 2004; Mom, Van den Bosch, and Volberda, 2009).

Research on how ambidexterity can be achieved has resulted in the emergence of four main types of ambidexterity (e.g., Simsek, Heavey, Veiga, and Souder, 2009): structural, contextual, sequential, and network ambidexterity. *Partitional ambidexterity, structural ambidexterity,* or *ambidexterity through structural differentiation* refers to the strategy of dividing the organization into exploratory and exploitative units (e.g., De Visser et al., 2010; Jansen, Tempelaar, Van den Bosch, and Volberda, 2009). One advantage of this method is that the two processes are completely separated from each other, and exploratory units are not corrupted by exploitative units (as exploration generally tends to drive exploitation out as it produces results in the shorter term – e.g., Benner and Tushman, 2003). One disadvantage is the cost resulting from creating two versions of the same unit. Another problem is that they cannot benefit from their commonalities. For instance, the same solutions may need to be developed in the two units separately (i.e., "reinventing the wheel") due to a lack of sufficient communication between them. The use of cross-functional teams can help alleviate this issue (e.g., Jansen et al., 2009). *Contextual, simultaneous,* or *harmonic ambidexterity* refers to the organization and its subparts (e.g., organizational units, individual managers) simultaneously engaging in exploration and exploitation activities (e.g., Carmeli and Halevi, 2009; Gibson and Birkinshaw, 2004; Mom, Fourné, and Jansen, 2015). Although this is a very direct method of achieving organizational ambidexterity, it comes with certain difficulties. For instance, simultaneously engaging in exploration and exploitation activities requires individuals capable of "hosting contradictions" (See Mom et al., 2009; Smith and Tushman, 2005). Likewise, especially at lower levels of analysis, this might be very difficult to achieve due to a more restricted pool of resources (Cao et al., 2009; Gupta et al., 2006). In the case of *sequential* or *temporal ambidexterity*, the organization balances exploration and exploitation by alternating between periods of the former and the latter (e.g., Boumgarden, Nickerson, and Zenger, 2012; Siggelkow and Levinthal, 2003). Finally, *network ambidexterity* is achieved through interorganizational links, such as interorganizational partnerships, mergers, and alliances, whereby one organization focuses on exploration and the other on exploitation, or they reciprocally alternate (e.g., Simsek et al., 2009; Stettner and Lavie, 2014; Tiwana, 2008).

More recently, the concept of ambidexterity has also been extended to understand different kinds of strategic renewal or strategic renewal in other fields. For instance, building on the more general theory of ambidexterity, academics in service research have developed a specific type of ambidexterity called *sales–service ambidexterity* to better explain performance in that area of research (e.g., Yu, Patterson, and de Ruyter, 2013). In information systems, the concept of *IT ambidexterity* is discussed as a mechanism of strategic renewal (e.g., Lee, Sambamurthy, Lim, and Wei, 2015). In the area of marketing, the concept of *brand ambidexterity* has been developed to explain the long-term survival and performance of brands (e.g., Beverland, Wilner, and Micheli, 2015; Nguyen, Yu, Melewar, and Hemsley-Brown, 2016).

In their chapter "Towards a cognitive dimension in the organizational ambidexterity framework", Päivi Karhu and Paavo Ritala review the ambidexterity literature and conceptually extend it by taking a novel perspective. In particular, they introduce "cognitive ambidexterity" as a manager's ability to deal with contradictory dualities in their decision-making. To this end, they integrate literature on organizational ambidexterity and dualities such as paradoxes, as well as management cognition, and discuss the role of cognition in achieving spatial, temporal, and contextual ambidexterity.

Innovation

The concept of innovation is central to the literature on strategic renewal, as strategic renewal generally occurs through a series of innovations or, occasionally, through one large innovation (e.g., Agarwal and Helfat, 2009). Several kinds of innovation are discussed in the literature. One key distinction is the size of change an innovation entails. For instance, *radical innovation* (e.g., Alexander and Van Knippenberg, 2014), *breakthrough innovation* (e.g., Kaplan and Vakili, 2015), *discontinuous innovation* (e.g., Birkinshaw, Bessant, and Delbridge, 2007), *disruptive innovation* (e.g., Christensen, Raynor, and McDonald, 2015), and *exploratory innovation* (Jansen, Van den Bosch, and Volberda, 2006; Mueller, Rosenbusch, and Bausch, 2013; Tuncdogan, Boon, Mom, Van den Bosch, and Volberda, 2017) are closely related concepts, and they require what is called a "long jump" (see Levinthal, 1997). In contrast, *incremental innovation* (e.g., Menguc, Auh, and Yannopoulos, 2014) and *exploitative innovation* (Jansen et al., 2006, Jansen, Van Den Bosch, and Volberda, 2005; Mueller et al., 2013) do not involve fundamental changes but smaller refinements. Innovations also differ in terms of what they influence. For instance, *product innovations* are different from *process innovations*: "while product innovation refers to new end products or services introduced by a firm, process innovation reflects changes in the way firms create and deliver such products and services" (Piening and Salge, 2015, p. 82). Other conceptually related streams of research include those on *architectural innovation*, which refers to "a change in the relationships between a product's components that leaves untouched the core design concepts of components" (Brusoni, Prencipe, and Pavitt, 2001, p. 598), and on *technological innovation*, which is defined as "the implementation of an idea for a new product or a new service or the introduction of new elements in an organization's production process or service operation" (Damanpour and Evan, 1984, p. 394).

In their chapter "Knowledge management practices for stimulating incremental and radical product innovation", Petra Andries, Sophie de Winne, and Anna Bos-Nehles build on data from 4951 organizations that participated in the Flemish part of the Community Innovation Survey to provide a better understanding of product innovation. More specifically, they conceptually develop and empirically test a multiple-mediation model that seeks to explain the effects of different HRM practices on knowledge transfer and creation and, through those, on incremental and radical product innovation.

Strategic renewal

Strategic renewal can also be examined from a macro-perspective, in which case it is conceptualized as an overarching construct. Studies taking this perspective generally include strategic renewal as an outcome in their models

(Albert et al., 2015; Kwee et al., 2011; Williams et al., 2017). In their chapter "Boards of directors and strategic renewal: how do human and relational capital matter", Bas Bosboom, Mariano Heyden, and Jatinder Sidhu integrate resource dependence theory and the knowledge-based view to examine how board capital (i.e., human and relational capital) influences strategic renewal (i.e., path-breaking corporate strategies). Their findings highlight the fact that outside board directorships are positively associated with strategic renewal. Further results indicate that board tenure and director-type heterogeneity have non-linear effects on strategic renewal. The findings reveal that directors bring different types of knowledge to the firm, and board capital matters in complex ways for understanding renewal.

Psychological antecedents and micro-foundations of strategic renewal

Strategy research spawned from the field of economics, and the initial focus was relatively more on the industry level of analysis (e.g., Porter, 1979, 1981). Industry analysis was useful to help companies choose profitable industries, but was unable to explain differences among different incumbent firms within an industry, so over time the focus shifted more towards lower and lower levels of analysis. Most recently, there has been a growing interest in the psychological micro-foundations of organizational phenomena at the team and individual manager levels of analysis (e.g., Felin, Foss, Heimeriks, and Madsen, 2012; Healey and Hodgkinson, 2017; Hodgkinson and Healey, 2011, 2014); this is also known as *behavioral strategy* research (Powell, Lovallo, and Fox, 2011; Sibony, Lovallo, and Powell, 2017; Tuncdogan, 2014). One benefit of this stream of research is that it can provide a more detailed explanation of phenomena at higher levels of analysis (e.g., Helfat and Peteraf, 2015; Teece, 2007). Another benefit is that the variance explained through the use of psychological theories is different from economic or organizational theories (Levinthal, 2011; Tuncdogan et al., 2015). In other words, the use of psychological theories complements economic and organizational theories and increases our overall ability to explain the variance we observe.

In their chapter "Emotion and strategic renewal", Quy Huy and Christina Scheef conceptually examine the relationship among different kinds of emotion management actions and their effects on the strategic renewal process. More specifically, they ponder the different influences of emotion management actions that stimulate (1) authenticity, (2) pride, (3) aspirational discontent, (4) hope, and (5) passion among the employees in the strategic renewal process of the firm.

Following that, in "The micro-foundations of strategic renewal: Middle managers' job design, strategic change culture, organizational effectiveness unit, and innovative work behavior", Tomislav Hernaus and Matej Černe use insights from the field of organizational psychology to provide deeper insight into the micro-foundations of innovative work behaviors. Specifically, they conceptualize managers' innovative work behavior (IWB; idea generation, championing, and implementation) and theorize how it may be enhanced by the interplay between job design and strategic change culture. Furthermore, their propositions account for a bottom-up emergence relationship between managers' IWB and strategic renewal, assuming a potential moderating role of organizational effectiveness unit characteristics in this association.

Next, in "Regulatory focus as a mediator of environmental dynamism and decentralization on managers' exploration and exploitation activities", Tom Mom, Aybars Tuncdogan, and Frans van den Bosch draw upon the regulatory focus theory – a motivational theory of goal attainment – to examine the effects of environmental dynamism and decentralization on exploration and exploitation at the individual manager level. The hypotheses are tested using a sample of 224 managers working at a "Big Four" consultancy and accountancy firm.

Finally, in "Should I stay or should I go? The individual antecedents of noticing and embracing strategic change", Daniella Laureiro-Martinez conceptually investigates strategic change from a neuropsychological point of view. In particular, she considers the question of why it is difficult to change and discusses the role of failing to recognize the need for change and reacting with the wrong behavior as two key impediments to successful strategic renewal.

Strategic renewal beyond organizational and national boundaries

An organization may not always have to develop the capabilities to achieve strategic renewal within its own organizational boundaries. Instead, it can collaborate with other partners (e.g., Ingram, 2017; Teng, 2007; Zheng and Yang, 2015) or even acquire smaller firms (e.g., Bauer, Matzler, and Wolf, 2016; Cefis and Marsili, 2015) for this purpose. There is a growing stream of research examining the benefits of crossing organizational boundaries to achieve strategic renewal goals such as ambidexterity (e.g., Stettner and Lavie, 2014; Yang, Fang, Fang, and Chou, 2014). Firms may also choose to cross national boundaries for a number of other reasons. For instance, crossing national boundaries can help them build the human capital necessary for strategic renewal, increase the size of their target market, and capitalize on opportunities in new markets (e.g., Chung, Park, Lee, and Kim, 2015; Gnizy, Baker, and Grinstein, 2014; Patel, Fernhaber, McDougall-Covin, and van der Have, 2014).

In their chapter "Strategic renewal through mergers and acquisitions: The role of ambidexterity", Olimpia Meglio and Kathleen Marshall Park examine mergers and acquisitions as maneuvers for strategic renewal. More specifically, they build on the process perspective on mergers and acquisitions and use the concept of contextual ambidexterity to better understand how to achieve successful post-acquisition integration. They draw on the emergent strategic notions of capability gaps and common ground and explicate the roles and responsibilities of integration leaders and the mechanisms of integration.

Following that, in his chapter "Developing alliance capability for strategic renewal", Abdelghani Es-Sajjade reviews and synthesizes studies investigating the role of alliances in instigating strategic renewal. He points out that while conventional wisdom suggests a positive relationship between alliance experience and success, research shows that relying on experience alone can cause managers to emphasize apparent similarities and overlook important differences among several alliances. The alliance success of some firms has instead been attributed to alliance capability, which is developed by systemic organizational learning processes combining routine and ad hoc approaches.

Finally, in her chapter entitled "Innovation in foreign and domestic firms: The advantage of foreignness in innovation and the advantage of localness in innovation", C. Annique Un integrates the literature on global strategy and innovation management to explain how domestic firms and subsidiaries of foreign firms innovate. Building on the knowledge-based view, she argues that subsidiaries of foreign firms and domestic firms have access to different knowledge sources and manage their employees differently, resulting in their following different innovation paths. Specifically, she proposes that subsidiaries of foreign firms may benefit from what she calls the advantage of foreignness in innovation, in which access to global knowledge sources and the strategy of managing employees with encouragement to have a multicultural mindset support global innovation. She also argues that domestic firms may enjoy what she calls the advantage of localness in innovation, in which deep and contextualized local knowledge and the strategy of managing employees with encouragement to focus on the local market support local innovation.

Interdisciplinary perspectives and future directions

As a result of the vibrant dialogue within the strategic renewal literature, new perspectives are entering the strategic renewal field every day. Furthermore, strategic renewal is interesting not only from the perspective of strategic management scholars, but also for both academics and practitioners from a wide range of fields who are motivated to better understand this subject. Some of the other fields showing interest in this subject include marketing (e.g., Rubera, Chandrasekaran, and Ordanini, 2016), economics (e.g., Hsu, Tian, and Xu, 2014), public management (e.g., De Vries, Bekkers, and Tummers, 2016), hospitality management (e.g., Leonidou et al., 2015), and policy research (e.g., Uyarra and Flanagan, 2010). Finally, technological developments are revolutionizing organizational structures and decision-making (e.g., McAfee, Brynjolfsson, Davenport, Patil, and Barton, 2012) and are therefore enhancing our understanding of strategy concepts (e.g., Lioukas et al., 2016). In parallel with these issues, the chapters in this section provide interdisciplinary perspectives and point towards areas of future research in those directions.

In their chapter "Strategic renewal in services: the role of the top management team's social relations", Julia Nieves and Javier Osorio consider strategic renewal from a service research perspective. They focus on hotels to examine the link between human resources practices that promote top managers' social relationships and innovation results by contemplating the mediator role of dynamic capabilities. They find that behaviors oriented towards fomenting top managers' ties provide a set of resources to companies that improve the ability to detect and take advantage of opportunities in the environment and, consequently, achieve strategic renewal through the introduction of innovations.

Following that, in "Institutional complexity and strategic renewal", Saeed Khanagha and Patrick Vermeulen bring the institutional theory perspective into the discussion. They build a conceptual model regarding the effect of institutional complexity on strategic responses. More specifically, they build a moderated-mediation model in which institutional complexity affects the strategic response processes of reconciliation and elimination through its effects on perception and interpretation, and managers' cognition, motivation, and traits moderate the effect of institutional complexity.

Next, in their chapter "Patent-based measures in strategic management research: A review and assessment", Barton M. Sharp, Dinesh N. Iyer, and Derek Ruth take a methodological perspective towards patent-based measures, which are among the most common types of measures used in strategic renewal research (and possibly the most common type in interorganizational strategic renewal research). Specifically, they evaluate the use of patent-based measures as proxies for various innovation-related constructs. They first survey the literature and find an enormous variety of variables in published work with relatively little in the way of consistency. Then, they offer an empirical demonstration of how the choice of operational variables may affect theory development.

The following chapter by Emile Lancée entitled "Strategic renewal in the digital age: The digital marketing core as a starting point" brings the digital marketing perspective into the strategic renewal discussion. He emphasizes that although scholars have paid much attention to the conceptualization of marketing capability and its performance implications, there has been little research into the leading role of digital marketing elements and capabilities in strategic renewal. Furthermore, additional research efforts are necessary to demonstrate how relevant digital marketing components such as big data, technology, partners, channels, and related capabilities initiate the construction of new strategic avenues. Therefore, this study presents a conceptual framework entitled "The digital marketing core: Towards a better understanding of strategic renewal".

Finally, in their chapter "Dynamic game plans: Using gamification to entrain strategic renewal with environmental velocity", Ian P. McCarthy, Kirk Plangger, Karen Robson, Jan H. Kietzmann, and Leyland Pitt put forward the concept of gamification as a potential catalyst for strategic renewal. In particular, by using gamification as a management control approach for strategic renewal and environmental velocity to characterize industry dynamics, they explain how a gamified strategic renewal approach can be used to direct and adjust the pace of two different organizational behaviors – exploitation and exploration – to attain strategic renewal suited to different environmental velocity types.

Conclusions

In this chapter, we have introduced some of the key mechanisms of strategic renewal and discussed different levels of analysis at which strategic renewal happens. This chapter is meant as an introduction to the book, and it is aimed at introducing the chapters and the key strategic renewal vocabulary to the readers. The remainder of this book will provide a more detailed look at the core concepts, antecedents, and micro-foundations of strategic renewal.

Note

1 When submitting their chapters, some of the authors also provided us with abstracts. We used parts of those abstracts within the chapter definitions in this introductory chapter.

References

Agarwal, R., & Helfat, C. E. (2009). Strategic renewal of organizations. *Organization Science*, 20(2), 281–293.

Albert, D., Kreutzer, M., & Lechner, C. (2015). Resolving the paradox of interdependency and strategic renewal in activity systems. *Academy of Management Review*, 40(2), 210–234.

Alexander, L., & Van Knippenberg, D. (2014). Teams in pursuit of radical innovation: A goal orientation perspective. *Academy of Management Review*, 39(4), 423–438.

Alexiev, A. S., Jansen, J. J., Van den Bosch, F. A., & Volberda, H. W. (2010). Top management team advice seeking and exploratory innovation: The moderating role of TMT heterogeneity. *Journal of Management Studies*, 47(7), 1343–1364.

Barney, J. (1991). Firm resources and sustained competitive advantage. *Journal of Management*, 17(1), 99–120.

Barney, J. B. (2001). Resource-based theories of competitive advantage: A ten-year retrospective on the resource-based view. *Journal of Management*, 27(6), 643–650.

Barney, J. B. (2017). The evolutionary roots of resource-based theory. In *The SMS Blackwell Handbook of Organizational Capabilities*, (Ed. Helfat, C. E.), 269–271, Oxford, UK: Blackwell Publishing.

Barreto, I. (2010). Dynamic capabilities: A review of past research and an agenda for the future. *Journal of Management*, 36(1), 256–280.

Bauer, F., Matzler, K., & Wolf, S. (2016). M&A and innovation: The role of integration and cultural differences – A central European targets perspective. *International Business Review*, 25(1), 76–86.

Benner, M. J., & Tushman, M. L. (2003). Exploitation, exploration, and process management: The productivity dilemma revisited. *Academy of Management Review*, 28(2), 238–256.

Betz, K., Zapkau, F. B., & Schwens, C. (2017). A meta-analysis on the effects of exploration, exploitation, and ambidexterity on SME performance. Academy of Management Proceedings, 2017(1), 17060. Briarcliff Manor, NY 10510: Academy of Management.

Beverland, M. B., Wilner, S. J., & Micheli, P. (2015). Reconciling the tension between consistency and relevance: Design thinking as a mechanism for brand ambidexterity. *Journal of the Academy of Marketing Science*, 43(5), 589–609.

Birkinshaw, J., Bessant, J., & Delbridge, R. (2007). Finding, forming, and performing: Creating networks for discontinuous innovation. *California Management Review*, 49(3), 67–84.

Boumgarden, P., Nickerson, J., & Zenger, T. R. (2012). Sailing into the wind: Exploring the relationships among ambidexterity, vacillation, and organizational performance. *Strategic Management Journal*, 33(6), 587–610.

Brusoni, S., Prencipe, A., & Pavitt, K. (2001). Knowledge specialization, organizational coupling, and the boundaries of the firm: Why do firms know more than they make? *Administrative Science Quarterly*, 46(4), 597–621.

Brusset, X., & Teller, C. (2017). Supply chain capabilities, risks, and resilience. *International Journal of Production Economics*, 184, 59–68.

Cao, Q., Gedajlovic, E., & Zhang, H. (2009). Unpacking organizational ambidexterity: Dimensions, contingencies, and synergistic effects. *Organization Science*, 20(4), 781–796.

Carmeli, A., & Halevi, M. Y. (2009). How top management team behavioral integration and behavioral complexity enable organizational ambidexterity: The moderating role of contextual ambidexterity. *The Leadership Quarterly*, 20(2), 207–218.

Cefis, E., & Marsili, O. (2015). Crossing the innovation threshold through mergers and acquisitions. *Research Policy*, 44(3), 698–710.

Christensen, C. M., Raynor, M. E., & McDonald, R. (2015). What is disruptive innovation. *Harvard Business Review*, 93(12), 44–53.

Chung, C. C., Park, H. Y., Lee, J. Y., & Kim, K. (2015). Human capital in multinational enterprises: Does strategic alignment matter? *Journal of International Business Studies*, 46(7), 806–829.

Damanpour, F., & Evan, W. M. (1984). Organizational innovation and performance: The problem of "organizational lag". *Administrative Science Quarterly*, 29, 392–409.

De Visser, M., de Weerd-Nederhof, P., Faems, D., Song, M., Van Looy, B., & Visscher, K. (2010). Structural ambidexterity in NPD processes: A firm-level assessment of the impact of differentiated structures on innovation performance. *Technovation*, 30(5–6), 291–299.

De Vries, H., Bekkers, V., & Tummers, L. (2016). Innovation in the public sector: A systematic review and future research agenda. *Public Administration*, 94(1), 146–166.

Duncan, R. B. (1976). The ambidextrous organization: Designing dual structures for innovation. In R. H. Kilmann, L. R. Pondy, & D. Slevin (Eds.), *The Management of Organization*, vol. 1, 167–188. New York, NY: North-Holland.

Felin, T., Foss, N. J., Heimeriks, K. H., & Madsen, T. L. (2012). Microfoundations of routines and capabilities: Individuals, processes, and structure. *Journal of Management Studies*, 49(8), 1351–1374.

Friesl, M., Garreau, L., & Heracleous, L. (2018). When the parent imitates the child: Strategic renewal through separation and reintegration of subsidiaries. *Strategic Organization*, available at https://doi.org/10.1177/1476127018794850.

Gibson, C. B., & Birkinshaw, J. (2004). The antecedents, consequences, and mediating role of organizational ambidexterity. *Academy of Management Journal*, 47(2), 209–226.

Girod, S. J., & Whittington, R. (2017). Reconfiguration, restructuring and firm performance: Dynamic capabilities and environmental dynamism. *Strategic Management Journal*, 38(5), 1121–1133.

Gnizy, I., Baker, W. E, & Grinstein, A. (2014). Proactive learning culture: A dynamic capability and key success factor for SMEs entering foreign markets. *International Marketing Review*, 31(5), 477–505.

Gupta, A. K., Smith, K. G., & Shalley, C. E. (2006). The interplay between exploration and exploitation. *Academy of Management Journal*, 49(4), 693–706.

He, Z. L., & Wong, P. K. (2004). Exploration vs. exploitation: An empirical test of the ambidexterity hypothesis. *Organization Science*, 15(4), 481–494.

Healey, M. P., & Hodgkinson, G. P. (2017). Making strategy hot. *California Management Review*, 59(3), 109–134.

Helfat, C. E., & Peteraf, M. A. (2015). Managerial cognitive capabilities and the micro-foundations of dynamic capabilities. *Strategic Management Journal*, 36(6), 831–850.

Helfat, C. E., & Raubitschek, R. S. (2018). Dynamic and integrative capabilities for profiting from innovation in digital platform-based ecosystems. *Research Policy*, 47(8), 1391–1399.

Helfat, C. E., & Winter, S. G. (2011). Untangling dynamic and operational capabilities: Strategy for the (N) ever-changing world. *Strategic Management Journal*, 32(11), 1243–1250.

Hodgkinson, G. P., & Healey, M. P. (2011). Psychological foundations of dynamic capabilities: Reflexion and reflection in strategic management. *Strategic Management Journal*, 32(13), 1500–1516.

Hodgkinson, G. P., & Healey, M. P. (2014). Coming in from the cold: The psychological foundations of radical innovation revisited. *Industrial Marketing Management*, 43(8), 1306–1313.

Hsu, P. H., Tian, X., & Xu, Y. (2014). Financial development and innovation: Cross-country evidence. *Journal of Financial Economics*, 112(1), 116–135.

IBM. (2010). *Capitalizing on Complexity: Insights from the Global Chief Executive Officer Study*. IBM. Online resource, retrieved from: https://www-01.ibm.com/common/ssi/cgi-bin/ssialias?htmlfid=GBE03297USEN.

Ingram, P. (2017). Interorganizational learning. In *The Blackwell Companion to Organizations*, (Ed. Baum, J. A. C.) 642–663, Blackwell Publishing: Oxford, UK.

Jalali, Z., & Rezaie, H. (2016). Analyzing the effect of dynamic organizational capabilities (organizational learning) and knowledge management in achieving the objectives of health reform plan. *Human Resource Management*, 3(12), 1–14.

Jansen, J. J., Tempelaar, M. P., Van Den Bosch, F. A., & Volberda, H. W. (2009). Structural differentiation and ambidexterity: The mediating role of integration mechanisms. *Organization Science*, 20(4), 797–811.

Jansen, J. J., Van Den Bosch, F. A., & Volberda, H. W. (2005). Exploratory innovation, exploitative innovation, and ambidexterity: The impact of environmental and organizational antecedents. *Schmalenbach Business Review*, 57(4), 351–363.

Jansen, J. J., Van Den Bosch, F. A., & Volberda, H. W. (2006). Exploratory innovation, exploitative innovation, and performance: Effects of organizational antecedents and environmental moderators. *Management Science*, 52(11), 1661–1674.

Kaplan, S., & Vakili, K. (2015). The double-edged sword of recombination in breakthrough innovation. *Strategic Management Journal*, 36(10), 1435–1457.

Karim, S., & Capron, L. (2016). Reconfiguration: Adding, redeploying, recombining and divesting resources and business units. *Strategic Management Journal*, 37(13), E54–E62.

Karimi, J., & Walter, Z. (2015). The role of dynamic capabilities in responding to digital disruption: A factor-based study of the newspaper industry. *Journal of Management Information Systems*, 32(1), 39–81.

Katila, R., & Ahuja, G. (2002). Something old, something new: A longitudinal study of search behavior and new product introduction. *Academy of Management Journal*, 45(6), 1183–1194.

Koryak, O., Lockett, A., Hayton, J., Nicolaou, N., & Mole, K. (2018). Disentangling the antecedents of ambidexterity: Exploration and exploitation. *Research Policy*, 47(2), 413–427.

Kull, A. J., Mena, J. A., & Korschun, D. (2016). A resource-based view of stakeholder marketing. *Journal of Business Research*, 69(12), 5553–5560.

Kwee, Z., Van Den Bosch, F. A., & Volberda, H. W. (2011). The influence of top management team's corporate governance orientation on strategic renewal trajectories: A longitudinal analysis of Royal Dutch Shell plc, 1907–2004. *Journal of Management Studies*, 48(5), 984–1014.

Lavie, D., Stettner, U., & Tushman, M. L. (2010). Exploration and exploitation within and across organizations. *The Academy of Management Annals*, 4(1), 109–155.

Lee, O. K., Sambamurthy, V., Lim, K. H., & Wei, K. K. (2015). How does IT ambidexterity impact organizational agility? *Information Systems Research*, 26(2), 398–417.

Leonidou, L. C., Leonidou, C. N., Fotiadis, T. A., & Aykol, B. (2015). Dynamic capabilities driving an eco-based advantage and performance in global hotel chains: The moderating effect of international strategy. *Tourism Management*, 50, 268–280.

Levinthal, D. A. (1997). Adaptation on rugged landscapes. *Management Science*, 43(7), 934–950.

Levinthal, D. A. (2011). A behavioral approach to strategy – What's the alternative? *Strategic Management Journal*, 32(13), 1517–1523.

Levinthal, D. A., & March, J. G. (1993). The myopia of learning. *Strategic Management Journal*, 14(S2), 95–112.

Lioukas, C. S., Reuer, J. J., & Zollo, M. (2016). Effects of information technology capabilities on strategic alliances: Implications for the resource-based view. *Journal of Management Studies*, 53(2), 161–183.

March, J. G. (1991). Exploration and exploitation in organizational learning. *Organization Science*, 2(1), 71–87.

McAfee, A., Brynjolfsson, E., Davenport, T. H., Patil, D. J., & Barton, D. (2012). Big data: The management revolution. *Harvard Business Review*, 90(10), 60–68.

McGrath, R. G. (2001). Exploratory learning, innovative capacity, and managerial oversight. *Academy of Management Journal*, 44(1), 118–131.

Menguc, B., Auh, S., & Yannopoulos, P. (2014). Customer and supplier involvement in design: The moderating role of incremental and radical innovation capability. *Journal of Product Innovation Management*, 31(2), 313–328.

Mom, T. J., Fourné, S. P., & Jansen, J. J. (2015). Managers' work experience, ambidexterity, and performance: The contingency role of the work context. *Human Resource Management*, 54(S1), s133–s153.

Mom, T. J., Van Den Bosch, F. A., & Volberda, H. W. (2009). Understanding variation in managers' ambidexterity: Investigating direct and interaction effects of formal structural and personal coordination mechanisms. *Organization Science*, 20(4), 812–828.

Mueller, V., Rosenbusch, N., & Bausch, A. (2013). Success patterns of exploratory and exploitative innovation: A meta-analysis of the influence of institutional factors. *Journal of Management*, 39(6), 1606–1636.

Nason, R. S., & Wiklund, J. (2018). An assessment of resource-based theorizing on firm growth and suggestions for the future. *Journal of Management*, 44(1), 32–60.

Nguyen, B., Yu, X., Melewar, T. C., & Hemsley-Brown, J. (2016). Brand ambidexterity and commitment in higher education: An exploratory study. *Journal of Business Research*, 69(8), 3105–3112.

O'Reilly III, C. A., & Tushman, M. L. (2013). Organizational ambidexterity: Past, present, and future. *Academy of management Perspectives*, 27(4), 324–338.

Patel, P. C., Fernhaber, S. A., McDougall-Covin, P. P., & van der Have, R. P. (2014). Beating competitors to international markets: The value of geographically balanced networks for innovation. *Strategic Management Journal*, 35(5), 691–711.

Peteraf, M. A. (1993). The cornerstones of competitive advantage: A resource-based view. *Strategic Management Journal*, 14(3), 179–191.

Piening, E. P. (2013). Dynamic capabilities in public organizations: A literature review and research agenda. *Public Management Review*, 15(2), 209–245.

Piening, E. P., & Salge, T. O. (2015). Understanding the antecedents, contingencies, and performance implications of process innovation: A dynamic capabilities perspective. *Journal of Product Innovation Management*, 32(1), 80–97.

Porter, M. E. (1979). How competitive forces shape strategy. In *Strategic Planning Readings*, (Ed. Smit, P. J.), 102–117, Juta & Co: Kenwyn, UK.

Porter, M. E. (1981). The contributions of industrial organization to strategic management. *Academy of Management Review*, 6(4), 609–620.

Powell, T. C., Lovallo, D., & Fox, C. R. (2011). Behavioral strategy. *Strategic Management Journal*, 32(13), 1369–1386.

Rubera, G., Chandrasekaran, D., & Ordanini, A. (2016). Open innovation, product portfolio innovativeness and firm performance: The dual role of new product development capabilities. *Journal of the Academy of Marketing Science*, 44(2), 166–184.

Schilke, O. (2014). On the contingent value of dynamic capabilities for competitive advantage: The nonlinear moderating effect of environmental dynamism. *Strategic Management Journal*, 35(2), 179–203.

Schilke, O., Hu, S., & Helfat, C. E. (2018). Quo vadis, dynamic capabilities? A content-analytic review of the current state of knowledge and recommendations for future research. *Academy of Management Annals*, 12(1), 390–439.

Schmitt, A., Raisch, S., & Volberda, H. W. (2018). Strategic renewal: Past research, theoretical tensions and future challenges. *International Journal of Management Reviews*, 20(1), 81–98.

Sibony, O., Lovallo, D., & Powell, T. C. (2017). Behavioral strategy and the strategic decision architecture of the firm. *California Management Review*, 59(3), 5–21.

Siggelkow, N., & Levinthal, D. A. (2003). Temporarily divide to conquer: Centralized, decentralized, and reintegrated organizational approaches to exploration and adaptation. *Organization Science*, 14(6), 650–669.

Simsek, Z., Heavey, C., Veiga, J. F., & Souder, D. (2009). A typology for aligning organizational ambidexterity's conceptualizations, antecedents, and outcomes. *Journal of Management Studies*, 46(5), 864–894.

Smith, W. K., & Tushman, M. L. (2005). Managing strategic contradictions: A top management model for managing innovation streams. *Organization Science*, 16(5), 522–536.

Stettner, U., & Lavie, D. (2014). Ambidexterity under scrutiny: Exploration and exploitation via internal organization, alliances, and acquisitions. *Strategic Management Journal*, 35(13), 1903–1929.

Teece, D. J. (2007). Explicating dynamic capabilities: The nature and microfoundations of (sustainable) enterprise performance. *Strategic Management Journal*, 28(13), 1319–1350.

Teece, D. J. (2014). A dynamic capabilities-based entrepreneurial theory of the multinational enterprise. *Journal of International Business Studies*, 45(1), 8–37.

Teece, D. J., Pisano, G., & Shuen, A. (1997). Dynamic capabilities and strategic management. *Strategic Management Journal*, 18(7), 509–533.

Teng, B. S. (2007). Corporate entrepreneurship activities through strategic alliances: A resource-based approach toward competitive advantage. *Journal of Management Studies*, 44(1), 119–142.

Tiwana, A. (2008). Do bridging ties complement strong ties? An empirical examination of alliance ambidexterity. *Strategic Management Journal*, 29(3), 251–272.

Tuncdogan, A. (2014). *Decision Making and Behavioral Strategy: The Role of Regulatory Focus in Corporate Innovation Processes*. Rotterdam: Erasmus Research Institute of Management (No. EPS–2014–334–S&E).

Tuncdogan, A., Boon, A., Mom, T., Van Den Bosch, F., & Volberda, H. (2017). Management teams' regulatory foci and organizational units' exploratory innovation: The mediating role of coordination mechanisms. *Long Range Planning*, 50(5), 621–635.

Tuncdogan, A., Van Den Bosch, F., & Volberda, H. (2015). Regulatory focus as a psychological micro-foundation of leaders' exploration and exploitation activities. *The Leadership Quarterly*, 26(5), 838–850.

Tushman, M. L., & O'Reilly, C. A., III (1996). Ambidextrous organizations: Managing evolutionary and revolutionary change. *California Management Review*, 38(4), 8–29.

Uotila, J., Maula, M., Keil, T., & Zahra, S. A. (2009). Exploration, exploitation, and financial performance: analysis of S&P 500 corporations. *Strategic Management Journal*, 30(2), 221–231.

Uyarra, E., & Flanagan, K. (2010). From regional systems of innovation to regions as innovation policy spaces. *Environment and Planning C: Government and Policy*, 28(4), 681–695.

Volberda, H. W. (2017). Comments on "mastering strategic renewal: Mobilising renewal journeys in multi-unit firms". *Long Range Planning*, Special Issue, Rethinking the Role of the Center in the Multidivisional Firm: A Retrospective, 50(1), 44–47.

Volberda, H. W., Baden-Fuller, Ch., & Van den Bosch, F. A. J. (2001). Mastering strategic renewal: Mobilizing renewal journeys in multi-unit firms. *Long Range Planning*, Special Theme: Mastering Strategic Renewal: Lessons from Financial Services, 34(2), 159–178.

Wang, C. L., Senaratne, C., & Rafiq, M. (2015). Success traps, dynamic capabilities and firm performance. *British Journal of Management*, 26(1), 26–44.

Wilden, R., & Gudergan, S. P. (2015). The impact of dynamic capabilities on operational marketing and technological capabilities: Investigating the role of environmental turbulence. *Journal of the Academy of Marketing Science*, 43(2), 181–199.

Williams, C., Chen, P. L., & Agarwal, R. (2017). Rookies and seasoned recruits: How experience in different levels, firms, and industries shapes strategic renewal in top management. *Strategic Management Journal*, 38(7), 1391–1415.

Yang, S. M., Fang, S. C., Fang, S. R., & Chou, C. H. (2014). Knowledge exchange and knowledge protection in interorganizational learning: The ambidexterity perspective. *Industrial Marketing Management*, 43(2), 346–358.

Yu, T., Patterson, P. G., & de Ruyter, K. (2013). Achieving service-sales ambidexterity. *Journal of Service Research*, 16(1), 52–66.

Zheng, Y., & Yang, H. (2015). Does familiarity foster innovation? The impact of alliance partner repeatedness on breakthrough innovations. *Journal of Management Studies*, 52(2), 213–230.

Zollo, M., & Winter, S. G. (2002). Deliberate learning and the evolution of dynamic capabilities. *Organization Science*, 13(3), 339–351.

Part 2

Core concepts

2 Strategic renewal and dynamic capabilities

Managing uncertainty, irreversibilities, and congruence

David J. Teece

Introduction

In environments where there is change, firms facing competition must also change. As Lou Gerstner, the CEO who revived IBM in the 1990s, put it:

> In anything other than a protected industry, longevity is the capacity to change ... Remember that the enduring companies we see are not really companies that have lasted for 100 years. They've changed 25 times or 5 times or 4 times over that 100 years, and they aren't the same companies as they were. If they hadn't changed, they wouldn't have survived. ... The leadership that really counts is the leadership that keeps a company changing in an incremental, continuous fashion. It's constantly focusing on the outside, on what's going on in the marketplace, what's changing there, noticing what competitors are doing.
>
> (quoted in Davis and Dickson, 2014: 125)

Gerstner's comment highlights that change—sometimes of a fundamental nature—is a requirement for survival in the corporate world. Indeed, the grandest problem in the field of strategic management is understanding how firms build and maintain competitive advantage over the long run. *Built to Last*, by Collins and Porras (1994), epitomizes this quest, and similar books are legion. Despite important insights produced by this stream of work, there is not much in the way of a deep understanding behind it. Deep understanding requires theory development, and the lack of it compromises the ability of other scholars to build on past work and advance knowledge about complex business phenomena.

The dynamic capabilities framework delves for deeper understanding. At its core, the concept of dynamic capabilities is about how firms can proactively maintain evolutionary fitness over time (Teece, Pisano, and Shuen, 1997). The broader dynamic capabilities framework identifies concepts relevant to the growth and semi-continuous strategic renewal of the business enterprise (Teece, 2007, 2014). It is outlined here and offered as a framework to help management theorists and practitioners better understand the interdependencies that impact enterprise performance in complex organizational settings undergoing change.

While, in one sense, the necessary change can be thought of as continuous, it is also important to recognize that industries (and firms, viewed as systems) evolve according to what evolutionary biologists call "punctuated equilibria" (Eldredge and Gould, 1972). Epochs of stasis can be interrupted at any time by shocks that demand change. Technological innovation, new business models, and macro political and economic factors are among the most common sources of disruption. The fact that the need for change is not continuous can bring a false sense of relief. Because disruption can arise at any time, firms must stand *ready* to change even if they are not actively changing all the time.

As a new enterprise grows and begins to put structure in place so as to be "efficient," change becomes harder and more costly. After all, establishing routines and rules and striving for efficiency are what good administration is all about; but bureaucracies tend to become bound by their rules. Problems arise when the well-defined job is no longer the job that needs to be done given the competitive circumstances the firm faces.

In limited cases, such as when a venture is in start-up mode, a major transformation may not be that hard. Indeed, with today's "lean start-up" modality, the mantra is "start, pivot, grow, pivot, retest, pivot" as often as required (Ries, 2011). This is both desirable and possible because, early in the life of a business (whether as a standalone venture or inside an established firm), everything is fluid, software code can be repurposed, and irreversible physical investments probably haven't been made. However, change becomes far more challenging when a business grows to more than a handful of people and has made irreversible commitments of one form or another. Effectuating change in such circumstances is hard, in part, because it requires convincing organizational members that what they are doing is no longer relevant—and possibly unhelpful—despite the fact that it was once meritorious. Change requires the reordering of priorities and learning new ways of doing things. These new ways may not only be unfamiliar; they may be outside the existing skills, capabilities, desires, and/or passions of the organization's members. Accordingly, when strategic renewal is called for, many organizational participants take umbrage at being told or encouraged to do things differently.

It is not only organizational members that have issues. The leadership team may be afflicted as well. Too often it's the case that the leadership team doesn't see the opportunity or threat in the first place, and renewal efforts, when they eventually occur, are crisis driven. Even if managers see a threat or opportunity, they may avoid pursuing the necessary change because it will be difficult, could fail, and would distract the organization from its current activities, which may, for the moment, be earning a decent return. And even if top or middle management instigates change, the leadership team may fail to lead effectively.

All of the above points are widely discussed in the management literature. However, little fundamental research has been conducted in organizational behavior, or in organizational theory more generally. Sadly, the theory of the firm in economics ignores many issues of transformation and renewal. As a step toward filling the gap, this chapter seeks to offer an economic explanation of the renewal challenge and endeavors to tie the theory and practice of strategic renewal into the dynamic capabilities framework.

The chapter begins by briefly explaining core theoretical issues in organizational change. The next section defines strategic renewal and dynamic capabilities, including what they are and what they are not, followed by a brief overview of the dynamic capabilities framework. The subsequent section analyzes how the use of the dynamic capabilities framework can enrich the study of strategic renewal by placing attention on important aspects of renewal that are too often overlooked: the sensing and seizing required to envision and plan renewal, and the cost of renewal. This is followed by a focus discussion on closing capability gaps. A brief section summarizes and concludes.

Theories of organizational change

The strategic renewal literature endeavors to provide guidance for resuscitating firm-level competitive advantage. The next section offers the dynamic capabilities framework as a theoretical underpinning for further development of the strategic renewal model. First, this section briefly identifies the essence of the problem and summarizes some of what the fields of economics and organizational behavior have said about organizational change.

Uncertainty and irreversibilities as culprits

In a hypothetical static (stationary) state of the world, somehow insulated from innovation and from political, social, or economic developments, one doesn't need dynamic frameworks. However, in today's relatively open and deregulated real-world business environment, this hypothetical isn't particularly relevant. Its main value is as a foil, or straw man.

It is important to recognize that there is a continuum of circumstances since some environments are more exposed to change than others. Moreover, scientific and technological breakthroughs arrive stochastically, and the prevailing level of uncertainty at a point in time can be deep or shallow. The deeper the uncertainty, the greater the need to be prepared for change and the greater the payoff to effectuating it quickly, other things being equal. As Frank Knight pointed out nearly a century ago:

> With uncertainty present, doing things, the actual execution of activity, becomes in a real sense a secondary part of life; the primary problem or function is deciding what to do and how to do it.
>
> (Knight, 1921: 268)

In other words, in an uncertain business environment, making the right investments is of primary importance, while optimizing current activities for efficiency is less important.

Because many investments are irreversible, there are fundamental managerial challenges when operating under uncertainty. Consider a factory in Country A making a product for export to Country B. If Country B has a change in government that leads to the disruption of trade, the economic value of the plant may plunge to zero if the equipment has no valuable alternative use. An investment structured more flexibly could have reduced the loss; however, it would have likely been less "efficient" in specific production modalities.

The basic textbook microeconomic model of the firm assumes that different production technologies (typically defined by particular capital-labor ratios), are available to the firm and can be selected and switched on with alacrity as input prices change. This is tantamount to an assumption of perfect reversibility. Writ large, such an assumption takes away the renewal challenge.

As Nobel laureate Ken Arrow noted, in cases where a commitment is costlessly reversible, uncertainty poses no problem for the firm (Arrow, 1973). There is no need to peer into the future because, if today's plan proves unprofitable, the firm can try something different tomorrow without penalty. There is no path dependence, and strategic renewal is a straightforward affair. Clearly, this is a caricature of real-world circumstances, with the possible exception of early-stage (software) start-ups. The lean start-up model, with its admonition to jump in, learn fast, and pivot quickly, implicitly assumes that irreversibilities are nonexistent or modest.

At the other extreme are businesses making large, complex products that face major irreversibilities. While new aircraft, ship, and automobile designs can be changed during early development at relatively low cost, change steadily becomes more and more costly as the level of commitment deepens through, for example, the adoption of cospecialized tooling. Most businesses of any size face at least a few decisions where a major commitment is involved. As Jeff Bezos, Amazon's founder and CEO, notes:

> Some decisions are consequential and irreversible or nearly irreversible—one-way doors—and these decisions must be made methodically, carefully, slowly, with great deliberation and consultation. If you walk through and don't like what you see on the other side, you can't get back to where you were before. We can call these Type 1 decisions. But most decisions aren't like that—they are changeable, reversible—they're two-way doors. If you've made a suboptimal Type 2 decision, you don't have to live with the consequences for that long. You can reopen the door and go back through. Type 2 decisions can and should be made quickly by high judgment individuals or small groups.
>
> (Bezos, 2016)

Bezos adds, however, that the methodical caution applied to irreversible decisions should not become the default for the typical decision process:

> As organizations get larger, there seems to be a tendency to use the heavyweight Type 1 decision-making process on most decisions, including many Type 2 decisions. The end result of this is slowness, unthoughtful risk aversion, failure to experiment sufficiently, and consequently diminished invention. We'll have to figure out how to fight that tendency.
>
> (ibid.)

Irreversibilities are not simply a design or production challenge flowing from past purchases of physical capital. Past commitments to strategic plans create strategic inflexibilities, too. Investment in new capacity to secure market share and deter investment by competitors is one example involving physical capital (Ghemawat and Caves, 1986; Shaanan, 1994). Investments in intangibles, such as research and advertising, also involve irreversible resource commitments (Caves, 1984). Purchase contracts for corporate assets or for products may include termination penalties—a type of partial irreversibility.

In general, the more specialized the capital (i.e., the lower its next-best-use value), the greater the irreversibility. A petroleum refinery, for instance, can be built to optimally process a particular type of oil (e.g., light sweet crude), and switching to a different feedstock (e.g. heavy sour crude) can have high costs, if it is even possible without building additional processing units. Such costs are usually well known and can be accurately calibrated.

Commitments to strategies also create inflexibilities in terms of organizational structures, culture, and human capital. These are different—and probably more subtle but more significant—types of irreversibility. Dorothy Leonard-Barton (1992) noted that adherence to the source of a company's strength can, under new circumstances, become a "core rigidity" that inhibits corporate renewal. In short, it is often harder to repurpose an organization—or redirect a strategy—than to repurpose a technology. The latter may involve little more than writing a check; the former requires organizational reengineering and must be done by marshalling the same internal forces that are inhibiting change. This is why outside hires or consultants are often needed as change agents. Leadership from the top management team is also essential. Without it, all the king's horses and all the king's men will not suffice to bring about transformation and renewal. Decisions surrounding organizational change are particularly sensitive to the level of uncertainty and the magnitude of irreversibilities involved. Change is harder to effectuate the greater the irreversibilities, whether they arise from physical, organizational, or human capital. Commitment strategies can amplify these considerations, too.

Commitment not only to strategies but to business models is another source of inflexibility. As Christensen, Baumann, Ruggles and Sadtler (2006) noted:

Organizations are set up to support their existing business models. Because implementing a simpler, less expensive, more accessible product or service could sabotage their current offerings, it's almost impossible for them to disrupt themselves. Therefore, the catalytic innovations that will bring new benefits to the most people are likely to come from outside the ranks of the established players.

(Christensen et al., 2006: 95)

However, Markides (2006) points out that business models are rarely overturned completely; companies wedded to the status quo merely have their market share trimmed to accommodate the loss of some, but not all, market segments to the rival business model. Consumers with different preferences can select suppliers using the model that best suits their needs, and some of them will remain wedded to a sub-optimal status quo out of inertia. Thus, a firm with an outdated business model can sometimes bump along without engaging in renewal until some other factor tips it over into a crisis.

It is not enough to simply identify factors that are barriers to change. There are equally important factors that stand in the way of building new capabilities once the barriers have been identified and overcome. In order to understand these challenges better, a critical review of the (economic) theory is necessary because much of the apparatus of economics stands in the way of understanding change in complex organizational settings. The field of organizational behavior, discussed in a subsequent section, does little better.

Economic theory: neoclassical and behavioral elements

There is little rigorous economic (or organizational) theory to help us understand the transformation of firms, much less their strategic renewal. However, as noted above, there are nevertheless important insights from economic theory with respect to uncertainty and irreversibilities. These can be the beginnings of a useful framework. In a later section, the concept of cospecialization will also be explored to illustrate the relevance of economic concepts.

As noted, the mainstream (textbook) economic theories of the firm— whether based on a production function, or on transaction or agency costs— tend to assume that adjustment is easy. This was implicit when Coase (1937) argued that firms form to minimize transaction costs; when Cyert and March (1963) explained that firms are animated by how their decisions are made; when Alchian and Demsetz (1972) argued that information costs explain the rise of firms;[1] and when Hart and Moore (1990) developed their incomplete contracting theory of the firm. The structures of these and other models are static; organizational change is either not considered or is not assigned a cost.

Ironically, the production function paradigm, while quite sterile, is perhaps the only major approach to the firm that specifies how change is brought about. However, the production function is not really a theory of the firm in that it provides no account of why firms exist. In the production function representation of firms, how much they produce and the technology they use (as represented by isoquants) are functions of relative prices. In textbook versions, there are no irreversibilities, Hence, a change in the price of inputs leads to substitution effects that the theory implicitly assumes managers can bring about at zero cost. Even though some economists (dating back to at least Alfred Marshall) recognize that adjustment isn't instantaneous, successful adjustment in production theory is almost always assumed to (magically) occur. There are, in most representations, no cultural or organizational barriers to change and no doubt in the minds of plant operators and managers about what the new equilibrium production schedule should look like. Changes are automatic, leaving little or no scope for managers to do more than set output levels by applying simple optimization criteria.[2] UCLA economist Harold Demsetz is quite honest about this simplification and the silence with which economic theory cloaks complex managerial decisions, noting that: "Neoclassical theory's objective is to understand price-guided, not management-guided, resource allocation" (Demsetz, 1997: 426).

Demsetz is one of the few economists to note that economic theory has shown a

> neglect of information problems that do not involve agency relationships. These are associated with planning in a world in which the future is highly uncertain, and they include problems of product choice, investment and marketing policies, and scope of operations.
>
> (ibid.: 428)

He is rightfully critical of the dominance of agency theory (e.g., Jensen and Meckling, 1976) in the theory of the firm, but he places too much emphasis on information as the primary issue, and this is especially true with respect to strategic renewal. Just as agency problems between owners and managers are largely irrelevant to strategic renewal (provided that the risks of managerial featherbedding and self-aggrandizement have already been addressed by incentive design), it would be an oversimplification to single out information as the biggest challenge. Lapses of leadership, intuition, or strategic vision are more central.[3]

The instinct of the economist, when something is difficult to achieve, is often to model it as "costly." However, such an approach can deflect attention from the reasons behind such costs. The transformation and renewal of a business of any size and scope is indeed costly, and there is an emerging literature in economics that includes organizational change as part of formal models. Brynjolfsson and Milgrom (2013) review several economic models of the adoption of new business practices, some of which reflect that the cost of change is larger when it increases in speed or varies from an existing trajectory. But, unless one has more to say about the activities to be done and the reasons for doing them, noting that they involve costs is not particularly insightful.

The new behavioral economics is less sanguine than neoclassical theory. In behavioral theory, there are hidden traps in decision making, irrationality is possible, rules of thumb are ubiquitous, and hubris is common. Sensible outcomes are not, as a result, assured. Loss aversion, for example, can lead to a fear of cannibalizing existing business even when a new business would prove far more lucrative.

Laboratory studies show that a significant bias in favor of maintaining the status quo is built in to the individual human mind. As Samuelson and Zeckhauser (1988: 10) point out, the status quo biases of people occur because of inertia, habit, convenience, fear, or innate conservatism. The bias is not a mistake, in the sense of a calculation error, but rather a means of avoiding cognitive discomfort. Simply being aware that a bias exists is generally inadequate to overcome it (Kahneman, Lovallo and Sibony, 2011). Moreover, bias often become even more ingrained in a team setting (Roberto, 2002). Solutions to the problem are still a work in progress.

In summary, economic theory, including the growing field of behavioral economics, has, to date, offered occasional deep insights but few practical solutions. Economic research on irreversibilities and strategic commitment is a good starting point; but the mainstream economic literature too often assumes that change is easy and costless, and that many unexplained problems can be distilled to information costs.

The organizational behavior literature, discussed next, acknowledge the difficulties involved in organizational change but does not go far enough because the conceptual underpinnings of its framework are weakly specified.

Organizational behavior: congruence, cospecialization, and modularity

Organizational behavior scholars recognize that change is hard. The reason given is that organizations are, as Nadler and Tushman correctly pointed out, made up of interacting subsystems that "must approach a state of congruence" (Nadler and Tushman, 1980: 37). To the limited extent that economists address this phenomenon, it has been modeled as complementarity or super-modularity (Brynjolfsson and Milgrom, 2013).

In any complex system, it's not always clear what will happen when one element is changed. Congruence theory developed out of general systems theory. Systems theory views organizations as social systems existing in different environments with units that must be connected if the organization is to be effective (Churchman, 1968). Interest in the application of systems theory to organizations peaked in the early 1970s (Ashmos and Huber, 1987). The underlying logic was later redeveloped into a pragmatic model of organizational alignment by Nadler and Tushman.

Organizational congruence appears to be the idea that certain things work best with certain other things, and that failure is all but guaranteed when elements of a system are mismatched. A counter-example attributed to systems theorist Russell Ackoff puts it this way:

Suppose you could build a dream car that included the styling of a Jaguar, the power plant of a Porsche, the suspension of a BMW, and the interior of a Rolls Royce. Put them together and what have you got? Nothing. They weren't designed to go together. They don't fit. The same is true of organizations.

(Mercer Delta Consulting, 2004: 7)

Congruence must extend beyond internal elements to the external environment. Williamson (1991), for example, describes the prototypical Japanese manufacturer of the 1980s as a coherent system of relations between employees, subcontracting suppliers, and banks that is tightly integrated and difficult to replicate elsewhere. This congruence extends to government ties; in 1991, the top 100 Japanese corporations had one or more former government bureaucrats on their board, including many serving as chairman or CEO (Schaede, 1995: 299).

In organizational terms, this means that renewal initiatives that are not integrated into a coherent whole will face an uphill battle for success. Promoting innovation, while penalizing participants in new ventures that fail, will be self-defeating. Likewise, offering high-power incentives without suitable measures of performance will likely fail to raise productivity.

Congruence is an important reason why it can be difficult for one firm to replicate distinctive capabilities developed elsewhere. GM tried to reverse its decline in the 1980s and 1990s by copying high-productivity Japanese practices, even setting up a jointly owned plant with Toyota in 1984. GM executives, however, focused on tangible features, such as equipment and factory layout, and struggled for more than a decade to understand the importance of the implicit "relational contracts" with employees that enabled Toyota's high-productivity corporate culture (Helper and Henderson, 2014).

Much of the congruence literature tends to place almost exclusive emphasis on the congruence of elements *within* the firm. Nadler and Tushman (1997), to their credit, include strategy and environmental variables in their model:[4]

If we also consider strategy, this view expands to include the fit between the organization and its larger environment; an organization is most effective when its strategy is consistent with its environment (in light of organizational resources and history) and when the organizational components fit the tasks necessary to implement that strategy.

(Nadler and Tushman, 1997: 34)

The tighter the fit (or congruence), the higher the performance. This insight is powerful. It is quite similar to the dynamic capabilities concept of evolutionary fitness.

However, key elements of the Nadler–Tushman framework are underdeveloped. The model is concerned primarily with resources, tasks, and goals inside the firm and appears to be lacking some critical components. A business model, for example, defines the architecture of a business, specifying the value proposition to the customer and how the delivery of value is to be monetized (Teece, 2010a). The business model must align with the organization and with its strategy (Teece, 2014). Even if all internal components fit well together, the organization may fail if it doesn't fit what the market requires and its business model is misspecified.

An example of a business model's evolutionary congruence can be seen in the dental supply e-commerce platform SourceOne Dental. SourceOne's initial business model, SourceOne version 1.0, consisted of an online platform for dentists to purchase products ranging from lidocaine to dental floss directly from manufacturers. SourceOne version 1.5 added to the platform's product line by including products sold through dealers. SourceOne version 2.0 included partnering with state dental associations. These state-level voluntary associations of dentists don't sell dental supplies, but they are able to partner with an online platform and endorse it (and not necessarily all the products it makes available) to their members.

Added elements in each version added robustness to the business model. The initial model, offering only manufacturers' products (albeit at a 30% discount), offered too narrow a selection. The addition of products from dealers dramatically expanded the scope of the offering, which enhanced the platform's appeal. Version 2.0 enabled state dental associations to "white-label" the platform, greatly enhancing the platform's legitimacy with dentists. It was the additive (perhaps multiplicative) combination (congruence) of the supply sources and the strategic partnerships that enhanced the platform's acceptance.

While achieving "congruence" is undoubtedly important, it is critical to understand the main elements of a business that most need to be congruent, especially when the environment is characterized by deep uncertainty (Teece, Peteraf and Leih, 2016). It is not clear how the Nadler–Tushman congruence model guides the identification of which elements need to be congruent. The dynamic capabilities framework, discussed in greater detail below, endeavors to provide some of that guidance.

The dynamic capabilities framework emphasizes cospecialization rather than congruence. Cospecialization (Teece, 1986, 2010b, 2016a) exists when there is a large gap between the value generated by two or more assets that are essential to each other and used jointly versus the value of each asset in its next best use.

The opposite of cospecialization is modularity. With modularity, a resource can be replaced in a system (following specified interface compatibility protocols or standards) without affecting other elements. Congruence for a particular element isn't necessary if a modular structure with specified interoperability protocols (compatibility standards) makes that element easily separable.

A better framework is one that sees the necessary technical, operational, and institutional cospecialization between capabilities and strategy, and the separability of many ordinary capabilities from dynamic capabilities. Ordinary capabilities for administration, operations, and governance are generally not important for long-term advantage and can frequently be outsourced.

A company like Dell can outsource manufacturing, thereby avoiding congruence problems between manufacturing and sales. Standardized interfaces obviate the need for congruence.

In short, congruence, as it's generally conceived, is too general and offers little operational insight into organizational architecture, interface dynamics, or firm boundary choices. The congruence concept is also missing other important variables for understanding firm performance, including the imitability of resources and the appropriability of the returns to technology (Teece, 2006).

The strategic renewal literature is positioned closer to the other end of the spectrum from congruence, focusing on practical challenges with limited reference to the underlying theoretical insights available from the social sciences. It asks too few fundamental questions. The dynamic capabilities framework attempts to provide a richer approach for understanding and effectuating organizational change, drawing on theoretical insights from multiple disciplines while providing linkages to the tools needed to drill down into the issues facing each company.

Efficiency versus efficacy: two fundamental genres of transformation and renewal

Strategic renewal is periodically necessary for the long-term survival of an organization. It's the process that helps a firm maintain evolutionary (as compared to technical) fitness (Helfat et al., 2007). Once an organization is beyond the start-up phase, it must constantly change or renew in order to maintain its fit with the environment. Selecting, modifying, and enhancing an organization's ordinary capabilities engages dynamic capabilities. This is to some extent conditional on environmental contingencies; dynamic capabilities are often of lesser value in truly stable business environments (Teece et al., 2016; Wilden and Gudergan, 2015).

Certain types of change are harder than others. The easiest form of change in most cases is the improvement of technical efficiency and cost control. The focus is on improving bottom-line results. This can be accomplished by downsizing: slash overhead costs, cut less-profitable product lines, fire workers and managers. This type of medicine is often required in controlled doses, as there is a general tendency for costs to creep up faster than revenues, or for revenue declines to run ahead of internal adjustments. Beer and Nohria (2000) call this "Theory E change" for economic efficiency. Its quintessential practitioner was "Chainsaw Al" Dunlop. "Neutron Jack" Welch's early period at GE also involved this type of restructuring.

While it is by no means easy to implement Theory E changes, it requires far less analysis, insight, and change in capabilities and culture than does more fundamental strategic renewal. More importantly, it is often the wrong type of change. The manufacturers of radio valves could not slash costs as a way to success once the transistor emerged; sailing ships could not just become faster and outcompete steam where reliability and predictability of arrival counted.

In this sense, the "E" in "Theory E" could just as well stand for (relative) "ease" as for "efficiency." When done well, Theory E change can bring short-term success, and Beer and Nohria (2000) cite Dunlop's reign at Scott Paper in the early 1990s as a case in point.

The real business of change, i.e., the hard part, is not about cutting costs but about applying dynamic capabilities to strengthen ordinary capabilities and focus on the right investment priorities. This, in turn, involves diagnosing opportunities and threats (sensing), acting on the diagnoses (seizing), and transforming the organization so that the old doesn't stand in the way of the new. The criterion is no longer efficiency; it is efficacy. Management must explore whether the company has the right products, business model, strategy, and supporting culture. Beer and Nohria (2000: 137) call this "Theory O" change (for organizational capability) and see it as manipulating "the 'software' of an organization—the culture, behavior, and attitudes of employees." These are some of the required elements. An organization must also learn from and respond to external signals, without depending too much on analysis provided by outside consultants.

Beer and Nohria's approach seems consistent with that of dynamic capabilities. However, much more is required. The strategic renewal considered in the dynamic capabilities framework is much broader. Having a "Theory O" culture is pointless if the strategy, products, and business models are maladapted to each other or to the environment.

The dynamic capabilities framework sees both Theory E and Theory O changes as important, the latter perhaps more so. O'Reilly and Tushman (2004, 2008) would argue that organizations need to be "ambidextrous," doing both together. However, the relationship may be asymmetrical. A company that operates on Theory O may be able to make judicious use of Theory E when necessary, but the opposite seems less likely to be true. Moreover, in VUCA (volatile, uncertain, complex, and ambiguous) environments, where dynamic capabilities are most essential, Theory E capabilities are of less moment, and might, in fact, get in the way of renewal and change (Teece et al., 2016).

Dynamic capabilities and strategic renewal

The above discussion has hinted that the dynamic capabilities framework has the potential to provide the conceptual grounding that has been missing in the understanding of transformation and renewal. The framework posits that "strong dynamic capabilities and good strategy anchored by difficult-to-imitate resources are the basis for the sustained competitive advantage displayed by a handful of firms that have endured for decades" (Teece, 2014: 328). Strategic renewal is, in fact, an integral part of the dynamic capabilities framework.

The dynamic capabilities framework resides between two diametrically opposed theoretical perspectives in the social sciences. On one side is the frictionless organizational world of mainstream microeconomic theory, discussed above, in which production technologies can be switched at will and with negligible cost. At the other end of the spectrum lies extreme path dependence, captured by the organizational ecology view, which postulates that some kind of organizational inertia prevents most firms from changing in response to existential strategic threats.[5]

The focus here will be on cases where upper and middle managers take an active role in anticipating and responding to alterations in the business environment, which Volberda, Baden-Fuller and Van Den Bosch (2001) call the "transformational renewal journey."[6] Their perspective is consistent with dynamic capabilities. The resulting organizational change processes are far from frictionless. Organizations with strong dynamic capabilities achieve greater flexibility than others.

The definitions of both strategic renewal and dynamic capabilities vary somewhat in the literature as to their nature and scope. In the next section, I define more carefully how these constructs will be used.

Dynamic capabilities: a synopsis[7]

Teece et al. (1997: 516) define dynamic capabilities as "the firm's ability to integrate, build, and reconfigure internal and external competences to address rapidly changing environments." These capabilities enable a firm "to continuously create, extend, upgrade, protect, and keep relevant" its resource base (Teece, 2007: 1319). Although dynamic capabilities are limited by some scholars to replicable routines (e.g., Helfat and Winter, 2011), the more comprehensive capabilities framework, as described by Teece (2014), incorporates both routines and managerial decision-making in a model of value creation and capture. Organizational routines and the strategic decisions of managers are tight complements; it's only by developing a deep knowledge of the routines embedded in a unit that managers can innovate and grow (Karim and Mitchell, 2004).

High-level dynamic capabilities, in which the role of managers is particularly prominent, involve a range of functions that can be categorized into sensing, seizing, and transforming (Teece, 2007). Transforming encompasses the implementation of strategic renewal; but sensing and the planning aspects of seizing—acting in concert with the process of strategy formation—are prerequisites for transformation. Moreover, the transformation itself involves changing an organization's mid- and lower-level capabilities, which involves closing capability gaps (Teece, 2017).

The dynamic capabilities framework synthesizes the roles of management and organizational routines (Teece, 2012). In many ways, it is both substitute and complement to the Nadler–Tushman congruence model. The capabilities framework encompasses not only a firm's dynamic capabilities, but also its ordinary capabilities and other tangible and intangible resources (Teece, 2014). The framework also shows how a firm's strategy needs to be taken into account. Strong dynamic capabilities, to be effective, require good strategy.

At the heart of the notion of sustained advantage in the dynamic capabilities perspective is ongoing strategic renewal, with the organization being steadily retuned in ways large and small in response to, or anticipation of, changes in the business environment.

Capabilities are distinct from strategy, and the two need to be harmonized. A strategy can be defined as "a coherent set of analyses, concepts, policies, arguments, and actions that respond to a high-stakes challenge" (Rumelt, 2011: 6). Capabilities and strategy co-evolve; capabilities provide inputs to, and then help enact, the strategy. A firm with strong dynamic capabilities is able to flesh out the details around strategic intent and to implement strategic actions quickly and effectively. When dynamic capabilities are weak, strategy must compensate by avoiding goals that are not feasible with the capabilities available.

Dynamic capabilities are at the apex of the multi-level capability hierarchy (Winter, 2003). At the base are operational and other ordinary capabilities, the countless everyday activities, administration, and basic governance that allow any organization to pursue a given production program, or defined set of activities, more or less efficiently. Above these are a level of dynamic capability "microfoundations" that can adjust and recombine existing ordinary capabilities as well as develop new ones (Teece, 2007). These second-order dynamic capabilities include new product development, expansion into new sales regions, the assignment of product mandates across divisions in large companies, and other actions that constitute astute managerial decision making under uncertainty.

Guiding these are the high-level dynamic capabilities by which management, supported by organizational processes, senses likely avenues of technological and market development, devises business models to seize new or changed opportunities, and determines the best configuration for the organization based on its existing form and the new plans for the future. This chapter uses the term "dynamic capabilities" to refer primarily to these high-order dynamic capabilities, i.e., the sensing, seizing, and transforming competencies that orchestrate the firm's ordinary capabilities and its second-order dynamic capabilities. High-level dynamic capabilities are those on which top management is (or should be) most focused. They are the most relevant for innovation and for selection of business models that address the problems and opportunities the company is endeavoring to solve/meet. In short, asset orchestration, when done well, can provide a basis for sustainable competitive advantage for considerable periods (Teece, 2007).

Part of asset orchestration is squeezing the most out of available resources. Signature processes (Gratton and Ghoshal, 2005) can enhance the productivity of these resources in ways that are difficult for rivals to copy because they arise from a company's unique history of competitive experiences, organizational learning, and management decisions. An example of such a signature process is the Toyota Production System, which developed gradually during the 1950s and '60s and wasn't codified until 1992. The system provided Toyota with a source of competitive advantage for decades despite numerous attempts at imitation by rivals, who eventually developed their own "lean manufacturing" techniques that have turned efficient manufacturing and continuous improvement into non-signature, ordinary, capabilities that are necessary for any competitor in the industry to be viable.

A microfoundation that has recently been growing in importance is data analytics, which can be used to increase the performance of ordinary capabilities beyond what was hitherto possible. As Bill Ruh, the head of GE Digital, said in a recent interview:

> In 2013, we launched a digital analytics capability called PowerUp for wind energy. By optimizing each blade for the wind it was receiving, the software could get 5 percent more electricity out of a wind turbine ... [which] equals 20 percent more profit for the wind farm owner. And it's been improved further—to 20 percent more electricity, with the same hardware. Similarly, for a North American railroad, we enabled a one mile per hour average increase in locomotive performance. For the railroad, that was equal to US$200 million in added profit each year. You can use similar analytics to boost fuel productivity for an airline or a power utility.
>
> (Kleiner and Sviokla, 2017)

This was not the result of changes in business model or strategy, but rather the application of one set of capabilities (data analytics) to another. Ruh describes the principle succinctly, noting that "owning an asset in itself isn't enough. You have to figure out how to get more productivity out of it than anyone else can" (Kleiner and Sviokla, 2017). The assets don't even need to be owned. Airbnb, for example, has profited by figuring out how homes can be "shared" and made to function not unlike hotel space, which has given Airbnb a higher valuation than Hilton Worldwide Holdings.[8] Airbnb is, of course, also a success story for innovative business model design. Business models are an output of a company's "sensing" and "seizing" capabilities.

All firms engage in sensing, seizing, and transforming to some extent; but most don't do it well enough to remain fully adapted to a changing business environment. The remainder of this chapter will emphasize outcomes for the case of strong dynamic capabilities, with the understanding that not every firm can accomplish what's described here to its utmost effectiveness. The strengthening of dynamic capabilities should be part of most firms' renewal plans.

Strong dynamic capabilities depend to a large degree on entrepreneurial managers who can sense opportunities and shifts in the business environment, assemble and orchestrate the resources to fulfill the goals of strategy, and lead the organization through the changes required to exploit the most promising avenues for future growth (Teece, 2016b). These activities involve setting an overall vision and culture that serve as the internal environment for organizational routines. Key dimensions of a dynamic corporate culture are openness to new ideas and willingness to change. For strong dynamic capabilities, these values need to be embraced at the individual, team, and unit levels in a way appropriate to each setting (Goffee and Jones, 1996). Tolerance for a diversity of views within a company is important for innovation and adaptability (Nemeth, 1997). Nevertheless, misunderstandings or disagreements between upper and middle managers about the new strategy can derail the renewal process, which places a premium on the leadership's ability to communicate clearly and persuasively (Floyd and Lane, 2000). There is a growing body of literature on the factors affecting how the top-down efforts of upper management are enacted (e.g., Glaser, Fourné and Elfring, 2015; Heyden, Sidhu and Volberda, 2015).

Strategic renewal

Notwithstanding success in asset orchestration, the necessity of major transformation and renewal will sooner or later crop up. Agarwal and Helfat (2009: 282) define strategic renewal as "the process, content, and outcome of refreshment or replacement of attributes of an organization that have the potential to substantially affect its long-term prospects." This definition is broad enough to cover the technological, organizational, and managerial aspects of change. The changes undertaken can be incremental or radical, proactive or reactive. The changes can be led primarily by upper management and/or by middle managers (Volberda et al., 2001). For example, when Kraft and Heinz merged in 2015, the two cultures needed to be brought into alignment. Bernardo Hees, the CEO overseeing the process, took a hands-on role:

> I talked to over 500 people individually. We always have some people that want to resist change. We came early on and said: "Look, this will be a high-performance company ... You're not going to have an office anymore. You're going to be empowered to do big things. You don't need to ask so many layers to take a decision." Sometimes they say: "Hey, that's not for me."
>
> (cited in Gasparro, 2017)

An accumulation of incremental changes does not seem to eliminate the need for periodic radical changes (Romanelli and Tushman, 1994). Nevertheless, radical change may need to be implemented gradually, especially when the organization initially proves resistant (Stopford and Baden-Fuller, 1994). In rare cases, resistance can overwhelm the CEO, as happened recently at Infosys, where an outsider brought in to transform the company resigned after three years because of what he called a "continuous drumbeat of distractions and negativity."[9]

To make a major change easier for employees to accept, it can sometimes be broken into smaller initiatives graded from easy to hard. Tackling the easier steps first can build the confidence of the change teams and the acceptance of employees.

Incremental renewal can involve any aspect of the enterprise and its offerings. The change involved is minor, in the sense that it does not necessitate change in other elements of the organization. At the product level, this can range from changing the features of an existing product to experimenting with entirely new products outside the company's core. At the organizational level, it could involve, for example, revamping a function such as customer service to make it more responsive or instituting new communication channels between different parts of the company to improve knowledge sharing.

Discontinuous renewal involves changing one or more fundamental aspects of the company, which is likely to affect interdependencies throughout the organization. The change could be, for example, in the company's overall product direction, the organization chart, the boundaries of the firm, or the geographic location of major operations. Change on one or more of these dimensions is inevitably challenging and likely to affect most of the others to some extent. When changing proactively, the company has more time to prepare, implement, and fine tune strategies to deal with the anticipated changes in the business environment (and/or to shape the environment); however, the key decisions are taken in the absence of full knowledge about the external shift. Waiting instead to implement change reactively provides greater certainty about the external environment but runs the risk of being too late to make an effective response. For implementation purposes, a potential advantage of waiting is that a greater sense of urgency in the face of an actual (rather than a predicted) threat may increase employee buy-in for the change.

In practice, many companies have proved to be unable to change fast enough or deeply enough in the face of existential threats. This can occur when management's focus on its existing customers blinds it to future threats from entry at the low end (Christensen, 1997) or the high end (Utterback and Acee, 2003) of its market. It can also occur because of the entrenched nature of the current knowledge and competences embedded throughout the organization (Henderson, 2006; Henderson and Clark, 1990). In other words, a major strategic renewal must not only engage all levels of management but also align the embedded routines in the relevant parts of the organization.

Linking the renewal literature and the capabilities perspective

As the preceding definitions indicate, transformation implicates a core cluster of capabilities in the dynamic capabilities framework; yet the linkages between renewal and capabilities are seldom made explicit. The renewal literature has, to date, largely ignored capabilities even when invoking capabilities-related concepts. This is the case, for example, with mentions of ambidexterity, which has been identified (outside the renewal literature) as a dynamic capability (O'Reilly and Tushman, 2008). This section will explore some of the ways that the dynamic capabilities framework can be used to enrich existing approaches to strategic renewal, including the inclusion of high-level dynamic capabilities and the incorporation of cost considerations.

High-level capabilities

The strategic renewal literature has acknowledged its affinity with dynamic capabilities, but has generally relegated high-level capabilities to a limited role.

According to Agarwal and Helfat (2009: 283), for example, "strategic renewal contains a role for dynamic capabilities through modification of the organization's resource base." This, however, refers only to microfoundational dynamic capabilities—the product development and other repeatable processes that are, in a sense, the tools that management wields to implement the vision developed using high-level capabilities.

At the other extreme, Flier, Van Den Bosch, and Volberda (2003), treat dynamic capabilities as primarily a theory of management intentionality, contrasting it with the organizational ecology approach of routine-driven inertia. This view ignores the importance of the routines that support the effectiveness of a firm's high-level capabilities.

Much of the strategic renewal literature implicitly assumes the existence of the sensing and (planning-stage) seizing that must occur before meaningful transformation/renewal can occur. A notable exception is research by Stopford and Baden-Fuller (1994: 528), who found that top managers needed to "*sense* the need for a new direction before much of substance could be started ... they had no hard data on which to base their beliefs."

Volberda et al. (2001: 165) capture some of the sensing and seizing activities (although without identifying them as high-level dynamic capabilities), particularly in their description of the "directed renewal journey" in which "management sets goals, scans the environments, searches for alternatives, chooses one, and monitors the process." The organizational learning approach to renewal in Crossan and Berdrow (2003), in which a process similar to Nonaka's (1991) SECI model of knowledge creation leads to the integration of individual insights into collective understanding, can also be interpreted as relevant to sensing.[10]

In short, the cognitive and organizational precursors of renewal have been given short shrift in the strategic renewal literature. Application of the dynamic capabilities framework can enrich existing analyses of strategic renewal in these areas by highlighting the importance of fundamental processes that have been largely neglected.

The cost of strategic renewal

While the strategic renewal literature is clear about the benefits of success, it is much less well developed in analyzing the cost of achieving it. The dynamic capabilities framework is well-suited to addressing this topic because, to a large extent, dynamic capabilities determine the cost of renewal. This is the case because a hallmark of strong dynamic capabilities is organizational agility, i.e., the firm's ability to adjust smoothly and quickly (Teece et al., 2016). The easier the transformation, the lower the total cost of the renewal. An agile organization must be able to innovate, learn, absorb, and improve processes identified by management as important to the future of the organization. Agility is, of course, impacted, but not inexorably, by the amount of irreversible investments and switching costs that are at issue. The ability to recognize the presence (or absence) of irreversibilities is critical for the correct calibration of the investment decision process (a key part of capabilities for seizing). As discussed earlier, the harder an investment will be to reverse, the more careful the decision process should be.

It's well known that poorly executed change initiatives can sap morale and run into delays due to employees' attachment to existing routines, especially in a firm that is currently performing satisfactorily. But an analysis of delays or other costs is largely absent from the strategic renewal literature. The dynamic capabilities framework was created, in part, to explore these cost concerns:

> Change is costly and so firms must develop processes to minimize low pay-off change. The ability to calibrate the requirements for change and to effectuate the necessary adjustments would appear to depend on the ability to scan the environment, to evaluate markets and competitors, and to quickly accomplish reconfiguration and transformation ahead of competition.
>
> (Teece et al., 1997: 521)

Dynamic capabilities are inherently specific to each firm, and the costs of developing and implementing these capabilities vary considerably based on the irreversibilities involved, as discussed earlier. Different approaches to hypothesis generation and sensemaking, for example, also involve different levels of expense (Russell, Stefik, Pirolli and Card, 1993). A study of a Dutch multinational by Glaser et al. (2015) showed that a potential cost lies in how the sensing activities of top managers and middle managers are organized. If both top and middle managers are actively seeking new sources of knowledge and developing new ideas, then the middle managers are likely to end up with conflicting guidance that reduces their ability to engage in business unit renewal unless there is some degree of coordination between the top and middle levels about the focus of the sensing activities. Various approaches to embedding transformation capabilities are equally variable in terms of cost.

Transformation is hardest (most costly) for large, established enterprises with irreversible assets, entrenched routines, and complex organizational linkages. Software-based start-ups perhaps lie at the other extreme; pivoting from one business model to another and modifying code along the way. These small firms can experiment and then pivot as new understandings emerge because the switching costs of repurposing code are often relatively low.

The speed at which an organization is able to alter its course can be critical. In some cases, early entry in a new market will establish first-mover advantages. For an incumbent, a quick response to a rival's behavior may be necessary to avoid losing its existing market position.

There is no standard definition of strategic agility, although the common-sense understanding of agility (the power to move quickly and easily) is apt. Doz and Kosonen (2008: 65) define strategic agility as the capacity to continuously adjust strategic direction in a core business to create value.[11] Teece et al. (2016: 17) provide a more capability-oriented definition: the capacity of an organization to effectively redirect its resources to higher-yield activities as internal and external circumstances warrant.

Agility is costly to develop and maintain, but in dynamic environments it's even more costly if it is absent (Teece et al., 2016). There are multiple ways for organizations to achieve a degree of flexibility, including maintaining slack in certain resources to permit fast deployment and diversifying the range of product markets served. Some provide protection against negative shocks and others permit rapid response to positive opportunities. However, as has long been recognized, agility always comes with a trade-off. Stigler (1939: 311), for example, noted that plant-level flexibility will generally come at the expense of operational efficiency.

One means of enhancing both agility and efficiency is the use of stronger implicit relational contracts with employees. These informal understandings between the firm and its employees rely heavily on the firm's credibility and on the consistency and clarity with which it is exercised (Gibbons and Henderson, 2012). As this suggests, these implicit contracts take time and care to establish, and strategic renewal must contend with the informal bargaining cost and complexity of realignment of the employment relation (Wernerfelt, 2016). Far from presenting a trade-off, creating an environment in which employees feel responsible toward the competitiveness of the firm, are able to solve minor problems before they fester, and are eager to share insights gleaned from customers and competitors ideally makes the company both more nimble and more productive (Hamel and Prahalad, 1993).

The design of flexible organizations is part of high-level "seizing" capabilities and is just one example of how strong dynamic capabilities can yield organizational agility while minimizing the associated friction. The trade-off between efficiency and agility may never be eliminated; but organizations with strong dynamic capabilities can experience lower costs for maintaining a given level of organizational agility.

Closing capability gaps

Renewal almost always entails developing or acquiring new-to-the-company ordinary or microfoundational capabilities in order to pursue a new strategy. The new capabilities required may be generated internally or sourced externally. The ability to select the best mode for obtaining a new capability is itself a critical dynamic capability (Capron and Mitchell, 2009). Capability selection and capability augmentation through managerially guided investment activity is absent from other strategic management perspectives.

The firm may also need to strengthen its high-level dynamic capabilities as part of the renewal process. Stopford and Baden-Fuller (1994) analyzed the experience of ten firms that had undergone a strategic renewal and found that middle managers needed to learn new methods of team-based problem solving in order to make progress. These new methods of resolving dilemmas then became part of the foundation of the companies' new competitive advantage.

An important consideration in renewal is the gap between the existing capabilities of the firm and those that need to be developed to implement the new strategy. The ability to recognize what capabilities are needed for a new strategy and then to develop them efficiently and effectively are key parts of dynamic capabilities (Feiler and Teece, 2014). The search begins by examining the match between a proposed business model and the firm's existing capabilities. An analysis of existing capabilities needs an objective point of view that is detailed and realistic. Organizational instincts tend to compel the exaggeration of current capabilities.

Capability gaps are different from resource gaps. There may be budgets and people assigned to a project; but, if the people are not chosen correctly, performance will be placed in jeopardy. Moreover, teams need time and guidance to develop their routines and develop working relationships. There may be a new piece of specialized equipment, but it takes time for it to be embraced, fully understood, and integrated into new routines. Many projects and programs fail because of an organization's inability to develop and integrate the capabilities needed to deliver on a new objective. Creating a capability may not simply be a matter of assembling assets; it may involve the process of creating a new intangible asset (Brynjolfsson, Hitt and Yang, 1998).

One way of thinking about capability gaps is in terms of the "distance" separating the existing and the desired capabilities (Teece, 2017). The greater the distance to be covered, the greater the cost in terms of time, effort, and expense. Capability distance can be calculated on at least three dimensions: (i) technical distance can be thought of in terms of how closely related the goal-state technology is to the firm's existing knowledge in terms of skills, patent class, etc. (ii) market distance increases as the firm reaches for new pools of customers, whether in a higher or lower market segment or in a new geography with different cultural and/or regulatory norms; and (iii) business model distance involves dimensions such as the suitability of the existing cost structure, supply relationships, and revenue model for the target activity.

There are studies that address how to close each type of gap in isolation, but few to help understand how to manage all three at once. The changing of all three at once involves managing radical transformation. Any large organization is a complex system with social, economic, and other dimensions as well as systemic effects. The effort and attention needed to close multiple capability gaps is non-linear.

It is a challenge to actually understand the location and magnitude of capability deficiencies. Often it is only after an organization falls short in one of its strategic initiatives that the true size of the gap(s) will be apparent. The early phase of an innovative project may be satisfactory; but, as it progresses, problems begin to crop up, the senior team has to get more and more involved, and the goal slips further away. Management may have thought that a particular capability, such as supply-chain management, was in place only to discover that it was inadequate to the needs of a new product or strategy.

There are few well-documented processes for bringing new capabilities online, and almost all organizations lack internal reference points for how to do what has never done before. There may be individuals with some of the requisite knowledge, but management may not know who they are. Moreover, having never experienced it before, the organization may not know what "excellence" in the target capability looks like.

Some (mainly ordinary) capabilities have multiple options by which they may be acquired; but most boil down to some form of the make/buy/rent options:

- developing the new capability in the existing organization by selecting and developing people, teams, tools, then providing them the necessary training and/or learning resources;
- acquiring the new capability by purchasing an existing organization or by employing key individuals/consultants with the knowhow required to implement it, after which some learning by existing personnel will still be needed; or
- adding the new capability through more or less temporary contracts and consultants.

The "make" option takes time, effort, and skill, but may be the only viable option for microfoundation capabilities such as product development. A robust capability-building process requires the conscious attention of management. To position the organization for excellence in a new capability using the existing internal team can be particularly challenging because in-house learning processes are difficult to accelerate. Success also requires accountability, which is aided by the use of objective measures against agreed-upon goals.

The "buy" option can be problematic as a first step, though it is often the one taken. Buying often involves hiring; but whom to hire? The "buy" option to add or enhance capabilities should probably be lower ranked unless or until it is understood with reasonable precision what is needed, including what constitutes excellence in the target capability.

The "rent" option can be a powerful accelerator for capability deployment, especially when the capability is competitively available and unlikely to contribute to competitive advantage. An inappropriate candidate for outsourcing, for example, is pioneering R&D, particularly where the firm needs to "pace" the technology so that it develops in line with other parts of a system (Chesbrough and Teece, 1996). For cases where a capability needs to be built but is well understood at other organizations, the use of outside consultants can jump-start the internal establishment of the capability at a best-practice level. Open innovation (Chesbrough, 2003)—involving the external sourcing of ideas, concepts, and technologies—can also be used judiciously. A barrier to the success of using outside sources of skills and knowledge to close capability gaps can be resistance from the existing organization. The "rent" option therefore requires conscious direction by senior leaders to promulgate a strategic vision and set achievable goals and expectations for the changes involved.

The closing of capability gaps requires leadership by managers. An organization won't embrace transformation unless its managers are clearly committed. Employees will not engage in the necessary learning unless they are encouraged—and given the means—to do so. During the initial learning phase, effectiveness is more important than efficiency. A focus on the maintenance of financial performance over the creation of new capabilities actually impairs the ability to deliver better results in the longer run.

Building a capability is likely to take longer if it is conducted entirely in-house, but taking a shortcut via acquisition can be problematic. An acquired capability will still need to be learned and absorbed by the acquiring firm's existing employees, which reduces the time saved. Moreover, management, prior to the acquisition, needs a deep understanding of the capability and how excellence is measured, failing which a hasty acquisition could turn out to be inadequate.

Getting new capabilities into place across all needed functions and geographies adds another dimension to the challenge. This requires alignment. In common practice, "alignment" is often used to mean acquiescence on a particular issue. It rarely means what it needs to mean, namely mutual understanding and agreement on actions to be taken in support of strategic goals. Acquiescence is shallow and easily abrogated. Strategic alignment is deep, committed and accountable.

For senior managers, the maintenance of organizational coherence requires the ability to know the manner in which processes and functions can fit together. Managers must learn to synchronize the efforts of marketing, R&D, operations, quality assurance, etc., to understand their perspectives, and to effectively draw them into a coordinated whole in ways specific to a particular company at a particular stage in its trajectory. Being able to understand who the stakeholders are, to elicit their needs, to develop interactive business processes, to create internal documentation and communication systems are additional examples of capabilities that are difficult and probably inappropriate to outsource. In fact, these integrative capabilities are often invisible to organizations, with management being only vaguely aware of the learning that needs to take place. An integrative capability may emerge in the course of a project, but it may not persist without conscious recognition and nurturing. If consciously developed, such a capability can generalize and become a dynamic capability.

Building and implementing capabilities is hard; the silver lining is that, if well-built, they can be difficult for others to imitate. Put differently, the absence of a market for the most valuable capabilities means that long-term profits can flow from building relevant capabilities and harnessing them to a good strategy.

Conclusions

It is well accepted that the long-term growth and survival of a business is never guaranteed. Most firms fail, and very few survive for a generation, let alone a century. Those that do must innovate or otherwise morph so as to be able to satisfy, in the face of strong competition, an evolving customer demand. Despite the obvious importance of the survival issue, there is little fundamental research—and hence very little theory—on organizational renewal and long-run growth and survival. For instance, the important work of Collins and Porras (1994) is not grounded in any recognizable theory of business and economic change. Absent a theory, or even a framework, it is hard for knowledge to advance cumulatively. The goal of science is to produce theory that can offer a stable encapsulation of facts that generalize beyond the particular.

An undervalued aspect of successful scientific inquiry is the quality of the questions posed. Selecting consequential questions requires both creativity and discipline and is aided by a deep understanding of intellectual history. The renewal literature has been slow to ask fundamental questions and suffers from a paucity of good empirical research. As Stokes (1997: 73) has pointed out, empirical research can help develop a deeper theoretical understanding of phenomena.

Deepening our understanding of strategic renewal will add to the fundamental understanding of organizational evolution and will also have practical benefits for managers. The real world that managers face is far removed from the assumptions of both neoclassical economics (frictionless change) and organizational ecology (extreme path dependence that makes change well-nigh impossible). However, it is not adequate to say that the truth lies in the middle, because the truth for any particular organization is context-dependent.

Economic theory has also fallen short in analyzing strategic change. Nevertheless, it can provide useful insights into renewal. Both the cost of change and the opportunity cost of not changing must be taken into account. Arrow's brilliant observation that, absent uncertainty, the problem of change would go away serves to remind us that the economic factors driving renewal are too easily overlooked. In this chapter, an effort has been made to link theoretical concepts like uncertainty and irreversibilities to some of the practical challenges faced by managers attempting to guide their business into the future.

The dynamic capabilities framework is employed to help frame the renewal problem and to bring focus to the discussion of capability development and augmentation. Once identified as necessary, how are new capabilities developed? How can existing capabilities be enhanced? Because the literature on this issue is so scant, even the short discussion of the particular challenges included in this chapter may turn out, in due course, to be its main contribution.

Renewal begins by questioning constraints on an organization's ability to compete, to grow, and to prosper. It is necessary, through sensing, to determine what should change to improve the organization's future outlook. Abductive reasoning, which includes the development of conjectures to explain patterns in pools of data, can be used to create hypotheses about what to do (Hanson, 1958: 85; Teece et al., 2016). Managers must then identify a path by which the renewal goals can be reached and be prepared to modify its course as progress is made. Once a new course is set, new and augmented capabilities are almost always required. If they cannot be bought, they must be built.

Systems thinking is implicated in this process because of the interdependencies inside and outside any organization. The dynamic capabilities framework is a tool that can aid managers to adopt a systems mindset. The way in which the framework can be implemented at a given company depends on the particular issues (technology change, competitive pressure, institutional shift, etc.) to be addressed, as well as the current state of the firm's dynamic capabilities. While the literatures on each type of issue can provide detailed guidance about potential solutions, the dynamic capabilities framework can help provide the system-level perspective needed to ensure that a unidimensional change does not undermine strategic or organizational coherence. Absent such a mindset, the unintended consequences of renewal efforts may not only disturb but actually overwhelm the renewal process.

Addressing strategic renewal within the dynamic capabilities framework will help to identify and clarify links to other theories. It will also open new avenues of research to enrich current conceptions of the managerial activities and organizational routines that lead to successful strategic renewal.

Strategic renewal is critical to the creation of long-run competitive advantage, the underlying motivation behind the dynamic capabilities framework. Managers, consultants, and policy makers alike are perpetually interested in understanding how individual firms grow, renew themselves, and create durable advantage. Despite the attention it receives, this remains perhaps the most perplexing and fundamental question in business and economics.

Acknowledgments

I wish to thank Greg Linden and Mariano Heyden for helpful comments and other assistance.

Notes

1 Alchian and Demsetz (1972) argued that, while team production produces extra output, cooperative teamwork is difficult because of shirking and the difficulty of detecting who in a team is shirking—a problem of moral hazard. Monitoring is therefore necessary, which creates a role for managers, implying the need for a hierarchical organization. Note that "shirking" suggests that what needs to be prioritized is clear, when, under deep uncertainty, it is not. Hence, this perspective provides few insights into renewal.

2 Paul Samuelson, in his seminal book *Foundations of Economic Analysis* (1947), suggested that a firm would react more to input prices in the long run than in the short run because, over time, there will be more inputs that can be adjusted. He called this the Le Chatelier effect. Whether in the short run or long, economic theory assumes that firms always adjust; it's axiomatic.

3 Organizations have a range of manager personalities, each of whom is likely to excel in particular roles. Change leadership should be reserved for those most able

to inspire others. Leadership qualities may not be entirely innate because perceptions of charisma are driven in part by managers undertaking change-promoting behaviors (Nohe, Michaelis, Menges, Zhang and Sonntag, 2013).

4   A similar approach was put forth by Miles and Snow (1994).

5   Volberda, Baden-Fuller and Van Den Bosch (2001) call the organizational ecology view (e.g., Hannan and Freeman, 1977), at least in cases where the firm survives, a type of "emergent renewal journey" in which management is reactive to market changes and passive with regard to internal innovation. They cite the example ING in the early 1990s as a firm whose leadership was more focused on managing large mergers and acquisitions than on facilitating internal alignment. In the dynamic capabilities framework, management that is purely passive and reactive is suggestive of weak dynamic capabilities.

6   Volberda, Baden-Fuller and Van Den Bosch (2001) also identify two intermediate "journeys" in which the initiative for change derives more from middle managers ("facilitated renewal") or from top management ("directed renewal"). These distinctions, while important when discussing specific organizations, will not be discussed further in this article, which will focus primarily on a specific archetype of strong dynamic capabilities in which top management plays a guiding role. The dynamic capabilities framework can readily accommodate cases where top management fosters an internal selection environment that enables major change to originate at lower levels of management, as in the well documented example of Intel's shift from memory chips to microprocessors in the 1980s (Burgelman, 1994). However, the ideal in the dynamic capabilities framework is for all managers to be, to some extent, entrepreneurial (and empowered).

7   Dynamic capabilities is a very active research topic, and numerous variations of the framework co-exist. For a recent overview and synthesis of the large literature on the topic, see Wilden, Devinney and Dowling (2016). Their "House of Dynamic Capabilities" approach is largely consistent with the brief overview of my own research provided here.

8   Airbnb's March 2017 funding round put its valuation at $31 billion. Hilton's market capitalization in mid-July 2017 is $20.4 billion. The market capitalization of Marriott International is higher, at $38.6 billion.

9   "Resignation letter of Vishal Sikka," *The Hindu*, August 18, 2017. www.thehindu.com/business/resignation- letter-of-vishal-sikka/article19515587.ece.

10   See Schmitt, Raisch and Volberda (2016) for a discussion of the sometimes mutually exclusive ways that learning and capabilities have been represented in the strategic renewal literature.

11   Doz and Kosonen's analysis of strategic agility is essentially a reformulation higher-order dynamic capabilities. In an article (Doz and Kosonen, 2010: 371), they describe the three requirements for strategic agility as awareness of strategic developments, the ability of top management to act rapidly, and the ability to redeploy resources rapidly. These map directly on to sensing, seizing, and transforming.

References

Agarwal, R., & Helfat, C. E. 2009. Strategic renewal of organizations. *Organization Science*, 20(2), 281–293.

Alchian, A. A., & Demsetz, H. 1972. Production, information costs, and economic organization. *American Economic Review*, 62(5), 777–795.

Arrow, K. J. 1973. Information and Economic Behavior. Technical Report No. 14. Cambridge, MA: Harvard University. www.dtic.mil/cgi-bin/GetTRDoc?AD=AD 0768446.

Ashmos, D. P., & Huber, G. P. 1987. The systems paradigm in organization theory: Correcting the record and suggesting the future. *Academy of Management Review*, 12(4), 607–621.

Beer, M., & Nohria, N. 2000. Cracking the code of change. *Harvard Business Review*, 78(3), 133–141.

Bezos, J. 2016. 2015 Letter to shareholders. www.sec.gov/Archives/edgar/data/1018724/ 000119312516530910/d168744dex991.htm.

Brynjolfsson, E., Hitt, L. M., & Yang, S. 1998. Intangible assets: How the interaction of computers and organizational structure affects stock market valuations. In *Proceedings of the International Conference on Information Systems*, pp. 8–29. Atlanta, GA: Association for Information Systems.

Brynjolfsson, E., & Milgrom, P. 2013. Complementarity in organizations. In R. Gibbons & J. Roberts (Eds.), *The Handbook of Organizational Economics*, pp. 11–55. Princeton, NJ: Princeton University Press.

Burgelman, R. A. 1994. Fading memories: A process theory of strategic business exit in dynamic environments. *Administrative Science Quarterly*, 39(1), 24–56.

Capron, L., & Mitchell, W. 2009. Selection capability: How capability gaps and internal social frictions affect internal and external strategic renewal. *Organization Science*, 20(2), 294–312.

Caves, R. E. 1984. Economic analysis and the quest for competitive advantage. *American Economic Review*, 74(2), 127–132.

Chesbrough, H., & Teece, D. J. 1996. When is virtual virtuous: Organizing for innovation. *Harvard Business Review*, 74(1), 65–73.

Chesbrough, H. W. 2003. *Open Innovation: The New Imperative for Creating and Profiting from Technology*. Boston, MA: Harvard Business School Press.

Christensen, C. M. 1997. The *Innovator's Dilemma: When New Technologies Cause Great Firms to Fail*. Boston, MA: Harvard Business School Press.

Christensen, C. M., Baumann, H., Ruggles, R., & Sadtler, T. M. 2006. Disruptive innovation for social change. *Harvard Business Review*, 84(12), 94–101.

Churchman, C. W. 1968. *The Systems Approach*. New York, NY: Dell.

Coase, R. H. 1937. The nature of the firm. *Economica*, 4(16), 386–405.

Collins, J. C., & Porras, J. I. 1994. *Built to Last: Successful Habits of Visionary Companies*. New York, NY: HarperBusiness.

Crossan, M. M., & Berdrow, I. 2003. Organizational learning and strategic renewal. *Strategic Management Journal*, 24(11), 1087–1105.

Cyert, R. M., & March, J. G. 1963. *A Behavioral Theory of the Firm*. Englewood Cliffs, NJ: Prentice-Hall.

Davis, I., & Dickson, T. 2014. Lou Gerstner on corporate reinvention and values. *McKinsey Quarterly*, 2014(3), 123–129. www.mckinsey.com/~/media/McKinsey/ McKinsey%20Quarterly/Digital%20Newsstand/2014%20Issues%20McKinsey% 20Quarterly/Management%20the%20next%2050%20years.ashx (accessed January 23, 2017).

Demsetz, H. 1997. The firm in economic theory: A quiet revolution. *American Economic Review*, 87(2), 426–429.

Doz, Y., & Kosonen, M. 2008. *Fast Strategy: How Strategic Agility Will Help You Stay Ahead of the Game*. Harlow, England: Pearson/Longman.

Doz, Y. L., & Kosonen, M. 2010. Embedding strategic agility: A leadership agenda for accelerating business model renewal. *Long Range Planning*, 43(2), 370–382.

Eldredge, N., & Gould, S. J. 1972. Punctuated equilibria: An alternative to phyletic gradualism. In T. J. M. Schopf (Ed.), *Models in Paleobiology*, pp. 82–115. San Francisco, CA: Freeman, Cooper & Co.

Feiler, P., & Teece, D. 2014. Case study, dynamic capabilities and upstream strategy: Supermajor EXP. *Energy Strategy Review*, 3, 14–20.

Flier, B., Van Den Bosch, F. A., & Volberda, H. W. 2003. Co-evolution in strategic renewal behaviour of British, Dutch and French financial incumbents: Interaction of environmental selection, institutional effects and managerial intentionality. *Journal of Management Studies*, 40(8), 2163–2187.

Floyd, S. W., & Lane, P. J. 2000. Strategizing throughout the organization: Managing role conflict in strategic renewal. *Academy of Management Review*, 25(1), 154–177.

Gasparro, A. 2017. Kraft Heinz's CEO on cost-cutting, dealmaking and Oprah. *wsj.com*, May 16. www.wsj.com/articles/kraft-heinzs-ceo-on-cost-cutting-dealmaking-and-oprah-1494932401.

Ghemawat, P., & Caves, R. E. 1986. Capital commitment and profitability: An empirical investigation. *Oxford Economic Papers*, 38(S), 94–110.

Gibbons, R., & Henderson, R. 2012. Relational contracts and organizational capabilities. *Organization Science*, 23(5), 1350–1364.

Glaser, L., Fourné, S. P., & Elfring, T. 2015. Achieving strategic renewal: The multi-level influences of top and middle managers' boundary-spanning. *Small Business Economics*, 45(2), 305–327.

Goffee, R., & Jones, G. 1996. What holds the modern company together? *Harvard Business Review*, 74(6), 133–148.

Gratton, L., & Ghoshal, S. 2005. Beyond best practice. *MIT Sloan Management Review*, 46(3), 49–57.

Hamel, G., & Prahalad, C. K. 1993. Strategy as stretch and leverage. *Harvard Business Review*, 71(2), 75–84.

Hannan, M. T., & Freeman, J. 1977. The population ecology of organizations. *American Journal of Sociology*, 82(5), 929–964.

Hanson, N. R. 1958. *Patterns of Discovery: An Inquiry into the Conceptual Foundations of Science*. Cambridge: Cambridge University Press.

Hart, O., & Moore, J. 1990. Property rights and the nature of the firm. *Journal of Political Economy*, 98(6), 1119–1158.

Helfat, C. E., Finkelstein, S., Mitchell, W., Peteraf, M. A., Singh, H., Teece, D. J., & Winter, S. G. 2007. *Dynamic Capabilities: Understanding Strategic Change in Organizations*. Oxford, UK: Blackwell.

Helfat, C. E., & Winter, S. G. 2011. Untangling dynamic and operational capabilities: Strategy for the (N) ever-changing world. *Strategic Management Journal*, 32(11), 1243–1250.

Helper, S., & Henderson, R. 2014. Management practices, relational contracts, and the decline of general motors. *Journal of Economic Perspectives*, 28(1), 49–72.

Henderson, R. 2006. The innovator's dilemma as a problem of organizational competence. *Journal of Product Innovation Management*, 23(1), 5–11.

Henderson, R. M., & Clark, K. B. 1990. Architectural innovation: The reconfiguration of existing product technologies and the failure of established firms. *Administrative Science Quarterly*, 35(1), 9–30.

Heyden, M. L., Sidhu, J. S., & Volberda, H. W. 2015. The conjoint influence of top and middle management characteristics on management innovation. *Journal of Management*, 44(4), 1505–1529.

Jensen, M. C., & Meckling, W. H. 1976. Theory of the firm: Managerial behavior, agency costs and ownership structure. *Journal of Financial Economics*, 3(4), 305–360.

Kahneman, D., Lovallo, D., & Sibony, O. 2011. Before you make that big decision. *Harvard Business Review*, 89(6), 50–60.

Karim, S., & Mitchell, W. 2004. Innovating through acquisition and internal development: A quarter-century of boundary evolution at Johnson & Johnson. *Long Range Planning*, 37(6), 525–547.

Kleiner, A., & Sviokla, J. 2017. The thought leader interview: Bill Ruh. *Strategy+Business*. www.strategy-business.com/article/The-Thought-Leader-Interview-Bill-Ruh (accessed September 11, 2017).

Knight, F. 1921. *Risk, Uncertainty and Profit*. New York, NY: Augustus Kelley.

Leonard-Barton, D. 1992. Core capabilities and core rigidities: A paradox in managing new product development. *Strategic Management Journal*, 13(S1), 111–125.

Markides, C. 2006. Disruptive innovation: In need of better theory. *Journal of Product Innovation Management*, 23(1), 19–25.

Mercer Delta Consulting. 2004. The congruence model: A roadmap for understanding organizational performance. http://ldt.stanford.edu/~gwarman/Files/Congruence_Model.pdf (accessed April 19, 2017).

Miles, R. E., & Snow, C. C. 1994. *Fit, Failure and the Hall of Fame*. New York, NY: Macmillan.

Nadler, D. A., & Tushman, M. L. 1980. A model for diagnosing organizational behavior. *Organizational Dynamics*, 9(2), 35–51.

Nadler, D. A., & Tushman, M. L. 1997. *Competing by Design: The Power of Organizational Architecture*. New York, NY: Oxford University Press.

Nemeth, C. J. 1997. Managing innovation: When less is more. *California Management Review*, 40(1), 59–74.

Nohe, C., Michaelis, B., Menges, J. I., Zhang, Z., & Sonntag, K. 2013. Charisma and organizational change: A multilevel study of perceived charisma, commitment to change, and team performance. *Leadership Quarterly*, 24(2), 378–389.

Nonaka, I. 1991. The knowledge-creating company. *Harvard Business Review*, 69(6), 96–104.

O'Reilly, C. A., & Tushman, M. L. 2004. The ambidextrous organization. *Harvard Business Review*, 82(4), 74–81.

O'Reilly, C. A., & Tushman, M. L. 2008. Ambidexterity as a dynamic capability: Resolving the innovator's dilemma. *Research in Organizational Behavior*, 28, 185–206.

Ries, E. 2011. *The Lean Startup: How Today's Entrepreneurs Use Continuous Innovation to Create Radically Successful Businesses*. New York, NY: Crown Business.

Roberto, M. A. 2002. Lessons from Everest: The interaction of cognitive bias, psychological safety, and system complexity. *California Management Review*, 45(1), 136–158.

Romanelli, E., & Tushman, M. L. 1994. Organizational transformation as punctuated equilibrium: An empirical test. *Academy of Management Journal*, 37(5), 1141–1166.

Rumelt, R. 2011. *Good Strategy/Bad Strategy: The Difference and Why It Matters*. New York, NY: Crown Business.

Russell, D. M., Stefik, M. J., Pirolli, P., & Card, S. K. 1993. The cost structure of sensemaking. In *Proceedings of the INTERACT'93 and CHI'93 Conference on Human Factors in Computing Systems*, pp. 269–276. New York, NY: Association for Computing Machinery.

Samuelson, P. A. 1947. *Foundations of Economic Analysis*. Cambridge, MA: Harvard University Press.

Samuelson, W., & Zeckhauser, R. 1988. Status quo bias in decision making. *Journal of Risk and Uncertainty*, 1(1), 7–59.

Schaede, U. 1995. The "old boy" network and government-business relationships in Japan. *Journal of Japanese Studies*, 21(2), 293–317.

Schmitt, A., Raisch, S., & Volberda, H. W. 2016. Strategic renewal: Past research, theoretical tensions and future challenges. *International Journal of Management Reviews*, Advance online publication dated 1 September. doi: 10.1111/ijmr.12117.

Shaanan, J. 1994. Sunk costs and resource mobility: An empirical study. *Review of Industrial Organization*, 9(6), 717–730.

Stigler, G. 1939. Production and distribution in the short run. *Journal of Political Economy*, 47(3), 305–327.

Stokes, D. E. 1997. *Pasteur's Quadrant: Basic Science and Technological Innovation*. Washington, DC: Brookings Institution Press.

Stopford, J. M., & Baden-Fuller, C. W. 1994. Creating corporate entrepreneurship. *Strategic Management Journal*, 15(7), 521–536.

Teece, D., Peteraf, M., & Leih, S. 2016. Dynamic capabilities and organizational agility. *California Management Review*, 58(4), 13–35.

Teece, D. J. 1986. Profiting from technological innovation: Implications for integration, collaboration, licensing and public policy. *Research Policy*, 15(6), 285–305.

Teece, D. J. 2006. Reflections on "profiting from innovation". *Research Policy*, 35(8), 1131–1146.

Teece, D. J. 2007. Explicating dynamic capabilities: The nature and microfoundations of (sustainable) enterprise performance. *Strategic Management Journal*, 28(13), 1319–1350.

Teece, D. J. 2010a. Business models, business strategy and innovation. *Long Range Planning*, 43(2), 172–194.

Teece, D. J. 2010b. Technological innovation and the theory of the firm: The role of enterprise-level knowledge, complementarities, and (dynamic) capabilities. In N. Rosenberg & B.H. Hall (Eds.), *Handbook of the Economics of Innovation*, Vol. 1, pp. 679–730. Oxford: North-Holland.

Teece, D. J. 2012. Dynamic capabilities: Routines versus entrepreneurial action. *Journal of Management Studies*, 49(8), 1395–1401.

Teece, D. J. 2014. The foundations of enterprise performance: Dynamic and ordinary capabilities in an (economic) theory of firms. *Academy of Management Perspectives*, 28(4), 328–352.

Teece, D. J. 2016a. Co-specialization. In M. Augier & D. J. Teece (Eds.), *The Palgrave Encyclopedia of Strategic Management*. London: Palgrave Macmillan. doi: 10.1057/978-1-349-94848-2_471-1. Retrieved from: https://link.springer.com/referenceworkentry/10.1057/978-1-349-94848-2_471-1.

Teece, D. J. 2016b. Dynamic capabilities and entrepreneurial management in large organizations: Toward a theory of the (entrepreneurial) firm. *European Economic Review*, 86, 202–216.

Teece, D. J. 2017. A capability theory of the firm: An economics and (strategic) management perspective. Forthcoming in *New Zealand Economic Papers*.

Teece, D. J., Pisano, G., & Shuen, A. 1997. Dynamic capabilities and strategic management. *Strategic Management Journal*, 18(7), 509–533.

Utterback, J. M., & Acee, H. J. 2003. Nano-Technology: A Disruptive Technology? Working Paper ESD-WP-2003-01.15. Cambridge, MA: MIT Engineering Systems Division. https://dspace.mit.edu/bitstream/handle/1721.1/102743/esd-wp-2003-01.15.pdf?sequence=1 (accessed March 28, 2017).

Volberda, H. W., Baden-Fuller, C., & Van Den Bosch, F. A. 2001. Mastering strategic renewal: Mobilising renewal journeys in multi-unit firms. *Long Range Planning*, 34(2), 159–178.

Wernerfelt, B. 2016. *Adaptation, Specialization, and the Theory of the Firm: Foundations of the Resource-Based View*. Cambridge, UK: Cambridge University Press.

Wilden, R., Devinney, T. M., & Dowling, G. R. 2016. The architecture of dynamic capability research identifying the building blocks of a configurational approach. *Academy of Management Annals*, 10(1), 997–1076.

Wilden, R., & Gudergan, S. P. 2015. The impact of dynamic capabilities on operational marketing and technological capabilities: Investigating the role of environmental turbulence. *Journal of the Academy of Marketing Science*, 43(2), 181–199.

Williamson, O. E. 1991. Strategizing, economizing, and economic organization. *Strategic Management Journal*, 12(S2), 75–94.

Winter, S. G. 2003. Understanding dynamic capabilities. *Strategic Management Journal*, 24(10), 991–995.

3 Corporate strategic change towards sustainability

A dynamic capabilities view

Qiang Wu, Qile He, and Yanqing Duan

Introduction

Corporate sustainability cannot be achieved without change. Growing in acceptance is the notion that moving towards sustainability is a long-term journey in which the firm must proactively change its strategies and operations to address emerging social and environmental concerns (Hart, 1995; Porter and Kramer, 2006; Hart and Dowell, 2011). At the same time, extant studies argue that this proactive change is associated with the emergence of unique organizational capabilities (Russo and Fouts, 1997; Sharma and Vredenburg, 1998; Christmann, 2000). Drawing on the Resource-Based View (RBV), the studies conclude that these idiosyncratic capabilities enable the firm to implement new value-adding strategies and contribute to its sustained competitive advantage (Hart, 1995; Russo and Fouts, 1997; Hart and Dowell, 2011).

Some more recent literature calls for introducing Dynamic Capabilities View (DCV) to the area of corporate sustainable change (Aragon-Correa and Sharma, 2003; Hart and Dowell, 2011). Dynamic capabilities are defined as "the firm's ability to integrate, build, and reconfigure internal and external competences to address rapidly changing environments" (Teece *et al.*, 1997: 516). When highly dynamic and unpredictable environments make a firm's existing competences quickly obsolete, the firm should implement dynamic capabilities to rebuild its competitive resources base and strategic position in a timely and astute manner (Eisenhardt and Martin, 2000; Helfat *et al.*, 2007). Given that the context in which firms deal with various emerging sustainable issues is highly complex and ambiguous (Aragon-Correa and Sharma, 2003), dynamic capabilities should be applied to the process by which firms undertake sustainable development strategies (e.g. Aragon-Correa and Sharma, 2003; Hart and Dowell, 2011).

However, to date most of the literature on the dynamic capabilities view (DCV) links dynamic capabilities only with the environments that concentrate on firm's economic bottom line. How firms can apply dynamic capabilities to address the distinctive challenges involved in corporate sustainable change is yet to be fully explored. In line with the argument that different dynamic capabilities should be applied to different changing scenarios (Eisenhardt and Martin, 2000; Zollo and Winter, 2002), we thus attempt to make an theoretical extension to the view of dynamic capabilities in the context of corporate strategic change towards sustainability.

Drivers to corporate sustainability: two theoretical perspectives

Corporate sustainability is an ongoing transitional process in which firms simultaneously deliver economic, social and environmental values to both direct and indirect stakeholders (Porter and Van der Linde, 1995; Shrivastava, 1995; Dyllick and Hockerts, 2002; Hart and Milstein, 2003; Bansal, 2005). According to this definition, corporate sustainability needs firms to respond to emerging environmental and social issues and integrate them into their economic strategic visions to manage as a whole (Elkington & Rowlands, 1999; Florida and Davison, 2001). It also needs firms to consider the sustainability concerns not only from direct stakeholders (shareholders, customers, and governments), but also from fringe or indirect stakeholders such as non-governmental organizations (NGOs) and community groups (Hart and Milstein, 2003; Reinhard *et al.*, 2005). By doing so, proactive organizations, especially the quick movers towards sustainable management, can use the institutional sustainability pressure wisely to obtain their marketing competitive edge. For example, in a thematic analysis of the corporate social responsibility (CSR) reports of 100 global companies, Tate *et al.* (2010) find that the companies they investigate not only follow simple compliance with legal regulations but also proactively search for more responsible strategies to build their "healthier" social and environmental images in the market.

The question as to why firms should commit to sustainable development is explained by two contrasting perspectives that are prevalent in the literature of corporate sustainability. The first is institution-focused and concentrates predominantly on the social context within which firms operate. This view aims to explain how social values and belief systems affects a firm's legitimate status and drive them to pursue sustainability (e.g., Freeman, 1984; Cox *et al.*, 2004). The second perspective is more resource-based and turns the emphasis to the internal resources and capabilities of the firm. This approach explicitly focuses on the identification of the specific capabilities and strategies that help firms to simultaneously pursue economic, environmental, and social competence (e.g., Hart, 1995; Russo and Fouts, 1997; Porter and Kramer, 2006).

Institution-based perspectives of corporate sustainability

The institution-based perspective argues that, as government, customers, public media, and society as a whole have taken increasing interest in sustainability issues, failure to respond to this institutional pressure threatens a firm's legitimacy and survival (Bansal and Roth, 2000). To the contrary, proactive stakeholder engagement as a means to identify and prevent negative social and environmental impacts not only reduces firms' ethical and ecologic risks, but also helps gain access to scare resources and enhances reputation among stakeholders (Hart, 1995; Bansal and Roth, 2000; Bansal, 2005). Nevertheless, the external pressure for sustainability faced by the firm comes from a myriad of interest groups with conflicting preferences (Dixon and Fallon, 1989). This complex contextual situation seriously challenges the conventional management approach of the firm in three ways.

First, firms with limited resources cannot simultaneously meet all sustainability needs from a broad variety of stakeholders. They have to select and satisfy firstly those that are perceived as the most urgent and legitimate (Escobar and Vredenburg, 2011). Firms used to put much attention on the social and environmental standards enforced by official regulators (Hart and Sharma, 2004). But as NGOs and other civil society groups are becoming more and more active in sustainability concerns, in many cases their requests supersede governmental regulations to become a more serious challenge to the unsustainable operations of the firm (Reinhard et al., 2005). Unfortunately, firms often find it difficult to quickly sense these emerging concerns and manage them properly because they lack immediate communication channels with these so-called indirect stakeholders (Hart and Sharma, 2004).

Second, the institutional pressure of sustainability cannot be understood as a collection of agreed schemas, norms, and rules. Rather, it is a complex phenomenon full of conflicting views and interests (Dixon and Fallon, 1989; Gladwin et al., 1995). Different stakeholders may interpret sustainability differently based on their own needs. So sustainability is not a predetermined goal but a negotiated outcome of various interest groups (Reinhard et al., 2005). Any stakeholder involved, including regulators, customers, community members, and also firms themselves, play a certain role in defining what sustainability means and how the navigation towards sustainability should be directed (Gladwin et al., 1995). Following this viewpoint, firms cannot catch the trend of sustainability and minimize the related potential risks by simply listening and responding to the voices of stakeholders. They have to step into the sustainability debate so as to influence its transitional direction.

Third, firms embedded in different institutional contexts may face different sustainable development pressures (Escobar and Vredenburg, 2011). While the stakeholders in most northern regions tend to show increasing interest in eco-friendly production and social equality, those in most southern regions generally still require firms to concentrate on the more basic needs such as poverty, job opportunities, and income (Hart, 1997; Escobar and Vredenburg, 2011). However, when international outsourcing activities link the firms in different geographic regions into a global supply chain, those involved in the same supply chain should not only consider the institutional context in which they are embedded, but also care about the different sustainable development pressure faced by their business partners. On the one side, the supply firms need to modify their unsustainable practices according to the guidance of the purchasing firms as well as the related regulations set by the destination market (Lee and Klassen, 2008). On the other side, it is irresponsible behaviour if the customer firms in developed countries simply pass the sustainability burdens to their supply partners. Instead, they should work closely with their suppliers to find a viable way to reconcile the imbalance of the sustainability focuses between developed and less developed countries in social, environmental, and economic spheres (Vachon and Klassen, 2006).

Resource-based perspectives of corporate sustainability

Referring to the evolutionary theory (Nelson and Winter, 1982; Tushman and Anderson, 1986), resource-based perspectives view corporate sustainability as an ongoing, non-linear journey towards the intersection of environmental, social, and economic competence (Hart, 1995, Hart and Milstein, 2003). Initially, firms find it easy to source inexpensive ways to reduce waste and achieve huge cost savings through internal process improvement and innovation. When these so-called "low-hanging fruits" are exhausted, further improvement becomes difficult to accomplish by simply increasing the efficiency of the existing business practices and patterns. It requires huge investment and a great shift in organizational strategies and technologies (Hart, 1997; Russo and Fouts, 1997). Put another way, different capabilities are required at different stages of sustainable development. Thus focusing on firms' current capabilities and competence is necessary but not enough; it can only ensure a temporary success. Long-term competitive advantage requires firms to quickly develop and apply new capabilities in responding to the increasingly frequent occurrence of major and discrete shifts in social, environmental, technological, and regulatory domains (Hart and Dowell, 2011).

However, firms already exhibit superior performance are more likely to stick to their existing capabilities (Hart, 1995; Markides, 1998). As indicated by the resource-based view (RBV) (Barney, 1991), firm-specific capabilities represent a series of patterned, self-reinforced behaviours that are stabilized through the accumulation of relevant skills, expertise, and know-how (Helfat and Peteraf, 2003; Winter, 2003). They render organizations incapable of changing their familiar "way of doing" things in volatile environments in which the rules of competitive game constantly change (Levinthal and March, 1993; Repenning and Sterman, 2002). This "capabilities trap" becomes even more salient when firms are not clear about the exact returns they can derive from the input into sustainability activities (Berchicci and King, 2007).

As a consequence, firms face a paradoxical situation: on the one hand, the superior capabilities that are valuable, rare, inimitable, and non-substitutable form the basis of strategic strength and the competitive advantage of the firm; on the other hand, those very capabilities restrict the organization's flexibility and responsiveness towards the emerging sustainability challenges. Obviously, firms need to find new ways to unlock this dilemma.

The resource-based perspective indicates that firms striving for sustainability should look inside to overcome the internal "capabilities trap" that can result due to a certain strategic mind set and group of managerial routines. The institutional-based perspective suggests that firms should look outside, to continuously prioritize and cope with the emerging sustainability needs. Combining these two theoretical perspectives, the next section discusses the new challenges involved in corporate strategic change towards sustainability.

Corporate change towards sustainability: a distinctive strategic change

Strategic change is conceptualized as the change in the content of a firm's strategy to enable alignment with its external environment (Hofer and Schendel, 1978; Rajagopalan and Spreitzer, 1997). Because a firm's performance and competitive advantage depend on its strategic fit with the external environment (Rajagopalan and Spreitzer, 1997; Helfat et al., 2007), emerging opportunities and threats often influence the firm to change the scope of its strategy, as well as its resource deployments, to gain competitive advantage and increased synergy (Hofer and Schendel, 1978; Rajagopalan and Spreitzer, 1997).

Corporate change towards sustainability is interpreted as a strategic change under the growing external pressure for environment- and society-friendly development (Hart, 1995; Porter and Kramer, 2006). It requires the firm to incorporate sustainable principles into its business model and growth strategy to achieve economic competence, while minimizing environmental and social impact at the same time (Dyllick and Hockerts, 2002; Hart and Milstein, 2003; Bansal, 2005). Because external stakeholders are becoming increasingly concerned about sustainability issues, firms' strategies and operations have been widely considered as the foundation of their long-term economic viability and sustained competitive advantage (Hart, 1995; Russo and Fouts, 1997; Porter and Kramer, 2006; Hart and Dowell, 2011).

However, corporate strategic change towards sustainability is a far more complex development process that confronts firms with distinctive challenges that have not been encountered before. First, the external sustainability pressures come not only from direct stakeholders such as customers or governments, but also from indirect stakeholders such as non-governmental organizations (NGOs) or other interest groups (Freeman, 1984; Jennings and Zandbergen, 1995; Bansal and Roth, 2000; Hart and Sharma, 2004; Steurer et al., 2005). These different stakeholders hold different interests regarding sustainability (Dixon and Fallon, 1989; Gladwin et al., 1995). Sometimes, they compete with each other to attract firms' attention (Hoffman, 1999; McWilliams and Siegel, 2001). Obviously, it is very difficult for firms to simultaneously meet all sustainability needs from such a broad variety of stakeholders. Firms have to allocate their limited resources to those that are perceived as the most urgent and legitimate (Hart and Sharma, 2004; Escobar and Vredenburg, 2011). Second, corporate change towards sustainability requires firms to meet the intersection of economic, environmental, and social performance (Dyllick and Hockerts, 2002; Bansal, 2005), which is referred to as the "triple bottom line" by Elkington and Rowlands (1999). However, no external market exists in which firms can generate revenues directly from the environmental and social values they create for the public (Berchicci and King, 2007).

Hence, the linkage between a firm's sustainable actions and its economic performance is not straightforward. Therefore, to financially justify the strategic change towards sustainability, firms have to find new ways to transform their sustainability efforts into their private interests.

Considering these distinctive challenges, in the following sections we first review the general findings of the existing literature, and then introduce a conceptual framework to examine the role that dynamic capabilities can play in the process of aligning firms' strategic orientation with various internal and external sustainability interests.

The dynamic capabilities view (DCV)

The question of how firms sustain competitive advantage in a changing environment is a central focus in the field of strategic management. Researchers have long understood that technological discontinuities and environmental shifts require the alignment of internal resource and capabilities configuration within the firm with external environmental variations (Nelson and Winter, 1982; Tushman and Anderson, 1986). But only since the seminal work of Teece *et al.* (1997), has the concept of dynamic capabilities begun to be extensively discussed by a growing body of literature (Barreto, 2010). The agreed view of dynamic capabilities is that, as the exogenous factors such as technological innovation and changes in regulatory and competitive conditions constantly erode the usefulness of the existing resources and capabilities of the firm, long-term competitive advantage is more rooted in the development of dynamic capabilities that are defined as the abilities to purposely reconfigure resources and ordinary capabilities to address changing environments (Teece *et al.*, 1997; Winter, 2003; Helfat *et al.*, 2007).

The fast growth of the research regarding dynamic capabilities has provided a rich body of distinctive views and constructs (Barreto, 2010). Under the banner of the dynamic capabilities view (DCV), a number of studies give various definitions of dynamic capabilities. Table 3.1 summarizes some typical definitions of dynamic capabilities.

However, the fast growing body of literature about DCV is full of diverse assumptions and constructs that vary significantly in terms of the nature of dynamic capabilities, their specific characteristics and creation mechanisms in relevant contexts, and their relationship with a firm's performance and competitive advantage. Figure 3.1 graphically summarizes these disparate views and the associated key authors.

Nature of dynamic capabilities

In the DCV literature, dynamic capabilities are explained as a special kind of organizational capability that should be differentiated from ordinary organizational capabilities (Zollo and Winter, 2002; Winter, 2003; Zahra *et al.*, 2006). More specifically, dynamic capabilities enable firms to change their ordinary

Table 3.1 Definitions of dynamic capability

Reference	Definitions
Teece *et al.* (1997)	The firm's ability to integrate, build, and reconfigure internal and external competences to address rapidly changing environments.
Zollo and Winter (2002)	A dynamic capability is a learned and stable pattern of collective activity through which the organization systematically generates and modifies its operating routines in pursuit of improved effectiveness.
Zahra *et al.*, (2006)	The ability to reconfigure a firm's resources and routines in the manner envisioned and deemed appropriate by its principal decision maker(s).
Helfat *et al.* (2007)	The capacity of an organization to purposefully create, extend, or modify its resource base.
Teece (2007)	Dynamic capabilities can be disaggregated into the capacity (a) to sense and shape opportunities and threats, (b) to seize opportunities, and (c) to maintain competitiveness through enhancing, combining, protecting, and, when necessary, reconfiguring the business enterprise's intangible and tangible assets.

capabilities in order to address external turbulence (Teece *et al.*, 1997; Winter, 2003). This argument does not mean that ordinary capabilities are totally immobile and fail with any change or adjustment. However, the evolution of ordinary capabilities has to follow their own life-cycle trajectories (Helfat and Peteraf, 2003) and bears an inherent tendency towards self-enhancement (Schreyögg and Kliesch-Eberl, 2007).

Indeed, the self-enhancing adaption of ordinary capabilities is a double-bladed sword. On the one hand, it ensures organizations operate in a reliable and efficient manner (Hannan and Freeman, 1984). On the other hand, it leads to the "capabilities trap" that narrows the scope of firm's alternative strategic choices in major, discrete environmental shifts (Levinthal and March, 1993). To overcome this long-standing theoretical paradox, the concept of dynamic capabilities was introduced. Unlike the conception of ordinary capabilities as "the abilities to solve complex problems" (Amit and Schoemaker, 1993), dynamic capabilities are described as "the abilities to change the way the firm solves its problems" (Zahra *et al.*, 2006). For example, a product development process is an ordinary capability. But the ability to change the way the firm develops new products is dynamic capability (Zahra *et al.*, 2006). Firms can utilize both of these capabilities to meet present and future challenges. Ordinary capabilities are employed as "zero-order" capabilities in operational activities and allow a firm to "make a living" in the short term (Winter, 2003). Dynamic capabilities are the "higher-order" ones that operate in turbulent environments and deliberately change the adaption routines of the ordinary capabilities in order to break the "capabilities trap" for future challenges (Zollo and Winter, 2002).

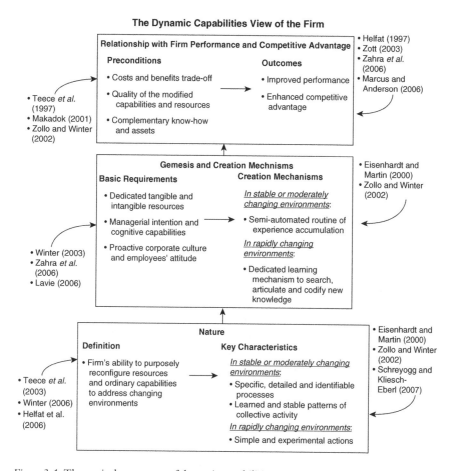

Figure 3.1 Theoretical constructs of dynamic capabilities

However, no matter how *dynamic* they are, dynamic capabilities are still conceptualized as organizational capabilities. Organizational capabilities are defined by Amit and Schoemaker (1993) as habitualized and reliable processes that are developed through interactions among a firm's resources for complex problem solving. In a similar vein, the literature about DCV also stresses the repeatability and reliability of dynamic capabilities by presenting them as specific and identifiable processes (Eisenhardt and Martin, 2000), learned, stable patterns of collective activity (Zollo and Winter, 2002), or capabilities to perform given tasks in an acceptable and repetitive manner (Teece *et al.*, 1997; Helfat *et al.*, 2007). But if dynamic capabilities are treated as reliable processes and replicable routines, they still need to follow stabilized action patterns and cannot become fully flexible for all kinds of external changes (Schreyögg and Kliesch-Eberl, 2007). The studies about DCV were quite aware of this problem and suggested that different changing scenarios require different dynamic capabilities.

Specific characteristics of dynamic capabilities in relevant contexts

The literature about DCV mainly relates dynamic capabilities with two changing scenarios: high-velocity environments *vs.* moderately changing or stable environments (Eisenhardt and Martin, 2000; Barreto, 2010). In high-velocity environments, disruptive technological change destroys the usefulness of the existing competencies and capabilities generated by past experience (Henderson and Clark, 1990; Teece, 2007), the sudden shift of marketing preference makes future business models unclear (Eisenhardt and Martin, 2000), and established firms are forced to follow a different set of technology and marketing principles introduced by radical innovation (Bourgeois and Eisenhardt, 1988; Henderson and Clark, 1990). In contrast, in moderately changing or stable environments in which market change can be predicted (Eisenhardt and Martin, 2000), incremental innovation requires minor changes to the established product design (Henderson and Clark, 1990), and the competence of the firm is reinforced by the exploitation of existing knowledge and skills bases (Gatignon *et al.*, 2002). It is suggested that the effective patterns and roles of dynamic capabilities vary greatly between these two contrasting environments (Eisenhardt and Martin, 2000; Schreyögg and Kliesch-Eberl, 2007).

In moderately dynamic or stable environments, dynamic capabilities are conceived as specific, detailed, and identifiable processes (Eisenhardt and Martin, 2000). These stable processes or routines can be used to systematically modify resource configurations in responding to the predictable market change (Eisenhardt and Martin, 2000; Zollo and Winter, 2002). But in high-velocity environments, dynamic capabilities are more recognized as a series of simple, experimental, and reactive actions based on real-time information and situation-specific knowledge (Eisenhardt and Martin, 2000). Open and non-routine searches for the extraordinary, unforeseen marketing signals allows firms to break away from the pre-set cognitive framing (Teece, 2000, 2007; Schreyögg and Kliesch-Eberl, 2007). Extensive cross-functional communication enables managers to quickly understand the changing situation and adapt to it (Zollo and Winter, 2002). And experimental actions following flexible and simple rules allow firms to make more improvisational and non-linear strategic decisions in fast-shifting and ambiguous markets (Eisenhardt and Martin, 2000; Okhuysen and Eisenhardt, 2002).

Genesis and creation mechanism of dynamic capabilities

The development of dynamic capabilities is costly and complex (Winter, 2003). Dedicated resources such as finance and manpower input is prerequisite but not sufficient (Winter, 2003; Zahra *et al.*, 2006). Equally important is managers' intentions and cognitive capabilities, as well as the proactive corporate culture and employee attitudes towards change (Winter, 2003; Zahra *et al.*, 2006). In addition, the evolution of dynamic capabilities is also influenced by the existing knowledge base and resource endowment of the firm (Winter, 2003; Lavie, 2006).

In moderately dynamic or stable environments, the genesis of dynamic capabilities relies heavily on previously built expertise (Eisenhardt and Martin, 2000). The semi-automated routine of experience accumulation within the existing knowledge domain is adequate to ensure the repetitive upgrading of dynamic capabilities for frequent and incremental changes (Zollo and Winter, 2002). However, in high-velocity environments where market conditions and rules of competition are subject to rapid change, dynamic capabilities should not bind to established rules and historical experience (Zollo and Winter, 2002). Rather, they should be more based on new, situation-specific knowledge (Eisenhardt and Martin, 2000). What firms need is a dedicated learning mechanism composed of a set of cognitive processes and activities to deliberately search for, articulate, and codify knowledge that is more relevant to the changing situation (Eisenhardt and Martin, 2000; Zollo and Winter, 2002).

Relationship between dynamic capabilities and a firm's performance and competitive advantage

Earlier research into DCV theoretically links the application of dynamic capabilities with enhanced competitive positions for the firm by arguing that firms with idiosyncratic dynamic capabilities can generate above-average economic rents, especially in changing environments (Teece et al., 1997; Makadok, 2001). In addition, through articulation and codification of the tacit knowledge embedded in operating routines, firms can understand and realize the causal linkage between the dynamic capabilities they operate and the performance outcomes obtained (Zollo and Winter, 2002).

More recent research complements the above assumptions by stating that, although the assertion that dynamic capabilities can enhance firm's performance and competitiveness is theoretically sound, this effect is indirect. First, as "higher-order" capabilities, dynamic capabilities have no direct impact on a firm's performance. Instead, they can influence performance only through reconfiguring the ordinary capabilities in which the quality of the modified capabilities plays a mediating role (Zott, 2003; Zahra et al., 2006). Second, the development of dynamic capabilities is a huge investment involving both economic and cognitive costs (Winter, 2003, Lavie, 2006). Whether dynamic capabilities should be used to improve a firm's performance depends on the relevant cost and benefit analysis (Winter, 2003). If dynamic capabilities are used based on wrong calculations, they may damage rather than improve a firm's performance (Zahra et al., 2006). Third, the possession of dynamic capabilities is a necessary, but not sufficient, condition for a firm's competitiveness (Eisenhardt and Martin, 2000). Firms with identical dynamic capabilities but different complementary know-how and assets may actually build differential resource positions and consequently have differentiated performance and competence levels (Helfat, 1997; Zott, 2003; Marcus and Anderson, 2006).

The discussion of dynamic capabilities provides three salient conclusions. First, the common feature of dynamic capabilities is that they are a special kind of capabilities aim to modify firm's existing resources and capabilities for the needs of environmental changes. Second, like other organizational capabilities, dynamic capabilities are still patterned processes and replicable routines and oriented towards specific tasks (Eisenhardt and Martin, 2000; Zollo and Winter, 2002). It is impossible to develop a general-purpose dynamic capability that is fully flexible for all kinds of external changes (Winter, 2003). Different competition contexts require different dynamic capabilities. Third, the development mechanisms of dynamic capabilities based on diverse external environments vary greatly, from experience accumulation to new knowledge creation (Zollo and Winter, 2002). Firms should consider the marketing conditions they are facing when designing the development routines of dynamic capabilities.

More recently, some studies suggest that dynamic capabilities should be applied to the process by which firms undertake corporate sustainability (e.g. Aragon-Correa and Sharma, 2003; Hart and Dowell, 2011). The argument is that corporate sustainability is an ongoing development process, in which the firm has to continuously evolve its capabilities and strategies to address the emerging sustainability challenges (Hart, 1995; Porter and Van der Linde, 1995; Shrivastava, 1995; Hart and Milstein, 2003, Porter and Kramer, 2006). The perspective of dynamic capabilities holds the promise for a better understanding of how firms adjust their capabilities for sustainable change (Hart and Dowell, 2011).

Traditional DCV literature links dynamic capabilities mainly with the environments that concentrate on a firm's economic bottom line, despite the fact that the external environment that drives corporate sustainability brings firms new challenges that have not been encountered before. Some recent studies examine the role of dynamic capability in corporate sustainable development, including research into the applications of dynamic capabilities in environmental management (e.g. Marcus and Anderson, 2006), green logistics, and purchasing management (Defee and Fugate, 2010; Reuter *et al.*, 2010), and the development of proactive sustainable strategies (e.g. Aragon-Correa and Sharma, 2003; Hart and Dowell, 2011). This research stream provides profound insights in how to apply dynamic capability to corporate sustainable development, but one issue still remains. Most of the studies assume the existence of the contingent dynamic capabilities in corporate sustainable development, but fail to elaborate their distinctive nature, despite the argument that different dynamic capabilities are required in different contexts (Eisenhardt and Martin, 2000; Zollo and Winter, 2002). There is thus a paucity of research explicating the nature and microfoundations of these contingent dynamic capabilities for corporate strategic change towards sustainability.

Towards a definition of dynamic capabilities for corporate sustainability

We define the application of dynamic capabilities to corporate sustainability thus: *firms' abilities to address the rapidly evolving sustainability expectations of stakeholders by purposefully modifying functional capabilities for the simultaneous pursuit of economic, environmental, and social competencies.*

This definition is underpinned by the DCV literature, but also incorporates the insights gained from research on corporate sustainability. The word *purposefully* indicates that the application of the dynamic capabilities for corporate sustainability should be linked directly with a firm's strategic objective and managerial intent, so as to systematically derive *sustainable development opportunities* from internal and external stakeholders' demand (Porter and Kramer, 2006; McWilliams and Siegel, 2011). Here, *sustainable development opportunities* are those that firms can use to pursue both environmental and social values for the public and economic values for themselves (McWilliams and Siegel, 2001). The definition is also in line with the concept of dynamic capabilities as the higher-order capabilities required to change the functional, or "ordinary" capabilities to match market changes (Zollo and Winter, 2002; Winter, 2003; Zahra *et al.*, 2006).

In the DCV literature, dynamic capabilities are treated as a multidimensional construct (Wang and Ahmed, 2007; Barreto, 2010). First, dynamic capabilities represent a firm's ability to monitor the constantly shifting environment (Schreyögg and Kliesch-Eberl, 2007), and to sense and seize new business opportunities (Teece, 2007). Second, dynamic capabilities also represent the antecedent organizational routines by which managers alter their resource deployment to generate new value-creation strategies (Eisenhardt and Martin, 2000). Following this theoretical viewpoint, the dynamic capabilities for corporate sustainability are disaggregated into three distinctive, but related capabilities to: (1) scan the emerging sustainable needs of various stakeholders, (2) sense opportunities or threats from the rapidly changing sustainable expectations, and (3) reconfigure existing functional capabilities for corporate sustainability. Below, we propose and delineate a conceptual framework to explain how these capabilities work together as an underlying mechanism to support firms' strategic change towards sustainability (see Figure 3.2).

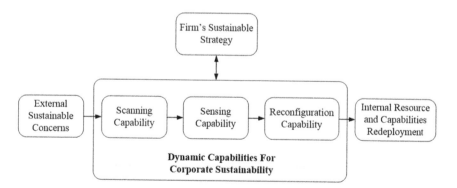

Figure 3.2 Conceptual framework of dynamic capabilities for corporate strategic change towards sustainability

Scanning capability

Teece (2007) suggests that the monitoring function of dynamic capabilities involves an analytical system to scan, learn, and interpret the signals reflecting emerging market and technological developments. Such a system represents a set of processes in which the external innovation ideas are received, integrated, and used to define future business model and investment priorities (Teece, 2007; Schreyögg and Kliesch-Eberl, 2007). Following this suggestion, the dynamic capability to scan the emerging sustainable needs is considered as an information-processing mechanism composed of two different searching processes, one for direct stakeholders and the other for indirect stakeholders.

In corporate sustainability, the pressure from direct stakeholders, such as customer requirements and governmental regulations, is always treated as the most relevant factor that affects a firm's legitimate status (Carroll, 1979; Porter and Van der Linde, 1995). Thus formal searching processes should be in place to communicate with those direct stakeholders, in order to recognize new sustainable trends, and analyze their impact on firms' current operations.

In addition, the sustainability concerns of indirect stakeholders cannot be neglected either (Bansal and Roth, 2000; Reinhard et al., 2005). Because indirect stakeholders normally reside outside of a firm's established communication or relationship networks, firms need to find new ways to systematically identify these "remote voices" (Hart and Sharma, 2004). On the one hand, in the case of the indirect stakeholders whose concerns are perceived as the most urgent and legitimate, firms should build direct communication channels with them (Hart and Sharma, 2004; Escobar and Vredenburg, 2011). On the other hand, in the case of the stakeholders that cannot be directly accessed initially, their concerns can also be sensed via the firm's existing communication network. For example, a firm can rely on its supply chain partners to gain information and insights about the stakeholders outside of its networking boundaries (Hart and Sharma, 2004; Ansett, 2008). In either case, the broad search for distant and unfamiliar signals requires deliberate managerial attention to delineate explicit search routines and processes in the organization's existing communication structure (Berchicci and King, 2007; Hart and Dowell, 2011).

It should be noted that the scanning capability is by no means a one-way mechanism for firms to receive information from various stakeholders. Instead, it is firm's ability to establish a trust-based collaborative relationship with a wide variety of stakeholders (Buysse and Verbeke, 2003; Sharma and Henriques, 2005). The firms with effective scanning capabilities are more likely to manage context-specific stakeholder pressures along its value chain (Sharma et al., 2007), and reduce negative social and environmental impacts in its pursuit of competitive advantage (Buysse and Verbeke, 2003).

Sensing capability

A firm's capability to sense external environmental changes and to identify relevant business opportunities and threats are often regarded as a unified theoretical construct (e.g. Gilbert, 2006; Teece, 2007). However, these two kinds of capabilities need to be delineated separately in the context of corporate sustainability, because understanding new sustainability expectations from external stakeholders does not mean firms can automatically seize profitable opportunities from them (McWilliams and Siegel, 2001). The focus of these expectations is on the improvement of corporate environmental and social performance. In many cases they do not tell firms how to link societal expectations with their own benefits (McWilliams and Siegel, 2001). These sustainability requirements often focus on improving a firm's environmental and social performance. In many cases they do not tell firms how to obtain their own financial benefits at the same time (McWilliams and Siegel, 2001). In this sense the sensing capability should be applied to not only recognize potential sustainability risks, but also to find the intersection between the firm's environmental and social goals and its economic interests. In other words, a firm's dynamic sensing capability is the ability to sense and capitalize on, rather than merely react to, emerging external sustainability challenges and opportunities in its business environment (Aragon-Correa, 1998; Dunphy *et al.*, 2003; Sharma *et al.*, 2007).

The development of the sensing capability needs a shared vision within the firm to unify the objectives and aspirations of its members (Oswald *et al.*, 1994; Tsai and Ghoshal, 1998). A shared vision enables a firm to generate internal pressure and mobilize the employees enthusiasm necessary for innovation and change (Hart, 1995; Graafland *et al.*, 2003; Worthington *et al.*, 2006). The shared vision facilitates organizational learning and employee creativity, initiates competitive actions to challenge the *status quo* (Storey, 1994; Chen and Hambrick, 1995; Hitt *et al.*, 2001), and enable firms to accumulate and harness the resources and skills necessary for developing and adopting proactive sustainability innovations (Hart, 1995; Graafland *et al.*, 2003).

In the context of corporate sustainability, the sensing capability should be performed to analyze new sustainable knowledge and information, and systematically link them with related organizational functions in various innovation activities. For example, to simultaneously reduce the negative sustainability impacts and operational cost through process reengineering, firms must combine strong process redesign capability with deep sustainability know-how (Russo and Fouts, 1997). Similarly, to obtain the differentiation advantage in "green" product markets, the knowledge about customers' sustainability preferences should be used to guide the R&D activities (Hart, 1995, 1997). Specifically, the sensing capability plays two dedicated roles: one for cross-functional knowledge sharing, and the other for knowledge articulation and codification. First, before the sustainable information and knowledge collected from diverse stakeholders are applied to subsequent actions, they must be well understood and meaningfully integrated into organization's existing knowledge structure. For this purpose, cross-functional knowledge exchange is necessary because novel sustainable knowledge should be forwarded to and interpreted by the individuals or planning units who are capable of making sense of them (Teece, 2007). For example, when new demands in the organic product market are received in the sales department, through knowledge sharing they can to be sent to product design teams for further analysis. Moreover, in more comprehensive sustainable innovations, profitable opportunities are often generated from the coordination of multiple functional departments. As an illustration, the study of Wells and Seitz (2005) showed that, when an engine remanufacturing programme was triggered by a new sustainable idea, its implementation involved the knowledge integration of at least 10 different departments to realize the anticipated environmental and cost benefits.

Second, once new sustainable knowledge has been successfully applied to organizational operations and repetitively justified, the resulting sustainable know-how sometimes need to be articulated and codified into explicit management approaches (Winter, 2003). In the literature about DCV and strategic management, these approaches are described as "best practices" (Christmann, 2000), combinative capabilities (Kogut and Zander, 1992), or proactive corporate approach (Aragon-Correa, 1998; Sharma and Vredenburg, 1998; Aragon-Correa and Sharma, 2003). In the research of corporate sustainable management, they are operationalized as environment management system (Florida and Davison, 2001), or responsive corporate social approaches (Wood, 1991; Porter and Kramer, 2006). These explicit approaches are the formalization of past experience accumulated in recurrent sustainable innovation activities. They offer stable action templates and simplify future task execution in similar situations.

Reconfiguration capability

Reconfiguring an organization's functional capabilities has been recognized as one of the fundamental roles of dynamic capabilities (Teece *et al.*, 1997; Winter, 2003; Zahra *et al.*, 2006). An organization's functional capabilities are complex, rigid operational routines guided by accumulated tacit skills (Helfat and Peteraf, 2003; Winter, 2003). Firms tend to stick to their established functional capabilities to ensure reliable and efficient organizational operation (Hannan and Freeman, 1984; Leonard-Barton, 1992; Levinthal and March, 1993), even when the changing business environment has begun to undermine its fundamental capabilities base (Repenning and Sterman, 2002; Schreyögg and Kliesch-Eberl, 2007). For example, to avoid the possible operational disturbance, many firms prefer the end-of-pipe approach to solve the imposed sustainable problems, despite the fact that this approach can entail huge, nonproductive cost (Hart, 1995; Russo and Fouts, 1997). Therefore, in corporate sustainable change, the reconfiguration capability refers to the firm's capability to discard, modify, or rebuild the well-entrenched organizational routines and practices that are unsustainable.

This reconfiguration capability aims to overcome the potential "capabilities trap" involved in corporate sustainable development. The "capabilities trap" means firms with superior performance tend to stick to their existing capabilities to ensure reliable and efficient organizational operation (Hannan and Freeman, 1984; Leonard-Barton, 1992; Levinthal and March, 1993). It makes an organization reluctant to drastically change its familiar "way of doing" things, even when the changing environmental conditions have begun to undermine its fundamental capabilities base (Repenning and Sterman, 2002; Schreyögg and Kliesch-Eberl, 2007). The "capabilities trap" problem is more salient in corporate sustainable management (Berchicci and King, 2007), because the link between sustainable actions and firm economic performance is not straightforward (McWilliams and Siegel, 2001, 2011). For example, to avoid the possible operational disturbance, some firms prefer the end-of-pipe approach to solve the imposed sustainability problems. Even this approach actually entails huge, non-productive cost (Hart, 1995; Russo and Fouts, 1997). Furthermore, even though firms tend to take more proactive actions to realize both sustainable and financial benefits, without the reliable estimation about the resulting impact on their existing operational routines, firms may still fail to make the right decisions (McWilliams and Siegel, 2001; Berchicci and King, 2007).

Indeed, organizational capabilities are complex operational routines guided by accumulated tacit skills and expertise (Helfat and Peteraf, 2003; Winter, 2003). The effective reconfiguration of these internal routines requires a clear understanding of their ambiguous nature (Schreyögg and Kliesch-Eberl, 2007). Firms should conduct a series of collective discussion and evaluation sessions to articulate how these routines are generated and organized (Winter, 2003), and what the results will be when these routines are changed.

Furthermore, the capabilities reconfiguration process should also consider the strong effect of functional interdependence that has been repetitively identified in corporate sustainable development (Hart, 1995, 1997). Functional interdependence means that the operational functions within an organization are interrelated. If one function is changed, its interactive patterns with other functions may be changed as well (Teece, 2007). Put differently, in corporate sustainability, what should be reconfigured includes not only organizational capabilities, but also their interactive patterns (Henderson and Cockburn, 1994; Hart, 1995). To rearrange these combinative patterns, firms should break the tacit routines embedded in the established communication channels and information filters between operational functional units (Galunic and Rodan, 1998; Galunic and Eisenhardt, 2001).

Drawing on a resource-based view of the firm (Barney, 1991; Barney *et al.*, 2011), these three particular dynamic capabilities (scanning, sensing, and reconfiguration) are not only valuable, socially complex, causally ambiguous, and deeply embedded within a firm, but also likely to be firm-specific and costly to imitate (Galunic and Eisenhardt, 2001; Hillman and Keim, 2001). As such, the three distinctive capabilities provide a foundation for successful corporate strategic change towards sustainability.

Interconnectedness of the three types of dynamic capabilities for corporate sustainability

It should be noted that the three dynamic capabilities for corporate sustainability are interconnected. Interconnectedness, as suggested by Hart (1995), consists of two seemingly controversial dimensions: path-dependence and

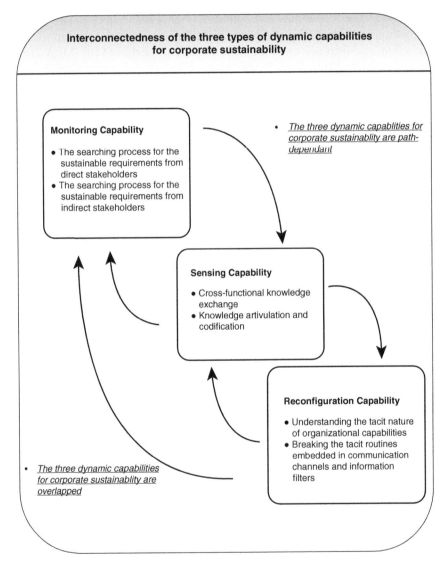

Figure 3.3 Interconnectedness of the three types of dynamic capabilities relevant to corporate sustainability

embeddedness. Path dependence suggests that there is a sequential logic to the implementation of the three dynamic capabilities. For instance, the capability to identify new opportunities and threats is relevant only if the scanning capability has been in place to recognize future sustainable trends. Similarly, the reconfiguration capability is relevant only when the sensing capability has already indicated what capabilities might be seriously challenged in further sustainable actions.

Although the logic of path dependence is obvious, the effect of embeddedness represents the other logic to the interconnections of the three dynamic capabilities. Embeddedness means that these capabilities are overlapped. For example, it can be argued that, because the sustainable information collected from different stakeholders is often contradictory (Dixon and Fallon, 1989; Gladwin *et al.*, 1995), the scanning capability should be combined with the sensing capability to identify and prioritize the most relevant sustainable needs. Similarly, the sensing capability cannot be separated from the reconfiguration capabilities because seizing sustainable opportunities requires firms to apply new knowledge to their existing operations to realize both private and public benefits (McWilliams and Siegel, 2011). In this process, without a comprehensive understanding about how its internal operations are organized and how they can be reconfigured, an organization cannot capture real sustainable opportunities and transform them into profitable outputs. Furthermore, the reconfiguration capability also relates to the scanning capability. Because the sensing capability requires deliberate managerial attention to establish a new information sharing mechanism with various external stakeholders (Berchicci and King, 2007; Hart and Dowell, 2011), the reconfiguration capability is thus needed to modify the existing communication practices and routines. In short, there are clear synergies across these three capabilities. Figure 3.3 summarizes the interrelatedness that exists among the three dynamic capabilities relevant to corporate sustainability.

Conclusions

The findings of this conceptual study regarding strategic change (or strategic renewal), especially towards corporate sustainability, are threefold. First, the study reviews and up-to-date DCV literature related to environmental complexity and strategic change. Second, the study identifies new challenges involved in contemporary corporate strategic change, especially towards sustainable development. Third, the study makes an early attempt to extend DCV to the understanding of corporate strategic change towards sustainability. The proposed conceptual framework can be used by future researchers to further explore the role of dynamic capabilities in facilitating corporate strategic change in a contemporary situation.

It is posited that corporate strategic change towards sustainability depends on the convergence between a firm's dynamic capabilities and the formation of its sustainability strategy. On the one hand, firms should establish their strategic objective and missions for long-term sustainable development (Porter and Kramer, 2006). On the other hand, the formation of firm's sustainability strategy requires its dynamic capabilities to sense the emerging sustainable opportunities from the external environment. The realization of firms' strategic sustainability objectives also needs dynamic capabilities to change unsustainable routines and practices.

Moreover, a firm's sustainability strategy can navigate the implementation focus of its dynamic capabilities. As suggested by Porter and Kramer (2006), the firm should not treat sustainable development as a series of unorganized, defensive actions. To make real benefits for society and confer competitive advantage, firms need to address the most relevant sustainability concerns in concert with their core strategies.

The theoretical framework developed in the study illustrates how dynamic capabilities potentially enable firms to follow certain managerial processes in order to sense and seize sustainable development opportunities. This framework stresses the interrelatedness of scanning, sensing, and reconfiguration capabilities in responding to stakeholder sustainability requirements and mobilizing firms' internal resources to simultaneously pursue economic, environmental, and social benefits. Given the fast-changing nature of stakeholder expectations, it is important for managers to realize that deploying dynamic capabilities for corporate sustainability is a continuous process. Firms should also build their long-term transformation vision for both CSR management and sustainable development. Moreover, firms should not become attached to their fixed organizational functions, but focus on the underlying changing routines and mechanism for sustainability-oriented innovation. During the change process, both intra- and inter-organizational knowledge exchange should be encouraged to break the conventional managerial cognition frame. It is worth noting, the framework developed in this paper is just a benchmarking guidance for firms to regulate their sustainability activities. Managers can use their own ways to utilize the framework based on their specific business and institutional environments.

References

Amit, R. and Schoemaker, P. J. H. 1993, Strategic assets and organizational rent. *Strategic Management Journal*, 14(1): 33–46.

Ansett, S. 2008, Mind the gap: A journey to sustainable supply chains. *Employee Responsibilities and Rights Journal*, 20(2): 295–303.

Aragon-Correa, A. and Sharma, S. 2003, A contingent natural-resource based view of proactive environmental strategy. *Academy of Management Review*, 28(1): 71–88.

Aragon-Correa, J. A. 1998, Strategic proactivity and firm approach to the natural environment. *Academy of Management Journal*, 48(5): 556–567.

Bansal, P. 2005, Evolving sustainably: A longitudinal study of corporate sustainable development. *Strategic Management Review*, 26(3): 197–218.

Bansal, P. and Roth, K. 2000, Why companies go green: A model of ecological responsiveness. *Academy of Management Journal*, 43(4): 717–736.

Barney, J. 1991, Firm resources and sustained competitive advantage. *Journal of Management*, 17(1): 99–121.

Barney, J. B., Ketchen, D. J., and Wright, M. 2011, The future of resource-based theory: Revitalization or decline? *Journal of Management*, 37(5): 1299–1315.

Barreto, I. 2010, Dynamic capabilities: A review of past research and an agenda for the future. *Journal of Management*, 36(1): 256–280.

Berchicci, L. and King, A. 2007, Postcards from the edge: A review of the business and environment literature. *Academy of Management Perspectives*, 1: 1513–1547.

Bourgeois, L. J. and Eisenhardt, K. 1988, Strategic decision processes in high velocity environments: Four cases in the microcomputer industry. *Management Science*, 34(7): 816–835.

Buysse, K. and Verbeke, A. 2003, Proactive environmental strategies: A stakeholder management perspective. *Strategic Management Journal*, 24(5): 453–470.

Carroll, A. B. 1979, A three-dimensional conceptual model of corporate performance. *The Academy of Management Review*, 4(4): 497–505.

Chen, M. J. and Hambrick, D. C. 1995, Speed, stealth, and selective attack: How small firms differ from large firms in competitive behavior. *Academy of Management Journal*, 38(2): 453–482.

Christmann, P. 2000, Effects of "best practices" of environmental management on cost advantage: The role of complementary assets. *Academy of Management Journal*, 43(4): 663–680.

Cox, A., Watson, G., Lonsdale, C., and Sanderson, J. 2004, Managing appropriately in power regimes: Relationship and performance management in 12 supply chain cases. *Supply Chain Management: An International Journal*, 9(5): 357–371.

Defee, C. C. and Fugate, B. S. 2010, Changing perspective of capabilities in the dynamic supply chain era. *The International Journal of Logistics Management*, 21(2): 180–206.

Dixon, J. A. and Fallon, L. A. 1989, The concept of sustainability: Origins, extensions, and usefulness for policy. *Society and Natural Resources*, 2: 73–84.

Dunphy, D., Griffiths, A., and Benn, S. 2003, *Organizational Change For Corporate Sustainability*, Routledge: New York, NY.

Dyllick, T. and Hockerts, K. 2002, Beyond the business case for corporate sustainability. *Business Strategy and the Environment*, 11(2): 130–141.

Eisenhardt, K. M. and Martin, J. A. 2000, Dynamic capabilities: What are they? *Strategic Management Journal*, 21(10/11): 1105–1121.

Elkington, J., & Rowlands, I. H. 1999, Cannibals with forks: the triple bottom line of 21st century business. *Alternatives Journal*, 25(4): 42–43.

Escobar, L. and Vredenburg, H. 2011, Multinational oil companies and the adoption of sustainable development: A resource-based and institutional theory interpretation of adoption heterogeneity. *Journal of Business Ethics*, 98(1): 39–65.

Florida, R. and Davison, D. 2001, Gaining from green management: Environmental management systems inside and outside the factory. *California Management Review*, 43(3): 64–85.

Freeman, R. E. 1984, *Strategic Management: A Stakeholder Approach*, Cambridge University Press: Cambridge, UK.

Galunic, D. C. and Eisenhardt, K. M. 2001, Architectural innovation and modular corporate forms. *Academy of Management Journal*, 44(6): 1229–1249.

Galunic, D. C. and Rodan, S. 1998, Resource recombinations in the firm: Knowledge structures and the potential for Schumpeterian innovation. *Strategic Management Journal*, 19(12): 1193–1201.

Gatignon, H., Tushman, M. L., Smith, W., and Anderson, P. 2002, A structural approach to assessing innovation: Construct development of innovation locus, type, and characteristics. *Management Science*, 48(9): 1103–1112.

Gilbert, C. G. 2006, Change in the presence of residual fit: Can competing frames coexist? *Organization Science*, 17: 150–167.

Gladwin, T. N., Kennelly, J. J., and Krause, T.-S. 1995, Shifting paradigms for sustainable development: Implications for management theory and research. *The Academy of Management Review*, 20(4): 874–908.

Graafland, J., Van de Ven, B., and Stofelle, N. 2003, Strategies and instruments for organizing CSR by small and large businesses in the Netherlands. *Journal of Business Ethics*, 47(1): 45–60.

Hannan, M. and Freeman, J. 1984, Structural inertia and organizational change. *American Sociological Review*, 49: 149–164.

Hart, S. L. 1995, A natural-resource-based view of the firm. *The Academy of Management Review*, 20(4): 986–1015.

Hart, S. L. 1997, Beyond greening: Strategies for a sustainable world. *Harvard Business Review*, 75(1): 66–77.

Hart, S. L. and Dowell, G. 2011, A natural-resource-based view of the firm: Fifteen years after. *Journal of Management*, 37(5): 1464–1479.

Hart, S. L. and Milstein, M. B. 2003, Creating sustainable value. *Academy of Management Executive*, 17(2): 56–69.

Hart, S. L. and Sharma, S. 2004, Engaging fringe stakeholder for competitive imagination. *The Academy of Management Executive*, 18(1): 7–18.

Helfat, C. E. 1997, Know-how and asset complementarity and dynamic capability accumulation: The case of R&D. *Strategic Management Journal*, 18(5): 339–360.

Helfat, C. E., Finkelstein, S., Peteraf, M. A., Mitchell, A., Singh, H., Teece, D. J., and Winter, S. G. 2007, *Dynamic Capabilities: Understanding Strategic Change In Organizations*, Blackwell: London.

Helfat, C. E. and Peteraf, M. A. 2003, The dynamic resource-based view: Capability lifecycles. Strategic Management Journal, 24(10): 997–1010.

Henderson, R. and Cockburn, I. 1994, Measuring competence? Exploring firm effects in pharmaceutical research. *Strategic Management Journal*, 15(Special Issue): 63–85.

Henderson, R. M. and Clark, K. B. 1990, Architectural innovation: The reconfiguration of existing product technologies and the failure of established firms. *Administrative Science Quarterly*, 35(1): 9–30.

Hillman, A. J. and Keim, G. D. 2001, Shareholder value, stakeholder management, and social issues: What's the bottom line? *Strategic Management Journal*, 22(2): 125–139.

Hitt, M. A., Ireland, R. D., Camp, S. M., and Sexton, D. L. 2001, Guest editors' introduction to the special issue strategic entrepreneurship: Entrepreneurial strategies for wealth creation. *Strategic Management Journal*, 22(6–7): 479–491.

Hofer, C. W. and Schendel, D. 1978, *Strategy Formulation: Analytical Concepts*, West Publications: St. Paul, MN.

Hoffman, A. J. 1999, Institutional evolution and change: Environmentalism and the U.S. chemical industry. *Academy of Management Journal*, 42(4): 351–371.

Jennings, P. D. and Zandbergen, P. A. 1995, Ecologically sustainable organizations: An institutional approach. *The Academy of Management Review*, 20(4): 1015–1053.

Kogut, B. and Zander, U. 1992, Knowledge of the firm, combinative capabilities, and the replication of technology. *Organization Science*, 3(3): 383–397.

Lavie, D. 2006, Capability reconfiguration: An analysis of incumbent responses to technological change. *Academy of Management Review*, 31(3): 153–174.

Lee, S. and Klassen, R. 2008, Drivers and enablers that foster environmental management capabilities in small- and medium-sized suppliers in supply chains. *Production and Operations Management*, 17(6): 573–592.

Leonard-Barton, D. 1992, Core capabilities and core rigidities: A paradox in managing new product development. *Strategic Management Journal*, 13(Special Issue): 111–126.

Levinthal, D. A. and March, J. G. 1993, The myopia of learning. *Strategic Management Journal*, 14(Special Issue): 95–113.

Makadok, R. 2001, Toward a synthesis of the resource-based and dynamic-capability views of rent creation. *Strategic Management Journal*, 22(5): 387–401.

Marcus, A. A. and Anderson, M. H. 2006, A general dynamic capability: Does it propagate business and social competencies in the retail food industry. *Journal of Management Studies*, 43(1): 19–46.

Markides, C. 1998, Strategic innovation in established companies. *Sloan Management Review*, 39(3): 31–42.

McWilliams, A. and Siegel, D. S. 2001, Corporate social responsibility: A theory of the firm perspective. *The Academy of Management Review*, 26(1): 117–127.

McWilliams, A. and Siegel, D. S. 2011, Creating and capturing value: Strategic corporate social responsibility, resource-based theory, and sustainable competitive advantage. *Journal of Management*, 37(5): 1480–1495.

Nelson, R. R. and Winter, S. G. 1982, *An Evolutionary Theory Of Economic Change*, Belknap Press/Harvard University Press: Cambridge, MA.

Okhuysen, G. A. and Eisenhardt, K. M. 2002, Integrating knowledge in groups: How formal interventions enable flexibility. *Organization Science*, 13(4): 370–386.

Oswald, S. L., Mossholder, K. W., and Harris, S. G. 1994, Vision salience and strategic involvement: Implications for psychological attachment to organization and job. *Strategic Management Journal*, 15(6): 477–489.

Porter, M. E. and Kramer, M. R. 2006, Strategy and society: The link between competitive advantage and corporate social responsibility. *Harvard Business Review*, 84(12): 78–85.

Porter, M. E. and Van der Linde, C. 1995, Green and competitive: Ending the stalemate. *Harvard Business Review*, 73(5): 120–134.

Rajagopalan, N. and Spreitzer, G. M. 1997, Toward a theory of strategic change: a multi-lens perspective and integrative framework. *The Academy of Management Review*, 22(1): 48–79.

Reinhard, S. E. L., Markus, K. A., and Martinuzzi, A. 2005, Corporations, stakeholders and sustainable development: A theoretical exploration of business-society relations. *Journal of Business Ethics*, 61(3): 263–281.

Repenning, N. P. and Sterman, J. D. 2002, Capability traps and self-confirming attribution errors in the dynamics of process improvement. *Administrative Science Quarterly*, 47(2): 265–295.

Reuter, C., Foerstl, K., Hartmann, E., and Blome, C. 2010, Sustainable global supplier management: The role of dynamic capabilities in achieving competitive advantage. *Journal of Supply Chain Management*, 46(2): 45–63.

Russo, M. V. and Fouts, P. A. 1997, A resource-based perspective on corporate environmental performance and profitability. *Academy of Management Journal*, 40(3): 534–559.

Schreyögg, G. and Kliesch-Eberl, M. 2007, How dynamic can organizational capabilities be? Towards a dual-process model of capability dynamization. *Strategic Management Journal*, 28(9): 913–933.

Sharma, S., Aragón-Correa, J. A., and Rueda-Manzanares, A. 2007, The contingent influence of organizational capabilities on proactive environmental strategy in the service sector: an analysis of North American and European ski resorts. *Canadian Journal of Administrative Sciences*, 24(4): 268–283.

Sharma, S. and Henriques, I. 2005, Stakeholder influences on sustainability practices in the Canadian forest products industry. *Strategic Management Journal*, 26(2): 159–180.

Sharma, S. and Vredenburg, H. 1998, Proactive corporate environmental strategy and the development of competitively valuable organizational capabilities. *Strategic Management Journal*, 19(8): 729–753.

Shrivastava, P. 1995, Environmental technologies and competitive advantage. *Strategic Management Journal*, 16(Special Issue): 183–200.

Steurer, R. Langer, M. E., Konrad, A., and Martinuzzi, A. 2005, Corporations, stakeholders and sustainable development I: A theoretical exploration of business–society relations. *Journal of Business Ethics*, 61(3): 263–281.

Storey, D. 1994, *Understanding The Small Business Sector*, Routledge: London, UK.

Tate, W. L., Ellram, L. M., and Kirchoff, J. O. N. F. 2010, Corporate social responsibility reports: a thematic analysis related to supply chain management. *Journal Supply Chain Management*, 46(1): 19–44.

Teece, D. J. 2000, *Managing Intellectual Capital: Organizational, Strategic, And Policy Dimensions*, Oxford University Press: Oxford, UK.

Teece, D. J. 2007, Explicating dynamic capabilities: the nature and microfoundations of (sustainable) enterprise performance. *Strategic Management Journal*, 28: 1319–1350.

Teece, D. J., Pisano, G., and Shuen, A. 1997, Dynamic capabilities and strategic management. *Strategic Management Journal*, 18(7): 509–533.

Tsai, W. and Ghoshal, S. 1998, Social capital and value creation: The role of intrafirm networks. *Academy of Management Journal*, 41(4): 464–476.

Tushman, M. L. and Anderson, P. 1986, Technological discontinuities and organizational environments. *Administrative Science Quarterly*, 31(3): 439–465.

Vachon, S. and Klassen, R. D. 2006, Extending green practices across the supply chain: the impact of upstream and downstream integration. *International Journal of Operations & Production Management*, 26(7): 795–820.

Wang, C. L. and Ahmed, P. K. 2007, Dynamic capabilities: A review and research agenda. *International Journal of Management Reviews*, 9(1): 31–51.

Wells, P. and Seitz, M. 2005, Business models and closed-loop supply chains: A typology. *Supply Chain Management*, 10(3/4): 249–251.

Winter, S. G. 2003, Understanding dynamic capabilities. *Strategic Management Journal*, 24(10): 991–995.

Wood, D. J. 1991, Corporate social performance revisited. *The Academy of Management Review*, 16(4): 691–718.

Worthington, I., Ram, M., and Jones, T. 2006, Exploring corporate social responsibility in the U.K. Asian small business community. *Journal of Business Ethics*, 67(2): 201–217.

Zahra, S. A., Sapienza, H. J., and Davidsson, P. 2006, Entrepreneurship and dynamic capabilities: A review, model and research agenda. *Journal of Management Studies*, 43: 917–955.

Zollo, M. and Winter, S. G. 2002, Deliberate learning and the evolution of dynamic capabilities. *Organization Science*, 13(3): 339–351.

Zott, C. 2003, Dynamic capabilities and the emergence of intra-industry differential firm performance: Insights from a simulation study. *Strategic Management Journal*, 24(2): 97–125.

4 Towards a cognitive dimension

The organizational ambidexterity framework

Päivi Karhu and Paavo Ritala

Introduction

Organizations face a continuous struggle for strategic renewal in the pursuit of breaking path dependencies under internal and external demands (Schmitt et al., 2016). One important perspective on strategic renewal is organizational ambidexterity – the organization's ability to manage contradictory strategic dualities, such as exploration and exploitation, at the same time. Interest in organizational ambidexterity has burgeoned during the past decade, with scholars appreciating its applicability and versatility (Birkinshaw and Gupta, 2013). Organizations and their managers are confronted with choices and tradeoffs among competing objectives all the time, and thus, the ambidexterity framework provides a readily applicable and normative perspective.

The definitions of organizational ambidexterity differ, and they have expanded over time (for review, see O'Reilly and Tushman, 2013; Papachroni et al., 2015; Raisch and Birkinshaw, 2008; Simsek et al., 2009). However, as the core feature, the definitions typically include engaging in opposing and contradictory activities and achieving a balance or fit between these (seemingly) conflicting demands. Traditionally, they have been viewed as exploitation and exploration, following March's (1991) typology. Fostering exploitation (performing routine tasks and sustaining the current activities) and exploration (renewing the organizational routines, creating new activities) can be seen as a paradox, as they are considered interdependent and non-substitutable activities for the firm (e.g., Gibson and Birkinshaw, 2004).

Recently, the organizational ambidexterity literature has started to look more broadly at managing different types of dualities. Dualities can be considered to provide an umbrella terminology for myriad organizational opposite demands, such as paradoxes and dilemmas (for reviews, see e.g., Putnam et al., 2016; Schad et al., 2016), which can be seen as decision-making pairs of which both alternatives are important but are to some degree in conflict with one another (Birkinshaw et al., 2016). Organizations are attempting to address many types of dualities (Gulati and Puranam, 2009) that resemble a similar juxtaposition to that of exploration and exploitation, where the conflict arises because resources and also managerial attention are limited. Such pressure to meet various but often inconsistent demands has only amplified with time as organizations are becoming more complex and managerial coordination activities more demanding (e.g., Benner and Tushman 2003; Graetz and Smith, 2008). Thus, organizations and managers must deal with a host of dualities, which are necessary for organizational renewal, including continuity and change (Evans, 1992, see also revolutionary and evolutionary change; Tushman and O'Reilly, 1996), efficiency and flexibility (Adler et al., 1999; Ghemawat and Ricart Costa, 1993), adaptability and alignment (Gibson and Birkinshaw, 2004), financial and social goals (Hahn et al., 2014; Margolis and Walsh, 2003; Smith et al., 2012), or functions and dysfunctions of processes, such as formalization (Vlaar et al., 2007). The fundamental challenge of such strategic dualities is that they often put forward contradictory tensions (Tushman and O'Reilly, 1996), whereas organizational ambidexterity helps to resolve these tensions, and the concept can thus be used to frame related research questions and designs (Birkinshaw and Gupta, 2013).

Encountering various strategic dualities places major demands on managerial decision-making, creating tensions that force managers to deal with controversial signals and mixed messages (e.g., Gibson and Birkinshaw, 2004; Lewis and Smith, 2014). Although some organizations adjust to this turmoil, many encounter various inertial forces (Kaplan, 2008). Knight (1921/1965 in Kaplan, 2008) proposed that this challenge does not stem from the environmental changes *as such* that make them tough to deal with, but rather managers' ineptness in judging what the contradictions mean (see also Bartunek, 1984; Lüscher and Lewis, 2008). Therefore, achieving organizational ambidexterity is first and foremost a managerial challenge (see also Birkinshaw and Gupta, 2013; O'Reilly and Tushman, 2008), and to understand the management of various types of dualities and related ambidextrous solutions, it is necessary to examine managerial cognition and decision-making.

In this book chapter, we elucidate several important implications. First, we address the lack of knowledge regarding the cognitive perspective in the endeavor to facilitate ambidexterity in an organization (Eisenhardt et al., 2010; Good and Michel, 2013). We integrate the findings from disparate research streams, drawing together the discussions from literature on organizational ambidexterity, duality and managerial cognition. This integration establishes a solider foundation for future empirical research on ambidexterity from a managerial standpoint. Second, we develop insights on the cognitive dimension in relation to different ways of building ambidexterity into an organization. In doing so, we aim to provide clarity on the broad, increasingly arbitrary (see O'Reilly and Tushman, 2013) juxtapositions of exploration and exploitation, as well as other dualities, especially at the individual level. Third, we introduce cognitive ambidexterity (following Chandrasekaran, 2009; Greenberg et al., 2013; Karhu et al., 2016, Neck, 2011) as an explanatory framework for how managers recognize and frame the duality-related tensions, and we further examine how this relates to different ambidexterity modes. Overall, we aim to enrich the organizational ambidexterity framework in the context of organizational renewal, and thus create a research agenda for better understanding of the managerial cognitive microfoundations of ambidexterity.

In what follows, we first highlight the existing ambidexterity literature that touches upon and calls for further research on cognitive issues. Second, we review the extant literature on organizational ambidexterity, including the core notion of exploration and exploitation, as well as dualities more broadly. We also discuss the suggested solutions for managing ambidexterity: spatial, temporal, and contextual. Finally, we discuss how the cognitive dimension informs and contributes to the discussion on organizational ambidexterity.

Case for the cognitive dimension: Research gaps and early contributions

Despite the large body of ambidexterity research, research into the underlying cognitive processes is still at an emergent stage. For instance, research around ambidexterity has traditionally focused on macro-level tensions; how the challenges unfold and are perceived at the micro-level have been left with less attention (Smith, 2014; Zhang et al., 2015). Exceptions in the duality and paradox literature include, e.g., Jarzabkowski and Lê (2017), Knight and Paroutis (2017) and Smith (2014). However, some ambidexterity scholars have also started to pinpoint cognitive and psychological aspects, as well as calls for further research on the area, which we briefly review here before moving further.

There is much research concerned with the various ways that managerial cognition affects corporate strategizing in general (e.g., Porac and Thomas, 2002; Walsh, 1995) as well as other organizational processes (Kaplan, 2011), however, only a handful of these studies focus directly on the mental aspect of cognition (for such studies, see Eggers and Kaplan, 2011; Gavetti, 2012; Helfat and Peteraf, 2015), especially in the context of organizational ambidexterity (see also Parker, 2014; Tuncdogan et al., 2015). A better comprehension of how cognition facilitates or hinders managers' achievement of this balance between opposite demands is also lacking (Eisenhardt et al., 2010). Eisenhardt et al. (2010) suggested that executives should empower the coexistence of contradictory cognitive agendas (Smith and Tushman, 2005), described as finding a balance between exploration and exploitation at the individual level (Eisenhardt et al., 2010; Good and Michel, 2013; Smith and Tushman, 2005). In addition, Birkinshaw and Gupta (2013) noted that if we are to really advance our understanding on how ambidexterity is achieved, much more insight into managerial capabilities is called for. According to them, we know that some organizations are more ambidextrous than others (as what comes to 'fit' versus 'balance' of exploration and exploitation), but we have to take a more detailed look at the way they make their decisions and how those decisions are implemented.

A small but mounting number of empirical studies suggest that individuals are a significant source of organizational ambidexterity (Gibson and Birkinshaw, 2004; Lubatkin et al., 2006; Mom et al., 2007, 2009). These studies emphasize the behavioral actions undertaken by managers to explore novel information and to exploit the current knowledge (Good and Michel, 2013). For example, O'Reilly and Tushman (2008) define ambidexterity as the paradoxical capability of the senior management, manifested as a set of senior team decisions with regards to the organizational structure, culture, linking mechanisms as well as the processes (see also Lewis et al., 2014; Smith et al., 2010). Studies by Mom and colleagues (2007, 2009) are some of the primary empirical examples at the individual level of analysis, pursuing an understanding of the extent to which individual managers balance exploration and exploitation behaviors.

As managers ascend the organizational ladder, the complexity and scope of their decision-making responsibilities upsurges (McKenzie et al., 2009). Therefore, the senior management team is particularly subject to cognitive ambidexterity challenges. Although the desire for a balance between exploitation and exploration has been recognized, along with the fact that the endeavor to pursue both is likely to cause tensions, there is little evidence showing how to manage this (Eisenhardt et al., 2010). This research gap is a key limitation to scholarship on ambidexterity, which is already delineated not only in organizational (Mom et al., 2009; Raisch et al., 2009) but also neuroscience (Aston-Jones and Cohen, 2005; Laureiro-Martínez et al., 2015) and psychology research (Laureiro-Martínez et al., 2010). As a response, researchers have increasingly focused on individuals', especially managers', exploration and exploitation activities and the psychological antecedents related to those (Good and Michel, 2013; Kauppila and Tempelaar, 2016; Laureiro-Martínez et al., 2015; Tuncdogan et al., 2015). However, as Laureiro-Martínez et al. (2015) addressed, we are still far from effusively understanding how exploration and exploitation decisions are met, and from providing the microfoundations for organizational ambidexterity.

Finally, the growing recognition of the applicability of ambidexterity has given rise to a proliferation of diverse and parallel definitions and perspectives that provide insights into the cognitive dimension. For instance, the ambidexterity literature borrows heavily from duality and managerial cognition literatures, including paradoxical leader (Lewis et al., 2014; Zhang et al., 2015), paradoxical thinking (Mom et al., 2009; O'Reilly and Tushman, 2004; Raisch et al., 2009; Smith, 2014; Smith and Tushman, 2005), paradoxical cognition (Smith and Tushman, 2005), and paradoxical vision (Andriopoulos and Lewis, 2010). Together, these streams have increased the understanding of how paradox or duality cognitive framing helps to understand and explain managerial challenges and solutions to ambidexterity.

Organizational ambidexterity

History of ambidexterity

Ambidexterity is a derivative of the Latin words *ambi* referring to "both" and *dexter*, signifying "right" or "favorable." In biological or medical science, ambidextrous people are equally skillful with both hands (see, e.g., Szaflarski et al., 2008). Thus, ambidexterity literally means being "right on both sides."

In management literature, Duncan (1976) introduced the term "organizational ambidexterity" to illustrate an organization's capacity to do two different things equally well. He described the dual structures companies inaugurate to deal with activities that encompass different managerial capabilities and time horizons. Twenty years later, Tushman and O'Reilly (1996) suggested that organizational ambidexterity, defined as "[t]he ability to simultaneously pursue both incremental and discontinuous innovation ... from hosting multiple contradictory structures, processes, and cultures within the same firm" (p. 24), was a prerequisite of long-term survival. Since then, there has been broad interest in and extensive research on the topic, including hundreds of empirical studies (e.g., Gibson and Birkinshaw, 2004; He and Wong, 2004), theory building papers (e.g., O'Reilly and Tushman, 2008), special issues of journals (*Academy of Management,* 2006; *Organization Science,* 2009), review articles (e.g., Birkinshaw and Gupta, 2013; Lavie et al., 2010; O'Reilly and Tushman, 2013; Raisch and Birkinshaw, 2008; Turner et al., 2013), books or book chapters (e.g., Sidhu and Reinmoeller, 2017; Zimmermann and Birkinshaw, 2016), doctoral dissertations (e.g., Chandrasekaran, 2009; Jansen, 2005; Tempelaar, 2010), as well as academic conference tracks and other professional meetings (O'Reilly and Tushman, 2013). Tushman and O'Reilly's (1996) ideas were well received in the business world, and they contributed to the broader managerial debate going on at the time about how companies might cope with what Christensen (1997) called disruptive technological innovations. However, the discussion in academia remained modest until a decade later, when the research started to quickly pick up speed.

The challenge of exploitation and exploration and other dualities in organizations

March's (1991) conceptual paper, which seems to have become a *pro forma* citation in the area of organizational ambidexterity, builds on the author's earlier notions on bounded rationality and problemistic search, and addresses the underlying incompatibilities between exploration and exploitation as different organizational learning modes. March's (1991) account of exploration and exploitation (as broadly defined) has been a useful theoretical anchor for several discussions, including those about strategic renewal and many others (Papachroni et al., 2015; Schmitt et al., 2016). In the past decade, a particularly decisive link has been adopted for the exploration and exploitation duality and organizational ambidexterity. March (1991) characterized *exploration* as including "things such as search, variation, risk taking, experimentation, play, flexibility, discovery, and innovation". *Exploitation*, in turn, includes such elements as "refinement, choice, production, efficiency, selection, implementation, execution" (March, 1991, p. 71).

Organizations often face the challenge of an asymmetric preference for short-term exploitation (Volberda and Lewin, 2003). Focusing on exploitation in the short term might sometimes enhance performance. Sooner or later, however, such over-emphasis might turn into a competence trap through overly specialized resources and cognitive maps (Volberda, 1996). Thus, the initial core competencies may develop into core rigidities (Leonard-Barton, 1992), and firms may not be responsive enough to environmental changes (Good and Michel, 2013; Levitt and March, 1988). However, exploration holds dysfunctional effects as well. Responding to every trend and short-term change, and avoiding routine behavior, may mean a company is wasting resources on insignificant or random environmental signals (Volberda, 2003). Eventually, this puts forward a vicious circle that turns into *a renewal trap* characterized by disputes with regards to insufficient controls, authority, undefined responsibilities, and a lack of direction or shared ideology (Volberda and Lewin, 2003). In the paradox literature, a one-sided response to the tension has been described as *suppression*, in which one element is favored at the expense of the other one(s) (Jarzabkowski et al., 2013; Lewis, 2000).

As a remedy, organizations need to "engage in enough exploitation to ensure the organization's current viability and engage in enough exploration to ensure its future viability" (Levinthal and March, 1993, p. 105). Accordingly, ambidextrous organizations are defined as those capable of "simultaneously exploiting existing competencies and exploring new opportunities" (Raisch et al., 2009, p. 685). Studies have proposed that organizations that manage to pursue exploration and exploitation simultaneously can achieve better financial performance (Gibson and Birkinshaw, 2004; He and Wong, 2004; Lubatkin et al., 2006).

Recently, organizational ambidexterity scholars have examined other types of dualities beyond exploitation and exploration (Birkinshaw and Gupta, 2013; see also Andriopoulos and Lewis, 2009, 2010; Smith and Tushman, 2005). At the same time, there is increasing cross-pollination between ambidexterity and the duality and paradox perspectives (Papachroni et al., 2015, 2016; Lewis and Smith, 2014), as well as the psychological and cognitive perspectives (e.g., Good and Michel, 2013; Lin and McDonough, 2014; Tuncdogan et al., 2015). This recent integration of literature streams has provided a broader outlook on the organizational and managerial mechanisms for dealing with exploitation or exploration and other organizational dualities.

Originally, March (1991) proposed exploration and exploitation to be two contradictory activities that can be considered as two ends of the same continuum that are competing for scarce resources and are technically incompatible (see also Walrave et al., 2011). However, this does not apply to all resources. For instance, information or knowledge resources can be limitless and accumulated (Shapiro and Varian, 1998). Further, a firm can acquire at least some organizational knowledge via simple learning from experience (Huber, 1991). Thus, if we accept that the company's resources are not always scarce, and that exploration and exploitation are not mutually exclusive, we can move away from the notion of the two ends of a continuum (Gupta et al., 2006). An alternative – and increasingly popular – view is to frame these seemingly opposite activities as complementary (e.g., Cao et al., 2009; Katila and Ahuja, 2002).

The *paradox* perspective follows a similar logic and suggests that tensions may be viewed as persistent, opposing, but interconnected poles, as opposed to a *dilemma*, which refers to a dichotomous, either-or solution by weighing the pros and cons. Paradoxes are defined as "contradictory yet interrelated elements that exist simultaneously and persist over time" in states of dynamic equilibrium (Smith and Lewis, 2011, p. 382). The paradox perspective helps to understand how various types of dualities can be managed in an ambidextrous fashion. The opposite demands of a duality (such as exploitation and exploration) can be approached as they would be compatible and interdependent rather than incompatible and separate (see also Farjoun, 2010). For instance, Nerkar (2003) illustrated that overcoming the dilemma trade-off (either-or) is not necessary if paradoxical thinking is used to achieve exploitation and exploration at the same time. Indeed, many ambidexterity scholars use the term "paradoxical thinking" as a condition needed to handle the contradictory demands (e.g., Andriopoulos and Lewis, 2009; Smith and Tushman, 2005). Lüscher and Lewis (2008) and Lewis and Smith (2014) discussed the duality categories comprising paradoxes and named them learning, organizing, performing, and belonging. In a review of the paradox research, Schad et al. (2016) discovered an emphasis on learning paradoxes, those that portray tensions between stability and change, old and new, or exploration and exploitation. This reflects the extensive interest in tensions that surface in attempts to facilitate ambidexterity and drive strategic renewal.

Three approaches to organize for ambidexterity

The literature has concentrated on three methods that empower ambidexterity within an organization: spatial, temporal, and contextual. In spatial ambidexterity, two activities are carried out in different organizational units or domains (Tushman and O'Reilly, 1996). In temporal ambidexterity, managers organize activities in temporal, sequential, or back-and-forth cycles among different dualities (Eisenhardt and Brown, 1998; Nickerson and Zenger, 2002; Siggelkow and Levinthal, 2003; Venkatraman et al., 2007). Contextual ambidexterity requires addressing different dualities, such as exploitation and exploration, simultaneously by the same individual or unit (Gibson and Birkinshaw, 2004; Raisch and Birkinshaw, 2008; Tushman and O'Reilly, 1996). In the following, we discuss the key characteristics of each approach.

Spatial ambidexterity

When confronted with competing activities and demands, organizations can maintain high levels of both activities through spatial ambidexterity (or *structural ambidexterity*, e.g., Tushman and O'Reilly, 1996). This happens by spatially dispersed units focussing on exploratory and exploitative activities (Jansen et al., 2009) or other types of dualities, such as competition and collaboration (Fernandez et al., 2014). This is possible when obtaining balance within the same organizational unit is not necessary or even conceivable (Gupta et al., 2006; Lubatkin et al., 2006; Papachroni et al., 2015). For example, individuals responsible for generating R&D may focus on exploration, while individuals responsible for accounting may emphasize the exploitation of efficiencies and economies of scale (Good and Michel, 2013). Jansen et al. (2009) described spatial ambidexterity as facilitating pragmatic boundaries (Carlile, 2004), which shelter experimental activities from overruling dominant managerial cognitions (see also dominant logic, Prahalad and Bettis, 1986) and inertia (Benner and Tushman, 2003). In spatial ambidexterity, the exploratory and exploitative endeavors coexist at separate locations, which gives a feel of freedom and ownership over particular work activities and allows structural flexibility to respond to contradictions locally in the task environments (Child, 1984; Jansen et al., 2009). This calls for leadership-based practices that make the senior management team accountable for responding and reconciling to the tensions that arise from the differences of opposite efforts (e.g., Mom et al., 2007, 2009; Raisch and Birkinshaw, 2008).

Thus, spatial ambidexterity refers to 1) managers' ability to recognize incompatible or complex tasks or processes that benefit from separation and 2) the unit of analysis, which is never a single person but two or more persons or business units, who engage in different types of activity (from the managerial perspective, such as exploratory or exploitative tasks).

Temporal ambidexterity

Temporal ambidexterity (Siggelkow and Levinthal, 2003; Tushman and O'Reilly, 1996) – also called cyclical (Simsek et al., 2009) or punctuated ambidexterity (Helfat and Raubitschek, 2000; Rothaermel and Deeds, 2004; Winter and Szulanski, 2001) – starts from the fundamental assumption of the noncomplementarity of competing demands (particularly exploration and exploitation). Temporal ambidexterity addresses these demands via temporal separation; that is, activities take place at different points in time (Papachroni et al., 2015). It serves as an in-between solution to the perceived contradictions: the negative effects of contradictions are neutralized by arranging them at different points in time for full concentration on either side of the duality for the time being.

Temporal ambidexterity originates in punctuated equilibrium (for a review, see Gersick, 1991), whose logic lies in the assumption that organizations develop during long periods of stability (i.e., exploitation) that are interrupted by episodes of change (i.e., exploration; Tushman and Romanelli, 1985). For managers, this means exploring and exploiting cycles based on seasonal peculiarities of the business (e.g., harvest season) or production cycles but also for their personal development to adjust to the change. In the dualities literature, Putnam et al. (2014) discussed an example: flexible work arrangements, where organizational actors cope with the tensions between fixed and variable hours by adopting fixed schedules during peak times and flexible schedules for the less busy times.

We suggest that temporal ambidexterity can be both proactive and reactive. First, after recognizing the duality tasks or processes that benefit from rotation (e.g., those that bring versatility to employees' tasks but are less burdening than simultaneous engagement), managers could temporally allocate such tasks in the organization. However, managers (and organizations in general) themselves are subject to such temporal changes due to the nature of the business (e.g., seasons or organizational renewal periods) and are required to react and adjust their operations and mindsets accordingly.

Contextual ambidexterity

The contextual ambidexterity (Gibson and Birkinshaw, 2004; He and Wong, 2004; Mom et al., 2007; see also harmonic ambidexterity, Simsek et al., 2009) approach suggests that ambidexterity is best attained by "building a set of processes or systems that enable and encourage individuals to make their own judgments about how to divide their time between conflicting demands for alignment and adaptability" (Gibson and Birkinshaw, 2004, p. 210). Studies on individual ambidexterity build on the premise that ambidextrous organizations require ambidextrous individuals who are adept to sensing the differing demands required for exploration and exploitation efforts (O'Reilly and Tushman, 2004). In this regard, Gibson and Birkinshaw (2004) characterized ambidextrous behavior as proactive and initiative-taking, involving recognizing opportunities outside one's core expertise, collaborating with others, playing various roles, and identifying opportunities to reap synergies. Further, Mom et al. (2009) characterized ambidextrous managers as multithinkers and taskers, who are capable of accommodating contradictions and willing to continuously improve and question their thinking.

Contextual ambidexterity often refers to the supportive organizational context that the senior executives put in place, so the front-line employees can address exploitation–exploration tensions within a single work unit, but poses cognitive demands on individuals at all levels of the organization (e.g., Zimmermann et al., 2015). In fact, ambidexterity has also been analyzed through the lenses of *individual ambidexterity* (e.g., Good and Michel, 2013), which refers to contextual ambidexterity at the individual level. Studies elaborating the role of the individual are sparse, probably due to the tendency to focus on structure instead of context (Good and Michel, 2013). Nevertheless, organizational ambidexterity researchers have acknowledged the central role of individuals (e.g., frontline employees, Jasmand et al., 2012; Yu et al., 2013) to better understand how to select, train, and develop employees to follow through on strategic initiatives in dynamic environments (Good and Michel, 2013). Thus, contextual ambidexterity (Gibson and Birkinshaw, 2004) accepts exploration and exploitation and other dualities as complementary. However, this is not because the fundamental conflicts would have been wiped away (Papachroni et al., 2015), but because individuals develop and apply the cognitive (and behavioral, Mom et al., 2009) capacity to distribute their time and attention between the two types of endeavors.

We suggest managers themselves have to manage both individual and contextual ambidexterity as the scope and complexity of their decision-making responsibilities are high (McKenzie et al., 2009). Therefore, managers need to be able to handle multiple tasks and roles themselves, but also to recognize the dualities the organization needs to respond to, and make judgments when assigning those tasks to particular individuals or business units.

Cognition and organizational ambidexterity

Management decision-making and cognitive microfoundations

The essential role of managers in all types of organizations and at all levels is to make decisions (Harrison and Pelletier, 2000). To do this, managers absorb, process, and diffuse knowledge about the problems and opportunities they have discovered. Managerial cognition (see also managerial cognitive capabilities, Helfat and Peteraf, 2015) refers to the mental models, belief systems (also called knowledge structures, e.g., Walsh, 1995), and mental processes, but also emotions (Hodgkinson and Healey, 2011). Thus, managerial cognitive frames explain why managers do not perceive the decisions in the same way but approach those differently and also attach divergent socioemotional information to the decisions (e.g., Smith and Tushman, 2005). The most essential challenge that managers come upon, though, is that the information to be processed is extremely complex and ambiguous, and the amount of it is immense (McCall and Kaplan, 1985). Tversky and Kahneman (1982) elaborated that "the frame that a decision-maker adopts is controlled partly by the formulation of the problem and partly by the norms, habits, and personal characteristics of the decision maker" (p. 453). Therefore, understanding the cognitive microfoundations that explain how managers make strategic decisions, and how managerial cognition facilitates different types of organizational ambidexterity, is important.

The cognitive aspect of decision-making comes close to the recent conceptualization of managerial dynamic capabilities (Helfat and Peteraf, 2015; see also ambidexterity as dynamic capability, Jansen et al., 2009). For instance, Adner and Helfat (2003) introduced dynamic managerial capabilities "to underpin the finding of heterogeneity in managerial decisions and firm performance in the face of changing external conditions" (p. 1011). Furthermore, Helfat and Peteraf (2015) defined managerial cognitive capability as "the capacity of an individual manager to perform one or more of the mental activities that comprise cognition" and suggested it as a foundation of dynamic managerial capabilities. These include mental undertakings such as attention, reasoning, perception, and problem solving, as well as communication.

The knowledge structures give stimuli to heuristics and biases that come into play when managers anticipate market changes, attempt to understand the consequences of different choices, and finally take action (Garbuio et al., 2011). In some way, managers "must see their way through what may be a bewildering flow of information to make decisions and solve problems" (McCall and

Kaplan, 1985, p. 280). Managers, and in fact all individuals who come to make decisions, tackle the described information challenge by using their knowledge structures (Walsh, 1995).

Cognitive ambidexterity framework

Based on the premises thus far, we characterize the core abilities related to *cognitive ambidexterity* through three complementary elements: (1) managers' ability to recognize the nature of the duality in their cognitive framing process, (2) managers' ability to build ambidexterity into their individual and organizational contexts spatially, temporarily, and contextually as a result of the framing of the decision, and (3) managers' ability to continuously assess the balance and dynamics between exploration and exploitation (or other dualities) and alter the ambidexterity mode to arrange dualities when needed. Together, these aspects of cognitive ambidexterity build on and refine its recent definition as "the ability to engage in parallel mental processes that are paradoxical or in contradiction" (Karhu et al., 2016).

Figure 4.1 depicts the role of cognitive ambidexterity in the broader organizational ambidexterity framework. In particular, two dimensions are highlighted: the complexity of the required managerial cognitive process and the simultaneity of the contradictory dualities (varying from low to high). This concerns each

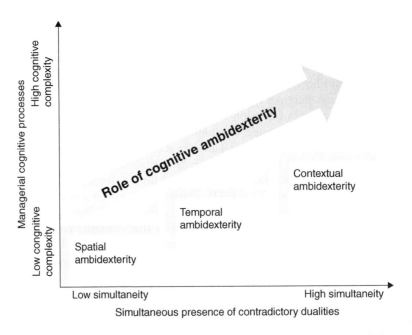

Figure 4.1 The cognitive ambidexterity dimension in the organizational ambidexterity framework

ambidexterity-building mechanism with different intensity levels (i.e., spatial, temporal, and contextual), and becomes gradually more and more significant when dualities are to be coped with simultaneously (i.e., individual-level contextual ambidexterity).

The presence of contradictory dualities increases as we move from the requirements of spatial ambidexterity toward contextual ambidexterity. Similarly, the complexity of cognitive processes increases, as the demands for parallel processing of competing dualities becomes more prominent in moving from separate solutions (structural or temporal ambidexterity) toward integrated, simultaneous solutions. Such simultaneity requires special cognitive abilities and tolerance for ambiguity from managers and decision-makers. In the following, we discuss these demands in conjunction with the three modes of ambidexterity.

Role of cognition in different modes of ambidexterity

For *spatial ambidexterity*, we suggest that managers adopt the ambidexterity type *as per* the cognitive complexity level of the duality (e.g., exploration and exploitation) as well as their respective compatibility. When managers cognitively frame the duality as a dilemma, they observe the decision-pair at hand as incompatible and begin to seek solutions to separate them spatially. A similar solution has also been discussed in the paradox literature (Poole and Van de Ven, 1989). Likewise, Tushman and O'Reilly (1996) argued for separate structures within the same organization to accommodate what are reflected as contradictory systems, competencies, and practices to enable both exploration and exploitation. For instance, the dominant culture of exploitative incremental innovation often reacts hostilely toward explorative discontinuous innovation as they compete for scarce resources (Papachroni et al., 2015). In consequence, spatial separation demands managers' cognitive comprehension of the opposites and the benefits of separating (rather than merging) those activities. O'Reilly and Tushman (2004) emphasized the role of the senior management team to act as the "corporate glue" and keep the organization together by managing the tensions that arise between dualities.

For *temporal ambidexterity*, managers have to identify the contrasting activities and decide how to compartmentalize those in time. For adopting this type of ambidexterity, the activities constituting the duality must, first of all, be separable and, secondly, offer more value separately than when carried out concurrently. Similarly, in paradox literature, Poole and Van de Ven (1989) discussed temporal separation. Alternatively, when duality arises from exogenous sources, managers can comprehend duality as exploratory (turbulent) or exploitative (stable) periods, for instance, to which the organization is exposed from the environment. In such a case, the theoretical stance is a contingency approach, which is based on choice (Clegg et al., 2002), where actors vacillate between both demands, and the focus on one (e.g., exploration) puts pressure on being attentive to the other (e.g., exploitation). Studies on emotions in contradictory situations show that these can cause stress, burnout, and turnover in the workplace (Putnam et al., 2016). Furthermore, research shows that a recurrent vacillation between the two poles builds up feelings of frustration, even anger (Apker et al., 2005), principally as various tensions intensify (or attenuate) one another (Putnam et al., 2016). Therefore, temporal ambidexterity requires careful consideration when applied.

Finally, when managers are able to frame contradictions as fortifying each other and thus complementary, the managers decide on *contextual ambidexterity* solutions, which forces managers and also their subordinates to deal with compound dualities, which, in order to obtain the synergy benefits, cannot be divided in space or time but have to be realized in chorus. The challenge is thus not to move from one configuration to another but to sustain numerous competencies instantaneously (Gilbert, 2006). This brings the focus onto individual ambidexterity (i.e., contextual ambidexterity at the individual level), which obliges handling parallel mental activities, in other words, the development of paradoxical cognition. The managerial cognition literature suggests developing a paradoxical cognition for holding exploration and exploration activities as mutually reinforcing and thereby succeeding in contextual ambidexterity. In the paradox literature, Lewis (2000) outlined strategies for managing a paradox (acceptance, confrontation, and transcendence) that together serve as the means to proactively address tensions (Lewis and Smith, 2014; see also Gaim and Wåhlin, 2016; Jarzabkowski and Lê, 2017). *Acceptance* involves "learning to live with the paradox" (Lewis, 2000, p. 764; Poole and Van de Ven, 1989, p. 566); *confronting* the tensions means to socially discuss them to construct a more accommodating understanding (Lewis, 2000). *Transcendence* is the ability to think paradoxically and engage in a range of diverse activities, roles, and learning (Mom et al., 2009; O'Reilly and Tushman, 2004; Raisch et al., 2009; Smith, 2014; Smith and Tushman, 2005). McKenzie et al. (2009) referred to transcendence as a nonconventional mental capacity that allows one to recognize and hold contradictions until something triggers the transcending of the tensions. Illustrating a transcendence approach, Eisenhardt and Westcott (1988) described how adopting a paradoxical frame (instead of concentrating on one end of the pole) empowered Toyota's senior leaders to create a new strategic practice, the "just in time" process, by contrasting the goals of carrying no inventory, while maintaining access to any component that may be needed at the right time. However, as valuable as it sounds, transcendence is a stressful mental activity, which calls for the capacity to step back and employ an eagle-eye perspective on the conflicting alternatives, and to embrace all options (McKenzie et al., 2009).

To summarize, Table 4.1 depicts a pragmatic framework for managerial framing of dualities and the resulting ambidexterity types, the related mechanisms in the paradox literature, as well as cognitive requirements and solutions. Here, we parallel spatial and temporal ambidexterity with managerial "dilemma framing", where the decision alternatives are seen as incompatible in the same spatial or temporal context. In this case, a manager perceives the

Table 4.1 Links among the paradox, ambidexterity, and managerial cognition literature streams

Ambidexterity literature	Managerial framing of duality	Mechanisms in paradox literature	Cognitive requirements	Role of cognitive ambidexterity
Spatial ambidexterity (Dual structures)	Dilemma (Either–or) Duality as two ends of a continuum	Differentiate structurally Resolve A and B by arranging them at different spatial locations	Top management team as the "corporate glue" governing exploration and exploitation operated by different units/persons Organizing for high specialization of individuals in the organization	Identification of dualities in the organization Recognizing the incompatible nature of the duality Comprehension of the big picture; which dualities to separate
Temporal ambidexterity (Punctuated equilibrium or structure-building and structure-changing periods)	Dilemma (Either–or) Duality as two ends of a continuum	Differentiate temporally Situate A and B at different temporal locations	Compartmentalization of opposites and vacillation between poles of the duality focusing on one at the time	Identification of opposites Recognizing the incompatible nature of the duality that benefits from rotation Understanding the endo- and exogenous triggers for such rotation
Contextual ambidexterity/ Individual ambidexterity	Paradox (Both-and) Duality as orthogonal dimensions	Acceptance and confrontation: accept the paradox of A and B and learn to live with it by socially discussing it Transcendence: find a new perspective which eliminates the opposition between A and B	Coping with cognitive complexity and acceptance of competing cognitive agenda Out-of-box mindset Ability to play multiple roles	Development of paradoxical cognition to allow duality-mindset Connecting dispersed ideas to overcome "doing two things at the same time" by "doing better things"

duality as a trade-off (either-or) and seeks structural solutions, or temporal solutions when the poles of duality benefit from or require such a rotation. For contextual ambidexterity, the managerial framing of the duality is perceived as paradoxical, and they choose contextual solutions to arrange the tasks simultaneously in order to benefit from synergies. The other columns in the table summarize the cognitive requirements for managers for each ambidexterity mode, as well as the role of "cognitive ambidexterity" – related managerial abilities and activities.

Discussion and implications

In this chapter, we have discussed the cognitive dimension of organizational ambidexterity, and furthermore, cognitive ambidexterity, as managerial microfoundations of organizational ambidexterity. In doing so, we contribute to the persisting gap in the literature: how are the various modes of ambidexterity selected, and how can these be organized in an optimal way? This issue was pinpointed by Simsek (2009), who noted that research on ambidexterity typically uses only one theoretical lens to illustrate it, such as the dual structures of spatial ambidexterity or organizational context for contextual ambidexterity. However, in reality several ambidexterity modes are employed simultaneously at different levels of an organization (see also Birkinshaw and Gupta, 2013), and for this reason we need to better understand the foundations of the decision-making processes to better grasp the complexity of ambidextrous solutions in organizations. We contribute to this discussion by putting forward an underlying dimension of organizational ambidexterity – cognitive ambidexterity, as a managerial condition for organizing ambidextrous behavior. By integrating theoretical insights from the ambidexterity, dualities, and managerial cognition literatures, we shed light on the cognitive microfoundations of how managers frame their ambidexterity decisions. In the following, we discuss implications for the organizational ambidexterity literature, as well more broadly to strategic renewal literature.

Cognitive dimension in the organizational ambidexterity framework

We suggested that management cognition plays an important role across the different ambidexterity modes (see Figure 4.1 and Table 4.1). The selection of the right ambidexterity mode itself has roots in the discussion on whether exploration and exploitation (and other dualities) are fundamentally compatible or incompatible activities in particular decision-making scenarios. The nature (compatibleness or incompatibleness) of the two alternatives of a duality is assessed through the managerial framing process, which produces an inquiry for either dilemma solutions (separation temporarily or spatially) or paradoxical thinking (contextual ambidexterity). This is rooted in managerial cognitive processes, through which managers formulate their personal perception of the decision at hand based on their personal beliefs and attitudes. In addition, personal emotions (e.g., Hodgkinson and Healey, 2011) play a role in the managerial framing process. It may be that managers, therefore, are likely to separate exploration and exploitation not only because they are actually incompatible but also because they are perceived and framed as incompatible.

Previous research suggests that implementing paradoxical solutions increases the cognitive complexity, but on the other hand warns about the harmful effects of cognitive simplicity in a complex, fast changing world (Levy et al., 2007). In this regard, ambidexterity and paradox scholars are increasingly advocating for synergetic and higher-order managerial thinking, and thus a reduced use of structural or temporal separation of exploitation and exploration (e.g., Aubry and Lièvre, 2010; Gebert et al., 2010; Lewis and Smith, 2014).

Implementing contextually ambidextrous solutions is a cognitively complex endeavor. This requires managerial abilities to reformulate problems, tolerate ambiguity, and considerer additional alternative perspectives. In order to deal with such issues, managers tend to search for more widespread and new information, spend more time interpreting it, detect deeper dimensions, and simultaneously obtain myriad competing but also complementary elucidations of their observations (Levy et al., 2007). Adopting transcendence-type solutions requires even more complex thinking. In this regard, Gavetti (2012) noted that some managers are well-equipped to establish associations (i.e. analogs) between knowledge structures in different contexts, which allows them to access and utilize cognitively distant, yet greater, business opportunities. Further, when there are changes in the source context, the managerial capacity to utilize this and build analogies to different target contexts improves in the long run (Gary et al., 2012). Through employment of cognitive frames that accept the contradictions, the managers and management teams can strive for more complex strategic actions, such as supporting the development of new competencies, as well as deepening existing ones (Mihalache et al., 2014). Thus, if skillfully applied, contextual ambidexterity could be good solution for resolving key strategic dualities and paradoxes.

However, some scholars have discovered that it is a tenuous process to hold the opposites together, and the endeavor reverts to favoring one pole over the other (Langley and Sloan, 2011; Putnam et al., 2016). In this light, it is notable that "wearing two hats at the same time" (Gibson and Birkinshaw, 2004) can be expected to cause a major cognitive burden. Therefore, managers are advised not to target paradoxical solutions without careful consideration. Rather, it might be reasonable to also aim at simplicity rather than complexity and specialization, especially when the structural solutions are feasible in facilitating the co-existence of the dualities in the organization to guarantee that exploration actions can be carried out. Thus, we advocate a more pragmatic contingency approach where the best-fitting organizational ambidexterity solutions are a result of the individual context, which refers to the decision-makers' personal cognitive abilities as well as the organizational context regarding a particular duality.

Cognitive ambidexterity and strategic renewal

The contradictions and tensions managers face during decision-making processes are manifold. They are not only an unintended outcome of managerial decisions but can also result from the market and stakeholder demands. While some scholars have suggested that organizations get increasingly rigid as they age and grow, others have demonstrated that longstanding firms can retain their competitive edge through strategic renewal (Lewin and Volberda, 1999; Schmitt et al., 2016).

Mental and cognitive models are present in any renewal process, becoming even more significant in the situation when individuals are required to simultaneously cope with contradictory demands. Indeed, organizational ambidexterity solutions – structural, temporal, contextual, or individual – cannot fully facilitate the strategic renewal if the members of the organization are not mentally and cognitively engaged in the change process. Furthermore, especially when the ambidexterity solutions are contextual and require individual and team level engagement of both sides of the duality, the demands for cognitive processing and judgment increase. Therefore, we call for further research focusing on the role of cognition in the strategic renewal process.

Managerial implications

Managerial decision-making becomes more complex due to the ever-rising demands of different internal and external stakeholders. This chapter sheds light on the interface of organizational ambidexterity, strategic dualities, and managerial cognition, which together help practitioners to better understand why dualities should be acknowledged, the potential situations where dualities emerge, and how the perception of these dualities affects their resolution. This chapter promotes a pragmatic contingency approach where organizational ambidexterity solutions – spatial, temporal, and contextual – should be chosen based on the use of a thoughtful managerial framing process. Some renewal demands might be best solved via strict trade-offs where different processes are separated and the problem-solving is left to specialized experts, while sometimes behavioral adjustments and contextually flexible arrangements help to react quickly to various impulses and to reap synergies. Nevertheless, we expect that managers could make better choices over ambidextrous solutions, if they critically reflect on the cognitive demands, challenges, and opportunities of those solutions.

References

Adler, P. S., Goldoftas, B., & Levine, D. I., 1999. Flexibility versus efficiency? A case study of model changeovers in the Toyota production system. *Organization Science* 10 (1), 43–68.

Adner, R., & Helfat, C. E. 2003. Corporate effects and dynamic managerial capabilities. *Strategic Management Journal*, 24 (10), 1011–1025.

Andriopoulos, C., & Lewis, M. W. 2009. Exploitation–exploration tensions and organizational ambidexterity: Managing paradoxes of innovation. *Organization Science*, 20 (4), 696–717.

Andriopoulos, C., & Lewis, M. W., 2010. Managing innovation paradoxes: Ambidexterity lessons from leading product design companies. *Long Range Planning* 43 (1), 104–122.

Apker, J., Propp, K. M., & Zabava Ford, W. S., 2005. Negotiating status and identity tensions in healthcare team interactions: An exploration of nurse role dialectics. *Journal of Applied Communication Research* 33 (2), 93–115.

Aston-Jones, G., & Cohen, J. D., 2005. An integrative theory of locus coeruleus–norepinephrine function: Adaptive gain and optimal performance. *Annual Review Neuroscience* 28, 403–450.

Aubry, M., & Lièvre, P., 2010. Ambidexterity as a competence of project leaders: A case study from two polar expeditions. *Project Management Journal* 41 (3), 32–44.

Bartunek, J. M., 1984. Changing interpretive schemes and organizational restructuring: The example of a religious order. *Administrative Science Quarterly* 29 (3), 355–372.

Benner, M. J., & Tushman, M. L., 2003. Exploitation, exploration, and process management: The productivity dilemma revisited. *Academy of Management Review* 28 (2), 238–256.

Birkinshaw, J., Crilly, D., Bouquet, C., & Lee, S. Y., 2016. How do firms manage strategic dualities? A process perspective. *Academy of Management Discoveries* 2 (1), 51–78.

Birkinshaw, J., & Gupta, K., 2013. Clarifying the distinctive contribution of ambidexterity to the field of organization studies. *The Academy of Management Perspectives* 27 (4), 287–298.

Carlile, P. R. 2004. Transferring, translating, and transforming: An integrative framework for managing knowledge across boundaries. *Organization Science*, 15 (5), 555–568.

Cao, Q., Gedajlovic, E., & Zhang, H., 2009. Unpacking organizational ambidexterity: Dimensions, contingencies, and synergistic effects. *Organization Science* 20 (4), 781–796.

Chandrasekaran, A., 2009. Multiple levels of ambidexterity in managing the innovation–improvement dilemma: Evidence from high technology organizations. Doctoral dissertation, University of Minnesota.

Child, J., 1984. *Organization: A guide to problems and practice*. Sage: Newbury Park, CA.

Christensen, C. M., 1997. *The innovator's dilemma: When new technologies cause great firms to fail*. Boston, MA: Harvard Business School Press.

Clegg, S. R., Da Cunha, J. V., & Cunha, M. P., 2002. Management paradoxes: A relational view. *Human Relations* 55 (5), 483–503.

Duncan, R. B., 1976. The ambidextrous organization: Designing dual structures for innovation. In Pondy, L. R., & Slevin, D. P. (Eds.), *The management of organization*, Vol. 1. New York, NY: North Holland, pp. 167–188.

Eggers, J. P., & Kaplan, S. 2013. Cognition and capabilities: A multi–level perspective. *Academy of Management Annals*, 7 (1), 295–340.

Eisenhardt, K. M., & Brown, S. L. 1998. Competing on the edge: Strategy as structured chaos. *Long Range Planning*, 31 (5), 786–789.

Eisenhardt, K. M., Furr, N. R., & Bingham, C. B., 2010. CROSSROADS–Microfoundations of performance: Balancing efficiency and flexibility in dynamic environments. *Organization Science* 21 (6), 1263–1273.

Eisenhardt, K. M., & Westcott, B. J., 1988. Paradoxical demands and the creation of excellence: The case of just–in–time manufacturing in paradox and transformation.

In Quinn, R., & Cameron, K. (Eds.), *Toward a theory of change in organization and management*. Cambridge, MA: Ballinger, pp. 169–193.

Evans, P., 1992. Balancing continuity and change: The constructive tension in individual and organizational development. In Bennis, W., Mason, R. O., & Mitroff, I. I. (Eds.), *Executive and organizational continuity: Managing the paradoxes of stability and change*, 253–283, San Francisco, CA: Jossey–Bass.

Farjoun, M., 2010. Beyond dualism: Stability and change as a duality. *Academy of Management Review* 35 (2), 202–225.

Fernandez, A. S., Le Roy, F., & Gnyawali, D. R., 2014. Sources and management of tension in co–opetition case evidence from telecommunications satellites manufacturing in Europe. *Industrial Marketing Management* 43 (2), 222–235.

Gaim, M., & Wåhlin, N., 2016. In search of a creative space: A conceptual framework of synthesizing paradoxical tensions. *Scandinavian Journal of Management* 32 (1), 33–44.

Garbuio, M., King, A. W., & Lovallo, D., 2011. Looking inside psychological influences on structuring a firm's portfolio of resources. *Journal of Management* 37 (5), 1444–1463.

Gary, M. S., Wood, R. E., & Pillinger, T., 2012. Enhancing mental models, analogical transfer, and performance in strategic decision making. *Strategic Management Journal* 33 (11), 1229–1246.

Gavetti, G., 2012. Toward a behavioral theory of strategy. *Organization Science* 23 (1), 267–285.

Gebert, D., Boerner, S., & Kearney, E., 2010. Fostering team innovation: Why is it important to combine opposing action strategies? *Organization Science* 21 (3), 593–608.

Gersick, C. J., 1991. Revolutionary change theories: A multilevel exploration of the punctuated equilibrium paradigm. *Academy of Management Review* 16 (1), 10–36.

Ghemawat, P., & Ricart Costa, J. E., 1993. The organizational tension between static and dynamic efficiency. *Strategic Management Journal* 14 (2), 59–73.

Gibson, C. B., & Birkinshaw, J., 2004. The antecedents, consequences, and mediating role of organizational ambidexterity. *Academy of Management Journal* 47 (2), 209–226.

Gilbert, C. G., 2006. Change in the presence of residual fit: Can competing frames coexist? *Organization Science* 17 (1), 150–167.

Good, D., & Michel, E. J., 2013. Individual ambidexterity: Exploring and exploiting in dynamic contexts. *The Journal of Psychology* 147 (5), 435–453.

Graetz, F., & Smith, A. C., 2008. The role of dualities in arbitrating continuity and change in forms of organizing. *International Journal of Management Reviews* 10 (3), 265–280.

Greenberg, D., McKone Sweet, K., & Wilson, H. J., 2013. Entrepreneurial leaders: Creating opportunity in an unknowable world. *Leader to Leader* 67, 56–62.

Gulati, R., & Puranam, P., 2009. Renewal through reorganization: The value of inconsistencies between formal and informal organization. *Organization Science* 20 (2), 422–440.

Gupta, A. K., Smith, K. G., & Shalley, C. E., 2006. The interplay between exploration and exploitation. *Academy of Management Journal* 49 (4), 693–706.

Hahn, T., Preuss, L., Pinkse, J., & Figge, F., 2014. Cognitive frames in corporate sustainability: Managerial sensemaking with paradoxical and business case frames. *Academy of Management Review* 39 (4), 463–487.

Harrison, E. F., & Pelletier, M. A., 2000. The essence of management decision. *Management Decision* 38 (7), 462–470.

He, Z. L., & Wong, P. K., 2004. Exploration vs. exploitation: An empirical test of the ambidexterity hypothesis. *Organization Science* 15 (4), 481–494.

Helfat, C.,& Raubitschek, R., 2000. Product sequencing: Co–evolution of knowledge, capabilities and products. *Strategic Management Journal* 21 (10/11), 961–979.

Helfat, C. E., & Peteraf, M. A., 2015. Managerial cognitive capabilities and the microfoundations of dynamic capabilities. *Strategic Management Journal* 36 (6), 831–850.

Hodgkinson, G. P., & Healey, M. P., 2011. Psychological foundations of dynamic capabilities: Reflexion and reflection in strategic management. *Strategic Management Journal* 32 (13), 1500–1516.

Huber, G. P., 1991. Organizational learning: The contributing processes and the literatures'. *Organizational Science* 2 (1), 88–115.

Jansen, J., 2005. Ambidextrous organizations: A multiple–level study of absorptive capacity, exploratory and exploitative innovation and performance. Doctoral dissertation. Erasmus University Rotterdam.

Jansen, J. J., Tempelaar, M. P., Van Den Bosch, F. A., & Volberda, H. W., 2009. Structural differentiation and ambidexterity: The mediating role of integration mechanisms. *Organization Science* 20 (4), 797–811.

Jarzabkowski, P., Lê, J., & Van de Ven, A. H., 2013. Responding to competing strategic demands: How organizing, belonging, and performing paradoxes coevolve. *Strategic Organization* 11 (3), 245–280.

Jarzabkowski, P. A., & Lê, J. K., 2017. We have to do this and that? You must be joking: Constructing and responding to paradox through humor. *Organization Studies* 38 (3–4), 433–462.

Jasmand, C., Blazevic, V., & de Ruyter, K., 2012. Generating sales while providing service: A study of customer service representatives' ambidextrous behavior. *Journal of Marketing* 76 (1), 20–37.

Kaplan, S., 2008. Framing contests: Strategy making under uncertainty. *Organization Science* 19 (5), 729–752.

Kaplan, S., 2011. Research in cognition and strategy: Reflections on two decades of progress and a look to the future. *Journal of Management Studies* 48 (3), 665–695.

Karhu, P., Ritala, P., & Viola, L., 2016. How do ambidextrous teams create new products? Cognitive ambidexterity, analogies, and new product creation. *Knowledge and Process Management* 23 (1), 3–17.

Katila, R., & Ahuja, G., 2002. Something old, something new: A longitudinal study of search behavior and new product introduction. *Academy of Management Journal* 45 (6), 1183–1194.

Kauppila, O. P., & Tempelaar, M. P., 2016. The social-cognitive underpinnings of employees' ambidextrous behaviour and the supportive role of group managers' leadership. *Journal of Management Studies* 53 (6), 1019–1044.

Knight, E., & Paroutis, S., 2017. Becoming salient: The TMT leader's role in shaping the interpretive context of paradoxical tensions. *Organization Studies* 38 (3–4), 403–432.

Knight, F. H., 1921. *Risk, uncertainty and profit.* New York, NY: Hart, Schaffner and Marx.

Langley, A., & Sloan, P., 2011. Organizational change and dialectic processes. In Boje, D. D., Burnes, B., & Hassard, J. (Eds.), T*he Routledge companion to organizational change.* London: Routledge, pp. 261–275.

Laureiro-Martínez, D., Brusoni, S., Canessa, N., & Zollo, M., 2015. Understanding the exploration–exploitation dilemma: An fMRI study of attention control and decision-making performance. *Strategic Management Journal* 36 (3), 319–338.

Laureiro-Martínez, D., Brusoni, S., & Zollo, M., 2010. The neuroscientific foundations of the exploration – Exploitation dilemma. *Journal of Neuroscience, Psychology, and Economics* 3 (2), 95.

Lavie, D., Stettner, U., & Tushman, M. L., 2010. Exploration and exploitation within and across organizations. *The Academy of Management Annals* 4 (1), 109–155.

Leonard-Barton, D. (1992). Core capabilities and core rigidities: A paradox in managing new product development. *Strategic Management Journal*, 13 (S1), 111–125.

Levinthal, D. A., & March, J. G., 1993. The myopia of learning. *Strategic Management Journal* 14 (S2), 95–112.

Levitt, B., & March, J. G., 1988. Organizational learning. *Annual Review of Sociology* 14 (1), 319–340.

Levy, O., Beechler, S., Taylor, S., & Boyacigiller, N. A., 2007. What we talk about when we talk about "global mindset": Managerial cognition in multinational corporations. *Journal of International Business Studies* 38 (2), 231–258.

Lewin, A. Y., & Volberda, H. W., 1999. Prolegomena on coevolution: A framework for research on strategy and new organizational forms. *Organization Science* 10 (5), 519–534.

Lewis, M. W., 2000. Exploring paradox: Toward a more comprehensive guide. *Academy of Management Review* 25 (4), 760–776.

Lewis, M. W., Andriopoulos, C., & Smith, W. K., 2014. Paradoxical leadership to enable strategic agility. *California Management Review* 56 (3), 58–77.

Lewis, M. W., & Smith, W. K. 2014. Paradox as a metatheoretical perspective: Sharpening the focus and widening the scope. *The Journal of Applied Behavioral Science*, 50 (2), 127–149.

Lin, H. E., & McDonough, E. F., 2014. Cognitive frames, learning mechanisms, and innovation ambidexterity. *Journal of Product Innovation Management* 31 (S1), 170–188.

Lubatkin, M. H., Simsek, Z., Ling, Y., & Veiga, J. F., 2006. Ambidexterity and performance in small–to medium–sized firms: The pivotal role of top management team behavioral integration. *Journal of Management* 32 (5), 646–672.

Lüscher, L. S., & Lewis, M. W., 2008. Organizational change and managerial sensemaking: Working through paradox. *Academy of Management Journal* 51 (2), 221–240.

March, J. G., 1991. Exploration and exploitation in organizational learning. *Organization Science* 2 (1), 71–87.

Margolis, J. D., & Walsh, J. P., 2003. Misery loves companies: Rethinking social initiatives by business. *Administrative Science Quarterly* 48 (2), 268–305.

McCall, M.W. Jr., & Kaplan, R. E., 1985. Whatever it takes: Decision makers at work. *The Academy of Management Review* 10 (4), 868–870.

McKenzie, J., Woolf, N., Van Winkelen, C., & Morgan, C., 2009. Cognition in strategic decision making: A model of non–conventional thinking capacities for complex situations. *Management Decision* 47 (2), 209–232.

Mihalache, O. R., Jansen, J. J., Van den Bosch, F. A., & Volberda, H. W., 2014. Top management team shared leadership and organizational ambidexterity: A moderated mediation framework. *Strategic Entrepreneurship Journal* 8 (2), 128–148.

Mom, T. J., Van Den Bosch, F. A., & Volberda, H. W., 2007. Investigating managers' exploration and exploitation activities: The influence of top-down, bottom-up, and horizontal knowledge inflows. *Journal of Management Studies* 44 (6), 910–931.

Mom, T. J., Van Den Bosch, F. A., & Volberda, H. W., 2009. Understanding variation in managers' ambidexterity: Investigating direct and interaction effects of formal structural and personal coordination mechanisms. *Organization Science* 20 (4), 812–828.

Neck, H., 2011. Cognitive ambidexterity: The underlying mental model of the entrepreneurial leader. In Greenberg, D., McKone–Sweet, K., & Wilson, H. J. (Eds.), *The new entrepreneurial leader: Developing leaders who shape social and economic opportunity*. pp. 24–42, Berrett–Koehler Publishers: Oakland, CA.

Nerkar, A., 2003. Old is gold? The value of temporal exploration in the creation of new knowledge. *Management Science* 49 (2), 211–229.

Nickerson, J. A., & Zenger, T. R., 2002. Being efficiently fickle: A dynamic theory of organizational choice. *Organization Science* 13 (5), 547–566.

O'Reilly, C. A., & Tushman, M. L., 2004. The ambidextrous organization. *Harvard Business Review* 82 (4), 74–83.

O'Reilly, C. A., & Tushman, M. L., 2008. Ambidexterity as a dynamic capability: Resolving the innovator's dilemma. *Research in Organizational Behavior* 28, 185–206.

O'Reilly, C. A., & Tushman, M. L., 2013. Organizational ambidexterity: Past, present, and future. *The Academy of Management Perspectives* 27 (4), 324–338.

Papachroni, A., Heracleous, L., & Paroutis, S., 2015. Organizational ambidexterity through the lens of paradox theory building: A novel research agenda. *The Journal of Applied Behavioral Science* 51 (1), 71–93.

Papachroni, A., Heracleous, L., & Paroutis, S., 2016. In pursuit of ambidexterity: Managerial reactions to innovation–Efficiency tensions. *Human Relations* 69 (9), 1791–1822.

Parker, S. K., 2014. Beyond motivation: Job and work design for development, health, ambidexterity, and more. *Annual Review of Psychology* 65, 661–691.

Poole, M. S., & Van de Ven, A. H., 1989. Using paradox to build management and organization theories. *Academy of Management Review* 14 (4), 562–578.

Porac, J. F., & Thomas, H., 2002. Managing cognition and strategy: Issues, trends and future directions. In Pettigrew, A., & Thomas, H., Whittington, R. (Eds.), *Handbook of strategy and management*. London: Sage, pp. 165–181.

Prahalad, C. K., & Bettis, R. A., 1986. The dominant logic: A new linkage between diversity and performance. *Strategic Management Journal* 7 (6), 485–501.

Putnam, L. L., Fairhurst, G. T., & Banghart, S., 2016. Contradictions, dialectics, and paradoxes in organizations: A constitutive approach. *The Academy of Management Annals* 10 (1), 65–171.

Putnam, L. L., Myers, K. K., & Gailliard, B. M., 2014. Examining the tensions in workplace flexibility and exploring options for new directions. *Human Relations* 67 (4), 413–440.

Raisch, S., & Birkinshaw, J., 2008. Organizational ambidexterity: Antecedents, outcomes, and moderators. *Journal of Management* 34 (3), 375–409.

Raisch, S., Birkinshaw, J., Probst, G., & Tushman, M. L., 2009. Organizational ambidexterity: Balancing exploitation and exploration for sustained performance. *Organization Science* 20 (4), 685–695.

Rothaermel, F. T., & Deeds, D. L., 2004. Exploration and exploitation alliances in biotechnology: A system of new product development. *Strategic Management Journal* 25 (3), 201–221.

Schad, J., Lewis, M. W., Raisch, S., & Smith, W. K., 2016. Paradox research in management science: Looking back to move forward. *The Academy of Management Annals* 10 (1), 5–64.

Schmitt, A., Raisch, S., & Volberda, H. W., 2016. Strategic renewal: Past research, theoretical tensions and future challenges. *International Journal of Management Reviews*, 20 (1), 81–98.

Shapiro, C., & Varian, H. R., 1998. *Information rules*. Boston, MA: Harvard Business School Press.

Sidhu, J. S., & Reinmoeller, P., 2017. *The ambidextrous organization: Management paradox today*, 1st edition. Routledge: Abingdon, UK.

Siggelkow, N., & Levinthal, D. A., 2003. Temporarily divide to conquer: Centralized, decentralized, and reintegrated organizational approaches to exploration and adaptation. *Organization Science* 14 (6), 650–669.

Simsek, Z., 2009. Organizational ambidexterity: Towards a multilevel understanding. *Journal of Management Studies* 46 (4), 597–624.

Simsek, Z., Heavey, C., Veiga, J. F., & Souder, D., 2009. A typology for aligning organizational ambidexterity's conceptualizations, antecedents, and outcomes. *Journal of Management Studies* 46 (5), 864–894.

Smith, W. K., 2014. Dynamic decision making: A model of senior leaders managing strategic paradoxes. *Academy of Management Journal* 57 (6), 1592–1623.

Smith, W. K., Besharov, M. L., Wessels, A. K., & Chertok, M., 2012. A paradoxical leadership model for social entrepreneurs: Challenges, leadership skills, and pedagogical tools for managing social and commercial demands. *Academy of Management Learning & Education* 11 (3), 463–478.

Smith, W. K., Binns, A., & Tushman, M. L., 2010. Complex business models: Managing strategic paradoxes simultaneously. *Long Range Planning* 43 (2), 448–461.

Smith, W. K., & Lewis, M. W., 2011. Toward a theory of paradox: A dynamic equilibrium model of organizing. *Academy of Management Review* 36 (2), 381–403.

Smith, W. K., & Tushman, M. L., 2005. Managing strategic contradictions: A top management model for managing innovation streams. *Organization Science* 16 (5), 522–536.

Szaflarski, J. P., Binder, J. R., Possing, E. T., McKiernan, K. A., Ward, B. D., & Hammeke, T. A., 2008. Language lateralization in left–handed and ambidextrous people: FMRI data. *American Academy of Neurology* 59, 238–244.

Tempelaar, M. (2010). Organizing for ambidexterity: Studies on the pursuit of exploration and exploitation through differentiation, integration, contextual and individual attributes. Doctoral dissertation, Erasmus University Rotterdam (No. EPS–2010–191–STR).

Tuncdogan, A., Van Den Bosch, F., & Volberda, H., 2015. Regulatory focus as a psychological micro–foundation of leaders' exploration and exploitation activities. *The Leadership Quarterly* 26 (5), 838–850.

Turner, N., Swart, J., & Maylor, H., 2013. Mechanisms for managing ambidexterity: A review and research agenda. *International Journal of Management Reviews* 15 (3), 317–332.

Tushman, M. L., & O'Reilly, C. A., 1996. The ambidextrous organizations: Managing evolutionary and revolutionary change. *California Management Review* 38 (4), 8–30.

Tushman, M. L., & Romanelli, E., 1985. Organizational evolution: Interactions between external and emergent processes and strategic choice. *Research in Organizational Behavior* 8, 171–222.

Tversky, A., & Kahneman, D., 1982. Evidential impact of base–rates. In Kahneman, D., Slovic, P., & Tversky, A. (Eds.), *Judgment under uncertainty: Heuristics and biases*. Cambridge, MA: Cambridge University Press, pp. 153–160.

Venkatraman, N., Lee, C. H., & Iyer, B., 2007. Strategic ambidexterity and sales growth: A longitudinal test in the software sector. Unpublished manuscript (earlier version presented at the Academy of Management Meetings, 2005).

Vlaar, P. W., Van Den Bosch, F. A., & Volberda, H. W., 2007. Towards a dialectic perspective on formalization in interorganizational relationships: How alliance managers capitalize on the duality inherent in contracts, rules and procedures. *Organization Studies* 28 (4), 437–466.

Volberda, H. W., 1996. Toward the flexible form: How to remain vital in hypercompetitive environments. *Organization Science* 7 (4), 359–374.

Volberda, H. W., 2003. Strategic flexibility: Creating dynamic competitive advantages. In Faulkner, D. O., & Campbell, A. (Eds.), *The Oxford handbook of strategy (Volume II: Corporate Strategy)*. Oxford: Oxford University Press, Ch. 32, pp. 447–506.

Volberda, H. W., & Lewin, A. Y., 2003. Co-evolutionary dynamics within and between firms: From evolution to co-evolution. *Journal of Management Studies* 40 (8), 2111–2136.

Walrave, B., Van Oorschot, K. E., & Romme, A. G. L., 2011. Getting trapped in the suppression of exploration: A simulation model. *Journal of Management Studies* 48 (8), 1727–1751.

Walsh, J. P., 1995. Managerial and organizational cognition: Notes from a trip down memory lane. *Organization Science* 6 (3), 280–321.

Winter, S. G., & Szulanski, G., 2001. Replication as strategy. *Organization Science* 12 (6), 730–743.

Yu, T., Patterson, P. G., & de Ruyter, K., 2013. Achieving service–sales ambidexterity. *Journal of Service Research* 16 (1), 52–66.

Zhang, Y., Waldman, D. A., Han, Y. L., & Li, X. B., 2015. Paradoxical leader behaviors in people management: Antecedents and consequences. *Academy of Management Journal* 58 (2), 538–566.

Zimmermann, A., & Birkinshaw, J., 2016. Reconciling capabilities and ambidexterity theories: A multi-level perspective. In Teece, D. J., & Leih, S. (Eds.), *The Oxford handbook of dynamic capabilities*. Oxford University Press: Oxford, UK.

Zimmermann, A., Raisch, S., & Birkinshaw, J., 2015. How is ambidexterity initiated? The emergent charter definition process. *Organization Science* 26 (4), 1119–1139.

5 Knowledge management practices for stimulating incremental and radical product innovation

Petra Andries, Sophie De Winne, and Anna Bos-Nehles

Introduction

According to Agarwal and Helfat (2009, p. 282) strategic renewal includes "the process, content, and outcome of refreshment or replacement of attributes of an organization that have the potential to substantially affect its long-term prospects". This is a broad definition, which can include many forms of renewal activities, in response to both external opportunities/threats and internal strengths/weaknesses. Examples of renewal activities currently receiving much attention are innovation activities, creating opportunities for both incremental and radical innovation. Crucial to innovation and the subsequent development of sustainable competitive advantage is the organization's ability to create and transfer knowledge (Nonaka, 1991, 1994). This ability depends upon the extent to which the organization succeeds in combining and exchanging existing knowledge among employees (Nahapiet and Ghoshal, 1998). Several studies have shown that the implementation of knowledge management practices that stimulate individual employees to develop their knowledge base (e.g. job rotation, training, financial incentives for new ideas), exchange their knowledge with others (e.g. teamwork, employee participation, suggestion schemes) or make their knowledge part of the organizational memory (e.g. input of knowledge in lessons learned databases) can be fruitful in this respect (e.g. Chen and Huang, 2009; Greiner, Böhmann and Krcmar, 2007; Lopez-Cabrales, Perez-Luno and Cabrera, 2009; Wang and Noe, 2010; Zhou, Hong and Liu, 2013). These practices incite a learning process, the creation of fresh insights and the discovery of new opportunities among employees, important antecedents of new knowledge creation and innovation.

Although there is theoretical and empirical evidence for the contribution of knowledge management practices to innovation performance, several studies have shown that there might be some contingencies at play, and that the relationship between knowledge management practices and innovation might be more complex than assumed thus far. Greiner et al. (2007), for example, show that there should be an alignment between knowledge management practices and the business strategy. Lopez-Cabrales et al. (2009), in turn, conclude that knowledge features mediate the relationship between knowledge management practices and innovation, and that not all knowledge management practices equally contribute to innovation. More specifically, they show that the uniqueness of knowledge plays a mediating role in the relationship between knowledge management practices and the organization's innovation activity. They also demonstrate that especially *collaborative human resource management (HRM) practices* (e.g. group-oriented HRM practices such as cross-functional teams and job rotation) contribute to the uniqueness of knowledge and subsequently to innovation. *Knowledge-based HRM practices* (e.g. HRM practices focused on internal development of knowledge such as employee empowerment and training in firm-specific knowledge), in turn, do not influence the uniqueness of knowledge and therefore do not show a relationship with innovation. More recently, Zhou et al. (2013) have shown that both a commitment-oriented HRM system (emphasizing internal cohesiveness) and a collaborative-oriented HRM system (building external connections) positively influence the firm's innovation. They also found a negative interaction effect between both systems. The authors rely on ambidexterity theory to explain the findings, and state that "if the organization ambidextrously invests in both commitment and collaboration oriented HRM systems, each system may divert the resources devoted to the other system" (Zhou et al., 2013, p. 279). Therefore, they suggest that organizations should take their innovation strategy into account (i.e. focus on incremental or radical innovation) to decide upon investments in the HRM system or try to find a balanced equilibrium if they decide to focus on both innovation strategies.

These studies show that the right choice of practices depends on whether organizations favor radical and incremental innovation and that the type of knowledge that is transferred and created might be an important mediating variable. We want to add to this discussion in two ways. First, we focus on the complexity of innovation strategies and the distinction between incremental and radical innovation in particular. Both activities demand different mindsets and approaches, which March (1991) refers to as "exploitation" and "exploration". Whereas *exploitative innovation* is incremental, builds further on existing knowledge and implies efficiency and refinement, *exploratory innovation* has a more radical character and requires the incorporation of diverse viewpoints, experimentation and risk taking (Lavie, Stettner and Tushman, 2010). As mentioned by Zhou et al. (2013), ambidexterity (i.e. the ability to be equally successful in incremental and radical innovation) might be very hard to realize given these opposing demands. Second, we expect that the type of innovation (incremental versus radical) asks for other types of knowledge to be created and shared. In developing the hypotheses, we therefore specifically focus on the concepts of related and unrelated knowledge. Whereas *related knowledge* refers to information, ideas and expertise that are closely related to the existing knowledge of the individual, *unrelated knowledge* is not (closely) related to the existing knowledge of the individual.

In this study, we hypothesize that certain knowledge management practices improve incremental product innovation performance, while others are more appropriate for radical product innovation. Using a sample of 822 Flemish manufacturing and service companies, we find that incentives oriented at the transfer and creation of related knowledge stimulate incremental innovation performance, whereas incentives oriented at the transfer and creation of unrelated knowledge stimulate radical innovation performance.

This study enriches the theoretical understanding of the relationship between knowledge management practices and innovation performance, by pointing to the potential roles of related and unrelated knowledge. It also warns against a "one-size-fits-all" approach to stimulating knowledge transfer and creation, and shows that companies should carefully select practices that fit with their innovation strategy.

Literature review and hypotheses

The role of related and unrelated knowledge for incremental and radical innovation

In line with Greiner et al. (2007), we argue that practices focusing on stimulating employees to develop, transfer, communicate and exchange their knowledge (rather than practices focusing on codifying knowledge) are the most optimal choice for innovation. The central objective of these practices is leveraging the value of tacit knowledge, i.e. the highly personal knowledge of individuals that is rooted in action, firm-specific and difficult to formalize and communicate (Nonaka, 1991). Tacit knowledge is considered to be the crucial ingredient of innovation and a source of sustained competitive advantage because it is unique, valuable, scarce and inimitable (Oliver, 1997), and can only be acquired and exchanged through experience and interaction with others (e.g. via observation, imitation, practice) (Nonaka, 1991).

Although tacit knowledge is beneficial for innovation, it is also generally accepted that the improvement of existing products and technologies requires different types of tacit knowledge than the creation of radically new products and competencies. On the one hand, exploratory innovation requires the integration of divergent opinions and viewpoints into a new synthesis or artifact (Pelz and Andrews, 1966; Schön, 1963). Whereas some have argued that exploration requires the integration of knowledge from outside the firm (see overview by Lavie et al., 2010), others have shown that the integration of divergent knowledge and viewpoints from different individuals and different parts of the firm can also foster explorative innovation (de Visser et al., 2010). Truly novel solutions and insights hence build on the transfer between individuals of unrelated knowledge, which can be defined as information, ideas and expertise that are not (closely) related to the existing knowledge of the individual.

On the other hand, this knowledge diversity appears less beneficial for exploitative, incremental innovation. Instead, exploitative innovation results from the refinement and more efficient use of the existing knowledge base

(Lavie et al., 2010; March, 1991; O'Reilly and Tushman, 2004). This refinement is best achieved through the transfer and creation of related knowledge, which can be defined as information, ideas and expertise that are closely related to the existing knowledge of the individual. Bringing together diverse knowledge and viewpoints is not beneficial for incremental innovation, since it triggers conflicting expectations and an overload of opinions from diverse individuals (de Visser et al., 2010; Song, Thieme and Xie, 1998). This can disrupt existing work routines and decision making, which in turn hampers the ability for continuous optimization and refinement of existing products and technologies (de Visser et al., 2010; Song and Xie, 2000). Overall, it can therefore be expected that knowledge management practices aimed at the transfer and creation of related knowledge will contribute to incremental product innovation performance, while knowledge management techniques aimed at the transfer and creation of unrelated knowledge will contribute particularly to radical product innovation performance.

In what follows, we elaborate on the above reasoning for specific knowledge management practices that were questioned in the sixth edition of the Community Innovation Survey (CIS, 2011) and that can be related to the personalization strategy as mentioned by Greiner et al. (2007). More specifically, these are all knowledge management practices focusing on stimulating employees to develop, transfer, communicate and exchange their knowledge.

Knowledge management practices for the transfer and creation of related knowledge

Brainstorm sessions. Organizing brainstorm sessions is a management technique to generate ideas and stimulate creative thoughts (Nunamaker, Applegate and Konsynski, 1987). This can be done both individually and in a group setting. According to Nunamaker et al. (1987) individual brainstorm sessions are highly effective in terms of the number and quality of ideas that are generated. Yet, because they are individually organized, there is no exchange of knowledge between employees. We therefore argue that the new ideas will be based upon the existing knowledge of the individuals and thus especially concern related knowledge.

Brainstorm sessions in groups, in turn, rely on a number of people to generate ideas. Although the basic premise is that a group of people working together will be more creative in problem solving as compared to individuals, previous research has shown that this is not always the case. Brainstorming in groups seems to be very difficult to organize because a lot of ideas have to be generated by different people in a relatively small amount of time. We argue that brainstorm sessions in groups primarily lead to the transfer and creation of related knowledge. First, previous research has shown that groups are inclined "to focus on information they have in common rather than on sharing unique expertise" (Stasser, 1999; cited by Paulus and Yang, 2000, p. 77). Next, although diversity of participants in brainstorm sessions might be important for the number and newness of ideas, group comfort and cohesion are as – or even more – important (Wilson, 2006). People might be unwilling to state some of their ideas because they are afraid of being negatively evaluated by others (Paulus and Yang, 2000). This process is called evaluation apprehension and will be more likely when people do not know each other. Group comfort and cohesion might prevent evaluation apprehension and are higher when employees know each other. Finally, Wilson (2006) argues that ideas should be expressed very quickly, one by one, and without undue elaboration or stories to prevent production blocking (Diehl and Stroebe, 1991). Listening to others' ideas may distract people and hinder them in developing own new ideas. Therefore, too much interaction might be pernicious. These mechanisms imply that especially related knowledge will be transferred and created in brainstorm sessions in groups, and that the transfer and creation of unrelated knowledge might be hindered.

In sum, we argue that the nature of brainstorm sessions – whether they are individual or collective – makes them especially suitable for the transfer and creation of related knowledge, which in turn leads to incremental innovation. We thus hypothesize that:

H1: The use of brainstorm sessions stimulates the transfer and creation of related knowledge and therefore has a positive effect on incremental product innovation performance.

Financial and non-financial incentives for new ideas. Financial (e.g. bonus) and non-financial incentives (e.g. extra holidays) for new ideas are extrinsic rewards. According to the expectancy theory (Vroom, 1964), financial and non-financial incentives can steer employees to act or behave in a certain way because they know that their efforts will be valued and rewarded by the organization. More specifically, financial and non-financial incentives for new ideas can motivate employees to generate new ideas (in the case of individual incentives) or to share their knowledge with other employees (in the case of group incentives) because the incentives send a signal of recognition towards the employee and show that the organization values knowledge sharing behavior (Cabrera and Cabrera, 2005). Yet, although financial and non-financial incentives may stimulate employees to generate new ideas or to share their knowledge, they may especially instigate them to look for related knowledge, which inherently incorporates lower uncertainty and hence higher chances of reaping these financial and non-financial benefits (see for example Holmström, 1989 on the tendency of risk-averse managers to reallocate resources from R&D investments to less risky projects). This in turn can be expected to improve especially incremental innovation performance. This leads to the following hypothesis:

H2: The use of financial and non-financial incentives for new ideas stimulates the transfer and creation of related knowledge and therefore has a positive effect on incremental product innovation performance.

Knowledge management practices for the transfer and creation of unrelated knowledge

Job rotation. Job rotation implies "a lateral transfer of employees among a number of different positions and tasks within jobs where each requires different skills and responsibilities" (Huang, 1999, p. 75). It helps members of an organization to understand – through experience – the business from a multiplicity of perspectives (Nonaka, 1994, p. 29) and allows for building redundancy of information into an organization. According to Nonaka (1994), redundancy of information facilitates interaction among organizational members and consequently makes it easier to transfer tacit knowledge among them, a necessary condition for new knowledge creation and innovation. Cabrera and Cabrera (2005), in turn, argue from a social capital perspective that the opportunity to share and subsequently create knowledge is determined by the extent to which employees share the same language and narratives. The likelihood that employees share the same language and narratives is enhanced when people frequently change positions and jobs throughout the organization.

Moreover, when this rotation concerns a transfer between different departments and business units (as we measured it), the employee is continuously provided with new information from new and different perspectives, i.e. unrelated knowledge. When combined with the employee's existing knowledge, this new unrelated knowledge will lead to a process of new and unique knowledge creation (Lopez-Cabrales et al., 2009), and subsequently to radical product innovation. We therefore hypothesize that:

> *H3: The use of job rotation stimulates the transfer and creation of unrelated knowledge and therefore has a positive effect on radical product innovation performance.*

Cross-functional or multidisciplinary teams. Cross-functional or multidisciplinary structures bring together specialists from different departments within a single team structure for a particular innovation project (Griffin, 1997). Cabrera and Cabrera (2005) argue that teamwork gives employees the opportunity to work closely and frequently with others and therefore encourages tacit knowledge sharing. According to Noe, Hollenbeck, Gerhart and Wright (2003), when team members have a shared responsibility and are accountable for the results, action learning occurs. To achieve a positive result the team members seek out information and share what they find with others. Teamwork thus stimulates tacit knowledge sharing, and subsequently knowledge creation and innovation.

The integration of several domain specialists in a cross-functional or multidisciplinary team is especially effective for transferring unrelated knowledge, because social ties are created between employees from different groups (Allen, 2001; Cabrera and Cabrera, 2005; Hargadon, 2003). The connection of previously unrelated tacit knowledge sets will contribute to new knowledge creation, and subsequently to radical product innovation. In line with previous empirical findings by de Visser et al. (2010), we therefore hypothesize that:

> *H4: The use of cross-functional teams stimulates the transfer and creation of unrelated knowledge and therefore has a positive effect on radical product innovation performance.*

Method

In 2011, the sixth edition of the Community Innovation Survey (CIS) was conducted in several member states of the European Union. The survey sought to develop insights into the innovative behavior of companies and included a one-off module on knowledge management practices. For the Flemish part of the CIS2011 survey, a representative sample of 4,951 – mostly private – Belgian manufacturing and service firms was selected. Top management of the organizations received a 20 page questionnaire, inquiring about different innovation-related issues in the period 2008–2010. The response rate was 49% (2,418 firms). A comparison between respondents and non-respondents showed no bias in terms of innovation. Due to missing values for the variables used in our models, the analyses were restricted to a final sample of 822 firms. Descriptive statistics are given in Table 5.1.

Variables and descriptive statistics

Dependent variables: Radical and incremental innovation performance

We follow the work by Mohnen and Mairesse (2002), Faems, Van Looy and Debackere (2005) and Laursen and Salter (2006), who measured product innovation success on the innovated product's share in total sales. We use two different dependent variables, representing radical product innovation performance and incremental product innovation performance. We measure the successful development of radically new products or services as the share of turnover in 2010 from goods and services that were new to the market and that were introduced during the period 2008 to 2010. We label this variable *Rad_Inno*. The average firm in the sample obtained about 7.9% of its turnover from goods and services that were new to the market. Similarly, *Incr_Inno* represents the successful development of incremental product or service innovations and is measured as the share of turnover in 2010 from goods and services that were new to the firm but that were already available on the market and that were introduced during the period 2008 to 2010. The average firm in the sample obtained about 7.2% of its turnover from incremental goods and services innovations. The two dependent variables have the advantage of directly measuring the commercial success of innovative output.

Table 5.1 Descriptive statistics (822 observations)

	Mean	Std. Dev.	Min	Max.
Rad_Inno	7.906566	19.69737	0	100
Incr_Inno	7.18176	16.9883	0	100
Brainstorm	.7907543	.4070178	0	1
Crossfunc	.6277372	.4837022	0	1
Jobrot	.3613139	.4806737	0	1
Finin	.2664234	.4423573	0	1
Nfinin	.2262774	.4186755	0	1
RD_Intensity	.1407204	2.094078	0	58.6
Group	.6751825	.4685917	0	1
Collab	.3807786	.4858739	0	1
Size	161.4064	394.601	1	4825
Age	26.33333	18.59939	1	110
Serv	.4586375	.4985896	0	1
Hitech	.4355231	.4961272	0	1

Independent variables: Knowledge management practices

The CIS2011 asked companies about their use of various knowledge management practices in line with a personalization strategy during the period 2008–2010 (see also Cabrera and Cabrera, 2005; Nonaka, 1994). *Brainstorm* is a binary variable that indicates whether or not a company used brainstorming sessions. *Crossfunc* measures whether or not a company used multidisciplinary or cross-functional teams. *Jobrot* is a binary variable that indicates whether or not a company used job rotation between different departments or different companies within the group. *Finin* indicates whether or not a company used financial incentives for the development of new ideas. Finally, the dummy variable *Nfinin* indicates whether or not a company used non-financial incentives for the development of new ideas, such as extra holidays, public recognition and more interesting work.

As shown in Table 5.1, the use of practices varies widely. While 80% of the firms used brainstorming sessions (*Brainstorm*) and 63% used cross-functional teams (*Crossfunc*), only 27% used financial incentives (*Finin*) and 23% used non-financial incentives (*Nfinin*). Job rotation (*Jobrot*) was used by 36% of the firms in our sample.

Control variables

A limitation of many existing studies is that they focus solely on the impact of knowledge management practices without controlling for other factors that affect innovation performance (or firm performance in general) (see critique by Shadur and Snell, 2002). In order to avoid possible omitted variable bias that could lead to an over- or underestimation of the effects of employee stimuli, we include a number of control variables in our models.

R&D intensity. We expect a positive effect of internal innovation efforts on a company's innovation performance. In line with previous work, we therefore control for the firm's internal innovation efforts by including the variable *RD_Intensity*, measured as the firm's internal R&D expenditures in 2010 divided by its turnover in 2010. The average firm in our sample spends about 14% of its turnover on internal R&D. Due to the skewed distribution of this variable, we transformed it by taking the natural logarithm of 1 + RD_*Intensity* (see for example Czarnitzki and Kraft, 2010 for previous use of this measure). We labeled this variable *Ln_RD_Intensity*.

Group. A company that is part of a larger group may have easier access to resources in terms of capital and knowledge and hence have a better chance to introduce innovations than stand-alone companies (Mention, 2011). For product innovations, group members may also benefit from better access to markets through their affiliates' distribution system. Therefore we included the dummy variable *Group*, which takes the value 1 if the company belongs to a larger group, and the value 0 if it is an independent company. Approximately 68% of the observations in our sample belong to a group.

Collaboration. Innovation is best achieved through a combination of internal and external communication (Damanpour, 1991; Teece, 2007; Van de Ven, 1986). Collaboration with outsiders is positively connected to innovative outcomes (Kessler and Chakrabarti, 1996; Phelps, 2010) because it increases knowledge diversity and heterogeneity, which many authors consider indispensable for innovation (see for example Kane and Alavi, 2007). We control for this by including the dummy variable *Collab* in our analyses. It takes the value 1 if the company engaged in collaborations for the development of new products or processes during the period 2008–2010, and the value 0 if it did not. Approximately 38% of the observations in our sample collaborate with external parties to develop innovations.

Size. Since the seminal writings of Schumpeter (1939), the relationship between size and firm performance has been much debated (Ahuja, Lampert and Tandon, 2008; Cohen, 1995). Several theoretical arguments have been brought forward to substantiate the potential innovative advantages of both small and large firms (see for example Acs and Audretsch, 1990). While many empirical studies report a positive link between size and innovation (e.g. Skuras, Tsegenidi and Tsekouras, 2008; Un, Cuervo-Cazurra and Asakawa, 2010), others report a negative (Knudsen, 2007; Spithoven, Frantzen and Clarysse, 2010) or quadratic relation (Arvanitis, 2008). To control for the size of the company we use the number of employees in 2010 (*Size*). The average firm in our sample has 161 employees, while the biggest firm in the sample has more than 4,800 employees. For the regression analysis we used the natural logarithm of 1 + *Size*. We label this variable *Ln_Size* and also include its square to analyze possible curvilinear effects.

Age. The firms' age is also used as control variable, as younger firms may be more innovative than older ones (e.g. De Jong and Vermeulen, 2006; Schneider and Veugelers, 2010). In particular, younger firms may achieve a higher share of sales with new products simply because they have fewer established products than older firms. Based on the firm's founding date, we obtained the firm's age (*Age*). The average age of the respondent firms is 26. The oldest firm in the sample is 110 years old. For the regression analysis we used the natural logarithm of 1 + *Age*. We label this variable *Ln_Age*.

Industry. The literature indicates an industry effect on both innovation and innovation success (Ettlie and Rosenthal, 2011; Spithoven et al., 2010) and especially points to differences between the manufacturing sector and the service sector (Evangelista and Vezzani, 2010). Based on the main NACE[1] code of each firm, we construct the dummy variable *Serv*, which takes a value zero for manufacturing firms and a one for service firms. About 54% of the companies in our sample are manufacturing companies, while 46% are service firms. Using the same NACE code, we construct another dummy variable *Hitech*, which takes a value zero for firms active in low-tech and medium-low-tech sectors and a one for firms active in medium-high-tech and high-tech sectors.[2] About 44% of the companies in our sample are classified as high-tech, while 66% are classified as low-tech firms. Table 5.2 contains the correlations between the variables.

Results

Table 5.3 provides an overview of our OLS regression results.[3] *Brainstorming* has positive effects for both radical and incremental innovation. Hypothesis 1 is thus confirmed. Yet, contrary to our expectations, it seems that brainstorm sessions might be fruitful for the transfer and creation of unrelated knowledge, and subsequently radical innovation, as well. *Financial incentives* have a positive and significant effect on incremental innovation. *Non-financial incentives* do not influence incremental innovation. Hypothesis 2 is thus partially – only for financial incentives – confirmed. *Cross-functional teams* have, in line with hypothesis 3, a positive significant effect on radical innovation. Finally, we do not find evidence for a relationship between *job rotation* and radical innovation. Hypothesis 4 is thus not confirmed.

As for the control variables, we find a significant positive effect of *R&D intensity* and *high-technology activities* on radical innovation but not on incremental innovation. *Age* and *size* have a significant negative effect on radical innovation but not on incremental innovation. No curvilinear effect is found for the square of *size*. *Collaboration* has a positive significant effect on both incremental and radical innovation. Finally, contrary to our expectations, *membership of a group* and *industry (service versus manufacturing)* do not have an impact on incremental nor on radical innovation.

Table 5.2 Correlations (822 observations)

	1	2	3	4	5	6	7	8	9	10	11	12	13
1. Rad_Inno	1.00												
2. Incr_Inno	0.09	1.00											
3. Brainstorm	0.13	0.11	1.00										
4. Crossfunc	0.19	0.05	0.22	1.00									
5. Jobrot	0.07	0.08	0.02	0.18	1.00								
6. Finin	0.03	0.09	0.03	0.09	0.23	1.00							
7. Nfinin	0.10	0.07	0.09	0.12	0.28	0.42	1.00						
8. Ln_RD_Intensity	0.32	0.07	0.03	0.11	0.04	0.05	0.04	1.00					
9. Group	−0.01	0.02	0.05	0.22	0.07	0.06	0.03	0.01	1.00				
10. Collab	0.28	0.21	0.13	0.25	0.04	0.00	0.05	0.21	0.12	1.00			
11. Ln_Size	−0.03	0.05	0.05	0.30	0.18	0.12	0.02	−0.06	0.43	0.21	1.00		
12. Ln_Age	−0.16	0.01	−0.06	−0.01	0.01	0.00	−0.05	−0.14	0.02	−0.05	0.33	1.00	
13. Serv	0.00	−0.02	0.02	0.04	−0.03	−0.04	0.06	0.08	−0.04	0.14	−0.24	−0.22	1.00
14. Hitech	0.19	0.06	0.05	0.09	0.05	0.02	0.01	0.20	−0.02	0.17	−0.24	−0.20	0.12

Table 5.3 Regression results (822 observations)

	Rad_Inno	Incr_Inno
Brainstorm	3.30**	3.65**
Crossfunc	4.64***	−1.33
Jobrot	1.30	2.08
Finin	−.90	2.90**
Nfinin	2.44	.51
Ln_RD_Intensity	22.33*	1.14
Group	−1.29	−.04
Collab	6.99***	7.28***
Ln_Size	−6.61*	.99
(Ln_Size)²	.67	−.13
Ln_Age	−2.31**	.83
Serv	−1.60	.48
Hitech	2.55*	.88
R^2	0.2005	0.0661

* Significant at $p < 0.10$.
** Significant at $p < 0.05$.
*** Significant at $p < 0.01$.

Discussion

In this study, we focused on innovation as one potential outcome of strategic renewal. Firms' innovation strategies are known to be complex, encompassing not only the improvement of existing products and technologies, but also the creation of new products and competencies (Chang, 2015). Chang (2015) articulates the need for ambidexterity if both types of innovation are focused upon and shows how high performance work systems (HPWS) can positively influence organizational units' human capital and subsequently the units' ambidexterity. Moreover, this positive influence is stronger if the organization also has a positive social climate, i.e. "a climate of trust, cooperation, shared codes and languages" (Chang, 2015, p. 81). Prieto-Pastor and Martin-Perez (2015), in turn, show how high-involvement HR systems positively influence employees' ambidextrous learning and subsequently the firm's ambidextrous learning. Moreover, they provide evidence of a positive moderating effect of management support in the relationship between high-involvement HR systems and employees' ambidextrous learning. Although both studies show the importance of human and social capital as well as management support for ambidexterity, they do not go into the different types of knowledge that are required for incremental and radical innovation, nor do they go into how these different types of knowledge can be stimulated by individual practices.

On the other hand, whereas many studies show how overall innovation performance benefits from stimulating knowledge transfer and creation, most do not take into account the complexity of innovation strategies and the distinction between incremental and radical innovation (Zhou et al., 2013). In addition, they focus solely on the impact of knowledge management practices without controlling for other factors that are known to affect innovation performance. By overcoming these limitations, this study contributes to the knowledge management, innovation and HRM literature. In particular, it enriches the theoretical understanding of the relationship between knowledge management practices and innovation performance, by distinguishing between the crucial roles of related and unrelated knowledge (see Figure 5.1). Our study suggests that knowledge management practices can stimulate the transfer and creation of related or unrelated knowledge, which in turn affect incremental and radical innovation performance respectively.

In particular, we found that brainstorm sessions affect both incremental and radical innovation performance. This suggests that this knowledge management practice can stimulate the transfer and creation of both related and unrelated knowledge. We did not expect brainstorm sessions to enhance both incremental and radical innovation. However, this finding can probably be explained by differences in the professionalism with which the brainstorm sessions are implemented in the organizations and in the composition of participants in the session. We expected related knowledge to be transferred and created by means of brainstorm sessions. Yet, Paulus and Yang (2000) argue that they can also be an effective means to enhance radical innovation under the right conditions. They, for example, conclude that using a group-writing procedure can effectively overcome the potential problems of production blocking or evaluation apprehension, which hinder the creation of unrelated knowledge. Next, the composition of the group might play a role as well. If the group only includes employees with a similar function, related knowledge

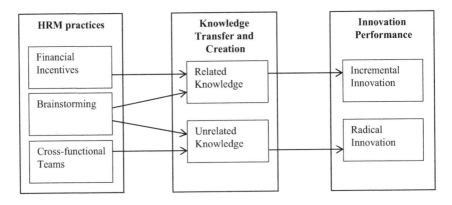

Figure 5.1 Conceptual model

will be transferred and created. However, if the group consists of different domain specialists and is professionally organized, the likelihood that unrelated knowledge is transferred and created increases. Cross-functional teams appear to induce mostly unrelated knowledge transfer and creation, which in turn increase radical innovation performance. When offered financial rewards, employees apparently tend to put forward related ideas for incremental innovation, which has a higher chance of success – and hence financial rewards – as compared to unrelated ideas for radical innovation. Contrary to our expectations, non-financial incentives have no influence. According to the expectancy theory (Vroom, 1964), incentives are motivating only if they are considered valuable by the employee. Because the generation of new ideas will lead to innovation and added value for the organization in monetary terms, it is possible that employees want their share of this added value and therefore prefer money above non-financial incentives. Finally, we do not find evidence for a relationship between job rotation and radical innovation. It is possible that job rotation will only have an influence if it is flanked by collaborative practices such as team work or collective brainstorm sessions. That way the accumulated knowledge through job rotation will also be exchanged with other employees, which might be a crucial condition for radical innovation.

Our findings are relevant for practitioners since they warn against a "one-size-fits-all" approach to knowledge management. It shows that companies should carefully select incentives for knowledge creation that fit with their innovation strategy and goals, whether this encompasses incremental innovation, radical innovation or a combination of both.

Limitations and suggestions for further research

In this study, we examined the impact of knowledge management practices in the period 2008–2010 on innovation performance in 2010. Whereas this design allows for the generation of insights into the short-term performance implications of these stimuli, we acknowledge that this time-frame is too short to fully grasp the long-term performance effects. We therefore stress the importance of future research that systematically assesses the performance implications of stimuli for knowledge creation and transfer across different time-frames.

Whereas we focused on the presence/absence of various knowledge management practices, we did not consider the extent to which they are dispersed throughout the company, nor the way in which they are implemented. Future research might focus on implementation issues such as the level at which these initiatives are introduced, i.e. the individual or group level. More detailed information on this topic might be especially valuable for the brainstorm sessions and financial incentives. Previous research has discussed the differential effects of both practices depending on the level of implementation (Bartol and Srivastava, 2002; Diehl and Stroebe, 1991). It might be worthwhile to study the impact of these issues on the contribution of knowledge management practices to incremental versus radical innovation.

In this study we focused upon four knowledge management practices and studied their independent effects on innovation. Future studies might focus upon the interaction between these practices. It is likely that the positive impact of cross-functional teams on radical innovation will be higher when these teams get financial incentives for innovative results or when professional brainstorm sessions are organized within these teams. On the other hand, the combination of cross-functional teams and individual financial incentives might be destructive for radical innovation. Insights into the interdependencies of practices might help practitioners to develop a strong knowledge management system, existing in "powerful connections" and avoiding "deadly combinations" of practices (Delaney and Huselid, 1996; Delery, 1998).

Further research might also focus upon other knowledge management practices, and their impact upon incremental versus radical innovation. We focused on financial practices and practices related to job design. Other practices could be considered as well, such as the use of collective situational tests in selection procedures, training in problem solving, formal suggestion schemes or mentoring and coaching practices. Each of these practices has been related to innovation before. Yet, their impact on incremental versus radical innovation has not yet been studied. Literature on the relationship between HRM and innovation might be inspiring here (e.g. Seeck and Diehl, 2016).

We studied knowledge management practices resulting from a personalization strategy because Greiner et al. (2007) showed them to be more fruitful for innovation as compared to practices resulting from a codification strategy. Although we follow their reasoning for radical innovation in which tacit knowledge plays a prominent role, it might be possible that some knowledge codification practices focusing on the storage of explicit knowledge might be interesting for incremental innovation as well. Future research could dig into this relationship.

We argue that the type of knowledge that is transferred and created plays a determining role in stimulating incremental versus radical innovation. We thereby focus on related versus unrelated knowledge. Yet, we did not measure these constructs. Future research might try to develop a measurement instrument to capture the related versus unrelated nature of knowledge and to actually test the mediating role of these constructs in the relationship between knowledge management practices, and incremental versus radical innovation as visualized in Figure 5.1.

This study involves knowledge management practices of Flemish firms. Replication of our findings in other regions and countries is necessary to test their generalizability.

Notes

1 NACE, which is short for "Nomenclature générale des Activités économiques dans les Communautés Européennes", refers to the industrial classification used by Eurostat and is the subject of legislation at the European Union level, which imposes the use of the classification uniformly within all the member states.

2 Based on the sector's average R&D intensity (R&D expenditures/value added) Eurostat classifies the NACE codes into high-tech, medium-high-tech, medium-low-tech and low-tech sectors. See http://epp.eurostat.ec.europa.eu/cache/ITY_SDDS/Annexes/htec_esms_an2.pdf.
3 Despite the fact that our dependent variables are left censored, we did not apply Tobit regressions but used OLS as a valid alternative (see also Angrist and Pischke, 2008).

References

Acs, Z. J. & Audretsch, D. B. 1990. *Innovation and small firms*. Cambridge, MA: MIT Press.

Agarwal, R. & Helfat, C. E. 2009. Strategic renewal of organizations. *Organization Science*, 20(2): 281–293.

Ahuja, G., Lampert, C. M., & Tandon, V. 2008. Moving beyond Schumpeter: Management research on the determinants of technological innovation. *Academy of Management Annals*, 2(1): 1–98.

Allen, T. J. 2001. Organizing for product development. MIT Sloan Working Paper, 422901.

Angrist, J. D. & Pischke, J. S. 2008. *Mostly harmless econometrics: An empiricist's companion*. Princeton, NJ: Princeton University Press.

Arvanitis, S. 2008. Explaining innovative activity in service industries: Micro data evidence for Switzerland. *Economics of Innovation & New Technology*, 17(3): 209–225.

Bartol, K. M. & Srivastava, A. 2002. Encouraging knowledge sharing: The role of organizational reward systems. *Journal of Leadership and Organization Studies*, 9(1): 64–76.

Cabrera, E. F. & Cabrera, A. 2005. Fostering knowledge sharing through people management practices. *The International Journal of Human Resource Management*, 16: 720–735.

Chang, Y. Y. 2015. A multilevel examination of high-performance work systems and unit-level organisational ambidexterity. *Human Resource Management Journal*, 25(1): 79–101.

Chen, C. J. & Huang, J. W. 2009. Strategic human resource practices and innovation performance. The mediating role of knowledge management capacity. *Journal of Business Research*, 62: 104–114.

CIS. (2011). For more information see http://ec.europa.eu/eurostat/web/microdata/community-innovation-survey.

Cohen, W. M. 1995. Empirical studies of innovative activity. In Stoneman, P. (Ed.). *Handbook of the economics of innovation and technological change*, pp. 182–264. Oxford: Blackwell.

Czarnitzki, D. & Kraft, K. 2010. On the profitability of innovative assets. *Applied Economics*, 42(15): 1941–1953.

Damanpour, F. 1991. Organizational innovation: A meta-analysis of the effects of determinants and moderators. *Academy of Management Journal*, 34: 555–590.

De Jong, J. P. J. & Vermeulen, P. A. M. 2006. Determinants of product innovation in small firms: A comparison across industries. *International Small Business Journal*, 24: 587–609.

de Visser, M., de Weerd-Nederhof, P., Faems, D., Song, M., Van Looy, B. & Visscher, K. 2010. Structural ambidexterity in NPD processes: A firm-level assessment of the impact of differentiated structures on innovation performance. *Technovation*, 30: 291–299.

Delaney, J. & Huselid, M. 1996. The impact of human resource management practices on perceptions of organizational performance. *Academy of Management Journal*, 39(4): 949–969.

Delery, J. 1998. Issues of fit in strategic human resource management: Implications for research. Human Resource Management Review, 8(3): 289–309.

Diehl, M. & Stroebe, W. 1991. Productivity loss in brainstorming groups: Towards the solution of the riddle. *Journal of Personality and Social Psychology*, 53(3): 497–509.

Ettlie, J. E. & Rosenthal, S. R. 2011. Service versus manufacturing innovation. *Journal of Product Innovation Management*, 28(2): 285–299.

Evangelista, R. & Vezzani, A. 2010. The economic impact of technological and organizational innovations. A firm-level analysis. *Research Policy*, 39: 1253–1263.

Faems, D., Van Looy, B. & Debackere, K. 2005. Interorganizational collaboration and innovation: Toward a portfolio approach. *Journal of Product Innovation Management*, 22(3): 238–250.

Greiner, M. E., Böhmann, T. & Krcmar, H. 2007. A strategy for knowledge management. *Journal of Knowledge Management*, 11: 3–15.

Griffin, A. 1997. PDMA research on new product development practices: Updating trends and benchmarking best practices. *Journal of Product Innovation Management*, 14: 429–458.

Hargadon, A. 2003. *How breakthroughs happen: The surprising truth about how companies innovate*. Boston, MA: Harvard Business School Press.

Holmström, B. 1989. Agency costs and innovation. *Journal of Economic Behavior & Organization*, 12(3): 305–327.

Huang, H. J. 1999. Job rotation from the employees' point of view. *Research and Practice in Human Resource Management*, 7: 75–85.

Kane, G. C. & Alavi, M. 2007. Information technology and organizational learning: An investigation of exploration and exploitation processes. *Organization Science*, 18(5): 796–812.

Kessler, E. H. & Chakrabarti, A. K. 1996. Innovation speed: A conceptual model of context, antecedents, and outcomes. *Academy of Management Review*, 21(4): 1143–1191.

Knudsen, M. P. 2007. The relative importance of interfirm relationships and knowledge transfer for new product development success. *Journal of Product Innovation Management*, 24(2): 117–138.

Laursen, K. & Salter, A. 2006. Open for innovation: The role of openness in explaining innovative performance among UK manufacturing firms. *Strategic Management Journal*, 27(2): 131–150.

Lavie, D., Stettner, U. & Tushman, M. L. 2010. Exploration and exploitation within and across organizations. *The Academy of Management Annals*, 4(1): 109–155.

Lopez-Cabrales, A., Perez-Luno, A. & Cabrera, R. V. 2009. Knowledge as a mediator between HRM practices and innovative activity. *Human Resource Management*, 48: 485–503.

March, J. G. 1991. Exploration and exploitation in organizational learning. *Organization Science*, 2: 71–87.

Mention, A.-L. 2011. Co-operation and co-opetition as open innovation practices in the service sector: Which influence on innovation novelty? *Technovation*, 31: 44–53.

Mohnen, P. & Mairesse, J. 2002. Accounting for innovation and measuring innovativeness: An illustrative framework and an application. *American Economic Review*, 92(2): 226–230.

Nahapiet, J. & Ghoshal, S. 1998. Social capital, intellectual capital, and the organizational advantage. *The Academy of Management Review*, 23: 242–266.

Noe, R. A., Hollenbeck, J. R., Gerhart, B. & Wright, P. M. 2003. *Gaining a competitive advantage*. New York City, NY: Irwin/McGraw-Hill.

Nonaka. 1991. The knowledge-creating company. *Harvard Business Review*, November–December: 96–104.

Nonaka, I. 1994. A dynamic theory of organizational knowledge creation. *Organization Science*, 5: 14–37.

Nunamaker, J. F., Applegate, L. M. & Konsynski, B. R. 1987. Facilitating group creativity: Experience with a group decision support system. *Journal of Management Information Systems*, 3: 5–19.

O'Reilly, C. A. & Tushman, M. L. 2004. The ambidextrous organization. *Harvard Business Review*, 82(4): 74–81.

Oliver, C. 1997. Sustainable competitive advantage: Combining institutional and resource-based views. *Strategic Management Journal*, 18: 697–713.

Paulus, P. B. & Yang, H. C. 2000. Idea generation in groups: A basis for creativity in organizations. *Organizational Behavior and Human Decision Processes*, 82(1): 76–87.

Pelz, D. & Andrews, F. 1966. Autonomy, coordination, and stimulation in relation to scientific achievement. *Behavioral Science*, 11: 89–97.

Phelps, C. C. 2010. A longitudinal study of the influence of alliance network structure and composition on firm exploratory innovation. *Academy of Management Journal*, 53(4): 890–913.

Prieto-Pastor, I. & Martin-Perez, V. 2015. Does HRM generate ambidextrous employees for ambidextrous learning? The moderating role of management support. *The International Journal of Human Resource Management*, 26(5): 589–615.

Schneider, C. & Veugelers, R. 2010. On young highly innovative companies: Why they matter and how (not) to policy support them. *Industrial and Corporate Change*, 19(4): 969-1007.

Schön, D. A. 1963. Champions for radical new inventions. *Harvard Business Review*, 41(2): 77–86.

Schumpeter, J. A. 1939. *Business cycles: A theoretical, historical, and statistical analysis of the capitalist process*. New York, NY: McGraw-Hill.

Seeck, H. & Diehl, M.-R. 2016. A literature review on HRM and innovation – Taking stock and future directions. *The International Journal of Human Resource Management*, 28(6): 913–944.

Shadur, M. A. & Snell, S. A. 2002. Knowledge management strategies, human resources and firm innovation: An empirical study of Australian firms in knowledge intensive industries. Paper presented at the Academy of Management Meeting, Denver, CO, August 2002.

Skuras, D., Tsegenidi, K. & Tsekouras, K. 2008. Product innovation and the decision to invest in fixed capital assets: Evidence from an SME survey in six European Union member states. *Research Policy*, 37: 1778–1789.

Song, X. M., Thieme, R. J. & Xie, J. 1998. The impact of cross-functional joint involvement across product development stages: An exploratory study. *Journal of Product Innovation Management*, 15: 289–303.

Song, X. M. & Xie, J. 2000. Does innovativeness moderate the relationship between cross-functional integration and product performance? *Journal of International Marketing*, 8(4): 61–89.

Spithoven, A., Frantzen, D. & Clarysse, B. 2010. Heterogeneous firm-level effects of knowledge exchanges on product innovation: Differences between dynamic and lagging product innovators. *Journal of Product Innovation Management*, 27(3): 362–381.

Stasser, G. 1999. The uncertain role of unshared information in collective choice. In Thompson, L. & Levine, J. (Eds.). *Shared knowledge in organizations*, pp. 49–69. Mahwah, NJ: Erlbaum.

Teece, D. J. 2007. Explicating dynamic capabilities: The nature and microfoundations of (sustainable) enterprise performance. *Strategic Management Journal*, 28(13): 1319–1350.

Un, C. A., Cuervo-Cazurra, A. & Asakawa, K. 2010. R&D collaborations and product innovation. *Journal of Product Innovation Management*, 24(5): 673–689.

Van de Ven, A. H. 1986. Central problems in the management of innovation. *Management Science*, 32(5): 590–607.

Vroom, V. H. 1964. *Work and motivation*. New York, NY: Wiley.

Wang, S. & Noe, R. A. 2010. Knowledge sharing: A review and directions for future research. *Human Resource Management Review*, 20: 115–131.

Wilson, C. E. 2006. Brainstorming pitfalls and best practices. *Interactions*, 13(5): 50–63.

Zhou, Y., Hong, Y. & Liu, J. 2013. Internal commitment or external collaboration? The impact of human resource management systems on firm innovation and performance. *Human Resource Management*, 52(2): 263–288.

6 Boards of directors and strategic renewal

How do human and relational capital matter?

Bas Bosboom, Mariano L.M. Heyden, and Jatinder S. Sidhu

Introduction

Firms need to manage their knowledge base in order to pre-emptively develop capabilities to cope with changes in their environment (Agarwal & Helfat, 2009; Schmitt, Raisch, & Volberda, 2016b). An organization's board of directors is the highest authority in the firm entrusted with safeguarding its strategy and has been shown to be crucial for infusing the firm with knowledge from its environment (Heyden, Oehmichen, Nichting, & Volberda, 2015). As directors are increasingly held accountable for the long-term outcomes of strategy (Aguilera, 2005; Hendry & Kiel, 2004; Hendry, Kiel, & Nicholson, 2010; Huse, 2005; Roberts, McNulty, & Stiles, 2005), boards have become more actively involved in contributing their knowledge resources to strategy-making (Hendry et al., 2010; Pugliese et al., 2009). Continuously enriching the firm's knowledge base, in turn, has been shown to be crucial for the pursuit of strategic renewal – path-creation changes in strategy (Baden-Fuller & Volberda, 1997; Burgelman, 1983; Flier, Van Den Bosch, & Volberda, 2003). Yet, studies linking boards of directors to renewal are scarce.

Boards of directors constitute an important repository of and conduit for tacit knowledge (Haynes & Hillman, 2010; Heyden et al., 2015; Oehmichen, Schrapp, & Wolff, 2016). Hillman, Cannella, and Paetzold (2000) captured these roles through the concept of board capital. *Board capital* essentially breaks down into *human capital* (board member characteristics) and *relational capital* (board members' network ties), which both can potentially cascade into the knowledge base of the firm as boards contribute to strategy-making. As directors draw on their human and relational capital to define strategic priorities and sanction resource allocations, they play an important role in shaping the extent to which firm strategy reinforces current path dependencies or encourages the creation of new paths (Hillman & Dalziel, 2003). Yet, the mechanisms through which human and social capital influence strategic renewal remain undertheorized. Thus the question remains: *How do a board of directors' knowledge resources, as embodied in their human and relational capital, influence strategic renewal?*

In this study we integrate board capital theory with the knowledge-based view to hypothesize how human and relational capital relate to strategic renewal – as reflected in path-breaking product-market diversification. Our hypotheses, tested on a panel of manufacturing firms in the US, shed light on the knowledge-related mechanisms through which board capital features relate to strategic renewal. Our main findings suggest that the number of outside board seats is an important determinant of strategic renewal, in addition to director tenure and director type heterogeneity. However, the latter two associations appear to be non-linear, highlighting the complex ways in which boards matter for strategic renewal. Taken together, our study indicates that firms should carefully consider whom to appoint on the board of directors, where the board should reflect a diversity of directors (different types of directors with differing organizational tenure) in order to positively contribute to strategic renewal (Minichilli, Zattoni, & Zona, 2009; Oehmichen, Heyden, Georgakakis, & Volberda, 2017).

In taking this approach we offer several contributions with this chapter. First, while previous research on boards of directors has focused on their influence on corporate performance, research has found weak, none, or contradictory relationships (Bhagat & Black, 2001; Peng, 2004). This study extends research on corporate boards to theorize about their specific roles in corporate decision-making and their contribution to the strategic renewal of their firms, and as such helps clarify the microfoundations of renewal by looking at boards (Foss, 2011; Oehmichen et al., 2017; Schmitt et al., 2016b). Boards are an important governance mechanism that influences firm strategy (Castañer & Kavadis, 2013). Next, we contribute to board capital theory by taking knowledge-based arguments as the central resource that directors bring to the firm and that affect a firm's strategic renewal. As such, we integrate knowledge-based arguments, to theorize how board members absorb and interpret information as well as accumulate knowledge (Oehmichen et al., 2017). Finally, the study adds to practical understanding by increasing our insights into which (knowledge) characteristics of directors contribute to strategic renewal and through which mechanisms. This is important, as the superiority of a specific board composition is still unclear (Boone, Field, Karpoff, & Raheja, 2007). These contributions can subsequently increase understanding and provide prescriptive avenues for the appointment procedures of directors (Oehmichen et al., 2016).

Conceptual background and hypotheses

Strategic renewal

Firms operating in dynamic industries are confronted with constantly changing customer demands and technological change, as well as increasing competitive forces due to globalization. These firms need to actively look for ways to renew themselves over the long run (Flier et al., 2003). Scholars have tried to tap into the dimensions of strategic renewal. Agarwal and Helfat (2009), for instance, have broken down strategic renewal into content, process, and outcome dimension. Others have tried to capture strategic renewal in context, content, and process dimensions (e.g., Volberda, Baden-Fuller, & van Den Bosch, 2001). Capron and Mitchell (2009) further distinguish renewal modes into "internal development" and "external sourcing". Finally, building on Burgelman (1991), Floyd and Lane (2000) conceptualized strategic renewal as an evolutionary process in which knowledge and innovation lead to a change in an organization's core competencies in order to align organizational strategy with changing environmental circumstances (see also Schmitt, Barker Iii, Raisch, & Whetten, 2016a).

Despite different interpretations, at its core, "[s]trategic renewal research analyzes how these organizations alter their path dependence by transforming their strategic intent and capabilities" (Schmitt et al., 2016b). Strategic renewal is important, as changing environmental conditions and competition pressure companies to balance efficiency and flexibility at the same time (Danneels, 2002). Breaking through existing path-dependencies is important to overcome rigidities as a result of a firm's history and close gaps between existing core competencies and the ever-changing conditions to achieve a competitive advantage (Burgelman, 1991; Huff, Huff, & Thomas, 1992). Hence, breaking through path-dependencies by means of exploring new opportunities is important for a firm's survival (Bettis & Hitt, 1995).

The exploration of new opportunities is entrusted to the highest strategic decision-makers of the organization – its board of directors (Tuggle, Schnatterly, & Johnson, 2010). Several scholars have stressed that non-executive directors play a critical role in strategy-making (Heyden et al., 2015; Hillman & Dalziel, 2003). Charan (2011) argued that the boardroom is a potential source of thinking about new ways that lead to growth, while Maassen and Van Den Bosch (1999) found that directors are convinced that they play an increasingly important role in defining and implementing strategy and may thus potentially influence journeys of strategic renewal. Thus, if boards matter for strategy, and they contribute to knowledge variety, then board capital can influence renewal. However, the influence of boards on strategic renewal is poorly understood.

Boards and strategic renewal

The "board of directors is an important mechanism in determining a firm's strategies and aligning the interests of insiders, controlling shareholders and minority shareholders" (Mínguez-Vera & Martin, 2011: 2852). Traditionally, research on corporate boards and their roles has incorporated an agency-theory perspective, arguing that the main function of board members is to control the executives of the firm in order to prevent opportunistic behavior and make sure that they act in line with the interests of the firm and its shareholders (Daily, Dalton, & Cannella, 2003). These roles implied that directors took a limited part in strategy because of their distance from daily operations as well as the perceived need to remain independent (Charan, 2011; Hendry & Kiel, 2004).

Recently, scholars and managers acknowledge that boards of directors do more than just monitoring executives. It is believed that directors could and should be involved in strategy and strategic decision-making activities as well (Forbes & Milliken, 1999; Maassen & Van Den Bosch, 1999; Roberts et al., 2005; Yawson, 2006). As such, scholars have pointed to the ability of directors to bring resources to the firm (Hillman & Dalziel, 2003), with resources being "anything that could be thought of as a strength or weakness of a given firm" (Wernerfelt, 1984: 172). A board's ability to bring resources to the firm and consequently manage interdependencies with its external environment to help reduce uncertainty, is one of the basic propositions of Resource Dependence Theory (RDT). The role of boards in reducing environmental uncertainty is based on Pfeffer's seminal (1972) work on the role of directors, which argues that directors bring and broker key resources from the organization's environment (Drees & Heugens, 2013; Hillman, Withers, & Collins, 2009). We focus here on knowledge as this key resource.

Although empirical studies have found a relation between board members as providers of resources and firm performance (Boyd, 1990; Dalton, Daily, Johnson, & Ellstrand, 1999), scholars have so far not focused on the insights RDT can offer to strategic renewal research. Intuitively, strategic renewal is directly related to resources in several ways. Paths that are initiated to break through current dependencies are expected to require resources such as financial capital and physical capital, as well as human capital. An important constituent of strategy is knowledge and hence knowledge is expected to play a significant role in strategic renewal. In sum, from an RDT perspective, board members are seen as providers of resources to organizations, of which knowledge can be considered to be the most important resource when it comes to strategic renewal. This provision of resources encompasses, among others, building external relations and diffusing innovation, as well as aiding in formulating strategy or other important decisions (Haunschild & Beckman, 1998; Judge & Zeithaml, 1992).

In determining the ways in and mechanisms through which board members gather and assimilate knowledge to aid the firm in their strategic renewal activities, Hillman and Dalziel (2003) provide a useful classification. They introduce the concept of *board capital*, which is believed to provide channels of communication and conduits for information between the firm and external organizations. This concept then breaks down into *human capital* and *relational capital*, which both provide directors with knowledge, based on which strategic renewal can be fostered. Human capital relates to the individual characteristics of directors such as their expertise, experience, and reputation. Relational capital, on the other hand, refers to the network of ties to other firms and external contingencies that board members have. Companies are able to enrich their knowledge base through their external networks (as embodied through outside directorships) and are thus more favorably positioned to formulate and implement discontinuous strategic pathways (Phan, Lee, & Lau, 2003). In addition, external ties can facilitate access to strategic information and opportunities to learn best practices from other firms (Burt, 1980). We proceed to hypothesize how outside board directorships, board tenure, board insider representation, and director type heterogeneity relate to strategic renewal.

Outside board directorships and strategic renewal

As mentioned, relational capital concerns the networks of ties that board members possess, often captured by outside directorships, which refers to "a situation in which a person affiliated with an organization has a position on the board of directors of another firm" (Mizruchi, 1996: 271) and thereby positions the firm in an external network (Boyd, 1990). However, evidence on the benefits of outside directorships is mixed (Boeker & Goodstein, 1991; Peng, 2004; Phan et al., 2003). Outside directorships are believed to hold the potential to tap into the knowledge base of partners and incorporate resources from the external environment (Bezemer, Maassen, Van den Bosch, & Volberda, 2007; Haunschild & Beckman, 1998). However, it may also make directors "busy", reducing their ability to contribute to individual firms (Ferris, Jagannathan, & Pritchard, 2003; Harris & Shimizu, 2004; Jiraporn, Davidson III, DaDalt, & Ning, 2009). Nevertheless, outside directorships provide valuable information about competitor practices, industry conditions, and other stakeholders, as well as increasing the board's ability to reduce environmental uncertainty (Pfeffer & Salancik, 1978). Consequently, boards with higher relational capital (as a function of the number of external board seats held by their directors) have a better ability to grasp more information and accumulate knowledge from other firms' practices. Hence we hypothesize that:

HYPOTHESIS 1 (H1): *The number of outside board directorships held by directors is positively related to strategic renewal.*

Board tenure and strategic renewal

A key part of human capital is the accumulated experience board members bring and embody. Accordingly, from a knowledge-based logic, we can expect that the greater a director's tenure, the greater their accumulated knowledge base of the specific industry environment, market segments, and product lifecycles, and thus the better they can inform strategy. By the same token, Hillman and Dalziel (2003) have argued that the greater a director's experience, the greater its ability to provide the firm with resources, especially knowledge. Furthermore, Fiske and Taylor (2013) argue that higher experience (which comes through increased tenure) will provide decision-makers with more comprehensive access to a richer repository of knowledge.

However, other scholars argue that decisionmakers with higher positional tenure will tend to exhibit stronger commitment to existing paradigms, greater rigidity, and less openness and responsiveness to stimuli from the external environment (Katz, 1982; Miller, 1991). Hence, directors tend to be more open-minded at the beginning of their tenure and become committed to their actions (by repeating and reinforcing them) as their tenure increases (Rubin & Brockner, 1975; Staw, 1976). In addition, directors with short tenures, although open to new experience, lack the rich bases from which to draw knowledge (Golden & Zajac, 2001). As their tenure increases, these repositories will increase and hence directors will be better able to bring resources (in the form of knowledge) to the firm. However, directors face a turning point in their tenure, where commitment to existing paradigms as well as the status quo and slower decision-making hampers their ability to provide the firm with knowledge. When tenure increases, sources of knowledge and information become narrower and more restricted. Accordingly, we hypothesize that:

HYPOTHESIS 2 (H2): *The relation between board tenure and strategic renewal will be curvilinear (an inverted u-shape).*

Insiders on the board and strategic renewal

"When an organization appoints an individual to the board, it expects the individual will come to support the organization" (Pfeffer & Salancik, 1978: 163). Consequently, each board member is expected to add value to the organization by means of their specific type of knowledge and unique set of attributes (Kesner, 1988; Kosnik, 1990). By observing these attributes, one can predict what kind of resources a certain director is likely to bring to the board, where differences among directors are best visible in terms of their individual experience or occupational attributes (Baysinger & Butler, 1985). One common method of classifying board members is by distinguishing inside and outside directors (Hillman et al., 2000; Wagner, Stimpert, & Fubara, 1998).

Inside directors have ties to the focal firm, and thus serve, or have served, as managers, employees, officers, owners, or have familial connections to the firm (Cochran, Wood, & Jones, 1985; Hillman et al., 2000). As such, inside directors are expected to provide firm-specific information (Fama & Jensen, 1983a; Harris & Helfat, 1997) that comes from personal experience not available to outsiders (Baysinger & Hoskisson, 1990), as well as general strategy and direction. *Outside directors*, in comparison, are not current or former employees, officers, or family members and hence do not have a close relationship with the focal firm beyond their role on the board (Wagner et al., 1998). As such, they primarily provide resources that deal with external factors, such as alternative strategic approaches and technologies employed by other firms (Heyden et al., 2015). Extending this classification and corresponding resource-dependence logic, it is argued that more insiders on the board of directors will mean that the board will be more internally focused. More outside board members will mean that focus will tend to be centered on practices and experiences from external knowledge inputs. Hence, it is argued that the more outsiders on a specific board of directors, the more the focal firm will be able to break through current path-dependencies. Thus, we hypothesize that:

HYPOTHESIS 3 (H3): *Higher proportion of insiders on the board of directors will be negatively related to strategic renewal.*

Director type diversity and strategic renewal

Diversity in organizational groups, more generally, has been shown to affect group processes and performance both positively and negatively (Jackson, Joshi, & Erhardt, 2003). Diversity is conceptualized as "a characteristic of social grouping that reflects the degree to which objective or subjective differences exist between group members" (Van Knippenberg & Schippers, 2007: 516). Hillman et al. (2000) suggested that directors can essentially be distinguished into four separate roles that each aid the firm and bring distinct resources to it, and diversity among these roles matters. Director type heterogeneity captures both human as well as relational capital. As was argued previously, *Inside directors* are expected to provide firm-specific information as well as general strategy and direction. *Outside directors*, on the other hand, primarily provide resources that deal with external factors such as expertise on competition and decision-making. Outside directors can further be divided into three distinct types of directors that each bring distinct external own resources to the firm.

Business experts are active or retired executives of other for-profit organizations or directors who serve on other boards as well. They provide expertise on competition and decision-making as well as providing alternative viewpoints on both internal and external problems. Since we can observe that it is common practice for large corporations to have business experts serving on their board, the benefits associated with this type of outside director can be expected to be substantial. *Support specialists* in turn provide the firm with specialized knowledge, for instance on regulations. As such, these directors can inform insiders and business experts on these specific issues and thereby reduce the transaction costs for obtaining knowledge. Nowadays, almost every firm has at least one lawyer and one accountant serving on its board of directors. Finally, *community influencers* provide non-business perspectives on issues and problems, as well as having the ability to represent the companies' interests outside competitive product or supply markets (Hillman et al., 2000). Al Gore, the former politician and environmental activist, who served on Apple's board of directors, is an example of a community influencer.

Some scholars argue that homogenous groups may function better than heterogeneous groups since people tend to favor in-group members versus out-group members, trust them more, and are also more willing to cooperate with them (Van Knippenberg & Schippers, 2007). However, work group diversity can have positive effects as well. Diverse groups are likely to possess a broader range of knowledge, skills, and abilities, which may foster the initiation of innovative types of solutions since these groups need to integrate diverse types of knowledge and perspectives (Van Knippenberg, De Dreu, & Homan, 2004). Empirical testing of this relationship, however, has produced inconsistent and unclear findings. We argue that too much heterogeneity will cause teams (such as boards) to become dysfunctional as too many different views and perspectives will eventually lead to conflict (Jehn, Northcraft, & Neale, 1999). On the other hand, too little heterogeneity in the boardroom may lead to situations in which too few resources can potentially be brought to the organization, thus impeding path-breaking activities. Hence, we hypothesize that diversity in director type will be related to renewal through new-to-the-firm product market diversification in a non-linear way.

HYPOTHESIS 4 (H4): *The relation between director type heterogeneity and strategic renewal undertaken will be curvilinear (an inverted u-shape).*

Data and methods

Setting and data collection

The empirical research was conducted by collecting data from 100 US-based, publicly listed firms, all of which are knowledge-intensive firms with concrete product offerings. The primary benefit of collecting data from such a particular sample is the relative similarity in resource bases, as a result of which these firms will face similar resource dependencies that have to be managed. Furthermore, the computer industry is characterized by a relatively high level of managerial discretion, meaning that managers and directors traditionally have leeway in their actions and decision-making. Data was gathered for a five-year time span (2003–2007) in the SIC35 two-digit code, and information about the firms' activities was obtained by using COMPUSTAT historical data. Data about the board members and their characteristics was obtained by analyzing Definitive Proxy Statements/SEC filings (14A) as published and stored by the US Securities and Exchange Commission. In addition, information about the board members was supplemented by using the "People Index" on the "Investing" website of *Business Week*.

Measurement and validation of constructs

Dependent Variable. Strategic renewal was conceptualized as the set of path-breaking activities that a particular organization undertakes. Research on strategic renewal has identified and elaborated on several exemplifications of what constitutes renewal. As such, Capron and Mitchell (2009) distinguish between external and internal modes of strategic renewal. The former comprises activities such as alliances and acquisitions, where the latter consists of internal training of personnel and, most notably, internal product development. A main component of what constitutes strategic renewal is a firm's ability to enter a new market or market segments (Floyd & Lane, 2000). Therefore, in line with Volberda et al. (2001), *new-to-the-firm diversification* has been used as a proxy for strategic renewal. The measure was calculated by using the log of the change in unrelated diversification per year ($t_1 - t_0$) at the three digit SIC level and positive scores were considered, to capture exploratory renewal (i.e. increase in product-market diversification). Here, diversification relates to an increase by a firm in the kinds of business it operates, which can be related to either products, geographical markets, or knowledge (Palepu, 1985).

Independent Variables. The *number of outside board seats* was a proxy to tap into the influence of outside directorships and was computed by taking the sum of all outside seats of the board members in a particular year and dividing it by the number of directors, in order to obtain an average number of board seats for the focal firm in a given year. Information on the specific number of board seats was obtained through the SEC-filings.

To measure the *percentage of insiders on the board*, the number of insiders on the board of directors was divided by the total number of board members (both insiders and outsiders). Based on the SEC-filings and historical background obtained via the *Business Week* investing homepage, board members were classified into either being an insider (a director who has ties to the focal firm) or outsider (a director who does not have family or working ties to the focal firm). The average *tenure* of a particular director could directly be obtained from the Proxy Statements and complementary biographies, which state the year in which he or she first became directors of the company (as well as, in some cases, the year in which he or she started working for the company). Subsequently, the sum of the tenures of all directors was divided by the number of board members to obtain the average tenure of the board in a given year.

Finally, the *director type heterogeneity* was determined by using Hillman et al.'s (2000) classification of insiders, business experts, support specialists, and community influencers and subsequently computing a corresponding Blau (1977) heterogeneity index ($1 - \Sigma p_k^2$), where p is the proportion of the group members in the kth category. Values can range between zero and $(K - 1)/K$, with a high score indicating director type heterogeneity, and a low score indicating director type homogeneity. Blau's index was used since it is the most commonly used measure for diversity as variety (Bunderson & Sutcliffe, 2002). In determining the director type, biographies listed in the Proxy Statement as well as on *Business Week*'s People Index have been used.

Control Variables. We mainly drew on data from COMPUSTAT to control for several important variables. The first variable for which this study controls is *year*, by including year dummies, and *industry effects* via dummies, by including 3-digit SIC codes representing different industries. The present study also controls for the *size of the firm* through the logarithm of the total number of employees, as it can be argued that larger firms possess more resources with which to introduce new products. On the other hand, larger firms might be characterized by a certain inertia and path-dependence, hampering their ability to launch new products and to innovate. Furthermore, the study controls for *dynamism*, which reflects the instability of a firm's environment and environmental munificence, referring to the abundance of resources needed by the firm in a specific environment (Castrogiovanni, 2002; Schmitt et al., 2016a). This was computed as the volatility in three-digit industry sales. Prior performance is known to be a referent for decision-makers, which they turn to in case of risky decisions. In addition, it is believed that poor performance may shift the board's attention to problem-solving. *Prior performance* was measured as the log of a firm's EBITDA (earnings before interest, tax, depreciation and amortization). A firm's investments in Research & Development (R&D) is expected to affect its ability to innovate as well as to absorb external knowledge and, hence, to engage in forms of new-to-the-firm diversification (Capron & Mitchell, 2009). In order to control for the difference in this ability, *R&D to sales* was taken as a proxy, and computed by dividing the investments in R&D by the total company sales.

Chair duality was computed as a dummy variable, with 0 referring to the situation of a discrete CEO and chairman of the board, and with 1 referring to the CEO being chairman of the board at the same time (Haynes & Hillman, 2010). Chair duality was taken as a control measure since it directly affects the number of insiders on a particular board. Data was collected by using SEC-filings. We also controlled for board size as the total number of board members also directly influences the possible number of outside board seats, as well as the knowledge structure of that particular board. Hence, *board size* was taken as a control variable and computed by counting the number of board members on a particular board. Finally, the last control variable incorporated in this study is the *average board career horizon*. There is a difference between decision-makers at the beginning of their career and those approaching the end of their career concerning the level of risk-taking (Matta & Beamish, 2008) and openness to innovative and explorative activities (Heyden, Reimer, & Van Doorn, 2017). The variable was computed as 75 (which was the estimated average termination of careers) – the current tenure of a director.

Analysis and results

The relationship between board members' characteristics and strategic renewal, operationalized as new-to-the-firm diversification, was estimated by using OLS regression analysis. The sample included firm and board data from 2003 to 2007, and after the elimination of observations with missing data, the sample size was 490 (N = 490). Table 6.1 presents the descriptive statistics and correlations of all variables weighted in the regression analysis. Subsequently, Table 6.2 provides an overview of the results of the regression analysis.

Table 6.1 Descriptive statistics and correlation matrix (2003–2007)

	M	SD	1	2	3	4	5	6	7	8	9	10	11	12	13
1. new-to-the-firm diversification	-0.387	0.693	1												
2. Firm size	0.274	1.937	-0.166**	1											
3. Dynamism	0.107	4.328	-0.123**	0.542	1										
4. Firm performance	3.703	2.186	-0.096*	0.857**	0.552	1									
5. R&D/sales	0.249	2.322	0.079*	-0.120**	-0.024	-0.009	1								
6. Chair duality	0.588	0.493	-0.151**	0.111**	0.058	0.107**	0.052	1							
7. Board size	7.363	1.997	-0.045	0.671**	0.392**	0.663**	-0.059	0.090*	1						
8. Average board career horizon	14.781	4.109	0.118**	-0.035	0.034	0.065	0.015	-0.144**	-0.031	1					
9. Average tenure	9.521	4.382	-0.210**	-0.072	-0.069	-0.171**	0.005	0.062	-0.087*	-0.508**	1				
10. Director type hetero-geneity	0.496	0.151	0.062	0.157**	0.046	0.226**	0.034	0.187**	0.035	0.045	-0.246**	1			
11. Number of seats	16.827	11.062	0.015	0.681**	0.445**	0.700**	-0.033	0.071	0.762**	-0.060	-0.112**	0.116**	1		
12. Director type squared	0.023	0.026	-0.092*	-0.094*	-0.079*	-0.100*	-0.054	0.048	-0.066	0.203**	-0.052	0.032	-0.131**	1	
13. Average tenure squared	19.165	39.616	-0.427**	-0.178**	-0.090*	-0.231**	-0.034	0.004	-0.219**	-0.222**	0.578**	-0.205**	0.032	-0.179**	1
14. % Insiders	0.232	0.112	-0.008	-0.394**	-0.150**	-0.450**	0.073	-0.166**	-0.359**	-0.182**	0.435**	-0.381**	-0.389**	-0.132**	0.261**

** Correlation is significant at the 0.01 level one-tailed.
* Correlation is significant at the 0.05 level one-tailed. Industry and year dummies included but omitted here due to space constraints.

Table 6.2 OLS Regression analysis: Directors and strategic renewal

	Model 1				Model 2			
	B	S.E.	Beta	Sign.	B	S.E.	Beta	Sign.
Constant	−0.322	0.298		0.281	−0.454	0.302		0.133
Firm size	−0.058	0.033	−0.163	0.080	−0.089	0.030	−0.250	0.003
Dynamism	−0.019	0.009	−0.117	0.031	−0.014	0.008	−0.090	0.070
Firm performance	−0.009	0.030	−0.029	0.758	−0.021	0.027	−0.066	0.447
R&D/sales	0.015	0.013	0.051	0.243	0.007	0.012	0.025	0.538
Chair duality	−0.122	0.068	−0.087	0.076	−0.127	0.064	−0.091	0.045
Board size	0.049	0.022	0.140	0.024	−0.027	0.024	−0.077	0.256
Average board career horizon	−0.001	0.009	−0.004	0.938	0.013	0.008	0.076	0.125
Average tenure	−0.033	0.009	−0.208	0.000	0.018	0.010	0.112	0.066
Director type heterogeneity	0.217	0.216	0.047	0.314	0.132	0.205	0.029	0.522
Number of seats					0.016	0.004	0.249	0.000
Director type squared					−2.642	1.134	−0.098	0.020
Average tenure squared					−0.008	0.001	−0.481	0.000
% Insiders					−0.025	0.349	−0.004	0.944

Industry and year dummies included but omitted here due to space constraints.

Model 1, the base model, is found to be significant ($p < 0.000$) in comparison to the null model that assumes all parameters in Model 1 are equal to 0. Model 2 is also found to be significant ($p < 0.000$), compared to Model 1. This significance indicates that the main (interaction) effects included in the second model (the independent variables) significantly improve the analysis of the dependent variable. Furthermore, Model 2 presents an explanation of the variance (adjusted R-square) of .281. Model 1 includes the basic control variables as well as year and industry effects. Dynamism is significant ($p < 0.05$) and negative, meaning that with an increase in dynamism (volatility of 3-digit industry sales), new-to-the-firm diversification activities decrease. Furthermore, board size ($p < 0.05$) and average director tenure ($p < 0.000$) are respectively positively and negatively associated with path-breaking activities undertaken by the organization.

Hypothesis 1 posited a positive linear relationship between the total number of outside board seats within a particular firm and new-to-the-firm diversification. In Model 2, it is found that this effect is significant ($p < 0.000$) and positive ($B = 0.016$), which supports hypothesis 1. An increase in the total number of board seats with one unit will lead to an increase in new-to-the-firm diversification. The relationship between average director tenure and strategic renewal was posited to be curvilinear under hypothesis 2. Model 2 found a significant interaction effect of average tenure ($p < 0.000$) with a corresponding beta of −0.481, indicating an inverted u-shape relationship between the two variables and thus supporting hypothesis 2. This means that in the beginning of their positional tenure, an increase in tenure will be positively related to new to the firm diversification, whereas after a certain point in time, an increase in tenure will negatively affect the dependent variable. Hypothesis 3 stipulates a negative relationship between the percentage of insiders on the board of directors of the focal firm and new-to-the-firm diversification. Although the relationship was found to be negative (B = −0.025), the effect is not significant ($p = 0.944$). Hence, the results of the regression analysis did not support hypothesis 3. Finally, hypothesis 4 predicted a curvilinear relationship between director type heterogeneity in the boardroom and new-to-the-firm diversification. Model 2 found support for this relationship ($p < 0.05$), meaning that too much or too little heterogeneity in director type is not associated with strategic renewal.

Discussion and conclusions

In this study we have provided a preliminary examination of how boards of directors influence strategic renewal through their human and relational capital. Combining RDT and knowledge-based perspectives, our study resonates with the emerging view of boards as actively involved in strategy-making, as highlighted by the likes of Charan (2011), Heyden et al. (2015), and Tuggle et al. (2010), who found that the boardroom is a potential source of both creativity and opportunities for growth. In addition, the study supports Hillman and Dalziel (2003) and Huse (1998), as well as Zahra and Pearce (1989) who argued that boards play a critical role within the organization, from an RDT perspective. In order to capture the knowledge component of boards of directors, we built on what Hillman and Dalziel (2003) term *board capital*, which breaks down into relational and human capital. These two sub-constructs both tap into distinct characteristics of board members and four corresponding hypotheses were developed and tested in this paper.

Starting with relational capital, board members are expected to provide the firm with resources via the relationships they build with other actors. This study used board outside directorships as a manifestation of relational capital and found that the number of outside board seats of directors positively relates to new-to-the-firm product market diversification. Via these external networks with other organizations, directors gain knowledge about competitors' best practices, innovations, and product ideas. This finding is in line with those of Bezemer et al. (2007) and Haunschild and Beckman (1998), as well as Pfeffer and Salancik (1978), who were influential in building the case on how the board's external network matters. However, although higher relational capital is found to contribute to strategic renewal, it is intuitively appealing to argue that this relationship does not hold across a certain number of board seats. We have argued that too many outside board seats may cause individual directors, and even entire boards, to dysfunction, since they have to devote their time and knowledge to various other companies and institutions simultaneously (Ferris et al., 2003; Fich & Shivdasani, 2006; Harris & Shimizu, 2004). Although not yet applied to US corporations, we can see that other countries are restricting the number of board seats that directors have. A good example is the "Code Tabaks-blat 2003" in The Netherlands, which limits the number of supervisory board positions of an individual director to five (Bezemer et al., 2007). Our findings provide support for the former part of the debate in relation to strategic renewal, that is, board outside directorships are positively associated with strategic renewal.

Human capital, on the other hand, taps into individual characteristics of directors to include their experience and expertise. In general, the study finds that human capital positively influences the strategic renewal of organizations. It was argued that the percentage of insiders on a board of directors would negatively influence strategic renewal, meaning that outside directors are better able to provide the firm with the specific knowledge that may initiate renewal journeys. This line of reasoning corresponds with traditional agency theory, which argues that insiders will have a primary focus on the firm itself (Fama & Jensen, 1983b) and are less capable monitors or controllers of managerial decisions. As such, the study supports Tuggle et al. (2010) who posited that inside directors have a more restrictive view on new products and new markets than other board members. However, this study did not find this relationship to be significant. This could be related to the sample size or specific characteristics of the industry the sample firms operated in. Another explanation could be that the commonly used insider-outsider categorization (Fama, 1980; Pfeffer, 1972; Wagner et al., 1998) may require more nuance to understand their collaborative role.

In order to capture these possible different dimensions of outside directors, this paper has adopted Hillman and Dalziel's (2003) classification of three different types of outside directors. It is argued that each type brings different resources to the firm. Stretching this argument, this paper posits that each different director type supports the firm in their strategic renewal activities by providing a different kind of knowledge. As such, boards seem to benefit from a diverse mixture of director type, but too little or too much may be counterproductive (see also Georgakakis, Dauth, & Ruigrok, 2016). In short, it is found that director type heterogeneity indeed influences strategic renewal, in line with Tuggle et al. (2010) who found that functional background heterogeneity positively influences the discussion of entrepreneurial issues. The curvilinear relationship also supports Cannella, Park, and Lee (2008) who argued that heterogeneity is a "mixed blessing", since heterogeneity of demographic traits can lead to greater diversity of knowledge bases (Wiersema & Bantel, 1992), but too much heterogeneity can lead to potential conflicts and difficulties in decision-making (cf. Oehmichen et al., 2017).

Managerial implications

The present study contributes to research on boards and board members as well as strategic renewal in several ways. In general, it is found that boards matter to strategic renewal. This study investigates this by combining and integrating the generally under-researched resource-dependence theory and relating it to strategic renewal. As such, it complements and extends agency theoretical views on boards and their impact, to include their significant contributions to strategy. The study finds that both human and relational capital influence strategic renewal, by identifying knowledge as one of the most valuable resources that contribute to strategic renewal from a resource-dependency perspective. In sum, it is found that directors each bring different resources to the firm and as such boards should reflect a diversity of directors (heterogeneity in the boardroom). In addition, the study finds that the number of outside seats of a board of directors positively influences new-to-the-firm diversification of that particular firm. These results indicate that organizations might encourage their board members to hold similar positions within other firm simultaneously, up to a point (Ferris et al., 2003; Fich & Shivdasani, 2006; Harris & Shimizu, 2004).

Furthermore, the results of the study indicate that firms should look beyond the common insider/outsider classification when it comes to determining whom to appoint on the board of directors. Since different types of directors tap into different resource and knowledge bases, it is important to find a balance of director types on a particular board of directors, which is in line with the findings of Baysinger & Butler, 1985. Firms might benefit from and contribute to strategic renewal by appointing a diversity of insiders, business experts, support specialists, and community influencers. In addition, it is argued by many scholars that a director's tenure does increase his or her experience, expertise, and subsequently the pool of resources from which he or she can draw information and accumulate knowledge. However, the present study finds that for younger director, increases in tenure will positively contribute to strategic renewal, whereas older directors do not seem to benefit from increases in tenure. Hence, this curvilinear relationship urges boards to pay close attention to whom to appoint to the board in terms of tenure. In short, heterogeneity in the boardroom is a mixed blessing (Cannella et al., 2008), since too little heterogeneity will impede creative thinking and possible innovation, whereas too much heterogeneity can lead to conflict and impede decision-making. Hence, firms need to find a balance in the boardroom in order to create the optimal conditions for strategic renewal.

Limitations and directions for future research

Several limitations of this study merit discussion. First, the sample included US-listed firms with tangible products. Intuitively, these firms could be expected to place great emphasis on innovation and new product offerings, since they need to maintain their competitiveness in their highly turbulent and complex environments. It thus might be worthwhile to analyze whether the results hold across different industries, in order to test the generalizability of the findings. Furthermore, the sample only included US-listed firms. Corporate activities in the United States are characterized by several foundations, such as a one-tier board structure in which executives and non-executives form one board of directors (Heyden et al., 2015; Oehmichen et al., 2016). On the other hand, two-tier board structures (as commonly found in Continental Europe) distinguish between management boards (all consisting of executives) and supervisory boards (which consist of non-executives). Again, it would be worthwhile to empirically test the relationships in different settings and contexts, for instance in Europe, in order to test the generalizability of the results.

As was argued in this paper, strategic renewal is an appealing construct that consists of many different conceptions and operationalizations. This study took new-to-the-firm diversification as a proxy for strategic renewal in order to test the posited relationships. However, referring to Capron & Mitchell, 2009, this proxy does not address a specific mode of renewal by which firms diversify. Hence, new-to-the-firm diversification could relate to both internal development (for instance by R&D initiatives) as well as external sourcing activities such as mergers and acquisitions and the formation of strategic alliances. Future research might address these issues to empirically test how human and relational capital influence different modes and examples of renewal. In addition, the study focused on boards of directors as an important set of actors in the renewal process. However, future studies could consider aspects of external governance (Aguilera, Desender, Bednar, & Lee, 2015; Heyden, Kavadis, & Neuman, 2014) in addition to those of other key actors, such as top and middle managers, who are expected to play key roles in effectuating the board's contributions to strategy (Floyd & Lane, 2000; Heyden, Fourné, Koene, Werkman, & Ansari, 2017; Heyden, Reimer, & Van Doorn, 2017; Heyden, Sidhu, & Volberda, 2018; Raes, Glunk, Heijltjes, & Roe, 2007; Raes, Heijltjes, Glunk, & Roe, 2011).

Finally, having found a significant relationship between board capital and strategic renewal, the study fails to address a very important issue: the success of the renewal activities. As such, future studies could contribute to the existing literature by examining the extent to which new-to-the-firm diversification (as well as other proxies of strategic renewal) contribute to corporate performance. In this light, Danneels (2002) argued that new products with a closer fit to the existing competencies of the firm tend to be more successful. In addition, this research might shed light on the debate as to which firms are more successful financially: those that engage in related diversification or those that engage in unrelated diversification.

The study reveals that an increasing number of outside board seats will positively influence strategic renewal. However, it can be argued that there is a maximum number of outside seats that can be taken by directors in order for them to remain flexible and make the best contributions. As such, firms and practitioners could benefit from research that identifies how many outside board seats lead to the optimal integration, absorption, and application of knowledge when it comes to strategic renewal.

References

Agarwal, R. & Helfat, C. E. 2009. Strategic renewal of organizations. *Organization Science*, 20(2): 281–293.

Aguilera, R. V. 2005. Corporate governance and director accountability: An institutional comparative perspective. *British Journal of Management*, 16(S1): S39–S53.

Aguilera, R. V., Desender, K., Bednar, M. K., & Lee, J. H. 2015. Connecting the dots: Bringing external corporate governance into the corporate governance puzzle. *The Academy of Management Annals*, 9(1): 483–573.

Baden-Fuller, C. & Volberda, H. W. 1997. Strategic renewal: How large complex organizations prepare for the future. *International Studies of Management & Organization*, 27(2): 95–120.

Baysinger, B. & Hoskisson, R. E. 1990. The composition of boards of directors and strategic control: Effects on corporate strategy. *Academy of Management Review*, 15(1): 72–87.

Baysinger, B. D. & Butler, H. N. 1985. Corporate governance and the board of directors: Performance effects of changes in board composition. *Journal of Law, Economics, & Organization*, 1(1): 101–124.

Bettis, R. A. & Hitt, M. A. 1995. The new competitive landscape. *Strategic Management Journal*, 16(S1): 7–19.

Bezemer, P. J., Maassen, G. F., Van Den Bosch, F. A., & Volberda, H. W. 2007. Investigating the development of the internal and external service tasks of non-executive directors: The case of the Netherlands (1997–2005). *Corporate Governance: An International Review*, 15(6): 1119–1129.

Bhagat, S. & Black, B. 2001. Non-correlation between board independence and long-term firm performance. *The Journal of Corporation Law*, 27: 231.

Blau, P. M. 1977. *Inequality and heterogeneity: A primitive theory of social structure.* New York, NY Free Press.

Boeker, W. & Goodstein, J. 1991. Organizational performance and adaptation: Effects of environment and performance on changes in board composition. *Academy of Management Journal*, 34(4): 805–826.

Boone, A. L., Field, L. C., Karpoff, J. M., & Raheja, C. G. 2007. The determinants of corporate board size and composition: An empirical analysis. *Journal of Financial Economics*, 85(1): 66–101.

Boyd, B. 1990. Corporate linkages and organizational environment: A test of the resource dependence model. *Strategic Management Journal*, 11(6): 419–430.

Bunderson, J. S. & Sutcliffe, K. M. 2002. Comparing alternative conceptualizations of functional diversity in management teams: Process and performance effects. *Academy of Management Journal*, 45(5): 875–893.

Burgelman, R. A. 1983. A process model of internal corporate venturing in the diversified major firm. *Administrative Science Quarterly*, 28(2): 223–244.

Burgelman, R. A. 1991. Intraorganizational ecology of strategy making and organizational adaptation: Theory and field research. *Organization Science*, 2(3): 239–262.

Burt, R. S. 1980. Cooptive corporate actor networks: A reconsideration of interlocking directorates involving American manufacturing. *Administrative Science Quarterly*, 25(4): 557–582.

Cannella, A. A., Park, J.-H., & Lee, H.-U. 2008. Top management team functional background diversity and firm performance: Examining the roles of team member colocation and environmental uncertainty. *Academy of Management Journal*, 51(4): 768–784.

Capron, L. & Mitchell, W. 2009. Selection capability: How capability gaps and internal social frictions affect internal and external strategic renewal. *Organization Science*, 20(2): 294–312.

Castañer, X. & Kavadis, N. 2013. Does good governance prevent bad strategy? A study of corporate governance, financial diversification, and value creation by French corporations, 2000–2006. *Strategic Management Journal*, 34(7): 863–876.

Castrogiovanni, G. J. 2002. Organization task environments: Have they changed fundamentally over time? *Journal of Management*, 28(2): 129–150.

Charan, R. 2011. *Boards that deliver: Advancing corporate governance from compliance to competitive advantage.* Hoboken, NJ: John Wiley & Sons.

Cochran, P. L., Wood, R. A., & Jones, T. B. 1985. The composition of boards of directors and incidence of golden parachutes. *Academy of Management Journal*, 28(3): 664–671.

Daily, C. M., Dalton, D. R., & Cannella, A. A. 2003. Corporate governance: Decades of dialogue and data. *Academy of Management Review*, 28(3): 371–382.

Dalton, D. R., Daily, C. M., Johnson, J. L., & Ellstrand, A. E. 1999. Number of directors and financial performance: A meta-analysis. *Academy of Management Journal*, 42(6): 674–686.

Danneels, E. 2002. The dynamics of product innovation and firm competences. *Strategic Management Journal*, 23(12): 1095–1121.

Drees, J. M. & Heugens, P. P. M. A. R. 2013. Synthesizing and extending resource dependence theory: A meta-analysis. *Journal of Management*, 39(6): 1666–1698.

Fama, E. F. 1980. Agency problems and the theory of the firm. *Journal of Political Economy*, 88(2): 288–307.

Fama, E. F. & Jensen, M. C. 1983a. Agency problems and residual claims. *Journal of Law and Economics*, 26(2): 327–349.

Fama, E. F. & Jensen, M. C. 1983b. Separation of ownership and control. *Journal of Law & Economics*, 26(2): 301–325.

Ferris, S. P., Jagannathan, M., & Pritchard, A. C. 2003. Too busy to mind the business? Monitoring by directors with multiple board appointments. *The Journal of Finance*, 58(3): 1087–1112.

Fich, E. M. & Shivdasani, A. 2006. Are busy boards effective monitors? *The Journal of Finance*, 61(2): 689–724.

Fiske, S. T. & Taylor, S. E. 2013. *Social cognition: From brains to culture.* Newbury Park, CA: Sage.

Flier, B., Van Den Bosch, F. A., & Volberda, H. W. 2003. Co-evolution in strategic renewal behaviour of British, Dutch and French financial incumbents: Interaction of environmental selection, institutional effects and managerial intentionality*. *Journal of Management Studies*, 40(8): 2163–2187.

Floyd, S. W. & Lane, P. J. 2000. Strategizing throughout the organization: Managing role conflict in strategic renewal. *Academy of Management Review*, 25(1): 154–177.

Forbes, D. P. & Milliken, F. J. 1999. Cognition and corporate governance: Understanding boards of directors as strategic decision-making groups. *Academy of Management Review*, 24(3): 489–505.

Foss, N. J. 2011. Invited editorial: Why micro-foundations for resource-based theory are needed and what they may look like. *Journal of Management*, 37(5): 1413–1428.

Georgakakis, D., Dauth, T., & Ruigrok, W. 2016. Too much of a good thing: Does international experience variety accelerate or delay executives' career advancement? *Journal of World Business*, 51(3): 425–437.

Golden, B. R. & Zajac, E. J. 2001. When will boards influence strategy? Inclination × power = strategic change. *Strategic Management Journal*, 22(12): 1087–1111.

Harris, D. & Helfat, C. 1997. Specificity of CEO human capital and compensation. *Strategic Management Journal*, 18(11): 895–920.

Harris, I. C. & Shimizu, K. 2004. Too busy to serve? An examination of the influence of overboarded directors. *Journal of Management Studies*, 41(5): 775–798.

Haunschild, P. R. & Beckman, C. M. 1998. When do interlocks matter?: Alternate sources of information and interlock influence. *Administrative Science Quarterly*, 43(4): 815–844.

Haynes, K. T. & Hillman, A. 2010. The effect of board capital and CEO power on strategic change. *Strategic Management Journal*, 31(11): 1145–1163.

Hendry, K. & Kiel, G. C. 2004. The role of the board in firm strategy: Integrating agency and organisational control perspectives. Corporate Governance: An International Review, 12(4): 500–520.

Hendry, K. P., Kiel, G. C., & Nicholson, G. 2010. How boards strategise: A strategy as practice view. *Long Range Planning*, 43(1): 33–56.

Heyden, M. L., Fourné, S. P., Koene, B. A., Werkman, R., & Ansari, S. S. 2017. Rethinking "Top-down"and "bottom-up" roles of top and middle managers in organizational change: Implications for employee support. *Journal of Management Studies*, 54(7): 961–985.

Heyden, M. L., Kavadis, N., & Neuman, Q. 2014. External corporate governance and strategic investment behaviors of target CEOs. *Journal of Management*, 43(7): 2065–2089.

Heyden, M. L., Oehmichen, J., Nichting, S., & Volberda, H. W. 2015. Board background heterogeneity and exploration-exploitation: The role of the institutionally adopted board model. *Global Strategy Journal*, 5(2): 154–176.

Heyden, M. L., Reimer, M., & Van Doorn, S. 2017. Innovating beyond the horizon: CEO career horizon, top management composition, and R&D intensity. *Human Resource Management*, 56(2): 205–224.

Heyden, M. L., Sidhu, J. S., & Volberda, H. W. 2018. The conjoint influence of top and middle management characteristics on management innovation. *Journal of Management*, 44(4), 1505–1529.

Hillman, A. J., Cannella, A. A., & Paetzold, R. L. 2000. The resource dependence role of corporate directors: Strategic adaptation of board composition in response to environmental change. *Journal of Management Studies*, 37(2): 235–256.

Hillman, A. J. & Dalziel, T. 2003. Boards of directors and firm performance: Integrating agency and resource dependence perspectives. *Academy of Management Review*, 28(3): 383–396.

Hillman, A. J., Withers, M. C., & Collins, B. J. 2009. Resource dependence theory: A review. *Journal of Management*, 35(6): 1404–1427.

Huff, J. O., Huff, A. S., & Thomas, H. 1992. Strategic renewal and the interaction of cumulative stress and inertia. *Strategic Management Journal*, 13(S1): 55–75.

Huse, M. 1998. Researching the dynamics of board—Stakeholder relations. *Long Range Planning*, 31(2): 218–226.

Huse, M. 2005. Accountability and creating accountability: A framework for exploring behavioural perspectives of corporate governance. *British Journal of Management*, 16(S1): S65–S79.

Jackson, S. E., Joshi, A., & Erhardt, N. L. 2003. Recent research on team and organizational diversity: SWOT analysis and implications. *Journal of Management*, 29(6): 801–830.

Jehn, K. A., Northcraft, G. B., & Neale, M. A. 1999. Why differences make a difference: A field study of diversity, conflict and performance in workgroups. *Administrative Science Quarterly*, 44(4): 741–763.

Jiraporn, P., Davidson III, W. N., DaDalt, P., & Ning, Y. 2009. Too busy to show up? An analysis of directors' absences. *The Quarterly Review of Economics and Finance*, 49(3): 1159–1171.

Judge, W. Q. & Zeithaml, C. P. 1992. Institutional and strategic choice perspectives on board involvement in the strategic decision process. *Academy of Management Journal*, 35(4): 766–794.

Katz, R. 1982. Project communication and performance: An investigation into the effects of group longevity. *Administrative Science Quarterly*, 27(1): 81–104.

Kesner, I. F. 1988. Directors' characteristics and committee membership: An investigation of type, occupation, tenure, and gender. *Academy of Management Journal*, 31(1): 66–84.

Kosnik, R. D. 1990. Effects of board demography and directors' incentives on corporate greenmail decisions. *Academy of Management Journal*, 33(1): 129–150.

Maassen, G. & Van Den Bosch, F. 1999. On the supposed independence of two-tier boards: Formal structure and reality in the Netherlands. *Corporate Governance: An International Review*, 7(1): 31–37.

Matta, E. & Beamish, P. W. 2008. The accentuated CEO career horizon problem: Evidence from international acquisitions. *Strategic Management Journal*, 29(7): 683–700.

Miller, D. 1991. Stale in the saddle: CEO tenure and the match between organization and environment. *Management Science*, 37(1): 34–52.

Mínguez-Vera, A. & Martin, A. 2011. Gender and management on Spanish SMEs: An empirical analysis. *The International Journal of Human Resource Management*, 22(14): 2852–2873.

Minichilli, A., Zattoni, A., & Zona, F. 2009. Making boards effective: An empirical examination of board task performance. *British Journal of Management*, 20(1): 55–74.

Mizruchi, M. S. 1996. What do interlocks do? An analysis, critique, and assessment of research on interlocking directorates. *Annual Review of Sociology*, 22(1): 271–298.

Oehmichen, J., Heyden, M. L. M., Georgakakis, D., & Volberda, H. W. 2017. Boards of directors and organizational ambidexterity in knowledge intensive firms. *International Journal of Human Resource Management*, 28(2): 283–306.

Oehmichen, J., Schrapp, S., & Wolff, M. 2016. Who needs experts most? Board industry expertise and strategic change—A contingency perspective. *Strategic Management Journal*, 38(3): 645–656.

Palepu, K. 1985. Diversification strategy, profit performance and the entropy measure. *Strategic Management Journal*, 6(3): 239–255.

Peng, M. W. 2004. Outside directors and firm performance during institutional transitions. *Strategic Management Journal*, 25(5): 453–471.

Pfeffer, J. 1972. Size and composition of corporate boards of directors: The organization and its environment. *Administrative Science Quarterly*, 17(2): 218–228.

Phan, P. H., Lee, S. H., & Lau, S. C. 2003. The performance impact of interlocking directorates: The case of Singapore. *Journal of Managerial Issues*, 15(3): 338–352.

Pfeffer, J. & Salancik, G. 1978. *The external control of organizations: A resource dependence perspective*, Redwood City, CA: Stanford University Press.

Pugliese, A., Bezemer, P. J., Zattoni, A., Huse, M., Van Den Bosch, F. A., & Volberda, H. W. 2009. Boards of directors' contribution to strategy: A literature review and research agenda. *Corporate Governance: An International Review*, 17(3): 292–306.

Raes, A. M., Glunk, U., Heijltjes, M. G., & Roe, R. A. 2007. Top management team and middle managers making sense of leadership. *Small Group Research*, 38(3): 360–386.

Raes, A. M., Heijltjes, M. G., Glunk, U., & Roe, R. A. 2011. The interface of the top management team and middle managers: A process model. *Academy of Management Review*, 36(1): 102–126.

Roberts, J., McNulty, T., & Stiles, P. 2005. Beyond agency conceptions of the work of the non-executive director: Creating accountability in the boardroom. *British Journal of Management*, 16(S1): S5–S26.

Rubin, J. Z. & Brockner, J. 1975. Factors affecting entrapment in waiting situations: The Rosencrantz and Guildenstern effect. *Journal of Personality and Social Psychology*, 31(6): 1054.

Schmitt, A., Barker III, V. L., Raisch, S., & Whetten, D. 2016a. Strategic renewal in times of environmental scarcity. *Long Range Planning*, 49(3): 361–376.

Schmitt, A., Raisch, S., & Volberda, H. W. 2016b. Strategic renewal: Past research, theoretical tensions and future challenges. *International Journal of Management Reviews*, 20(1): 81–98.

Staw, B. M. 1976. Knee-deep in the big muddy: A study of escalating commitment to a chosen course of action. *Organizational Behavior and Human Performance*, 16(1): 27–44.

Tuggle, C. S., Schnatterly, K., & Johnson, R. A. 2010. Attention patterns in the boardroom: How board composition and processes affect discussion of entrepreneurial issues. *Academy of Management Journal*, 53(3): 550–571.

Van Knippenberg, D., De Dreu, C. K., & Homan, A. C. 2004. Work group diversity and group performance: An integrative model and research agenda. *Journal of Applied Psychology*, 89(6): 1008.

Van Knippenberg, D. & Schippers, M. C. 2007. Work group diversity. *Annual Review of Psychology*, 58: 515–541.

Volberda, H. W., Baden-Fuller, C., & van Den Bosch, F. A. 2001. Mastering strategic renewal: Mobilising renewal journeys in multi-unit firms. *Long Range Planning*, 34(2): 159–178.

Wagner III, J. A., Stimpert, J., & Fubara, E. I. 1998. Board composition and organizational performance: Two studies of insider/outsider effects. *Journal of Management Studies*, 35(5): 655–677.

Wernerfelt, B. 1984. A resource-based view of the firm. *Strategic Management Journal*, 5(2): 171–180.

Wiersema, M. F. & Bantel, K. A. 1992. Top management team demography and corporate strategic change. *Academy of Management Journal*, 35(1): 91–121.

Yawson, A. 2006. Evaluating the characteristics of corporate boards associated with layoff decisions. *Corporate Governance: An International Review*, 14(2): 75–84.

Zahra, S. A. & Pearce, J. A. 1989. Boards of directors and corporate financial performance: A review and integrative model. *Journal of Management*, 15(2): 291–334.

Part 3

Psychological antecedents and micro-foundations of strategic renewal

7 Emotion and strategic renewal

Quy Huy and Christine Scheef

Introduction

New competition, shorter product lifecycles, globalization, and frequent techno-logical disruptions create market environments in which organizations' ability to renew themselves is critical for their sustained success and long-term survival (Agarwal & Helfat, 2009). Strategic renewal, however, constitutes a major challenge for organizations as it requires fundamental changes to the core business as well as the development of new competences (Agarwal & Helfat, 2009). Such organizational events can elicit strong emotions among large groups of employees that can influence the way those groups think and behave in relation to the strategic transformation (Barsade, 2002; Sanchez-Burks & Huy, 2009; Volberda *et al.*, 2001). The composition of collective emotions might be diverse with groups of distinct roles, values, and interests as they perceive implications differently (Cyert & March, 1963). For instance, some employees may react with fear to the unknown, others with hope and relief, and others with anger or contempt as they feel that their ideas have not been heard. Thus, emotion represents an important dimension in major renewal projects (Huy, 1999, 2005, 2011).

Although anecdotal evidence and scholars have documented the (often harmful) effects of emotions, research that investigates how to manage these collective emotions, so as to reduce their harmful effects and increase their effects on desired strategic outcomes, still remains in its infancy (Huy, 2012). This chapter aims to elaborate on the role of emotion in strategic renewal. Specifically, we propose a prescriptive model of how emotion management at the organizational level can enhance strategic renewal goals. We posit that organizations should focus on the development of an emotional capability, which we refer to as "an organization's abilities to acknowledge, recognize, monitor, discriminate, and attend to its members' emotions and it is mani-fested in the organization's routines related to feelings" (Huy, 1999, p. 325). The key elements of emotional capability are emotion-management actions that inspire employees to mobilize their resources to achieve organizational goals (Huy, 1999). Building on prior research on emotional capability (e.g., Huy, 1999, 2002, 2005, 2011), we will discuss specific emotion-management actions that create an emotional context in which a large number of employees feel or express authenticity, aspirational discontent, hope, pride, and passion and how those emotion management actions influence key strategic renewal processes such as receptivity for change, collective mobilization, and innovativeness.

Strategic renewal research benefits from the use of multiple lenses (Agarwal & Helfat, 2009). This chapter aims to make two contributions to the strategic renewal literature. First, this chapter nuances a dominantly indifferent or negative role of emotion in strategic renewal and suggests emotion-management practices that can enable strategic transformation. While knowledge of strategic renewal has accumulated, the micro-foundations of strategic renewal have received little attention. Understanding how emotions influence an organization's strategic transformations contributes to establishing more realistic assumptions about humans involved in strategic actions (Powell *et al.*, 2011). Second, most research on emotions has addressed individual or collective emotions and their effects on behavior. However, much less is known about how these emotions affect firm-level processes and outcomes (Huy, 2012). In this chapter, we elaborate on the role of organizations in dealing with the individual or collective emotions of their employees during strategic renewal and its effects on renewal outcomes.

The chapter is organized as follows. First, strategic renewal will be defined as a distinct form of organizational change. We then review the role of emotion in strategic change at the individual and collective level. Then, we propose a set of emotion-management actions that help organizations to facilitate strategic renewal. These sets of emotion-management actions aim to elicit authenticity, pride, discontent, hope, and passion among large parts of the workforce. We discuss how these specific emotions influence key strategic renewal processes such as employees' receptivity to change, collective mobilization and innovativeness.

Employees' individual and collective emotion in the context of strategic renewal

Strategic renewal is critical for the sustained success of organizations. Broadly speaking, strategic renewal can be defined as a firm's ability to modify or replace core competences to ensure its long-term performance (Agarwal & Helfat, 2009; Lechner & Floyd, 2012). Strategic renewal is a specific type of strategic change (Agarwal & Helfat, 2009). Specifically, strategic change can happen by eliminating or extending a division, whereas strategic renewal, per definition, includes an element of refreshment or replacement of strategic attributes of the organization, such as goals, products, and services, resources or capabilities (Agarwal & Helfat, 2009). Prior research has primarily focused on drivers of strategic renewal efforts such as capability development and learning processes (Crossan & Bredrow, 2003), technological change (Volberda & Lewin, 2003), and leadership processes enabling strategic renewal (Cho & Hambrick, 2006; Kwee *et al.*, 2011).

While research on strategic renewal has accumulated, the behavioral perspective has received less attention. The goal of the field of behavioral strategy is to bring more realistic assumptions about cognition, emotion, and social behavior to strategic management research (Powell *et al.*, 2011). For example, we know little about the role of emotion and how emotion management can affect firm-level processes and outcomes (Huy, 2012).

Research on emotion in organizations suggests that emotion represents an important dimension in major change processes (Huy, 2005, 2011). Emotions are inherent to change in that they are aroused not by the presence of favorable or unfavorable conditions in themselves, but by actual or expected *changes* in these conditions (Frijda, 1988). Emotions affect how employees interpret change and how they behave. Employees are emotionally invested in the organization and their emotional reactions to new strategic directions can be particularly intense and diverse (Kanter, 1983). Some employees may react with anxiety to the unknown, others with fear about potential negative consequences of the change, and again others with hope that the organization will move forward. In the strategic change literature, employees' emotions are most frequently discussed with a negative connotation. Strategic change causes a massive redistribution of resources and power that can trigger strong defense mechanisms such as fear, anxiety or defensiveness (Schein, 1992). However, emotions may also serve as motivator and help employees to get ready for the transformation (Frijda, 1996). Much less research has addressed how emotions can be managed to reduce the harmful effects, or how emotions can have a positive impact on the desired outcomes (Huy, 2012).

The intensity of the emotional response with which an employee experiences the strategic renewal process likely varies with the subjective meaning of the event for the employee (Frijda, 1988). For example, radical and incremental renewal may not cause the same emotions and coping mechanisms. Incremental renewal refers to incremental alteration to the core businesses or experimentation outside the core business (Agarwal & Helfat, 2009). This is a proactive, gradual renewal process that continuously replaces smaller parts of the organization and its strategy (Agarwal & Helfat, 2009). Employees can infer changes from past patterns and have certain expectations about future changes in their organization. The emotional response is likely to be less strong for most employees as they are used to changes and the changes are less close to their core beliefs.

Radical renewal or discontinuous strategic transformation refers to replacing or fundamentally altering important parts of company's strategy and core business (Agarwal & Helfat, 2009). For instance, globalization and digitalization place strong pressure on organizations to reinvent themselves, which involves large scale change as well as change in multiple dimensions, such as organizational structure, culture, and strategy. These radical strategic renewal activities alter existing attributes or create new attributes of the firm's strategy that are considered to be relatively distant from the current firm strategy (Agarwal & Helfat, 2009). These changes often challenge employees' basic assumptions about the organization (Bartunek, 1984). Challenging these assumptions represents an attack to the core identity of the organization. and implies high levels of uncertainty about employees' future roles (Tripsas & Gavetti, 2000), which likely elicit intense emotional responses or strong defense mechanisms (Schein, 1992). Therefore, we would expect that emotion management plays a crucial part, particularly in the context of radical strategic renewal.

Emotions in organizations, however, have implications that extend beyond those related to specific individuals. Collective emotions in response to strategic change can influence the ways in which various groups think and behave in relation to the organization and other groups within it (Barsade, 2002; Sanchez-Burks & Huy, 2009). The composition of collective emotions might be diverse with groups of distinct roles, values, and interests, as they perceive implications differently (Cyert & March, 1963). For instance, the marketing department might feel proud as they consider that the organization moves into the strategic direction that they championed. However, other parts of the organization might feel angry or contemptuous because they believe that their ideas have not been heard. Yet, still within the marketing department, the majority would feel hopeful but a minority of marketers might react with fear. Being able to recognize the composition of diverse emotions in groups and the organization is called emotional aperture (Sanchez-Burks & Huy, 2009). These different collective emotions lead to mobilization for or against strategic renewal, and it is important that supervisors recognize these emotions among their employees.

Prior research suggests that top management and middle managers as change agents likely play a crucial part in the change process. Top managers can give the emotion–management actions legitimacy and send a strong signal to the organization with their support. Middle managers need to recognize clues that signal fear, anxiety, or sarcasm among their employees and then also address those emotions. Yet, Huy (2002) argues that it is not enough that middle managers pay attention to their employees' emotions but that they, at the same time, need to have themselves a high emotional commitment to the organization to facilitate organizational change and to stimulate continuous improvement. Therefore, how organizations recognize and manage employees' diverse emotions during change is crucial and can facilitate or hinder the progress of change projects (Huy, 1999).

Building an organizational emotional context to facilitate strategic renewal

Individual or collective emotions can also become organizational through the enactment of what is called organizational emotional capability, which refers to "an organization's abilities to acknowledge, recognize, monitor, discriminate, and attend to its members' emotions and it is manifested in the organization's routines related to feelings" (Huy, 1999, p. 325). The key elements of emotional capability are emotion-management actions that inspire employees to mobilize their resources for the achievement of organizational goals. We define emotional capability as a set of deliberate and collective (organization or group-level) emotion-management actions that seek to elicit a mindful emotional state among employees. In this chapter, we will discuss specific emotion-management actions that create an emotional context in which a number of employees feel or express emotion such as hope, pride, passion, aspirational discontent, and authenticity, and how these emotion-management actions facilitate some of the processes underlying strategic renewal.

Emotion-management actions reflect the collective knowledge and skills needed to manage the emotions of employees when necessary to realize strategic renewal. Emotional capability theory posits that organizations that develop procedures related to emotion management and that provide systematic training on this subject to various managers likely reduce the need to rely on the innate competence of individuals' emotional intelligence and their individual dispositions (Huy, 1999).

Our research builds on cognitive appraisal theory of emotion (Smith & Ellsworth, 1985) suggesting that emotions are elicited by the cognitive evaluation of an event, which, in our case, are the organizational emotion management actions. Therefore, cognitive appraisal theory along with emotional capability theory serve as bases to identify emotion-management practices that elicit emotional states relevant for strategic renewal. We build on prior research (Huy, 1999, 2005, 2011) to discuss the following specific emotion-management actions that create an emotional context in which a number of employees feel or express aspirational discontent, hope, passion, pride, and authenticity. We posit that these emotion-management actions influence key strategic renewal processes such as receptivity for change, collective mobilization, and innovativeness.

It is important to note that we define emotion-management actions as intentional actions that seek to elicit desirable emotions and resulting behavior; however, we do not require these actions to be perceived equally and/or elicit the same specified emotion among all employees. The basic intention is to create an emotional context in which there is a large number of employees who appreciate the goal of the emotion-management actions and who experience these emotions, at least for some time, during the strategic renewal processes (Huy, 1999, 2005). For instance, in different cultural or organizational contexts emotion-management practices can be perceived differently.

Authenticity

Broadly speaking, authenticity refers to "owning one's personal experiences, be they thoughts, emotions, needs, preferences, or beliefs, processes captured by the injunction to know oneself" and behaving in accordance with the true self (Harter, 2002, p. 382). Thus, authenticity describes a feeling of being sincere to oneself and others and that one's thoughts, emotions, and behavior are aligned. During renewal phases employees are likely to feel reluctant to express their true thoughts and feelings – out of fear for their job security – and might disguise those that result in emotional dissonance. Emotional dissonance is the internal conflict generated between genuinely felt emotions and the emotions that are expected to be displayed in organizations (Wharton & Erickson, 1993). When authenticity is missing in the organization, employees perceive emotion-management actions as fake and manipulative, quickly creating a climate of mistrust and rendering emotion-management actions ineffective. Emotion-management actions that facilitate authenticity are those actions that are aligned with the organization's rhetoric in the pursuit of an organizational goal (Huy, 2005). Authenticity is particularly important as it helps to build a climate of trust and transparency in the organization. Specifically, the organization should take actions to make employees feel that they can express their honest thoughts and feelings and behave in accordance with their thoughts and feelings during strategic renewal processes (Huy, 2005).

Thus, it is important that organizations use emotion-management actions to provide employees with a safe space where they can express their true thoughts and feelings. For example, Huy (2002) found in his research that during a massive downsizing and relocation of the work location, employees opposed the new strategic direction arguing that it would not make sense from a customer service perspective. In fact, those employees were worried about their jobs and the effects of relocation for their families; however, they did not dare to express those true thoughts and feelings until middle managers organized information sessions in small groups, where they encouraged employees to express their feelings about how change would affect them. Only after these sessions did the employees start to realize how similar their feelings were, and they started to laugh and sympathize with each other. Further, it is important that leaders themselves show consistent behavior, for example, by not only repeatedly communicating the importance of a new business or functional unit but also by making regular visits in the physical world to demonstrate support on the ground (Huy & Shipilov, 2012). Thus, top management and middle managers as change leaders play a critical part in facilitating emotion-management practices that elicit authenticity.

Although the organization seeks to encourage all employees to express their honest thoughts and feelings and act in alignment with them, these honest expressions should be subject to respecting others (Huy, 2005). Respect is reflected in social norms of civility, sensitivity, and politeness rather than rudeness, insensitivity, and impoliteness. When authenticity is perceived highly in the organization, the other emotion-management actions can be developed on a solid foundation (Huy, 2005; Huy & Shipilov, 2012) and positively contribute to the strategic renewal process.

Proposition 1: Emotion-management actions that stimulate authenticity among employees positively contribute to the firm's strategic renewal process.

Pride

Pride is an emotional state of pleasure elicited usually by a specific accomplishment or achievement (Tracy & Robins, 2007). The feeling of pride can help to counterbalance the feeling of fear and anxiety during strategic renewal.

Particularly in radical strategic renewal, to achieve the goal, the negative feelings and threats to employees' core values and identity should be encountered by the organization by recognizing and valuing the distinct competences and experiences of its employees during and after the renewal process. Experiencing pride can be a strong motivator, boost self-esteem, and may reinforce the behavior that generated the proud feeling (Tracy & Robins, 2007; Williams & DeSteno, 2008). When employees are recognized for an accomplishment in the change process, they may feel motivated to pursue further action in the same domain and increase their efforts toward change. Research has shown that the experience of pride after accomplishing a task promotes improved performance at subsequent tasks (Herrald & Tomaka, 2002). For instance, during IBM's strategic transformation process, the top management provided economic rewards and social status for managers who developed capabilities related to the new identity of an electronic computing company (Agarwal & Helfat, 2009). In this way, IBM recognized managers' accomplishments and instilled a feeling of pride.

The pursuit of renewal goals is often a quite challenging and demanding transformation journey that usually exacts short-term costs such as high efforts, the unlearning of skills and acquisition of new ones, or even embarrassment due to initial failures. Pride is an important goal-directed emotion that helps persons to remain focused and increase persistence on tasks, particularly in face of initial cost (Williams & DeSteno, 2008). The feeling of pride also stimulates the development of difficult skills (Tracy & Robins, 2004). Emotion-management actions that elicit pride to recognize and value employees' competences and accomplishments will encourage employees to make sacrifices and make stronger efforts to achieve the proposed renewal. Thus, we posit that pride helps to decrease employees' resistance to change and to mobilize employees during strategic renewal processes.

Organizations can instill pride in several ways. Besides financial compensation and promotions, peer appreciation and praise can also be powerful stimuli for pride (Huy & Shipilov, 2012). Organizations can, for example, organize "moments of pride" during annual celebrations where top performers or change leaders are recognized and receive gifts and prizes. Alternatively, top-performing employees or teams can be publicly announced to praise their achievements. This form of psychic reward can be as stimulating as financial rewards for employees and serve as a powerful motivator (Huy & Shipilov, 2012).

While deserved pride stems from a specific accomplishment or event and has arguably a positive effect on strategic renewal, hubristic pride, which is in essence an unconditional positive view of one's self and associated with narcissism, likely has a detrimental effect on strategic renewal efforts. This form of pride risks turning into hubris and the feeling of being satisfied with the current situation, increasing the resistance to change (Tracy & Robins, 2007). Elicitors of hubristic pride are usually only loosely coupled with specific achievements but rather connected to one's ability attribution in general (Tracy & Robins, 2007). Therefore, it is important to bear in mind that the emotion-management actions to elicit deserved pride should be linked to specific achievements in the renewal process rather than to managers' general abilities or competences.

Proposition 2: Emotion-management actions that stimulate deserved pride among employees positively contribute to the firm's strategic renewal process.

Discontent

Discontent is an emotional state of dissatisfaction with one's own situation or with the situation of a group of people (Hafer & Olson, 1993). Although intuitively appealing, dissatisfaction at work does not always mean that it is detrimental for performance. Research on job satisfaction commonly assumes that high level of satisfaction lead to organizational effectiveness while low levels are detrimental for organizations and its employees (Zhou & George, 2001). However, this is not always supported by empirical research and some studies show that, under certain circumstances, dissatisfaction can have a positive effect on creativity and innovation in the organization (e.g., Zhou & George, 2001).

In the context of strategic renewal, established organizations may face complacency among its employees. Some employees may feel satisfied with the organization's performance and, therefore, feel less need to make an effort to continuously improve themselves. Others may feel unhappy with the organization's performance; however, do not know how to improve their performance. We posit that organizations should actively address those feelings of complacency at the beginning of the strategic renewal process and actively stimulate discontent that increases employees' aspirations for superior performance.

In the organizational context, aspirational discontent describes a feeling of unhappiness that the organization has not realized its full potential and, importantly, that the organization could do better if it wants to. Top management should implement emotion-management actions that seek to elicit discontent/dissatisfaction among employees that the organization can do better to achieve a higher level of value for their stakeholders. This helps employees understand the reasons for the proposed strategic renewal, inspire the need for change, and, therefore, likely increase employees' receptivity to change.

For example, as part of IBM's transformation from a hardware-based computing company to a business computing service company, the top management identified key weaknesses in the existing capabilities, such as a deficit in software expertise, and actively communicated and addressed these weaknesses in the renewal process (Agarwal & Helfat, 2009). Further, the top management shaped the perception of the employees by constantly communicating the need to move forward and the necessity for change to keep ahead of the curve and avoid obsolescence (Taylor & Helfat, 2009). The top management also provided economic incentives to employees for developing electronic capabilities (Taylor & Helfat, 2009). These practices helped employees understand that the organization was not doing as well as it could do, and increased their readiness to embrace strategic renewal.

There are multiple ways in which middle managers can instill discontent among employees during strategic renewal. For instance, middle managers can regularly share objective data on market share and sales in relation to their direct competitors or specific business units that are underperforming with their business units, and emphasize that there is no real reason for performing worse than the competition (when this is indeed the case). In addition, middle managers should provide resources to employees to identify areas where the organization is doing worse than the competition and, thus, actively involve employees from the beginning of the renewal process.

While eliciting discontent among employees that the organization could do better is important, it is not enough to mobilize employees for change. The organization also needs to instill hope among its employees that the proposed strategic renewal is doable and feasible for them to achieve, which we discuss in the following section.

Proposition 3: Emotion-management actions that stimulate aspirational discontent among employees positively contribute to the firm's strategic renewal process.

Hope

Hope is an emotional state that is elicited by appraisal of future positive prospects for the self (Ortony *et al.*, 1988). Hope buffers people against apathy and depression and strengthens their capacity to persist under adversity; it bolsters people's beliefs that they have both the will and the means to accomplish goals (Snyder *et al.*, 1991). Transforming the core business of an organization as part of the renewal process challenges the fundamental beliefs, work habits, and routines of its employees and comes with high levels of uncertainty (Bartunek, 1984; Tripsas & Gavetti, 2000). As discussed above, such a transformation likely triggers feelings such as fear and depression among many employees, to the extent that they feel that their current competencies and skill sets may not match with the capabilities needed to compete successfully in the new industry (Capron & Mitchell, 2009).

We posit that organizations can counteract those negative feelings during strategic transformation processes by instilling hope among its employees. In the organizational context, hope describes employees' feelings that today's actions will improve the organization's future. In other words, the emotion-management actions elicit hope in the employees that there is a feasible set of actions to achieve the change goals successfully. These actions create a feeling of optimism and encouragement among the employees that the proposed strategic renewal is feasible and that there is a reasonable chance that the organization will succeed. For example, constant and extensive communication of concrete sets of actions to transform the core business from the top and middle management will help to decrease resistance to the strategic renewal project and make employees more receptive to change. Further, prior research on strategic renewal suggests that organizations likely face a competence gap between employees' current skill set and the desired future skill set (Capron & Mitchell, 2009). This gap can be overcome by either internal development or external sourcing. When employees perceive that organizations propose workshops and continuous learning opportunities, they likely feel more optimistic that the transformation is feasible and will increase long-term wellbeing for themselves and the organization.

Instilling hope will also help organizations to increase collective mobilization for continuous renewal, as employees feel involved in the change and able to shape their own future. Employees perceive that the organization takes actions to create a better collective future for the company and its employees. For example, Huy (2002) found that some middle managers as change agents managed to elicit hope among their employees by promoting wide participation of and active consultation with employees from a very early stage of the transformation project onwards. Giving some ownership of the change project to the employees makes them likely to feel more confident about their future (Beer *et al.*, 1990).

There are various ways in which organizations can instill hope among its employees during strategic renewal. For instance, when the top management announces performance targets, it should also communicate concrete and realistic actions that the organization should perform to reach the aspired targets. Further, organizations should directly address the competence gap between current and future skill sets and propose feasible improvements to employees to make the transition. It is also important to clearly communicate how the new strategic direction will create more value for the different stakeholder groups including employees.

While hope can facilitate receptivity to change and collective mobilization in strategic renewal processes, it may be less valuable to foster creativity and innovativeness, as hope also promotes group thinking (Janis, 1972). Faced with high uncertainty, anxious employees are likely to become more narrow-minded and, therefore, less exploratory and creative in their work. The organization needs to consider another set of emotion-management actions to stimulate employees' innovativeness as discussed below.

Proposition 4: Emotion-management actions that stimulate hope among employees positively contribute to the firm's strategic renewal process.

Passion

Passion is a positive emotional state that describes a strong inclination toward an activity that is liked and valuable to oneself and in which one invests significant energy and time (Amiot *et al.*, 2006; Vallerand *et al.*, 2003). Passion goes beyond liking, for example, one's job, but involves a strong positive feeling about exercising a task (Ho *et al.*, 2011). Thus, passion describes a feeling of deep personal engagement.

Research on passion suggests that it fuels intrinsic motivation, which is an important precondition for creativity (Amabile, 1988). Further, passion elicits an intense flow-like state of strong engagement in one's activity (Csikszentmihalyi, 1990). People who experience flow or timelessness are likely to be more creative and lose a sense of time while performing the activity. Flow replenishes people's energy as they undertake long and challenging work to reach a distant vision with uncertain outcomes (Csikszentmihalyi, 1997). It is therefore critical that organizations allocate attention to unleashing employees' creativity by enacting a set of emotion-management actions that elicit employees' passion for their work (Huy, 2005).

Research on entrepreneurship has also discussed the importance of passion in the entrepreneurial process (Baron, 2008; Cardon *et al.*, 2009; Ho & Pollack, 2013). Passion fuels goal-directed behavior, persistence, and creative problem-solving that enhances the recognition of opportunities and innovativeness (Cardon *et al.*, 2009). Strategic renewal bears some similarity to an entrepreneurial context, in that the organization is searching for new opportunities outside its core business and requires that managers engage in more creative work and search for new ideas. Employees fired by passion produce more out-of-the-box and novel ideas and are more persistent despite failures (Cardon *et al.*, 2009). Thus, we posit that emotion-management actions that elicit passion help to engage employees in the renewal process and foster creative thinking that goes beyond the core business.

Emotion-management actions can elicit passion in employees when they are involved in the often interesting, stimulating, engaging processes of formulating and implementing strategic renewal in the organization. Passion is not a disposition but depends on the activities that are perceived as important to the employee (Vallerand *et al.*, 2003). For instance, the emotion-management actions should allow employees to perform work that is interesting to them and where they feel engaged in their task. The fulfillment of a passionate activity increases persistence in the task to prolong the pleasant affect (Murnieks *et al.*, 2012), which likely leads to more mobilization for strategic renewal among the workforce, and creative thinking as discussed above. To create an emotional context to elicit passion, organizations can, for example, involve many middle managers to develop the strategy plan, creating cross-functional teams and offsite events so that they can exchange and debate different perspectives and come up with ambitious renewal targets. Being involved in the strategy development task is often highly interesting and stimulating for those middle managers, who may perceive this as a managerial development opportunity whereby they can learn what other departments are doing, but also have to negotiate and build an ambitious collective plan that they have ownership for implementing successfully.

Proposition 5: Emotion-management actions that stimulate passion among employees positively contribute to the firm's strategic renewal process.

Conclusions and future research

In this chapter, we have discussed specific emotions and how organizations can enact emotion-management practices that elicit specific emotional states among large parts of its employee base to initiate, support, and facilitate the strategic renewal processes. This represents increasing employees' receptivity to change, enhancing their collective mobilization for change, and inspiring their creativity to reinvent selective attributes of the core business. Developing an emotional capability will no doubt require a new awareness of the importance of emotion in organizational life and, generally, a more positive attitude toward emotion within organizations. Thus far, most research and anecdotal evidence on strategic renewal focuses on the detrimental effects of emotion in change processes and undermines the positive effects that specific emotions can have on the renewal process (Huy, 2012). We provide a fresh perspective by discussing the beneficial influence of both positive and negative emotions – if authentically managed by the organization.

Building up emotion-management practices is likely to require a long-term and sustained organizational effort, and commitment from the top. Organizations need to prioritize and start to steadily develop those practices to facilitate continuous strategic renewal. Thus far, however, we have not discussed the emotional sequencing of the emotion-management actions targeted at eliciting different emotional states (Huy, 2005). Limited organizational resources and attention suggest that the relative emphasis of a particular set of emotion-management actions should vary according to the particular stage of the strategic transformation project (Huy, 2005). Initially, it is important to achieve credibility among a large proportion of the employees, communicating the idea that the emotion-management practices are intrinsically well-meant and respectful. Authenticity plays a crucial role in building up such a climate of trust and transparency in the organization. A perceived lack of authenticity and respect for each other can quickly render emotion-management actions ineffective. When authenticity is perceived highly, the other pillars of emotional capability can be developed on a solid foundation (Huy, 2005). Thus, when faced with limited resources, organizations should initially prioritize the development of respectful authenticity.

Further, in the initial stage of the renewal process, it is important to create awareness among employees that renewal is crucial for the long-term survival of the organization. Creating discontent among employees about the organization's performance and targeting employees' ambitions, the emotion-management actions that aim to elicit discontent help to make complacent employees ready for change, and enable collective mobilization as energetic group action is often required to realize ambitious renewal projects. At the same time, it is important to address employees' fears about the uncertain renewal process and to instill hope among employees that the proposed strategic transformation is feasible and doable. The sets of emotion-management actions that aim to elicit hope at the beginning of the renewal process help to convert fearful employees into ambitious and positive employees in the later stages of strategic renewal (Huy, 2005). Hope plays a crucial part in mobilizing groups of employees and actions arousing hope should dominate the main phase of strategic renewal.

Stimulating a feeling of pride among employees or groups of employees who have successfully accomplished renewal targets or have made a significant contribution to the renewal process, is another important means by which to reduce employees' resistance to change and achieve collective mobilization. Recognizing achievements throughout the renewal process will encourage those employees to make sacrifices and even stronger efforts to achieve the proposed renewal, and motivate others to join the effort in order to likewise receive recognition. Actions arousing passion prevail during the beginning phase of renewal. Creativity and innovativeness is particularly important in the development of the strategy plan and for those managers who are involved in the development. Thus, those emotion-management actions eliciting passion should be emphasized at the beginning and selectively applied on key individuals.

As strategic renewal is a continuous process (Agarwal & Helfat, 2009), the ending phase of one renewal cycle will eventually be followed by another starting phase of a new cycle of strategic renewal. Effective implementation of an organization's emotional capability requires knowing both the distinct effect of each set of emotion-management actions and its aggregated effect according to a temporal order (Huy, 2005).

To implement emotion-management actions successfully, it is important to make the middle managers with supervisory responsibility aware of the importance of actively and appropriately managing the emotions of their employees. Organizations could initially identify leaders who are authentic and whom employees trust, and help those managers to develop emotion-management practices. Organizations could offer them training and suggestions as to how and when to build emotion-management practices that emphasize authenticity, pride, passion, hope, and aspirational discontent. Further, middle managers need to develop their emotional aperture, which is the ability to perceive various shared emotion in collectives (Sanchez-Burks & Huy, 2009). This will help middle managers to assess the effectiveness of the implemented emotion-management actions. Lastly, this group of middle managers can then serve as a role models or mentors for other managers to build up an emotional capability across the organization.

We encourage future research on strategic renewal to take a behavioral perspective and investigate the proposed role of emotions in greater depth using qualitative and quantitative approaches. For instance, there is still little empirical research on emotional capability, including qualitative (Huy, 2002; Huy & Shipilov, 2012) and quantitative research (Akgün *et al.*, 2009). Future research could study how organizational practices related to emotional capability are developed and adapted over time. Triangulation of private interviews, survey method, and company reports and/or ethnographic studies should help researchers to validate self-reported data and to enrich our knowledge of emotion-management actions. For example, emotion management actions eliciting pride can be assessed not only by survey methods but also by counting company events where employees or groups of employees receive acknowledgement for their achievements. Combining various methods would enhance the validity of the measurement.

Future research could also explore emotion-management actions and their organizational consequences. We still need to develop reliable measurement for the different sets of emotion-management actions and link emotion-management actions to strategic renewal outcomes such as innovativeness, as well as identifying important moderating and mediating effects. For example, while emotion-management actions are suggested to elicit specific emotions among a large number of employees, empirical research could further test the mediating effect of emotions.

Future research can also examine the roles of various organizational actors, such as middle and top managers, in perceiving and managing their own and others' emotions during strategic renewal. For instance, researchers could follow an organization throughout an entire strategic renewal process, conduct private interviews and ethnographic and observation studies, to triangulate information and identify key actors and underlying mechanisms that make emotion-management actions effective in the renewal process. For example, Huy and Shipilov (2012) used case studies to analyze the role of emotion management in the context of use of social media in organizations. They carefully selected the target organizations to have contrasting cases and triangulated data using personal interviews, company documentation, and survey method. Their results show that it is important to initially invest in building emotional capital within employees' communities. The study shows that only executives who have built emotional capital can reap real benefits from the use of social media in terms of better information flows, closer collaboration, and higher employee motivation.

To conclude, the field of strategic renewal can be enriched by exploring the diversity of positive and negative emotions, how those emotions (individually and collectively) influence the renewal process, and how an organization's emotional capability can help to deal with those emotions to achieve both employees' well-being and high organizational performance and long-term survival.

References

Agarwal R, Helfat CE. 2009. Strategic renewal of organization. *Organization Science* 20(2): 281–293.

Akgün AE, Keskin H, & Bzrne J. 2009. Organizational emotional capability, product and process innovation, and firm performance: An empirical analysis. *Journal of Engineering and Technology Management* 26(3): 103–130.

Amabile TM. 1988. A model of creativity and innovation in organizations. In *Research in organizational behavior*. Cummings LL & Staw BM (eds.), 123–167, JAI Press: Greenwich, CT.

Amiot CE, Vallerand RJ, & Blanchard C. 2006. Passion and psychological adjustment: A test of the person-environment fit hypothesis. *Personality and Social Psychology Bulletin* 32(2): 220–229.

Baron RA. 2008. The role of affect in the entrepreneurial process. *Academy of Management Review* 33(2): 328–340.

Barsade SG. 2002. The ripple effect: Emotional contagion and its influence on group behavior. *Administrative Science Quarterly* 47: 644–675.

Bartunek JM. 1984. Changing interpretive schemes and organizational restructuring: The example of a religious order. *Administrative Science Quarterly* 29: 355–437.

Beer M, Eisenstat RA, & Spector B. 1990. Why change programs don't produce change. *Harvard Business Review* 68(6): 158.

Capron LW & Mitchell W. 2009. Selection capability: How capability gaps and internal social frictions affect internal and external strategic renewal. *Organization Science* 20(2): 294–312.

Cardon MS, Wincent J, Singh J, & Drnovsek M. 2009. The nature and experience of entrepreneurial passion. *Academy of Management Review* 34(3): 511–532.

Cho TS & Hambrick DC. 2006. Attention as the mediator between top management team characteristics and strategic change: The case of airline deregulation. *Organization Science* 17(4): 453–469.

Crossan M & Bredrow I. 2003. Organizational learning and strategic renewal. *Strategic Management Journal* 24(11): 1087–1105.

Csikszentmihalyi M. 1990. *Flow: The psychology of optimal experience.* Harper Perennial: New York, NY.

Csikszentmihalyi M. 1997. *Finding flow: The psychology of engagement with everyday life.* Basic Books: New York, NY.

Cyert RM & March JG. 1963. *A behavioral theory of the firm.* Prentice-Hall: Englewood Cliffs, NJ.

Frijda NH. 1988. The laws of emotion. *American Psychologist* 43: 349–358.

Frijda NH. 1996. *Passions: Emotion and socially consequential behavior.* Lawrence Erlbaum Associates: Mahwah, NJ.

Hafer CL & Olson JM. 1993. Beliefs in a just world, discontent, and assertive actions by working women. *Personality and Social Psychology Bulletin* 19(1): 30–38.

Harter S. 2002. Authenticity. In *Handbook of positive psychology.* Snyder CR & Lopez SJ (eds.), 382–394, Oxford University Press: London.

Herrald MM & Tomaka J. 2002. Patterns of emotion-specific appraisal, coping, and cardiovascular reactivity during an ongoing emotional episode. *Journal of Personality and Social Psychology* 83: 434–450.

Ho VT & Pollack JM. 2013. Passion isn't always a good thing: Examining entrepreneurs' network centrality and financial performance with a dualistic model of passion. *Journal of Management Studies* 51(3), 433–459.

Ho VT, Wong S, & Lee CH. 2011. A tale of passion: Linking job passion and cognitive engagement to employee work performance. *Journal of Management Studies* 48(1): 26–47.

Huy QN. 1999. Emotional capability, emotional intelligence, and radical change. *Academy of Management Review* 24(2): 325–345.

Huy QN. 2002. Emotional balancing of organizational continuity and radical change: The contribution of middle managers. *Administrative Science Quarterly* 47: 31–69.

Huy QN. 2005. An emotion-based view of strategic renewal. *Advances in Strategic Management* 22: 3–37.

Huy QN. 2011. Emotions and strategic change. In *The Oxford handbook of positive organizational scholarship*. Cameron KS & Spreitzer GM (eds.), 811–824, Oxford University Press: Oxford, UK.

Huy QN. 2012. Emotions in strategic organization: Opportunities for impactful research. *Strategic Organization* 10(3): 240–247.

Huy QN & Shipilov A. 2012. The key to social media success within organizations. *MIT Sloan Management Review* 54(1), 73–81.

Janis IL. 1972. *Victims of groupthink*. Houghton Mifflin: Boston, MA.

Kanter RM. 1983. Change masters and the intricate architecture of corporate culture change. *Management Review* 72(10): 18.

Kwee Z, Van den Bosch FAJ, & Volberda HW. 2011. The influence of top management team's corporate governance orientation on strategic renewal trajectories: A longitudinal analysis of Royal Dutch Shell plc, 1907–2004. *Journal of Management Studies* 48: 5.

Lechner C, Floyd SW. 2012. Group influence activities and the performance of strategic initiatives. Strategic Management Journal 33: 478–495.

Murnieks CY, Mosakowski E, & Cardon MS. 2012. Pathways of passion: Identity centrality, passion, and behavior among entrepreneurs. *Journal of Management*, 40(6): 1583–1606.

Ortony A, Clore GL, & Collins A. 1988. *The cognitive structure of emotions*. Cambridge University Press: Cambridge, UK.

Powell TC, Lovallo D, & Fox CR. 2011. Behavioral strategy. *Strategic Management Journal* 32(13): 1369–1386.

Sanchez-Burks J & Huy QN. 2009. Emotional aperture and strategic change: The accurate recognition of collective emotions. *Organization Studies* 20(1): 22–34.

Schein EH. 1992. *Organizational culture and leadership*. Jossey-Bass: San Francisco, CA.

Smith CA & Ellsworth PC. 1985. Patterns of cognitive appraisal in emotion. *Journal of Personality and Social Psychology* 48(4): 813–838.

Snyder CR, Harris C, Anderson JR, Holleran SA, Irving LM, Sigmon ST, Yoshinobu L, Gibb J, Langelle C, & Harney P. 1991. The will and the ways: Development and validation of an individual-difference measure of hope. *Journal of Personality and Social Psychology* 60(4): 570–585.

Taylor A & Helfat CE. 2009. Organizational linkages for surviving technological change: Complementary assets, middle management, and ambidexterity. *Organization Science* 20(4): 718–739.

Tracy JL & Robins RW. 2004. Putting the self into self-conscious emotions: A theoretical model. *Psychological Inquiry* 15: 103–125.

Tracy JL & Robins RW. 2007. The psychological structure of pride: A tale of two facets. *Journal of Personality and Social Psychology* 92(3): 506–525.

Tripsas M & Gavetti G. 2000. Capabilities, cognition, and inertia: Evidence from digital imaging. *Strategic Management Journal* 21(10/11): 1147–1161.

Vallerand RJ, Blanchard C, Mageau GA, Koestner R, Ratelle C, Léonard M, Gagné M, & Marsolais J. 2003. Les passions de l'âme: On obsessive and harmonious passion. *Journal of Personality and Social Psychology* 85(4): 756–767.

Volberda HW, Van den Bosch FAJ, Flier B, & Gedajlovic E. 2001. Following the herd or not? *Long Range Planning* 34(2): 209–229.

Volberda HW & Lewin A. 2003. Co-evolutionary dynamics within and between firms: From evolution to coevolution. *Journal of Management Studies* 40(8): 2111–2136.

Wharton AS & Erickson RJ. 1993. Managing emotions on the job and at home: Understanding the consequences of multiple emotional roles. *Academy of Management Review* 18: 457–486.

Williams LA & DeSteno D. 2008. Pride and perseverance: The motivational role of pride. *Journal of Personality and Social Psychology* 94(6): 1007–1017.

Zhou J & George JM. 2001. When job dissatisfaction leads to creativity: Encouraging the expression of voice. *Academy of Management Journal* 44(4): 682–696.

8 The micro-foundations of strategic renewal

Middle managers' job design, strategic change culture, organizational effectiveness unit, and innovative work behavior

Tomislav Hernaus and Matej Černe

Introduction

Organizational capability to innovate has been recognized as a critical factor in creating and maintaining organizational competitiveness (e.g., Helfat et al., 2007; Tushman and O'Reilly, 1996). Practitioner readings and governmental strategies have highlighted the importance of innovation, and additionally emphasized its key role in climbing out of economic downturns, particularly in the light of environmental dynamism and complexity in contemporary business environments. The importance of strategic renewal, i.e., the process, content, and outcome of refreshment or replacement of the attributes of an organization that have the potential to substantially affect its long-term prospects (Agarwal and Helfat, 2009), has been emphasized in the recent strategic management literature (Martin-Rios and Parga-Dans, 2016; Schmitt, Raisch and Volberda, 2018). One way for organizations to become more innovative is through their managers' explorative and exploitative endeavors (Glaser, Fourné, and Elfring, 2015), which are important as organizations rely on their employees to introduce new products/services, build new technologies, improve business processes, or apply new working methods. Managers might contribute to organizational innovation and strategic renewal by practicing innovative work behaviors (IWBs) on their own (i.e., devising and implementing creative ideas) or indirectly by encouraging their employees to be creative and innovative. While both alternatives have not yet been examined thoroughly, we decided to address the former one – being the road less taken.

Individual innovativeness, defined as a set of individual behaviors that stimulates job-level innovation (De Jong and Den Hartog, 2007), thus far has mostly been studied in relation to research and development (R&D) professionals or "creative" individuals within large organizations and multinationals (Sanders and Lin, 2015). Primarily, these processes have been covered by micro-innovation (e.g., new product development) or creativity and organizational behavior literature focusing on employees' IWB, while the literature on strategy and entrepreneurship typically adopt a company- or top-management-team perspective and thereby neglect the micro-processes (Helfat and Peteraf, 2015; Kwee, Van Den Bosch, and Volberda, 2011) that represent the micro-foundations of strategic renewal. The field needs a broader array of theoretically sophisticated and practically useful frameworks for understanding the role of the micro-foundations of strategic renewal. Specifically, the role of managers' (especially middle managers') IWB has been surprisingly underexamined in the strategic management literature (Kwee, Van Den Bosch, and Volberda, 2011; Rouleau and Balogun, 2010; Wooldridge, Schmid, and Floyd, 2008), as has designing managers' work settings in the job-design research domain (Munyon et al., 2010; Page, 2011). Therefore, the main purpose of this chapter is to apply existing job design knowledge to the strategic management field by developing a research framework that will explain the complex nature of the managers' innovation process at the micro (individual) level, and how middle managers might optimize their contribution to strategic renewal initiatives. An overview of the micro-foundations research framework with individual- and organizational-level constructs relevant for strategic renewal is presented in Figure 8.1.

The main study contributions are three-fold. First, cross-level and interrelated antecedents have been recognized that primarily shape managers' IWB as a positive workplace outcome. Specifically, we derived from the job characteristics theory (Hackman and Oldham, 1980), job demands-resources framework (Demerouti et al., 2001; Schaufeli & Bakker, 2004), and the recent literature examining the role of job design for stimulating employees' IWB (Battistelli, Montani, and Odoardi, 2013; Černe et al., 2017) in order to conceptualize propositions regarding the link between managers' job characteristics and IWB, and further stipulate the role of both informal strategic change culture and a formal organizational effectiveness unit. Second, by

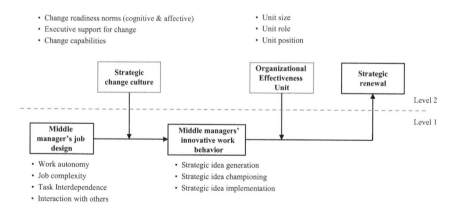

Figure 8.1 Proposed research framework

accounting for bottom–up processes of aggregation, we built upon the multi-level theory (cf. Kozlowski et al., 2013; Mathieu and Chen, 2011) in order to theorize about how managers' IWB gets translated into organizational efforts toward strategic renewal. Furthermore, we examined a potentially important top-down boundary condition in this link, related to the positioning and characteristics of an organizational effectiveness unit. Finally, our study is practically relevant for boosting corporate entrepreneurship and creating institutional enablers of strategic renewal. The role of job design at the individual (middle managers') level, as well as that of an organizational effectiveness unit as a center of excellence providing professional and administrative support (Hrebiniak, 2005; Lawler, 2005), were recognized to be important drivers of or enablers for implementing creative and innovative strategic ideas developed by middle managers.

Middle managers' job design and strategic renewal

Job design as a micro-organizational behavior topic has drawn much attention from psychologists, economists, and sociologists over the last hundred years (e.g., Oldham and Fried, 2016; Parker, Morgeson, and Johns, 2017). It represents the content and organization of one's work tasks, activities, relationships, and responsibilities (Parker, 2014), and affects various work behaviors and performance results. This human resource management (HRM) tool is also useful for balancing job demands (challenges and hindrances) and job resources to create motivating and/or avoid over-stressed managerial work positions.

Managerial roles at different hierarchical levels within an organization are subject to a variety of diverse demands, constraints, and opportunities (Dierdorff, Rubin, and Morgeson, 2009; Stewart, 1982). While executive jobs have been already identified as having extreme levels of job demands (e.g., Hambrick, Finkelstein and Mooney, 2005) and being central to the notion of the strategy process (Paroutis and Pettigrew, 2007), managers at middle hierarchical levels as boundary-spanners might also have important consequences for how strategy forms within organizations (Wooldridge, Schmid and Floyd, 2008). By having necessary information (both from the top and bottom of the pyramid) and certain resources at their disposal, they are well positioned to drive intra-preneurial initiatives and contribute to strategic renewal.

Middle managers, similar to top executives (e.g., Munyon et al., 2010) mostly function under high levels of almost every job characteristic. Their enriched jobs should contribute positively to change-oriented behavior (Marinova et al., 2015), including strategy development programs and plans. This might be particularly valid for managerial job resources (e.g., work autonomy) and challenges (e.g., job complexity, task interdependence, and interaction with others) that are expected to mitigate the risks of excessive managerial job hindrances (e.g., work pressure, role ambiguity, emotional demands). In other words, through deliberate job re-design actions, middle managers can be encouraged to initiate, support, and implement new strategic ideas.

Work autonomy – the degree to which an individual is given freedom and discretion in carrying out a task (Breaugh, 1985; Hackman and Oldham, 1980) – has been found to be a key issue for professional knowledge workers (Jackson, DeNisi, and Hitt, 2003). Highly autonomous employees, and managers likewise, are more likely to engage in risk taking, alternative thinking, and problem solving (Amabile, 1988; Oldham and Cummings, 1996; Tierney and Farmer, 2002). Autonomy provides an individual with freedom to decide how, when, and with whom to work (West and Farr, 1989). Managers who are perceived as having high decision autonomy are most likely to feel energetic, dedicated, and absorbed in their work, which would ultimately proactively shape more opportunities (e.g., Van Den Broeck et al., 2010) to voice ideas about strategic renewal. However, usually employees (and very often even managers) do not perform their tasks with absolute autonomy, and many of their work-related goals are achievable only through interdependent efforts of their team (e.g., Hertel, Konradt, and Orlikowski, 2004).

Task interdependence – a situation in which one's performance on one task depends on the task performance of the other (Van der Vegt and Janssen, 2003) – is a critical characteristic of managerial jobs focused on interpersonal networking and managing work relationshsips. Highly interdependent tasks provide a favorable setting for extra-role performance (Pearce and Gregersen, 1991). Mangerial boundary-spanning activities might be linked to outcomes closely related to strategic renewal (e.g., Fourne, Jansen, and Mam, 2014; Glaser, Fourné, and Elfring, 2015). Because creative ideas benefit from managers being socially connected (Shalley and Gilson, 2004) and obtaining inputs from others across the creative process, we expect that high levels of task interdependence should result in the superior creative inputs required for strategic renewal.

In terms of the role of ***interaction with others***, already Gottfredson (1997) has indicated that dealing with other people increases the cognitive demands of the job. However, this does not mean necessarily that jobs should be designed for teamwork; it means that work requires that one consults other people before delivering one's own work tasks. People are more productive, more relaxed, and more engaged when they personally interact with their peers (DUP, 2015). Interactions with others are common in "boundary-spanning" jobs, such as that of middle managers, where they have frequent communication with two different hierarchical levels: top managers and low-level managers. This role conflict in itself can produce creative tensions conducive to strategic renewal, but interaction with others also enables managers to obtain information from others and take perspective from others' viewpoints, thereby contributing to a superior level of ideas produced in contribution to more successful strategic renewal solutions.

Finally, ***job complexity*** reflects the cognitive demands of the job (Campbell and Gingrich, 1986; Schaubroeck, Ganster, and Kemmerer, 1994) and is increasingly recognized as an important feature of contemporary jobs with significant motivational implications (e.g., Humphrey, Nahrgang, and Morgeson, 2007). Cognitive job loading might be important, especially for implementing ideas about strategic renewal, as middle managers are often required to improve working procedures (Frese, Teng, and Wijnen, 1999) to translate strategic plans into actions more efficiently. Recent studies showed that having complex tasks provides mental challenges (Parker and Ohly, 2008) and offers opportunities for change-oriented behavior (e.g., Marinova et al., 2015). Similarly, we assume that more complex middle management jobs might be favorable to the development of proposals for strategic renewal.

However, if organizations want to strengthen the strategizing practices at multiple levels (e.g., Paroutis and Pettigrew, 2007), they should move beyond a component-based approach and instead take the composite approach to stimulate positive job design influences. Through the development of managerial job design bundles as preconditions for strategic renewal, middle managers might become more persistent and more likely to consider different alternatives, i.e., to be innovative in terms of strategy process within an organization:

P1: Particular aspects of middle managers' job design (specifically: high work autonomy, high task interdependence, high interaction with others, and high job complexity) serve as foundations of strategic renewal.

The mediating role of managers' innovative work behavior

Large-scale changes (i.e., disruptive innovations or strategic transformations) start with small steps (i.e., employees' creative thoughts and proactive behaviors) at the individual level. Employees who have been recognized as an essential part of the innovation process represent a creative pool with the potential to develop and foster innovation at multiple levels (e.g., Foss, Lyngsie, and Zahra, 2013). However, creativity is a necessary yet only partial antecedent of innovation, which also includes the finalizing step – the implementation of creative ideas. Taken together, employees' creative ideas and subsequent implementation efforts constitute innovative work behavior – IWB (De Jong and Den Hartog, 2010; Janssen, 2000).

IWB in general, and creativity at the individual level and innovation implementation at the group level specifically, provides the foundation for organizations to pursue innovative efforts in different domains of work. Although job design has been recognized as a crucial predictor of individual innovation (e.g., Hammond et al., 2011), and middle managers were identified as the most entrepreneurial people (Glaser, Fourné, and Elfring, 2015; Morris and Jones, 1999) who reconcile top-level executives' perspectives with strategy implementation issues surfacing at lower organizational levels (e.g., King, Fowler, and Zeithaml, 2001), we still lack evidence of how and when middle managers' jobs translate into innovative behavior and contribute to the broader strategic context (e.g., Wooldridge, Schmid, and Floyd, 2008). Nonaka and Takeuchi (1995) highlighted the central role of middle managers for championing innovations, which then create new knowledge that fuels organizational growth. Middle managers are placed in the primary position of converting raw information and business concepts that meet the goals enunciated by top management (Nonaka, 1991). Thus, we decided to answer a recent call (Sprafke, 2013) and to consider a potential upward mediation model (1–1–2), i.e., bridging factors among an individual-level predictor (job design), individual-level intervening mechanism (innovative work behavior), and an organizational-level outcome (strategic renewal).

Our assumption is that middle managers' IWB will lead to better ideas, ownership of their ideas, and more effort exerted toward their implementation, which should result in better solutions and inputs for organizational-level strategic renewal. However, whether or not middle managers will exhibit IWB (i.e., strategic idea generation, strategic idea championing, and strategic idea implementation) depends on the job-related context. Each job characteristic involves different cognitive processes, affecting creativity in unique ways through intrinsic motivation- and domain-relevant skills (Coelho and Augusto, 2010). Factors such as work autonomy, task interdependence or interaction with others (Amabile, 1998), and job complexity (Campbell, 1988) have been frequently identified as key components of a stimulating creative or innovative work environment (see Hernaus, 2016).

In particular, if we give employees freedom and provide them with higher levels of control of their work (high *work autonomy*), they will be more able to provide creative and innovative inputs. The same is true for middle managers. Autonomous work settings are expected to encourage positive levels of IWB targeted for strategy development because decision-making autonomy makes employees feel self-determined and free from external controls or constraints (Deci, Connell, and Ryan, 1989). The more decisions they can make on their own, the more effort will be put into implementing their own creative ideas. In other words, the person–job integration process of innovation implementation is assured by the decentralization of decision-making in order to promote autonomy (Drach-Zahavy et al., 2004). This would enable managers to propose ideas related to strategic renewal of their organizations, to develop a sense of ownership for them, and, ultimately, to contribute to their realization, either directly through providing personal effort or through channeling employees' resources.

Research reviewed by Bachrach et al. (2006) suggested that *task interdependence* may increase communication, helping, and information-sharing; boost extra-role performance; and raise expectations of help and norms of cooperation. It is a particularly important feature of the implementation phase of IWB, where team design is a predictive job trait (e.g., Axtell, Holman, and Wall, 2006). Task interdependence triggers two psychological states of experienced responsibility: responsibility for one's personal work and outcomes and responsibility for others' work and their personal outcomes, for which one initiates task interdependence (Kiggundu, 1983). Highly interdependent managers generate solutions faster, complete more tasks, and perform better than managers who are not highly dependent upon others (Thomson, 2011). Task interdependence increases the knowledge of other employees and the interaction between employees, which enhance the generalization and implementation of new ideas and the relevance that managers' IWB might hold for organizational-level strategic renewal. Task interdependence leads to employees accepting greater responsibility for other employees' task performance, and to advice-seeking and knowledge-sharing behaviors when confronted with problems (Sanders and Lin, 2015). This should improve the managers' IWB and thereby contribute to better solutions related to overall strategic renewal plans.

Interaction with others is another, related job characteristic conducive to IWB, and ultimately an enabler of strategic renewal initiatives. It requires job incumbents to consult other people before delivering formal work tasks. Communication with co-workers and/or interaction outside an organization makes a job more complex and challenging, which can increase employee motivation (Humphrey, Nahrgang, and Morgeson, 2007; Kiggundu, 1983) and make work more satisfying for an employee (Ryan and Deci, 2001). Interactions with others also influence various aspects of the creative process (e.g., Amabile, 1983; Woodman, Sawyer, and Griffin, 1993). For instance, interaction with co-workers can be helpful for coping with work-related problems (Terry, Nielsen, and Perchard, 1993); it can make employees feel relaxed and more engaged (DUP, 2015), as well as resulting in extra work effort, and should therefore also enhance middle managers' IWB, thus contributing to strategic renewal.

Finally, *job complexity* is an important job-design element in the sense that having challenging work stimulates creativity (Amabile et al., 1996) and innovation. Previous studies have already demonstrated that job complexity promotes creativity (Shalley, Gilson, and Blum, 2009) and personal initiative (Frese, Garst, and Fay, 2007). Undoubtedly, job complexity in contemporary organizations is increasing with technological change and globalization. It follows that intelligence and mental ability turn out to be increasingly important in predicting job performance or creativity. Managers who handle complex tasks are more satisfied with their job, more intrinsically motivated, and more productive (Janssen, 2001). This contributes positively to the levels of IWB. More challenging and problem-solving-oriented managerial jobs should, in addition to directly contributing to strategic renewal, also encourage employees to be more creative and exhibit IWB (Cummings and Oldham, 1997), making it likely for this behavior to spillover to the organizational level in terms of generating suggestions for strategic renewal. Taken together, because of these job-design inputs stimulating middle managers' IWB, they will be more likely to come up with the creative and innovative inputs needed for strategy development.

Strategic renewal is an organizational-level phenomenon heavily dependent upon the ideas and innovations of managers. The extant literature informs us that it is predicted by managers' corporate governance orientation (Kwee, Van Den Bosch, and Volberda, 2011). Therefore, the role of individuals, i.e., managers, in strategic renewal is crucial. When job design will enable them to exhibit IWB, this is likely to also boost their contributions toward strategic renewal. This is due to their superior engagement across the stages of IWB. Those middle managers who generate creative ideas and are able to implement them at their workplace are likely to produce better ideas for the benefit of the organization as a whole (Criscuolo, Salter, and Ter Wal, 2014). Furthermore, as idea championing has been linked to several beneficial outcomes at levels higher than the individual (cf., Černe, Kaše, and Škerlavaj, 2016; Perry-Smith and Mannucci, 2017), if middle managers promote ideas to their superiors, this is likely to result in more of their ideas being implemented in organizational-level initiatives toward strategic renewal. Finally, middle managers who implement creative ideas at their workplace show the confidence they and their colleagues have in their ideas, and demonstrate that these are not as risky to implement (cf., Baer, 2012; Škerlavaj, Černe, and Dysvik, 2014). This might make the strategy-formulation process more convincing, and include more opportunities for middle management contributions in strategic renewal.

P2: Innovative work behavior mediates the relationship between middle managers' job design (high work autonomy, high task interdependence, high interaction with others, and high job complexity) and strategic renewal.

The moderating roles of strategic change culture and an organizational effectiveness unit

Whether the proposed individual-level relationships will have implications for organizational-level strategic renewal outcome also depends upon cross-level boundary conditions – organizational culture and structural choices. Specifically, informal strategic change culture (consistent of cognitive and affective change readiness norms, executive support for change, and change capabilities; Armenakis et al., 1993; Caldwell et al., 2008; Johnson, 1992; Rafferty, Jimmieson, and Armenakis, 2013) and a formal organizational effectiveness unit (characterized by size, role, and position within the organization; Burke, 2004) have been recognized as enablers of strategic renewal.

The extant literature informs us that beneficial outcomes of job design such as creativity and innovation depend heavily on contextual, higher-level contingencies such as organizational culture or climate (Ahmed, 1998; Somech and Drach-Zahavy, 2013). For example, a study by Černe et al. (2017) showed that the effects of task interdependence on employees' IWB are contingent upon the presence of a mastery climate characterized by learning, collaboration, and development. Research by Wallace et al. (2016) found that autonomy-stimulated thriving at work only resulted in employee innovation when accompanied by a climate of employee involvement. Job complexity, too, only resulted in creative performance in conditions characterized by a supportive work context (Shalley, Gilson, and Blum, 2009). We propose that the same logic is true for middle managers' IWB and organizational-level strategic renewal. As IWB can be understood as a risky behavioral effort (Lee, 2008), whether stimulating job-design elements *per se* (autonomy, interdependence, interaction with others, and complexity) would ultimately result in strategy-desired outcomes, is contingent upon a shared meaning or the overall attitude of individuals within an organization and its general strategic orientation toward change and innovation (Dobni, 2008).

Specifically, the extent to which middle managers perceive executive support for innovation and change (e.g., Siegel and Kaemmerer, 1978) or experience tolerance for risk tasking within their organizations (e.g., Hornsby, Kuratko, and Zahra, 2002; Kuratko et al., 2005) might determine the extent to which they feel enabled to take on corporate entrepreneurship roles (e.g., Daellenbach, McCarthy, and Schoenecker, 1999; Wooldridge, Schmid, and Floyd, 2008). Therefore, when organizations have not developed such a culture or change capabilities, formal managerial job demands and requirements, placed together by job design and job descriptions, will likely only remain on paper, thereby not resulting in increased levels of middle managers' IWB. This is further supported by the logic of studies reporting detrimental outcomes of job-design initiatives when not accompanied by an appropriate supporting culture or climate (e.g., Černe et al., 2017). On the other hand, when organizations or units develop a culture or a climate that is beneficial toward change, this is likely to boost the positive outcomes of managerial job-design characteristics. In general, the way employees perceive the extent to which culture within an organization is supportive of change influences a number of creative and novel behaviors (Černe, Jaklič, and Škerlavaj, 2013). Middle managers within such a context are more likely to be better able to perceive the leaders as supportive of their novel, different ideas. The managers thus might not be afraid to experiment and suggest novel, unusual ideas and implement them at their workplace. In turn, this may lead to generating new ideas and managerial innovations (cf., Birkinshaw, Hamel and Mol, 2008; Volberda, Van Den Bosch, and Heij, 2013) that can provide a basis for strategic renewal.

P3: Strategic change culture moderates the relationship between middle managers' job design and strategic renewal that is mediated by IWB.

To the best of our knowledge, the importance of formal structural mechanisms for translating the creative and innovative efforts of individuals into strategic renewal actions is still underreported. While we know that institutionalized research and development (R&D) structures (such as R&D departments or new product development teams; e.g., Argyres and Silverman, 2004; Sosa and Mihm, 2008) or different approaches of organizational design (i.e., functional design, cross-functional teams, ambidextrous design, and unsupported teams; cf., Tushman et al., 2005) can boost radical and incremental product/service innovation, a somewhat different approach is needed for achieving strategic renewal. Strategy innovations or innovations of business models should be either developed by managerial elites (e.g., Pettigrew, 1992; Whittington, 2003), and/or supported by a group of strategy and design professionals who might facilitate the strategizing activities of top and middle managers within an organization.

Much of the organizational design (OD) work is concerned with strategy implementation, especially when a change in strategy has been planned and is underway (Burke, 2004). As strategy development has become a continuous, not periodic, process (Breene, Nunes, and Shill, 2007), organizations increasingly require corporate staff departments (such as strategic management offices or organizational design/development units) that will formally handle the reins of strategy execution. We follow Lawler (2005) and suggest that an organizational effectiveness (OE) unit – a multidisciplinary center of excellence that focuses on business strategy, organization design, and human capital development – should be put in place. As a type of corporate strategy group, it should be concerned with more than just efficiency or central support services; also facilitating the strategy review as well as providing valuable strategy-informed design knowledge and skills (e.g., Hrebiniak, 2005; Lawler, Boudreau, and Mohrman, 2006). Thus, an OE unit should represent an integral part of the strategizing process that will provide necessary support to middle managers in their strategic renewal efforts. A positive top-down boundary condition can be expected if an OE unit is not buried within the human resource function (Burke, 2004; Pasmore, 1994); in other words, it would help if internal consultancy experts have direct access to executives. Additionally, while previous studies have indicated that organization departments have relatively small staffs (e.g., Glueck, 1971; Lawler, 2005), more people resources for the OE unit might result in stronger involvement and better services being offered to middle managers' strategy development efforts, initially driven by having an enriched job design. Otherwise, creative strategic ideas proposed by corporate entrepreneurs might not receive adequate attention to be integrated into the new business model and eventually implemented.

P4: An organizational effectiveness unit moderates the relationship between middle managers' job design and strategic renewal that is mediated by IWB.

Discussion and implications

The study contributes to the strategic renewal literature by recognizing cross-level and inter-related antecedents that contribute to establishing appropriate middle management job design, leading to creative and innovative performance behavior, and ultimately enabling the bottom-up emergence of effort that drives organizational-level strategic renewal. In other words, we emphasize that enriched job design (managerial job resources and challenges) should be clearly addressed as a direct antecedent of IWB and an indirect antecedent of organizational-level strategic renewal. Such an approach is theoretically and practically important because it offers a comprehensive overview that helps researchers and practitioners in search of a relevant "mixture of ingredients" for enhancing strategizing at multiple levels of an organization. In addition, by highlighting the role of middle managers in building up the strategic renewal case, we raised the issue of distributed activity (e.g., Orlikowski, 2002; Paroutis and Pettigrew, 2007) that presumes not only top management as the sole hierarchical level responsible for contributing to strategic decisions in organizations.

Specifically, we initially conceptualized propositions regarding the link between middle management job characteristics and IWB, and further stipulated the role of a strategic change culture in organizations (Armenakis, Harris, and Mossholder, 1993; Caldwell et al., 2008; Johnson, 1992; Rafferty, Jimmieson, and Armenakis, 2013). Thus, we made a step beyond focusing merely on employees' IWB, by explicitly focusing on the managers, and how designing their jobs might contribute to their innovativeness under the informal, socially shaped boundary conditions. Risk-taking and a change-oriented culture within an organization might provide a solid ground for reaching higher levels of managerial innovativeness when aligned with specific job-design bundles.

Next, by relating to ideas of bottom-up emergence and aggregation processes, discussed in the multi-level theory of management and organization (Kozlowski et al., 2013), we extended the idea of the emergence of middle managers' innovativeness and conceptualized about what their IWB means for organizational-level outcomes in the form of strategic renewal. The role of a formal structural boundary condition (i.e. an organizational design unit) has been examined as a potential enabler of strategizing practices. This contributes to the theory of strategic renewal by proposing its micro-foundations related to creativity and innovation, frequently examined in the creativity and organizational innovation literatures (cf., Amabile, 1988; Axtell, Holman and Wall, 2006; Baer, 2012; Škerlavaj, Černe, and Dysvik, 2014), but not well integrated with the strategic management topics yet.

Finally, this study also has important practical implications both at the individual and organizational level. We suggest that organizations should design resourceful and challenging jobs (i.e., high on autonomy, collaboration, and complexity) to focus the attention of middle managers on work activities related to strategic renewal. For instance, organizations can apply specific techniques, such as managerial job rotation, which has the potential to enlarge or enrich the middle managers' work experience, as well as managerial job-crafting via seeking resources and/or challenges, thus encouraging proactive individuals to re-adjust their job characteristics (e.g., job complexity, task identity, and task interdependence) according to their personal needs and abilities. Otherwise, without the necessary resources or challenges, middle managers might feel overburdened with excessive job demands, and therefore not be interested in or capable of providing creative and innovative contributions. While managerial resources in particular might come out of their job design, they can be additionally provided by an organizational effectiveness unit that can offer useful advice and necessary support for strategic renewal initiatives. Thus, we also advance our knowledge about the role and importance of internal OD practitioners (e.g., Burke, 2004; Lawler, 2005) as structural resources for achieving strategic renewal in organizations.

References

Agarwal, R., & Helfat, C. E. 2009. Strategic renewal of organizations. *Organization Science*, 20(2), 281–293.

Ahmed, P. K. 1998. Culture and climate for innovation. *European Journal of Innovation Management*, 1(1), 30–43.

Amabile, T. M. 1983. The social psychology of creativity: A componential conceptualization. *Journal of Personality and Social Psychology*, 45(2), 357–376.

Amabile, T. M. 1988. A model of creativity and innovation in organizations. In B. M. Stew & L. L. Cummings (eds.), *Research in organizational behavior*, 123–167, Greenwich, CT: JAI.

Amabile, T. M. 1998. How to kill creativity. *Harvard Business Review*, 76(5), 76–87.

Amabile, T. M., Conti, R., Coon, H., Lazenby, J., & Herron, M. 1996. Assessing the work environment for creativity. *Academy of Management Journal*, 39(5), 1154–1184.

Argyres, N. S., & Silverman, B. S. 2004. R&D, organization structure, and the development of corporate technological knowledge. *Strategic Management Journal*, 25(8–9), 929–958.

Armenakis, A. A., Harris, S. G., & Mossholder, K. W. 1993. Creating readiness for organizational change. *Human Relations*, 46(6), 681–703.

Axtell, C. M., Holman, D. J., & Wall, T. D. 2006. Promoting innovation: A change study. *Journal of Occupational and Organizational Psychology*, 79(3), 509–516.

Bachrach, D. G., Powell, B. C., Collins, B. J., & Richey, R. G. 2006. Effects of task interdependence on the relationship between helping behavior and group performance. *Journal of Applied Psychology*, 91(6), 1396–1405.

Baer, M. 2012. Putting creativity to work: The implementation of creative ideas in organizations. *Academy of Management Journal*, 55(5), 1102–1119.

Battistelli, A., Montani, F., & Odoardi, C. 2013. The impact of feedback from job and task autonomy in the relationship between dispositional resistance to change and innovative work behaviour. *European Journal of Work and Organizational Psychology*, 22(1), 26–41.

Birkinshaw, J., Hamel, G., & Mol, M. J. 2008. Management innovation. *Academy of Management Review*, 33(4), 825–845.

Breaugh, J. A. 1985. The measurement of work autonomy. *Human Relations*, 38(6), 551–570.

Breene, R. T. S., Nunes, P. F., & Shill, W. E. 2007. The chief strategy officer. *Harvard Business Review*, 85(10), 84–93.

Burke, W. W. 2004. Internal organization development practitioners where do they belong? *The Journal of Applied Behavioral Science*, 40(4), 423–431.

Caldwell, D. F., Chatman, J., O'Reilly III, C. A., Ormiston, M., & Lapiz, M. 2008. Implementing strategic change in a health care system: The importance of leadership and change readiness. *Health Care Management Review*, 33(2), 124–133.

Campbell, D. J. 1988. Task complexity: A review and analysis. *Academy of Management Review*, 13(1), 40–52.

Campbell, D. J., & Gingrich, K. F. 1986. The interactive effects of task complexity and participation on task performance: A field experiment. *Organizational Behavior and Human Decision Processes*, 38(2), 162–180.

Černe, M., Hernaus, T., Dysvik, A., & Škerlavaj, M. 2017. The role of multilevel synergistic interplay among team mastery climate, knowledge hiding, and job characteristics in stimulating innovative work behavior. *Human Resource Management Journal*, 27(2), 281–299.

Černe, M., Jaklič, M., & Škerlavaj, M. 2013. Authentic leadership, creativity, and innovation: A multilevel perspective. *Leadership*, 9(1), 63–85.

Černe, M., Kaše, R., & Škerlavaj, M. 2016. This idea rocks! Idea championing in teams. In M. Škerlavaj, M. Černe, A. Dysvik, & A. Carlsen (eds.), *Capitalizing on creativity at work: Fostering the implementation of creative ideas in organizations*, 53–63, Cheltenham, UK: Edward Elgar.

Coelho, F., & Augusto, M. 2010. Job characteristics and the creativity of frontline service employees. *Journal of Service Research*, 13(4), 426–438.

Criscuolo, P., Salter, A., & Ter Wal, A. L. 2014. Going underground: Bootlegging and individual innovative performance. *Organization Science*, 25(5), 1287–1305.

Cummings, A., & Oldham, G. R. 1997. Enhancing creativity: Managing work contexts for the high potential employee. *California Management Review*, 40(1), 22–38.

Daellenbach, U. S., McCarthy, A. M., & Schoenecker, T. S. 1999. Commitment to innovation: The impact of top management team characteristics. *R&D Management*, 29(3), 199–208.

Deci, E. L., Connell, J. P., & Ryan, R. M. 1989. Self-determination in a work organization. *Journal of Applied Psychology*, 74(4), 580–590.

De Jong, J., & Den Hartog, D. 2010. Measuring innovative work behaviour. *Creativity and Innovation Management*, 19(1), 23–36.

De Jong, J. P., & Den Hartog, D. N. 2007. How leaders influence employees' innovative behaviour. *European Journal of Innovation Management*, 10(1), 41–64.

Demerouti, E., Bakker, A. B., Nachreiner, F., & Schaufeli, W. B. 2001. The job demands-resources model of burnout. *Journal of Applied Psychology*, 86(3), 499.

Dierdorff, E. C., Rubin, R. S., & Morgeson, F. P. 2009. The milieu of managerial work: An integrative framework linking work context to role requirements. *Journal of Applied Psychology*, 94(4), 972–988.

Dobni, C. B. 2008. Measuring innovation culture in organizations: The development of a generalized innovation culture construct using exploratory factor analysis. *European Journal of Innovation Management*, 11(4), 539–559.

Drach-Zahavy, A., Somech, A., Granot, M., & Spitzer, A. 2004. Can we win them all? Benefits and costs of structured and flexible innovation–implementations. *Journal of Organizational Behavior*, 25(2), 217–234.

DUP. 2015. *Global human capital trends 2015: Leading in the new world of work*. New York, NY: Deloitte University Press.

Frese, M., Garst, H., & Fay, D. 2007. Making things happen: Reciprocal relationships between work characteristics and personal initiative in a four-wave longitudinal structural equation model. *Journal of Applied Psychology*, 92(4), 1084–1102.

Foss, N. J., Lyngsie, J., & Zahra, S. A. 2013. The role of external knowledge sources and organizational design in the process of opportunity exploitation. *Strategic Management Journal*, 34(12), 1453–1471.

Fourne, S. P. L., Jansen, J. J., & Mom, T. J. M. 2014. Strategic agility in MNEs: Managing tensions to capture opportunities across emerging and established markets. *California Management Review*, 56(3), 13–38.

Frese, M., Teng, E., & Wijnen, C. J. 1999. Helping to improve suggestion systems: Predictors of making suggestions in companies. *Journal of Organizational Behavior*, 20(7), 1139–1155.

Glaser, L., Fourné, S. P., & Elfring, T. 2015. Achieving strategic renewal: The multi-level influences of top and middle managers' boundary-spanning. *Small Business Economics*, 45(2), 305–327.

Glueck, W. F. 1971. *Organization planning and development* (No. 106). New York, NY: AMACOM.

Gottfredson, L. S. 1997. Why g matters: The complexity of everyday life. *Intelligence*, 24 (1), 79–132.

Hackman, J. R., & Oldham, G. R. 1980. *Work redesign*. Reading, MA: Addison Wesley.

Hambrick, D. C., Finkelstein, S., & Mooney, A. C. 2005. Executive job demands: New insights for explaining strategic decisions and leader behaviors. *Academy of Management Review*, 30(3), 472–491.

Hammond, M. M., Neff, N. L., Farr, J. L., Schwall, A. R., & Zhao, X. 2011. Predictors of individual-level innovation at work: A meta-analysis. *Psychology of Aesthetics, Creativity, and the Arts*, 5(1), 90–105.

Helfat, C. E., Finkelstein, S., Mitchell, W., Peteraf, M., Singh, H., Teece, D., & Winter, S. 2007. *Dynamic capabilities: Understanding strategic change in organizations*. New York, NY: Wiley.

Helfat, C. E., & Peteraf, M. A. 2015. Managerial cognitive capabilities and the micro-foundations of dynamic capabilities. *Strategic Management Journal*, 36(6), 831–850.

Hernaus, T. 2016. Job design at the crossroads: From "creative" jobs to "innovative" jobs. In M. Škerlavaj, M. Černe, A. Dysvik, & A. Carlsen (eds.), *Capitalizing on creativity at work: Fostering the implementation of creative ideas in organizations*, 17–28, Cheltenham, UK: Edward Elgar.

Hertel, G., Konradt, U., & Orlikowski, B. 2004. Managing distance by interdependence: Goal setting, task interdependence, and team-based rewards in virtual teams. *European Journal of Work and Organizational Psychology*, 13(1), 1–28.

Hornsby, J. S., Kuratko, D. F., & Zahra, S. A. 2002. Middle managers' perception of the internal environment for corporate entrepreneurship: Assessing a measurement scale. *Journal of Business Venturing*, 17(3), 253–273.

Hrebiniak, L. G. 2005. *Making strategy work: Leading effective execution and change*. Upper Saddle River, NJ: Prentice Hall.

Humphrey, S. E., Nahrgang, J. D., & Morgeson, F. P. 2007. Integrating motivational, social, and contextual work design features: A meta-analytic summary and theoretical extension of the work design literature. *Journal of Applied Psychology*, 92(5), 1332–1356.

Jackson, S. E., DeNisi, A., & Hitt, M. A., eds. 2003. *Managing knowledge for sustained competitive advantage: Designing strategies for effective human resource management*. New York, NY: John Wiley & Sons.

Janssen, O. 2000. Job demands, perceptions of effort-reward fairness and innovative work behaviour. *Journal of Occupational and Organizational Psychology*, 73(3), 287–302.

Janssen, O. 2001. Fairness perceptions as a moderator in the curvilinear relationships between job demands, and job performance and job satisfaction. *Academy of Management Journal*, 44(5), 1039–1050.

Johnson, G. 1992. Managing strategic change – Strategy, culture and action. *Long Range Planning*, 25(1), 28–36.

Kiggundu, M. N. 1983. Task interdependence and job design: Test of a theory. *Organizational Behavior and Human Performance*, 31(2), 145–172.

King, A. W., Fowler, S. W., & Zeithaml, C. P. 2001. Managing organizational competencies for competitive advantage: The middle-management edge. *The Academy of Management Executive*, 15(2), 95–106.

Kozlowski, S. W., Chao, G. T., Grand, J. A., Braun, M. T., & Kuljanin, G. 2013. Advancing multilevel research design capturing the dynamics of emergence. *Organizational Research Methods*, 16(4), 581–615.

Kuratko, D. F., Ireland, R. D., Covin, J. G., & Hornsby, J. S. 2005. A model of middle-level managers' entrepreneurial behavior. *Entrepreneurship Theory and Practice*, 29(6), 699–716.

Kwee, Z., Van Den Bosch, F. A., & Volberda, H. W. 2011. The influence of top management team's corporate governance orientation on strategic renewal trajectories: A longitudinal analysis of Royal Dutch Shell plc, 1907–2004. *Journal of Management Studies*, 48(5), 984–1014.

Lawler, E. E. III. 2005. From human resource management to organizational effectiveness. *Human Resource Management*, 44(2), 165–169.

Lawler, E. E. III, Boudreau, J. W., & Mohrman, S. A. 2006. *Achieving strategic excellence: An assessment of human resource organizations.* Stanford, CA: Stanford Business Books.

Lee, J. 2008. Effects of leadership and leader-member exchange on innovativeness. *Journal of Managerial Psychology*, 23(6), 670–687.

Marinova, S. V., Peng, C., Lorinkova, N., Van Dyne, L., & Chiaburu, D. 2015. Change-oriented behavior: A meta-analysis of individual and job design predictors. *Journal of Vocational Behavior*, 88, 104–120.

Martin-Rios, C., & Parga-Dans, E. 2016. Service response to economic decline: Innovation actions for achieving strategic renewal. *Journal of Business Research*, 69 (8), 2890–2900.

Mathieu, J., & Chen, G. 2011. The etiology of the multilevel paradigm in management research. *Journal of Management*, 37(1), 395–403.

Morris, M. H., & Jones, F. F. 1999. Entrepreneurship in established organizations: The case of the public sector. *Entrepreneurship: Theory and Practice*, 24(1), 71–91.

Munyon, T. P., Summers, J. K., Buckley, M. R., Ranft, A. L., & Ferris, G. R. 2010. Executive work design: New perspectives and future directions. *Journal of Organizational Behavior*, 31(2/3), 432–447.

Nonaka, I. 1991. The knowledge-creating company. *Harvard Business Review*, 69(6), 96–104.

Nonaka, I., & Takeuchi, H. 1995. *The knowledge-creating company: How Japanese companies create the dynamics of innovation.* Oxford, UK: Oxford University Press.

Oldham, G. R., & Cummings, A. 1996. Employee creativity: Personal and contextual factors at work. *Academy of Management Journal*, 39(3), 607–634.

Oldham, G. R., & Fried, Y. 2016. Job design research and theory: Past, present and future. *Organizational Behavior and Human Decision Processes*, 136, 20–35.

Orlikowski, W. J. 2002. Knowing in practice: Enacting a collective capability in distributed organizing. *Organization Science*, 13(3), 249–273.

Page, D. 2011. I-deals in further education? A new approach to managerial job design. *Management in Education*, 25(4), 182–187.

Parker, S. K. 2014. Beyond motivation: Job and work design for development, health, ambidexterity, and more. *Annual Review of Psychology*, 65(1), 661–691.

Parker, S. K., Morgeson, F. P., & Johns, G. 2017. One hundred years of work design research: Looking back and looking forward. *Journal of Applied Psychology*, 102(3), 403–420.

Parker, S. K., & Ohly, S. 2008. Designing motivating jobs: An expanded framework for linking work characteristics and motivation. In R. Kanfer, G. Chen, & R. D. Pritchard (eds.), *Work motivation: Past, present and future*, 233–284, York, UK: Routledge.

Paroutis, S., & Pettigrew, A. 2007. Strategizing in the multi-business firm: Strategy teams at multiple levels and over time. *Human Relations*, 60(1), 99–135.

Pasmore, W. A. 1994. *Creating strategic change: Designing the flexible, high-performing organization*. New York, NY: John Wiley & Sons.

Pearce, J. L., & Gregersen, H. B. 1991. Task interdependence and extrarole behavior: A test of the mediating effects of felt responsibility. *Journal of Applied Psychology*, 76(6), 838–844.

Perry-Smith, J. E., & Mannucci, P. V. 2017. From creativity to innovation: The social network drivers of the four phases of the idea journey. *Academy of Management Review*, 42(1), 53–79.

Pettigrew, A. M. 1992. On studying managerial elites. *Strategic Management Journal*, 13, 163–182.

Rafferty, A. E., Jimmieson, N. L., & Armenakis, A. A. 2013. Change readiness a multilevel review. *Journal of Management*, 39(1), 110–135.

Rouleau, L., & Balogun, J. 2010. Middle managers, strategic sensemaking and discursive competence. *Journal of Management Studies*, 48(5), 953–983.

Ryan, R. M., & Deci, E. L. 2001. On happiness and human potentials: A review of research on hedonic and eudaimonic well-being. *Annual Review of Psychology*, 52(1), 141–166.

Sanders, K., & Lin, C.-H. V. 2015. Human resource management and innovative behaviour: Considering interactive, informal learning activities. In H. Shipton, P. Budhwar, P. Sparrow, & A. Brown (eds.), *Human resource management, innovation and performance*, 32–47, New York, NY: Palgrave Macmillan.

Schaubroeck, J., Ganster, D. C., & Kemmerer, B. E. 1994. Job complexity, "Type A" behavior, and cardiovascular disorder: A prospective study. *Academy of Management Journal*, 37(2), 426–439.

Schaufeli, W. B., & Bakker, A. B. 2004. Job demands, job resources, and their relationship with burnout and engagement: A multi-sample study. *Journal of Organizational Behavior*, 25(3), 293–315.

Schmitt, A., Raisch, S., & Volberda, H. W. 2018. Strategic renewal: Past research, theoretical tensions and future challenges. *International Journal of Management Reviews*, 20(1), 81–98.

Shalley, C. E., & Gilson, L. L. 2004. What leaders need to know: A review of social and contextual factors that can foster or hinder creativity. *The Leadership Quarterly*, 15(1), 33–53.

Shalley, C. E., Gilson, L. L., & Blum, T. C. 2009. Interactive effects of growth need strength, work context, and job complexity on self-reported creative performance. *Academy of Management Journal*, 52(3), 489–505.

Siegel, S. M., & Kaemmerer, W. F. 1978. Measuring the perceived support for innovation in organizations. *Journal of Applied Psychology*, 63(5), 553–562.

Škerlavaj, M., Černe, M., & Dysvik, A. 2014. I get by with a little help from my supervisor: Creative-idea generation, idea implementation, and perceived supervisor support. *The Leadership Quarterly*, 25(5), 987–1000.

Somech, A., & Drach-Zahavy, A. 2013. Translating team creativity to innovation implementation: The role of team composition and climate for innovation. *Journal of Management*, 39(3), 684–708.

Sosa, M., & Mihm, J. 2008. Organization design for new product development. In C. H. Loch & S. Kavadias (eds.), *Handbook of new product development management*, 181–214, London, UK: Routledge.

Sprafke, N. 2013. Dynamic capabilities and job design: Applying employee empowerment to organizational renewal. 29th EGOS Colloquium, Montreal.

Stewart, R. 1982. A model for understanding managerial jobs and behavior. *Academy of Management Review*, 7(1), 7–13.

Terry, D. J., Nielsen, M., & Perchard, L. 1993. Effects of work stress on psychological well-being and job satisfaction: The stress-buffering role of social support. *Australian Journal of Psychology*, 45(3), 168–175.

Thomson, L. L. 2011. *Making the team: A guide for managers.* Upper Saddle River, NJ: Prentice Hall.

Tierney, P., & Farmer, S. M. 2002. Creative self-efficacy: Its potential antecedents and relationship to creative performance. *Academy of Management Journal*, 45(6), 1137–1148.

Tushman, M. L., & O'Reilly, C. A. 1996. Ambidextrous organizations: Managing evolutionary and revolutionary change. *California Management Review*, 38(4), 8–30.

Tushman, M. L., Smith, W., Wood, R., Westerman, G., & O'Reilly, C. A. 2005. *Innovation streams and ambidextrous organizational designs: On building dynamic capabilities.* Boston, MA: Harvard Business School Working Paper.

Van Den Broeck, A., De Cuyper, N., De Witte, H., & Vansteenkiste, M. 2010. Not all job demands are equal: Differentiating job hindrances and job challenges in the job demands–resources model. *European Journal of Work and Organizational Psychology*, 19 (6), 735–759.

Van der Vegt, G. S., & Janssen, O. 2003. Joint impact of interdependence and group diversity on innovation. *Journal of Management*, 29(5), 729–751.

Volberda, H. W., Van Den Bosch, F. A., & Heij, C. V. 2013. Management innovation: Management as fertile ground for innovation. *European Management Review*, 10(1), 1–15.

Wallace, J. C., Butts, M. M., Johnson, P. D., Stevens, F. G., & Smith, M. B. 2016. A multilevel model of employee innovation understanding the effects of regulatory focus, thriving, and employee involvement climate. *Journal of Management*, 42(4), 982–1004.

West, M. A., & Farr, J. L. 1989. Innovation at work: Psychological perspectives. *Social Behaviour*, 4, 15–30.

Whittington, R. 2003. The work of strategizing and organizing: For a practice perspective. *Strategic Organization*, 1(1), 117–125.

Woodman, R. W., Sawyer, J. E., & Griffin, R. W. 1993. Toward a theory of organizational creativity. *Academy of Management Review*, 18(2), 293–321.

Wooldridge, B., Schmid, T., & Floyd, S. W. 2008. The middle management perspective on strategy process: Contributions, synthesis, and future research. *Journal of Management*, 34(6), 1190–1221.

9 Regulatory focus as a mediator of environmental dynamism and decentralization on managers' exploration and exploitation activities

Tom Mom, Aybars Tuncdogan, and Frans van den Bosch

Introduction

Research on the exploration of new possibilities and the exploitation of existing certainties in organizations increasingly draws the attention of both management academics and practitioners (Gupta et al., 2006; March, 1991; Simsek, 2009). As this research has usually focused on the corporate or business unit level of analysis, improving understanding of exploration and exploitation at the individual level is still needed. This is 'vitally important', as Raisch and Birkinshaw (2008, p. 397) put it, 'because choices about how to resolve tensions [between exploration and exploitation] at one level of analysis are often resolved at the next level down'. Consequently, several researchers including Gupta et al. (2006, p. 703), Lavie et al. (2010, p. 143), Raisch and Birkinshaw (2008, p. 397), Simsek (2009, p. 612), and Smith and Tushman (2005, p. 533) explicitly suggest further investigating exploration and exploitation at the individual level of analysis as a promising direction for future research.

We contribute to this by investigating a manager's exploration and exploitation activities (O'Reilly & Tushman, 2004). That is, we aim at increasing insight into the variation of a manager's exploration and exploitation activities by investigating the effects of *different types* of antecedents, as well as the *relationships* between these antecedents. Current literature on exploration and exploitation builds on insights from fields like innovation, strategic management, organizational learning, and organization design, and has focused on *organizational* and *environmental types of antecedents* (see e.g. Gupta et al., 2006; Raisch & Birkinshaw, 2008; Simsek et al., 2009). This paper contributes to current literature on exploration and exploitation by building upon regulatory focus theory (Brockner & Higgins, 2001; Higgins, 1997, 1998; Shah et al., 1998), which is a *motivational type of antecedent*. Recently, regulatory focus theory – which defines the gains versus losses orientation of an individual – increasingly appears in management and organization studies (Wallace et al., 2009) and has been utilized to interpret a wide range of inadequately understood phenomena, such as the germination of employee commitment in organizations (Johnson et al., 2010), managers' inattention to emerging competitive threats (McMullen et al., 2009), opportunistic behavior of managers in corporate alliances (Das & Kumar, 2010), the use of contracts (Weber & Mayer, 2011), and transformational and transactional leadership behaviors (Kark & van Dijk, 2007). Recent studies (e.g., Tuncdogan et al., 2015 – also see 2017) suggest that regulatory focus may help understand exploration and exploitation as well, particularly at the individual level of analyses, given its versatile applications in related areas like those of individuals' creativity (Friedman, & Förster, 2001), performance (Neubert et al., 2008; Keller, & Bless, 2006) and behavioral change (Fuglestad et al., 2008; Liberman et al., 1999).

This study also investigates an organizational and environmental type of antecedent of managerial exploration and exploitation to create a more all-encompassing insight into drivers of variation in managers' exploration and exploitation activities. Regarding organizational antecedents, centralization-decentralization emerges most consistently in studies of the components of the organization structure (Miller & Dröge, 1986; Zmud, 1982), and it plays a prominent role in studies on firm and unit level exploration and exploitation as well (Benner & Tushman, 2003; Jansen et al., 2006; Tushman & O'Reilly, 1996). We investigate (de)centralization at the individual level of analysis in terms of a manager's decision-making authority (cf. Ghoshal et al., 1994; Sheremata, 2000). Regarding environmental antecedents, researchers particularly point to dynamism as a fundamental aspect of the environment (Dess & Beard, 1984), shaping the extent to which organizations, and units focus on and invest in exploration and/or exploitation (Floyd & Lane, 2000; Jansen et al., 2005; Simsek, 2009). In this study we focus on dynamism at the individual level by investigating the dynamism of a manager's direct internal and external surrounding environment (cf. Burgelman, 1991, 2002) as an antecedent of that manager's exploration and exploitation activities.

The remainder of this paper is structured as follows. In the next section, we will introduce the relevant concepts and develop the conceptual model and hypotheses. Next, in the methods section, specifics of the data and the measures utilized in the study will be elucidated. After that, we will discuss how the analysis was done and the results achieved. Finally, we will conclude by discussing implications for theory and management practice, and by reviewing limitations and interesting pathways for future research.

Theory and hypotheses

Managers' exploration and exploitation activities

Discussions on exploration and exploitation, in terms of a manager's activities, can be found in various literatures; most notably those on organizational learning, innovation, and strategic management (Gupta et al., 2006; O'Reilly & Tushman, 2004; Raisch & Birkinshaw 2008). March (1991) proposed exploration and exploitation as two different learning activities of firms and their organization members. Studies of organizational learning indicate that the essence of a manager's exploration activities is about creating variety in experience (Holmqvist, 2004; McGrath, 2001; Mom et al., 2007), associated with renewing and broadening their knowledge base, skills, and expertise (cf. Fang et al., 2009; Levinthal & March, 1993). A manager's exploitation activities are argued to be essentially about increasing reliability in experience (Holmqvist, 2004; Mom et al., 2007), associated with refining, deepening, and applying their existing knowledge base, skills, and expertise (cf. Fang et al., 2009; Levinthal and March, 1993).

Studies on innovation and strategic management characterize a manager's exploration activities as those associated with a long-term future time frame, and novelty. Examples include conducting autonomous strategic initiatives that emerge outside the scope of the current strategy (Burgelman, 2002), and that involve creating new firm competencies (Floyd & Lane, 2000) and pursuing radical innovations to switch from existing products or concepts to new ones, or to meet the needs of new or emergent customers (Danneels, 2002; Smith & Tushman, 2005). Managers' exploitation activities are characterized as those associated with an immediate or near-future time frame and the improvement of existing certainties. Examples include conducting induced strategic initiatives that take place within the scope of the current strategy (Burgelman, 2002) and that involve leveraging and deploying existing firm competencies, and conducting relatively minor adaptations of existing products and business concepts to better meet existing customers' needs (Danneels, 2002; Smith & Tushman, 2005).

Regulatory focus theory

Regulatory focus is a theory of goal attainment (Brockner & Higgins, 2001; Higgins, 1997; Pennington & Roese, 2003). Research suggests two types of regulatory foci: *promotion focus* is enacted when people concentrate on the gains they can make as they act (i.e., 'If I work hard, I can buy a new car'). In contrast, *prevention focus* emerges when people are afraid of losses and struggle to prevent them (i.e., 'I must work hard not to lose this job'). The individual's perception, set of emotions, attention, and behaviors differ depending on the regulatory focus he or she is predominantly experiencing (Förster & Higgins, 2005; Shah et al., 1998; Weber & Mayer, 2011). Regarding managers, for instance, McMullen et al. (2009) argue that prevention focus and promotion focus results in managers showing attention to different issues; more prevention-focused managers would be more likely to notice and respond to an emerging threat than would more promotion-focused managers. Regulatory focus has an important influence on the behavior of an individual, especially with respect to how the individual approaches a situation. A more promotion-focused individual uses an eager approach and tries to achieve 'maximal goals', by concentrating on maximizing gains (Higgins, 1997; Pennington & Roese, 2003). On the contrary, a more prevention-focused individual prefers a vigilant approach and focuses on 'minimal goals', via putting emphasis on minimizing losses and shortcomings.

Research shows that an individual's regulatory focus is influenced by the situation or context the individual resides in (Keller & Bless, 2006; Shah et al., 1998). In an organizational context, organizational and environmental factors are argued to have an effect on the regulatory focus of the organization members (Brockner & Higgins, 2001; Kark & van Dijk, 2007; McMullen et al., 2009). That is, through its effect on a manager's regulatory focus, the context – both internal and external to the firm – has an effect on the behavior of that manager. For instance, Kark and van Dijk (2007) argue that the organization structure and dynamism, and change in the organizational environment, elicit a manager's regulatory focus, impacting that manager's leadership behavior.

The literature on regulatory focus indicates that promotion focus and prevention focus are two different regulatory foci (Higgins, 1997). This literature also indicates that their motivational effects are generally polar and competing (Uskul et al., 2009; Spanjol & Tam, 2010; Zhao & Pechmann, 2007). In line with this, studies have indicated that the two regulatory foci tend to suppress each other; i.e., an increase in a person's promotion focus is associated with a decrease in that person's prevention focus and the other way around (Sengupta & Zhou, 2007; Shah & Higgins, 2001; Zhou & Pham, 2004). We follow this previous research by referring to a manager's regulatory focus as that manager's '*relative' regulatory focus* (Lockwood et al., 2002, p. 861; see also Uskul et al., 2009; Spanjol & Tam, 2010; Zhao & Pechmann, 2007) to denote that an increase of a manager's promotion focus is associated with a decrease of that manager's prevention focus and the other way around.

Regulatory focus and managers' exploration and exploitation activities

The literature indicates that managers whose regulatory focus is closer to promotion than prevention are more prone to engage in exploration activities and less in exploitation activities compared to managers whose regulatory focus is closer to prevention than promotion. Promotion-focused individuals are more tolerant of ambiguity, risk, and change than prevention-focused individuals (Brockner & Higgins, 2001; Fuglestad et al., 2008; Hamstra et al., 2010; Herzenstein et al., 2007; Liberman et al., 1999). Contrary to prevention-focused individuals, promotion-focused individuals are also more willing to diverge from their norms (Fuglestad et al., 2008; Liberman et al., 1999), engage in entrepreneurial activities (Hmielski & Baron, 2008), and concentrate on the large picture (Förster & Higgins, 2005). In contrast, prevention-focused individuals are more inclined to partake in exploitation activities, as they favor reliable outcomes (Brockner & Higgins, 2001; Hamstra et al., 2010; Liberman et al., 1999), aim at keeping the status quo (Fuglestad et al., 2008; Liberman et al., 1999), and concentrate their attention on details (Förster & Higgins, 2005) and on refinement of the task towards perfection (Crowe & Higgins, 1997; Wan et al., 2009).

A recent study by McMullen and colleagues (2009) presents us with another example suggesting a link between regulatory focus and exploration and exploitation activities. Their review of the literature shows that threats are more likely to draw the attention of prevention-focused managers and draw it more intensively, and in contrast, promotion-focused managers are regularly indifferent in the face of an approaching threat, as they are primarily enticed by potential gain opportunities (e.g., Higgins, 1997; Brockner & Higgins, 2001). Consequently, promotion-focused managers will have a higher inclination towards exploration activities, which increases the probability of future gains. In contrast, prevention-focused managers will have a propensity for allocating more attention towards exploitation activities, thereby eliding the potential hazards to organizational survival in the short term.

Finally, in regulatory focus theory, a tendency for thinking towards the distant future is shown to be more associated with promotion focus, whereas the near future as well as retrospective thinking are associated with prevention focus (Mogilner et al., 2008; Pennington & Roese, 2003). Time-frame orientation, likewise, is an important aspect of exploration and exploitation, where exploration activities are essential to long-term gains and exploitative ones to short-term survival (Levinthal & March, 1993; Tushman & O'Reilly, 1996). This again suggests that a more promotion-focused person, who wants to achieve better results in the long term, is more likely to undertake more exploration activities than a more prevention-focused person, who is more sensitive towards threats, pitfalls, and critical feedback (Crowe & Higgins, 1997; Förster et al., 2001; McMullen et al., 2009), and is therefore more likely to engage more in exploitation activities. The above arguments suggest the following hypotheses:

> HYPOTHESIS 1a: A manager will conduct *more exploration* activities when that manager's relative regulatory focus is closer to promotion focus than prevention focus.

> HYPOTHESIS 1b: A manager will conduct *less exploitation* activities when that manager's relative regulatory focus is closer to promotion focus than prevention focus.

A manager's decision-making authority as an organizational type of antecedent

Current literature on exploration and exploitation has focused on organizational and environmental types of antecedents; see for instance Gupta et al. (2006), Raisch and Birkinshaw (2008), and Simsek (2009). Regarding organizational antecedents, we focus in this study on (de)centralization because it emerges most consistently in studies of the components of the organization structure (cf. Miller and Dröge, 1986). Decentralization also plays a prominent role in exploration and exploitation studies focusing on levels such as the firm (e.g., Tushman & O'Reilly, 1996), business unit (e.g., Jansen et al., 2006), and team (e.g., McGrath, 2001;

Perretti & Negro, 2006). To investigate decentralization at the manager level of analysis, we focus on a manager's decision-making authority (Ghoshal et al., 1994; Sheremata, 2000). A manager's decision-making authority refers to the extent to which a manager has authority to decide what tasks the manager performs and how, and how to solve problems and set goals (Atuahene-Gima, 2003; Dewar et al., 1980).

Increasing a manager's decision-making authority enable that manager to conduct more exploration activities as the increased self-control and the delegated authority to solve problems enable the manager to tap into the needed pool of information and other resources to develop and implement the 'creative' and 'high-quality ideas' (Sheremata, 2000, p. 394) necessary for exploration (Voss et al., 2008). In contrast, decreasing a manager's decision-making authority reduces the ability of the manager to make and execute high-risk exploratory decisions (Singh, 1986), as with little authority granted, the decisions can involve only limited risk, which means low exploration (March, 1991; Jansen et al., 2006), as 'a bias against risk is effectively a bias against exploration' (March, 2006, p. 206). Furthermore, regarding exploitation, Hage & Aiken (1967, p. 88) point out that 'as freedom to make work decisions diminishes, rule observation increases' due to the expansion of the superiors' control on the activities of the individual (Ghemawat & Ricart I Costa, 1993, p. 64). In other words, as a manager's decision-making authority decreases, that manager becomes more likely to be forced to follow the existing framework of the organization by engaging in exploitation activities (Singh, 1986).

Not only the ability, but also the motivation to undertake exploration and exploitation decisions and activities are affected by changing levels of decision-making authority (Cao et al., 2010, p. 1278; Miller, 1987). When considered through the perspective of regulatory focus theory, changes in motivation due to increased decision-making come to the manager with higher intentions to pursue ideals, and therefore, according to Higgins (1997), a promotion-focused situation. For instance, the increased authority triggers the individual to engage in more resource access and acquisition (Ermer et al., 2008; Murray et al., 2006; Sapolsky, 2005), which induces promotion focus by allowing the person to further satisfy his or her needs to achieve 'maximal goals' (Friedman & Förster, 2001; Higgins, 1997). Moreover, with this augmented pool of resources, the risk of losing one resource becomes relatively less of a threat than it used to be, which diminishes the effect of the jeopardy on the person's prevention-focus level (Brockner & Higgins, 2001, p. 48). In other words, we anticipate that higher decision-making authority makes a manager less prone to feel endangered by a threat that he or she would previously regard as significant, and, thus, causes the manager to become less prevention focused. Therefore, the increased decision-making authority shifts the manager's relative regulatory focus towards promotion focus rather than prevention focus, increasing the tendency towards exploration activities and decreasing the tendency towards exploitation activities.

Summarizing, we expect that increasing the levels of a manager's decision-making authority will be positively associated with that manager's exploration activities and negatively associated with that manager's exploitation activities *in two ways*. First, by altering the abilities of the manager, and second, by altering the motivation of the manager. Because we expect the motivational mechanism (regulatory focus) to explain a different part in the variance of the manager's exploration and exploitation activities than the structural mechanism, we expect that regulatory focus will mediate only part of the relations. Hence, we claim that part of the effect will be due to the structural consequences of decision-making authority (i.e., on the ability or inability to take an exploration or exploitation action), and the other part of the effect will be due to the motivational consequences of it, through the effect on the manager's regulatory focus induced by the decision-making authority bestowed upon that person.

HYPOTHESIS 2a: Increasing the decision-making authority of a manager shifts that manager's relative regulatory focus closer to promotion focus rather than prevention focus.

HYPOTHESIS 2b: The *positive* relationship between a manager's decision-making authority and that manager's *exploration* activities is partially mediated by that manager's regulatory focus.

HYPOTHESIS 2c: The *negative* relationship between a manager's decision-making authority and that manager's *exploitation* activities is partially mediated by that manager's regulatory focus.

Dynamism of a manager's environment as an environmental type of antecedent

Adapting to the dynamics of the surrounding environment is of crucial importance not only for an organization but for a manager as well (Floyd & Lane, 2000). We focus in this study on dynamism, as organization theory on the environment typically concentrates on its dynamism feature (i.e. Andersen, 2004; Harris, 2004; Heavey et al., 2009). Similarly, dynamism is among the most often included environmental type of antecedent in firm and unit level exploration and exploitation research as well (e.g. Jansen et al., 2005; Levinthal and March, 1993; Sidhu et al., 2004). Environmental dynamism refers to the amount and rate of change and to the unpredictability of change or the degree of instability of the surrounding environment (Dess & Beard, 1984). A manager's surrounding environment refers to the manager's direct environment both internal and external to the firm (Burgelman, 1991). Research points out that managers of the same firm or unit may face different levels of dynamism in their direct environment as they may have responsibilities regarding different products, services, or processes, and may operate in specific work contexts featuring different levels of, for instance, uncertainly and interdependencies (Burgelman, 1991; Floyd & Lane, 2000; Griffin et al., 2007).

The literature points out that more exploration activities are necessary to stay aligned with a dynamic environment, while more exploitative activities are necessary in a stable environment (Jansen et al., 2006; Levinthal & March, 1993). Increasing levels of dynamism in a manager's environment raise the necessity for that manager to increase variety in experience, to broaden his or her knowledge base (He & Wong, 2004), as well as to regularly renew it (Floyd & Lane, 2000; Tushman & O'Reilly, 1996) to deal with the increasing amount, rate, and unpredictability of change associated with dynamic environments (Jansen et al., 2006; Lewin et al., 1999). Thus, when the level of dynamism in their environment increases, managers would conduct more exploration activities in an attempt to adapt to their environment. In contrast, decreasing levels of dynamism in a manager's environment, i.e., more stability, raise the necessity for that manager to increase reliability in experience and to refine, deepen, and more efficiently apply his or her existing knowledge base and skills (Floyd & Lane, 2000; Tushman & O'Reilly, 1996) as in a stable environment the activities that have proven to be effective for the manager do not change (Lewin et al., 1999). Thus, in order to reap the benefits of the proven and well known, managers would adapt to decreasing levels of environmental dynamism by conducting more exploitation activities.

The effect of environmental dynamism on a manager's exploration versus exploitation activities is not limited to the adaptation mechanism explained above. Part of the effect runs through how environmental dynamism alters the goal attainment strategy of that manager, by situationally inducing a particular regulatory focus on him or her. Research indicates that dynamic environments situationally induce promotion focus through their ambiguous structure (Keller & Bless, 2006; Shah et al., 1998), motivating managers to deviate from the original plan, while stable environments are associated with inducing prevention focus, motivating managers to stick to the original plan (Hmielski & Baron, 2008). Furthermore, in a dynamic environment, the manager would need to show attention to the state of environmental variables more often as these variables change regularly. Because attention is limited, this would restrain managers from showing a large amount of attention to threat-related, prevention-focused concerns (McMullen et al., 2009), such as exploiting to survive in the short term (Levinthal & March, 1993). Hence, it can be argued that in dynamic environments managers are shifted away from prevention focus towards promotion focus.

Considering that regulatory focus influences one's goal–attainment strategy to improve the chances of survival through recognizing the cues of the environment (Friedman & Förster, 2001) to act appropriately to the environment, it is plausible that in stable environments the individual has situationally induced (Keller & Bless, 2006; Shah et al., 1998) the prevention focus, which is associated with stability (Liberman et al., 1999), and in dynamic environments the promotion focus, which is associated with change (ibid.). Phrased differently, promotion focus increases a manager's motivation to engage in a more diverse set of activities (exploration) to increase chances of survival within a dynamic environment, whereas prevention focus increases a manager's motivation to engage in more reliable and proven activities (exploitation) to ensure survival within the stable environment.

These motivational mechanisms are expected to affect managers' exploration and exploitation activities in the same direction as the adaptation mechanisms we discussed in the beginning of this section. Nevertheless, the motivational mechanisms have different theoretical explanations than the adaptation mechanisms. Therefore, we expect not only that the manager's exploration and exploitation activities will be directly related to the dynamism of the manager's environment, but we also expect this effect to be partially mediated by that manager's regulatory focus.

HYPOTHESIS 3a: Increasing dynamism of a manager's environment shifts that manager's relative regulatory focus closer to promotion focus rather than prevention focus.

HYPOTHESIS 3b: The *positive* relationship between dynamism of a manager's environment and that manager's *exploration* activities is partially mediated by that manager's regulatory focus.

HYPOTHESIS 3c: The *negative* relationship between dynamism of a manager's environment and that manager's *exploitation* activities is partially mediated by that manager's regulatory focus.

The resulting conceptual model can be illustrated as in Figure 9.1.

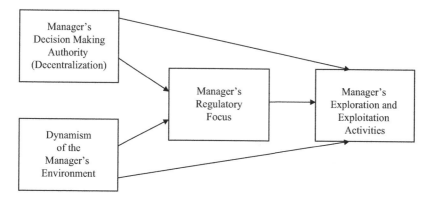

Figure 9.1 Conceptual framework

Method

Sample and data collection

To test the hypotheses we draw upon a sample of a large variety of managers from one of the 'big four' accountancy and professional services firms. Managers active in the accountancy and professional services sector provide an interesting case for researching exploration and exploitation, as their firms are confronted with pressures to explore – e.g., due to changes regarding regulation, technologies, competition, and customer demands– and with pressures to exploit – due to short term competitive pressures in terms of an increased focus on efficiency, cutting costs, and imitation – (Banker et al., 2005; Chang et al., 2009; Semadeni & Anderson, 2010). In line with this, several previous empirical studies investigating issues related to exploration and exploitation take the accountancy and professional services sector purposefully as an empirical setting as well (e.g., Van Den Bosch et al., 2005; Groysberg & Lee, 2009; Swart & Kinnie, 2010). This study's target firm consists of three organizational units; two divisions and a central internal support unit. The first division provides services in accounting and auditing, taxes, and legal issues. The second division provides consulting and financial advisory services.

The survey was sent, in consultation with corporate management, to a sample of 653 managers who vary in terms of demographic characteristics such as age, tenure in the firm, functional tenure, education, and organizational characteristics such as hierarchical level and organizational unit. We ensured that the distribution of the sample managers over the hierarchical levels, organization units, and the demographic characteristics corresponded to the distribution of all managers in the firm (Chi-square tests; $p < .05$; $\alpha = .05$) to decrease the probability that bias due to the sampling procedure may be a problem. To ensure confidentiality, we agreed not to reveal the names of the respondents and to allow the return of the completed surveys to us without interference from corporate management. We received 229 completed surveys corresponding to a response rate of 35%. List-wise deletion of cases with missing values resulted in a final sample of 224. We examined differences between respondents and non-respondents to test for non-response bias. Chi-square tests ($p < .05$; $\alpha = .05$) indicate that the distribution of the respondents over the hierarchical levels, organization units, and demographic characteristics corresponds to the population's distribution. We also compared early and late respondents in terms of model variables (*t*-test; $p < .05$) as late respondents can be expected to be similar to non-respondents (Armstrong & Overton, 1977). No significant differences appeared, indicating that non-response bias may not be a problem.

Measures and validation

Dependent Variable. We use the scales of managers' exploration and exploitation activities set out by Mom et al. (2007). The seven-item exploration scale

(α = .91) captures the extent to which a manager engaged in exploration activities last year. In line with our conceptualization, the scale refers to activities relating to such things as creating variety in experience, learning new knowledge and skills, searching new product and market possibilities, adapting for the long-term, renewing products, services, or processes, and experimenting. The seven-item exploitation scale (α = .87) captures the extent to which the manager engaged in exploitation activities last year. In line with our conceptualization, the scale refers to activities relating to such things as increasing reliability in experience, using and deepening existing knowledge and skills, serving existing customers with exiting products or services, achieving short-term goals, and fitting into existing firm policies. All items were measured on a seven-point Likert scale (1 = to a very small extent to 7 = to a very large extent). Appendix I shows the items of this study's variables.

To check for convergent and discriminant validity, we performed exploratory and confirmatory factor analyses. Exploratory factor analysis with Varimax rotation with all 14 items, based on the survey data, revealed that two summated scales could be constructed; one exploration scale with the seven exploration items and one exploitation scale with the seven exploitation items. Eigenvalues for each factor were greater than 2.82, all items loaded on their appropriate factors at greater than .61, and no item cross-loading was greater than .25. We conducted confirmatory factor analysis (CFA) of the 14 items to check for discriminant validity of the constructs. Results indicate that the two-factor model fits the data well (NFI = .91, CFI = .95, RMSEA < .07). Moreover, a comparison of a one-factor model with a two-factor model shows a significant improvement in fit ($\Delta\chi^2$ significant at p < .001) further providing evidence of discriminant validity (Bagozzi & Phillips, 1982).

Mediating Variable. In order to calculate our measure of *relative regulatory focus*, we followed the procedures used in prior regulatory focus research. That is, we first measure both foci using a scale for promotion focus and a scale for prevention focus, and subsequently subtract the sores on the prevention subscale from the scores on the promotion subscale (see e.g., Uskul et al., 2009; Spanjol & Tam, 2010; Zhao & Pechmann, 2007). As Lockwood and colleagues (2002, p. 861) explain: 'we come to a measure of relative regulatory focus by subtracting scores on the prevention goal subscale from scores on the promotion goal subscale'. On this relative scale of regulatory focus, higher values represent more promotion focus and lower values represent more prevention focus.

We measured both foci based on the measures of Wallace and Chen (2006) and Wallace et al. (2009) as these scales have particularly been developed to measure regulatory foci of individuals in 'organization contexts' (Wallace et al., 2009, p. 805). As pointed out by Wallace et al. (2009), the three-item promotion focus measure (α = .84) captures a manager's motivation 'to promote positive outcomes at work' (Wallace et al., 2009, p. 814) last year. Likewise, the three-item prevention focus measure (α = .88) captures a manager's motivation 'to prevent negative outcomes at work' (Wallace et al., 2009, p. 814). All items were measured on a seven-point Likert scale (1 = to a very small extent to 7 = to a very large extent). Validity checks are reported in the 'validation' paragraph. Appendix 1 shows the items of this study's variables.

Independent Variables. To measure the extent of a manager's *decision-making authority*, we followed others like Jansen et al. (2006) and Richardson et al. (2002) by using a four-item scale originally developed by Aiken and Hage (1968) and further validated by Dewar et al. (1980), assessing the extent to which the manager has decision-making authority in choosing which tasks to perform and how, to set goals, to solve problems, and to undertake action without superior's approval (α = .91). Finally, to measure the level of *dynamism of a manager's environment*, we followed others like Jansen et al. (2006) and Volberda (1998) by using a four-item scale based on Dill (1958), measuring the intensity and rate of change a manager faces in his or her direct both internal and external working environment (α = .87).

Control Variables. We controlled for the effects of *age* and *tenure in the firm*, which are indicators of experience and can affect the exploration and exploitation activities of the manager (Tushman & O'Reilly, 1996). Likewise, we controlled for the effect of *tenure in the current function* for its potential effects on exploration and exploitation activities (Gibson & Birkinshaw, 2004), and for possible effects of *education*, as this has an effect on cognitive abilities (Papadakis et al., 1998), which may in turn affect the choice of exploration and exploitation activities (Adler et al., 1999). To control for educational effects, we included a dummy variable; 1 = managers with master degrees or higher, 0 = managers with bachelor degrees or lower. We controlled for the effects of the person's *hierarchical level* in the company including two dummy variables based on the firm's system of position classification; one dummy reflecting the most senior managers and another reflecting middle managers, making operational level managers the reference group. Finally, we included two dummy variables to reflect the organizational unit the manager resides in; one dummy for the accounting, tax and legal division, and another for the consulting and financial advisory division, making managers of the central and support unit the reference group. By doing so we intend to control for contextual factors possibly affecting a manager's exploration and exploitation activities (Gibson & Birkinshaw, 2004).

Validation. We conducted convergent and discriminant validity checks on all of this study's items. First we conducted an exploratory factor analysis (Principle Components Analysis, Varimax rotation with Kaiser normalization) including all items (i.e., the exploration, exploitation, promotion focus, prevention focus, decision-making authority, and dynamism items). KMO measure of sampling adequacy was .847, showing that partial correlations among the variables included in this study were small, and Bartlett's test of sphericity was significant (χ^2 = 3992.35; p < .001), meaning that the sample was well fit for exploratory factor analysis. Our model suggested a total of six separate factors (exploration, exploitation, promotion focus, prevention focus, decision-making authority, and dynamism). As expected, the exploratory factor analysis yielded a six-factor result, with eigenvalues greater than 1.56, and where each item loaded at least 0.6 on its corresponding concept's dimension and 0.3 or less on other dimensions. Moreover, using confirmatory factor analyses (CFA) to compare a one-factor model with a two-factor for every possible pair of factors shows a significant improvement in fit for each pair ($\Delta \chi^2$ significant at $p < .001$) further providing evidence of discriminant validity (Bagozzi & Phillips, 1982).

Analysis and results

The descriptive statistics and correlations for the variables used in this study are exhibited in Table 9.1. The independent and mediating variables and some of the control variables significantly relate to each other. To examine multicollinearity, we calculated variance inflation factors (VIF) for each of the regression equations. The VIFs ranged from 1.08 to 2.47, and thus were well below 10, which is the common cut-off point for multicollinearity (Neter et al., 1996).

Tests of hypotheses

We used regression analyses and Sobel tests (Sobel & Leinhardt, 1982) to test the hypotheses. Model 2 of Table 9.2 shows that the manager's relative regulatory focus variable (of which higher scores correspond to relatively more promotion focus than prevention focus) positively relates to the manager's exploration activities variable ($\beta = .16$; $p < .01$), *supporting Hypothesis 1a*. Model 4 shows that manager's relative regulatory focus negatively relates to manager's exploitation activities ($\beta = -.18$; $p < .01$), *supporting Hypothesis 1b*. Moreover, as expected, a manager's decision-making authority positively relates to that manager's relative regulatory focus (Model 5: $\beta = .17$; $p < .05$), *supporting Hypothesis 2a*, and also to that manager's exploration activities, both in Model 1 ($\beta = .17$; $p < .01$) and Model 2 ($\beta = .14$; $p < .05$). The result of Model 2 provides support for the direct structural effect of a manager's decision-making authority on that manager's exploration. The Sobel test indicates that there is a significant mediation effect as well (Sobel $t = 1.89$; $p < .10$), *supporting Hypothesis 2b*, i.e. the motivational effect. That is, the positive effect of a manager's decision-making authority on a manager's exploration activities is partially mediated by that manager's regulatory focus. Model 3 shows that there is no significant relationship between a manager's decision-making authority and that manager's exploitation activities; hence *Hypothesis 2c is not supported*. In line with our expectations, the dynamism of manager's environment positively relates to that manager's relative regulatory focus (Model 5: $\beta = .28$; $p = .001$), *supporting Hypothesis 3a*, and also to that manager's exploration activities, both in Model 1 ($\beta = .44$; $p < .001$) and Model 2 ($\beta = .39$; $p < .001$). The result of Model 2 provides support for the adaptation effect of dynamism of a manager's environment on that manager's exploration. he Sobel test indicates that there is

Table 9.1 Means, standard deviations, minimum and maximum values, and correlations

	Mean	St. dev.	Min.	Max.	1	2	3	4	5	6	7	8	9	10	11	12
1. Manager's Exploration Activities	4.23	1.16	1.00	7.00												
2. Manager's Exploitation Activities	4.91	.85	3.00	7.00	-.35											
3. Manager's Decision Making Authority	3.52	1.65	1.00	7.00	.37	-.23										
4. Dynamism of a Manager's Environment	4.17	1.46	1.00	7.00	.52	-.38	.26									
5. Manager's Relative Regulatory Focus*	1.39	2.02	-4.67	6.00	.35	-.31	.23	.33								
6. Age	37.47	8.67	26.00	61.00	-.03	-.03	.07	.12	-.01							
7. Tenure in firm	7.60	7.38	.00	39.00	-.12	.14	-.03	-.04	-.05	.70						
8. Tenure in current function	4.35	3.38	.50	24.00	-.25	.02	-.10	-.10	-.03	.26	.25					
9. Education: Master of above	.58	.50	.00	1.00	-.02	-.07	-.07	.09	.12	-.02	-.02	.05				
10. Hierarchical level: Top	.17	.37	.00	1.00	.10	.02	.08	.19	.05	.41	.31	.08	-.13			
11. Hierarchical level: Middle	.38	.49	.00	1.00	.17	-.06	.13	.05	.05	.12	.05	-.05	.07	-.35		
12. Division: Accountancy and legal	.64	.48	.00	.00	-.18	.25	-.23	-.20	-.05	-.07	.09	-.03	-.12	-.01	.17	
13. Division: Consultancy and finance	.21	.41	.00	1.00	.20	-.30	.21	.21	.14	.04	-.10	-.05	.15	.13	-.11	-.69

Notes: n = 224; All correlations above |.12| are significant at p <=.05; *Higher scores correspond to relatively more promotion focus than prevention focus

Table. Results of hierarchical regression analyses

Dependent variable	Manager's Exploration Activities				Manager's Exploitation Activities				Manager's Relative Regulatory Focus	
	Model 1		Model 2		Model 3		Model 4		Model 5	
	b (s.e.)	β	b (s.e.)	β	b (s.e.)	β	b (s.e.)	β	b (s.e.)	β
Intercept	3.25 (4.3)***		3.37 (.43)***		6.10 (.36)***		6.10 (.36)***		−1.31 (1.91)	
Main effect										
Manager's decision making authority	.12 (.04)	.17**	.10 (.04)	.14*	−.05 (.03)	−.09	−.03 (.03)	−.06	.21 (.08)	.17*
Dynamism of a manger's environment	.35 (.05)	.44***	.31 (.05)	.39***	−.18 (.04)	−.31***	−.15 (.04)	−.26***	.39 (.10)	.28***
Manager's relative regulatory focus[a]			.09 (.03)	.16**			−.08 (.03)	−.18**		
Control variables										
Age	−.02 (.01)	−.15†	−.02 (.01)	−.14†	−.01 (.01)	−.12	−.01 (.01)	−.12	−.01 (.02)	−.06
Tenure in firm	.00 (.01)	−.00	.00 (.01)	−.00	.02 (.01)	.17†	.02 (.01)	.17†	−.00 (.03)	−.01
Tenure in current function	−.05 (.02)	−.15**	−.05 (.02)	−.16**	−.01 (.02)	−.03	−.01 (.02)	−.03	.01 (.04)	.02
Education: Master or above	−.13 (.13)	−.06	−.17 (.13)	−.07	.00 (.01)	.00	.04 (.11)	.02	.43 (.27)	.11
Hierarchical level: Top	.47 (.21)	.15*	.46 (.21)	.15**	.20 (.18)	.09	.21 (.17)	.09	.09 (.33)	.02
Hierarchical level: Middle	.59 (.15)	.25***	.58 (.15)	.25***	.08 (.13)	−.05	−.07 (.12)	−.04	.13 (.31)	.03
Division: Accountancy and legal	−.22 (.18)	−.09	−.27 (.18)	−.11	.04 (.15)	.02	.08 (.15)	.04	.57 (.38)	.14
Division: Consultancy and finance	.12 (.21)	.04	.07 (.21)	.02	−.41 (.18)	−.20*	−.36 (.18)	−.17*	.62 (.44)	.13
R–squared	.42		.44		.23		.26		.16	
Adjusted R-squared	.39		.41		.20		.22		.12	
F improvement of fit	15.33***		15.17***		6.42***		6.75***		3.98***	

Notes: Unstandardized coefficients are reported, with standard errors in parentheses, as well as standardized coefficient; N = 224; † p <= .10; *p <= .05; **p <= .01; ***p <= .001;
[a]Higher scores correspond to relatively more promotion focus than prevention focus.

a significant mediation effect as well, i.e. the motivational effect (Sobel t = 3.59; p = .001), *supporting Hypothesis 3b*. That is, the positive effect of dynamism of a manager's environment on that manager's exploration activities is partially mediated by that manager's regulatory focus. Finally, dynamism of a manager's environment negatively relates to that manager's exploitation activities, both in Model 3 (β = −.31; p < .001) and Model 4 (β = −.26; p < .001). The result of Model 4 provides support for the adaptation effect. The Sobel test indicates that there is a significant mediation effect as well, i.e. the motivational effect (Sobel t = 3.07; p = .01), *supporting Hypothesis 3c*. That is, the negative effect of dynamism of a manager's environment on that manager's exploitation activities is partially mediated by that manager's regulatory focus.

Discussion

As a response to various recent calls for further research on individual level exploration and exploitation (e.g., Gupta et al., 2006; Lavie et al., 2010; Raisch & Birkinshaw, 2008; Simsek, 2009; Smith & Tushman, 2005) as well as on models that specify relations between different types of antecedents of exploration and exploitation (Raisch & Birkinshaw, 2008; Simsek, 2009), this chapter aims to contribute to existing literature by increasing insight into the variation of management exploration and exploitation activities by investigating regulatory focus as a motivational antecedent. It does this by developing a model and associated hypotheses that specify the relationships between organizational, environmental, and motivational types of antecedents, and by testing the hypotheses based on a sample of managers. The chapter's contributions raise several important issues for both theory and practice.

First, current literature on exploration and exploitation has focused primarily on organizational and environmental types of antecedents (see e.g., Raisch & Birkinshaw, 2008; Simsek et al., 2009 for recent overviews). However, in organizational research, especially at the individual level of analysis, motivational antecedents present another important trajectory of research (i.e., de Clercq et al., 2011; Katz, 1964; March, 2006, p. 205). In this chapter we build upon regulatory focus theory (Brockner & Higgins, 2001; Higgins, 1997, 1998; Shah et al., 1998), to contribute to the emerging literature on individual level exploration and exploitation (e.g., Tuncdogan et al., 2015, 2017) by better understanding a motivational type of antecedent of the manager's exploration and exploitation activities; i.e., a manager's regulatory focus. In line with our expectations, the results of this study illustrate a relationship between the regulatory focus of the manager and that manager's exploration and exploitation activities. That is, our first hypotheses and associated results indicate that a manager conducts more exploration activities when that manager's relative regulatory focus becomes closer to promotion than prevention focus, and that a manager conducts more exploitation activities when that manager's regulatory focus becomes closer to prevention than promotion focus. By showing this, we contribute to increased conceptual and empirically validated understanding of how individual differences in terms of managers' goal attainment guide the selection of managers' different kinds of behavior in terms of the extent to which they engage in exploration and exploitation activities (Leana & Barry, 2000).

Second, we investigated an organizational and environmental type of antecedent of managers' exploration and exploitation as well, to create a more all-encompassing insight into drivers of variation in managers' exploration and exploitation activities. Furthermore, we took a step in answering various recent calls for models that specify relations between different types of antecedents (e.g., Raisch & Birkinshaw, 2008; Simsek, 2009).

Hypotheses 2a and 3a and associated results indicate that increasing the decision-making authority of a manager and increasing the dynamism of a manager's environment shift the manager's relative regulatory focus closer to promotion rather than prevention. These findings may contribute to calls for more regulatory focus research in organizational contexts (i.e., Brockner & Higgins, 2001, p. 61; McMullen et al., 2009, p. 176; Wallace et al., 2009, p. 828). For instance, Wallace and colleagues (2009, p. 828) have noted that 'It would be quite beneficial to examine the effects that organizational and contextual variables (...) have on one's regulatory focus.' A benefit of such research would be that 'If such relationships are identified it might be possible to (...) instill one type of regulatory focus or the other by creating certain climates, depending on the complexities and requirements of the job or specific tasks' (p. 828). Regarding these issues, an important implication of this study for the literature and for management practice is showing that by varying a manager's decision-making authority or by varying the dynamism of a manager's environment – for instance, by changing the manager's job description or features of the manager's work context (cf. Griffin et al., 2007) – it is possible to alter the manager's relative regulatory focus, and, hence, the manager's motivation towards specific kinds of behavior, i.e., exploration or exploitation activities.

Furthermore, our partially mediating hypotheses and associated results indicate that a manager's decision-making authority and the dynamism of the manager's environment not only relate directly to that manager's exploration and exploitation activities, but also indirectly through that manager's regulatory focus. Through this richer explanation and empirical assessment, we contribute to a greater clarity and better understanding for the exploration and exploitation literature of how different types of antecedents relate to managers' exploration and exploitation activities (Raisch & Birkinshaw, 2008; Simsek, 2009). By introducing regulatory focus and investigating its relationships with the organizational and environmental type of antecedents, we conceptually explained and empirically indicated *motivational effects* of these antecedents on managers' exploration and exploitation activities besides the *direct structural and adaptation effects*. In doing so, we are able to more precisely explain variations in managers' exploration and exploitation activities. That is, separation of the motivational effects permits the refinement of prior apprehension of the organizational and environmental antecedents. This finding represents an important implication for managerial practice as well. For example, consider the scenario of a company implementing a new enterprise resource planning (ERP) system for its managers to better coordinate. On one hand, the top management team of the company may want the managers to use this system in an exploratory manner, and find new ways to solve managerial problems. On the other hand, in line with their information-security-related concerns, the IT department may want to follow the principle of least privilege (i.e., Saltzer & Schroeder, 1975), stating that users of an IT system should be granted the minimum possible decision-making authority on the system. Our model would suggest that, even if the level of decision-making authority of a manager is sufficient for the desired level of exploration activities, the manager may be shifted towards a prevention focus because of the restricted level of decision-making authority related to IT issues, and, therefore, may be reluctant to use the system in an innovative manner. Once we realize this double effect by understanding the model proposed in this study, we can think of ways to lessen the problem. For example, in this scenario, the IT policy can be framed in a promotion-focused manner in order to induce promotion focus on the individual (Weber & Mayer, 2011).

Interestingly, and contrary to our expectations, a manager's decision-making authority was not significantly related to that manager's exploitation activities. Although research points to relationships between (de)centralization and exploitation at the firm and unit levels of analyses (e.g., Jansen et al., 2006; Tushman & O'Reilly, 1996), our study indicates from an individual level perspective that changing the level of a manager's decision-making authority does not affect the extent to which that manager conducts exploitation activities. As managers typically see their job as 'getting things done', managers with high and managers with low levels of decision-making authority are apparently equally able and motivated to engage in exploitation activities. To further clarify the relationship between (de)centralization and exploitation at the individual level of analysis, other dimensions of (de)centralization could be investigated, such as the participation of a manager in decision-making (Hage & Aiken, 1967).

Third, as pointed out by Gupta et al. (2006, p. 693) 'a central issue of debate' in the literature on exploration and exploitation pertains to the 'relationship between exploration and exploitation'. March (1991) points to exploration and exploitation competing for scarce resources and being associated with different mind-sets and organizational routines while arguing that, in general, the two are incompatible. This chapter may add to this debate, particularly regarding the individual level of analysis. Regarding 'conflicting mindsets' (cf. March, 1991) associated with exploration and exploitation, this paper points to the importance of a manager's regulatory focus to understand conflicting mind-sets at the individual level. That is, the concept of an individual's 'relative' regulatory focus (e.g., Lockwood et al., 2002) indicates that their motivational effects are generally opposite and competing (Uskul et al., 2009; Spanjol & Tam, 2010; Zhao & Pechmann, 2007) and that they tend to suppress each other; i.e., an increase of a person's promotion focus is associated with a decrease of that person's prevention focus and the other way around (Sengupta & Zhou, 2007; Shah & Higgins, 2001; Zhou & Pham, 2004). Gupta et al. (2006) argue that the debate on the relationship between exploration and exploitation may also depend on the level of analysis applied by researchers. They argue that, at the lowest level of analysis, exploration and exploitation cannot be pursued synchronously, but must be pursued sequentially. An implication regarding the sequential pursuit of exploration and exploitation and conflicting mind-sets, also for management practice, would be the importance of organizational mechanisms that change a manager's relative regulatory focus over time to both enable and motivate the manager to sequentially conduct exploration and exploitation tasks. In this connection, Adler et al. (1999) suggest the enrichment of jobs to include improvement as well as efficiency goals, and parallel organizational structures in which people move back and forth between a more mechanistic structure for routine tasks and a more organic structure for non-routine tasks.

Limitations and future research

Our study has limitations, suggesting issues for future research. To further comprehend the exploration and exploitation activities of a manager within the context of organizations, future studies should consider including other contextual variables in this model, as well as conducting multi-level research. These could be variables that are both contextual and multi-level at the same time. For example, group regulatory focus (Faddegon et al., 2008; Rietzschel, 2011) poses interesting opportunities especially in explaining further variation in a manager's regulatory focus as a member of the group. Such work would bolster the development of overarching models like that of Simsek (2009), which is urgently necessary in this field (Raisch & Birkinshaw, 2008). Furthermore, our study involves cross-sectional, single informant data and uses perceptual scales highlighting issues of common method bias and causal reciprocity. Regarding the issue of common method bias, we performed Harman's one-factor test on items included in the regression models. If common method bias were a serious problem in the study, we would expect a single factor to emerge to account for most of the covariance in the dependent and independent variables (Podsakoff and Organ 1986). We did not find such a single factor. The issue of common method bias could be addressed in future studies by measuring exploration and exploitation at the managerial level of analysis using objective measures.

Table 9.3. APPENDIX 1 – Survey measures and items*

A manager's exploration activities (based on Mom et al., 2007).
To what extent did you, last year, engage in work related activities that can be characterized as follows:

Searching for new possibilities with respect to products/services, processes or markets

Evaluating diverse options with respect to products/services, processes or markets

Focusing on strong renewal of products/services or processes

Activities of which the associated yields or costs are currently unclear

Activities requiring quite some adaptability of you

Activities requiring you to learn new skills or knowledge

Activities that are not (yet) clearly existing company policy

A manager's exploitation activities (based on Mom et al., 2007).
To what extent did you, last year, engage in work related activities that can be characterized as follows:

Activities of which a lot of experience has been accumulated by yourself

Activities which you carry out as if it were routine

Activities which serve existing (internal) customers with existing services/ products

Activities of which it is clear to you how to conduct them

Activities primarily focused on achieving short-term goals

Activities which you can properly conduct by using your present knowledge

Activities which clearly fit into existing company policy

A manager's promotion focus (based on Wallace & Chen, 2006; Wallace et al., 2009).
To what extent did you focus, last year, on:

Accomplishing achievements which go to a large extent beyond the formal requirements of the job

Showing the willingness to go beyond what the situation requires

Exhibiting zeal about the job and a consequent willingness to work hard and energetically

A manager's prevention focus (based on Wallace & Chen, 2006; Wallace et al., 2009).
To what extent did you focus, last year, on:

Following rules at work

Completing work in the approved manner

Completing assigned tasks adequately

A manager's decision making authority (based on Dewar et al., 1980)

I can undertake little action until my supervisor approves a decision

If I want to make my own decisions, I will be quickly discouraged

I have to ask my supervisor before I do almost everything

Any decision I make has to have my supervisor's approval

Dynamism of a manager's environment (based on Dill, 1958; Jansen et al., 2006)

My (internal or external) clients regularly ask for complete new products and services

In my business, changes are intense

Where I work, we are continuously forced to change our product/service offerings

Where I work, hardly anything will be changed within a year ®

*All items were measured on a seven-point scale (1 = 'to a very small extent' or 'strongly disagree' to 7 = 'to a very large extent' or 'strongly agree').

References

Adler, P. S., Goldoftas, B., and Levine, D. I. 1999. Flexibility versus efficiency? A case study of model changeovers in the Toyota Production System. *Organization Science*, 10, 43–68.

Aiken, M. and Hage, J. 1968. Organizational interdependence and intraorganizational structure. *American Sociological Review*, 33, 912–930.

Andersen, T. J. 2004. Integrating decentralized strategy making and strategic planning processes in dynamic environments. *Journal of Management Studies*, 41, 1271–1299.

Armstrong, J. S. and Overton T.S. 1977. Estimating nonresponse bias in mail surveys. *Journal of Marketing Research*, 14, 396–402.

Atuahene–Gima, K. 2003. The effects of centrifugal and centripetal forces on product development speed and quality: How does problem solving matter. *Academy of Management Journal*, 46, 359–373.

Bagozzi, R.P and Phillips, L. W. 1982. Representing and testing organizational theories: A holistic construal. *Administrative Science Quarterly*, 27, 459–489.

Banker R. D., Chang, H., and Natarajan, R. 2005. Productivity change, technical progress and relative efficiency change in the public accounting industry. *Management Science*, 51, 291–304.

Benner, M. J. and Tushman, M. L. 2003. Exploitation, exploration, and process management: The productivity dilemma revisited. *Academy of Management Review*, 28, 238–256.

Brockner, J. and Higgins, E. T. 2001. Regulatory Focus Theory: Implications for the study of emotions at work. *Organizational Behavior and Human Decision Processes*, 86, 35–66.

Burgelman, R. A. 1991. Interorganizational ecology of strategy making and organizational adaptation: Theory and field research. *Organization Science*, 2, 239–262.

Burgelman, R. A. 2002. Strategy as vector and the inertia of coevolutionary lock–in. *Administrative Science Quarterly*, 47, 325–357.

Cao Q., Simsek Z., and Zhang, H. 2010. Modeling the joint impact of the CEO and the TMT on organizational ambidexterity. *Journal of Management Studies*, 47, 1272–1296.

Chang, H., Galantine, C., and Thevaranjan, A. 2009. Returns to scale pattern and efficient firm size in the public accounting industry: An empirical investigation. *Journal of the Operational Research Society*, 60, 1495–1501.

Crowe, E. and Higgins, E. T. 1997. Regulatory focus and strategic inclinations: Promotion and prevention in decision making. *Organizational Behavior and Human Decision Processes*, 69, 117–132.

Danneels, E. 2002. The dynamics of product innovation and firm competences. *Strategic Management Journal*, 23, 1095–1121.

Das, T. K. and Kumar, R. 2010. Regulatory focus and opportunism in the alliance development process. *Journal of Management*. Doi: 10.1177/0149206309356325

De Clercq, D., Castaner X., and Belausteguigoitia, I. 2011. Entrepreneurial initiative selling within organizations: Towards a more comprehensive motivational framework. *Journal of Management Studies*. Doi: 10.1111/j.1467–6486.2010.00999.x

Dess G. G. and Beard, D. W. 1984. Dimensions of organizational task environments. *Administrative Science Quarterly*, 29, 52–73.

Dewar, R. D., Whetten, D. A., and Boje, D. 1980. An examination of the reliability and validity of the Aiken and Hage Scales on centralization, formalization, and task routines. *Administrative Science Quarterly*, 25, 120–128.

Dill, W. R. 1958. Environment as an influence on managerial autonomy. *Administrative Science Quarterly*, 2, 409–443.

Ermer, E., Cosmides, L., and Tooby, J. 2008. Relative status regulates risky decision-making about resources in men: Evidence for the co–evolution of motivation and cognition. *Evolution and Human Behavior*, 29, 106–118.

Faddegon, K., Scheepers, D., and Ellemers, N. 2008. If we have the will, there will be a way: Regulatory focus as a group identity. *European Journal of Social Psychology*, 38, 880–895.

Fang, C., Lee, J., and Schilling, M. A. 2009. Balancing exploration and exploitation through structural design: The isolation of subgroups and organizational learning. *Organization Science*, 21, 625–642.

Floyd, S. W. and Lane, P. J. 2000. Strategizing throughout the organization: Managing role conflict in strategic renewal. *Academy of Management Review*, 25, 154–177.

Förster, J., Grant, H., Idson L. C., and Higgins, E. T. 2001. Success/Failure feedback, expectancies, and approach/avoidance motivation: How regulatory focus moderates classic relations. *Journal of Experimental Social Psychology*, 37, 253–260.

Förster, J. and Higgins, E. T. 2005. How global versus local perception fits regulatory focus. *Psychological Science*, 16, 631–636.

Friedman, R. S. and Förster, J. 2001. The effects of promotion and prevention cues on creativity'. *Journal of Personality and Social Psychology*, 81, 1001–1013.

Fuglestad, P. T., Rothman, A. J., and Jeffery, R. W. 2008. Getting there and hanging on: The effect of regulatory focus on performance in smoking and weight loss interventions. *Health Psychology*, 27, 260–S270.

Ghemawat, P. and Ricart I Costa, J. E. 1993. The organizational tension between static and dynamic efficiency. *Strategic Management Journal*, 14, 59–73.

Ghoshal, S., Korine, H., and Szulanski, G. 1994. Interunit communication in multinational corporations. *Management Science*, 40, 96–110.

Gibson, C. B. and Birkinshaw, J. 2004. The antecedents, consequences, and mediating role of organizational ambidexterity. *Academy of Management Journal*, 47, 209–226.

Griffin, M. A., Neal, A., and Parker, S. K. 2007. A new model of work performance: Positive behavior in uncertain and interdependent contexts. *Academy of Management Journal*, 50, 327–347.

Groysberg, B. and Lee, L. 2009. Hiring stars and their colleagues: Exploration and exploitation in professional service firms. *Organization Science*, 20, 740–758.

Gupta, A. K., Smith, K. G., and Shalley, C. E. 2006. The interplay between exploration and exploitation. *Academy of Management Journal*, 49, 693–706.

Hage, J. and Aiken, M. 1967. Relationship of centralization to other structural properties. *Administrative Science Quarterly*, 12, 72–92.

Hamstra, M. R. W., Bolderdijk, J. W., and Veldstra, J. L. 2010. Everyday risk taking as a function of regulatory focus. *Journal of Research in Personality*, 45, 134–137.

Harris, R. D. 2004. Organizational task environments: An evaluation of convergent and discriminant validity. *Journal of Management Studies*, 41, 857–882.

He, Z. and Wong, P. 2004. Exploration vs. exploitation: An empirical test of the ambidexterity hypothesis. *Organization Science*, 15, 481–494.

Heavey, C., Simsek, Z., Roche, F., and Kelly, A. 2009. Decision comprehensiveness and corporate entrepreneurship: The moderating role of managerial uncertainty preferences and environmental dynamism. *Journal of Management Studies*, 46, 1289–1314.

Herzenstein, M., Posavac, S., and Brakus, J. 2007. Adoption of new and really new products: The effects of self–regulation systems and risk salience. *Journal of Marketing Research*, 44, 251–260.

Higgins, E. T. 1997. Beyond pleasure and pain. *American Psychologist*, 12, 1280–1300.

Higgins, E. T. 1998. Promotion and prevention: Regulatory focus as a motivational principle. In Zanna, M. P. (Ed.), *Advances in Experimental Social Psychology*, Vol. 30, 1–45. San Diego, CL: Academic Press.

Hmielski, K. M. and Baron, R. A. 2008. Regulatory focus and new venture performance: A study of entrepreneurial opportunity exploitation under conditions of risk versus uncertainty. *Strategic Entrepreneurship Journal*, 2, 285–299.

Holmqvist, M. 2004. Experiential learning processes of exploitation and exploration within and between organizations: An empirical study of product development. *Organization Science*, 15, 70–81.

Jansen, J. J. P., Van den Bosch, F. A. J., and Volberda, H. W. 2005. Exploratory innovation, exploitative innovation, and ambidexterity: The impact of environmental and organizational antecedents. *Schmalenbach Business Review*, 57, 351–363.

Jansen, J. J. P., Van den Bosch, F. A. J., and Volberda, H. W. 2006. Exploratory innovation, exploitative innovation, and performance: Effects of organizational antecedents and environmental moderators. *Management Science*, 52, 1661–1674.

Johnson, R. E., Chang, C., and Yang, L. 2010. Commitment and motivation at work: The relevance of employee identity and regulatory focus. *Academy of Management Review*, 35, 226–245.

Kark, R. and van Dijk, D. 2007. Motivation to lead, motivation to follow: The role of the self– regulatory focus in leadership processes. *Academy of Management Review*, 32, 500–528.

Katz, D. 1964. The motivational basis of organizational behavior. *Behavioral Science*, 9, 131–146.

Keller J. and Bless, H. 2006. Regulatory fit and cognitive performance: The interactive effect of chronic and situationally induced self–regulatory mechanisms on test performance. *European Journal of Social Psychology*, 36, 393–405.

Lavie, D., Stettner, U., and Tushman, M. L. 2010. Exploration and exploitation within and across organizations. *Academy of Management Annals*, 4, 109–155.

Leana, C. R. and Barry, B. 2000. Stability and change as simultaneous experiences in organizational life. *Academy of Management Review*, 25, 753–759.

Levinthal, D. A. and March, J. G. 1993. The myopia of learning. *Strategic Management Journal*, 14, 95–112.

Lewin, A. Y., Long, C. P., and Carroll, T. N. 1999. The coevolution of new organizational forms. *Organization Science*, 10, 535–550.

Liberman, N., Idson, L. C., Camacho, C. J., and Higgins, E. T. 1999. Promotion and prevention choices between stability and change. *Journal of Personality and Social Psychology*, 77, 1135–1145.

Lockwood, P., Jordan, C. H., and Kunda, Z. 2002. Motivation by positive or negative role models: Regulatory focus determines who will best inspire us. *Journal of Personality and Social Psychology*, 83, 854–864.

March, J. G. 1991. Exploration and exploitation in organizational learning. *Organization Science*, 2, 71–87.

March, J. G. 2006. Rationality, foolishness, and adaptive intelligence. *Strategic Management Journal*, 27, 201–214.

McGrath, R. G. 2001. Exploratory learning, innovative capacity, and managerial oversight. *Academy of Management Journal*, 44, 118–131.

McMullen, J. S., Shepherd, D. A., and Patzelt, H. 2009. Managerial (in)attention to competitive threats. *Journal of Management Studies*, 46, 157–181.

Miller, D. 1987. Strategy making and structure: Analysis and implications for performance. *Academy of Management Journal*, 30, 7–32.

Miller, D. and Dröge, C. 1986. Psychological and Traditional Determinants of Structure. *Administrative Science Quarterly*, 31, 539–560.

Mogilner, C., Pennington, G. L., and Aaker, J. 2008. Time will tell: The distant appeal of promotion and imminent appeal of prevention. *Journal of Consumer Research*, 34, 670–681.

Mom, T. J. M., Van Den Bosch, F. A. J., and Volberda, H. W. 2007. Investigating Managers' Exploration and Exploitation Activities: The Influence of Top–Down, Bottom–Up, and Horizontal Knowledge Inflows. *Journal of Management Studies*, 44, 910–931.

Murray, C. M., Eberly, L. E., and Pusey, A. E. 2006. Foraging strategies as a function of season and rank among wild female chimpanzees (Pan troglodytes). *Behavioral Ecology*, 17, 1020–1028.

Neter J., Kutner, M. H., Nachtsheim, C. J., and Li, W. 1996. *Applied Linear Statistical Models*. New York, NY: McGraw–Hill.

Neubert, M. J., Kacmar, K. M., Carison, D. S., Chonko, L. B., and Roberts, J. A. 2008. Regulatory focus as a mediator of the influence of initiating structure and servant leadership on employee behavior. *Journal of Applied Psychology*, 93, 1220–1233.

O'Reilly, C. A. and Tushman, M. L. 2004. The ambidextrous organization. *Harvard Business Review*, 82, 74–81.

Papadakis, V. M., Lioukas, S., and Chambers, D. 1998. Strategic decision–making processes: The role of management and context. *Strategic Management Journal*, 19, 115–147.

Pennington, G. L. and Roese, N. J. 2003. Regulatory focus and temporal distance. *Journal of Experimental Social Psychology*, 39, 563–576.

Perretti, F. and Negro, G. 2006. Filling empty seats: How status and organizational hierarchies affect exploration versus exploitation in team design. *Academy of Management Journal*, 49, 759–777.

Podsakoff, P. M. and Organ, D. W. 1986. Self–reports in organizational research: Problems and prospects. *Journal of Management*, 12, 531–544.

Raisch, S. and Birkinshaw, B. 2008. Organizational ambidexterity: Antecedents, outcomes, and moderators. *Journal of Management*, 34, 375–409.

Richardson, H. A., Vandenberg, R. J., Blum, T. C., and Roman, P. M. 2002. Does decentralization make a difference for the organization? An examination of the boundary conditions circumscribing decentralized decision–making and organizational financial performance. *Journal of Management*, 28, 217–244.

Rietzschel, E. F. 2011. Collective regulatory focus predicts specific aspects of team innovation. *Group Processes & Intergroup Relations.* Doi: 10.1177/1368430210392396

Saltzer, J. H. and Schroeder, M. D. 1975. The protection of information in computer systems. *Proceedings of the IEEE*, 63, 1278–1308.

Sapolsky, R. M. 2005. The influence of social hierarchy on primate health. *Science*, 308, 648–652.

Semadeni, M. and Anderson, B. S. 2010. The follower's dilemma: Innovation and imitation in the professional services industry. *Academy of Management Journal*, 53, 1175–1193.

Sengupta, J. and Zhou, R. 2007. Understanding impulsive eaters' choice behaviors: The motivational influences of regulatory focus. *Journal of Marketing Research*, 95, 297–308.

Shah, J., and Higgins, E. T. 2001. Regulatory concerns and appraisal efficiency: The general impact of promotion and prevention. *Journal of Personality and Social Psychology*, 80(5), 693.

Shah, J., Higgins, T., and Friedman R. S. 1998. Performance incentives and means: How regulatory focus influences goal attainment. *Journal of Personality and Social Psychology*, 74, 285–293.

Sheremata, W. S. 2000. Centrifugal and centripetal forces in radical new product development under time pressure. *Academy of Management Review*, 25, 389–408.

Sidhu, J. S., Volberda, H. W., and Commandeur, H. R. 2004. Exploring exploration orientation and its determinants: Some empirical evidence. *Journal of Management Studies*, 41, 913–932.

Simsek, Z. 2009. Organizational ambidexterity: Towards a multilevel understanding. *Journal of Management* Studies, 46, 597–624.

Simsek, Z., Heavey, C. B., Veiga, J. F., and Souder, D. 2009. A typology for aligning organizational ambidexterity's conceptualizations, antecedents, and outcomes. *Journal of Management Studies*, 46, 864–894.

Singh, J. V. 1986. Performance, slack, and risk–taking in organizational decision making. *Academy of Management Journal*, 29, 562–585.

Smith, W. K. and Tushman, M. L. 2005. Managing strategic contradictions: A top management model for managing innovation streams. *Organization Science*, 16, 522–536.

Sobel, M. E. and Leinhardt, S. 1982. Asymptotic confidence intervals for indirect effects in structural equation models. *Sociological Methodology, American Sociological Association*, 13, 290–312.

Spanjol, J. and Tam, L. 2010. To change or not to change: How regulatory focus affects change in dyadic decision–making. *Creativity and Innovation Management*, 19, 346–363.

Swart, J. and Kinnie, N. 2010. Organizational learning, knowledge assets and HR practices in professional service firms. *Human Resource Management Journal*, 20, 64–79.

Tuncdogan, A., Boon, A., Mom, T., Van Den Bosch, F., and Volberda, H. 2017. Management teams' regulatory foci and organizational units' exploratory innovation: The mediating role of coordination mechanisms. *Long Range Planning*, 50, 621–635.

Tuncdogan, A., Van den Bosch, F., and Volberda, H. 2015. Regulatory focus as a psychological micro–foundation of leaders' exploration and exploitation activities. *The Leadership Quarterly*, 26, 838–850.

Tushman, M. L. and O'Reilly, C. A. 1996. Ambidextrous organizations: Managing evolutionary and revolutionary change. *California Management Review*, 38, 8–30.

Uskul, A. K., Sherman, D. K., and Fitzgibbon, J. 2009. The cultural congruency effect: Culture, regulatory focus, and the effectiveness of gain– vs. loss– framed health messages. *Journal of Experimental Social Psychology*, 45, 535–541.

Van den Bosch, F. A. J., Baaij, M. G., and Volberda, H. W. 2005. How knowledge accumulation has changed strategy consulting: Strategic options for established strategy consulting firms. *Strategic Change*, 14, 25–34.

Volberda, H. W. 1998. *Building the Flexible Firm: How to Remain Competitive.* Oxford: Oxford University Press.

Voss, G. B., Sirdeshmukh, D., and Voss, Z. G. 2008. The effects of slack resources and environmental threat on product exploration and exploitation. *Academy of Management Journal*, 51, 147–164.

Wallace, C. and Chen, G. 2006. A multilevel integration of personality, climate, self–regulation, and performance. *Personnel Psychology*, 59, 529–557.

Wallace, J. C., Johnson, P. D., and Frazier, M. L. 2009. An examination of the factorial, construct, and predictive validity and utility of the regulatory focus at work scale. *Journal of Organizational Behavior*, 30, 805–831.

Wan, E. W., Hong, J., and Sternthal, B. 2009. The effect of regulatory orientation and decision strategy on brand judgements. *Journal of Consumer Research*, 35, 1026–1038.

Weber, L. and Mayer, K. J. 2011. Designing effective contracts: Exploring the influence of framing and expectations. *Academy of Management Review*, 36, 53–75.

Zhao, G. and Pechmann, C. 2007. The impact of regulatory focus on adolescents' response to antismoking advertising campaigns. *Journal of Marketing Research*, 44, 671–687.

Zhou, R., & Pham, M. T. 2004. Promotion and Prevention across Mental Accounts: When Financial Products Dictate Consumers & Investment Goals. *Journal of Consumer Research*, 31(1), 125–135.

Zmud, R. W. 1982. Diffusion of modern software practices: Influence of centralization and formalization. *Management Science*, 28, 1421–1431.

10 Should I stay or should I go?

The individual antecedents of noticing and embracing strategic change

Daniella Laureiro-Martinez

Introduction

Research on strategic renewal has focused mainly on understanding the relevant organizational processes and outcomes that promote change (Agarwal & Helfat, 2009; Baden-Fuller & Volberda, 1997; Volberda, Baden-Fuller, & Van Den Bosch, 2001a; Volberda, Van Den Bosch, Flier, & Gedajlovic, 2001b). There are multiple organization-level factors at play, including structure (Gulati & Puranam, 2009; Puranam, Singh, & Chaudhuri, 2009) and a range of power, social, and political dynamics (Capron & Mitchell, 2009). But while these factors may *promote* change, ultimately it is individuals who do the actual changing—or don't. The general consensus seems to be that "You can't build an adaptable organization without adaptable people—and individuals change only when they have to, or when they want to" (e.g., Hamel, 2012). We know that individuals have a substantial impact on the effectiveness of the various modes of renewal, particularly at top management level (Eggers & Kaplan, 2009; Salvato, 2009; Tripsas, 2009). However, we know far less about the individual-level antecedents that account for how people adapt to change, and ultimately help or hinder strategic renewal.

Agarwal and Helfat (2009) suggest that strategic renewal includes "the process, content, and outcome of refreshment or replacement of attributes of an organization that have the potential to substantially affect its long-term prospects" (p. 282). This chapter takes an individual-level perspective on the process aspect, drawing on constructs from neuroscience and psychology that have already been applied to management, and presenting them as part of an integrated model. The contribution of this chapter is the proposition of a model, which explains the individual-level antecedents of the process of refreshment or replacement of an organization's attributes that have the potential to substantially affect its long-term prospects.

In this chapter, first, I propose a process framework of two key individual antecedents to strategic renewal. Next, relying on recent advances in neuroscience, psychology, and decision-making neurosciences, I outline two cognitive abilities involved in strategic renewal. Some examples follow, and the chapter concludes with some ideas for future research.

Individual antecedents of strategic change and innovation

There's no doubt about it: change is hard. Comfortable, familiar options easily beat the possibility of finding better alternatives. In fact, just *thinking* about change can feel painful (Laureiro-Martínez, Brusoni, & Canessa, 2015a). Two opposing needs are in tension when one considers the idea of change: on one hand, the desire to avoid losses by staying with the current alternatives. On the other hand, the desire to seek higher gains by exploring novel alternatives. But why is it so difficult to change? To answer this question, this section proposes a process model in which different individual-level abilities combine to respond to strategic change at the organizational level.

This model starts from the premise that a process of strategic change (e.g. a product innovation, adapting to a new market) can be divided into two phases: "business as usual" and renewal. They can appear sporadically, with renewal punctuating business as usual, or follow each other in reiterative cycles. Each phase comprises sub-activities that are either explorative or exploitative. Organizational-level behaviors are mirrored by, and depend on, parallel behaviors at the individual level. These two levels and their respective activities are shown in in the upper and lower parts of Figure 10.1.

Figure 10.1 depicts the key aspects of the model. Along the horizontal axis, events take place along a temporal dimension. Along the vertical axis, the individual level serves as an antecedent of organizational-level behaviors. When the organization's business as usual process encounters strategic change (the lightning

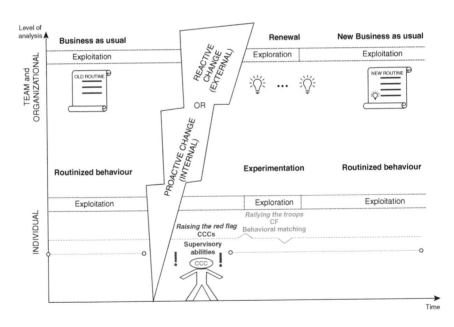

Figure 10.1 Key aspects of the model

bolt) it enters a phase of strategic renewal. At the individual level, change is detected by cognitive controls (CCs) and a behavioral change is matched thanks to cognitive flexibility (CF). Individual behavior shifts from exploitation to exploration, as does the associated organizational behavior. During the exploration phase the organization searches for new routines that can be adapted to the situation. Once they are found, both the individual and organizational behaviors revert to exploitation, and a new phase of business as usual begins.

The model puts forward a sequence of events. During the business as usual phase, the organization initiates or encounters a change of some sort and enters a renewal phase. The change can be reactive, responding to external change, or proactive, driven by internal events. During renewal, routines are no longer adequate and must be modified. Exploiting old routines is put on hold, and replaced by the exploration of novel behaviors that might work under the changed conditions, and could potentially be turned into new routines. After the change is embraced, and provided suitable new routines are found, the organization moves into its *new* business as usual process, in exploitation mode.

Turning to the individual level, two essential types of ability work together to allow people to notice, embrace, and adapt to change. The first, *cognitive control capabilities* (CCCs), serve to "raise the red flag." They are noticing the situation has changed, or will change, and alerting multiple other abilities. The other, *cognitive flexibility* (CF), serves to "rally the troops"—that is, to match the right mental processing resources to the needs of the situation. For a summary table with the definitions of the key concepts of the model see Table 10.1.

During the business as usual phase, individuals act according to existing mental models (Hodgkinson, 1997) and perform routinized behaviors. They operate in a less-mindful mode—although this is not to say that their behavior is mindless (Levinthal & Rerup, 2006). During renewal phases, existing mental models need to be updated, and individuals need to explore new behaviors, in more mindful ways.

The key to these individual-level processes is attention. The focus of attention (March & Simon, 1958) that guides behavior at the individual level is different in each phase. During business as usual, the focus of attention is narrower. During renewal, focus expands to encompass a broader scope of information, whether in the active search for new alternatives or simply the awareness of a broader range of possibilities. The notion that broad attention is important in situations that are dynamic, ill-structured, ambiguous, and unpredictable is acknowledged in the management literature (Levinthal & Rerup, 2006; Ocasio, 2011; Weick & Sutcliffe, 2006).

Abilities such as attention control, which take charge of managing other cognitive processes, are a central field of study in psychology and neurosciences that has gone through much progress recently. There has been much interest in understanding how individuals flexibly deploy attention and match their behaviors to environmental conditions.

Table 10.1 Summary of the definitions of the main concepts used in this chapter

Concept	Definition
Exploration and exploitation	Defined by Laureiro-Martínez, Brusoni, Canessa, and Zollo (2015b) "Exploration entails disengaging from the current task to enable experimentation, flexibility, discovery, and innovation. Exploitation aims at optimizing the performance of a certain task and is associated with high-level engagement, selection, refinement, choice, production, and efficiency" (p. 320).
Attention – individual level	Defined by Jonathan D Cohen, Aston-Jones, and Gilzenrat (2004, p. 71) "[attention is] the cognitive system that allows [the mind] to successfully process some sources of information to the exclusion of others, in the service of achieving some goals to the exclusion of others."
Attention – organizational level	Defined by Ocasio (1997) "Attention is here defined to encompass the noticing, encoding, interpreting, and focusing of time and effort by organizational decision-makers on both (a) issues; the available repertoire of categories for making sense of the environment: problems, opportunities, and threats; and (b) answers: the available repertoire of action alternatives: proposals, routines, projects, programs, and procedures" (p. 89).
Cognitive control capabilities	Defined by Laureiro-Martinez (2014) "the supervisory cognitive mechanisms through which individuals monitor and control their own attention and cognitive processes" (p. 1114).
Cognitive flexibility	Defined by Laureiro-Martinez and Brusoni (2018) "as the ability to match the type of cognitive processing with the type of problem at hand. This matching depends on two conditions being met. First, decision-makers need to be able to describe the type of problem they face, which requires the identification of different elements, views, and perspectives of a situation. Second, decision-makers need to consider different possibilities, which requires active reflection on the elements identified to find possible connections and judge their appropriateness" (p. 1032).

I now turn to each of the two proposed individual-level abilities described above in more depth. For a summary table with the definitions of the key concepts of the model see Table 10.1.

Who raises the red flag?

Organizational members can be proactive initiators or reactive recipients of organizational change. In either case, the first step is noticing change. When change is imminent, understanding who raises the red flag helps us isolate which individual-level ability is involved in this very first stage.

The individual-level antecedents of noticing change are the CCCs: a family of top-down mental processes that include the supervisory cognitive abilities through which individuals monitor and control their own attention and other mental processes (Laureiro-Martinez, 2014). They are responsible for initiating appropriate actions and inhibiting inappropriate ones; selecting relevant information; acquiring rules of behavior; planning future steps; and thinking in abstract ways (Loring & Meador, 1999).

CCCs are called on when we must concentrate and pay attention, or when "flying on autopilot," relying on instinctive responses, or following well-established behaviors and routines would be inadequate or impossible (Laureiro-Martinez, 2014; Miller & Cohen, 2001). CCCs require high effort and thus can be easily depleted (Baumeister, Bratslavsky, Muraven, & Tice, 1998; Muraven, Tice, & Baumeister, 1998). Important inter-individual differences in the use of CCCs to solve managerially relevant problems have been found (Laureiro-Martinez, 2014).

Who rallies the troops?

Noticing change is necessary for adaptation, but not sufficient. In order for adaptation to take place, the individual must not just notice change, but also react to it with the right processes.

Once organizational members notice change, they have a choice. They can continue to act according to past mental models and their associated old routines, or they can embrace change. At the cognitive level, the individual-level ability in charge of mustering the right "mental resources" is the necessary step that—coupled with noticing change—will lead to an adaptive response to change.

CF is the ability in charge of this behavioral matching (Laureiro-Martinez & Brusoni, 2017). It is closely allied to CCCs, and complements them.[1] While CCCs monitor the environment and provide alerts in case of change, CF is responsible for matching the cognitive processes that best suit the situation's needs.

It might be, for example, that a situation presents a novel challenge for which there are no alternative behaviors ready, and therefore requires more deliberation until a new alternative is discovered. In the words of Levinthal and Rerup (2006, p. 507): "A particularly conscious mindful exercise of mapping a context to appropriate routines occurs in the context of novel situations." CF recruits the right "team" (set of abilities) for the task at hand.

When conditions change, CF maps the characteristics of the novel situation with the appropriate type of cognitive processes. CF can be understood as a behavioral switch, responsible for "changing perspectives or approaches to a problem, flexibly adjusting to new demands, rules, or priorities" (Diamond, 2013, p. 137). Faced with unfamiliar challenges, CF will activate more deliberative processes—also called "Type 2" or "more-mindful" processes, in the words of Levinthal and Rerup (2006). However, if it turns out that a change actually requires some behaviors that have been explored in the past, for which viable routines might exist, CF will deactivate the need to deliberate and rely on more automatic ("Type 1" or "less-mindful") processes instead.

Two other aspects of CF are relevant to strategic change. One involves changing how we think about something, switching temporal or individual perspective (e.g. thinking outside the box, seeing others' points of view), and being flexible enough to adjust to new situations and priorities, to admit past solutions were wrong, or to take advantage of sudden, unexpected opportunities (Diamond, 2013).

CF can also be influential through its absence. Lack of CF results in "attentional inertia": the tendency to continue to focus attention on what had previously been relevant (Chatham, Yerys, & Munakata, 2012; Kirkham, Cruess, & Diamond, 2003; Kloo & Perner, 2005).

Should I stay or should I go? Individual-level behaviors

So the red flags have been raised and the troops rallied. What happens next? It all depends on where attention is directed, which in turn determines whether individuals opt for exploitation or exploration.

CCCs prevent attentional inertia by controlling attentional processes (Laureiro-Martinez, 2014).[2] Depending on what type of cognitive processes are needed, CCCs signal the need to broaden the scope of attention to capture more elements, or narrow it down to fewer. The focus of attention, in turn, originates from neuromodulatory abilities guided by CCCs (Jonathan D. Cohen et al., 2004; Laureiro-Martínez, Brusoni, Canessa, & Zollo, 2014).

Different cognitive processes vary in the degree to which they rely on attention, from highly automatic to highly deliberate.[3] Each phase of change has a different focus of attention that guides behavior at the individual level. During business as usual, the focus of attention is narrower, later expanding during renewal. These two types of attention correspond to two higher-level behavioral categories:[4] exploration and exploitation.

> The essence of exploitation is the refinement and extension of existing competences, technologies, and paradigms. Its returns are positive, proximate, and predictable. The essence of exploration is experimentation with new alternatives. Its returns are uncertain, distant, and often negative.
>
> (March, 1991, p. 81)

Past studies have consistently found that neuromodulatory systems involved in assessing reward and uncertainty are also involved in balancing explorative and exploitative behaviors (Jonathan D. Cohen, McClure, & Yu, 2007; Daw, O'Doherty, Dayan, Seymour, & Dolan, 2006). Recent studies have looked at how experienced decision makers deal with explorative and exploitative decisions in a changing environment. They found that exploration relies on brain regions associated mainly with anticipation of rewards, while exploration depends on regions associated mainly with attentional control (Laureiro-Martínez et al., 2014).

The localization of these two types of behavior in the brain is informative in at least two ways. First, it allows us to understand what cognitive functions are more relevant for each type of behavior. Second, it allows us to advance theory by resolving a longstanding and much-debated issue: whether exploration and exploitation are two distinct behaviors (Gupta, Smith, & Shalley, 2006). Recent findings show that, at the individual level, when facing an environment that is constantly changing (i.e. non-stationary environments), exploration and exploitation are separate behaviors that involve different cognitive processes. These neurological findings on the activation of different brain regions provide evidence of the separation between two important constructs in the innovation literature (Laureiro-Martínez et al., 2014).

I began this chapter by asking why it is so difficult to change. The reason is that change requires two important abilities, and therefore there are two major stumbling blocks along the road to change. The most likely one is failing to recognize the need for change (failure of CCCs), while the second, less likely, possibility is reacting with the wrong behavior (failure of CF).

Bear in mind that, so far, we have only considered the individual level. Once an individual has resolved to embrace a change, others must do the same—or, at least, refrain from resisting it. To complicate the picture further, team and organizational dynamics must be conducive in order for strategic change to take place, as we shall briefly see in the next section.

Great oaks from little acorns: How individual-level behaviors affect organizational actions

> There is nothing more difficult to take in hand, more perilous to conduct, or more uncertain in its success, than to take the lead in the introduction of a new order of things.
>
> Niccolo Machiavelli. *The Prince* (1532)

A well-accepted model of how individual behaviors translate into organizational actions is that of Crossan, Lane, and White (1999). It focuses on processes of organizational learning, but can also be applied to processes of strategic change that ultimately rely on organizational learning.

The model proposes three different levels within organizations: individual, group, and the overall organization. These three levels interact through multiple social and psychological processes that constitute two kinds of feedback loop: from the individual to the group and on to the organization, and the same in reverse (organization–group–individual). These loops are important, as from the interactions created between different levels emerge complex dynamics across the organization (Crossan et al., 1999).

How can individual behaviors translate into organizational strategic change? The bridge between cognitive abilities and behavior at the individual and organizational level was proposed 60 years ago by March and Simon (1958) through the focus of attention. The focus of attention, they propose, is not only the guide for behavior at the individual level, but through individual behaviors it affects routines and translates[5] into organizational action. One of the simplest outcomes resulting from an individual noticing change, and being willing to embrace it, would be that they would collect more information and gain more knowledge. In fact, Mom, Van Den Bosch, and Volberda (2007) found that higher levels of exploration and exploitation from managers are associated with their acquisition of horizontal, top-down, and bottom-up knowledge.

Let's look at an example. An important aspect of strategic renewal is innovation: strategic renewal has been referred to as the revitalization of a company's business, and innovation has been identified as inducing renewal (Narayanan, Yang, & Zahra, 2009). Elsewhere, together with Brusoni and Zollo (Laureiro-Martínez, Brusoni, & Zollo, 2010), I presented the case of Menlo Park Edison, a world-class innovation lab led by one of the greatest inventors of all time in the second half of the 19th century. The lab dealt with the uncertainties of developing multiple new products in a changing environment. In our story, we illustrated how individual-level abilities can add up to team- and organizational-level outcomes. From the detailed accounts of Edison's work emerges a story involving multiple switches between exploration and exploitation, both at the organizational and at the individual level, based on environmental needs. Edison's own attention shifted from being narrow to broad, and while there is no evidence on the cognitive abilities involved in these shifts, one could propose that Edison's CCCs served to alert him of possibilities that needed more attention. His CF, in turn, triggered processing modes that allowed him to switch behavior.

This case shows how, in situations of severe uncertainty, when business as usual is not sufficient, a renewal phase unfolds, in which the attention of an individual and their fellow team members is switched from exploitation to exploration. Not only is individuals' behavior aimed at balancing exploration and exploitation, but so too are the behaviors of those around them.

More specifically, managers, and more broadly organizational upper-echelons, are considered to have latitude of action in making strategic choices and even setting entirely new strategic directions for their organizations (Hambrick, 2007; Volberda et al., 2001a). Their proposed exploratory actions can be relatively radical or discontinuous strategic transformations (Agarwal & Helfat, 2009; Kwee, Van Den Bosch, & Volberda, 2011; March, 1991), while the exploitative strategic renewal actions they suggest will involve organizational actions that focus on the current range of activities within the current geographic scope of a firm (Agarwal & Helfat, 2009; Kwee et al., 2011; March, 1991).

In these examples, the emphasis was on the "forward" loops from individual to group and on to organization. But this is only one side of the coin. The reverse feedback loops are equally important, in at least two ways: signaling change and not blocking it.

Take signaling change first. It might be the individual (such as Edison) who notices change. But it might equally be someone else (perhaps a colleague exposed to a different environment) or even an artifact (such as an artificial intelligence tool). In other words, the red flag will not necessarily come from the individual in charge of initiating strategic change—but it must reach them if change is to succeed.

Also, there are several things that can interrupt and even block change initiatives. These include top management, existing routines that are never questioned, and internal politics and power games. Clearly, not all organizations that face strategic change have a leader as visible and impactful as Edison, so it is vital that organizational processes ensure that change initiatives are not blocked without being at least considered (Reast, Lindgreen, Vanhamme, & Maon, 2010). The lesson is that for change to succeed, organizations should carefully nurture feedback loops in both directions. Interestingly, what might block the loops from the individual to the organization—as stated earlier—is more likely to be failing to recognize the need for change. In contrast, what might block the loops from the organization to the individuals is not so much recognizing the need to change, but reacting with the right behavior (Tripsas & Gavetti, 2000; Vuori & Huy, 2016).

Conclusions and recommendations

In this chapter, I have proposed a model that builds upon two essential, co-dependent abilities that individuals need in order to notice and embrace change. CCCs notice change and "raise the red flag" to alert multiple other abilities, while CF serves to "rally the troops" by matching the right mental processing resources to situational needs. So far, these abilities have received very little attention in the management literature, and none at all from the strategic renewal community, to the best of my knowledge.

It might be that CCCs and CF interact with, and are affected by, other individual characteristics, which have already been studied by the scholarly strategic renewal community. Given the importance of CCCs and CF in noticing and embracing change, it is imperative that future research on the microfoundations of strategic change advances our understanding of these possible interactions and complementarities among individual-level factors. For example, in a recent case study, Kwee et al. (2011) are among the few to longitudinally track an organization's strategic renewal trajectories. Their rich organizational data, covering almost 100 years, complemented with in-depth interviews, does not tackle the cognitive antecedents of strategic change. Nevertheless, it does support some inferences about the complementarity of the factors uncovered in their findings and the abilities proposed here. In a nutshell, their paper finds that individuals' corporate governance orientation styles (Anglo-Saxon or Germanic-Rhine, also called market-oriented and network-oriented systems respectively) influence a firm's strategic renewal trajectories over time, revealing an important antecedent of strategic renewal. CCCs and CF could be seen as important antecedents that do not necessarily depend on culture or nationality, but interact with it by regulating the balance between the desire to avoid losses and the desire to seek gains (i.e. regulatory focus). Tuncdogan, Van Den Bosch, and Volberda (2015) proposed regulatory focus as an important ability in mediating exploratory and exploitative preferences. It might be that when faced with a change in the environment that throws up a new problem, some individuals' CCCs notice a change and their CF tries to map the new problem with the right type of cognitive processing. However, due to their regulatory focus, rather than switching to exploration (which corresponds to the principle of avoiding bad outcomes/punishment if they do not change), they decide to keep exploiting (which corresponds to a principle of seeking good outcomes/reward).

Change events can carry a powerful emotional charge, which creates halo effects and difficulties in measurement. Hence, it is very difficult to measure the broad mix of emotional processes involved in change processes using self-reported measures (see Quy Huy and Christine Scheef's chapter in this book). In general, individuals are poor at uncovering processes they are aware of (e.g. multiple emergent behavioral switches that can signal changes in the type of processing and might be accompanied by implicit attitudes and biases). Moreover, the timescales over which certain cognitive processes take place might be simply beyond our capacity to verbalize, let alone mark on a Likert scale in a survey. Many studies of strategic change are carried out long after the event, leaving data at the individual level open to memory and retrospective biases and ex-post interpretations and reconstructions.

However, there are different approaches to studying individuals. One is taking a cognitive perspective—for example, through neuroscience. Theories and findings from neuroscience could serve as building blocks for the study not only of individual-level aspects, but also of how individuals interact across different levels and functions. Using cognitive neuroscientific techniques would allow for greater precision, reliability, and cumulativeness in the analysis of certain types of problem (Laureiro-Martínez, Venkatraman, Cappa, Zollo, & Brusoni, 2015c). A universal advantage of the neuroscientific approach is the chance to work in a highly controlled study environment where observations can be obtained at a very fine-grained level, with the non-trivial disadvantage of short observation periods. There are many areas in which the cognitive sciences, psychology, and neurosciences in particular, can help the study of innovation and strategic renewal. Below I propose three important avenues for future research.

First, we could explore the interaction between contextual factors from the external environment and individual-level abilities, or among multiple antecedents themselves. How can organizational design help resolve the trade-offs between exploration and exploitation? Most of the so-called structural solutions (e.g. Baden-Fuller & Volberda 1997; Raisch & Birkinshaw 2008) have focused on the organizational level, proposing solutions centered on business unit separation. A less-traveled road would be to explore which organizational structures could be provided to facilitate the work of individuals who might be more prone to exploration, exploitation, or both. These organizational structures could be simulated in a neuroscientific study (whether using fMRI (functional Magnetic Resonance Imaging), EEG (electro encephalography), or other tools) and complemented with field data (for a discussion on the use of some of these methods see a book chapter on using Think Aloud and fMRI to take a closer look at managerial cognition in Laureiro-Martínez, 2017).

Second, I believe understanding temporal dynamics is another very important area. Here, neuroscientific methods may prove less useful, given the short time-frames usually involved, but other methods to trace the cognitive processing, like think aloud techniques, could be of use. In a complementary manner, neuroscientific advances have much to contribute regarding our temporal perspectives and abilities to discount future alternatives. An important question is how the framework I propose in this chapter could be longitudinal, and take into account a firm's successive strategic renewal trajectories over the years (Volberda & Lewin, 2003). We know very little, if anything, about how these abilities are deployed over time, and future research on strategic renewal will benefit from a longitudinal perspective on the antecedents proposed in this chapter (Kwee et al., 2011).

Third, we could explore aggregation dynamics by empirically examining the proposed framework across different levels of analysis. Lab or field studies could be very suitable here. This could throw light on how the feed-forward and feedback loops described earlier are enacted differently depending on how CCCs and CF are engaged.

To conclude, scholars generally agree on the importance of individuals as key drivers of change, and interest is growing in understanding individual antecedents of strategic renewal. But there have been few theoretical, and even fewer empirical, efforts to connect the field to new learning in psychology and neurosciences about the abilities that allow individuals to flexibly deploy attention and match their behaviors to environmental conditions. The abilities proposed here are critical for many of the most important skills that mark success in our times: creativity, flexibility, self-control, and discipline (Diamond, 2013). Their impact extends well beyond strategic change moments, touching many other aspects of leadership. Given the renaissance of interest in the individual antecedents of renewal (Tuncdogan et al., 2017), I identify a critical opportunity for future researchers to better explore how the abilities proposed here impact strategy making.

Acknowledgments

I am thankful for the feedback received from the book editors, one anonymous reviewer, Sen Fang, and the participants at the Frontiers in Managerial and Organizational Cognition Conference of the Academy of Management in ETH Zurich, in June 2017.

Notes

1 Cognitive flexibility (CF) and cognitive control capabilities (CCCs) work together. Indeed, it is very difficult to distinguish them empirically, and studies focus on one or the other depending on their specific objective. Some authors would classify CF as one core CCC. Some others would see CF as a higher-level ability that depends on CCCs as an antecedent. This discussion is beyond the scope of this chapter: For our purposes here, it is not necessary to understand the hierarchy of these abilities. We simply need to understand their differential but complementary function, and accept that both are needed to notice and embrace change.

2 Among many other functions. We focus here on attention control as it is a crucial component of CCCs that acts as the cognitive gatekeeper, governing what can access other mental resources. If something does not receive attention, it is unlikely to be further processed.

3 From this perspective, the distinction between deliberate and automatic processing is not dichotomous and absolute but, rather, graded and relative: some processes are more automatic than others, and processes vary in their automaticity based on the context in which they occur.

4 For simplicity, here I use a dual classification rather than a continuum. I would like to highlight that the definitions of exploration and exploitation provided by neuroscientists (Aston-Jones & Cohen, 2005) are compatible with those of March (1991) and many in the management literature. For a comparison of definitions of exploration and exploitation at different levels of analysis and different contexts see page 97 of Laureiro-Martinez et al. (2010).

5 Though clearly not directly, but with many complexities derived from the interactions among individual and organizational aspects. In order to sustain the focus on the individual-level antecedents of strategic change, these important complexities are left out of the current theorizing.

References

Agarwal, R., & Helfat, C. E. 2009. Strategic renewal of organizations. *Organization Science*, 20(2), 281–293.

Aston-Jones, G., & Cohen, J. D. 2005. An integrative theory of locus coeruleus–norepinephrine function: Adaptive gain and optimal performance. *Annual Review of Neuroscience*, 28, 403–450. doi: 10.1146/annurev.neuro.28.061604.135709.

Baden-Fuller, C., & Volberda, H. W. 1997. Strategic renewal: How large complex organizations prepare for the future. *International Studies of Management & Organization*, 27(2), 95–120.

Baumeister, R. F., Bratslavsky, E., Muraven, M., & Tice, D. M. 1998. Ego depletion: Is the active self a limited resource? *Journal of Personality and Social Psychology*, 74, 1252–1265.

Capron, L., & Mitchell, W. 2009. Selection capability: How capability gaps and internal social frictions affect internal and external strategic renewal. *Organization Science*, 20(2), 294–312.

Chatham, C. H., Yerys, B. E., & Munakata, Y. 2012. Why won't you do what I want? The informative failures of children and models. *Cognitive Development*, 27(4), 349–366.

Cohen, J. D., Aston-Jones, G., & Gilzenrat, M. S. 2004. A systems–level perspective on attention and cognitive control. Guided activation, adaptive gating, conflict monitoring,and exploitation versus exploration. Chapter 6. In M. I. Posner (Ed.), *Cognitive Neuroscience of Attention* (pp. 71–90). New York, NY: Guilford Publications.

Cohen, J. D., McClure, S. M., & Yu, A. 2007. Should I stay or should I go? How the human brain manages the trade–off between exploitation and exploration. *Philosophical Transactions of the Royal Society*, 362, 933–942. doi: 10.1098/rstb.2007.2098.

Crossan, M. M., Lane, H. W., & White, R. E. 1999. An organizational learning framework: From intuition to institution. *Academy of Management Review*, 24(3), 522–537.

Daw, N. D., O'Doherty, J. P., Dayan, P., Seymour, B., & Dolan, R. J. 2006. Cortical substrates for exploratory decisions in humans. *Nature*, 441(15), 876–879. doi: 10.1038/nature04766.

Diamond, A. 2013. Executive functions. *Annual Review of Psychology*, 64, 135–168.

Eggers, J. P., & Kaplan, S. 2009. Cognition and renewal: Comparing CEO and organizational effects on incumbent adaptation to technical change. *Organization Science*, 20(2), 461–477.

Gulati, R., & Puranam, P. 2009. Renewal through reorganization: The value of inconsistencies between formal and informal organization. *Organization Science*, 20(2), 422–440. doi: 10.1287/orsc.1090.0421.

Gupta, A. K., Smith, K. G., & Shalley, C. E. 2006. The interplay between exploration and exploitation. *Academy of Management Journal*, 49(4), 693–706.

Hambrick, D. C. 2007. Upper echelons theory: An update. *Academy of Management Review*, 32(2), 334–343.

Hamel, G. 2012. *What matters now: How to win in a world of relentless change, ferocious competition, and unstoppable innovation*. San Francisco, CA: Jossey–Bass.

Hodgkinson, G. P. 1997. Cognitive inertia in a turbulent market: the case of UK residential state agents. *Journal of Management Studies*, 34(6 (Special Issue)), 921–945.

Kirkham, N. Z., Cruess, L., & Diamond, A. 2003. Helping children apply their knowledge to their behavior on a dimension-switching task. *Developmental Science*, 6(5), 449–467.

Kloo, D., & Perner, J. 2005. Disentangling dimensions in the dimensional change card-sorting task. *Developmental Science*, 8(1), 44–56.

Kwee, Z., Van Den Bosch, F. A., & Volberda, H. W. 2011. The influence of top management team's corporate governance orientation on strategic renewal trajectories: a longitudinal analysis of Royal Dutch Shell plc, 1907–2004. *Journal of Management Studies*, 48(5), 984–1014.

Laureiro-Martinez, D. 2014. Cognitive control capabilities, routinization propensity, and decision–making performance. *Organization Science*, 25(4), 1111–1133.

Laureiro-Martínez, D. 2017. How do managers really think? Using think aloud and fMRI to take a closer look at managerial cognition. In G. Hodgkinson, K. J. Sund, & C. Galavan (Eds.), *Methodological Challenges and Advances in Managerial and Organizational Cognition* (pp. 279–314). Bradford, UK: Emerald.

Laureiro-Martinez, D., & Brusoni, S. 2017. Cognitive flexibility and decision–making. Manuscript in preparation.

Laureiro-Martinez, D., & Brusoni, S. 2018. Cognitive flexibility and adaptive decision–making: Evidence from a laboratory study of expert decision–makers. *Strategic Management Journal*, 39, 1031–1058. doi: 10.1002/smj.2774.

Laureiro-Martínez, D., Brusoni, S., & Zollo, M. 2010. The neuroscientific foundations of the exploration–exploitation dilemma. Journal of Neuroscience, Psychology, and Economics, 3(2), 95–115.

Laureiro-Martínez, D., Brusoni, S., Canessa, N., & Zollo, M. 2014. Understanding the exploration-exploitation dilemma: An fMRI study of attention control and decision-making performance. *Strategic Management Journal*, 36(3): 319–338.

Laureiro-Martínez, D., Brusoni, S., & Canessa, N. (2015a). Cognition and Emotions in Exploration: A Deeper Look Into the Microfoundations of Strategic Change. In *Academy of Management Proceedings* (Vol. 2015, No. 1, p. 14079). Briarcliff Manor, NY: Academy of Management.

Laureiro–Martínez, D., Brusoni, S., Canessa, N., & Zollo, M. 2015b. Understanding the exploration–exploitation dilemma: An fMRI study of attention control and decision-making performance. *Strategic Management Journal*, 36(3), 319–338.

Laureiro–Martínez, D., Venkatraman, V., Cappa, S., Zollo, M., & Brusoni, S. 2015c. Cognitive neurosciences and strategic management: Challenges and opportunities in tying the knot. In *Cognition and Strategy (Advances in Strategic Management, Volume 32)* (pp. 351–370). Bradford, UK: Emerald Group Publishing Limited.

Levinthal, D., & Rerup, C. 2006. Crossing an apparent chasm: Bridging mindful and less–mindful perspectives on organizational learning. *Organization Science*, 17(4), 502–513.

Loring, D. W., & Meador, K. J. 1999. *INS Dictionary of Neuropsychology.* Oxford, UK: Oxford University Press.

March, J. G. 1991. Exploration and exploitation in organizational learning. *Organization Science*, 2(1), 71–87.

March, J. G., & Simon, H. A. 1958. *Organizations.* New York, NY: Wiley.

Miller, E. K., & Cohen, J. D. 2001. An integrative theory of prefrontal cortex function. *Annual Review of Neuroscience*, 24, 167–202.

Mom, T. J. M., Van Den Bosch, F. A. J., & Volberda, H. W. 2007. Investigating managers' exploration and exploitation activities: The influence of top–down, bottom–up, and horizontal knowledge inflows. *Journal of Management Studies*, 44(6), 910–931.

Muraven, M., Tice, D. M., & Baumeister, R. F. 1998. Self–control as limited resource: Regulatory depletion patterns. *Journal of Personality and Social Psychology*, 74, 774–789.

Narayanan, V., Yang, Y., & Zahra, S. A. 2009. Corporate venturing and value creation: A review and proposed framework. *Research Policy*, 38(1), 58–76.

Ocasio, W. 1997. Towards an attention–based view of the firm. *Strategic Management Journal*, 18(Summer Special Issue), 187–206.

Ocasio, W. 2011. Attention to attention. *Organization Science*, 22(5), 1286–1296. doi: 10.1287/orsc.1100.0602.

Puranam, P., Singh, H., & Chaudhuri, S. 2009. Integrating acquired capabilities: When structural integration is (un) necessary. *Organization Science*, 20(2), 313–328.

Raisch, S., & Birkinshaw, J. 2008. Organizational ambidexterity: Antecedents, outcomes, and moderators. *Journal of Management*, 34(3), 375–409. doi: 10.1177/0149206308316058.

Reast, J., Lindgreen, A., Vanhamme, J., & Maon, F. 2010. The Manchester super casino: Experience and learning in a cross–sector social partnership. *Journal of Business Ethics*, 94, 197–218.

Salvato, C. 2009. Capabilities unveiled: The role of ordinary activities in the evolution of product development processes. *Organization Science*, 20(2), 384–409.

Tripsas, M. 2009. Technology, identity, and inertia through the lens of "The Digital Photography Company". *Organization Science*, 20(2), 441–460.

Tripsas, M., & Gavetti, G. 2000. Capabilities, cognition and inertia: Evidence from digital imaging. *Strategic Management Journal*, 21, 1147–1161.

Tuncdogan, A., Acar, O. A., & Stam, D. 2017. Individual differences as antecedents of leader behavior: Towards an understanding of multi–level outcomes. *The Leadership Quarterly*, 28(1), 40–64.

Tuncdogan, A., Van Den Bosch, F., & Volberda, H. 2015. Regulatory focus as a psychological micro–foundation of leaders' exploration and exploitation activities. *The Leadership Quarterly*, 26(5), 838–850.

Volberda, H. W., Baden-Fuller, C., & Van Den Bosch, F. A. 2001a. Mastering strategic renewal: Mobilising renewal journeys in multi–unit firms. *Long Range Planning*, 34(2), 159–178.

Volberda, H. W., & Lewin, A. Y. 2003. Co-evolutionary dynamics within and between firms: From evolution to co-evolution. *Journal of Management Studies*, 40(8), 2111–2136.

Volberda, H. W., Van Den Bosch, F. A., Flier, B., & Gedajlovic, E. R. 2001b. Following the herd or not?: Patterns of renewal in the Netherlands and the UK. *Long Range Planning*, 34(2), 209–229.

Vuori, T. O., & Huy, Q. N. 2016. Distributed attention and shared emotions in the innovation process: How Nokia lost the smartphone battle. *Administrative Science Quarterly*, 61(1), 9–51.

Weick, K. E., & Sutcliffe, K. M. 2006. Mindfulness and the quality of organizational attention. *Organization Science*, 17(4), 514–524. doi: 10.1287/orsc.1060.0196.

Part 4

Strategic renewal beyond organizational and national boundaries

11 Strategic renewal through mergers and acquisitions

The role of ambidexterity

Olimpia Meglio and Kathleen Marshall Park

Introduction*

In an increasingly complex and globalized world, long-term survival requires companies to continually respond to changing conditions. Strategic renewal has gained momentum as a topic of interest among strategic management scholars by capturing a broad array of the processes of strategic change (Agarwal & Helfat, 2009). The term "strategic renewal" generally refers to the activities a firm undertakes to alter its path dependence—a requisite but not entirely irrevocable reliance on what has happened previously—following two alternative forms: selection or adaptation (Volberda, Baden-Fuller, & van den Bosch, 2001). The selection perspective sees strategic renewal as highly restricted by resource endowment and structural inertia. That is, successful firms focus on strengthening and exploiting their existing core competencies. By contrast, the adaptation perspective suggests that firms overcome their rigidities by concurrently exploring and exploiting their resources and capabilities (Volberda et al., 2001), that is, by relying on organizational ambidexterity (Lavie, Stettner, & Tushman, 2010; Simsek, Heavey, Veiga, & Souder, 2009). We embrace the adaptation perspective and investigate strategic renewal through mergers and acquisitions (also referred to as M&As or simply as acquisitions) and the role of organizational ambidexterity in the acquisitions process.

Mergers and acquisitions have demonstrably served as mechanisms for multiple strategic objectives, from pursuing growth to enabling innovation, from achieving synergies to entering new markets. Despite ambiguous evidence about their success (King, Dalton, Daily, & Covin, 2004; Risberg & Meglio, 2012), figures show a cyclical growth of acquisitions in frequency and volume (Park & Gould, 2017). The acquisitions momentum can arguably be attributed to M&A crucially serving as instruments of strategic renewal (Agarwal & Helfat, 2009), as they constitute a means for resources and capabilities reconfiguration (Capron & Mitchell, 2009). Such reconfiguration relies primarily on the exploration and exploitation of resources and capabilities, which in turn leads into the role of ambidexterity in enhancing solutions specifically in post-merger or post-acquisition integration. The study of ambidexterity in the post-acquisition phase represents a recent addition to the literature (Meglio, King, & Risberg, 2015), enhancing understanding of acquisitions in a process as well as a strategic renewal approach. Despite the demonstrated and enduring popularity of M&A, scant literature to date analyzes mergers and acquisitions in the light of strategic renewal (Capron & Mitchell, 2009) and ambidexterity (Meglio et al., 2015) combined.

In this chapter we therefore discuss how strategic renewal can occur through mergers and acquisitions and how ambidexterity contributes to firms successfully reconfiguring resources and capabilities during post-acquisition integration. To achieve this aim we first discuss traditional notions of relatedness and fit, and their applications in integration typologies. We next advance the notions of capability gaps and common ground to better analyze acquisitions as implements of strategic renewal. Then, we apply the concept of ambidexterity as a means to achieve resources and capabilities reconfiguration during the integration process. Finally, we propose a typology of integration demands and ambidexterity solutions at different levels of analysis. We discuss limitations and implications for research and practice in conclusion.

Mergers and acquisitions: Relatedness, fit, and integration typologies

Acquisitions represent an enduring theme in the strategic management literature (Jemison & Sitkin, 1986). M&A have been prominent in strategy—and before that in economics and finance—for over a century. The inherent complexity of acquisitions has prompted scholars to develop typologies of acquisitions, primarily for research purposes, but also to draw more effective managerial implications and help practitioners in both the decision-making and integration processes. Different classifications have been developed over time; for example, one distinguishes between related and unrelated mergers and acquisitions (see Larsson, 1990 for a critical reflection on the Federal Trade Commission classification).

The degree of relatedness is a longstanding construct in M&A research and has been extensively employed in many studies investigating the relationship between acquisition occurrence and post-acquisition performance (e.g., Datta, 1991). Although the relatedness-performance research stream has been substantial, it has produced often ambiguous and inconclusive results (see King et al., 2004 for a meta-analysis).

High degrees of relatedness between the acquiring and target firms are generally associated with high potential synergies (Carow, Heron, & Saxton, 2004), but high relatedness could in turn require a longer time for the acquisition implementation, particularly in the presence of organizational turmoil. Such turmoil becomes especially likely if achieving cost savings—and reaping synergistic benefits—requires the elimination of redundancies and downsizing of the workforce. For some types of cost savings, the considerations are likely to be similar for either unrelated or related acquisitions. For example, a merged firm will only need one chief financial officer. Meanwhile, differences exist in how to improve revenues. Unrelated targets have less interdependence, allowing for lower levels of integration and simplified planning (Coff, 2002). In contrast, related acquisitions derive value from coordinating inter-dependencies, integrating target resources, and divesting excess capacity (Barkema & Schijven, 2008). To sum up, relatedness can identify potential benefits during the pre-acquisition stage and anticipate integrative demands in the post-acquisition one.

Over time, parallel to the blurring of boundaries among industries, the differentiation of relatedness and unrelatedness has lost meaning. That is, when scholars analyze acquisitions as a means of reconfiguring strategic resources and capabilities, whether within or between traditional industry groupings or within or across functions, the categorization of acquisitions according to relatedness loses explanatory power and meaningfulness. The concept of relatedness has been progressively replaced by the notion of fit—strategic, organizational, or cultural. Fit accounts for benefits arising from both overlapping and complementary resources, thereby addressing a broader variety of intercorporate combinations. For instance, recent research suggests that combinations of firms with orthogonal, complementary, or simply in essence dissimilar strengths and weaknesses are the types of combinations most likely to create value (Harrison, Hitt, Hoskisson, & Ireland,1991; King et al., 2004; King, Slotegraaf, & Kesner, 2008). Strategic acquisitions with juxtaposed resources may experience fewer difficulties in integration than acquisitions with overlapping resources, which can require a more complex integration. To sum up, the notion of fit provides a more nuanced understanding of potential advantages accruing in a deal and opens up a broader spectrum of integrative solutions.

In addition to classic notions of relatedness and contemporary comprehensions of fit, post-acquisition integration in general has been an enduring theme in the M&A literature. Since the pivotal article by Jemison and Sitkin (1986), management scholars have increasingly recognized that integration processes contribute to creating value from acquisitions. A plethora of studies have extensively investigated post-acquisition integration processes. Some studies have focused their attention on single integration issues such as the level of integration (Shrivastava, 1986), the degree of integration (Pablo, 1994), or the type of integration such as task and human (Birkinshaw, 1999). Meanwhile other studies have aimed at developing integration typologies. These typologies have attempted to capture both the variety of acquisitions and the array of integrative techniques, sometimes by oversimplifying post-acquisition issues, tensions, and demands. Among the initial typologies, the work of Haspeslagh and Jemison (1991) has emerged as particularly prominent and enduring. Building on foundations of strategic interdependence and organizational autonomy, Haspeslagh and Jemison (1991) identify four approaches acquiring companies can follow in integrating value-creating acquisitions. The Haspeslagh and Jemison (1991) and ensuing typologies (see for instance Nahavandi & Malekzadeh, 1993; Napier, 1989; Puranam & Srikanth, 2007) are all organized around dual dimensions addressing the degree of similarity/relatedness between the merging companies and the degree of integration required.

While these typologies have garnered much attention from scholars for their simplicity, over time dissatisfaction has arisen with the breadth and depth of insights thereby available. For instance, Angwin and Meadows (2015) critically assess methodological and practical concerns affecting existing typologies. From a methodological standpoint, they raise concerns regarding the accuracy of differentiation of extant typology dimensions (Angwin & Meadows, 2015). While present integration typologies tend to polarize autonomy/preservation and symbiosis/amalgamation as mutually exclusive, empirical results show that preservation and symbiosis can coexist in integrating a target (Zaheer, Castañer, & Souder, 2013). Such coexistence may occur due to the strategic fit between the merging companies involving either resource similarity or complementarity (Larsson, 1990). Similarity and complementarity—although not incompatible for strategic fit—require different integrative solutions, depending on the business unit/function. These concerns have practical implications, as single integration typologies can scarcely capture the actual assortment of solutions that acquiring firms rely upon in practice while integrating target firms. In his examination of acquisitions involving pharmaceutical and biotechnology companies, Schweizer (2005) finds it essential to combine integration typologies in a hybrid approach, resolving conflicting tensions and time frames within different functions and units of the merging companies. This requisite hybridization proposes the advantages of further examining factors influencing process decision-making and implementation.

Mergers and acquisitions as tools for strategic renewal: Capability gaps and common ground

A way to address the limitations described above is to offer an extended process view of acquisitions that does justice to the complexities of these deals in the stages both preceding and following the legal acquisition date. Existing notions of relatedness and fit and also extant integration typologies are typically too coarse-grained to capture the interrelationships between the merging companies before the deals, as well as the integrative solutions required in the aftermath. To further an understanding of acquisitions and to build on current conceptualizations prioritizing resource centrality and interdependencies (e.g., Agarwal & Helfat, 2009), we examine acquisitions as tools for reconfiguring resources and capabilities toward achieving strategic renewal. As previously mentioned, strategic renewal has been seen as the activities a firm undertakes to alter its path by concurrently pursuing exploration and exploitation (Volberda et al., 2001). Strategic management scholars refer to strategic renewal as the refurbishment or replacement of organizational attributes to enhance longer-term organizational success (Agarwal & Helfat, 2009). Therefore, by associating acquisitions with strategic renewal, we underscore the impact of acquisitions in revitalizing resources and capabilities ranging from new technology and product development to business process innovations (Capron & Mitchell, 2009; Puranam, Singh, & Chaudhuri, 2009). This view has been studied from the 1990s onward. Scholars have focused on, for instance, (1) resource redeployment following horizontal acquisitions in Europe and North America (Capron, 2013); (2) redeployment of brands, sales forces, and general marketing management expertise (Capron & Hulland, 1999); and (3) asset divestiture following horizontal acquisitions (Capron, Mitchell, & Swaminathan, 2001).

Taken together, these studies reveal that resource redeployment and post-acquisition integration processes have been studied mainly in horizontal acquisitions in US and European companies. In addition to the paucity of geographic coverage and the relative lack of attention to types of acquisitions other than horizontal/related, there have been temporal and complexity lacunae in the resource-grounded conceptualizations of acquisitions and the resultant decisions for specific modes of internal or external development.

Capron and Mitchell (2009) crucially broadened the domain of resource-related analysis in the acquisitions context in two ways: by including the pre-acquisition phase and by replacing the idea of bundles of resources and capabilities with that of capability gaps. Following Helfat and Lieberman (2002), Capron and Mitchell (2009) take as a starting point the postulated set of resources and capabilities necessary for a firm to compete in a given context. The capability gaps—between a firm and its competitors and between what the firm needs and what it presently has toward competing effectively—influence the choice between internal and external sourcing modes. Even more specifically, the knowledge of the capability gap becomes central in sourcing decisions involving choosing among building, borrowing, or buying (Capron & Mitchell, 2012).

According to Capron and Mitchell (2009), sourcing decisions should take into account the extent of capability gaps measured in terms of both closeness–distance and strength–weakness. A firm faces a small gap when its current capabilities are similar to needed capabilities in terms of relevant technical and organizational characteristics (capability closeness) and when the firm already possesses a strong position in the targeted capability area relative to its competitors (capability strength). Firms face their most serious capability gaps when their existing capabilities are dissimilar from needed capabilities (capability distance) and when a firm has only limited strengths in the targeted capability area relative to competitors (capability weakness). Sometimes capability closeness and weakness can coexist. For instance, an acquiring firm's desired capabilities may derive from common technology and organizational processes with the target firm, yet the combined firm may still not have an effective set of capabilities relative to the competition within its industry niche.

While the capability gaps concept enables us to better understand acquisition choices as relating to various sourcing options, a deeper analysis is necessary to understand how the differences between acquiring and target firm resources and capabilities influence post-acquisition integration. We believe that common ground—knowledge both shared and known to be shared—offers an additional, illuminative contextual factor.

The notion of common ground dates back to Clark (1996), who provided an everyday example in how the seemingly simple action of two people talking to each other creates a surprising number of coordination demands. The demands depend in part on whether we are talking with people whom we already know or have just met. Whether we are talking with newer or more longstanding contacts, we have to follow what the other person is saying while preparing our reaction and concurrently managing taking turns speaking. In many ways, a conversation thus becomes a microcosm of the larger concepts of coordination and common ground. The common ground concept has been used to ease post-merger integration (Bauer, Matzler, & Wolf, 2016; Puranam et al., 2009) and to investigate whether shared knowledge and beliefs between the acquiring and target sides may trigger a self-coordination among employees. The existence of common ground between merging firms reduces the need for coercive integration and instead enables a successful intermeshing by allowing interdependent actors to adjust their actions appropriately to each other (Puranam et al., 2009).

Taking into account both capability gaps and common ground furthers our understanding of the relationship between merging companies and resulting integrative solutions. We propose that ambidexterity represents a useful lens for elucidating how integrative demands—at the organizational, group, and individual levels of analysis—can be effectively handled. By explicating and applying the ambidexterity construct in M&A, we dig deeper into and offer a more fine-grained view of the post-acquisition integration process.

Postacquisition integration and ambidexterity

Since the seminal article by Duncan (1976), the metaphor of organizations being equally adept at using both hands—referred to as organizational ambidexterity—has been employed to reconcile competing organizational demands (Lavie et al., 2010; Simsek et al., 2009) in addressing seemingly opposite yet coexisting imperatives. The ambidexterity perspective has been applied to dualities such as exploitation and exploration (March, 1991), incremental and discontinuous innovation (Tushman & O'Reilly, 1996), alignment and adaptability (Gibson & Birkinshaw, 2004), and market and political capabilities (Li, Peng, & Macaulay, 2013). Due to the versatility of the concept (Birkinshaw & Gupta, 2013), it has been suggested that ambidexterity has acquired the status of a new paradigm—a concept within which theories can be formulated and tested (Raisch & Birkinshaw, 2008). Following this tradition, Meglio and colleagues (2015), have recently used ambidexterity to study trade-offs between task and human integration in acquisitions, as these two types of integration often present conflicting goals and time frames.

In the ambidexterity literature, solutions for balancing competing demands take the form of structural, temporal, or contextual ambidexterity

(O'Reilly & Tushman, 2013). *Structural* ambidexterity requires physically separating units with different orientations to different locations (Benner & Tushman, 2003). *Temporal* ambidexterity suggests that conflicting goals can take place within the same business unit, but only in a cyclical or sequential manner (Siggelkow & Levinthal, 2003). The first solution, if applied to a post-acquisition context, resembles the choice of separation/hands-off, with no integration taking place between the merging companies. The second one can be conceived as an intermediate solution within a gradual approach to the post-acquisition integration. Both solutions describe the integration approach at the organizational level of analysis. Therefore, they do not provide any real advancement to our understanding of how to reconcile task and human integration during the post-merger integration. To achieve this aim, we need to introduce the idea that competing demands are orthogonal, or capable of co-existing. Under such circumstances, tensions can be best addressed by *contextual* ambidexterity, which involves simultaneously pursuing conflicting demands using organizational processes and managerial intervention to achieve the needed balance (Gibson & Birkinshaw, 2004). Contextual ambidexterity refers to the routines and processes used by organizations to mobilize, coordinate, and integrate dispersed exploratory and exploitative efforts and to allocate, reallocate, combine, and recombine resources and assets (Jansen, Tempelaar, van den Bosch, & Volberda, 2009).

Previous studies suggest that the individual level of analysis is essential to combining exploration- and exploitation-related activities within a certain period of time (see Gibson & Birkinshaw, 2004). We contend that this level of analysis is important also in the post-acquisition context to enable hybrid integration approaches. During the integration process, this is primarily achieved through integration leadership and integration mechanisms that help to concurrently achieve task and human integration (Meglio et al., 2015). As such it involves the organizational, the group, and the individual levels of analysis. In the next subsection we analyze the contribution of ambidexterity at different levels of analysis.

Ambidexterity and integrative solutions: The role of integration leader

Here we assess the integration process in a manner addressing the full spectrum of integrative choices, moving beyond the simplistic dichotomy between absorption and preservation. We build our analysis by incorporating the notions of capability gaps and common ground between the merging companies as discussed above.

In the case of broad capability gaps, the acquiring firm neither possesses nor is familiar with the resources and capabilities of the target firm. Maintaining separation between units or functions of the acquiring and target firms preserves tacit and embedded knowledge and minimizes disruptions. In these situations, separation offers a means of sustaining invaluable knowledge resources already entrenched in people and routines. Then lower levels of intervention—that is, at the group or individual levels—are not required.

In the case of small capability gaps, the range of prospective integration solution broadens. In such circumstances, it is important to introduce the notion of common ground. If substantial common ground exists between acquiring and target firm personnel at the time of the acquisition, personnel from the merging firms will more easily adjust to each other through informal mechanisms. It may then suffice to coordinate interdependences between the merging firms, obviating the need for intensive structural integration and thereby avoiding the attendant disruptions. In cases of weaker common ground, structural integration becomes a more effective solution. This integration choice can be accomplished through contextual ambidexterity relying on integration leadership and mechanisms (Meglio et al., 2015).

Integration leaders are key figures in the acquisitions process and experience. In guiding and coordinating the integration process, integration leaders play multiple shifting roles. As organizational mavericks, they promote a cooperative atmosphere; as transformational leaders, they sustain commitment; as organizational buffers, they alleviate pressures on integration teams; and as network facilitators, they bond previously separate personnel and divisions (Pisano & Dagnino, 2008). According to Mom and colleagues (2009) ambidextrous managers present three common traits: they host contradictions (Tushman & O'Reilly, 1996); they are multi-taskers (Birkinshaw & Gibson, 2004); and they continually refine and renew their knowledge, skills, and expertise (Floyd & Lane, 2000).

That integration leaders possess these traits has been documented in the literature. For example, Teerikangas and colleagues (2011) present empirical findings from several cross-border acquisitions on the tasks performed by integration managers. They find that integration managers affect acquisition performance by finding specific ways of capturing additional value while also avoiding value-leakage. The ability to balance the competing demands of simultaneously actively enhancing value and avoiding value loss is in line with the description of ambidextrous managers as embodying contradictions (Mom, van den Bosch, & Volberda, 2009). Moreover, Mom and colleagues (2009) find that ambidextrous managers are particularly effective at performing informal and formal liaison roles, which are extremely relevant and valuable in an ambiguous context such as a post-acquisition phase. This is supported by Nemanich and Vera (2009), who investigate integration leaders as transformational leaders and identify psychological safety, openness to diverse opinions, and participation in decision-making as essential to fostering value-adding ambidexterity during post-acquisition integration. Integration leaders rely on a repertoire of mechanisms to promote contextual ambidexterity in acquisitions, as further described below.

Ambidexterity and integrative solutions: The role of integration mechanisms

The idea of investigating the integration process as a problem of achieving coordination between the merging firms at different levels—organizational, group, and individual—and requiring different integration mechanisms, dates back to Larsson (1990). Integration mechanisms have been described as the micro-mechanisms for balancing tensions between task and human integration (Meglio et al., 2015). Considering integration mechanisms enables expanding on the solutions between full autonomy and tight coordination, and, in so doing, facilitates exploring the impact of lower-level decisions on human and task integration. Integration mechanisms provide the tools to achieve acquisition goals, and each mechanism largely focuses on either exploration or exploitation. While Meglio and colleagues (2015) focus on the contribution of integration mechanisms to task or human integration, here we discuss integration mechanisms in connection with capability gaps and common ground. Below, we explicate the following mechanisms: restructuring, formal planning, management information system, socialization, mutual consideration, transition teams, and HR management systems.

Restructuring focuses either on eliminating redundancies arising from similar, overlapping assets and capabilities or improving coordination between complementary assets and capabilities. This mechanism is particularly suited for when capability gaps are small and tight structural integration is required. In contrast, in the presence of common ground, a focus on soft integration mechanisms is vital to minimize disruptive effects arising from uncertainty among employees regarding work security or career prospects, disruption of social connections, and the need to unlearn old procedures and learn new ones.

Formal planning is the essence of the integration process as it sets priorities, allocates resources, and defines time intervals to attain goals. In so doing, formal planning allows for tracking integration progress. Like restructuring, this mechanism is particularly effective when capability gaps are small. In the presence of common ground, an excessive emphasis on operational and financial milestones can contribute to employee stress and hinder human integration. These hindrances can be mitigated by integration leaders having clear rationales for change and quickly and effectively communicating these rationales to affected employees (Ullrich & van Dick, 2007).

The integration of *management information systems* (MIS) focuses on improving the coordination of operations through the standardization of budget and data systems. Again this is particularly suitable in cases of small capability gaps, when the need for structural integration is high. Focusing excessively on operations and updating work routines is associated with employee dissatisfaction (Ullrich & van Dick, 2007), especially in the presence of common ground.

Coordinated by an integration manager, *transition teams* are typically responsible for single integrative goals. These teams generally include people from both the acquiring and target firms to bring multiple perspectives and experiences toward the achievement of the designated goals. Such teams have been found to be particularly effective when capability gaps are broad. Transition teams resolve competing demands by providing a social context for coordinating post-acquisition integration activities (Gilson, Mathieu, Shalley, & Ruddy, 2005). The integration leader/manager and the supporting integration transition teams enable contextual ambidexterity during integration.

Socialization aims at forging a shared organizational identity, facilitating trust in relationships, and minimizing conflicts between personnel from the acquiring and target sides of the merging firms (Björkman, Stahl, & Vaara, 2007). Socialization could take the form of cultural seminars for inculcating organizational learning and knowledge transfer (Bresman, Birkinshaw, & Nobel, 1999; Kaše, Paauwe, & Zupan, 2009; Prieto & Pilar Pérez Santana, 2012), personnel rotation, or membership in cross-unit teams, task forces, and committees (Björkman et al., 2007). Taken together, these solutions are particularly valuable when capability gaps are broad yet resources and capabilities are complementary between the acquiring and target firms. Likewise *mutual consideration* aims to minimize conflict and resistance by focusing employees on tasks rather than politics by using intercultural learning seminars (Vaara, 2003) and communication techniques (Bastien, 1987) for promoting fundamental sociocultural integration (Stahl et al., 2013).

Negative employee reactions to uncertainty created by acquisition announcements and integration reinforce the need to carefully consider human resource (HR) management. HR management comprises a comprehensive set of tools to deal with personnel issues such as career planning, retaining talented people, and instilling new competences through training programs (see Zhang et al., 2015). Patel and colleagues (2013) find that competing demands framed as alignment and adaptability can be addressed through HR management approaches, fostering multilateral support and trust.

HR management systems are crucial to handle the seemingly inevitable personnel turnover during acquisitions (Krug, 2003; Krug, Wright, & Kroll, 2014) and avoid losing associated employee knowledge and expertise (Ranft, 2006; Ranft & Lord, 2002). Aguilera and Dencker (2004) suggest that HR managers take part in the planning and due diligence stages of acquisitions to identify key personnel for retention. Weber and Tarba (2010) highlight the importance of training and development during acquisition integration to renew employee competencies and compensate for employee turnover. An increase in turnover can signal a negative ambiance surrounding the acquisition; hence, an emphasis on socialization during the integration period can help to reduce personnel turnover (Antila, 2006).

Along with the introduction of formal integration mechanisms in the merging firms, as described above, informal organizational processes also shape the integration process. These informal processes—for instance, impromptu conversations and team building interactions—aid knowledge transfer through the creation of additional communication channels, group identity, and common ground (Puranam et al., 2009). Integration leaders can use both formal and informal approaches through contextual ambidexterity, relying on selected mechanisms to address competing demands at the individual, group (for instance, a team of scientists in a R&D lab), and organizational levels. Integration instruments, formal as well as informal, represent the micro-mechanisms balancing ambidextrous exploitation and exploration—an essential dualism in the post-merger/post-acquisition integration of the combining firms.

Discussion

In our explication of strategic renewal through contextual ambidexterity in the implementation of mergers and acquisitions, we have contributed to the emergent conjunction of research on ambidexterity, acquisitions, and sustaining and revitalizing strategic momentum. In further advancing understanding of this conjunction, researchers could pursue an empirical examination of single deals and also deals in the context of an acquisitions program. The evolving research on programmatic acquisitions (e.g., Laamanen & Keil, 2008) suggests that different integration solutions could become salient in serial acquisitions in contrast to more temporally distinct and isolated single deals. Integration solutions are intrinsically dynamic and can be prospectively envisioned as positioned along a continuum from rare and single deals to rapidly simultaneously or sequentially occurring multiple deals. In addition, future research could develop propositions from inductive theorizing and further conceptualization of the ambidexterity and renewal phenomena, and could also formulate and investigate hypotheses using an empirically deductive approach from nascent models.

Strategic renewal has gained increasing scholarly attention accompanied by a heightened awareness of acquisition as a tool for reconfiguring and revitalizing resources and capabilities. Extant research supports the idea that firms may overcome their inertia and assure competitive advantage over time by acquiring bundles of resources and capabilities addressing the previously described capability gaps (Capron & Mitchell, 2012). However, as attested by considerable research previously cited, post-acquisition integration vitally contributes to the accrual of benefits from acquisitions. Conversely, anticipated benefits can be partially or totally offset by ineffective integration processes—which can be minimized or avoided through a theoretically salient and pragmatically appealing reliance on the formal and informal mechanisms of contextual ambidexterity during post-acquisition integration.

The M&A literature abounds with integration models simplifying dilemmas and solutions by streamlining the relationship between the merging companies into two overarching concepts such as strategic and organizational fit. These models, although seemingly elegantly parsimonious, have ultimately proven too coarse-grained to capture the actual range of integration demands and decisions. In sum, effective integrative solutions are far from ideal types and instead require hybrid approaches. We have noted the evolution in acquisition and integration typologies and classification systems, building from the initial process approaches in the early 1990s to the increasingly nuanced understandings embracing the strategic complexity intrinsic to single or serial acquisitions. We have here further propelled the idea that acquisitions should be classified according to the capability gaps between the merging companies and the existence of common ground. We have also suggested that contextual ambidexterity represents a key capability to resolve competing demands and more effectively integrate the merging firms. Integration leaders and integration mechanisms are the building blocks of contextual ambidexterity toward addressing integrative demands within the veridical complexities of mergers and acquisitions from inception through implementation.

Implications for research

The application of ambidexterity in the acquisitions context is still new and promises additional developments at the theoretical level. The considerations we have expressed can be further advanced into a conceptual model and propositions relevant to different industries and geographical contexts. While ambidexterity is intuitively seen as crucial in the high technology and energy industries, it would be interesting to investigate how it applies to mature industries such as automotive or steel, both heavily involved in huge consolidation processes, or in emerging markets, which are still under-researched. Another important development would be to further review and refine acquisition typologies based on the notions of capability gaps, integrative solutions, and common ground. How common ground interacts with integration imperatives deserves deeper theoretical and empirical exploration.

From a methodological standpoint we advocate the investigation of acquisitions phenomena contemporaneously and longitudinally—that is, in real time and over time. These temporal dimensions are especially crucial in the study of acquisition programs involving multiple, sometimes overlapping, deals with transformative implications for the acquiring firm. The contribution of ambidexterity—and how integration leaders influence deals through the use of integration mechanisms—could emerge from an integration process investigation. An additional line of inquiry, again in the context of acquisition programs, could be to detect whether an integration capability benefit arises from an ambidextrous approach.

Implications for practice

Our analysis also conveys critical managerial implications. It signals the value of appointing an integration manager or team of managers early in the integration process to ensure as much as possible effective interventions and communications into the intercultural dynamics, interactions, and desired degrees of assimilation or separation between the merging firms. Moreover, our analysis indicates the transformative leadership skill sets needed for those recruited as integration managers for performing the tasks with which they are charged.

In closing, we have affirmed acquisitions as an essential tool for strategic renewal for resource reconfiguration and revitalization between the acquiring and target firms. We have further contributed by explicating that for navigating the inherent complexities in acquisitions, and in particular in the post-acquisition integration, contextual ambidexterity and its pillars—integration leaders and mechanisms—are crucial to ensuring effective solutions. We position our framework as part of an emergent mandate for future research further exploring the interplay of ambidexterity and strategic renewal in the mergers and acquisitions context.

Note

* This chapter is the outcome of an intense collaboration between the authors and builds upon and extends Meglio and colleagues' (2015) previous work on contextual ambidexterity and mergers and acquisitions. The order of authors therefore reflects the actual contribution to the ideation and writing of the chapter.

References

Agarwal, R., & Helfat, C. E. 2009. Strategic renewal of organizations. *Organization Science*, 20(2): 281–293.

Aguilera, R. V., & Dencker, J. C. 2004. The role of human resource management in cross-border mergers and acquisitions. *International Journal of Human Resource Management*, 15(8): 1355–1370.

Angwin, D. N., & Meadows, M. 2015. New integration strategies for post-acquisition management. *Long Range Planning*, 48(4): 235–251.

Antila, E. M. 2006. The role of HR managers in international mergers and acquisitions: A multiple case study. *International Journal of Human Resource Management*, 17(6): 999–1020.

Barkema, H. G., & Schijven, M. 2008. Toward unlocking the full potential of acquisitions: The role of organizational restructuring. *Academy of Management Journal*, 51(4): 696–722.

Bastien, D. T. 1987. Common patterns of behavior and communication in corporate mergers and acquisitions. *Human Resource Management*, 26(1): 17–33.

Bauer, F., Matzler, K., & Wolf, S. 2016. M&A and innovation: The role of integration and cultural differences—A central European targets perspective. *International Business Review*, 25(1, Part A): 76–86.

Benner, M. J., & Tushman, M. L. 2003. Exploitation, exploration, and process management: The productivity dilemma revisited. *Academy of Management Review*, 28(2): 238–256.

Birkinshaw, J. 1999. Acquiring intellect: Managing the integration of knowledge-intensive acquisitions. *Business Horizons*, 42(3): 33–40.

Birkinshaw, J., & Gibson, C. 2004. Building ambidexterity into an organization. *MIT Sloan Management Review*, 45(4): 47–55.

Birkinshaw, J., & Gupta, K. 2013. Clarifying the distinctive contribution of ambidexterity to the field of organization studies. *Academy of Management Perspectives*, 27(4): 287–298.

Björkman, I., Stahl, G. K., & Vaara, E. 2007. Cultural differences and capability transfer in cross-border acquisitions: The mediating roles of capability complementarity, absorptive capacity, and social integration. *Journal of International Business Studies*, 38(4): 658–672.

Bresman, H., Birkinshaw, J., & Nobel, R. 1999. Knowledge transfer in international acquisitions. *Journal of International Business Studies*, 30(3): 439–462.

Capron, L. 2013. Cisco's corporate development portfolio: A blend of building, borrowing and buying. *Strategy & Leadership*, 41(2): 27–30.

Capron, L., & Hulland, J. 1999. Redeployment of brands, sales forces, and general marketing management expertise following horizontal acquisitions: A resource-based view. *Journal of Marketing*, 63(2): 41–54.

Capron, L., & Mitchell, W. 2009. Selection capability: How capability gaps and internal social frictions affect internal and external strategic renewal. *Organization Science*, 20(2): 294–312.

Capron, L., & Mitchell, W. 2012. *Build, Borrow or Buy: Solving the Growth Dilemma*. Boston, MA: Harvard Business Review Press.

Capron, L., Mitchell, W., & Swaminathan, A. 2001. Asset divestiture following horizontal acquisitions: A dynamic view. *Strategic Management Journal*, 22: 817–844.

Carow, K., Heron, R., & Saxton, T. 2004. Do early birds get the returns? An empirical investigation of early-mover advantages in acquisitions. *Strategic Management Journal*, 25(6): 563–585.

Clark, H. 1996. *Using Language*. Cambridge, UK: Cambridge University Press.

Coff, R. W. 2002. Human capital, shared expertise, and the likelihood of impasse in corporate acquisitions. *Journal of Management*, 28(1): 107–128.

Datta, D. K. 1991. Organizational fit and acquisition performance: Effects of postacquisition integration. *Strategic Management Journal*, 12: 281–298.

Duncan, R. B. 1976. The ambidextrous organization: Designing dual structures for innovation. In R. H. Kilmann, L. R. Pondy, & D. P. Slevin (Eds.), *The Management of Organization Design, Volume 1: Strategies and Implementation*: 167–188. New York, NY: North Holland.

Floyd, S. W., & Lane, P. J. 2000. Strategizing throughout the organization: Managing role conflict in strategic renewal. *Academy of Management Review*, 25(1): 154–177.

Gibson, C. B., & Birkinshaw, J. 2004. The antecedents, consequences and mediating role of organizational ambidexterity. *Academy of Management Journal*, 47(2): 209–226.

Gilson, L. L., Mathieu, J. E., Shalley, C. E., & Ruddy, T. M. 2005. Creativity and standardization: Complementary or conflicting drivers of team effectiveness? *Academy of Management Journal*, 48(3): 521–531.

Harrison, J. S., Hitt, M. A., Hoskisson, R. E., & Ireland, R. D. 1991. Synergies and post-acquisition performance: Differences versus similarities in resource allocations. *Journal of Management*, 17(1): 173.

Haspeslagh, P. C., & Jemison, D. B. 1991. *Managing Acquisitions: Creating Value Through Corporate Renewal*. New York, NY: Free Press.

Helfat, C. E., & Lieberman, M. B. 2002. The birth of capabilities: Market entry and the importance of pre-history. *Industrial & Corporate Change*, 11(4): 725–760.

Jansen, J. J. P., Tempelaar, M. P., van den Bosch, F. A. J., & Volberda, H. W. 2009. Structural differentiation and ambidexterity: The mediating role of integration mechanisms. *Organization Science*, 20(4): 797–811.

Jemison, D. B., & Sitkin, S. B. 1986. Corporate acquisitions: A process perspective. *Academy of Management Review*, 11(1): 145–163.

Kaše, R., Paauwe, J., & Zupan, N. 2009. HR practices, interpersonal relations, and intrafirm knowledge transfer in knowledge-intensive firms: A social network perspective. *Human Resource Management*, 48(4): 615–639.

King, D. R., Dalton, D. R., Daily, C. M., & Covin, J. G. 2004. Meta-analyses of post-acquisition performance: Indications of unidentified moderators. *Strategic Management Journal*, 25(2): 187–200.

King, D. R., Slotegraaf, R. J., & Kesner, I. 2008. Performance implications of firm resource interactions in the acquisition of R&D-intensive firms. *Organization Science*, 19(2): 327–340.

Krug, J. A. 2003. Why do they keep leaving? *Harvard Business Review*, 81(2): 14–15.

Krug, J. A., Wright, P., & Kroll, M. 2014. Top management turnover following mergers and acquisitions: Solid research to date but much still to be learned. *Academy of Management Perspectives*, 28: 147–163.

Laamanen, T., & Keil, T. 2008. Performance of serial acquirers: Toward an acquisition program perspective. *Strategic Management Journal*, 29(6): 663–672.

Larsson, R. 1990. *Coordination of Action in Mergers and Acquisitions: Interpretive and Systems Approaches Towards Synergy*. Lund, Sweden: Lund University Press.

Lavie, D., Stettner, U., & Tushman, M. L. 2010. Exploration and exploitation within and across organizations. *Academy of Management Annals*, 4(1): 109–155.

Li, Y., Peng, M. W., & Macaulay, C. D. 2013. Market–political ambidexterity during institutional transitions. *Strategic Organization*, 11(2): 205–213.

March, J. G. 1991. Exploration and exploitation in organizational learning. *Organization Science*, 2(1): 71–87.

Meglio, O., King, D. R., & Risberg, A. 2015. Improving acquisition outcomes with contextual ambidexterity. *Human Resource Management*, 54(S1): s29–s43.

Mom, T. J. M., van den Bosch, F. A. J., & Volberda, H. W. 2009. Understanding variation in managers' ambidexterity: Investigating direct and interaction effects of formal structural and personal coordination mechanisms. *Organization Science*, 20(4): 812–828.

Nahavandi, A., & Malekzadeh, A. R. 1993. Leader style in strategy and organizational performance: An integrative framework. *Journal of Management Studies*, 30(3): 405–425.

Napier, N. K. 1989. Mergers and acquisitions, human resource issues and outcomes: A review and suggested typology. *Journal of Management Studies*, 26: 271–289.

Nemanich, L. A., & Vera, D. 2009. Transformational leadership and ambidexterity in the context of an acquisition. *Leadership Quarterly*, 20(1): 19–33.

O'Reilly, C. A., III, & Tushman, M. L. 2013. Organizational ambidexterity: Past, present and future. *Academy of Management Perspectives*, 27(4): 324–338.

Pablo, A. L. 1994. Determinants of acquisition integration level: A decision-making perspective. *Academy of Management Journal*, 37: 803–836.

Park, K. M., & Gould, A. M. 2017. The overlooked influence of personality, idiosyncrasy and eccentricity in corporate mergers and acquisitions: 120 years and six distinct waves. *Journal of Management History*, 23(1): 7–31.

Patel, P. C., Messersmith, J. G., & Lepak, D. P. 2013. Walking the tightrope: An assessment of the relationship between high-performance work systems and organizational ambidexterity. *Academy of Management Journal*, 56(5): 1420–1442.

Pisano, V., & Dagnino, G. B. 2008. Unpacking the champion of acquisitions: The key figure in the execution of the post-acquisition integration process. In C. L. Cooper &

S. Finkelstein (Eds.), *Advances in Mergers and Acquisitions*, Vol. 7: 51–69: Emerald Group Publishing.

Prieto, I. M., & Pilar Pérez Santana, M. 2012. Building ambidexterity: The role of human resource practices in the performance of firms from Spain. *Human Resource Management*, 51(2): 189–211.

Puranam, P., Singh, H., & Chaudhuri, S. 2009. Integrating acquired capabilities: When structural integration is (un)necessary. *Organization Science*, 20(2): 313–328.

Puranam, P., & Srikanth, K. 2007. What they know vs. what they do: How acquirers leverage technology acquisitions. *Strategic Management Journal*, 28(8): 805–825.

Raisch, S., & Birkinshaw, J. 2008. Organizational ambidexterity: Antecedents, outcomes, and moderators. *Journal of Management*, 34(3): 375–409.

Ranft, A. L. 2006. Knowledge preservation and transfer during post-acquisition integration. *Advances in Mergers and Acquisitions*, 5: 51–67.

Ranft, A. L., & Lord, M. D. 2002. Acquiring new technologies and capabilities: A grounded model of acquisition implementation. *Organization Science*, 13(4): 420–441.

Risberg, A., & Meglio, O. 2012. Merger and acquisition outcomes—Is it meaningful to talk about high failure rates? In Y. Weber (Ed.), *The Handbook of M&A Research*: 147–171. Cheltenham, UK: Edward Elgar.

Schweizer, L. 2005. Organizational integration of acquired biotechnology companies into pharmaceutical companies: The need for a hybrid approach. *Academy of Management Journal*, 48(6): 1051–1074.

Shrivastava, P. 1986. Postmerger integration. *Journal of Business Strategy*, 7(1): 65–76.

Siggelkow, N., & Levinthal, D. A. 2003. Temporarily divide to conquer: Centralized, decentralized, and reintegrated organizational approaches to exploration and adaptation. *Organization Science*, 14(6): 650–669.

Simsek, Z., Heavey, C., Veiga, J. F., & Souder, D. 2009. A typology for aligning organizational ambidexterity's conceptualizations, antecedents and outcomes. *Journal of Management Studies*, 46(5): 864–894.

Stahl, G. K., Angwin, D. N., Very, P., Gomes, E., Weber, Y., Tarba, S. Y., Noorderhaven, N., Benyamini, H., Bouckenooghe, D., Chreim, S., Durand, M., Hassett, M. E., Kokk, G., Mendenhall, M. E., Mirc, N., Miska, C., Park, K. M., Reynolds, N.-S., Rouzies, A., & Sarala, R. M. 2013. Sociocultural integration in mergers and acquisitions: Unresolved paradoxes and directions for future research. *Thunderbird International Business Review*, 55(4): 333–356.

Teerikangas, S., Véry, P., & Pisano, V. 2011. Integration managers' value-capturing roles and acquisition performance. *Human Resource Management*, 50(5): 651–683.

Tushman, M. L., & O'Reilly, C. A., III. 1996. Ambidextrous organizations: Managing evolutionary and revolutionary change. *California Management Review*, 38(4): 8–29.

Ullrich, J., & van Dick, R. 2007. The group psychology of mergers and acquisitions: Lessons from the social identity approach. In C. L. Cooper, & S. Finkelstein (Eds.), *Advances in Mergers and Acquisitions*, Vol. 6: 1–15: Bradford, UK: Emerald Group Publishing.

Vaara, E. 2003. Post-acquisition integration as sensemaking: Glimpses of ambiguity, confusion, hypocrisy, and politicization. *Journal of Management Studies*, 40(4): 859–894.

Volberda, H. W., Baden-Fuller, C., & van den Bosch, F. A. J. 2001. Mastering strategic renewal: Mobilising renewal journeys in multi-unit firms. *Long Range Planning*, 34(2): 159–178.

Weber, Y., & Tarba, S. Y. 2010. Human resource practices and performance of mergers and acquisitions in Israel. *Human Resource Management Review*, 20(3): 203–211.

Zaheer, A., Castañer, X., & Souder, D. 2013. Synergy sources, target autonomy, and integration in acquisitions. *Journal of Management*, 39(3): 604–632.

Zhang, J., Ahammad, M. F., Tarba, S., Cooper, C. L., Glaister, K. W., & Wang, J. 2015. The effect of leadership style on talent retention during merger and acquisition integration: Evidence from China. *International Journal of Human Resource Management*, 26(7): 1021–1050.

12 Developing alliance capability for strategic renewal

Abdelghani Es-Sajjade

Introduction

Alliances are a powerful means to strategic renewal. Nissan's alliance with Renault allowed it to recover from near-bankruptcy, becoming the world's fourth-largest automaker in 2013. Firms have, however, initiated alliances with varying success and much research has therefore been dedicated to explaining differences in alliance performance. An alliance is any independently initiated inter-firm link that involves exchange, sharing, or co-development (Gulati, 1995). This includes joint ventures, R&D or production agreements, marketing or distribution agreements, or technology exchange.

The increase in alliances over the past decades and the consequent growth of complex alliance portfolios has shifted management attention from focusing on individual contracts to adopting a holistic view in order to utilize firm-wide capabilities that are needed to achieve strategic objectives. Strategic renewal is the rationale behind the formation of many alliances, as alliances have been used to regain competitive advantage, improve innovation performance, and increase market share (Brouthers et al., 2015; Hamel, 1991; Mowery et al., 1996). In order to realize strategic renewal through alliances, firms require alliance capability, which is a nebulous phenomenon due to the complexity surrounding its constituents (Callahan & MacKenzie, 1999). Alliance capability is defined as the ability to capture, share, and apply alliance-management knowledge (Heimeriks et al., 2008). Those firms that succeed in developing alliance capability will possess something that is valuable, rare, imperfectly inimitable, non-substitutable, and, to some extent, causally ambiguous (Anand & Khanna, 2000). If alliance capability is this important for strategic renewal, then how can firms develop it?

"Knowing how to do alliances" or "alliance capability" is a higher-order routine that has the potential to improve the performance of the firm's alliance portfolio by integrating accumulated experience and deliberate learning processes (Heimeriks et al., 2007; Kale & Singh, 2007). To understand how firms develop alliance capability for strategic renewal, studies will be discussed on the roles of alliance experience, deliberate learning mechanisms, and organizational learning as a multi-level system (Contractor & Reuer, 2014; Heimeriks, 2009;

Heimeriks et al., 2012; Kale & Singh, 2007; Niesten & Jolink, 2015). Exploring and comparing these theoretical perspectives is important for several reasons. First, knowledge is considered to be the primary antecedent of sustained competitive advantage, which makes knowledge management within and across alliances critical to strategic renewal (Grant, 1996; Kogut & Zander, 1992; Nelson & Winter, 1982; Nonaka, 1994). Second, organizational learning theory focuses on learning processes on different levels within an organization that reveal how individual- and group-level learning within alliances relates to firm-level strategic renewal (Draulans et al., 2003; Huber, 1991; Levitt & March, 1988; Vera & Crossan, 2003). Third, these perspectives are useful as they reveal how knowledge resources underlying alliance capability need to be integrated, deployed, and reconfigured for the creation of strategic value (Barney, 1991; Heimeriks, 2009; Teece et al., 1997; Zollo & Winter, 2002). The ideas that follow from this discussion will hopefully provide insights that motivate future research and guide managerial practice to a more accurate understanding and a more effective implementation of alliances for strategic renewal.

How firms develop alliance capability for strategic renewal

Knowing how to initiate and manage alliances can be an important contributor to strategic renewal and thus it is important we understand what this "knowing how" means (Gordon et al., 2017). Knowledge is considered to be a critical strategic resource because of its contribution to sustained competitive advantage (Grant, 1996; Winter, 2003). As a resource, however, knowledge does not *per se* result in sustained competitive advantage. Instead, knowledge resources serve as the content for a complex process through which capabilities are developed (Eisenhardt & Martin, 2000; Teece, Pisano & Shuen, 1997).

A substantial amount of research has focused on how a firm's experience relates to alliance performance (Anand & Khanna, 2000; Gulati, 1999). Due to the lack of specificity in stand-alone experience as a proxy for alliance performance, a more recent stream of literature has emerged that focuses on higher-order learning processes as mechanisms to build alliance capability (Heimeriks et al., 2007, 2012; Kale & Singh, 2007; Zollo & Singh, 2004). From this research we can derive that it is not automatic, experienced-based learning (experiential learning), but instead managed, purposeful knowledge management that contributes to alliance capability. It is useful to juxtapose the experiential and deliberate learning perspectives to explore their differences and complementarities.

Experiential learning

Practice makes perfect and earlier studies have therefore suggested that firms with more alliance experience achieve more success than less-experienced firms (Anand & Khanna, 2000). As Harbison and Pekar (1998: 41) argued:

"the more alliances you do, the better you get at them." This is based on a learning-by-doing logic, but if the accumulation of experience leads to alliance capability, then what is experience, exactly?

Gulati (1999) proposes that alliance experience pertains to the rate with which firms enter new alliances. Zollo et al. (2002) complement this view by arguing that the more heterogeneous a firm's prior experience with alliances, the more valuable the knowledge gained from this experience. This in turn increases chances for success in new alliances. In an effort to disentangle multiple sources of alliance experience, Hoang and Rothaermel (2005) included two levels of experience in their research, namely: general, diverse-partner experience and partner-specific experience. The results of this study reveal that the first level demonstrated a positive but diminishing effect on alliance performance. These diminishing returns can be interpreted as follows: the benefits of alliance experience should not be taken for granted as they rely upon the degree to which firms can actively mobilize and leverage their experience. More surprisingly, partner-specific alliance experience may even decrease alliance performance. The inconsistency in results within this stream of literature forms an obstacle to uncovering the drivers of alliance capability. As it seems, a mere focus on experience does not offer managers the prescriptions they need to manage alliances as a means to strategic renewal.

The inconclusive evidence regarding the role of alliance experience has several reasons behind it. First, organizational memory is highly dependent on the social construction of meanings and patterns of retention (Lyles, 1985). Memories may therefore not be exact replications of anterior events and a multitude of memories of the same event may exist in the same organization: "Memories are not necessarily grounded in realities and there may be more than one memory about a single learning event" (Lyles, 1985: 5). Second, it is often taken for granted that "lessons learned" are accurate and applicable in circumstances that seem similar but are not necessarily so (Heimeriks, 2009). This can result in a misunderstanding of causality between action and outcome by decision makers, especially for experienced and successful firms with plenty of resources. In recent studies it is therefore proposed that firms should avoid myopic learning caused by an overemphasis on stand-alone experience. Instead, firms should experiment with learning mechanisms to deliberately create, retrieve, and apply relevant knowledge contributing to alliance success (Heimeriks, 2009; Heimeriks & Duysters, 2007; Kale & Singh, 1999, 2007; Volberda et al., 2003).

Deliberate learning

Stand-alone experience does not automatically lead to alliance success (Barkema & Schijven, 2008; Heimeriks, 2009; Sampson, 2005). Instead, firms should have mechanisms in place supporting deliberate learning, to purposefully develop and disseminate knowledge throughout the firm (Niesten & Jolink, 2015; Zollo & Singh, 2004).

Deliberate learning is necessary, as managing alliances is complex and cannot be handled as a routine activity due to the multiple sub-activities that need to be managed sequentially or simultaneously, such as: selection, negation, formation, governance, knowledge management, relationship management, and termination. Moreover, managers take considerable risk by assuming that alliances over different timeframes or in different industries can be managed in the same way. Instead, the causal ambiguity and complexity of alliances make deliberate learning mechanisms essential in order to foster knowledge transfer (Heimeriks & Duysters, 2007). Deliberate learning mechanisms are conceptualized as purposeful approaches that help develop and disseminate alliance-related knowledge throughout the firm, to ultimately deploy relevant knowledge when and where it is needed (Zollo & Singh, 2004).

Several empirical studies suggest a positive relationship between deliberate learning mechanisms and alliance capability. In a study on collaborative know-how (Simonin, 1997) it is shown that experience alone is insufficient for optimizing the rents from inter-firm collaboration. Instead, the development of collaborative know-how is essential in order for the lessons learned to be utilized for future alliance success. Kale and Singh (1999) therefore define alliance capability as the coordinative capacity and processes for the articulation, codification, sharing, and internalization of alliance knowledge. This study also reveals that the relationship between alliance experience and success loses significance when alliance learning process variables are added; i.e. the link between experience and performance is mediated by the use of deliberate learning mechanisms.

The dedicated alliance function

An important deliberate learning mechanism through which firms develop alliance capability is the dedicated alliance function that oversees and coordinates alliance activity. The establishment of a dedicated function is not always based on an intended strategy, as the need for this function can emerge from interactions between an organization and its environment, which allow ideas and actions from multiple sources to integrate into a pattern or decision (Es-Sajjade, 2010). Kale et al. (2002) argue that firms possessing an alliance function enjoy greater alliance success as measured by both greater stock market returns following alliance announcements and by managerial assessments. An alliance function contributes to alliance capability through several mechanisms such as organized learning, resource-configuration, and increased external visibility. Research has revealed that the dedicated alliance function captures alliance knowledge to make it available and applicable to future alliances by offering tools and consultancy depending on the phase of a particular alliance, or depending on specific requests from internal organizational clients (Es-Sajjade, 2010). Examples of support given by a dedicated alliance function include 1-on-1 coaching, cross-cultural training for international alliances, training sessions, and risk escalation process charts. The alliance learning process is most effective when the alliance function combines different tools.

In a related study (Kale & Singh, 2007) the benefits of an alliance function are further elaborated through the inclusion of knowledge-management processes. The authors suggest that an alliance learning process, which includes articulation, codification, and sharing of alliance-related knowledge, mediates between an alliance function and alliance performance. These insights demonstrate that establishing a dedicated function – a considerable investment – does not automatically lead to the development of alliance capability. Instead, the dedicated alliance function should be utilized as a hub for other learning mechanisms to help firms manage their alliance portfolios (Heimeriks et al., 2008), e.g.: tool based solutions (e.g. codified best practices); training solutions (e.g. in-house training courses); and third-party solutions (e.g. consultants). These findings suggest that depending on a firm's alliance portfolio size, different mechanisms are conducive to enabling a shift from low to medium, or from medium to high performance. Moreover, it is also proposed that some mechanisms, such as joint business planning and in-house training solutions, are so-called "hygiene-factors", which can contribute to portfolio expansion, but not to higher alliance performance. The conditions of how and when a dedicated function contributes to capability development and enhanced performance remain an important direction for future research (Contractor & Reuer, 2014). These studies are important to shed light on how firms can utilize the dedicated function by combining it with other learning mechanisms for the purpose of within- and between-firm learning (Heimeriks et al., 2012).

The process of alliance learning

After discussing the differences between experiential and deliberate learning, it is imperative to shed light on the actual process of learning. Organizational learning in the context of alliances occurs when there is progress in thought and action on the level of individuals, groups, and the organization. This progress contributes to the development of alliance capability; an important mediator between alliance experience and alliance performance. Landmark studies by Crossan et al. (1999) and Vera and Crossan (2004) have elaborated this multilevel perspective on organizational learning and explained how learning takes place at the individual, group, and organization levels and how each level influences the other.

Quite intuitively, they start at the individual level by showing how individuals form interpretations of the conscious factors of their learning experiences and share these interpretations at the level of groups. If these interpretations are integrated at the level of groups, they may alter the collective understanding, which creates an opportunity for further learning at the level of the organization. If the organization adopts the changed collective understanding of one or several groups by making it a part of its systems, routines, and structures then the learning is institutionalized. Interestingly though, learning does not only move forward from the individual, through the group, to the organization level, but there is also a backward flow which reinforces what has already been learned (Bontis et al., 2002). Between these two flows there are tensions as the forward flow is geared toward new learning while the backward flow is focused on existing practices, which is known as the "exploration/exploitation paradox" (Lewis, 2000; Smith & Lewis, 2011). In research on alliances, the learning processes at the individual, group, and organization levels have been referred to as *articulation, codification,* and *transfer* (Kale & Singh, 2007).

Articulation, codification, and transfer of alliance knowledge

The first step of the alliance learning process, knowledge *articulation,* is crucial to the creation of new knowledge (Nonaka, 1994). Articulation is the process of externalizing individually held, tacit knowledge into explicit knowledge (Nonaka, 1994). An important element of articulation is that it happens in social settings where knowledge and experience are shared with others through interaction and dialogue. Articulation contributes to learning within the field of alliances in several ways (Kale & Singh, 2007). Firstly, it prevents the loss of knowledge due to employee turnover. Articulated knowledge can be stored in archives, databases, portals, or intranets and can serve as frame of reference for others. Secondly, it facilitates the sense-making process that takes place posterior to key events, which provides managers with a better perception of causal links between action and outcome. Articulation can occur through several methods: debriefing of alliance managers, progress reports/presentations, or logbooks of alliance-related events and outcomes.

The second step, *codification* of knowledge, can be defined as the organizing of knowledge into sets of identifiable rules and relationships that can be easily shared within the firm. Codified knowledge is "alienable from the individual who wrote the code" (Kogut & Zander, 1992: 6). Codification makes possible the diffusion of knowledge required for the coordination and implementation of complex activities such as an alliance (Kogut & Zander, 1992; Nonaka, 1994). A definition better suited to the context of alliance management is the one formulated by Kale and Singh (2007: 985): "codification involves creating and using knowledge objects or resources such as alliance guidelines, checklists, or manuals to assist action or decision making in future alliance situations." Other forms of output of knowledge codification include: partner selection protocols, best practice documents, intranet documentation, and alliance manuals (Heimeriks et al., 2008). Studies have reported codified knowledge as contributing to alliance performance (Heimeriks et al., 2008; Kale & Singh, 2007).

The codification and articulation processes are obviously linked as the latter is a prerequisite for the former. Unfortunately, however, most articulated knowledge is never codified, which brings unnecessary costs upon firms as it prevents them from transforming simple individual experiences into manuals and other alliance-related tools that offer the content (what), the methodology (how), and the rationale (why) (Zollo & Winter, 2002) of alliances. Managers get bogged down in today's thinking due to continuous dynamics and high workloads. This prevents them from taking a step back after important events, such as the closure of certain phases in the alliance, to formally capture new experiences and insights by means of codification. Codification offers managers tools, manuals, and guidelines that give them access to previous experiences. An important additional benefit is that it helps managers to grasp the causal links between decisions, actions, and outcomes even if this was not the intention behind the codification effort (Zollo & Winter, 2002). The cognitive process associated with codification allows managers to expose the logical steps of their argumentation and to uncover their assumptions. This enables firms to come up with best practices of their own, contextualized in their unique path-dependent experiences, instead of replicating other firms' best practices, which may never work under different circumstances (Kale & Singh, 2007).

Notwithstanding these benefits of codification, managers should also understand the limitations. For example, codified documents can inhibit creative thinking and ad hoc problem solving as managers and employees strictly follow prior practices. The convenient practice of rigorously following what is written down could lead to missing blind spots or areas of improvement. Furthermore, in many cases the individuals who performed the codification are not those who use its output, which prevents individuals from a complete or optimal understanding of causal links between decisions, actions, and outcomes.

The third and final step in the alliance learning process is the *transfer* of knowledge. Knowledge is now articulated, codified, and needs to be shared with relevant individuals and units within the firm in order to translate new alliance-related knowledge into meaningful action and replicable behavior (Argyris & Schön, 1978). This is an essential step in the alliance learning process through which knowledge moves to the organizational level and becomes part of an organization's practices and routines (Levitt & March, 1988). If knowledge transfer is managed effectively it can be a direct link to strategic renewal, as it relates to the capacity of a firm to integrate new knowledge into value-creating routines that can help improve performance (Tsai, 2001; Zahra & George, 2002). For this purpose, the alliance function can "act as a focal point for learning and leveraging both explicit and tacit lessons from prior and ongoing alliances" (Kale et al., 2002: 752). Yet, the process through which an alliance function performs this task, i.e. how it specifically coordinates and facilitates the transfer of knowledge from individual, to group, to organizational level, requires further investigation (Contractor & Reuer, 2014).

For the purpose of knowledge transfer, an important distinction between learning mechanisms should be made, viz. between group-level and organization-level learning (Heimeriks et al., 2007), because both levels involve different types of knowledge and serve different ends. Group-level learning pertains to the *integration* of knowledge and is driven by interaction (formal or informal) between individuals. Organization-level learning is achieved by the deployment of *institutionalizing* routines and structures. The more experienced a firm gets in managing alliances the more likely it is to have organization-level learning mechanisms in place. Although organization-level learning can generate efficiency gains in managing alliances, it can also lead to an overreliance on existing practices and routines. Such overreliance can result in erroneous inferences and, consequently, in *superstitious learning* (Levitt & March, 1988; Heimeriks, 2009). Superstitious learning happens when "the subjective experience of learning is compelling, but the connections between actions and outcomes are misspecified" (Levitt & March, 1988: 325). Within the context of alliances this occurs when experienced firms confuse experience with competence by naively championing "best practices" across different alliances, contexts, and timeframes without a careful note that reminds participants to at least consider idiosyncratic conditions and requirements (Heimeriks, 2009). Firms can protect against the inertial effects of institutionalizing mechanisms by balancing between the use of integrating mechanisms and institutionalizing mechanisms. This would make the institutionalizing mechanisms more flexible and open to discussion and reduce therewith the threat of management myopia. Moreover, firms that focus solely on institutionalizing mechanisms (top-down, experience driven) to the exclusion of integration mechanisms (bottom-up, discovery driven) may find themselves at stable but suboptimal performance levels. Maintaining a balance between organization-level and group-level learning, therefore, is crucial to the development of alliance capability and its effectiveness in strategic renewal.

Discussion

The systematic approach to organizational learning in alliances discussed in the previous sections is in clear opposition to earlier views in which organizational learning has been described as a random, trial-and-error process (Lant et al., 1992). Indeed, the advanced learning mechanisms underlying the development of alliance capability in firms that excel in alliance performance reveal organizational learning as a strategic priority, and even as a means to strategic renewal (Contractor & Reuer, 2014; Heimeriks, 2009; Heimeriks et al., 2007; Heimeriks & Duysters, 2007; Kale & Singh, 2007; Niesten & Jolink, 2015). In order for alliance learning to contribute to strategic renewal, it needs to acknowledge and address issues stemming from tensions between new knowledge and existing routines that are core to strategic renewal (Crossan & Berdrow, 2003). Figure 12.1 depicts the organizational learning process underlying the development of alliance capability as a means to strategic renewal.

As firms gain experience in alliances, learning proceeds from the individual, to the group, to the organizational level. It is this third step of the alliance process – transfer of alliance knowledge to the organizational level – where new knowledge is institutionalized. At this level, structures, systems, procedures, routines, and strategy take shape formally and are expected to be adopted at other levels in the organization. These building blocks of firm-level alliance capability are expected to evolve based on a) the nature, context, and dynamism of each new alliance, and b) the development of the firm's overall alliance portfolio. Longitudinal work using quantitative panel data or inductive, theory-building studies are encouraged in order to reveal the in-depth process of how the transfer of alliance knowledge contributes to different strategic

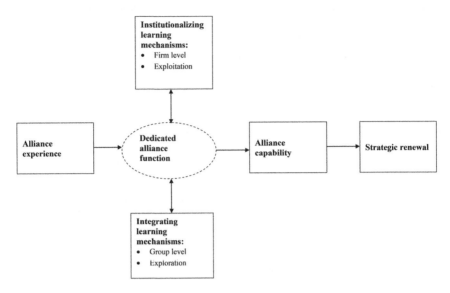

Figure 12.1 The development of alliance capability for strategic renewal

renewal trajectories such as regaining competitive advantage, improving innovation performance, and increasing market share (Brouthers et al., 2015; Hamel, 1991; Mowery et al., 1996). Such work has great potential because it could offer important insights into 1) when and how alliance knowledge contributes to strategic renewal, and 2) whether firms opts to allow knowledge to be transferred in the first place or, instead, decide to reject the transfer based on certain decision making criteria.

Although it is appealing for managers to emphasize institutionalizing mechanisms, equal attention needs to be given to new knowledge at the level of individuals and groups involved in alliances (Heimeriks, 2009). This is a considerable challenge, particularly if previous approaches to managing alliances have brought the firm considerable success and wealth. The risk of superstitious learning, however, should temper the confidence with which firms approach each new alliance (Heimeriks et al., 2008). Using a combination of different learning mechanisms can help address this risk. Although researchers have suggested the importance of higher-order routines that allow for ad hoc problem solving when a situation deviates from the norm (Heimeriks et al., 2012), it remains unclear why firms developed these higher-order routines and how they did so exactly. This is important as it may inform other firms of how to overcome management myopia; a persistent reliance on zero-order routines that blindly repeats previous successes. Furthermore, future research can help reveal specific examples or typologies of combinations of learning mechanisms that have been useful in certain alliances serving strategic renewal purposes.

Another mechanism for developing alliance capability is the dedicated alliance function that is created by firms to have a specific locus carrying the responsibility for developing alliance capability (Es-Sajjade, 2010; Heimeriks, 2009; Kale et al., 2002). The expected benefits of a dedicated alliance function are not always realized as the development of alliance capability requires more than a single-role function; i.e. traditional responsive consultancy. Instead, the alliance function should proactively manage the balance between institutionalizing and integrating mechanisms by offering a wide range of learning services depending on the contextual and temporal requirements of each respective alliance as it moves through different phases (Es-Sajjade, 2010). While prior conceptual studies and cross-sectional research have proposed that the dedicated alliance function could lead to alliance capability and superior performance (Kale et al., 2002; Kale & Singh, 2007), in-depth process studies are needed to reveal the complex process from local (within-alliance and within-function) and distributed learning (across alliances and functions) to strategic renewal (suboptimal to superior performance).

Recommendations for alliance practice

This preceding analysis includes important suggestions for alliance management practice. For example, managers are advised to overcome the tendency of trying to repeat past successes in the complex and high-risk venture of alliances. The effectiveness of routines depends on the predictability and stability of the environment and it is well known that the environment of alliances lacks both criteria. Instead managers should carefully and deliberately build and manage a learning system that balances the absorption of new knowledge and the capitalization of existing knowledge. They could, for example, combine mechanisms such as alliance experts, alliance management guidelines, discussion sessions, and formal training, depending on the unique requirements of each individual alliance and its respective developmental phases. If this is done in a creative and careful way, it could lead to the development of alliance capability as a powerful tool for strategic renewal. Figure 12.2 depicts the combination of different learning mechanisms at Dow Chemical.

The list of learning tools included in the figure is not exhaustive, as Dow Chemical's dedicated alliance function has an impressive portfolio of tools to offer on the level of individuals and groups, using documents, training, consultancy, and coaching. Moreover, the director of the function explained that they not only make the knowledge available, they also guide alliance managers in how and when to use it. An interesting and effective knowledge-management approach of the function is that it allows clients (colleagues involved in alliances who need learning tools) to request tailor-made service. This is an important illustration of balancing between exploitation (offering existing tools) and exploration (creation of new tools based on individual/group needs).

It is important, therefore, for alliance function managers and alliance managers to carefully consider if and how they use existing knowledge in new alliances to

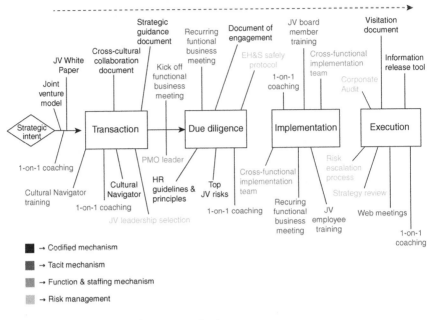

Figure 12.2 Dow Chemical's learning mechanisms

protect against false generalizing. Although there could be opportunities for using tools that have worked before, managers should consider contingencies that could make these tools less effective, such as deal size, geographic scope, and strategic intent. The selection and relevance of tools should be discussed in detail between the alliance management function and the alliance manager in an early stage of the alliance life cycle in order to decide the extent to which this particular alliance can utilize existing tools versus needing to create new ones. Alliances as a means to strategic renewal are about capitalizing on previous learning with mild confidence, versus receptiveness to new knowledge with strong competence.

Another useful illustration of alliances for strategic renewal is the STI alliance (Kahle et al., 2005). This collaborative effort of Sony, Toshiba, and IBM began with initial discussion between Sony and IBM, quickly gaining the support from both companies' CEOs. Sony was preparing for an effective response to Microsoft's rapid market gain in the game console business with its Xbox product. Moreover, Nintendo was back in the game with its Wii console targeted at families. Sony realized it had to develop new capabilities by building a console with superior CPU performance, which could be achieved by means of an alliance with technology partners with complementary capabilities. The objective was to develop a revolutionary multiprocessor that would benefit each firm in their respective product and service portfolio, best known for enabling the production of the Sony Playstation 3, a product based on the strategic objective of building a machine with "100 times the performance of the Playstation 2." In the STI alliance, Sony acted as the content provider, IBM contributed the technology, and Toshiba performed the role of high-volume manufacturing technology partner. The creation of the Cell processor allowed Sony to reinforce its presence as a producer of high-performance, reliable gaming hardware. Sony and its partners could have simply used existing routines and processes to manage the STI alliance. Instead, they captured new insights and allowed these to feed back into each respective organization, for example by establishing the "Sony Toshiba IBM Center of Competence for the Cell Processor." The center offers workshops, lectures, and training and is aimed at building a wider community around the creation of the Cell processor.

Conclusions

This discussion provides researchers and managers interested in managing alliances for strategic renewal with some suggestions on how to organize internal learning processes to benefit from experience and prepare for precariousness. These suggestions include important challenges and responsibilities associated with managing tensions between routines and ad hoc approaches, as it can be tempting for managers to simply follow the same routines over different alliances in a firm's alliance portfolio. While firms have initiated alliances with varying levels of success, theory has yet to shed light on best practices showing how particular combinations of learning mechanisms that balance exploration and exploitation contribute to alliance success and strategic renewal.

References

Anand, B. and T. Khanna. 2000. Do firms learn to create value? The case of alliances. *Strategic Management Journal*, 21(3): 295–316.

Argyris, C. and D. A. Schön. 1978. *Organizational learning: A theory of action perspective.* Reading, MA: Addison-Wesley.

Barkema, H. G. and M. Schijven. 2008. How do firms learn to make acquisitions? *Journal of Management*, 34: 594–634.

Barney, J. 1991. Firm resources and sustained competitive advantage. *Journal of Management*, 17: 99–120.

Bontis, N., M. M. Crossan, and J. Hulland. 2002. Managing an organizational learning system by aligning stocks and flows. *Journal of Management Studies*, 39(4): 437–469.

Brouthers, K. D., G. Nakos and P. Dimitratos. 2015. SME entrepreneurial orientation, international performance, and the moderating role of strategic alliances. *Entrepreneurship Theory and Practice*, 39(5): 1161–1187.

Callahan, J. and S. MacKenzie. 1999. Metrics for strategic alliance control. *R&D Management*, 29: 365–378.

Contractor, F. J. and J. J. Reuer. 2014. Structuring and governing alliances: New directions for research. *Global Strategy Journal*, 4: 241–256.

Crossan, M., H. Lane, and R. White. 1999. An organizational learning framework: From intuition to institution. *Academy of Management Review*, 24(3): 522–538.

Crossan, M. M. and I. Berdrow. 2003. Organizational learning and strategic renewal. *Strategic Management Journal*, 24: 1087–1105.

Draulans, J., A. P. de Man, and H. W. Volberda. 2003. Building alliance capability: Management techniques for superior alliance performance. *Long Range Planning*, 36(2): 151–166.

Eisenhardt, K. M. and J. A. Martin. 2000. Dynamic capabilities: What are they? *Strategic Management Journal*, 21(10/11): 1105–1122.

Es-Sajjade, A. 2010. *The origins of alliance capability: How Dow Chemical learns from its joint venture experience.* Rotterdam, Netherlands: Erasmus University Rotterdam.

Gordon, M. E. G., B. Kayseas, and P. W. Moroz. 2017, January. Indigenous controlled joint ventures and the transformation of opportunity structure constraints. In Academy of Management Proceedings (Vol. 2017, No. 1, p. 17625). Academy of Management.

Grant, R. M. 1996. Toward a knowledge-based theory of the firm. *Strategic Management Journal*, Winter Special Issue, 17: 109–122.

Gulati, R. 1995. Does familiarity breed trust? The implications of repeated ties for contractual choice in alliances. *The Academy of Management Journal*, 38: 85–112.

Gulati, R. 1999. Network location and learning: The influence of network resources and firm capabilities on alliance formation. *Strategic Management Journal*, 20: 397–420.

Hamel, G. 1991. Competition for competence and interpartner learning within international strategic alliances. *Strategic Management Journal*, 12(S1): 83–103.

Harbison, J. R. and P. Pekar Jr. 1998. *Smart alliances: A practical guide to repeatable success.* San Francisco, CA: Jossey- Bass Publishers.

Heimeriks, K. 2009. Confident or competent? How to avoid superstitious learning in alliance portfolios. *Long Range Planning*, 42: 96–114.

Heimeriks, K., K. Elko, and J. Reuer. 2008. Building capabilities for alliance portfolios. *Long Range Planning*, 42: 96–114.

Heimeriks, K. H., G. Duysters, and W. Vanhaverbeke. 2007. Learning mechanisms and differential performance in alliance portfolios. *Organization Science*, 5: 373–408.

Heimeriks, K. H., M. Schijven, and S. Gates. 2012. Manifestations of higher-order routines: The underlying mechanisms of deliberate learning in the context of post-acquisition integration. *Academy of Management Journal*, 55(3): 703–726.

Hoang, H. and F. T. Rothaermel. 2005. The effect of general and partner-specific alliance experience on joint R&D project performance. *Academy of Management Journal*, 48: 332–345.

Huber, G. P. 1991. Organizational learning: The contributing processes and the literatures. *Organization Science*, 2: 88–115.

Kahle, J. A., M. N. Day, H. P. Hofstee, C. R. Johns, T. R. Maeurer, and D. Shippy. 2005. Introduction to the cell multiprocessor. *IBM Journal of Research and Development*, 49(4.5): 589–604.

Kale, P., Dyer, J. H., and Singh, H. 2002. Alliance capability, stock market response, and long-term alliance success: The role of the alliance function. *Strategic Management Journal*, 23(8): 747–767.

Kale, P., & Singh, H. 1999. Alliance Capability & Success: A Knowledge-Based Approach. In *Academy of management proceedings* (Vol. 1999, No. 1, pp. 01–06). Briarcliff Manor, NY: Academy of Management.

Kale, P. and H. Singh. 2007. Building firm capabilities through learning. *Strategic Management Journal*, 28: 981–1000.

Kogut, B. and U. Zander. 1992. Knowledge of the firm, combinative capabilities and the replication of technology. *Organization Science*, 3: 383–397.

Lant, T. K., F. J. Milliken, and B. Batra. 1992. The role of managerial learning and interpretation in strategic persistence and reorientation: An empirical exploration. *Strategic Management Journal*, 13(8): 585–608.

Levitt, B., & March, J. G. 1988. Organizational learning. *Annual review of sociology*, 14(1): 319–338.

Lewis, M. W. 2000. Exploring paradox: Toward a more comprehensive guide. *Academy of Management Review*, 25(4): 760–776.

Lyles, M. 1985. The impact of organizational learning on joint venture formations. *International Business Review*, 3(4): 459–467.

Mowery, D. C., J. E. Oxley, and B. S. Silverman. 1996. Strategic alliances and interfirm knowledge transfer. *Strategic Management Journal*, 17(S2): 77–91.

Nelson, R. and S. Winter. 1982. *An evolutionary theory of economic change*. Cambridge, MA: Harvard University Press.

Niesten, E. and A. Jolink. 2015. The impact of alliance management capabilities on alliance attributes and performance: A literature review. *International Journal of Management Reviews*, 17(1): 69–100.

Nonaka, I. 1994. A dynamic theory of organizational knowledge creation. *Organization Science*, 5: 14–37.

Sampson, R. 2005. Experience effects and collaborative returns in R&D alliances. *Strategic Management Journal*, 26: 1009–1031.

Simonin, B. 1997. The importance of collaborative know-how: An empirical test of the learning organization. *The Academy of Management Journal*, 40: 1150–1174.

Smith, W. K., & Lewis, M. W. 2011. Toward a theory of paradox: A dynamic equilibrium model of organizing. *Academy of management Review*, 36: 381–403.

Teece, D. J., G. Pisano, and A. Shuen. 1997. Dynamic capabilities and strategic management. *Strategic Management Journal*, 18: 509–533.

Tsai, W. 2001. Knowledge transfer in intraorganizational networks: Effects of network position and absorptive capacity on business unit innovation and performance. *Academy of management Journal*, 44(5): 996–1004.

Vera, D. and M. Crossan. 2003. Organizational learning and knowledge management: Toward an integrative framework. In *Handbook of organizational learning and knowledge management*. Easterby-Smith, M. and Lyles, M. A. (eds). Oxford: Blackwell: 122–141.

Vera, D. and M. Crossan. 2004. Strategic leadership and organizational learning. *Academy of Management Review*, 29(2): 222–240.

Winter, S. G. 2003. Understanding dynamic capabilities. *Strategic Management Journal*, 24(10): 991–995.

Zahra, S. A. and G. George. 2002. Absorptive capacity: A review, reconceptualization, and extension. *Academy of Management Review*, 27(2): 185–203.

Zollo, M., J. Reuer, and H. Singh. 2002. Interorganisational routines and performance in strategic alliances. *Organization Science*, 6: 701–713.

Zollo, M. and H. Singh. 2004. Deliberate learning in corporate acquisitions: Post-acquisition strategies and integration capability in U.S. bank mergers. *Strategic Management Journal*, 25: 1233–1256.

Zollo, M. and S. G. Winter. 2002. Deliberate learning and the evolution of dynamic capabilities. *Organization Science*, 13(3): 339–351.

13 Innovation in foreign and domestic firms

The advantage of foreignness in innovation and the advantage of localness in innovation

C. Annique Un

Introduction

Firms need to innovate to be able to renew their competitive capabilities. Changes in customer preferences and competitors' actions and strategies would eventually render any competitive advantage obsolete (Schumpeter, 1954; Teece, 2007). As a result, a large literature analyzing renewal via innovation has emerged, discussing a plethora of antecedents from both within and outside the firm that affect innovation (see reviews in the handbooks edited by Dodgson, Gann, and Phillips, 2013; Hall and Rosenberg, 2010; Nelson and Fagerberg, 2005). Additionally, this renewal via innovation has now become more imperative than ever, because the general opening of economies and exposure to international competition that has accompanied globalization has increased the pressures to innovate, with firms no longer being shielded from competition in their home country (Cuervo-Cazurra and Un, 2007; Stienstra, Baaij, Van den Bosch, and Volberda, 2004; Yergin and Stanislaw, 2002).

Therefore, to provide a better understanding of these dynamics of renewal in the face of global competition, in this chapter I analyze the differences in innovation strategies between domestic firms and subsidiaries of foreign firms competing in the same country. I do this by linking the literature on global strategy with the literature on innovation management, and I build on the knowledge-based view (Grant, 1996, 2013; Kogut and Zander, 1992, 1993; Nonaka, 1994; Szulanski, 1996) to explain the mechanisms. Specifically, I introduce a theoretical framework that explains how domestic firms and subsidiaries of foreign firms have access to different knowledge sources and manage their employees differently, resulting in their following different innovation paths. I propose three ideas. First, I propose that subsidiaries of foreign multinational enterprises (MNEs) may enjoy what I call the *advantage of foreignness in innovation,* in which they benefit from access to global knowledge sources and manage their employees to have a multicultural mindset, which supports their global innovation (Un, 2016). I also argue that domestic firms may benefit from what I call *the advantage of localness in innovation,* in which they have deep and contextualized local knowledge and manage their employees to focus on the local market, which supports their local innovation. Second, I propose that as a result of these advantages, domestic firms and subsidiaries of foreign MNEs may generate different types of innovations that provide them with a relative competitive advantage in the host country, depending on whether the innovations are created for end-user customers or other firms, and whether the industry is global or local in nature. Third, I argue that although the strength of these advantages diminishes over time as subsidiaries and domestic companies imitate each other and learn how to serve customers better, the relative advantages remain because each type of firm faces a particular constraint in its ability to imitate the other type of firm.

These ideas contribute to the literature on innovation and strategic renewal by explaining differences in the innovation strategies of firms in global competition. Unlike other studies that have focused on discussing the innovation strategies of multinationals (Bartlett and Ghoshal, 2001; Doz and Wilson, 2012; Hedlund, 1986), I compare the innovativeness of subsidiaries of foreign MNEs and domestic firms competing in the same country. This comparison is important because multinationals have to compete not only against each other in host countries, but also against domestic firms in other countries (Bartlett and Ghoshal, 2001; Doz and Wilson, 2012). In the latter case, the literature has argued that subsidiaries of foreign MNEs suffer from a liability of foreignness that reflects their competitive disadvantages in comparison to domestic firms (Hymer, 1976; Zaheer, 1995). Unlike this approach, however, I explain how both subsidiaries of foreign MNEs and domestic companies may enjoy advantages in the realm of innovation, and how these advantages are driven by differences in their knowledge bases and in the management of their employees.

The rest of the chapter is organized as follows. In the next section I briefly review studies on innovation in global competition and explain how this paper fits within the broader body of literature. I then discuss the advantage of foreignness in innovation, followed by an explanation of the advantage of localness in innovation. I explain the conditions under which either subsidiaries of foreign MNEs or domestic companies are likely to achieve an ultimate advantage over each other in the host country. I follow with a discussion of the dynamics of the advantages, and conclude with a review of the contributions of this theoretical framework.

Innovation in global competition

Theoretical basis: The knowledge-based view

The knowledge-based view of the firm (KBV), which is an extension of the broader resource-based view of the firm, positions knowledge as the key resource that firms can manage to achieve a competitive advantage (Kogut and Zander, 1992; Nonaka, 1994). In the KBV, firms are superior to markets in searching for, creating, and transferring knowledge (Grant, 2013; Kogut and Zander, 1992). Since individuals inside the firm are the ones who explore and exploit knowledge (Tuncdogan, Van den Bosch, and Volberda, 2015; Un, 2007; Un, Cuervo-Cazurra, and Asakawa, 2010), the firm can provide them with the incentives, mindsets, and organizational framework to help them search, integrate, and transform tacit knowledge into explicit knowledge (e.g., Kogut and Zander, 1992; Nonaka, 2007), which results in innovations (Carlile, 2002; Nonaka, 2007). Additionally, the firm facilitates intra-firm knowledge transfer within and across national borders (Kogut and Zander, 1993; Szulanski, 1996) via mechanisms such as transnational teams and the rotation of employees across different units and country subsidiaries (Nohria and Ghoshal, 1997; Adenfelt and Lagerström, 2008; Williams and Nones, 2009). I build on this theory to analyze how domestic firms and subsidiaries of foreign MNEs innovate, because knowledge is the key basis for innovation and competition.

Innovation in global competition

Much of the literature in international business that analyzes innovation has focused on how multinationals innovate thanks to their global reach. This literature discusses how firms can benefit from the tension between global integration and local responsiveness to innovate and compete globally (Bartlett and Ghoshal, 2001; Doz and Wilson, 2012), and argues that they adopt new innovation structures such as heterarchy, transnational, meta-national, team-based, and collaborative to achieve global innovation (Bartlett and Ghoshal, 2001; Doz, Santos, and Williamson, 2001; Doz and Wilson, 2012; Hedlund, 1986). Extensions of this literature have analyzed the mechanisms that help multinationals to transfer innovations and knowledge across countries (Kogut and Zander, 1993; Nohria and Ghoshal, 1997) and how subsidiaries can become sources of innovations for the MNE (Frost, Birkinshaw, and Ensign, 2002; Frost and Zhou, 2005). A further extension of this literature analyzes how subsidiaries within the MNE compete against each other to become innovation leaders (Phene and Almeida, 2008). However, although it provides many valuable insights, this literature has neglected to compare differences in innovativeness between subsidiaries of foreign MNEs and host-country domestic firms, even though subsidiaries of foreign MNEs in a given country compete not only against subsidiaries of other foreign MNEs, but also, and in many cases more intensively, against host-country firms.

Therefore, to contribute to the literature, in this chapter I focus on this comparison and study differences in innovativeness between subsidiaries of foreign MNEs and domestic firms competing in the same country. Such comparison has usually focused on analyzing differences in performance rather than differences in innovation. Starting with Hymer (1976), studies argue that subsidiaries of MNEs face disadvantages in the form of additional costs of doing business abroad, which include investments that the host-country firms have already made and costs related to dealing with discrimination by the host-country government (Buckley and Casson, 2009). Thus, the monopolistic or ownership advantages transferred to the host country are supposed to help offset these costs to enable subsidiaries of foreign MNEs achieve success abroad. Building on these ideas, later studies relabeled these costs as the liability of foreignness (Zaheer, 1995), arguing that subsidiaries suffer a liability of foreignness because they are less integrated in the host-country social network, and as a result of being social outsiders to the country have less local knowledge than domestic firms. Thus, subsidiaries of foreign MNEs are less able to meet the needs of host-country customers, especially end users; less able to counteract host-country competitors' moves; and less able to reduce discrimination by the host- country government. As a result of all this, subsidiaries of foreign MNEs achieve lower performance (Zaheer, 1995), experience lower survival rates (Zaheer and Mosakowski, 1997), and face more labor lawsuits (Mezias, 2002) than host-country firms.

Nevertheless, other studies argue that subsidiaries of foreign MNEs also enjoy advantages that domestic firms do not, and that these can potentially compensate for the liability of foreignness in the form of monopolistic (Hymer, 1976) or ownership advantages (Dunning, 1977). Kronborg and Thomsen (2009), for example, argue that foreign firms have advantages in industry knowledge that give them a higher chance of survival than certain types of host-country firms. Nachum (2010) argues that only host-country MNEs can match the advantages of foreignness enjoyed by subsidiaries of foreign MNEs. Other studies argue that subsidiaries of foreign MNEs, as social outsiders, can take beneficial actions that host-country firms are unwilling to take because they are constrained by their local embeddedness. For example, Siegel, Pyun, and Cheon (2011) argue that subsidiaries of foreign MNEs can take advantage of the local labor market discrimination to hire highly quali- fied female executives and achieve higher performance. Un (2011) proposes that subsidiaries of foreign MNEs are more effective in transforming their investments in research and development (R&D) into innovations because their employees are likely to have higher abilities to search for and integrate a larger variety of knowledge.

The advantage of foreignness in innovation and the advantage of localness in innovation

Building on these studies and focusing on the realm of firm renewal via innovation, I discuss how subsidiaries of foreign MNEs and domestic firms use alternative ways to achieve an advantage in innovation, which I call the advantage of foreignness in innovation and the advantage of localness in innovation, respectively. Table 13.1 summarizes the ideas I discuss now.

The advantage of foreignness in innovation

I propose that subsidiaries of foreign MNEs can achieve an advantage of for- eignness in innovation that enables them to generate more globally focused

Table 13.1 The advantage of foreignness in innovation and the advantage of localness in innovation

	Advantage of foreignness in innovation	Advantage of localness in innovation
Definition	Subsidiaries of foreign firms are able to create more globally focused innovations than domestic firms.	Domestic firms are able to create more locally relevant innovations than subsidiaries of foreign firms.
Focus	Receive innovations from the parent company created in the home country. Receive innovations from other subsidiaries of the multinational, especially global centers of excellence. Create innovations that address the needs of multiple operations of the multinational rather than those of the local country.	Create innovations that address the needs of local customers and that are better than the products offered by competitors in the host country. Create innovations that are less complex in knowledge and more locally focused.
Management of employees	Select employees with a multicultural mindset. Select employees with foreign language skills. Develop employees with a multicultural mindset via employee rotation across countries.	Select employees with a focus on the local market. Develop employees to have a deep understanding of the local conditions and how to innovate to address this environment.

innovations. Two characteristics explain this advantage of foreignness in innovation: the global knowledge transfer from the MNEs, and the management of employees to have a multicultural mindset.

The advantage of foreignness in innovation via global knowledge transfer

Subsidiaries of foreign MNEs benefit from the global knowledge transfer of a large variety of knowledge sources in the MNE, supporting their global innovativeness. Since different countries create different types of knowledge (Mudambi, Piscitello, and Rabbiosi, 2014; Scott-Kennel and Giroud, 2015), MNEs can provide their subsidiaries with a larger variety of knowledge that enables them to create more new combinations of knowledge, and thereby more innovations. Subsidiaries of foreign MNEs can receive valuable knowledge that helps them innovate from two main sources: the parent company, and other subsidiaries of the multinational located in different countries.

First, subsidiaries are more innovative than domestic firms, in part because they receive global knowledge and innovations from the parent MNE. Companies tend to become MNEs when they have developed innovations in the home country that they can use in other countries (Vernon, 1966; Buckley and Casson, 2009). Vernon (1966), for example, argues that firms expand into foreign markets primarily to exploit their superior innovations created in and for the domestic market. Once the domestic market is saturated with these innovations, firms export their products and then make foreign direct investments to produce products there. Buckley and Casson (2009) argue that firms only enter foreign markets where their knowledge and technologies are superior to those of the host-country competitors. These transferred innovations include, in the case of firms from advanced countries, product innovations as a result of serving sophisticated consumers at home (Vernon, 1966). They also include, in the case of firms from emerging economies, process innovations and business model innovations as a result of serving low-income consumers at home (Govindarajan and Ramamurti, 2011). Hence, the parent company can provide its subsidiaries with the knowledge and technologies it acquires from interacting with its home-country knowledge sources. As a result, subsidiaries enjoy an advantage of foreignness in innovation, primarily because the parent firms transfer knowledge and innovations to them (Li and Lee, 2015; Un and Cuervo-Cazurra, 2008; Un, 2011).

Second, subsidiaries can also receive global innovations from other subsidiaries of the MNE. Because they are located in multiple countries, the subsidiaries of an MNE are exposed to different types of knowledge (Doz and Wilson, 2012). This wider exposure to diversity of knowledge can help the subsidiary create more knowledge combinations, which result in more innovations. To facilitate this, the parent firm may allow more autonomy to its subsidiaries to search for and create new knowledge, not only for the host-country market, but also for other subsidiaries and the parent company (Gupta and Govindarajan, 2000; Najafi-Tavani, Zaefarian, Naudé, and Giroud, 2015). This worldwide learning and innovation is enabled via several organizational mechanisms that support subsidiary knowledge acquisition, accumulation, creation, and transfer within the MNE's network of subsidiaries. These include the use of incentive systems, training and job rotation, and transnational teams (Adenfelt and Lagerström, 2008; Fey and Furu, 2008; Williams and Nones, 2009). Fey and Furu (2008), for example, show that in the MNEs where managers are compensated for their knowledge-transferring behavior and firm-wide performance, there is more knowledge transfer. Monteiro, Arvidsson, and Birkinshaw (2008) argue that some subsidiaries are more isolated than others from the knowledge-transfer activities in the MNEs, with those subsidiaries that are perceived as more capable playing more active roles, while those perceived as less capable suffer from the liability of internal isolation; however, this isolation can be reduced through the use of training and job rotation (Williams and Nones, 2009). As individuals from particular subsidiaries become exposed to individuals in other subsidiaries, they develop social ties, which facilitates their knowledge sharing because people tend to share more knowledge with people they know than those they do not know (Nahapiet and Ghoshal, 1998). Finally, the use of transnational teams is an effective organizational mechanism by which the MNE can acquire and transfer knowledge across countries (Lagerström and Andersson, 2003). Team members perform tasks that cut across different parts of the MNE, and they not only acquire knowledge from the various countries in which they are based, but also share and integrate their knowledge to create new knowledge to complete those tasks (Adenfelt and Lagerström, 2008). An extension of this line of thinking includes studies that explain the role of subsidiaries as sources of knowledge that facilitate the competitive advantage of MNEs. This literature argues that beyond the initial entry point, the parent company expects its foreign subsidiaries to proactively acquire knowledge and generate innovations to compete in the host country and contribute to the competitiveness of other subsidiaries and the parent firm (Birkinshaw and Morrison, 1995; Nair, Demirbag, and Mellahi, 2016). To facilitate this, subsidiaries are expected to compete for resources in the corporate factor market on the basis of their contributions to the MNE, which include knowledge and innovations that can be used by other subsidiaries (Frost, Birkinshaw, and Ensign, 2002; Un, 2011). Subsidiaries with higher innovative capabilities are designated as centers of excellence, providing knowledge, innovations, and technology to other firms in the network of subsidiaries, and as a result they receive more attention and resources from the parent MNE (Bouquet and Birkinshaw, 2008).

The advantage of foreignness in innovation via the management of employees to have a multicultural mindset

In addition to receiving innovations from the MNE, subsidiaries of foreign firms manage their employees to imbue them with a multicultural mindset that supports the creation of innovations. By the use of the term "multicultural", I refer to employees' ability to manage differences in cultural, social, economic, political, institutional, and other differentiating characteristics of individuals, teams, organizations, and countries (Un, 2016). To be able to operate within the network of subsidiaries, subsidiaries tend to manage their employees in particular ways: they typically hire employees who are cognitively multicultural, and they also further develop these multicultural mindsets via job rotation, job design, and investment in language training. Since it is individuals who explore and exploit knowledge (Tuncdogan et al., 2015; Un, 2010), these multicultural capabilities enable employees to search for new knowledge and ideas from a larger variety of sources of knowledge, resulting in more innovations.

First, subsidiaries of foreign MNEs are more likely to hire employees who are cognitively multicultural. Since subsidiaries have to interact with the parent company and with other country subsidiaries (for a review, see Li, Jiang, and Shen, 2016), one of the characteristics that they look for in employees is likely to be the ability to work across national boundaries. Subsidiaries are also more likely to hire individuals who have international experiences (Holtbrügge and Mohr, 2011). These experiences help develop the multicultural mindset that facilitates knowledge transfer (Lücke, Kostova, and Roth, 2014) and creativity (Leung and Chiu, 2008; Maddux and Galinsky, 2009).

Subsidiaries are also more likely to hire employees who possess foreign language skills and related multicultural skills. To be able to work in a multinational, employees have to be able to communicate in the language of the parent company and/or a common language used in the MNE, which may not necessarily be the language of the home country, the parent company, or of any of the subsidiaries, but rather a common language like English (for a review, see Froese, Kim, and Eng, 2016). Language abilities are critical, since the transfer of knowledge and technologies relies on interpersonal communication and interaction (Peltokorpi, 2015). Language skills enable employees in the subsidiary to understand and absorb such knowledge, decontextualizing and recontextualizing it for use in the host country. Language abilities enable individuals not only to more effectively transfer knowledge, but also to become more cognitively multicultural. Language is an important cultural resource (for a review of language and culture, see Brannen, Piekkari, and Tietze, 2014) and as people learn a foreign language they also tend to learn about the country in which the language is used. This knowledge enables employees to have a greater understanding and appreciation of how things are done in other countries, making them more cognitively multicultural. This multiculturalism enables employees to be aware of and able to search in a greater variety of sources of knowledge, resulting in more combinations of new knowledge from a wider variety of global sources, and thereby more innovations.

Second, subsidiaries of foreign MNEs are more likely to train employees to be more cognitively multicultural. Once hired by a subsidiary, employees might be given training on how the MNE is organized and how the particular subsidiary is connected to the parent company and other subsidiaries in terms of roles and responsibilities. Therefore, to work effectively in the MNE, subsidiaries may provide development practices such as job rotation, job design, and language training that enable employees to have the necessary multicultural mindset (Lewis, Goodman, Fandt, and Michlitsch, 2007). Managers who are rotated globally across subsidiaries gain knowledge of how these subsidiaries operate in the particular country, dealing with the cultural, institutional, and competitive pressures of the country, while working together with the rest of the MNE. This international experience enables managers to gain knowledge about the alternative knowledge sources available in other countries (Li and Scullion, 2010), such as the clients and suppliers of the particular subsidiary, further building their multicultural capabilities. Subsidiaries can also develop their employees' multicultural capabilities by designing their tasks in such a way that they have to interact with individuals located in other countries, for example by assigning them to transnational teams to work on developing transnational products or to solve problems that affect other subsidiaries (Adenfelt and Lagerström, 2008; Subramaniam and Venkatraman, 2001). Through their participation in transnational teams, employees become exposed to other employees operating in different cultural and institutional contexts, and learn about their knowledge and ideas, which later on can be important sources of knowledge for generating innovations. Finally, subsidiaries of foreign MNEs may provide additional cultural training, such as language training (Puck, Kittler, and Wright, 2008). By learning a new language or improving upon the language skills that they already had when they were hired, these individuals sharpen their abilities to interact and communicate with employees from other countries (Peltokorpi, 2015). As a result, these development practices enable the employees to further develop their multicultural mindset, which is useful for integrating knowledge from different countries and sources, and therefore for innovating.

The advantage of localness in innovation

I argue that domestic firms enjoy an advantage of localness in innovation that enables them to create locally adapted innovations. This advantage of localness in innovation arises from two sources: a deeper understanding of the needs and preferences of local customers and the characteristics of local competitors, and the management of employees to be locally embedded and understand trends and changes in these needs.

The advantage of localness via local knowledge focus

Domestic companies have more local-market knowledge than subsidiaries of foreign MNEs because of their focus on acquiring and using local knowledge to serve the local market. For domestic companies, the home market is their main market (Mata and Freitas, 2012), and for many of those who are not engaged in foreign markets via exports or foreign direct investments, the domestic market is their only market. As a result, the knowledge that they have is primarily about the needs of local customers, the actions of local competitors, and the regulatory and social requirements governing their operation. Since these companies emerged in their home market, their initial innovations were made to meet local needs and preferences (Vernon, 1966), keeping in mind the nature of the local competition for such innovations and any regulatory and social requirements governing how these innovations are produced and marketed. As the local market evolves and customer preferences change over time, such as with the growth in consumers' disposable income, changes in the nature of local competition, or new regulatory requirements, domestic firms continue to incorporate these changes and generate innovations that enable them to be locally adapted (Allred and Steensma, 2005).

Additionally, this focus on knowledge of the domestic market enables managers and employees of domestic firms to deal with relatively lower complexity in terms of the knowledge they have to gather and integrate in the process of innovation. Nooteboom (2000), for example, argues that integrating knowledge from sources with low cognitive distance or difference is easier than integrating knowledge from sources with higher cognitive distance. Since local knowledge sources have low cognitive distance (Bertrand and Mol, 2013), it is easier to integrate than knowledge from domestic and foreign sources. Therefore, domestic firms can devote their attention and resources to gathering a deep understanding of the unmet needs and preferences of local consumers, as well as of how competitors are trying to meet these needs. This knowledge gathering can be done easily via their established relationships with local knowledge sources, such as customers, suppliers, competitors, and universities (Un, Cuervo-Cazurra, and Asakawa, 2010). As such, the local-market knowledge base of domestic firms, and the latter's ease of access to additional local-market knowledge, enables firms to modify and innovate their products and services to precisely meet local market needs.

The advantage of localness via the management of employees to be locally embedded

The way in which domestic firms manage their employees to be locally embedded and establish tight relationships and connections with customers, suppliers, competitors, etc., helps them create locally appropriate innovations. Since the domestic market is the main or only market of the firm (Mata and Freitas, 2012), domestic firms are more likely to select employees with deep local-market knowledge that can help the company better compete and innovate its products to satisfy local customer needs (Un, 2016). Domestic firms are likely to hire employees on the basis of their ability to help the company in the domestic market, such as their existing work experience in the domestic market and their contacts with key customers, suppliers, and distributors that can help the company improve its competitiveness (Bhatta-charya and Michael, 2008). Therefore, employees of domestic firms are likely to be local individuals who have relatively limited multicultural capabilities, because the international market and international knowledge sources have lower importance for domestic firms than the local market. Moreover, local individuals with deep local-market knowledge are also more likely to want to work for these domestic firms, since people tend to want to work for firms that match their interests and capabilities (Chatman, 1991; Yu, 2014).

Additionally, domestic firms are more likely to provide incentives for employees to focus only on acquiring local-market knowledge. Employees are likely to be rewarded for understanding and meeting the needs and preferences of local customers (Inderst and Ottaviani, 2009), performing better than local competitors, finding suppliers who can provide products and services efficiently and effectively, and dealing with regulatory and social pressures. This can include providing ideas that enable the firm to create innovations that are better adapted to the needs and desires of local customers. Employees of domestic firms are also likely to be developed towards a deep understanding of the local conditions and how to innovate to address these, for example by providing them with training on how to establish tight connections with local customers and distributors to obtain new ideas from them (Fu, 2015), or encouraging them to collaborate with end-user consumers to obtain new ideas. It is especially useful to collaborate with lead users, who can provide the firm with an understanding of new ways to develop and adapt a product to address unmet consumer needs (Harhoff, Henkel, and von Hippel, 2003).

Competition in a host country and the relative advantages of foreignness and localness

Since both domestic firms and subsidiaries of foreign firms can enjoy an advantage in innovation, although for different reasons and with different characteristics, one question that remains is: under which conditions does one type of firm have an advantage over the other? I propose two conditions that help identify when the advantage of foreignness or the advantage of localness helps a particular firm achieve a relative advantage in the host country: whether the products of the industry are primarily sold to end-user consumers or primarily sold to other companies, and whether the industry of operation is mostly a global one or mostly a local one.

Competing in business-to-consumer or business-to-business industries

In industries in which the customers are mostly end-user consumers, I propose that the advantage of localness supersedes the advantage of foreignness. There are large and subtle differences in consumer needs and preferences across countries, which induce companies to create products that are tailored to those needs. Needs and preferences of end-user consumers tend to be influenced not only by sociocultural issues such as religion, culture, language, ethnic group, etc., but also by geographic issues such as weather, distribution, distance, etc.; economic issues such as poverty, house size, access to electricity and water, etc.; and political issues such as political system, civil society, consumer rights, etc. (Khavul and Bruton, 2013). Since domestic firms have more tacit and explicit knowledge about these local issues, they are better able to innovate to meet the needs of these customers in the context in which they use the innovations (Bhattacharya and Michael, 2008). In contrast, subsidiaries' lower level of local-market knowledge and weaker relationships with local knowledge resources make them less likely to have the necessary tacit knowledge about local customer needs required to generate locally relevant innovations (Williams and Du, 2014). Moreover, end-user customers may even discriminate against products produced by subsidiaries of foreign MNEs (for a review, see Siamagka and Balabanis, 2015), because they suffer from consumer ethnocentrism, preferring products created by domestic firms over those produced by foreign firms (Cleveland, Rojas-Méndez, Laroche, and Papadopoulos, 2016).

In contrast, when the firms' customers are other companies, I propose that the advantage of foreignness of subsidiaries is likely to supersede the advantage of domestic firms' localness. The innovations that subsidiaries of foreign MNEs create and receive from the parent firm and other subsidiaries are likely to be applicable to the needs of customers across different countries rather than only one country in particular. Companies, in contrast to end-user consumers, tend to have needs that remain consistent across national boundaries. There are fewer differences in industrial needs, as production processes tend to be standardized across countries, with best practices developed in one country being transferred to firms in other countries via mechanisms such as consultancy. In such conditions, subsidiaries of foreign MNEs can benefit from worldwide learning and innovation and global efficiency (Bartlett and Ghoshal, 2001; for a review see Motohashi, 2015), integrating and standardizing the innovations created by the different country subsidiaries and the parent company. When serving domestic customers, the subsidiaries can benefit from the knowledge and innovations received via the MNE to provide more sophisticated innovations and products to their customers. For example, a subsidiary may use innovations that have already been created in the parent company or in other national subsidiaries, and offer them to their industrial clients in the host country. Meanwhile, domestic competitors may not be able to access such innovations or may suffer a delay as innovations take time to diffuse from the multinational to the domestic competitors via demonstration, common suppliers, and employee mobility (Blomström and Kokko, 1998).

Competing in global or local industries

When the industry is mostly global in nature, I propose that the advantage of foreignness supersedes the advantage of localness in innovation. In a global industry, firms compete in the majority of countries with a particular product in order to survive and gain economies of scale or economies of scope across foreign markets (Makhija, Kim, and Williamson, 1997). Since firms operating in global industries need to make large investments to compete, and thus their costs cannot be recouped by selling in only one country, they tend to sell in as many countries as possible (Motohashi, 2015). The need for scale economies means that products are transferred from country to country. In some of these industries the products are of high value relative to their weight and thus transportation costs are not relevant, further facilitating the globalization of the industry. Moreover, firms operating in global industries can more easily sell their products in the foreign countries with fewer tariffs to limit their sales (Makhija et al., 1997). As such, subsidiaries of foreign MNEs may enjoy an advantage in these industries as they benefit from links to operations in multiple countries and economies of scale. They can receive or create innovations that are designed for sale in different countries without adapting them to the particular needs of any individual country. Most domestic firms would be at a disadvantage in global industries, and only the host-country multinationals are able to counter this advantage of foreignness for the subsidiaries of foreign MNEs (Nachum, 2010).

In contrast, when the industry is mostly locally responsive in nature, I propose that domestic companies have an advantage over subsidiaries of foreign MNEs. A local industry has several characteristics: products and services have to be tailored to individual countries, R&D investment has to be local, and extensive local market knowledge is needed to tailor innovations to the needs of local customers (Doz and Wilson, 2012). Since domestic firms have more local-market knowledge, have already invested in R&D in that market, and can more easily access the knowledge of local customers, suppliers, and universities to gather the necessary knowledge to create local innovations, they may enjoy an advantage over MNE subsidiaries (Andersson, Forsgren, and Holm, 2002; Hymer, 1976; Zaheer, 1995). The innovations and products of domestic firms are better adapted to the local market and thus may be more appropriate in industries that are locally responsive (Bhattacharya and Michael, 2008). Subsidiaries of foreign MNEs are at a disadvantage when the industry is local, because they would face higher costs to tailor products and duplicate efforts in product design and R&D development across national boundaries (Doz and Wilson, 2012).

Competition and relative advantage

The combination of these two dimensions leads to a two-by-two matrix that helps to better understand the conditions under which the two types of firm can achieve a relative advantage over each other. Table 13.2 illustrates the possible combinations of these two dimensions and the proposed relative advantage of each type of firm.

Two cases are easier to identify based on the previous explanations. First, when the companies are competing in a global industry that serves other companies, subsidiaries of foreign firms are likely to enjoy an advantage of foreignness in innovation that supersedes the advantage of localness for domestic firms. In this case, subsidiaries can benefit both from the innovations developed in multiple countries, and the similarity in the needs of companies across national boundaries, which helps subsidiaries provide customers with innovations and solutions developed elsewhere (Bartlett and Ghoshal, 2001; Doz and Wilson, 2012). Second, when companies are competing in a local industry that serves end-user consumers, domestic firms are likely to enjoy an advantage of localness in innovation that supersedes the advantage of foreignness of subsidiaries. In this

Table 13.2 Competition between local firms and subsidiaries of multinationals by industry characteristics

		Type of customer	
		End-user consumers	Businesses
Type of industry	Global	Advantage of localness slightly supersedes advantage of foreignness	Advantage of foreignness supersedes advantage of localness
	Local	Advantage of localness supersedes advantage of foreignness	Advantage of foreignness slightly supersedes advantage of localness

case, competition differs significantly across countries, and customers tend to demand products and services that are better adapted to the particular needs of consumers (Bhattacharya and Michael, 2008), helping domestic firms do better with the more locally adapted products.

The other two cases are less clear-cut, but they can be theoretically ranked. Hence, I first propose that for firms that operate in global industries serving end-user customers, domestic firms are likely to have an advantage of localness in innovation that supersedes the advantage of foreignness for subsidiaries. Domestic firms are able to create products better adapted to the particular needs of customers, although some subsidiaries of foreign MNEs may invest in the adaptation of their global innovations to the particular needs of the host country, especially when the host country is large enough to justify the investments this entails (Bartlett and Ghoshal, 2001). In such a case, some subsidiaries of foreign companies may have an advantage over many, but not all, of the domestic firms. Large domestic firms, especially those that are also MNEs, may have developed products that are better than those of the subsidiaries of foreign MNEs and remain the dominant competitors in their home market (Nachum, 2010). Second, I propose that for firms that compete in local industries serving other companies, subsidiaries of foreign MNEs may achieve a slight advantage of foreignness in innovation that is superior to the advantage of localness in innovation. Subsidiaries of foreign MNEs can make innovations that prove better at satisfying the needs of other companies, and achieve an advantage in the host country because the quality of the products is superior to those provided by domestic companies, even if the latter's products are better adapted to the particular needs of the local companies that buy them (Hout and Ghemawat, 2010). Thus, although some domestic companies may be able to compete on the basis of better location or better speed of service provided to other companies, the foreign products maybe preferred by many of the customers, because they enable them to achieve higher efficiency in the production process. For example, foreign machinery may be superior to that available from local providers, with the customer company then adapting the machinery to its own production needs (Ghemawat and Hout, 2016).

Competitive dynamics and the reduction in relative advantages

No firm can sustain an advantage indefinitely. Changes in customer needs and demands, advances in technology, changes in regulation, entry of new competitors, and imitation by existing competitors eventually render an advantage obsolete (for a review on innovation and imitation, see Jenkins, 2014). Thus, both the advantage of foreignness in innovation as well as the advantage of localness in innovation will diminish over time, as each type of company learns how to serve their customers better and how to imitate the advantages of their competitors (Lieberman and Asaba, 2006). Therefore, we can expect that the advantage that each type of company has at the beginning of their competitive interaction, particularly when subsidiaries enter the market, will diminish (Reed and DeFillippi, 1990). The interesting question is whether the advantages may eventually disappear. I propose that this is not likely to be case, because there are limitations to the ability of both types of firms to completely imitate the advantage of the other.

Reduction in advantages over time

First, I argue that the advantages are likely to diminish over time as both types of firms imitate each other's advantages and learn to serve customers better. As a result of these processes we may encounter situations in which, over time, the innovations are imitated and the products sold to local customers converge in their innovativeness.

On the one hand, subsidiaries of foreign companies counter the advantage of localness in innovation by learning to understand the particular needs of local customers through imitating the local adaptation that domestic companies have accomplished. They can investigate in detail the different dimensions of the needs of local customers, and how their current products are or are not meeting all these needs, as well as learning what the products of their competitors are, how they differ from the current products offered by the firm, and how they provide new and different features that are better suited to the needs of local customers. This market and competitor research can help subsidiaries identify areas that could be easily adapted in terms of their products or the way these are marketed (Jolly and Masetti-Placci, 2016), distributed, and sold in the host country, and that would in effect reduce some of the advantage of localness that domestic firms enjoy. Additionally, subsidiaries can gain experience from interacting directly with customers in the host country, and this experience can help them better understand the needs of customers and what they can easily adapt to satisfy those needs (Andersson et al., 2002; Ernst, Kahle, Dubiel, Prabhu, and Subramaniam, 2015). Direct learning about customer needs is another important source of product innovation (Bhattacharya and Michael, 2008). In this way, subsidiaries of foreign companies reduce the advantage of localness and the better adaptation of domestic firms' innovations to local customer needs. In some cases, subsidiaries may even create new products that are designed for the local market based on the needs of customers there, in effect behaving like domestic firms; this is likely to happen only when the potential market in the host country is large enough for subsidiaries to justify the creation of a new product and the offerings of local competitors do not seem to be satisfying the potential market (Bartlett and Ghoshal, 1986; Hout and Ghemawat, 2010). In such cases, subsidiaries are actually developing an advantage of localness, behaving like domestic companies by introducing innovations that are designed for the local market.

On the other hand, domestic firms can counter the advantage of foreignness by imitating some of the features of the products of subsidiaries, adapting the new ideas and features to the local context to maintain their advantage there. Domestic companies may not have the global reach of subsidiaries of foreign

MNEs, and may not be able to learn from the needs of customers in other countries, but they can achieve this indirectly by incorporating the innovations that subsidiaries of foreign companies have created by reverse engineering their products (Malik and Kotabe, 2009). This imitation can help domestic firms reduce the advantage of foreignness, especially in countries in which there is limited protection of property rights, and thus the domestic companies are less likely to face lawsuits for breach of intellectual property, or in the case of innovations that are not subject to patents, whereby the firm imitates the design and look of the product without copying the trademarked designs or brands (Luo, Sun, and Wang, 2011). Additionally, domestic companies may just imitate parts of the foreign product that can help their own products achieve superior functionality and efficiency, while leaving the rest of the product unchanged and better adapted to the conditions of the local market (Shih, 2010), thus reducing the advantage of foreignness in innovation.

Limitations to the reduction in advantages

Despite this potential convergence in the innovativeness of subsidiaries of foreign firms and domestic companies, and thus the reduction of the advantage of foreignness and the advantage of localness in innovation, I propose that there are particular characteristics in the innovation processes of both subsidiaries and domestic firms that will prevent a full convergence and the achievement of parity between products.

Subsidiaries of foreign companies are subject to the need to coordinate and integrate with other parts of the company. As a result, they face limitations in their ability to fully adapt to the conditions of the local market and create products and services that are uniquely tailored to the local market. Although the adaptation of products to the conditions of the local market can help subsidiaries of foreign firms achieve a degree of responsiveness to local conditions and thus enable them to counter the advantage of localness in innovation, this adaptation is costly. It requires subsidiaries of foreign firms to invest in the redesign and, in some cases, the innovation of the products and their tailoring to the local conditions (Bartlett, 2009). These costs of adaptation or innovation need to be paid for by an increase in sales that makes the investments profitable; however, subsidiaries face domestic competitors that have better adapted products, which may limit the ability of the products of the subsidiaries of foreign MNEs to achieve high levels of sales. Additionally, the adaptation of products to the local market is accompanied by an increase in complexity in the management of the multinational, as headquarters have to keep track of the differences in products across countries and coordinate the variety of products and their different versions (Bartlett and Ghoshal, 2001; Doz and Wilson, 2012; Hedlund, 1986). Local adaptation and innovation may also create challenges if customers in one country learn about the features and attributes of products in other countries and find that they prefer those products to the ones offered locally. Finally, the adaptation of foreign products to local conditions may end up being counterproductive for some customers, who may actually value the differentiation and uniqueness of the foreign products and may not appreciate products that are similar to those offered by domestic companies (Hout and Ghemawat, 2010). As a result of these constraints, subsidiaries of foreign firms may not be able to fully imitate or develop products that are fully adapted to local needs, and thus may maintain a degree of foreignness in their innovations.

Domestic companies, unless they become multinationals themselves, are limited in their ability to compensate for the global innovation of subsidiaries of foreign firms, because they are under pressure to produce products that are distinct and well adapted to the local market in order to maintain their perception of responsiveness and distinctiveness. The imitation of foreign products can be a quick way to upgrade the innovativeness of domestic firms, especially when the firms are far away from the technological frontier (Shih, 2010). However, there are limitations to the imitation of foreign products, in the form of customers knowing that domestic products are merely a copy of foreign products rather than actual innovations, and thus requiring the price to be substantially lower to compensate for the lower perceived innovativeness status. Additionally, imitation via reverse engineering can help the domestic company understand the features of the product and which ideas can be incorporated in their own products to improve their quality, but reverse engineering cannot provide information about the production process used to create those products (Malik and Kotabe, 2009). The production process in many cases is the actual source of many innovations, as it enables the creation of high-quality products at a low price (Pisano and Shih, 2012; Un and Asakawa, 2015). Reverse engineering the products does not reveal how to achieve their quality, and thus domestic firms face a limitation in their imitation of foreign products. Moreover, reverse engineering products is costly and requires firms to invest in the purchase and analysis of foreign products, and the associated modification needed to their own products and production processes to be able to incorporate the innovations; this may conflict with a well-tuned product and process and thus create additional coordination and management costs. Finally, domestic firms that imitate foreign products may have to deal with customer perceptions that they are offering cheaper, locally made versions of the "real" products, and even if the products retain some distinct local innovativeness, customers may not identify this, thereby limiting the ability of domestic firms to charge a premium for their own innovation efforts (Ghemawat and Hout, 2016).

Conclusions

In this chapter I have analyzed differences in the abilities of subsidiaries of foreign MNEs and domestic companies to renew their competitive advantage via innovation. I have explained how subsidiaries enjoy an advantage of foreignness in innovation while domestic companies enjoy an advantage of localness in innovation. I have also explained how these advantages are driven by the differences in the knowledge focus of the two types of firms as well as by the differences in how they manage their employees. I concluded with an explanation of how these advantages provide an ultimate competitive advantage depending on the characteristics of the industry, whether it is global or local in nature, and of the customers, whether they are end-user consumers or other businesses, and how these relative advantages change over time as companies imitate each other.

The ideas presented in this chapter contribute to a better understanding of strategic renewal in global competition in several ways. First, unlike much of the literature that has discussed the traditional determinants of innovation, such as R&D investments, R&D collaboration, and firm acquisitions (Cuervo-Cazurra and Un, 2010; Kapoor and Lim, 2007; Un and Asakawa, 2015), I explain how differences in the knowledge bases of firms and the management of employees enable them to achieve an innovation-based advantage, contributing to the knowledge-based view of the firm (Grant, 2013; Kogut and Zander, 1992). The ideas also contribute to calls for more research on the micro-foundation of the firm's competitive strategy, as individuals inside the firms are the ones who explore and exploit knowledge, forming the basis of the firms' absorptive capacity and thus their ability to undertake strategic renewal (Helfat and Peteraf, 2015; Martinkenaite and Breunig, 2016; Volberda, Foss, and Lyles, 2010).

Second, I have discussed how subsidiaries of foreign firms can achieve an advantage of foreignness in innovation over domestic firms, not only from the transfer of innovations from the MNE, but also from how they manage their employees to develop a multicultural mindset to create their own innovations. This contributes to studies that call for more analyses on the advantages of the foreignness of subsidiaries (e.g., Edman, 2016; Nachum, 2010; Siegel et al., 2011; Un, 2016). As such, this study also complements a larger body of literature on the liability of foreignness (e.g., Husted, Montiel, and Christmann, 2016; Zaheer, 1995). Moreover, I complement these studies by also analyzing the advantages of localness for the host-country domestic firms, which is not typically explored in studies of the liabilities of foreignness (e.g., Mezias, 2002; Zaheer and Mosakowski, 1997).

Third, I discussed how the advantages of foreignness and localness in innovation differ depending on the characteristics of the customers that the firms serve and their industry of operation. Whereas domestic firms are more likely to enjoy their advantage of localness in innovation when serving customers who are end users of the firms' products and services, subsidiaries of foreign firms are more likely to enjoy their advantage of foreignness in innovation when they serve business customers. This provides a more nuanced discussion of the conditions under which one type of firms has an advantage over another (Bartlett and Ghoshal, 2001; Doz and Wilson, 2012). Moreover, whereas the advantage of foreignness is likely to supersede the advantage of localness in global industries, the advantage of localness is likely to supersede the advantage of foreignness in local industries. This discussion extends studies that have explored the advantages and liabilities of foreignness (Edman, 2016; Husted et al., 2016), by providing another condition under which one type of advantage supersedes another. Finally, I discussed the temporary nature of the advantage of foreignness and the advantage of localness in innovation. As foreign and domestic firms compete in the same country, they may end up imitating each other, eroding each other's advantages. However, these advantages are not likely to disappear completely. As subsidiaries of foreign MNEs interact with local customers, suppliers, universities, and competitors, they gain more local-market knowledge, and thus, they incorporate such knowledge in their innovations to meet local needs. As a result, their products and services may become more similar to those offered by local firms. However, these products are not likely to become exactly the same as those of local firms, nor to completely erode these firms' advantage of localness, especially when subsidiaries of foreign firms serve other firms rather than end-user customers and operate in the global industry. This is particularly important since these subsidiaries need to maintain their integration with the MNE to achieve global efficiency and worldwide learning and innovation (Bartlett, 2009; Doz and Wilson, 2012). Thus, this discussion extends studies on the liability of foreignness that suggest that subsidiaries of foreign MNEs imitate the behavior of host-country firms to achieve local legitimacy (e.g., Husted et al., 2016). Similarly, although domestic firms may imitate certain aspects of the products and services of the subsidiaries of foreign MNEs, they cannot completely replicate the advantages of foreignness unless they become MNEs themselves (Nachum, 2010; Un, 2016). Even so, they may not enjoy the same level of advantage of foreignness (Mata and Freitas, 2012). As a result, although firms may imitate certain elements of each other's sources of competitive advantage, their respective advantages of foreignness and localness are not likely to disappear completely over time.

In sum, companies can achieve strategic renewal via innovation, but the processes by which they achieve it will differ depending on whether they are foreign or domestic firms, since these are likely to manage their employees differently, resulting in differences in their abilities to innovate and compete.

References

Adenfelt, M., and Lagerström, K. 2008. The development and sharing of knowledge by centres of excellence and transnational teams: A conceptual framework. *Management International Review*. 48(3): 319–338.

Allred, B. B., and Steensma, H. K. 2005. The influence of industry and home country characteristics on firms' pursuit of innovation. *Management International Review*. 45(4): 383–412.

Andersson, U., Forsgren, M., and Holm, U. 2002. The strategic impact of external networks: Subsidiary performance and competence development in the multinational corporation. *Strategic Management Journal*. 23(11): 979–997.

Bartlett, C. A. 2009. *Philips Versus Matsushita: The Competitive Battle Continues*. Harvard Business School Cases. Cambridge, MA: Harvard Business School.

Bartlett, C. A., and Ghoshal, S. 1986. Tap your subsidiaries for global reach. *Harvard Business Review.* November–December: 87–94.

Bartlett, C. A., and Ghoshal, S. 2001. *Managing Across Borders: The Transnational Solution,* 2nd edition. Boston, MA: Harvard Business School Press.

Bertrand, O., and Mol, M. 2013. The antecedents and innovation effects of domestic and offshore R&D outsourcing: The contingent impact of cognitive distance and absorptive capacity. *Strategic Management Journal.* 34(6): 751–760.

Bhattacharya, A. K., and Michael, D. 2008. How local companies keep multinationals at bay. *Harvard Business Review.* 86(3), 20–33.

Birkinshaw, J. M., and Morrison, A. J. 1995. Configurations of strategy and structure in subsidiaries of multinational corporations. *Journal of International Business Studies.* 26(4): 729–753.

Blomström, M., and Kokko, A. 1998. Multinational corporations and spillovers. *Journal of Economic Surveys.* 12(3): 247–278.

Bouquet, C., and Birkinshaw, J. 2008. Weight versus voice: How foreign subsidiaries gain attention from corporate headquarters. *Academy of Management Journal.* 51(3): 577–601.

Brannen, M. Y., Piekkari, R., and Tietze, S. 2014. The multifaceted role of language in international business: Unpacking the forms, functions and features of a critical challenge to MNC theory and performance. *Journal of International Business Studies.* 45(5): 495–507.

Buckley, P. J., and Casson, M. C. 1976. *The Future of the Multinational Enterprise.* London: Macmillan.

Buckley, P. J., and Casson, M. C. 2009. The internalisation theory of the multinational enterprise: A review of the progress of a research agenda after 30 years. *Journal of International Business Studies.* 40(9): 1563–1580.

Carlile, P. R. 2002. A pragmatic view of knowledge and boundaries: Boundary objects in new product development. *Organization Science.* 13(4): 442–455.

Chatman, J. A. 1991. Matching people and organizations: Selection and socialization in public accounting firms. *Administrative Science Quarterly.* 36(3): 459–484.

Cleveland, M., Rojas-Méndez, J. I., Laroche, M., and Papadopoulos, N. 2016. Identity, culture, dispositions and behavior: A cross-national examination of globalization and culture change. *Journal of Business Research.* 69(3): 1090–1102.

Cuervo-Cazurra, A., and Un, C. A. 2007. Regional economic integration and R&D investment. *Research Policy.* 36(2): 227–246.

Cuervo-Cazurra, A., and Un, C. A. 2010. Why some firms never invest in formal R&D. *Strategic Management Journal.* 31(7): 759–779.

Dodgson, M., Gann, D. M., and Phillips, N. 2013. *The Oxford Handbook of Innovation Management.* Oxford: Oxford University Press.

Doz, Y., Santos, J., and Williamson, P. 2001. *From Global to Meta-National – How Companies Win in the Knowledge Economy.* Boston, MA: Harvard University Press.

Doz, Y., and Wilson, K. 2012. *Managing Global Innovation: Frameworks for Integrating Capabilities Around the World.* Boston, MA: Harvard Business Press.

Dunning, J. H. 1977. Trade, location of economic activity and the MNE: A search for an eclectic approach. In *The International Allocation of Economic Activity* (pp. 395–418). London: Palgrave Macmillan.

Edman, J. 2016. Reconciling the advantages and liabilities of foreignness: Towards an identity-based framework. *Journal of International Business Studies.* http://link.springer.com/article/10.1057/jibs.2016.29.

Ernst, H., Kahle, H. N., Dubiel, A., Prabhu, J., and Subramaniam, M. 2015. The ante-cedents and consequences of affordable value innovations for emerging markets. *Journal of Product Innovation Management*. 32(1): 65–79.

Fey, C. F., and Furu, P. 2008. Top management incentive compensation and know-ledge sharing in multinational corporations. *Strategic Management Journal*. 29(12): 1301–1323.

Froese, F., Kim, K., and Eng, A. 2016. Language, cultural intelligence, and inpatriate turnover intentions: Leveraging values in multinational corporations through inpatriates. *Management International Review*. 56(2): 283–301.

Frost, R. S., Birkinshaw, J. M., and Ensign, P. 2002. Centers of excellence in multi-national corporations. *Strategic Management Journal*, 23: 997–1018.

Frost, T. S., and Zhou, C. 2005. R&D co-practice and 'reverse' knowledge integration in multinational firms. *Journal of International Business Studies*. 36(6): 676–687.

Fu, F. Q. 2015. Motivate to improve salesforce performance: The sales training perspective. *Performance Improvement*. 54(4): 31–35.

Ghemawat, P., and Hout, T. 2016. Can China's companies conquer the world? *Foreign Affairs*. 95(2): 86–98.

Govindarajan, V., and Ramamurti, R. 2011. Reverse innovation, emerging markets, and global strategy. *Global Strategy Journal*. 1(3–4): 191–205.

Grant, R. 2013. Reflections on knowledge-based approaches to the organization of production. *Journal of Management & Governance*. 17(3): 541–558.

Grant, R. M. 1996. Toward a knowledge-based theory of the firm. *Strategic Management Journal*. 17: 109–122.

Gupta, A. K., and Govindarajan, V. 2000. Knowledge flows within multinational corporations. *Strategic Management Journal*. 21(4): 473–497.

Hall, B. H., and Rosenberg, N. 2010. *Handbook of the Economics of Innovation*. North Holland: Elsevier.

Harhoff, D., Henkel, J., and von Hippel, E. 2003. Profiting from voluntary information spillovers: how users benefit by freely revealing their innovations. *Research Policy*. 32 (10): 1753–1770.

Hedlund, G. 1986. The hypermodern MNC - a heterarchy? *Human Resource Management*. 25(1): 9–35.

Helfat, C. E., and Peteraf, M. A. 2015. Managerial cognitive capabilities and the micro-foundations of dynamic capabilities. *Strategic Management Journal*. 36(6): 831–850.

Holtbrügge, D., and Mohr, A. 2011. Subsidiary interdependencies and international human resource management practices in German MNCs. *Management International Review*. 51(1): 93–115.

Hout, T. M., and Ghemawat, P. 2010. China vs. the world. *Harvard Business Review*. 88 (12): 94–103.

Husted, B. W., Montiel, I., and Christmann, P. 2016. Effects of local legitimacy on certification decisions to global and national CSR standards by multinational sub-sidiaries and domestic firms. *Journal of International Business Studies*. 47(3): 382–397.

Hymer, S. 1976. *The International Operations of National Firms: A Study of Direct Invest-ment*. Cambridge, MA: MIT Press.

Inderst, R, and Ottaviani, M. 2015. Misselling through agents. *American Economic Review*. 99(3): 883–908.

Jenkins, M. 2014. Innovate or imitate? The role of collective beliefs in competences in competing firms. *Long Range Planning*. 47(4): 173–185.

Jolly, D., and Masetti-Placci, F. 2016. The winding path for foreign companies: Building R&D centers in China. *Journal of Business Strategy.* 37(2): 3–11.

Kapoor, R., and Lim, K. 2007. The impact of acquisitions on the productivity of inventors at semiconductor firms: A synthesis of knowledge-based perspectives. *Academy of Management Journal.* 50(5): 1133–1155.

Khavul, S., and Bruton, G. D. 2013. Harnessing innovation for change: Sustainability and poverty in developing countries. *Journal of Management Studies.* 50(2): 285–306.

Kogut, B., and Zander, U. 1992. Knowledge of the firm, combinative capabilities, and the replication of technology. *Organization Science.* 3: 383–397.

Kogut, B., and Zander, U. 1993. Knowledge of the firm and the evolutionary theory of the multinational corporation. *Journal of International Business Studies.* 24(4): 625–645.

Kronborg, D., and Thomsen, S. 2009. Foreign ownership and long-term survival. *Strategic Management Journal.* 30(2): 207–219.

Lagerström, K., and Andersson, M. 2003. Creating and sharing knowledge within a transnational team—the development of a global business system. *Journal of World Business.* 38(2): 84–95.

Leung, A. K-Y., and Chiu, C.-Y. 2008. Interactive effects of multicultural experiences and openness to experience on creativity. *Creativity Research Journal.* 20(4): 376–382.

Lewis, P., Goodman, S., Fandt, P., and Michlitsch, J. 2007. *Management: Challenges for Tomorrow's Leaders.* Stanford, CT: Thomson Learning, Inc.

Li, J., Jiang, F., and Shen, J. 2016. Institutional distance and the quality of the headquarters – Subsidiary relationship: The moderating role of the institutionalization of headquarters' practices in subsidiaries. *International Business Review.* 25(2): 589–603.

Li, J., and Lee, R. P. 2015. Can knowledge transfer within MNCs hurt subsidiary performance? The role of subsidiary entrepreneurial culture and capabilities. *Journal of World Business,* 50(4): 663–673.

Li, S., and Scullion, H. 2010. Developing the local competence of expatriate managers for emerging markets: A knowledge-based approach. *Journal of World Business.* 45(2): 190–196.

Lieberman, M. B., and Asaba, S. 2006. Why do firms imitate each other? *Academy of Management Review.* 31(2): 366–385.

Lücke, G., Kostova, T., and Roth, K. 2014. Multiculturalism from a cognitive perspective: Patterns and implications. *Journal of International Business Studies.* 45(2): 169–190.

Luo, Y., Sun, J., and Wang, S. L. 2011. Emerging economy copycats: Capability, environment and strategy. *Academy of Management Perspectives,* 25: 37–56.

Maddux, M. W., and Galinsky, A. D. 2009. Cultural borders and mental barriers: The relationship between living abroad and creativity. *Journal of Personality and Social Psychology.* 96(5): 1047.

Makhija, M., Kim, K., and Williamson, S. D. 1997. Measuring globalization of industries using a national industry approach: Empirical evidence across five countries and over time. *Journal of International Business Studies.* 28(4): 679–710.

Malik, O. R., and Kotabe, M. 2009. Dynamic capabilities, government policies, and performance in firms from emerging economies: Evidence from India and Pakistan. *Journal of Management Studies.* 46(3): 421–450.

Martinkenaite, I., and Breunig, K. J. 2016. The emergence of absorptive capacity through micro–macro level interactions. *Journal of Business Research.* 69(2): 700–708.

Mata, J., and Freitas, E. 2012. Foreignness and exit over the life cycle of firms. *Journal of International Business Studies.* 43(7): 615–630.

Mezias, J. M. 2002. Identifying liabilities of foreignness and strategies to minimize their effects: The case of labor lawsuit judgments in the United States. *Strategic Management Journal.* 23(3): 229–244.

Monteiro, L. F., Arvidsson, N., and Birkinshaw, J. 2008. Knowledge flows within multinational corporations: Explaining subsidiary isolation and its performance implications. *Organization Science.* 19(1): 90–107.

Motohashi, K. 2015. *Global Business Strategy: Multinational Corporations Venturing into Emerging Markets.* Berlin, Germany: Springer Open.

Mudambi, R., Piscitello, L., and Rabbiosi, L. 2014. Reverse knowledge transfer in MNEs: subsidiary innovativeness and entry modes. *Long Range Planning.* 47(1/2): 49–63.

Nachum, L. 2010. When is foreignness an asset or a liability? Explaining the performance differential between foreign and local firms. *Journal of Management.* 36(3): 714–739.

Nahapiet, J., and Ghoshal, S. 1998. Social capital, intellectual capital, and the organizational advantage. *Academy of Management Review.* 23(2): 242–266.

Nair, S. R., Demirbag, M., and Mellahi, K. 2016. Reverse knowledge transfer in emerging market multinationals: The Indian context. *International Business Review.* 25(1): 152–164.

Najafi-Tavani, Z., Zaefarian, G., Naudé, P., and Giroud, A. 2015. Reverse knowledge transfer and subsidiary power. *Industrial Marketing Management,* 48: 103–110.

Nelson, R. R., and Fagerberg, J. 2005. *The Oxford Handbook of Innovation.* Oxford: Oxford University Press.

Nohria, N., and Ghoshal, S. 1997. *The Differentiated Network: Organizing Multinational Corporations for Value Creation.* San Francisco, CA: Jossey-Bass.

Nonaka, I. 1994. A dynamic theory of organizational knowledge creation. *Organization Science,* 5: 14–37.

Nonaka, I. 2007. The knowledge-creating company. *Harvard Business Review,* 85(7/8): 162–171.

Nooteboom, B. 2000. Learning by interaction: Absorptive capacity, cognitive distance and governance. *Journal of Management & Governance.* 4(1/2): 69–92.

Peltokorpi, V. 2015. Corporate language proficiency and reverse knowledge transfer in multinational corporations: Interactive effects of communication media richness and commitment to headquarters. *Journal of International Management.* 21(1): 49–62.

Phene, A., and Almeida, P. 2008. Innovation in multinational subsidiaries: The role of knowledge assimilation and subsidiary capabilities. *Journal of International Business Studies.* 39: 901–919.

Pisano, G. P., and Shih, W. C. 2012. *Producing Prosperity: Why America Needs a Manufacturing Renaissance.* Boston, MA: Harvard Business Press.

Puck, J. F., Kittler, M. G., and Wright, C. 2008. Does it really work? Re-assessing the impact of pre-departure cross-cultural training on expatriate adjustment. *International Journal of Human Resource Management.* 19(12): 2182–2197.

Reed, R., and DeFillippi, R. J. 1990. Causal ambiguity, barriers to imitation, and sustainable competitive advantage. *Academy of Management Review.* 15(1): 88–102.

Schumpeter, J. A. 1954. *History of Economic Analysis.* Oxford, UK: Oxford University Press.

Scott-Kennel, J., and Giroud, A. 2015. MNEs and FSAs: Network knowledge, strategic orientation and performance. *Journal of World Business.* 50(1): 94–107.

Shih, W. 2010. *Reverse Engineering, Learning, and Innovation.* Harvard Business School Cases. Cambridge, MA: Harvard Business School.

Siamagka, N-T., and Balabanis, G. 2015. Revisiting consumer ethnocentrism: Review, reconceptualization, and empirical testing. *Journal of International Marketing*. 23(3): 66–86.

Siegel, J., Pyun, L., and Cheon, B. Y. 2011. *Multinational Firms, Labor Market Discrimination, and the Capture of Competitive Advantage by Exploiting the Social Divide*. Boston, MA: Harvard Business School. Working Papers.

Stienstra, M., Baaij, M., Van den Bosch, F., and Volberda, H. 2004. Strategic renewal of Europe's largest telecom operators (1992–2001): From herd behaviour towards strategic choice? *European Management Journal*. 22(3): 273–280.

Subramaniam, M., and Venkatraman, N. 2001. Determinants of transnational new product development: Testing the influence of transferring and deploying tacit overseas knowledge. *Strategic Management Journal*. 22(4): 359–378.

Szulanski, G. 1996. Exploring internal stickiness: Impediments to the transfer of best practice within the firm. *Strategic Management Journal*. 17(S2): 27–43.

Teece, D. J. 2007. Explicating dynamic capabilities: The nature and micro-foundations of (sustainable) enterprise performance. *Strategic Management Journal*. 28(13): 1319–1350.

Tuncdogan, A., Van den Bosch, F., and Volberda, H. 2015. Regulatory focus as a psychological micro-foundation of leaders' exploration and exploitation activities. *Leadership Quarterly*. 26(5): 838–850.

Un, C. A. 2007. Managing the innovators for exploration and exploitation. *Journal of Technology Management & Innovation*. 2(3): 4–20.

Un, C. A. 2010. An empirical multi-level analysis for achieving balance between incremental and radical innovations. *Journal of Engineering & Technology Management*. 27(1/2): 1–19.

Un, C. A. 2011. The advantage of foreignness in innovation. *Strategic Management Journal*. 32(11): 1232–1242.

Un, C. A. 2016. The liability of localness in innovation. *Journal of International Business Studies*. 47(1): 44–67.

Un, C. A., and Asakawa, K. 2015. Types of R&D collaborations and process innovation: The benefit of collaborating upstream in the knowledge chain. *Journal of Product Innovation Management*. 32(1): 138–153.

Un, C. A., and Cuervo-Cazurra, A. 2008. Do subsidiaries of foreign MNEs invest more in R&D than domestic firms? *Research Policy*. 37(10): 1812–1828.

Un, C. A., Cuervo-Cazurra, A., and Asakawa, K. 2010. R&D collaborations and product innovation. *Journal of Product Innovation Management*. 27(5): 673–689.

Vernon, R. 1966. International investment and international trade in the product cycle. *Quarterly Journal of Economics*. 80(2): 190–207.

Volberda, H. W., Foss, N., and Lyles, M. 2010. Absorbing the concept of absorptive capacity: How to realize its potential in the organization field. *Organization Science*. 21(4): 931–951.

Williams, C., and Du, J. 2014. The impact of trust and local learning on the innovative performance of MNE subsidiaries in China. *Asia Pacific Journal of Management*. 31(4): 973–996.

Williams, C., and Nones, B. 2009. R&D subsidiary isolation in knowledge-intensive industries: evidence from Austria. *R&D Management*. 39(2): 111–123.

Yergin, D., and Stanislaw, J. 2002. *The Commanding Heights*. New York City, NY: Simon and Schuster.

Yu, K. Y. T. 2014. Person – organization fit effects on organizational attraction: A test of an expectations-based model. *Organizational Behavior & Human Decision Processes.* 124(1): 75–94.

Zaheer, S. 1995. Overcoming the liability of foreignness. *Academy of Management Journal.* 38(2): 341–363.

Zaheer, S., and Mosakowski, E. 1997. The dynamics of the liability of foreignness: A global study of survival in financial services. *Strategic Management Journal.* 18(6): 439–463.

Part 5

Interdisciplinary perspectives and future directions

14 Strategic renewal in services

The role of the top management team's social relationships

Julia Nieves and Javier Osorio

Introduction

Strategic renewal involves the refreshment or replacement of attributes of an organization that have the potential to affect its long-term expectations (Agarwal and Helfat, 2009). The implementation of new organizational strategies, such as novelties or significant changes in marketing strategies, allows companies to respond to different external dynamics that can improve their competitive capability (Binns, Harreldl, O'Reilly, and Tushman, 2014; Klammer, Gueldenberg, Kraus, and O'Dwyer, 2016; Sáez-Martínez and González-Moreno, 2011). Marketing and promotion are essential tools for the success of hospitality firms (Williams, 2006). Consequently, making early efforts in marketing innovations is essential in order to keep hospitality firms from being outdone by their competitors. In fact, the literature not only contemplates innovation capability as a skill to produce new ideas, but suggests that innovative processes also represent a fundamental mechanism for organizational adaptation and renewal (Lawson and Samson, 2001; Nohria and Gulati, 1996).

The top management team is responsible for driving the necessary transformations to promote an organizational renewal that favours constant adaptation to changing conditions (Rosenbloom, 2000). Therefore, one of managers' most important functions is to aperceive opportunities and lead the appropriate actions so that the organization can exploit them through the transformation or reconfiguration of its resource base (Augier and Teece, 2009). This function requires the good strategic fit of both the resources controlled internally and those situated outside the organizational limits to which the company has access. Therefore, the degree of information and knowledge about the resources themselves will influence the efficient development of the management function, given that it affects the actions taken for their renewal. In a similar way, knowledge about the environment, that is, sensing capability, is going to determine the success of management decisions related to the strategic renewal of the organization (Ambrosini and Bowman, 2009). Thus, the social relationships of the top management team, defined as "the systems of relationships top managers have with employees and other actors outside of their organization" (Collins and Clark, 2003: 740) help to guarantee that companies will be more sensitive to changes, and this gives them advantages over other organizations that react more slowly or are less informed (Tippins and Sohi, 2003).

For years, researchers focused their attention on the manufacturing industry, considering services to be residual activities with very little capacity for change. However, in the past 20 years, the economic activity has undergone a profound structural transformation. The most developed countries have evolved toward a service economy, which has fostered a gradual increase in studies with significant contributions in this field. Nevertheless, the innovation literature has put greater emphasis on the manufacturing sector, neglecting services firms, and particularly non-knowledge-intensive services. In order to address this empirical gap, this study aims to explore the role of encouraging top managers' social relationships in the organizational renewal of services companies. Specifically, the aim of the study is to explore the influence of human resources (HR) practices that foment top managers' internal and external social relations on marketing innovation, contemplating the mediating role of sensing dynamic capability.

Theoretical framework and hypothesis

Dynamic capabilities as a source of competitive advantage

The theory of the dynamic capabilities points out that, given that markets are dynamic, rather than mere heterogeneity in the availability of resources it is companies' capacity to renew their resource base that explains differences in their performance over time (Morgan, Vorhies, and Mason, 2009). The dynamism of the environment causes the resources and capabilities that provide value to become obsolete, which means that competitive advantages can be transitory (Collis, 1994; Wu, 2004). In this regard, many studies propose the advantages of aligning the organizational resources and capabilities to the changes that occur in the environment (Danneels, 2002; Eisenhardt and Martin, 2000; Teece, 2007; Wang and Ahmed, 2007). However, some researchers support the idea that the dynamic capabilities are not a source of sustainable competitive advantages (Eisenhardt and Martin, 2000; Winter, 2003; Zahra, Zapienza, and Davidsson, 2006). Ambrosini, Bowman, and Collier (2009) argue that the impact of the dynamic capabilities on the company's results can even be negative when the changes made in the resource base are not aligned with the requirements of the environment. Winter (2003) argues that investing in dynamic capabilities will only imply partial protection from the obsolescence of the existing capabilities, which, at times, can provide relatively sustainable advantages. In addition, Eisenhardt and Martin (2000) consider that the dynamic capabilities are not a source of sustainable strategic advantages, given that the companies can reach the same set of resources through different processes or paths. These authors consider that the potential for long-term competitive advantage is linked to the use of the dynamic capabilities first, and in a more astute and fortuitous way, among competitors.

However, for Zahra et al. (2006), the fact that different companies can reach the same point, following different processes, does not diminish the potential advantage of having the ability to quickly adjust, redesign, or change. Zott (2003) agrees with this proposal, pointing out that, even in the case of equivalent dynamic capabilities between companies, differences in performance can exist due to the costs of the dynamic capabilities and the different synchronization in their use. Similarly, Wang and Ahmed (2007: 36) refer to the arguments of Eisenhardt and Martin (2000), asserting that the ability to apply capabilities "sooner, more astutely, and more fortuitously" is, in fact, the essence of dynamic capabilities. Moreover, Zahra et al. (2006) state that if the common capabilities on which the dynamic capabilities operate are mediocre and continue to be mediocre after the restructuring, they will not provide competitive advantages. For these authors, although the dynamic capabilities can allow companies to pursue opportunities in a novel and potentially effective way, this does not guarantee their success or survival. However, they consider that if two companies have equivalent common capabilities, the one that has greater dynamic capabilities will have more possibilities for dealing with challenges in the best way.

Meanwhile, Zott (2003) argues that the dynamic capabilities make it possible to achieve and maintain competitive advantages, and this author emphasizes the importance of the timing of the change. Similarly, Verona and Ravasi (2003) maintain that these capabilities are determinants in reaching and sustaining competitive advantages. Barney, Wright, and Ketchen (2001) point out that the dynamic capabilities are a source of sustainable competitive advantage, to the degree that a company's ability to quickly change and be alert to changes in the market can be difficult for others to imitate, although this does not mean that they maintain this advantage in all the market adjustments. Ambrosini and Bowman (2009) conclude that dynamic capabilities have a direct impact on the company's resource base, which, in turn, is a source of competitive advantage, temporary or sustainable, depending on the dynamism of the environment. In synthesis, the sustainable competitive advantages will be based on the company's capacity to create, increase, foment, protect, and maintain valuable resources and capabilities, that is, on dynamic capabilities that are unique and difficult to copy (Teece, 2007).

The role of managers in the construction of dynamic capabilities

Managers are responsible for the management of the organizational resources and, therefore, research on corporate strategy must be extended to the people responsible for decision making, as a way to understand whether what distinguishes companies depends on what their managers do differently (Adner and Helfat, 2003). For Helfat et al. (2007) and Zahra et al., 2006) the dynamic capabilities are the company's ability to intentionally create, increase, or modify its resources and capabilities in the way considered most appropriate by the management function. Thus, the important role played by managers in the framework of dynamic capabilities is revealed. Understanding and implementing the processes and structures underlying dynamic capabilities is a specific management task and requires detailed knowledge about the company and the environment in which the company cooperates and competes (Teece, 2007). The efficacious performance of the management function in developing dynamic capabilities allows the organization to successfully adapt to changes. However, changes in the resource base that are not aligned with the requirements of the environment can negatively affect the company's results (Ambrosini et al., 2009). Furthermore, the management team's particular perception of the environment determines its decisions and actions with regard to deploying dynamic capabilities (Ambrosini and Bowman, 2009). In this way, the dynamic capabilities could be subject to both the dynamism of the environment and to the managers' interpretation of the environment surrounding their organization (Aragón-Correa and Sharma, 2003).

Adequate understanding of the latent desires and needs expressed by clients, the capabilities and strategies of competitors, and the new technological and normative developments, are essential elements in the creation of dynamic capabilities (Morgan et al., 2009; Teece, 2007). This comprehension allows managers to be more efficient in selecting the best combination of resources to adjust the organization to the changing conditions of the environment (Morgan et al., 2009). Interorganizational relationships grant managers a greater ability to identify the demand for changes in the resource base, at the same time as allowing them to acquire a large variety of information and knowledge that favours the implementation of these changes in an opportune and appropriate way. Likewise, managers' knowledge about their own resources is a critical aspect in the development of dynamic capabilities, given that this knowledge allows them to make appropriate decisions about which resources are still valuable, which have to be renewed, and which should be removed (Danneels, 2010). Therefore, the interorganizational relationships that managers maintain are also fundamental for adequately redesigning the internal resources in order to align them with changes in the environment or in the internal strategies (Liao, Welsch, and Stoica, 2003; Tsai, Huang, and Ma, 2009).

Social-relationship-building HR practices and sensing dynamic capability

HR practices can lead to improved business results and constitute a solid source of sustainable competitive advantage because they are often specific, difficult to imitate, and causally ambiguous (Wright, Dunford and Snell, 2001). These practices can reinforce certain employee behaviours that are desirable for the organization (Collins and Clark, 2003; Chen and Huang, 2009). This, along with the growing importance of knowledge, has determined changes in HR management, with it becoming a less bureaucratic and more strategic function, so that organizations can use these practices to support organizational performance (Gloet, 2006). Specifically, companies can use a set of HR practices to systematically develop and manage the social relationships of the top management team (Collins and Clark, 2003). These organizational practices make it possible to access diverse information and knowledge that helps to improve decision making. Information has become a valuable asset that, when managed correctly, allows for better use of resources. It is not surprising, therefore, that many companies have focused their strategies on the effective use of information and knowledge sources.

Pavlou and El Sawy (2011: 243–244) define sensing capability "as the ability to spot, interpret, and pursue opportunities in the environment". This definition implies that sensing capability is contemplated as a dynamic capability because it is made up of three basic routines (generating market intelligence, disseminating market intelligence, and responding to market intelligence) related to the literature on dynamic capabilities. The ability to process information from the environment is critical due to the large quantity of data that must be managed, the continuous changes, and the importance of undertaking anticipatory actions (Hult, Ketchen, and Slater, 2005). Thus, companies that have greater knowledge than their rivals about clients' desires and needs or competitors' capabilities and strategies will be more effective at adapting to the market conditions (Morgan et al., 2009).

Managers' behaviour and capacity for action are influenced by both external and internal links (Adler and Kwon, 2002). This network of relationships is capable of integrating and mobilizing a set of current and potential resources (Nahapiet and Ghoshal 1998). Therefore, companies must not only establish opportunities for their managers to develop social links, but they must also promote their motivation and provide them with adequate resources (Adler and Kwon, 2002).

External ties are fundamental in generating and accumulating knowledge in a sustainable way because they make it possible to bring knowledge from the exterior to the internal organizational systems, thus producing new routines that evolve into new dynamic capabilities (Lee, Chen, and Shyr, 2011a). These relationships provide essential information about opportunities to acquire and integrate resources that make it possible to adapt to changes (Blyler and Coff, 2003). Therefore, a company's ability to develop and manage social relationships with other stakeholders not only produces knowledge transference, but it also creates new resources, generating dynamic capabilities (Kim and Boo, 2010). Lee, Lin, Chen, and Shyr (2011b) point out that organizations use external ties to improve the exchange of opinions and information, as well as to acquire specialized knowledge and experience that can be used efficiently to develop dynamic capabilities. Similarly, the study by Tsai et al. (2009) finds that interorganizational social capital is positively related to multinational corporations' capacity to redesign resources and activities in response to changes and opportunities in the global market. In addition, the studies by Wu (2006) and Desai, Sahu, and Sinha (2007) find that the capacity to establish and manage relationships with customers, suppliers, and other organizations is a determinant element of dynamic capabilities. Specifically, in the area of services, Agarwal and Selen (2009) show that dynamic capabilities are generated as a result of collaboration with other groups of interest.

However, Zollo and Winter (2002) argue that knowing what competitors do or what customers desire are critical elements in the competitive strategy of any company, but are not capable of creating or modifying the company's routines, given that they involve tacit knowledge, which is developed within the organization. In parallel, Blyler and Coff (2003) consider that social capital is a necessary condition, although not sufficient on its own, for the development of a dynamic capability. For Desai et al. (2007), these proposals do not contemplate the learning potential involved in interorganizational relationships. The empirical study by Kim and Boo (2010), consistent with the proposals of Zollo and Winter (2002), finds no relationship between service companies' ability to develop social relationships and the generation of dynamic capabilities.

The contradictory results pointed out above can be attributed to the fact that dynamic capabilities can adopt many forms, given that different capabilities are useful for different purposes (Helfat et al., 2007). Specifically, relationships with stakeholders outside the company make it possible to explore and perceive changes in the environment and access diverse knowledge coming from multiple sources. Therefore, fomenting external relationships gives managers a greater ability to identify the demand for changes in the resource base, at the same time that it favours the implementation of these changes in an opportune and appropriate way. These relationships can improve the organization's ability to alter its resource base in order to take advantage of opportunities the environment offers and respond to them.

Danneels (2010) highlights that it is not only the resource base that influences the development of dynamic capabilities, but also knowledge about these resources. Therefore, the more relationships the managers establish with the different areas and departments of the company, the more knowledge they will obtain about the resources they manage. In addition, intraorganizational relationships favour the development of dynamic capabilities by facilitating the acquisition, integration, combination, and liberation of the company's resources (Blyler and Coff, 2003; Festing and Eidems, 2011). These links make it possible to learn, coordinate, and integrate, which are critical aspects of the development of dynamic capabilities and favour the identification and comprehension of the resources themselves (Danneels, 2010). In this regard, Blyler and Coff (2003) argue that the absence of internal social relationships causes the resources to remain disconnected, which impedes their adaptation to volatile environments. Meanwhile, Liao et al. (2003) state that the intraorganizational spread of knowledge is fundamental in order to align organizations with their external environment, and it plays an important role in determining their capacity for response. Moreover, Tsai et al. (2009) establish a positive relationship between the interorganizational social capital and the reconfiguration of resources to respond to changes in the environment.

Consistent with these proposals, this study considers that the structure of managers' social relationships provides a set of knowledge resources to their companies that favours the ability to develop dynamic capabilities. Thus, we propose that HR practices that promote the social relationships, both external and internal, of the top management team, improve the organizational ability to develop dynamic sensing capabilities.

HYPOTHESIS (H1): HR practices that promote the top management team's social relationships have a positive influence on the development of dynamic sensing capabilities.

Sensing dynamic capability and marketing innovation

A basic notion of the theory of dynamic capabilities is that the capabilities related to the market are keys to understanding companies' performance (Newbert, 2007). Identifying the customers' needs and developing innovations that respond to these needs is an organization's main objective. Companies that are closer to clients and have a deep knowledge of their markets will be better able to carry out activities that respond to the clients' needs and preferences and to the actions of the competition (Berthon, Hulbert, and Pitt, 2004). Therefore, the dynamic sensing capability, as an indicative element of orientation towards the exterior, will make it possible for companies to identify the changing conditions and adjust to these changes by transforming their available resources.

"A marketing innovation is the implementation of a new marketing method involving significant changes in product design or packaging, product placement, product promotion or pricing" (OECD/Eurostat, 2005: 49). For years, studies on innovation focused on product innovation and process innovation, ignoring other forms of non-technological innovation (Damanpour and Aravind, 2011; Gallego, Rubalcaba, and Hipp, 2013; Hecker and Ganter, 2013; Volberda, Van Den Bosch, and Heij, 2013) such as marketing innovation. In recent years, researchers have paid increasing attention to marketing innovation, but few studies have addressed this construct in the area of the service industry. The close personal contact with clients that characterizes services companies grants special importance to innovative strategies related to product or service placement, promotion, and pricing (Medrano and Olarte-Pascual, 2016).

Technological advances have drastically modified the way services companies distribute their products. Specifically, in the area of tourism companies, the internet has created the conditions for users to directly access the reservation systems of tourism services providers (e.g., airlines, hotels). Consequently, companies have improved their negotiation capacity with the powerful tour operators (Buhalis, 2000; Buhalis and Licata, 2002). The company web page is an important tool for carrying out novel promotions of certain services and trying to foster its use as a sales channel. Novel loyalty programmes are also an important marketing innovation activity. These programmes give their holders advantages while providing the company with valuable information about clients' preferences, allowing it to develop actions designed to improve their loyalty. Likewise, the use of novel strategies to set prices for services is another type of marketing innovation. These actions allow the company to vary the price of services depending on the demand, or offer clients the possibility of adapting a certain service on the company web page and then checking its price (OECD/Eurostat, 2005).

Changes in demand produced by new lifestyles, larger incomes, or more free time have modified the tourist's behaviour and require new marketing innovation strategies. Thus, companies must develop a detailed understanding of clients' preferences in order to adapt to their needs and desires. In this scenario, awareness of the environment is a necessary activity to achieve timely recognition of market trends and ideas that orient and feed innovation processes (COTEC, 2007). Consistent with the aforementioned proposals, in this study we propose that a dynamic sensing capability allows companies to act by responding to external tendencies and events, which translates into introducing changes and making significant improvements related to marketing innovations.

H2: Dynamic sensing capabilities positively influence the introduction of marketing innovations.

The mediating role of dynamic sensing capabilities

An assumption underlying the research on strategic HR management is that HR practices do not directly affect organizational performance, but rather do so indirectly through their influence on the company's resources and capabilities (Collins and Smith, 2006; López-Cabrales, Pérez and Valle, 2009). Following this line of thought, specific HR practices that are difficult to imitate are a valuable resource that allow companies to better perform their strategic actions, ultimately improving organizational performance. Based on this approach, this study tries to link social-relationship-building HR practices to marketing innovation, through the mediating role of dynamic sensing capability. Thus, companies that promote top management's social relationships will be able to more precisely assess the opportunities around them, which gives them a greater capacity to adequately alter their resource base, that is, to produce dynamic capabilities that, in turn, improve the innovation results. Based on this proposal, the following research hypothesis is proposed:H3: The dynamic sensing capability mediates the relationship between social-relationship-building HR practices and marketing innovation.

Figure 14.1 provides an overview of the hypothesized relationships.

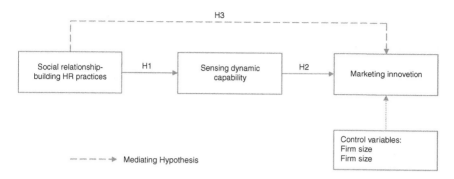

Figure 14.1 Research model

Method

Sample and data collection

The methodological procedure in this study involved the use of a cross-sectional survey through a self-administered questionnaire. The item and scale selection began with an exhaustive literature review that made it possible to identify the different measurement instruments related to the proposed research model. These measures were submitted to a pre-testing phase with five professionals in the sector studied to guarantee the correct comprehension of the questionnaire by the people who had to fill it out.

The study population that provided the necessary information for the evaluation of the proposed hypotheses is composed of tourist hotel lodging firms that run establishments with three or more stars in the Spanish territory and have a staff of more than 50 employees. Companies dedicated to tourist lodging were chosen because this sector is quite important in the Spanish economy. Spain is the second tourist destination in Europe and the fourth worldwide, with a total of 68.2 million visitors in 2015 (World Tourism Organization, 2016). In addition, the population under study is composed of a set of homogeneous companies with regard to the nature of their products and competitive environment (Martínez-Ros and Orfila-Sintes, 2009). Although the choice of only one industry can limit the generalization of the results, it reduces the potential problems presented by samples coming from diverse industries by eliminating possible distortions due to interindustry structural differences (Kyriakopoulos and Moorman 2004; Ordanini and Parasuraman, 2011).

The data from the hotel lodging companies were obtained from the 2011 Annual Hostelmarket report on hotels, restaurants, tourism, and leisure, which includes the contact data and economic and commercial information for the hotel and tourism sectors. After database purification, the population consisted of a total 525 companies. In this study, we decided to investigate all the sampling units by sending the questionnaire to all the companies that made up the population. Later, given that the questionnaires revealed that one company did not have 50 employees or more and another company did not have three or more stars, these two questionnaires were discarded, and the companies were excluded from the population, making a total of 523 companies in the population. The final sample consisted of 109 companies, 20.84% of the population. The professional and demographic variables contained in the questionnaire reveal that the majority of the interviewees have top management functions, have been in the company for more than 10 years, and have higher education.

Measurement

The measurement of all the variables was carried out through 7-point Likert-type scales. Appendix 1 (Table 14.2) shows the items for all the variables. Social-relationship-building HR practices were measured based on a scale developed by Collins and Clark (2003). To measure dynamic sensing capability, the scale proposed by Pavlou and El Sawy (2011) was adapted. The marketing innovation scale was measured taking into account information outlined in the Oslo Manual (OECD/Eurostat, 2005).

In this study, the effects of two variables were statistically controlled: size and age of the companies. The size and age of the company were measured by transforming to a natural logarithm the number of employees and the years since the establishment of the company, respectively. Although the existing research on the relationship between the size of the company and innovation presents disparate results (Leiblein and Madsen, 2009; Revilla and Fernández, 2012), studies carried out in the tourism sector are almost unanimous in presenting a positive association between size and innovation (Martínez-Ros and Orfila-Sintes, 2009; Pikkemaat and Peters, 2005). Moreover, the age of the company has been related to innovation because established companies have greater technical and financial capacity to adapt to changes (Amara, Landry, Becheikhb, and Ouimet, 2008; Jiménez-Jiménez and Sanz-Valle, 2010). Specifically, Ceylan (2013) finds that the age of the company is related to marketing innovation activities in the services sector.

Analyses and results

The exploratory factor analysis, carried out as a previous phase to the confirmatory factor analysis, confirmed the existence of only one dimension in the scales used to measure the latent constructs (Appendix 1, Table 14.2). Likewise, the scales have shown good psychometric properties. Their reliability was evaluated with Cronbach's alpha, composite reliability, and the average variance extracted (AVE). All of the Cronbach's alpha values for the variables used are above 0.9. The value of the composite reliability in all the constructs ranged between 0.91 and 0.92, above the recommended threshold of 0.7. In addition, the AVE was situated between 0.65 and 0.75, thus exceeding the minimum recommended threshold of 0.50. The convergent validity of the scales was tested because all of the loadings or standardized estimators of the regression weights of the latent variable on the indicators are statistically significant, positive, and above 0.64. Finally, discriminant validity was evaluated by checking that the AVE from each construct is greater than the square of the correlation between two constructs (Fornell and Larcker, 1981). To simplify the procedure, the square root of the AVE from each construct was calculated. Table 14.1 reports means, standard deviations, and correlations among the variables, indicating that all the constructs have the property of discriminant validity.

To test the proposed hypotheses, multiple linear regression analyses were performed. One of the assumptions that must be met to guarantee the validity of the regression model is the independence of the error terms. The Durbin-Watson (D-W) statistic provides information about the degree of independence existing between the residuals. If the value of the statistic is near two, it can be assumed that there is independence (Durbin and Watson, 1951). In addition, the Variance Inflation Factor (VIF) was examined for each independent variable in order to evaluate the risk of multicollinearity. The VIF values range between 1.015 and 1.743, which indicates that multicollinearity is not a problem (Hair, Anderson, Tatham, and Black, 1999).

Appendix 2 (Table 14.3) shows the regression analyses conducted to evaluate the proposed relationships. Model 1 reflects the results of the regression analysis on sensing capability. Models 2, 3, and 4 show the results of the regression analysis on marketing innovation. The results indicate that there is a positive and significant relationship between social-relationship-building HR practices and dynamic sensing capability. In addition, dynamic sensing capability positively influences marketing innovation. Therefore, H1 and H2 are accepted.

Table 14.1 Measurement information: Mean, standard deviation, correlations, (n = 109)

	Mean	Standard deviation	1	2	3	4	5
(1) Social-relationship-building HR practices	4.24	1.49	−0.811				
(2) Dynamic sensing capacity	4.54	1.28	.646**	−0.87			
(3) Marketing innovation	4.4	1.19	.548**	.697**	−0.833		
(4) Firm size	603.48	1992.50	.224**	.218*	.222*	n/a	
(5) Firm age	27.56	23.5	0.033	−0.029	−.057	−.095	n/a

**Correlation is significant at the 0.01 level (2-tailed).
*Correlation is significant at the 0.05 level (2-trailed).
The elements on the diagonal (values between parentheses) correspond to the square root of the AVE of the construct, n/a: not applicable.

This paper follows the Baron and Kenny procedure (1986) to analyse the mediating effect of dynamic sensing capability in the relationship between the social-relationship-building HR practices and marketing innovation. The first step is to analyse the link between social-relationship-building HR practices and marketing innovation. Appendix 2 (Model 3) shows that they are significantly related. The second step consists of examining the effect of social-relationship-building HR practices on the mediator variable. The results from Model 1 show that there is a direct and positive relationship. The third step consists of analysing the relationship between the mediator variable and the dependent variable. The data from Model 2 indicate a positive and significant relationship between dynamic sensing capability and marketing innovation. The fourth step is to include the mediator variable, dynamic sensing capability, in the model, to examine whether it reduces the effects of social-relationship-building HR practices to non-significance. As Model 4 shows, the coefficients are positive and significant for the relationship between sensing dynamic capability and marketing innovation. However, including the mediator variable in the model makes the relationship between social-relationship-building HR practices and marketing innovation non-significant. These results indicate that dynamic sensing capability fully mediates the relationship between social-relationship-building HR practices and marketing innovation. The data support hypothesis H3. Moreover, the results show that the size and age of the company do not present a significant relationship with marketing innovation.

Conclusions

This study aims to evaluate the role of HR practices that promote top management's social relationships in the strategic renewal of services companies. Specifically, the effect of these practices on dynamic sensing capability and marketing innovation is analysed. The literature points out that the dynamic capabilities play an important role in altering the resource base of a company in order to adapt to changing conditions, allowing it to maintain competitive advantages. However, the scant empirical research in the services area impedes the identification of the organizational variables that foster these capabilities. Moreover, the research on innovation in the services field has mainly focused on the analysis of product and process innovation, ignoring other non-technological types of innovation such as marketing innovation. This study tries to fill this empirical gap and contribute to knowledge about the factors that drive strategic renewal in services companies.

The results show a positive relationship between HR practices that encourage top management team's social relationships and dynamic sensing capability. Likewise, they reveal that these practices do not directly influence marketing innovation, but rather do so indirectly through the mediating role of dynamic sensing capability. Therefore, the results show that fomenting top management's social relationships, both internal and external, improves a company's ability to identify and deal with changes by altering its resource base, that is, by constructing dynamic sensing capability. Social links make it possible to access broad and diverse information that provides managers with a knowledge base favouring adequate decision making to address strategic and environmental changes. In addition, the mediating role of dynamic sensing capability in the relationship between social-relationships-building HR practices and marketing innovation seems to indicate that HR practices are a strategic resource that requires organizational capabilities to achieve innovation results.

The findings also show that dynamic sensing capability favours marketing innovation. It seems logical to assume that the ability to detect, interpret, and take advantage of opportunities in the environment guarantees that companies are more capable of adapting to changes, which translates into innovation results. The data show that dynamic sensing capability grants companies the ability to be alert to market trends and respond to them by introducing significant changes in their marketing activities.

From a theoretical point of view, this study adds knowledge to the existing debate in the literature about the possible existence of variables that mediate in the relationship between HR practices and organizational results. One line of research tends to consider that resources only have potential value, and that realizing this potential requires their alignment with other important organizational elements (Ketchen, Hult, and Slater, 2007; Morgan et al., 2009). From this perspective, companies need complementary capabilities in order to display these valuable resources in a way that fits the market's requirements (Wei and Wang, 2011; Wu, 2004). In line with these arguments, this study finds that social-relationship-building HR practices make up a specific asset of the company that requires sensing capabilities, as a strategic complementary action, to encourage marketing innovations. The results are consistent with the proposals of authors such as Liao, Kickut, and Ma (2009) and Wu (2006), for whom dynamic capabilities allow companies to take advantage of their resources and adapt them to changing opportunities in the environment.

Regarding the practical implications, the data show the determinant role of the top management team in the construction of dynamic sensing capabilities and, therefore, in marketing innovation. Therefore, it is fundamental for companies to systematically develop and maintain a policy that fosters the social relationships of its managers, both with agents in the environment and from other areas or departments in the organization. The access to external information gives companies a greater capacity to act, given that they are in a better position to identify changes and, therefore, adequately respond to them. A system of evaluation and incentives designed to foment the social relationships of top management fosters their motivation to build relationships with internal and external agents who provide advantages for the company. However, establishing efficient social relationships requires, in addition to motivation, adequate relational competencies or skills. Therefore, it is important to provide top management with training opportunities and facilitate discussion about appropriate strategies to develop personal contacts. Moreover,

Table 14.2 Appendix 1. Exploratory and confirmatory factor analysis

Item[a]	Factor loading	Std. λ_x
Social relationship-building HR practices. Cronbach's alpha = .916; composite reliability = .919; AVE = .658		
SR_1 The members of the top management team receive training to develop personal contacts with key employees in the company.	.508	–
SR_2 The members of the top management team are evaluated on their capacity to develop relationships with personnel from different areas in the company.	.685	.782
SR_3 The members of the top management team often discuss strategies for developing personal contacts with external stakeholders (e.g., travel agencies, tour operators, public organisations, clients, etc.).	.628	.830
SR_4 The members of the top management team are evaluated on their capacity to develop relationships with external stakeholders.	.800	.909
SR_5 This company provides incentives to the members of the top management team to develop personal work contacts with external stakeholders.	.632	.694
SR_6 We devote financial resources so that the members of the top management team can develop personal contacts related to work.	.706	.733
SR_7 The members of the top management team advise each other about the way to maintain personal contacts related to their work.	.741	.895
Dynamic sensing capability. Cronbach's alpha = .932; composite reliability = .925; AVE = .757		
SC_1 We frequently scan the environment to identify new business opportunities.	.895	.895
SC_2 We periodically review the likely effect of changes in our business environment on customers.	.935	.910
SC_3 We often review our service development efforts to ensure they are in line with what customers want.	.908	.927
SC_4 We spend a great deal of time implementing ideas for new services and improving our existing services.	.836	.736
Marketing innovation. Cronbach's alpha =.901; composite reliability =.917; AVE =.695		
MkI_1 We are dynamic in developing and using new sales channels (e.g., exploiting the potential of the internet as a sales channel, presence on social networks, etc.).	.886	.913
MkI_2 We frequently introduce new techniques or channels for promoting our services (new advertising channels, new customer loyalty cards, etc.).	.911	.955
MkI_3 We frequently introduce new methods for pricing our services.	.857	.841
MkI_4 Our competitors use our marketing methods as a point of reference.	.838	.658
MkI_5 The new marketing methods we have incorporated have been new to the sector.	.830	.644

a To fit the confirmatory factorial model, item SR_1 was eliminated from the social-relationship-building HR practices scale.

Table 14.3 Appendix 2. Results of linear regression analyses.

Independent variables	VIF	Model 1 Dynamic sensing capability Beta	t-value	Model 2 Marketing innovation Beta	t-value	Model 3 Beta	t-value	Model 4 Beta	t-value
					Dependent variable				
Social-relationships-building HR practices	1.74	.646	8.746 ***			.525	6.346 ***	.163	1.794
Dynamic sensing capability	1.74			.678	9.507 ***			.576	6.340 ***
Control variables:									
Firm size	1.07			.079	1.097	.112	1.349	.065	.911
Firm age	1.02			-.044	-.635	-.085	-1.047	-.052	-.0743
R^2		.417		.492		.317		.508	
Adjusted R^2		.411		.478		.298		.489	
F		76.501***		33.941***		16.262***		26.798***	
D-W		2.103		1.762		2.154		1.797	

Standardised coefficients; n= 109;
***p< 0.001; **p< 0.01; *p< 0.05.

assigning resources to foment internal relationships leads to more in-depth knowledge about internal assets, which favours the adoption of appropriate measures to alter these resources in order to adapt them to the changing circumstances.

This study presents some limitations that represent possibilities for future research. One limitation stems from the use of the key informant methodology. However, we tried to mitigate the possible perceptual bias by ensuring, to some degree, the reliability of the responses. For this reason, the informants in the sample have extensive professional experience in both the sector and the company, they hold positions of responsibility, and they have an overall view of the organization. Another study limitation is related to the generalization of the conclusions. The services sector consists of a set of industries with quite different characteristics, and this limits the possibility of generalizing the results obtained. However, we can extrapolate the results to the area of the population under study, that is, companies dedicated to running hotel establishments with more than 50 employees and in the category of three or more stars. Thus, future studies could apply the model to other services companies and carry out comparative studies. Finally, the study only considers social-relationship-building HR practices that the firm applies to top management. Consequently, future research could analyse how the application of these strategies to other employees, such as middle managers, would influence organizational performance.

References

Adler, P. S. & Kwon, S.-W. (2002). Social capital: Prospects for a new concept. *Academy of Management Review*, 27(1), 17–40.

Adner, R. & Helfat, C. E. (2003). Corporate effects and dynamic managerial capabilities. *Strategic Management Journal*, 12(10), 1011–1025.

Agarwal, R. & Helfat, C. E. (2009). Strategic renewal of organizations. *Organization Science*, 20(2), 281–293.

Agarwal, R. & Selen, W. (2009). Dynamic capability building in service value networks for achieving service innovation. *Decision Sciences*, 40(3), 431–475.

Amara, N., Landry, R., Becheikhb, N., & Ouimet, M. (2008). Learning and novelty of innovation in established manufacturing SMEs. *Technovation*, 28(8), 450–463.

Ambrosini, V. & Bowman, C. (2009). What are dynamic capabilities and are they a useful construct in strategic management? *International Journal of Management Reviews*, 11(1), 29–49.

Ambrosini, V., Bowman, C., & Collier, N. (2009). Dynamic capabilities: An exploration of how firms renew their resource base. *British Journal of Management*, 20(1), 9–24.

Aragón-Correa, J. & Sharma, S. (2003). A contingent resource-based view of proactive corporate environmental strategy. *Academy of Management Review*, 28(1), 71–88.

Augier, M. & Teece, D. J. (2009). Dynamic capabilities and the role of managers in business strategy and economic performance. *Organization Science*, 20(2), 410–421.

Barney, J. B., Wright, M., & Ketchen, Jr. D. J. (2001). The resource-based view of the firm: Ten years after 1991. *Journal of Management*, 27(6), 625–641.

Baron, R. M. & Kenny, D. A. (1986). The moderator–mediator variable distinction in social psychological research: Conceptual, strategic, and statistical considerations. *Journal of Personality and Social Psychology*, 51(6), 1173–1182.

Berthon, P., Hulbert, J. M. & Pitt, L. (2004). Innovation or customer orientation? An empirical Investigation. *European Journal of Marketing*, 38(9/10), 1065–1090.

Binns, A., Harreldl, J. B., O'Reilly, III, C., & Tushman, M. L. (2014). The art of strategic renewal. *MIT Sloan Management Review*, 55(2), 20–24.

Blyler, M. & Coff, R. W. (2003). Dynamic capabilities, social capital, and rent appropriation: Ties that split pies. *Strategic Management Journal*, 24(7), 677–686.

Buhalis, D. (2000). Marketing the competitive destination of the future. *Tourism Management*, 21(1), 97–116.

Buhalis, D. & Licata, M. C. (2002). The future eTourism intermediaries. *Tourism Management*, 23(3), 207–220.

Ceylan, C. (2013). Commitment-based HR practices, different types of innovation activities and firm innovation performance. *The International Journal of Human Resource Management*, 24(1), 208–226.

Chen, C. J. & Huang, J. W. (2009). Strategic human resource practices and innovation performance – The mediating role of knowledge management capacity. *Journal of Business Research*, 62(1), 104–114.

Collins, C. J. & Clark, K. D. (2003). Strategic human resource practices, top management team social networks, and firm performance: The role of human resource practices in creating organizational competitive advantage. *Academy of Management Journal*, 46(6), 740–751.

Collins, C. J. & Smith, K. G. (2006). Knowledge exchange and combination: The role of human resource practices in the performance of high-technology firms. *Academy of Management Journal*, 49(3), 544–560.

Collis, D. J. (1994). How valuable are organizational capabilities? *Strategic Management Journal*, 15(Issue S1), 143–152.

COTEC, fundación Cotec para la innovación tecnológica. (2007). Innovación en el sector hotelero, available at: www.ithotelero.com/wp-content/uploads/2013/08/proyecto13-cotec.pdf (accessed 24 August 2016).

Damanpour, F., & Aravind, D. (2011). Managerial innovation: Conceptions, processes, and antecedents. *Management and Organization Review*, 8(2), 423–454.

Danneels, E. (2002). The dynamics of products innovation and firm competences. *Strategic Management Journal*, 23(12), 1095–1121.

Danneels, E. (2010). Trying to become a different type of company: Dynamic capability at Smith Corona. *Strategic Management Review*, 32(1), 1–31.

Desai, D., Sahu, S., & Sinha, P. K. (2007). Role of dynamic capability and information-technology in customer relation management: A study of Indian companies. *Vikalpa*, 32(4), 45–62.

Durbin, J. & Watson, G. S. (1951). Testing for serial correlation in least squares regression. II. *Biometrika*, 38(1/2), 159–177.

Eisenhardt, K. M. & Martin, J. A. (2000). Dynamic capabilities what are they? *Strategic Management Review*, 21(10–11), 1105–1121.

Festing, M. & Eidems, J. (2011). A process perspective on transnational HRM systems—A dynamic capability-based analysis. *Human Resource Management Review*, 21(3), 162–173.

Fornell, C. & Larcker, D. F. (1981). Evaluating structural equation models with unobservable variables and measurement error. *Journal of Marketing Research*, 8(1), 39–50.

Gallego, J., Rubalcaba, L., & Hipp, C. (2013). Services and organisational innovation: The right mix for value creation. *Management Decision*, 51(6), 1117–1134.

Gloet, M. (2006). Knowledge management and the links to HRM. *Management Research News*, 29(7), 402–413.

Hair, Jr, J. F., Anderson, R. E, Tatham, R. L., & Black, W.C. (1999). *Análisis multivariante* [Multivariate data analysis], (5th edition), Prentice Hall Iberia, Madrid.

Hecker, A. & Ganter, A. (2013). The influence of product market competition on technological and management innovation: Firm-Level evidence from a large-scale survey. *European Management Review*, 10(1), 17–33.

Helfat, F. E., Finkelstein, S., Mitchell, W., Peteraf, M. A., Sing, H., Teece, D. J., & Winter, S. G. (2007). *Dynamic capabilities: Understanding strategic change in organizations*. Blackwell Publishing, Oxford.

Hult, G. T. M., Ketchen Jr., D. J. & Slater, S. F. (2005). Market orientation and performance: An integration of disparate approaches. *Strategic Management Journal*, 26 (12), 1173–1181.

Jiménez-Jiménez, D. & Sanz-Valle, R. (2010). Innovation, organizational learning, and performance. *Journal of Business Research*, 64(4), 408–417.

Ketchen, D. J., Hult, G. T., & Slater, S. F. (2007). Toward greater understanding of market orientation and the resource-based view. *Strategic Management Journal*, 28(9), 961–964.

Kim, J. & Boo, S. (2010). Dynamic capabilities and performance of meeting planners. *Journal of Travel & Tourism Marketing*, 27(7), 736–747.

Klammer, A., Gueldenberg, S., Kraus, S., & O'Dwyer, M. (2016). To change or not to change–antecedents and outcomes of strategic renewal in SMEs. *International Entrepreneurship and Management Journal*, doi: 10.1007/s11365-016-0420-9.

Kyriakopoulos, K. & Moorman, C. (2004). Tradeoffs in marketing exploitation and exploration strategies: The overlooked role of market orientation. *International Journal of Research in Marketing*, 21(3), 219–240.

Lawson, B. & Samson, D. (2001). Developing innovation capability in organisations: A dynamic capabilities approach. *International Journal of Innovation Management*, 5(3), 377–400.

Lee, P. Y., Chen, H. H., & Shyr, Y. H. (2011a). Driving dynamic knowledge articulation and dynamic capabilities development of service alliance firms. *The Services Industries Journal*, 31(13), 2223–2242.

Lee, P. Y., Lin, H. T, Chen, H. H., & Shyr, Y. H. (2011b). Dynamic capabilities exploitation of market and hierarchy governance structures: An empirical comparison of Taiwan and South Korea. *Journal of World Business*, 46(3), 359–370.

Leiblein, M. J. & Madsen, T. L. (2009). Unbundling competitive heterogeneity: Incentive structures and capability influences on technological innovation. *Strategic Management Journal*, 30(7), 711–735.

Liao, J., Kickut, J. R., & Ma, H. (2009). Organizational dynamic capability and innovation: An empirical examination of internet firms. *Journal of Small Business Management*, 47(3), 263–286.

Liao, J., Welsch, H., & Stoica, M. (2003). Organizational absorptive capacity and responsiveness: An empirical investigation of growth-oriented SMEs. *Entrepreneurship Theory and Practice*, 28(1), 63–85.

López-Cabrales, A. Pérez, A., & Valle, R. (2009). Knowledge as a mediator between HRM practices and innovative activity. *Human Resource Management*, 48(4), 485–503.

Martínez-Ros, E. & Orfila-Sintes, F. (2009). Innovation activity in the hotel industry. *Technovation*, 29(9), 632–641.

Medrano, N. & Olarte-Pascual, C (2016). The effects of the crisis on marketing innovation: An application for Spain. *Journal of Business & Industrial Marketing*, 31(3), 404–417.

Morgan, M. A., Vorhies, C. W., & Mason, C. H. (2009). Market orientation, marketing capabilities, and firm performance. *Strategic Management Journal*, 30(8), 909–920.

Nahapiet, J. & Ghoshal, S. (1998). Social capital, intellectual capital, and the organizational advantage. *Academy of Management Review*, 23(2), 242–266.

Newbert, S. L. (2007). Empirical research on the resource based view of the firm: An assessment and suggestions for future research. *Strategic Management Journal*, 28, 121–146.

Nohria, N. & Gulati, R. (1996). Is slack good or bad for innovation? *Academy of Management Journal*, 39(5), 1245–1264.

OECD/Eurostat. (2005). Guidelines for collecting and interpreting innovation data. available at: www.keepeek.com/Digital-Asset-Management/oecd/science-and-technology/oslo-manual_9789264013100-en (accessed 24 August 2016).

Ordanini, A. & Parasuraman, A. (2011). Service innovation viewed through a service-dominant logic lens: A conceptual framework and empirical analysis. *Journal of Service Research*, 14(1), 3–23.

Pavlou, P. A. & El Sawy, O. A. (2011). Understanding the elusive black box of dynamic capabilities. *Decision Sciences*, 42(1), 239–273.

Pikkemaat, B. & Peters, M. (2005). Towards the measurement of innovation—A pilot study in the small and medium sized hotel industry. *Journal of Quality Assurance in Hospitality & Tourism*, 6(3), 89–112.

Revilla, A. J. & Fernández, Z. (2012). The relation between firm size and R&D productivity in different technological regimes. *Technovation*, 32(11), 609–623.

Rosenbloom, R. S. (2000). Leadership, capabilities, and technological change: The transformation of NCR in the electronic era. *Strategic Management Journal*, 21(10/11), 1083–1103.

Sáez-Martínez, F. J. & González-Moreno, A. (2011). Strategic renewal, cooperation, and performance: A contingency approach. *Journal of Management and Strategy*, 2(4), 43–55.

Teece, D. J. (2007). Explicating dynamic capabilities: The nature and microfoundations of (sustainable) enterprise performance. *Strategic Management Journal*, 28(13), 1319–1350.

Tippins, M. J. & Sohi, R. S. (2003). IT competency and firm performance: Is organizational learning a missing link? *Strategic Management Journal*, 24(8), 745–761.

Tsai, M. T., Huang, Y. C., & Ma, R. (2009). Antecedents and consequences of global responsiveness: An empirical examination of MNCs in the global sourcing context. *International Business Review*, 18(6), 617–629.

Verona, G. & Ravasi, D. (2003). Unbundling dynamic capabilities: An exploratory study of continuous product innovation. *Industrial and Corporate Change*, 12(3), 577–606.

Volberda, H. W., Van Den Bosch, F. A. J., & Heij, C. V. (2013). Management innovation: Management as fertile ground for innovation. *European Management Review*, 10(1), 1–15.

Wang, C. L. & Ahmed, P. K. (2007). Dynamic capabilities: A review and research agenda. *International Journal of Management Review*, 9(1), 31–51.

Wei, Y. & Wang, Q. (2011). Making sense of a market information system for superior performance responsiveness. *Industrial Marketing Management*, 40(2), 267–277.

Williams, A. (2006). Tourism and hospitality marketing: Fantasy, feeling and fun. *International Journal of Contemporary Hospitality Management*, 18(6), 482–495.

Winter, S. G. (2003). Understanding dynamic capabilities. *Strategic Management Journal*, 24(19), 991–995.

World Tourism Organization. (2016), "UNWTO tourism highlights 2016 edition", available at: www.e-unwto.org/doi/pdf/10.18111/9789284418145 (accessed 10 October 2016).

Wright, P., Dunford, B., & Snell, S. (2001). Human resources and the resource-based view of the firm. *Journal of Management*, 27(6), 701–721.

Wu, J. (2004). *Knowledge stock, search competence and innovation performance in the U.S. electrical medical device industry*. Doctoral thesis, Purdue University, IN.

Wu, L. Y. (2006). Resources, dynamic capabilities and performance in a dynamic environment: Perceptions in Taiwanese IT enterprises. *Information & Management*, 43(4), 447–454.

Zahra, S. A., Zapienza, H., & Davidsson, P. (2006). Entrepreneurship and dynamic capabilities: A review, model and research agenda. *Journal of Management Studies*, 43(4), 917–955.

Zollo, M. & Winter, S. G. (2002). Deliberate learning and the evolution of dynamics capabilities. *Organization Science*, 13(3), 339–351.

Zott, C. (2003). Dynamic capabilities and the emergence of intraindustry differential firm performance: Insights from a simulation study. *Strategic Management Journal*, 24(2), 97–125.

15 Institutional complexity and strategic renewal

Saeed Khanagha and Patrick Vermeulen

Introduction

Strategic renewal is considered to be of critical importance for the survival of an organization (Volberda, Baden-Fuller, & Van Den Bosch, 2001). Agarwal and Helfat (2009: 282) define strategic renewal as: "the process, content, and outcome of refreshment or replacement of attributes of an organization that have the potential to substantially affect its long-term prospects" (2009: 282). Managers play a key role in recognizing changes in their environment that require the renewal of organizational strategies (Barr, Stimpert, & Huff, 1992). The way managers perceive their environment and the cognitive processes of enacting environmental change have received ample attention in the literature (e.g. Kiesler & Sproull, 1982).

However, organizations are being more and more frequently confronted with incompatible prescriptions from their environment. Hospitals, for instance, are expected to deliver high-quality care, but at the same time market forces demand them to be efficient as well. Similarly, banks that were once mainly in the business of making profits to support ongoing operations, also have to think about societally responsible investments. We refer to these situations as institutional complexity (cf. Greenwood, Raynard, Kodeih, Micelotta, & Lounsbury, 2011). In this chapter, we argue that institutional complexity forces firms into processes of strategic renewal. However, the nature of institutionally complex environments will be differentially perceived by different managers, which in turn will result in strategic responses that vary in the degree to which they reconcile the seemingly conflicting requirements.

A central insight among institutional scholars centers on the notion that fields or industries are characterized by multiple institutional logics (Friedland & Alford, 1991; Thornton, Ocasio, & Lounsbury, 2012). Institutional logics govern the behavior of individual and organizational actors by prescribing "how to interpret organizational reality, what constitutes appropriate behavior, and how to succeed" (Thornton, 2004: 70). Recently, research attention in institutional theory has centered on situations where organizations face *institutional complexity*. In such situations the prescriptions stemming from different logics are experienced as being (largely) incompatible, thereby creating challenges and tensions for the organizations involved (Greenwood et al., 2011; Raynard, 2016).

When organizations are confronted with incompatible prescriptions concerning "the proper thing to do", they inevitably experience tension, conflict, and confusion as they face trade-offs in securing legitimacy from different sources (Greenwood et al., 2011; Pache & Santos, 2010; Ruef & Scott, 1998; Seo & Creed, 2002). Overcoming such seemingly incompatible and competing requirements often points toward a need for renewing the organization in order to overcome contradictions, for example by securing novel synergies between competing demands (Smith, 2014). However, not all organizations recognize such a need correctly and in a timely manner and, even if they do, they may fail to take an appropriate approach toward the renewal process. Although institutional scholars have investigated the antecedents of organizational responses to institutional complexity (see Greenwood et al., 2011 for a review) and strategy researchers have explored the role of cognition in strategic renewal (e.g. Barr et al., 1992), the cognitive underpinnings of strategic renewal attempts under conditions of institutional complexity are underexplored.

In this chapter, we identify managerial factors that have a bearing on the perception and interpretation of institutional complexity and investigate the actual mechanisms through which variation of these variables will result in heterogeneity in organizations' strategic renewal attempts in response to institutional complexity. We develop a conceptual model and propositions on how managerial interpretations of institutional complexity shape trajectories of strategic renewal.

Theoretical background

Organizations in different sectors increasingly need to overcome challenges associated with contradictory institutional demands. For instance, several studies have demonstrated how healthcare organizations can become sites of contestation due to the contrasting demands of multiple logics that are not easily combined in practice (Dunn & Jones, 2010; Heimer, 1999; Reay & Hinings, 2009; Scott, Ruef, Mendel, & Caronna, 2000). Dunn and Jones (2010) for instance demonstrated how in the field of medical education the logics of science and care result in disagreements over the appropriate means for treating patients. In a similar vein, Reay and Hinings (2005, 2009) demonstrated how the contradictory values, practices, and principles generated by a market logic and a professional logic created institutional complexity for physicians. Also in the field of academic science the logics of science, commerce, and the state generate distinct—at times—conflicting prescriptions (Berman, 2012; Sauermann & Stephan, 2013). An effective organizational response to such institutional complexities requires adaptations in organizational structure and strategies (Greenwood et al., 2011).

Strategic renewal often requires a reshaping of organizational cognition regarding the nature of the organization's environment (Agarwal & Helfat, 2009). As such, strategic renewal includes cognitive tasks that demand substantive information processing, meaning that they cannot be addressed by simply activating pre-existing knowledge structures. Organizational attention toward and correct interpretation of the need for strategic renewal are crucial determinants of strategic change (Helfat & Peteraf, 2015). Different perceptions of the need for change by managers may lead to different strategies toward strategic renewal, ranging from evolutionary to transformational and radical approaches (Lavie, 2006). Particularly, when it comes to institutional complexity, managers' interpretations and perceptions play a significant role in determining the strategic response. As suggested by Raynard (2016), institutional complexities vary in terms of (1) the extent to which the prescriptive demands of logics are incompatible, (2) whether there is a settled or widely accepted prioritization of logics within the field, and (3) the degree to which the jurisdictions of the logics overlap. An accurate evaluation of these three dimensions, which are all influential on the effectiveness of a firm's strategic response (Raynard, 2016), has to do with how managers perceive and interpret these dimensions. Therefore, whether and how the organization can effectively manage strategic renewal in the face of institutional complexity is related to their managers' perception and interpretation of that institutional complexity (Helfat & Peteraf, 2014), specifically in terms of compatibility, prioritization, and jurisdictional overlap of the emerging complexities in the institutional environment.

Contextual organizational factors have an important influence on the interpretation of institutional complexity by the managers. Seminal work by Rousseau (1978) highlights how contextual factors provide a direct construction of meaning through socially acceptable beliefs, attitudes and needs, and acceptable reasons for action, and additionally focus managers' attention on certain information, making it more salient, and providing expectations concerning individual behavior its logical consequences. In particular, organizational identity and value systems are important aspects of the organizational context, which are known to be important determinants of strategic renewal processes (Tripsas, 2009). More specifically, organizational identity and value systems have the potential to affect the perception of complexity by filtering how institutional demands are conceptualized (Kodeih & Greenwood, 2014; Lok, 2010; Meyer & Hammerschmid, 2006). Besides contextual factors, CEO characteristics (e.g. age, tenure) and top management team (TMT) composition (homogeneous and heterogeneous) are likely to influence the perception of managers and the formation of strategic renewal activities (Cho & Hambrick, 2006; Helfat & Peteraf 2015). When it comes to institutional complexity, we will argue that CEO tenure in a certain institutional context alters a manager's perception of complexity and, therefore, may result in a different approach to and trajectory of strategic renewal. Similarly, diversity in the institutional background of the TMT may affect the perception of institutional complexity.

However, the way in which managers perceive and interpret institutional complexity strongly depends on a manager's cognition and motivation. We argue that the cognitive capabilities of managers (Helfat & Peteraf, 2015) are likely to influence the interpretation of institutional complexity and the subsequent formation of strategic renewal activities. Cognitive capabilities of managers play an important role because they allow managers to receive information from their environment through perceptual (attention-driven) processes and create a representation of this environment. Yet, institutional complexities give rise to increased levels of uncertainty, and dealing with such uncertainties calls for high levels of cognitive capabilities among senior managers (George & Chattopadhyay, 2006). The idea that even in the same organization strategic decisions makers have differential interpretations of the future and base their decisions on such interpretations has been noted in prior research (Kaplan & Orlikowski, 2013). In this chapter, we discuss the implications that this might have on organizational response to institutional complexity.

In doing so, we identify instances of managerial factors, such as cognitive variety, temporal depth, and regulatory focus that recent literature on strategic management identifies as determinants of strategic renewal. We argue that such characteristics have a bearing on the relation between the perception and interpretation of institutional complexity and strategic renewal. We investigate the actual mechanisms through which variation in these variables will result in heterogeneity in firm's strategic renewal attempts. We develop a conceptual model and propositions on how managerial interpretations of institutional complexity are affected by these factors and shape the trajectory of strategic renewal. To discuss the outcomes, we pay attention to particular aspects of strategic renewal that capture important elements of variation in strategic change and renewal (Smith, 2014). These dimensions include resource allocation (Bower & Gilbert, 2005), including issues of allocating financial, human, and attention-based resources; organizational design (i.e. Tushman & Nadler, 1992), including structure, processes, and metrics; and product design (i.e. Gatignon, Tushman, Smith & Anderson, 2002), including product, technology, and markets. In Figure 15.1, we summarize our model and in the next sections elaborate on its various parts.

The perception and interpretation of institutional complexity

Prior research assumes that organizations are not passive recipients of institutional prescriptions, but they interpret, translate, and, in some instances, transform them (Kraatz and Block (2008). For example, a strong or positive sense of organizational identity will influence the response to complexity by creating a confidence in the ability to ignore or comply with external demands (Gioia & Thomas, 1996; Greenwood et al., 2011). Despite the increasing

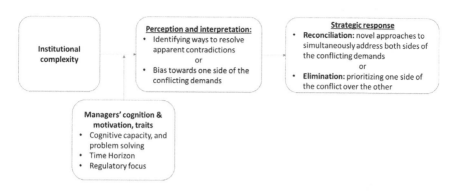

Figure 15.1 Theoretical model

importance of senior managers in determining the strategic responses of their organizations, prior research on complexity does not sufficiently incorporate the drivers and consequences of CEO traits and individual capabilities in determining organizational responses. For example, we know that institutional complexities come with different logics, each requiring different mental templates and approaches (Gröschl, Gabaldón, & Hahn, 2017). Managers faced with such complexities tend to filter the information through their cognitive frames to reduce the complexity along the mental templates of their cognitive frames, which then shapes the decisions and actions they take (Daft & Weick, 1984). But what if some managers are more capable than others in dealing with and reconciling such complexities?

Another issue is that institutional pressures come with possibilities for gains and losses and multiple demands may differ in their promise of positive or negative outcomes for the organizations. Some institutional demands may be associated with a positive situation in which gain is likely and over which one has a fair amount of control, while others are associated with a negative situation in which loss is likely and over which one has relatively little control (Dutton & Jackson, 1987). Prior research establishes that organizations facing a loss situation tend to rigidly pursue familiar and well-established patterns of behavior in an attempt to regain control over the situation (Staw, Sandelands, & Dutton, 1981). Conversely, Thomas, Clark, and Gioia (1993) showed that a perception of gains enhances the potential for taking actions to achieve these gains, making change or adoption more likely. We raise the issue of what happens if managers who are often not equally sensitive to both gains and losses, face competing demands with differential focus on gains or losses. For example, what happens if conformity to a new institutional pressure or practice is heavily contested by your most important source of legitimacy, hence engendering the perception of loss for a manager that is sensitive to losses?

Finally, issues related to temporality and time also become important in connection with the role of managers in strategic renewal. Prior institutional research suggests that time is indeed important when it comes to responses to institutional pressures. For instance, one logic can be used by a particular actor in different situations to achieve opposite goals, and the same actor may use different logics at different times depending on the perceived needs of the immediate situation (McPherson & Sauder, 2013). Zhao and his colleagues (2017) discuss why firms need to adjust their activities in accordance with temporarily shifting legitimacy expectations. Again, this stream of literature does not consider the role of managers' temporal orientation in organizations' responses to institutional complexity. The legitimacy implications of competing institutional pressures do not necessarily materialize in the same time horizon. Hence, if managers have a differential focus on the time horizon, then it is reasonable to expect variation in their response to institutional complexity.

The above discussion raises the point that it is important to consider managers and their cognitive and psychological traits when studying organizational responses to institutional complexity. Below, we investigate the actual mechanisms through which varying these variables will result in heterogeneity in a firm's strategic renewal attempts. We introduce three important managerial factors: cognitive variety, regulatory focus, and temporal orientation, and explain the ways in which these factors determine an organization's strategic renewal trajectory.

Propositions

1. Cognitive variety: Cognitive variety refers to the diversity of mental templates for problem solving in the organizational context (Eisenhardt, Furr, & Bingham, 2010: 1269). Cognitive variety is beneficial because it creates a greater range of solutions, derived from diverse templates, to apply to a given problem, and allows for the recombination of these templates that managers can use as basis for their decision-making. Moreover, cognitive variety creates tolerance for variety itself, thereby increasing the degree to which novel alternatives can be expected from the manager (Barber, 1988; Lachman, Lachman, & Butterfield, 1979; Schwartz, 1978).

Executives facing concurrent and potentially contradictory institutional demands from their environment, do not necessarily filter the information to reduce the complexity according to their mental templates. Instead, those with higher levels of cognitive variety may utilize multiple mental templates to find novel ways to recombine the possible solutions available to less complex situations and to come up with creative responses that fulfill contradictory demands concurrently. Cognitive variety allows managers to maintain a larger set of mental alternatives from which potential strategic actions can be chosen (Furr, 2009) and such a broader set of alternatives may also cause managers to refrain from committing to single options at an early stage (Staw et al., 1981). Organizations that narrowly hew to one specific institutional demand may be particularly vulnerable to obsolescence should the environment or the demands of institutional audiences change—that is, if the "selected" institutional demands were to become marginalized or displaced (Raynard, 2016: 318). Due to heterogeneity in cognitive variety, we expect that managers are likely to differ in their capacity to strategically reconfigure a firm's resources when confronted with institutional complexity.

For instance, cognitive variety may help managers to select different types of resource configurations. Resource reconfigurations refer to the selection, modification, and alignment of resources (cf. Helfat & Peteraf, 2015). Changes in the external environment frequently require firms to alter the configuration of strategic resources. In an institutionally complex environment, cognitive variety "determines the subset of resources perceived to be strategically valuable" (Kunc & Morecroft, 2010: 1166). In this way, managers may find it more feasible to simultaneously allocate their time and attention to the conflicting demands and to allocate financial and human resources to diverse expectations from institutional audiences in synergetic ways.

Different levels of cognitive variety held by senior managers in the face of institutional complexity may affect the ways through which organizations redesign their structures. Overcoming conflicting institutional demands points toward a need for particular organizational structures (Vermeulen, Zietsma, Greenwood, & Langley, 2016) that allow for collaboration between members advancing different institutional demands (Ramus, Vaccaro, & Brusoni, 2017). The literature on institutional complexity has distinguished between structurally differentiated or *compartmentalized hybrids*, wherein different units or subsidiaries of an organization deal with different logics, and *blended hybrids*, wherein elements of different logics are selectively coupled, integrated, or assimilated into one logic (Greenwood et al., 2011; Kraatz & Block, 2008; Skelcher & Smith, 2015; Zilber, 2002). Higher levels of cognitive variety may result in organizational designs that, rather than separating the conflicting demands, focus on creating integrative roles, stressing overall objectives, and solving problems jointly when it comes to conflicts in the institutional demands.

Overall, a key point is that responding to complexities in the institutional environment may require the flexible recombination of individually efficient mental templates to enable the emergence of novel solutions that address diverse requirements in a complex institutional environment. Therefore we expect that:

Proposition 1: Managers with higher levels of cognitive variety tend to respond to institutional complexity with a) concurrent allocation of organizational resources to conflicting requirements, and b) integrative approaches to organizational design.

2. Regulatory focus: Regulatory focus theory (RFT) (Higgins, 1997, 1998) proposes that individuals have two distinct motivational systems. A *promotion focus* is concerned with aspirations for growth, advancement, achievement, and ideals, and emphasizes gains (Crowe & Higgins, 1997). It is sensitive to the presence and absence of positive outcomes and focuses people on a promotion goal and approach tendencies (Higgins, 1997, 1998). Promotion focus leads individuals to a state of eagerness in which they desire to achieve "hits" and avoid "errors of omission" (i.e. to avoid closing off possibilities) (Higgins, 1998: 27). A *prevention focus* is concerned with prudence, safety, and obligations, and emphasizes losses (Crowe and Higgins, 1997). It is sensitive to the presence and absence of negative outcomes and focuses attention on a prevention goal and avoidance tendencies (Higgins, 1997, 1998). It drives individuals to a state of vigilance in which they insure against "errors of commission" and seek to avoid mistakes (Higgins, 1998: 27). Regulatory focus has been found to be influential on firms' and managers' strategic preferences and behavior (Ahmadi, Khanagha, Berchicci, & Jansen, 2017; Gamache, McNamara, Mannor, & Johnson, 2015; Tuncdogan, Boon, Mom, van Den Bosch & Volberda, 2017; Tuncdogan, Van Den Bosch, & Volberda, 2015)

In the context of institutional complexity, one should note that conflicting institutional demands can vary in their regulatory aspect. Particularly, Higgins (2000) suggests that such effects are accentuated when the characteristics of the situation are congruent with individuals' regulatory focus trait, a phenomenon called "regulatory fit". People experience regulatory fit when the manner in which they engage in an activity sustains their current orientation (Higgins, 2000; Higgins, Idson, Freitas, Spiegel & Molden, 2003). It is reasonable to believe that such tendencies are influential on managers' perception of institutional complexities and their consequent responses. A regulation that prohibits or enforces certain rules needs to be complied with mostly because of penalties or sanctions associated with it. Conversely, there are institutional demands that result in higher status and potential rewards when the firm complies with them. Individuals with certain regulatory orientations are more sensitive to the stimuli that correspond to their orientation. It means that a manager with a high level of promotion focus tends to be more receptive to an institutional requirement that emphasizes gains to be won through, for example, compliance with a demand. Hence, such managers may prioritize this demand over a competing one, which is not similarly rewarding if fulfilled. Conversely, a prevention-focused manager will pay more attention to the demands that are associated with potential losses. This will clearly influence managerial decisions when it comes to the allocation of resources, and it is expected that most of the attention and other resources will be allocated to the institutional demand that triggers the manager's individual motivational drive. The organizational design will reflect the same approach, in that the metrics and processes of the organization will remain or become more attuned to the demand that is more in line with the key decision makers' regulatory focus. Therefore we propose that:

> **Proposition 2:** Managers tend to respond to institutional complexity in accordance with their regulatory focus, i.e. a) a promotion-focused manager prioritizes organizational responses (resource allocation, organizational designs, and product designs) that accommodate the demand associated with higher potential rewards, and b) a prevention-focused manager prioritizes organizational responses that accommodate the demand associated with higher potential losses.

3. Temporal orientation: Temporal depth refers to the temporal distance (or time horizons) into the past and the future that executives typically consider when contemplating events that have happened or may happen (Nadkarni, Chen, & Chen, 2016). Temporal orientation influences fundamental aspects of a firm's strategic orientation (Das, 1987), and behaviors such as technological and capital investments (Laverty, 1996; Marginson & McAulay, 2008; Souder & Bromiley, 2012). Temporal depth has two distinct dimensions, past temporal depth (PTD) and future temporal depth (FTD), each of which is associated with different information processing filters (Bluedorn, 2002). PTD concerns how far back managers tend to go when considering past events and FTD how far ahead executives tend to look when considering the future (Bluedorn & Martin, 2008).

In the context of institutional complexity, the conflicting demands do not address the same time horizons. There are demands based on recent developments in the environment or those that have immediate or short-term consequences. There are then other demands, which are a result of long-term developments in the environment or that have consequences that will unfold in the longer term. A manager with short temporal depth has a higher tendency to consider the demands that are more recent or have more immediate consequences. Conversely a manager with a long temporal depth gives more attention to the longer-term development of demands in the past and their consequences in extended time horizons. A short temporal depth, therefore, may result in attentional bias to the urgent problems, flexibility and remobilization of resources in response to incidents, and product redesign in response to recent demands. A long temporal depth will favor more alignment with the visions that are less subject to modification, and therefore results in less flexibility in organization and offerings in response to recent changes. Therefore, we propose that:

> **Proposition 3:** Managers tend to respond to institutional complexity in accordance with their temporal orientation, i.e. a) a manager with short temporal depth will be more flexible in reallocation of resources, changing the organizational design, and altering the product design in response to recent events and future consequences and b) a manager

with long temporal depth will favor stability and alignment with demands that have been developed for a long time and are consequential in the long term.

Discussion and conclusions

The above discussion highlights that a consideration of managers and their individual tendencies and abilities may help us to form a more nuanced perspective of organizational responses to institutional complexity. Strategy and organization researchers have emphasized that beyond being seamless conduits of plans based on organizational capabilities, managers could matter separately from the effects of the organization and the environment (Eggers & Kaplan, 2009). These effects on strategic responses can be attributed to cognitive capabilities (Laureiro-Martinez, 2014), motivational drivers and regulatory focus (Gamache et al., 2015), and temporal orientation (Nadkarni et al., 2016). In this chapter, we highlighted the lack of consideration of these managerial factors in the current understanding of organizational response to institutional complexity and illuminated specific mechanisms through which such factors may result in differential responses by the organizations facing conflicting demands from their environment.

Concerning the effect of cognitive variety, our discussion highlights a possibility for the reconciliation of seemingly conflicting requirements into novel organizational responses. A general conclusion from prior research was that organizations filter the information according to the prevalent mental templates in their organizations in order to reduce the complexity. In line with recent research on the management of paradoxes (Smith, 2014), we argued for the importance of embracing the complexities by finding and exploiting synergies that are not apparent to the others. Understanding the creative responses of organizations to multiple logics has been a focus of prior studies (e.g. Binder, 2007). Our discussion highlights the cognitive variety of senior managers as an important determinant of such responses. On a broader level, one could argue that the coexistence of institutional complexity and cognitive variety is a driver of management innovation (Birkinshaw, Hamel, & Mol, 2008; Volberda, Van Den Bosch, & Mihalache, 2014).

When it comes to regulatory focus and temporal orientation, our argument discusses the potential biases of decision makers that may result in the favouring of some institutional demands over the others. The effects of biases in strategic planning has been long considered in the context of strategic management (e.g. Barnes, 1984) and reflected in contemporary research as well. Our research explains how biases in terms of temporal orientation and depth and regulatory focus may result in differential responses to institutional complexities. According to prior research, opportunity or threat perception are discussed as collective responses related to the strength and positive impressions about identity and, hence, one would expect certain behavior from firms whose identity is threatened by conflicting institutional demands. In contrast, our argument indicates that a manager who is oriented toward gains, may be less sensitive to the potential losses that may occur due to conformity and, therefore, orients the firm toward conformity notwithstanding the potential losses that may come with it. We also highlighted the importance of the temporal focus and temporal depth held by individual managers in terms of their decisions for compliance with conflicting institutional demands. While firms are expected to rationally navigate between temporally shifting demands for legitimacy, according to our argument in this chapter a long-term oriented manager may prioritize a long-term legitimacy demand, even though the short-term demand seems to be stronger. Table 15.1 summarizes the distinction between our propositions and those of prior research on institutional complexity.

It is important to note that the effects of managerial factors are to a high degree bounded by organizational contextual factors. For example, the notion of regulatory fit suggests that although complexity enacts the effect of regulatory focus, this effect is much stronger in the presence of matching organizational contexts (Ahmadi et al., 2017). This means that a promotion-focused manager will have a stronger motive to pursue gain-oriented decisions if the incentive systems and communications within the organization also emphasize the importance of gains and positive outcomes. Hence, future research needs to consider the combinations of managerial traits and organizational contextual factors, to generate a more complete understanding of the drivers of strategic response to institutional complexity.

Table 15.1 Implications of consideration of managerial effects

	Managers as seamless conduits of plans (Prior research on institutional complexity)	Managers as active agents
Different demands requiring different mental templates	• Organizations reduce the complexity by focusing on prevalent mental template.	• Managers reconcile the apparent contradictions through combining multiple mental templates.
Different institutional demands are associated with different levels of gains and loss	• Organizations will focus on conforming with the demands that indicate gains as well as those that indicate great threats to their identity.	• Managers prioritize the institutional demand that is more aligned with their motivational drivers.
Different institutional demands are associated with different temporal horizons	• Organizations navigate through temporarily shifting legitimacy requirements.	• Managers focus on the institutional demands that fit with their temporal orientation.

References

Agarwal, R., & Helfat, C. E. 2009. Strategic renewal of organizations. *Organization Science*, 20, 281–293.

Ahmadi, S., Khanagha, S., Berchicci, L., & Jansen, J. J. 2017. Are managers motivated to explore in the face of a new technological change? The role of regulatory focus, fit, and complexity of decision-making. *Journal of Management Studies*, 54(2), 209–237.

Barber, P. J. 1988. *Applied cognitive psychology: An information- processing framework*. New York: Methuen & Co.

Barnes, J. H. 1984. Cognitive biases and their impact on strategic planning. *Strategic Management Journal*, 5, 129–137.

Barr, P. S., Stimpert, J. L., & Huff, A. S. 1992. Cognitive change, strategic action, and organizational renewal. *Strategic Management Journal*, 13(S1), 15–36.

Berman, E. P. 2012. Explaining the move toward the market in US academic science: How institutional logics can change without institutional entrepreneurs. *Theory and Society*, 41, 261–299.

Binder, A. 2007. For love and money: Organizations' creative responses to multiple environmental logics. *Theory and Society*, 36(6), 547–571.

Birkinshaw, J., Hamel, G., & Mol, M. J. 2008. Management innovation. *Academy of Management Review*, 33(4), 825–845.

Bluedorn, A. C. 2002. *The human organization of time: Temporal realities and experience*. Palo Alto, CA: Stanford University Press.

Bluedorn, A. C., & Martin, G. 2008. The time frames of entrepreneurs. *Journal of Business Venturing*, 23(1), 1–20.

Bower, J. L., & Gilbert, C. G. (Eds.). 2005. *From resource allocation to strategy*. Oxford, UK: Oxford University Press.

Cho, T. S., & Hambrick, D. C. 2006. Attention as the mediator between top management team characteristics and strategic change: The case of airline deregulation. *Organization Science*, 17(4), 453–469.

Crowe, E., & Higgins, E. T. 1997. Regulatory focus and strategic inclinations: Promotion and prevention in decision-making. *Organizational Behavior and Human Decision Processes*, 69(2), 117–132.

Daft, R. L., & Weick, K. E. 1984. Toward a model of organizations as interpretation systems. *Academy of Management Review*, 9(2), 284–295.

Das, T. K. 1987. Strategic planning and individual temporal orientation. *Strategic Management Journal*, 8(2), 203–209.

Dunn, M. B., & Jones, C. 2010. Institutional logics and institutional pluralism: The contestation of care and science logics in medical education, 1967–2005. *Administrative Science Quarterly*, 55, 114–149.

Dutton, J. E., & Jackson, S. E. 1987. Categorizing strategic issues: Links to organizational action. *Academy of Management Review*, 12(1), 76–90.

Eggers, J. P., & Kaplan, S. 2009. Cognition and renewal: Comparing CEO and organizational effects on incumbent adaptation to technical change. *Organization Science*, 20 (2), 461–477.

Eisenhardt, K. M., Furr, N. R., & Bingham, C. B. 2010. CROSSROADS— Microfoundations of performance: Balancing efficiency and flexibility in dynamic environments. *Organization Science*, 21(6), 1263–1273.

Friedland, R., & Alford, R. R. 1991. Bringing society back in: Symbols, practices, and institutional contradictions. In W. W. Powell & P. J. DiMaggio (Eds.), *The new institutionalism in organizational analysis* (pp. 232–266). Chicago, IL: University of Chicago Press.

Furr, N. R. 2009. *Cognitive flexibility: The adaptive reality of concrete organization change.* Palo Alto, CA: Stanford University Press.

Gamache, D. L., McNamara, G., Mannor, M. J., & Johnson, R. E. 2015. Motivated to acquire? The impact of CEO regulatory focus on firm acquisitions. *Academy of Management Journal*, 58(4), 1261–1282.

Gatignon, H., Tushman, M. L., Smith, W., & Anderson, P. 2002. A structural approach to assessing innovation: Construct development of innovation locus, type, and characteristics. *Management Science*, 48(9), 1103–1122.

George, E., & Chattopadhyay, P. 2006. Cognitive underpinnings of institutional persistence and change: A framing perspective. *Academy of Management Journal*, 31(2), 347–365.

Gioia, D. A., & Thomas, J. B. 1996. Identity, image, and issue interpretation: Sensemaking during strategic change in academia. *Administrative Science Quarterly*, 41(3), 370–403.

Greenwood, R., Raynard, M., Kodeih, F., Micelotta, E. R., & Lounsbury, M. 2011. Institutional complexity and organizational responses. *The Academy of Management Annals*, 5, 317–371.

Gröschl, S., Gabaldón, P., & Hahn, T. 2017. The co-evolution of leaders' cognitive complexity and corporate sustainability: The case of the CEO of Puma. *Journal of Business Ethics*. https://doi.org/10.1007/s10551-017-3508-4

Heimer, C. A. 1999. Competing institutions: Law, medicine, and family in neonatal intensive care. *Law and Society Review*, 33, 17–66.

Helfat, C. E., & Peteraf, M. A. 2015. Managerial cognitive capabilities and the microfoundations of dynamic capabilities. *Strategic Management Journal*, 36, 831–850.

Higgins, E. T. 1997. Beyond pleasure and pain. *American Psychologist*, 52(12), 1280.

Higgins, E. T. 1998. Promotion and prevention: Regulatory focus as a motivational principle. *Advances in Experimental Social Psychology*, 30, 1–46.

Higgins, E. T. 2000. Making a good decision: Value from fit. *American Psychologist*, 55, 1217–1230.

Higgins, E. T., Idson, L. C., Freitas, A. L., Spiegel, S., & Molden, D. C. 2003. Transfer of value from fit. *Journal of Personality and Social Psychology*, 84(6), 1140.

Kaplan, S., & Orlikowski, W. J. 2013. Temporal work in strategy making. *Organization Science*, 24(4), 965–995.

Kiesler, S., & Sproull, L. 1982. Managerial response to changing environments: Perspectives on problem sensing from social cognition. *Administrative Science Quarterly*, 27(4), 548–570.

Kodeih, F., & Greenwood, R. 2014. Responding to institutional complexity: The role of identity. *Organization Studies*, 35, 7–39.

Kraatz, M. S., & Block, E. 2008. Organizational implica- tions of institutional pluralism. In R. Greenwood, C. Oliver, K. Sahlin, & R. Suddaby (Eds.), *The Sage handbook of organizational institutionalism* (pp. 243–275). Thousand Oaks, CA: Sage Publications.

Kunc, M. H., & Morecroft, J. D. 2010. Managerial decision making and firm performance under a resource-based paradigm. *Strategic Management Journal*, 31(11), 1164–1182.

Lachman, R., Lachman, J. L., & Butterfield, E. C.. 1979. *Cognitive psychology and information processing: An introduction.* Hillsdale, NJ: Lawrence Erlbaum Associates.

Laureiro-Martinez, D. 2014. Cognitive control capabilities, routinization propensity, and decision-making performance. *Organization Science*, 25(4), 1111–1133.

Laverty, K. J. 1996. Economic "short-termism": The debate, the unresolved issues, and the implications for management practice and research. *Academy of Management Review*, 21(3), 825–860.

Lavie, D. 2006. Capability reconfiguration: An analysis of incumbent responses to technological change. *The Academy of Management Review*, 31(1), 153–174.

Lok, J. 2010. Institutional logics as identity projects. *Academy of Management Journal*, 53, 1305–1335.

Marginson, D., & McAulay, L. 2008. Exploring the debate on short-termism: A theoretical and empirical analysis. *Strategic Management Journal*, 29(3), 273–292.

McPherson, C. M., & Sauder, M. 2013. Logics in action: Managing institutional complexity in a drug court. *Administrative Science Quarterly*, 58(2), 165–196.

Meyer, R. E., & Hammerschmid, G. 2006. Changing institutional logics and executive identities: A managerial challenge to public administration in Austria. *American Behavioural Scientist*, 49, 1000–1014.

Nadkarni, S., Chen, T., & Chen, J. 2016. The clock is ticking! Executive temporal depth, industry velocity, and competitive aggressiveness. *Strategic Management Journal*, 37(6), 1132–1153.

Tushman, M. L., & Nadler, D. A. 1992. Designing organizations that have good fit: A framework for understanding new architectures. In M. Gerstein, D. Nadler, & R. Shaw (Eds.) *Organizational Architecture: Designs for Changing Organizations* (39–56). San Francisco: Jossey-Bass.

Pache, A., & Santos, F. 2010. When worlds collide: The internal dynamics of organizational responses to conflicting institutional demands. *Academy of Management Review*, 35, 455–476.

Ramus, T., Vaccaro, A., & Brusoni, S. 2017. Institutional complexity in turbulent times: Formalization, collaboration, and the emergence of blended logics. *Academy of Management Journal*, 60(4), 1253–1284.

Raynard, M. 2016. Deconstructing complexity: Configurations of institutional complexity and structural hybridity. *Strategic Organization*, 14(4), 310–335.

Reay, T., & Hinings, C. R. 2005. The recomposition of an organizational field: Health care in Alberta. *Organization Studies*, 26, 349–382.

Reay, T., & Hinings, C. R. 2009. Managing the rivalry of competing institutional logics. *Organization Studies*, 30, 629–652.

Rousseau, D. M. 1978. Characteristics of departments, positions, and individuals: Contexts for attitudes and behavior. *Administrative Science Quarterly*, 23, 521–540.

Ruef, M., & Scott, W. R. 1998. A multidimensional model of organizational legitimacy: Hospital survival in changing institutional environments. *Administrative Science Quarterly*, 43, 877–904.

Sauermann, H., & Stephan, P. 2013. Conflicting logics? A multidimensional view of industrial and academic science. *Organization Science*, 24, 889–909.

Schwartz, B. 1978. *Psychology of learning and behavior*. New York City, NY: WW Norton & Co.

Scott, W. R., Ruef, M., Mendel, P. J., & Caronna, C. A. 2000. *Institutional change and healthcare organizations: From professional dominance to managed care*. Chicago, IL: University of Chicago Press.

Seo, M., & Creed, W. E. D. 2002. Institutional contradictions, praxis and institutional change: Adialectical perspective. *Academy of Management Review*, 27, 222–247.

Skelcher, C., & Smith, S. R. 2015. Theorizing hybridity: Institutional logics, complex organizations, and actor identities: The case of nonprofits. *Public Administration*, 93(2), 433–448.

Smith, W. K. 2014. Dynamic decision making: A model of senior leaders managing strategic paradoxes. *Academy of Management Journal*, 57, 1592–1623.

Souder, D., & Bromiley, P. 2012. Explaining temporal orientation: Evidence from the durability of firms' capital investments. *Strategic Management Journal*, 33(5), 550–569.

Staw, B. M., Sandelands, L. E., & Dutton, J. E. 1981. Threat rigidity effects in organizational behavior: A multilevel analysis. *Administrative Science Quarterly*, 26(4), 501–524.

Thomas, J. B., Clark, S. M., & Gioia, D. A. 1993. Strategic sensemaking and organizational performance: Linkages among scanning, interpretation, action, and outcomes. *Academy of Management Journal*, 36(2), 239–270.

Thornton, P. H. 2004. *Markets from culture: Institutional logics and organizational decisions in higher education publishing.* Stanford, CA: Stanford University Press.

Thornton, P. H., Ocasio, W., & Lounsbury, M. 2012. *The institutional logics perspective: A new approach to culture, structure and process.* Oxford: Oxford University Press.

Tripsas, M. 2009. Technology, identity, and inertia through the lens of "The Digital Photography Company". *Organization Science*, 20, 441–460.

Tuncdogan, A., Boon, A., Mom, T., van Den Bosch, F., & Volberda, H. 2017. Management teams' regulatory foci and organizational units' exploratory innovation: The mediating role of coordination mechanisms. *Long Range Planning*, 50(5), 621–635.

Tuncdogan, A., Van Den Bosch, F., & Volberda, H. 2015. Regulatory focus as a psychological micro-foundation of leaders' exploration and exploitation activities. *The Leadership Quarterly*, 26(5), 838–850.

Vermeulen, P. A. M., Zietsma, C., Greenwood, R., & Langley, A. 2016. Strategic responses to institutional complexity. *Strategic Organization*, 14(4), 277–286.

Volberda, H. W., Baden-Fuller, C., & Van Den Bosch, F. A. 2001. Mastering strategic renewal: Mobilising renewal journeys in multi-unit firms. *Long Range Planning*, 34(2), 159–178.

Volberda, H. W., Van Den Bosch, F. A., & Mihalache, O. R. 2014. Advancing management innovation: Synthesizing processes, levels of analysis, and change agents. *Organization Studies*, 35(9), 1245–1264.

Zhao, E. Y., Fisher, G., Lounsbury, M., & Miller, D. 2017. Optimal distinctiveness: Broadening the interface between institutional theory and strategic management. *Strategic Management Journal*, 38, 93–113.

Zilber, T. B. 2002. Institutionalization as an interplay between actions, meanings, and actors: The case of a rape crisis center in Israel. *Academy of Management Journal*, 45(1), 234–254.

16 Patent-based measures in strategic management research

A review and assessment

Barton M. Sharp, Dinesh N. Iyer, and Derek Ruth

Introduction

Innovation as a process is widely believed to be the key to growth and economic success for companies, geographic regions, and societies as a whole. A long tradition of research beginning with Solow (1957) indicates that innovation in the form of technical change has an enormously positive impact, accounting for a third or more of the growth in factor productivity and general economic welfare (Cameron, 1996). Innovation in the form of "new consumers' goods, the new methods of production or transportation, the new markets, [and] the new forms of industrial organization" is the source of "creative destruction", which adds economic value through the emergence of entirely new industries at the expense of older, less efficient ones (Schumpeter, 1950: 82). Within existing industries, firms with higher levels of innovation tend to experience such positive impacts as greater revenue growth (Thornhill, 2006) and higher likelihood of survival (Cefis & Marsili, 2005), although not necessarily higher profitability (Koellinger, 2008). Given the practical implications of innovation, it comes as little surprise that a large and growing body of academic literature has been devoted to its study. Some evidence for this can be found by searching the Web of Science Business and Management article databases for the topic of "innovation". That search reveals an average of nearly 2,500 articles per year published on the subject from 2006 to 2013, compared to an average of fewer than 600 articles per year from 1998 to 2005.

This growing focus is consistent with a number of theoretical perspectives that place knowledge at the heart of why organizations exist, either to provide a forum for the application of individual knowledge (Grant, 1996), or to serve as the incubator for new knowledge by providing a venue for existing knowledge to be recombined (Kogut & Zander, 1992). Without knowledge there is no value, and so understanding what organizations (and the people within them) know is critical to strategic management research. With that in mind, it is appropriate to consider the methods with which organizational knowledge is being studied. It is our intention with this chapter to offer an assessment of one aspect of the literature on knowledge and innovation – the ways in which authors have used variables based on data from patents as part of their empirical tests.

Patents are believed to be a reasonable representation of a firm's technical knowledge (Ahuja & Katila, 2001; Jaffe, Trajtenberg, & Henderson, 1993) and at least an intermediate output from their innovative efforts (Hagedoorn & Cloodt, 2003). The patent system, which grants inventors the right to forestall imitation of their ideas for a specified period of time, is designed to enhance knowledge creation through two primary mechanisms. First, the financial incentives associated with innovation are enhanced by the time-limited monopoly that the patent system permits. Second, the patent process requires that the details of the invention be published, which allows others to build on the work and accelerate future progress. Hence, they are a natural source of data regarding knowledge stocks and creation within organizations.

However, the data available in the patent system in its raw form often does not bear a direct relationship to the relevant theories associated with this field of academic research. It is at a given author's discretion to use the available data to develop empirical measures that proxy for the underlying theoretical constructs. Our primary purpose in this paper is to offer a review of how the United States Patent and Trademark Office (USPTO) database is being used to operationalize specific constructs in research, and to evaluate the extent to which strategic management researchers have been consistent in using patent data in reliable, valid ways. This allows us to make several substantial contributions to the literature. First, by conducting a thorough review of extant constructs and variables our study can serve as an invaluable reference to future researchers who wish to incorporate some element of innovation or knowledge into their empirical studies. Second, by gaining the big-picture perspective on how individual authors have made use of patent data in their work we will be able to offer an assessment and critique of practice in our field. Third, we offer suggestions for how to improve the quality and rigor of work in this area by helping ensure that the measures being used are truly reflective of their underlying constructs. We hope to encourage authors to be explicit about why particular operational variables have been chosen going forward.

Review of patent-based measures in strategic management research

To characterize and catalog the patent-based empirical measures being used in strategic management research, we began with a full-text search for the term "patent" in all papers published in the *Strategic Management Journal (SMJ)* during the eight-year window from 2008 through 2015 using the search function available from Wiley, the publisher of the *SMJ*. We chose *SMJ* for two primary reasons. First, given that our express focus is on the way in which patent-based measures are used in strategic management research, using the *SMJ* as our sampling frame ensures that all of the papers would be topically relevant. Second, given the status of the *SMJ* as a premier outlet in the field, we feel confident that the work published there represents the state-of-the-art. The initial full-text search resulted in a sample of 222 papers published over eight years that contained the word "patent". We then examined each paper to identify which of them contained patent-based variables as part of their empirical tests. For the purpose of this review we included only those papers that used data from the United States Patent and Trademark Office. Although a number of papers made use of patent data from other parts of the world, the data available varies from country to country. Out of 222 papers that contained the word "patent", 77 (34.7%) had empirical variables based on USPTO patent data. Those 77 papers comprise our sample for review.

We then scrutinized those 77 papers to identify 1) what patent-based variables they contained, 2) how those variables were calculated, 3) what underlying constructs the variables were proxies for, and 4) any discernible patterns regarding what people have measured using patent data. Across 77 papers, we found 286 patent-based variables, or an average of 3.7 patent variables per paper. The complete list of constructs and variables is cataloged here as an appendix (Table 16.3). In the hope of making this paper as useful as possible to future researchers who are interested in using patent measures in their own work, we have organized the variables into broad categories. Not all constructs and variables fell neatly into a category so some judgment calls had to be made, and those which could not be more precisely placed were left for a catch-all "Other" category.

The first category comprises largely constructs related to the idea of knowledge "stock" and variables based on patent counts. The second category is for constructs and variables that in some way address the breadth/focus or generality/specialization of technologies. The third category is for constructs and variables which describe the depth of knowledge or expertise in particular technologies. The fourth category captures variables and constructs related to the similarity or overlap in the technological stocks or capabilities of dyadic pairs of organizations. The fifth category is for constructs and variables related to the flow of technologies (between firms, from basic science to the firms, etc.). The sixth category broadly contains the constructs and variables related in some way to the performance, value, quality, or impact of a firm's technologies. The seventh category contains all variables related in some way to time (patent age, patenting speed, years of protection remaining, etc.). The eighth category is for variables that capture some geographical dimension related to technologies. The ninth category is for constructs and variables that describe the technological environment (such as within an industry or within a country). The tenth category is for constructs and variables related to individual inventors, and the final category is for variables that either 1) did not fit neatly into the other categories, 2) did not have a clear construct defined in the paper, or 3) were used simply as controls. The variables in each category are presented in order of year of publication such that some sense might be gained of how the patent variables being used in *SMJ* papers have changed over time.

We did find some agreement across authors for certain variables and constructs. For example, it is common practice among the papers that included a construct of technology "breadth" (or its opposite, specialization/focus) in their models to use calculations based on the number of technology classes spanned by a firm's patents as their measure (Fernhaber & Patel, 2012; Guler & Nerkar, 2012; Kotha, Zheng, & George, 2011; Ndofor, Sirmon, & He, 2011). Technology classes are useful for that purpose as they represent a standardized classification system whereby each patent granted includes a list of the various underlying technological domains that the patent touches. The assumption is that the more technology classes a company has represented across its patent portfolio, the broader their technological expertise (or the obverse, that the fewer classes represented, the more narrowly focused or specialized their technological expertise). However, the manner in which that technology class data was transformed into a variable capturing technological breadth or focus differed significantly across authors. For example, some authors used the technology class to calculate a Herfindahl index (Conti, 2014; Kaplan & Vakili, 2015; Ndofor, Sirmon, & He, 2015; and many others), while others based their variables on a Blau index (Kehoe & Tzabbar, 2015), or the simple total number of technology classes covered by a patent portfolio (Fernhaber & Patel, 2012; Toh, 2014), not to mention a number of other idiosyncratic measures that can be seen in the appendix.

A similar pattern of general agreement can be found among the measures of similarity or overlap in technologies between organizations. Most of the measures are again based on technology classes, with the actual variables being calculated as the Euclidean distance between the two vectors that describe the distribution of technology classes for each organization (Corredoira & Rosenkopf, 2010; Jiang, Tan, & Thursby, 2011; Kotha et al., 2011; and others). However, here too there were some other variants employed. For example, Diestre and Rajagopalan (2012) measure technological relatedness as simply "a count of the number of patent classes in which both firms had patenting activities" (p. 1122), and Sears and Hoetker (2014) use patterns of citations (where the patents received by one firm cite those held by another) as the basis for their technological overlap measures. We will return to the implications of these inconsistencies shortly.

What we find most striking in a careful examination of the catalog is the extent to which particular variables are used as proxies for multiple constructs across different papers, and the extent to which different authors use different operational variables for the same underlying constructs. For example, our summary in Table 16.1 shows a representative selection of constructs and variables that various authors have derived from data on the "number of patents" a particular firm has either applied for or been granted. The "number of patents" held by a particular firm is variously used as a measure of activity (Schildt, Keil, & Maula, 2012), performance (Keil, Maula, Schildt, & Zahra, 2008), stock (Kotha et al., 2011), capability (Arora & Nandkumar, 2012), quality (Park & Steensma, 2012), propensity to patent (Hess & Rothaermel, 2011), and technical advantage achieved (Soh, 2010). It is unresolved whether the number of patents held by a particular firm is a proper measure of what the firm knows, what it has achieved in the past, what it is capable of doing, or what it is likely to do. From a theoretical perspective those are meaningfully distinct constructs, and it seems unlikely on the face that they could all be validly measured using the same operational variable.

Another example of a single variable being interpreted to represent multiple constructs is the "forward citations" measure. This is operationalized as the number of times a firm's patents are cited by other patents. Forward citation counts are variously used to proxy for the quality (Agarwal, Ganco, & Ziedonis, 2009; Joshi & Nerkar, 2011; Makri, Hitt, & Lane, 2010), impact (Kotha et al., 2011; Valentini, 2012), and value (Levitas & McFadyen, 2009) of a firm's patent

Table 16.1 Example of patent-count-based measures

Paper	Construct	Variable
Schildt et al. (2012)	Patenting activity	Count of patents over the previous three years
Kotha et al. (2011)	Innovation quantity	Number of patents applied for in the previous two years
Clarkson, G., & Toh, P. (2010)	Total inventive effort	Total patents for firm i in year t
Keil et al. (2008)	Innovative performance	Number of successful patent applications
Leone, M., & Reichstein, T. (2012)	Patent stock	Number of patents prior to a licensing agreement
Kotha et al. (2011)	Knowledge stock	Number of patents applied for in previous three years. (Controls for firm size and resource availability; uses lower weights for previous two years, 0.6, 0.8)
Yu, J., Gilbert, B., & Oviatt, B. M. (2011)	Technological capability	Number of patents obtained by the firm in the previous five years
Arora, A., & Nandkumar, A. (2012)	Technical capability	Count of information security patents that startup firm has (measure is weighted by forward citations)
Park, H., & Steensma, H. (2012)	Quality of a venture	Log of number of patents granted before VC funding received
Hess, A. M., & Rothaermel, F. T. (2011)	Total patent propensity	Total patents
Nadkarni, S., Herrmann, P., & Perez, P. (2011)	Technology intensity	Total patents filed
Soh, P. (2010)	Technical advantage achieved by firm	Number of patents (by issue date rather than application date)

portfolio, as well as a firm's research and development (R&D) productivity (Kaul, 2012). Again, we are left with concerns regarding the extent to which a single variable can be expected to reliably represent such diverse underlying constructs.

Just as we find examples in which a single operational variable is used to proxy for multiple constructs, we also find instances where different variables have been used to measure the same construct in different papers. For example, several of the papers in our sample focus on dyadic relationships between partner firms (Jiang et al., 2011), in acquisitions (Makri et al., 2010), and in cases of interfirm mobility of human resources (Corredoira & Rosenkopf, 2010). One of the constructs of interest in many of those studies is technical similarity, or the extent to which the firms involved share certain technological resources or capabilities.

In Rothaermel and Boeker (2008), similarity is measured as the degree to which the patents held by two firms share commonality in citations. Firms are believed to be more similar when their patents cite the same external patents, or cite each other's patents. By contrast, Makri et al. (2010) measure the same construct, but use data on technology classes rather than citation patterns. In their model, the more overlap there is between technology classes listed in the patents held by two firms, the more technically similar the two firms are considered to be. Specifically, they calculate similarity as "the number of patents applied for by the target and acquirer that are in the same patent classes, multiplied by the total number of patents the acquirer has in all common classes divided by total acquirer patents" (Makri et al., 2010: 611). Jiang et al. (2011) also use the overlap in technology classes as a proxy for technical similarity, but use a significantly different formula. In their paper:

$$\text{Technological similarity} = \frac{T'_{it} T_{jt}}{\sqrt{T'_{it} T_{it}} \sqrt{T'_{jt} T_{jt}}} \tag{1}$$

where "T_{it} is a 470-dimension vector representing the number of semiconductor patents firm i applied for between 1980 and t, in each of the 470 USPTO patent classes" (Jiang, Tan, & Thursby, 2011: 64). We find yet a third approach to using technology class data to calculate technological similarity in Schildt et al. (2012). In order to calculate their measure of similarity they "multiplied the number of patents in patent class (k) for companies A and B, summed up the results from every patent class, and then divided the result by the geometric mean of patent portfolio sizes" (2012: 1163).

$$\text{Technological similarity} = \frac{\sum_k \sqrt{C_{k;A} \times C_{k;B}}}{\sqrt{\textit{Patents}_A + \textit{Patents}_B}} \tag{2}$$

So here we have one construct that is measured using four different operational variables across four different papers. To the extent that these measures are not perfectly correlated, we risk finding ourselves in a situation where the empirical results we get depend upon which variable we choose to use.

Even among those constructs where there appears to be a certain amount of consistency, subtle differences in the way the variables are operationalized could make it difficult to generalize results or understand how the insights from one paper add to or fit together with what we learn from other studies. For example, among the papers that use "technology class count" as the basis for variables measuring the breadth of a firm's technologies, some use the total count of unique technology classes included in a firm's patents (Fernhaber & Patel, 2012; Kotha et al., 2011), others use the average number of unique technology classes per patent (Guler & Nerkar, 2012), and still others use a Herfindahl index of the firm's technology classes (Ndofor et al., 2011). The total count measure and the average count measure are likely to diverge as the number of patents held by a particular firm increases. The Herfindahl-based measure will diverge from both in cases where the distribution of patents across technology classes is skewed, such as in a situation where a firm has many patents in a small number of technology classes but many technology classes in which the firm has a small number of patents.

In some cases, the authors themselves explicitly recognize that they are deviating from their cited precedents in developing their constructs and variables. For example, in describing the operationalization of a construct he calls "knowledge diversity", Berry (2014) says that he "... uses Hall et al.'s (2001) measure of originality" (p. 876). Similarly, Kim, Arthurs, Sahaym, and Cullen (2013) describe the variable they use to proxy for search scope as being "... the same as the 'originality' measure in the paper by Trajtenberg, Henderson, and Jaffe (1997)" (p. 1003). The result is that we have a single operational variable being used to proxy for three seemingly distinct constructs: the originality of a firm's technologies, the diversity of a firm's knowledge, and the scope of the firm's search for new technologies. While those three constructs may certainly be related, it seems fair to say that they are likely theoretically distinct. Therefore, measuring them with the same variable is potentially problematic from the perspective of validity.

As a whole, this review suggests that there are potential problems with the manner in which patent data is used to construct variables meant to proxy for various technology – or innovation-related constructs. In the absence of consistent, valid, and rigorously tested construct-variable pairings, there is a question as to how reliable the resulting body of theoretical knowledge can be. However, we cannot know, based simply on the catalog, whether the inconsistencies identified might be having a significant effect on the outcomes of our research. The next section represents a limited first step towards exploring that question.

Test of validity

One way to determine whether the wide discrepancies in constructs and variables based on patent data impact the empirical work we do to test our theories is to examine the convergent and discriminant validity of some of the measures. In theory, if multiple variables do in fact proxy for the same construct, each of those variables should be closely correlated in any given population. And, conversely, measures which effectively proxy for discrete constructs should be demonstrably distinct from one another. We test this for two constructs identified as having multiple operationalizations: (1) Technology breadth measured as total number of technology classes (Fernhaber & Patel, 2012; Kotha et al., 2011), average number of technology classes per patent (Guler & Nerkar, 2012), and the Herfindahl index (Ndofor et al., 2011); and (2) Radicalness measured as backward citations (Ahuja & Lampert, 2001) and number of technology classes (Shane, 2001).

To do this, we first developed a database using the bulk patent archive files available from Google (www.google.com/googlebooks/uspto-patents.html). We then randomly selected 500 companies that were issued patents in 2000 and collected all of the data for the patents issued to them in that year. The random selection of companies was made from a database table in which each row represents a single patent, meaning that companies that were issued multiple patents would appear multiple times in the list and thus were at higher risk of being randomly selected. This helps increase the chances that the companies in our random sample were issued enough patents to make the patent-based measures meaningful. We randomly drew rows from the database, rejecting any selection which duplicated a company already in our sample, until we had collected 500 unique companies. Missing data resulted in a final sample of 476 companies that were issued a total of 41,545 patents in 2000.[1] We then collected data on the backward citations and technology classes for each of those 41,545 patents and calculated firm-level measures of the breadth and radicalness of their year 2000 patent portfolios. Table 16.2 contains the descriptive statistics and pairwise correlations for each of those variables.

A few interesting observations can be drawn from the table. First, there is no significant correlation between the two measures of radicalness that were identified from the literature. This suggests a lack of convergent validity, or that the two variables are not in fact measuring the same thing. Second, we see a situation in which there is a highly significant correlation among all three extant measures of technology breadth, but not all in the same direction. The average number of technology classes represented (the total number of unique technology classes in which a firm patented divided by the total number of patents) is negatively correlated with both of the other measures. A firm in this sample that we might conclude had a broad range of technological expertise based on the average number of technology classes would actually exhibit low breadth when the measure used was the total number of technology classes or the Herfindahl index of technology classes. Finally, we see some suggestive (but by no means conclusive) evidence for a lack of discriminant validity in the significant correlation between one of the radicalness measures (average number of technology classes included on each patent) and two of the measures of technological breadth (number of unique classes divided by number of patents, and the Herfindahl index of technology classes). In sum, this suggests that the lack of consistency in the way we use patent data to measure important constructs could in fact be impacting our conclusions.

Table 16.2 Descriptive statistics and correlations

Variable	Mean	Std. Dev.	1	2	3	4	5	6
1. Patent Count	87.28	257.61	1.00					
Breadth Measures								
2. Total number of unique tech classes	23.00	36.76	0.85**	1.00				
3. Number of unique tech classes divided by number of patents	1.02	0.75	−0.34**	−0.44**	1.00			
4. Herfindahl index of technology classes	0.65	0.32	0.28**	0.50**	−0.12**	1.00		
Radicalness Measures								
5. Average number of backward citations per patent	12.27	16.49	−0.05	−0.07	−0.04	−0.01	1.00	
6. Average number of technology classes on each patent	1.70	0.57	0.01	0.04	0.62**	0.50**	−0.04	1.00

* $p<0.05$ ** $p<0.01$

Discussion and recommendations

Good theory is based on clearly defined constructs, variables that validly measure the underlying constructs, and the proposed relationships among them (Bacharach, 1989). The ability of any variable to stand for a particular construct is in turn a function of its content validity, dimensionality, reliability, convergent validity, discriminant validity, and predictive validity (Boyd, Bergh, Ireland, & Ketchen, 2013; Venkatraman & Grant, 1986). Given the surprising lack of consistency between the constructs under study and the variables used to measure them across the papers in our review, it is reasonable to conclude that the appropriateness of the patent-based variables currently being used to proxy for innovation-oriented constructs is questionable at best.

In their paper in the *Journal of Management Studies*, Aguinas and Edwards have expressed the "wish" that in the coming decade we "improve the construct validity of measures used in management research" (2014: 145) where "validity refers to the extent to which a measure represents the intended construct (Edwards, 2003; Schwab, 1980)" (2014: 148). In a situation like we found in our review of the strategic management literature, where a single, simple measure such as the number of patents held by a firm may stand as a proxy for seven or more distinct constructs across multiple papers, we clearly can have little confidence that the measure validly represents any of those underlying constructs. Aguinas and Edwards quote Ketchen et al. when they say that "even if a proxy appears to be reasonable *within the context of an individual study,* its use *among different studies* to represent different constructs creates serious problems" (2013: 37; emphasis in original). This points to an apparent lack of content validity. It is unreasonable to think that one variable can "closely … mesh with the theoretical framing" of seven disparate constructs (Boyd et al., 2013: 6). It is equally difficult to develop an internally consistent, scientifically sound body of knowledge without first ensuring that the constructs we are talking about and the measures used to proxy for them are sound and well vetted.

Our findings here have a number of implications. One, they lead us to question the extent to which we actually know what we think we know about the antecedents, processes, and consequences of innovation. Are the extant empirical findings a true reflection of the underlying phenomenon, or are they simply spurious artifacts of the particular patent-based measures chosen by the authors? This uncertainty represents a threat to the rigor and validity of research in this field. Another, and perhaps more troublesome issue, is the way in which these multiple unvalidated measures may increase the opportunity for research misconduct. A growing body of work across a range of academic disciplines is beginning to pull back the curtain on just how researchers may cut corners and employ questionable methods that often seem to shade findings in the direction of the authors' hypotheses (Bakker & Wicherts, 2011; Edwards & Smith, 1996; Fanelli, 2010; Fugelsang, Stein, Green, & Dunbar, 2004). A wily researcher working in the field of innovation may be tempted to "shop around" for a measure that supports their theory to the exclusion of other extant measures for the same construct which do not. The potential success of such a gambit is indicated by the negative correlation found above for two measures of technological breadth. This, again, threatens the foundations of our research as a scientifically sound field of inquiry.

The results of our study lead us to make a number of concrete recommendations aimed at scholars who plan to use patent measures in their future work. First and foremost, careful and explicit consideration must be given to the process of defining the constructs under study and selecting empirical measures that will proxy for those underlying constructs. Failure to do so puts us at risk of building a body of knowledge on a shaky foundation. Second, we encourage authors to use previously published operational variables rather than developing their own novel measures, unless the existing measures are deficient in some clearly explicated way. Knowledge advances as future work builds and expands on prior work, and a constantly shifting definition of operational variables can make it impossible to understand how various pieces of research relate to one another. We hope that this paper will aid in that effort by offering a thorough catalog of extant measures. Third, we call on the researchers active in this field to undertake a careful and thorough exploration of extant constructs and validation of the variables used to measure them. It will be a significant undertaking given the sheer number of constructs and variables in the literature, but it is important that we ensure to whatever extent possible that the variables we choose are valid and reliable measures of the constructs we set out to measure.

We also offer recommendations for reviewers and editors. Collectively, we must use a critical eye when considering whether authors have convincingly and explicitly made the case for the validity and appropriateness of their empirical measures. We must also be willing, when there are alternative measures that could have been used, to ask, "why these and not others?". Why measure radicalness using backward citations rather than technology class counts? Why might it be better to use average technology class counts versus using a Herfindahl index when measuring technological breadth? We must also question the discriminant validity of measures chosen. When authors include the number of patent counts owned by an organization in their model as a proxy for knowledge stock, is that really the construct they are capturing? Or are they actually measuring the firm's propensity to patent? Or the intensity of innovative activity? Researchers must be expected to fully and transparently justify the choices they make in support of their theory testing.

The current work does have limitations. First, we only examine the literature in a relatively recent timeframe. Given the time it takes for papers to be written, reviewed, and published, it is possible that a more coherent and consistent body of measures is about to emerge. Our timeframe also prevents us from speaking to any development or improvement in the state-of-the-art over a longer period. Further, we review only those papers published in the *Strategic Management Journal*. While certainly a premier outlet for strategic management research, we do not capture the entire breadth of work being pursued using patent data. We also do not capture the constructs and variables being studied using foreign patent data (Durand, Bruyaka, & Mangematin, 2008; Jensen, Thomson, & Yong, 2011; Lichtenthaler & Ernst, 2012; Mahmood, Zhu, & Zajac, 2011; Reitzig & Puranam, 2009; Reitzig & Wagner, 2010; Salomon & Jin, 2010). As such, we must be careful to not overgeneralize the results of our USPTO-based study.

Despite those limitations, we feel strongly that this work represents an important step towards greater rigor in patent-based innovation research. We have identified the population of patent-based variables currently used to measure important constructs within strategic management and highlighted specific examples of single constructs being measured using multiple different operational variables as well as examples of single operational variables being used to proxy for a multitude of different constructs. As well, we have offered a concrete example of how the choice of operational variable can materially impact the results of our empirical models and, in turn, the development of our theoretical understanding. We call on our peers in the field to further build on what we have done by pursuing rigorous, explicit validation of the available variables used to proxy for these innovation-oriented constructs.

Table 16.3 Appendix Catalog of patent-based measures in the *Strategic Management Journal*, 2008–2012

Author	Year	Construct	Variable
Stock/Count Variables			
Chung & Yeaple	2008	Knowledge stock	Patent count – US "we construct a moving stock using the perpetual inventory method; we use the yearly flow in 1976 as our starting point and depreciate the existing stock by 20 percent while adding additional patents each year" p. 1213
Chung & Yeaple	2008	Knowledge stock	Patent count – Host "we construct a moving stock using the perpetual inventory method; we use the yearly flow in 1976 as our starting point and depreciate the existing stock by 20 percent while adding additional patents each year" p. 1213
Ethiraj & Zhu	2008	Patent stock	"Moving three year sum of patents filed by the firm in the corresponding therapeutic class" p. 807
Keil et al.	2008	Patent stocks	"pre-sample mean patents and annually 30% depreciated stock of prior patents" p. 899
Keil et al.	2008	Yearly innovative performance	"the number of successful patent applications filed during each year" p. 898
Rothaermel & Boeker	2008	Patent propensity	A count of the total number of patents assigned between 1994 and 1997 to biotechnology and pharmaceutical firms in the sample
Agarwal et al.	2009	Patent Stock	"log patent stock is a count of patents awarded to a firm in a year t, measured as a log because of skewness" p. 1359
Aggarwal & Hsu	2009	Patent Stock	"Total stock of patents held by the firm up to the current year" p. 848
Wang, He, & Mahoney	2009	Patenting intensity	"Patenting intensity was calculated by dividing the aggregate number of a firm's patents by its total assets" p. 1273
Clarkson & Toh	2010	Inventive efforts *ijt*	"the number of patents firm i applied for in class j in year t that are subsequently granted." p. 1212
Clarkson & Toh	2010	Total inventive effort it	"the number of reexamination certificates issued to firms other than firm i in class j in year t−1" p. 1212

(Continued)

Table 16.3 (Cont.)

Author	Year	Construct	Variable
Corredoira & Rosenkopf	2010	Control for probability of citation	"the count of patents granted to the firm that have application dates during the year of observation." p. 167
Corredoira & Rosenkopf	2010	Focal firm knowledge stock	"It is the count of patents granted to the firm that have application dates in the five-year window previous to the year of observation. We utilized five-year windows to count the number of patents as a proxy for firms' knowledge stock to account for knowledge depreciation." p. 167
Corredoira & Rosenkopf	2010	Patents at risk of citation by dyad firm	"This variable represents the number of patents granted to the alter firm of the dyad during the 10-year window previous to the year of observation. In the case of the number of patents at risk of being cited, we utilized the 10-year window, which is the time it takes a patent to start receiving a negligible number of citations per year." (Jaffe et al., 1993). p. 167
Hoang & Rothaermel	2010	Overall competence in biotech	"We weighted each patent obtained by a pharmaceutical company in the relevant patent classes by its forward citations to capture the quality of a firm's patent portfolio [...] Thus, we calculated a cumulative variable for each pharmaceutical firm by summing the annual citation-weighted patent counts up to the year before the initiation of the focal project." p. 744
Makri et al.	2010	Invention Quantity	"the number of patents for which the firm applied three years pre ... and three years post M&A ... subtracting the [pre-M&A] value from the [post-M&A] value and then dividing that difference by the [post-M&A] value" p. 610
Soh	2010	Technical advantage achieved by firm	"patent applications and patents issued for Ethernet and Token Ring, according to the patent abstracts that cite these two technologies" p. 447
Adegbesan & Higgins	2011	Superior patent portfolio	Patent count: "Thus, by subtracting the number of patents assigned to the early-stage biotechnology firm with the

(*Continued*)

Table 16.3 (Cont.)

Author	Year	Construct	Variable
			fewest patents in each period, from the number assigned to each early-stage biotechnology firm in our sample in that period, we generated the variable superior biotech patent portfolio" p. 197
Hess & Rothaermel	2011	Innovation performance	"a five-year [forward] citation-weighting window [count of patents]" p. 900
Hess & Rothaermel	2011	Total patent propensity	"total patents" p. 902
Jiang et al.	2011	Inventive performance	"the annual count of nanotechnology patents applied for by the firm (nano patents)" p. 63
Jiang et al.	2011	Pre-sample dependent variable (nanotechnology)	"the number of nanotechnology patents applied for by a focal firm during the nine-year period before 1989." p. 65
Jiang et al.	2011	Pre-sample dependent variable (semiconductor)	"the number of semiconductor patents a focal firm applied for in year t-1" p. 65
Joshi & Nerkar	2011	Innovation historical average quantity	"This is measured as the [number of patents] received by the firm to its patents filed in the years 1976 to 1981" p. 1151
Joshi & Nerkar	2011	Innovation quantity	"the number of related patents generated by a given firm in a given year. Related patents are those patents that have a technology classification corresponding to one of the 10 classes representing optical disc technology" p. 1150
Kotha et al.	2011	Knowledge stock	"the number of patents applied in the previous three years" p. 1015
Kotha et al.	2011	Quantity of innovative output	"the number of new patents applied for in two subsequent years (t + 1, t + 2)." p. 1015
Nadkarni et al.	2011	Technology intensity	"Technological intensity was measured by R&D intensity […] and total patents filed by the firm" p. 520
Yu et al.	2011	Technological capability	"the number of patents obtained by each venture in a five-year window preceding each observation year" p. 434
Yu et al.	2011	Technology expertise of partners	"the aggregate number of patents obtained by partners during the five years preceding each observation year" p. 432

(Continued)

Table 16.3 (Cont.)

Author	Year	Construct	Variable
Arora & Nandkumar	2012	Technical capability	"the number of information security patents assigned to the start-up when it was formed as a proxy for the technical ability of the startup. As is standard in the literature, we weight these patents by the number of forward citations received" p. 239
Benner & Tripsas	2012	Technical capability	"a cumulative count of granted digital camera patents, coded by application date" p. 290
Diestre & Rajagopalan	2012	Technological capabilities	"the natural logarithm of the number of patents obtained by the pharmaceutical firm in the previous four years" p. 1124
Kaul	2012	Patents per R&D spend	"Unweighted stock of firm patents (depreciated at 15%), divided by stock of R&D spending (log)" p. 355
Kaul	2012	R&D productivity	"Citation weighted stock of firm patents (depreciated at 15%), divided by stock of R&D spending (log)" p. 355
Leone & Reichstein	2012	Patent stock	"the logarithm of the number of patents granted before the signing (potential signing in the case of a non-licensee) of a license agreement" p. 972
Macher & Boerner	2012	Knowledge stock	"logged number of clinical patents held by the pharmaceutical firm in the five years prior to the start of development" p. 1025
Moore, Bell, Filatotchev, & Rasheed	2012	Innovative firms	"the total number of patents that were awarded to each firm prior to IPO" p. 928
Park & Steensma	2012	Quality of a venture	"pre-funding number of patents" p. 9
Schildt et al.	2012	Patenting activity	"count of patents granted during three preceding years" p. 1163
Valentini	2012	Prior patenting	Count of prior patents
Berrone, Fosfuri, Gelabert, & Gomez-Mejia	2013	Control for ability to develop innovations, technology portfolio, propensity to patent, and time-varying firm-level differences	Total number of patents granted

(*Continued*)

Table 16.3 (Cont.)

Author	Year	Construct	Variable
Carnabuci & Operti	2013	Technological experience	Patents applied for during the prior three years
Ceccagnoli & Jiang	2013	Stock of technologies	"The measure is firm i's stock of U.S. patents as of year t that are potentially useful for industry k. We depreciated the stock of patents with a discount rate of 15 percent" p. 414
Hsu & Ziedonis	2013	Patent application stock	"defined as the number of applications filed by a focal start-up at time t that eventually result in the successful award of a U.S. patent. [Prior studies] employ similar measures." p. 769
Kim et al.	2013	Innovation output	"We measured innovation output of the focal firm by counting the total number of citations of its patents cited by subsequent patents from other firms within a four-year span from the focal year" p. 1002
Lahiri & Narayanan	2013	Innovation performance	"Using number of patents as a direct measure of the firms' innovation performance assumes that all innovations are equal. Hence, we use a weighted measure of innovation that assigns an impact factor to each patent in the firms' portfolio of granted patents for each year. Our measure of a patent's impact is the number of forward citations that the focal firm's patent receives from other patents." (Argyres & Silverman, 2004; Henderson, Jaffe, & Trajtenberg, 1998). p. 1050
Mindruta	2013	Patenting capabilities (firm)	"Six-year stock of patents weighted by citations (as of June 2010) and a 10% yearly depreciation rate." p. 655
Toh & Polidoro	2013	Inventiveness	Number of patents
Van de Vrande	2013	Innovative performance	"Weighted patent counts (WPC) is a count variable, where each patent i is weighed according to the subsequent citations C_i it receives, assuming that more important patents receive more citations and vice versa." p. 614
Van de Vrande	2013	Technological capital	"cumulative number of patents applied for by the focal firm in the five years prior to the observation year t" p. 615

(*Continued*)

Table 16.3 (Cont.)

Author	Year	Construct	Variable
Yanadori & Cui	2013	Firm innovation	"annual number of successful patent applications by a firm (Ahuja & Katila, 2001)" p. 1506
Yanadori & Cui	2013	Prior innovation performance	"the number of patents that were successfully granted to a firm in the past five years" p. 1507
Alcácer & Chung	2014	Prior experience by supplier	Supplier has prior patents – "a dummy variable equal to 1 if the supplier has successfully applied for one or more telecom-related patents prior to year t." p. 212
Arend, Patel, & Park	2014	Total number of patents	Total number of patents – "Yearly count of total number of patents where the firm is either the sole assignee or coassignee" p. 387
Arora, Belenzon, & Rios	2014	Centralized patents	"patents assigned to the parent" p. 320
Arora et al.	2014	Decentralized patents	"patents assigned to affiliates" p. 320
Arora et al.	2014	Internal patents	"Internal patents are those generated by internal divisions." p. 332
Arora et al.	2014	Patents stock	"Patents stock in year t is calculated as Patents stock $t = Pt + (1- \delta)$Patents stock $t - 1$ where Pt is the citation-weight flow of patents in year t ." p. 324
Berry	2014	Control 1 for knowledge assets	"count of prior year patents" p. 876
Berry	2014	Knowledge assets	"stock measure of prior country patents by the foreign operation in the host country" p. 876
Chatterji & Fabrizio	2014	Firm's accumulated knowledge stock	"measured with the depreciated stock of patents over the prior five-year period using a discount rate of 20 percent" p. 1436
Conti	2014	Firm knowledge stock	"Number of patents applied in the previous five years by the focal company." p. 1238
Sears & Hoetker	2014	Technological capabilities	"measure technological capabilities using a count of each firm's patents, which each represent a successfully realized innovation, weighted by the number of forward citations each has received to control for quality differences" (Hall, Jaffe, & Trajtenberg,

(Continued)

Table 16.3 (Cont.)

Author	Year	Construct	Variable
			2000; Kalaignanam, Shankar, & Varadarajan, 2007; Trajtenberg, 1990) p. 55
Stern, Dukerich, & Zajac	2014	Biotech patents	"the number of patents issued to the biotechnology company in the 12 months prior to the formation of the focal alliance." p. 521
Toh	2014	Inventive activities	"I control for Total Patents ijt for firm i at location j in year t to account for inventive activities inducing inventors to both operate in many technological areas and create wide scope technologies." p. 730
Yang, Narayanan, & De Carolis	2014	Technological capability	"the total number of citation-weighted patents the focal firm filed and owned between years t−4 and t." p. 152
Ganco, Ziedonis, & Agarwal	2015	Firm size/Firm patenting productivity	"annual number of U.S. patents awarded to the source firm". p. 668
Hashai	2015	Technological assets	"number of patent applications and the number of patent citations". p. 1390
Kehoe & Tzabbar	2015	Innovative productivity	"weighted patents by citations received in the five years after issuance". p. 717
Ndofor et al.	2015	Number of patents	"number of patents in the firm's patent portfolio". p. 1665
Ozmel & Guler	2015	Patent count	"number of patents granted to the venture during the past five years". p. 2048
Yayavaram & Chen	2015	Size of knowledge base	"measured as the total number of patents for which the firm had applied (and subsequently been granted) in the previous three years" p. 387
Younge, Tong, & Fleming	2015	Propensity to patent	"a measure of the number of granted patent applications in the current year." p. 697

Breadth/Scope/Diversity/Focus Variables

Author	Year	Construct	Variable
Makri et al.	2010	Invention Novelty	"we calculated an index of technological diversification similar to a Herfindahl index of concentration" p. 611
Makri et al.	2010	Technology Complementarity	"the number of patents in the same subcategory but in different patent classes in 1996." p. 612

(Continued)

Table 16.3 (Cont.)

Author	Year	Construct	Variable
Yang, Lin, & Lin	2010	Knowledge specialization	"Knowledge specialization is calculated by the maximum number of patents in any one technical class weighted by the total number of a firm's patents." p. 247
Jiang et al.	2011	Knowledge in Novel Technology Areas	"the number of new U.S. patent classes that a focal firm entered in the previous three years. A firm enters a new technology class when this firm applies for a patent in a class in which this firm has not patented in the previous five years." p. 63
Jiang et al.	2011	Total tech classes	"the number of patent classes a firm had entered over the past three years." p. 65
Joshi & Nerkar	2011	Innovation in other areas	"the number of patents filed by the firm in areas unrelated to optical disc technology" p. 1151
Joshi & Nerkar	2011	Technological focus	"the number of optical disc technology classes in which a firm files patents during a particular year" p. 1151
Kotha et al.	2011	Branching	"a count of the number of entries by a firm into 'new to the firm' niches measured at the patent main class level, consistent with Ahuja and Lampert (2001). We use the three digit main classification followed by USPTO to identify technology domains." p. 1015
Kotha et al.	2011	Breadth of tech capability	"the total number of technological classes in which a firm applied for patents, prior to the time window for the construction of the branching variable" p. 1016
Ndofor et al.	2011	Technology resources breadth	"Technological resource breadth was calculated using a Herfindahl-type index analogous to Hall et al.'s (2001) approach" p. 649
Diestre & Rajagopalan	2012	Breadth of knowledge applicability	"we combined these two types of information to create a patent-level measure of breadth by counting the number of distinct therapeutic areas in which 'similar' active ingredients (i.e., arising from knowledge bases that belong to the same patent class and subclass as the NBF's patent) had been applied in the past, assuming they would have similar applicability." p. 1123–1124

(Continued)

Table 16.3 (Cont.)

Author	Year	Construct	Variable
Fernhaber & Patel	2012	Patent breadth	"total number of technological classes where patents were filed" p. 1525
Guler & Nerkar	2012	Technological breadth	"the average number of subclasses that the organization is patenting within the pharmaceutical area" p. 542
Kaul	2012	Patent entropy	"Entropy of patent stock by patent class; models use residual from OLS regression of raw entropy on firm size, patent stock" p. 355
Leone & Reichstein	2012	Search scope	"The proportion of a given year's citations that were previously unused by a firm in the prior five years (Katila & Ahuja, 2002)" p. 972
Leone & Reichstein	2012	Technological diversity	"the number of different primary IPC codes in which the firm has patented." p. 972
Leone & Reichstein	2012	Technological generality	"calculated as the share of cites received by a patent from different technological classes (Hall et al., 2001)" p. 972
Leone & Reichstein	2012	Technological specialization	"the Herfindahl index based on the share of patents in each IPC code" p. 973
Leone & Reichstein	2012	Unfamiliarity	"We regard a technology to be unfamiliar to the licensee if the licensee's prior patent history (previous six years) did not include any patent grants in the International Patent Classification (IPC) code listed in the patent(s) included in the license agreement. The variable is a dummy" p. 972
Schildt et al.	2012	Technological focus	"measured as a Herfindahl index, based on the patenting in the three years preceding the alliance … The maximum value of 1 represents a firm that has all of its patents filed in the same main patent class. Values approaching 0 represent a situation where every patent filed by the company is in a distinct patent class of its own." p. 1163
Valentini	2012	Generality	The percentage of citations received by patent i that belongs to class j out of n patent classes (see equation, p. 340)

(*Continued*)

Table 16.3 (Cont.)

Author	Year	Construct	Variable
Carnabuci & Operti	2013	Combination of inherently unrelated components	"we use the firm's Average Cumulative "Combination Usage [...] computed as the average frequency with which the combinations in a firm's patent portfolio at time t have appeared across all of the patents granted by the USPTO since 1975" p. 1602
Carnabuci & Operti	2013	Knowledge diversity	"We measure knowledge diversity using Teachman's entropy index (1980)" p. 1601
Carnabuci & Operti	2013	Recombinant creation	"To measure the extent to which a firm innovates by creating new technological combinations, we computed the share of subclass coassignments that had not been used by the firm in the prior five years (Katila & Ahuja, 2002)" p. 1599
Carnabuci & Operti	2013	Recombinant reuse	"This variable measures the extent to which a firm innovates by reusing technological combinations known to the firm. Accordingly, we counted the number of times each pair of subclasses cooccurring in a firm's patents within a given year had already been used by the firm during the previous five years. In line with Katila and Ahuja (2002), we normalized the count of repeated technological combinations using the total number of combinations created by that firm in that year to account for differences in the size of the firms' portfolio of technological combinations and, hence, in their potential for recombination" p. 1599
Carnabuci & Operti	2013	Technological components available for recombination	Number of technology subclasses
Ganco	2013	Patenting breadth	"the log of the average number of patent main classes for the inventor in the focal year to capture an inventor's specialization" p. 678
Kim et al.	2013	Search scope	"Technological search scope refers to the degree to which a focal patent cites prior art from a variety of technological domains. Our measure is the same as the 'originality' measure in the paper by Trajtenberg, Henderson, and Jaffe (1997)." p. 1003

(Continued)

Table 16.3 (Cont.)

Author	Year	Construct	Variable
Lahiri & Narayanan	2013	Focus of technological resources (alliance portfolio)	"we construct the cumulative Herfindahl Index of primary three-digit technology classes under which partner firms filed patents. Each technology class was weighted by the percentage of the portfolio's total patents to arrive at the Herfindahl Index." p. 1052
Lahiri & Narayanan	2013	Focus of technological resources (own)	"This measure is based on the Herfindahl Index of primary three-digit technology classes under which individual patents were filed. Each technology class was weighted by the percentage of the firm's total patents to arrive at the Herfindahl Index." p. 1052
Mindruta, Denisa	2013	Breadth of knowledge base	"an entropy index of diversification based on the distribution of a firm's patents in technology domains defined by the inventive International Patent Classification Reform (IPCR) patent classes." p. 653
Van de Vrande	2013	Internal technological diversity	"using the Herfindahl index of the distribution of patents over the patent classes of interest" p. 615
Van de Vrande	2013	Partner technological diversity	"using the Herfindahl index of the distribution of the partners' patents over the different patent classes" p. 615
Alcácer & Chung	2014	Suppliers' technological capabilities	Patents – "the number of 'patent families' in successful telecom-related U.S. patent applications filed by supplier i, in year t" p. 212
Arend et al.	2014	Diversifying, alliance-based knowledge development activity	Diversifying, alliance-based KDA – "Count of patents filed by a firm in collaboration with another organization [another firm, university, or public research institute] in year t in diversifying technology domains; a technology domain is diversifying if the firm has not filed a patent in one of 628 IPC-4 technology classes in the past five years (t − 5 to t − 1)" p. 387
Arend et al.	2014	Diversifying, internal knowledge development activity	Diversifying, internal KDA – "Count of patents filed by a firm as a sole assignee in year t in diversifying technology domains; a technology domain is diversifying if the firm has not filed a patent in one of 628 IPC-4 technology classes in the past five years" (t − 5 to t − 1) p. 387

(*Continued*)

Table 16.3 (Cont.)

Author	Year	Construct	Variable
Arend et al.	2014	Focused, alliance-based knowledge development activity	Focused, alliance-based KDA – "Count of patents filed by a firm in collaboration with another organization (another firm, university, or public research institute) in year t in focused technology domains; a technology domain is focused if the firm filed a patent in one of 628 IPC-4 technology classes in the past five years" (t – 5 to t – 1) p. 387
Arend et al.	2014	Focused, internal knowledge development activity	Focused, internal KDA – "Count of patents filed by a firm as a sole assignee in year t in focused technology domains; a technology domain is focused if the firm filed a patent in one of 628 IPC-4 technology classes in the past five years" (t – 5 to t – 1) p. 387
Arora et al.	2014	Continuous measure of the level of decentralization of research	Share patents assigned, continuous – "measure of how centralized or decentralized a firm's patent portfolio is" p. 321
Arora et al.	2014	Discrete level of decentralization of research	Share patents assigned, discrete – "classifies a firm as centralized, hybrid, or decentralized based on the tertile of share patents assigned to which it belongs." p. 321
Berry	2014	Knowledge diversity	"used Hall et al.'s (2001) measure of originality – which is essentially a measure of technological diversity considering backward patent citations." p. 876
Conti	2014	Firm knowledge specialization	"Herfindahl index of concentration, within four-digit IPC classes, of patents produced from t−1 to t−5, equal to 1 when the number of accumulated patents is 0." p. 1238
Conti	2014	Invention in new technological area	"equal to '1' if the patented invention referred to a primary patent class different from the primary classes of patents applied for by that organization in the previous five years; and '0' otherwise" p. 1235
Mudambi & Swift	2014	Scope of knowledge creation	"The technological scope of the firm's patenting activity is estimated using a two-step process. First, the amount of knowledge that the firm has

(Continued)

Table 16.3 (Cont.)

Author	Year	Construct	Variable
			created in each technological subclass is estimated using the same methodology described above under 'Firm Knowledge Creation.' Second, the dispersion of this firm-level knowledge creation across technological subclasses is measured using an entropy index (Theil, 1967), as follows" (see equation on p. 133)
Patel & Chrisman	2014	Exploitative patents	"Exploitative … number of patents filed in the patent classes in which the firm has been active … over the past five years" p. 624
Patel & Chrisman	2014	Explorative patents	"explorative … patents are measured by the number of patents filed in the patent classes in which the firm … has not been active … over the past five years" p. 624
Toh	2014	Technological breadth	"I control for such Technological Breadth$_{ijt}$ measuring the number of patents' assigned technological subcategories, based on NBER's classification, associated with the location." p. 730
Toh	2014	Technological scope	"I create a Java-based language parser program to access patent texts on the USPTO Web site and code the dependence-independence nature of all individual claims with the following heuristics: a dependent claim always contains a reference to an earlier claim number within the same patent. References always include the word structure 'claim #' (where # is a number). The program identifies a dependent claim as one that incorporates this word structure. It captures all references in the form of 'as defined in claim #', 'according to claim #', 'as claimed in claim #', 'as set forth in claim #', or 'the method of claim #', etc. All other claims are coded as independent … Next, I aggregate this coding at the patent level and map patents to R&D locations based on inventors listed in the patents … Finally, I construct the measure Scope$_{ijt}$ as the

(*Continued*)

Table 16.3 (Cont.)

Author	Year	Construct	Variable
			average number of independent claims per patent that firm i in R&D location j applies for in year t." p. 727
Hashai	2015	Within-industry diversification	"the number of technological domains to which the firm's patent provides information on the main three-digit technology domain to which the USPTO has assigned the invention". p. 1391
Kaplan & Vakili	2015	Technological diversity	"To capture the breadth of recombination, we draw on Hall et al. (2001) … They use a Herfindahl index of the concentration of USPTO patent classes in the prior art cited by a focal patent in a measure that represents technological diversity (which they termed 'patent originality')." (see formula, p. 1445)
Kaplan & Vakili	2015	Topic-originating patents	"the identification of patents that originate novel ideas … *topic originating patents* is an indicator variable where 1 identifies those patents that are over the threshold". p. 1443
Kehoe & Tzabbar	2015	Technological breadth	"using a Blau index to capture diversity in the areas across which a firm has patented" p. 718
Ndofor et al.	2015	Technology resource breadth	"a herfindahl-type index analogous". p. 1663
Yayavaram & Chen	2015	Change in coupling among existing knowledge domains	"measured as the change in coupling between domains that were present in both time periods" (see formula, p. 386)
Yayavaram & Chen	2015	Coupling between new and existing knowledge domains	"measured as the changes resulting from the addition of couplings between these domains" (see formula, p. 386)
Yayavaram & Chen	2015	Relatedness existing-existing	"was measured for each firm as the weighted sum of relatedness between two classes that (1) existed in both time periods, and (2) were coupled with each other in either the early or later period, but not in both." p. 388
Yayavaram & Chen	2015	Relatedness existing-new	"was measured for each firm as the weighted sum of relatedness between two classes, only one of which existed in the first time period, whereas both existed and were coupled in the second." p. 388

(Continued)

Table 16.3 (Cont.)

Author	Year	Construct	Variable
Yayavaram & Chen	2015	Technological diversification	"We therefore controlled for Technological diversification based on the Herfindahl index of concentration" (see formula, p. 388)
Yayavaram & Chen	2015	Use of new knowledge domains	"Use of new knowledge domains was measured as the sum of the fractions for all technological classes k that were new to the firm's knowledge base in year t compared with year t - 3" (see formula p. 388)

Depth Variables

Author	Year	Construct	Variable
Kotha et al.	2011	Depth of tech capability	"the maximum number of patents in any one technological class as defined by the USPTO (Argyres & Silverman, 2004)" p. 1016
Fernhaber & Patel	2012	Patent depth	"average number of patents in each technological class" p. 1525
Leone & Reichstein	2012	Search depth	"The average of the number of times the citations in year t-1 were used in the prior five years of citations(Katila & Ahuja, 2002)" p. 972
Kaplan & Vakili	2015	Combination familiarity	"is measured as the time-discounted count of the previous use of the focal patent's subclass combination across all patents". p. 1446
Kaplan & Vakili	2015	Component familiarity	"is measured as the average time-discounted count of all previous usage of focal patent's subclasses across all patents". p. 1445–1446
Kaplan & Vakili	2015	Cumulative combination	"the same as combination familiarity but without the time discount". p. 1446

Similarity/Overlap Variables

Author	Year	Construct	Variable
Rothaermel & Boeker	2008	Technological similarity (common citation rates)	The extent to which the pharma-biotech dyad draws from the same external technology (see Equation on p. 55)
Rothaermel & Boeker	2008	Technological similarity (cross-citation rates)	The extent to which the pharma–biotech pair in each dyad cite each other's patents (see Equation on p. 55)
Rothaermel & Boeker	2008	Technological similarity (patenting propensity)	"First, we centered each biotechnology and pharmaceutical firm's patenting propensity by their respective industry average in the same manner in which

(*Continued*)

Table 16.3 (Cont.)

Author	Year	Construct	Variable
			we created the centered ratios for the complementarity index described above. Next, for each dyad, we created its patenting distance measure by taking the absolute difference of the centered patenting ratios." p. 59 (see Equation on p. 55)
Agarwal et al.	2009	Technological proximity	"Technological proximity between the source and recipient firms. Calculated as angular separation between the normalized vectors representing proportions of patents in each patent class" p. 1360
Ahuja, Polidoro, & Mitchell	2009	Differences between firms' technical resources	Technical Resources "Chemical patents contains the ratio between the chemical patents that each firm possessed in a given year, from the lesser to the greater number." p. 950
Ahuja et al.	2009	Technical similarity	"For each firm in the sample, we counted the number of patent applications in each technological class in a given year. Then, for each firm, we computed the proportion of all patents in each technological class. To capture the resource similarity between firms i and j in year t, we created the variable technical similarity." p. 949
Chatterji	2009	Technological similarity	Percentage of spawned firm patents which fall in the parent firm's top three technology classes
Corredoira & Rosenkopf	2010	Technological distance (absorptive capacity)	"reflects the dyad's common patenting patterns. For each patent with an application date on the 10-year window previous to the year of observation, we tabulated to which technological class and subclass it was assigned, and created a vector with the percentage of patents assigned to each class/subclass for each firm. Then, we calculated the technological distance between two firms as the Euclidean distance between the vectors just described." p. 166
Makri et al.	2010	Technology Similarity	"Technology similarity between two firms was operationalized using the number of patents in the same three-digit patent classes in 1996." p. 611

(Continued)

Table 16.3 (Cont.)

Author	Year	Construct	Variable
Yang et al.	2010	Technical distance	"we first construct the distribution of a firm's patents across the 16 technical domains and then compute the proportion of the firm's patents that fall within each technology class. After representing all the firms in their technological space, we calculate the technical distance by the Euclidean distance between a pair of firms in either alliances or acquisitions." p. 247
Jiang et al.	2011	Knowledge from partners diverse in technological distance	"We measure this diversity by the variance of technological distance between a focal firm and all its partners." p. 63
Jiang et al.	2011	Technological similarity	"Tit is a 470-dimension vector representing the number of semiconductor patents firm i applied for between 1980 and t, in each of the 470 USPTO patent classes ... Then for each year, we calculated the technological distances between a focal firm and its partners in the portfolio and the variance of these values." p. 64
Kotha et al.	2011	Distance	"we follow the technique used by Rosenkopf and Almeida (2003). For each patent, we tabulated the technological classes to which the patent was assigned. Aggregating the set of patents for each firm by year, we summarized the percentage of assignments in each patent class. We then calculated the Euclidean distances between these patent class vectors for each firm by comparing it to the preceding year." p. 1015
Diestre & Rajagopalan	2012	Technological relatedness	"a count of the number of patent classes in which both firms had patenting activities (overlap) during this time window" p. 1122
Schildt et al.	2012	Technological similarity	Overlap in terms of patent class (see equation, p. 1163)
Van de Vrande	2013	Variance in relative technological proximity	"technological proximity between two firms (i and j) is computed as the uncentered correlation between their respective vectors of technological

(*Continued*)

Table 16.3 (Cont.)

Author	Year	Construct	Variable
			capital (measured as the number of patent applications in technology class k) ... variance in relative technological proximity is then calculated as the variance of technological proximity for each firm per year." p. 614
Sears & Hoetker	2014	Acquirer technological overlap	"=R/Ka ... where Ka = the number of unique patents in the acquirer's knowledge base, which consists of the acquirer's patents and patents cited by the acquirer's patents in the seven years prior to the acquisition announcement date ... R = redundancy in knowledge bases, the number of patents in the intersection of the acquirer and target's knowledge bases" p. 55
Sears & Hoetker	2014	Target technological overlap	"=R/Kt ... where ... Kt,= the number of unique patents in the target's knowledge base, which consists of the target's patents and patents cited by the target's patents in the seven years prior to the acquisition announcement date ... R, = redundancy in knowledge bases, the number of patents in the intersection of the acquirer and target's knowledge bases" p. 55
Kaplan & Vakili	2015	Technological distance	"we use the technological distance measure proposed by Trajtenberg et al. (1997)" (see formula, p. 1445)
Flow Variables			
Agarwal et al.	2009	Knowledge spillover	"The dependent variable is the count of citations made by patents of a recipient firm to patents of a source firm in a given year." p. 1357
Chatterji	2009	Technological knowledge inheritance	Percent of spawned firm patents which cite parent firm patents
Corredoira & Rosenkopf	2010	Drawing on knowledge of another firm	Citation Count "For each focal-alter dyad, this variable is a count of the number of times the focal firm cited the alter firm on patents granted with application dates on the year of observation." p. 163

(Continued)

Table 16.3 (Cont.)

Author	Year	Construct	Variable
Corredoira & Rosenkopf	2010	Propensity to cite hiring firm patents	"We include the one-year lagged value of the dependent variable. This controls for the focal firm's past propensity to cite the patents of the hiring firm." p. 167
Jiang et al.	2011	(1) Exploring knowledge from other firms (semiconductor patents)	"the number of [semiconductor] patents granted to other firms and cited by the focal firm's semiconductor patents applied for in year t" p. 65
Jiang et al.	2011	(2) Exploring knowledge from other firms (non-semiconductor patents)	"the number of non-semiconductor patents granted to other firms and cited by the focal firm's semiconductor patents applied for in year t" p. 65
Jiang et al.	2011	Knowledge from public science	"the number of semiconductor patents citing scientific articles applied for by the focal firm in year t-1" p. 65
Joshi & Nerkar	2011	Licensee	"a binary variable that takes a value of 1 when a firm is engaged in the inbound licensing of essential patents from one or more of the three optical disc industry patent pools, and 0 when it is not engaged in such inbound licensing" p. 1150
Leone & Reichstein	2012	Technology collaborator	"measured by a firm's co-patenting activity prior to the license agreement" p. 9792
Schildt et al.	2012	Dyadic propensity for learning	"the sum of the partners' unique patents cited by the patents filed by a focal firm in a specific month" p. 1162
Alcácer & Chung	2014	Extent to which a supplier's customers can provide a window on the technological frontier	Customer patents – "equal to the maximum number of patent families in the telecom-related patent applications of any one of supplier i's customers in year t −1." p. 212
Arora et al.	2014	External patents	"External patents are those obtained through acquisitions." p. 332
Arora et al.	2014	Firm's reliance on externally-acquired technology	Share patents acquired, "the share of patents within the total stock of the firm's patents that came to the firm via an acquisition, as opposed to having been generated by the firm (including its firm's affiliates)" p. 323

(*Continued*)

Table 16.3 (Cont.)

Author	Year	Construct	Variable
Arora et al.	2014	Patents flow	"the citation-weight flow of patents in year t" p. 324
Toh	2014	Knowledge inputs	"counts citations in patents, to control for span of knowledge inputs" p. 730
Toh	2014	Use of science in prior art	Scienceijt "to capture the science-based prior art used to generate the technologies, measured as the average proportion of nonpatent-based citations made in patents" p. 730

Performance/Value/Quality/Impact Variables

Author	Year	Construct	Variable
Agarwal et al.	2009	Patent portfolio quality	"Log of the number of citations the source firm received from all sample firms within the preceding five years, as measured by the application year." p. 1360
Levitas & McFadyen	2009	Patent value	"We count the number of times each of a firm's patents is cited in the years following the date of patent filing … We then divide each patent's citation count by the mean patent citation count for all patents produced by all U.S. publicly traded biotechnology firms we identified in that patent's year of filing and technological class … For each year, we then add together all of the firm's standardized patent citation values. This represented the patent 'flow' created by the firm in that single year … We then add to this yearly value the previous four years' flows to generate a 'stock' of patent value." p. 665
Makri et al.	2010	Invention Quality	"we calculated the number of citations for five years after the grant date on all patents for which a firm applied in our three-year pre-M&A window … and then divided that by the total number of patents during each of those three years (i.e., we created an annual citations-perpatent ratio). We did the same for the [post-M&A] window and, using the procedure described above for the invention quantity change measures, we constructed three change measures for 1999, 2000, and 2001 using the three to five year invention quality values pre and post M&A." p. 610

(*Continued*)

Table 16.3 (Cont.)

Author	Year	Construct	Variable
Joshi & Nerkar	2011	Innovation historical average quality	"This is measured as the citations received by the firm to its patents filed in the years 1976 to 1981 divided by the number of patents it filed in the same period." p. 1151
Joshi & Nerkar	2011	Innovation quality	"is the citation count of related patents (Trajtenberg, 1990) generated by a given firm from its grant date to the end of our study period in 2006." p. 1150
Kotha et al.	2011	Impact	"the average number of citations, net of self-citations, received by patents filed by the firm in years $t+1$ and $t+2$ (citations received/count of patents) observed in five subsequent years." ($t + 2$ to $t + 6$ and $t + 3$ to $t + 7$, respectively). p. 1015
Guler & Nerkar	2012	Innovative performance	"the number of patents that led to new drugs" p. 541
Leone & Reichstein	2012	Ability to generate high value inventions	"Average number of cites received by the firm to already granted patents" p. 972
Valentini	2012	Impact	"the number of forward citations received by a focal patent" p. 340
Valentini	2012	Originality	The percentage of citations made by patent i that belongs to class j out of n patent classes (see equation, p. 340)
Chatterji & Fabrizio	2014	Innovative output of the firm	"we employ a production function model to estimate the elasticity of innovation (output) to knowledge inputs including R&D investment, accumulated knowledge stock, and firm employment" (see formula, p. 1434)
Conti	2014	Inventive breakthroughs	"a dichotomous variable that takes a value of '1' if the patent is in the top 5 percent in terms of forward citations received, with respect to all patents applied for in the same year (by application date) and in the same technological class (i.e., four-digit International Patent Classification (IPC) classes). The variable equals '0' otherwise" p. 1235

(Continued)

Table 16.3 (Cont.)

Author	Year	Construct	Variable
Conti	2014	Inventive failures	"I measured a failure according to whether the invention received no forward citations. Therefore, I used a dummy variable that takes the value of '1' if a patent received no citations and '0' otherwise" p. 1235
Eesley, Hsu, & Roberts	2014	Innovator firm	"The variable innovator ranges from 0 to 3 depending on how innovative the firm is. A firm receives a 3 if it indicated that innovation was critical for its success, if it held at least one patent at the time of the survey, and if the idea for the venture came from a research lab." (corporate or university). p. 1805
Eesley et al.	2014	Originality of patent	"the average patent 'originality' score for a firm's patents. The originality measure, a common one in the innovation literature, is a concentration index of the diversity of patent classes that a focal patent cites, with a patent citing a more diverse set of patent classes said to be more original" (Hall, Jaffe, & Trajtenberg, 2001) p. 1805
Ganco, Ziedonis, & Agarwal	2015	Patenting quality	"average annual citations per patent in a five-year window". p. 668
Kaplan & Vakili	2015	Breakthrough innovations	"the number of 'forward citations' & 'dummy variable indicating the breakthroughs'" p. 1444
Steensma, Chari, & Heidl	2015	Forward citations	"the number of forward citations within a five-year window subsequent to the grant date of the sample patent." p. 1195

Temporal Variables

Author	Year	Construct	Variable
Ethiraj & Zhu	2008	Patent protection remaining	Remaining years on patent
Heeley & Jacobson	2008	Technological recency	"Remaining patent protection years for the innovator" p. 807
Joshi & Nerkar	2011	Average time to grant	"the average time taken for patents in that filing year to be granted" p. 1151
Joshi & Nerkar	2011	Technological maturity	"the average backward citation lag of the patent portfolio of a firm in a particular filing year." p. 1151
Ndofor et al.	2011	Patent Age	Average age of the firm's patents

(*Continued*)

Table 16.3 (Cont.)

Author	Year	Construct	Variable
Leone & Reichstein	2012	General invention speed	"the average time between granted patent applications, prior to signing the license agreement" p. 972
Leone & Reichstein	2012	Time to invention	"measured in months is extracted by considering license date as the onset of risk, and date of application for first patent filed after the signing of the license agreement as the transition time" p. 972
Toh & Polidoro	2013	Desperation for innovation	Count of patents nearing expiration
Van de Vrande	2013	Average technological age	"calculated as the average age of the partners' patents" p. 615
Chatterji & Fabrizio	2014	Age of technology area	"For each physician–firm coinvented patent, we categorized the patent as belonging to a nascent (<0), new (0–5 years old), or established (5+ years old) technology class and aggregated nascent, new, and established class co-inventions separately into three measures of firm–physician collaboration" p. 1436
Ndofor et al.	2015	Average patent age	"average age of the firm's patent portfolio". p. 1665
Steensma et al.	2015	Average age of prior art at risk	"the difference between the application year of the focal patent and grant year of the prior art." p. 1195

Geographic Variables

Author	Year	Construct	Variable
Agarwal et al.	2009	Same region	"Dummy = 1 if cited and citing firms have headquarters in the same consolidated statistical area (CSA)." p. 1360
Toh & Polidoro	2013	Geographic diversity	"a firm's number of distinct geographic locations (states or foreign countries) based on information in patents about where inventors reside." p. 1169
Berry	2014	Multicountry knowledge generation	"the foreign patents that have been granted to U.S. MNCs by the USPTO that have inventors from more than one country." p. 876
Ganco et al.	2015	Number of inventors in the region	"annual number of inventors in other semiconductor firms' patens (minus the source-firm's) for inventors located in the same region as the focal firm". p. 668

(*Continued*)

Table 16.3 (Cont.)

Author	Year	Construct	Variable
Environment Variables			
Chung & Yeaple	2008	Technical similarity (at the country-industry-year level of analysis)	Technology classifications: "Technical similarity is then the extent that two countries' industry vectors overlap – the uncentered correlation between a pair of countries' industry technical stocks" p. 1214
Oriani & Sobrero	2008	Technological uncertainty	"Inverse of the median age in years of the U.S. patent references cited on the front page of the patent (Technology Cycle Time) calculated at the industry level" p. 353
Oriani & Sobrero	2008	Technology cumulativeness	"Patent backward self-citations/patent total backward citations calculated at the industry level" p. 353
Clarkson & Toh	2010	Extent of crowding in technology space	"the inventive effort (patent count) of firms other than firm i in class j in year t−1" p. 1213
Clarkson & Toh	2010	Strategic stakes in technological resources	Number of re-examination certificates issued to firms other than firm i in class j at t-1
Dushnitsky & Shapira	2010	Industry Technology Opportunities	"for each industry, the natural logarithm of the average number of citation-weighted patents applied for by firms in a given year" p. 1004
Soh	2010	Size of technological community	"Patent data by assignee name indicate the total number of firms committed to the development of Ethernet and Token Ring technologies, which offers a proxy for the size of each technological community." p. 447
Jiang et al.	2011	Technological opportunity	"We used a count of all nanotechnology patents granted by USPTO in year t-1 as a proxy of opportunities to invent in the field." p. 65
Arora & Nandkumar	2012	Technological opportunity	"the total citation weighted and lagged ISM patents relevant to the submarket," p. 241
Arora & Nandkumar	2012	Technology supply	"Log of 1+ weighted security technology patents by universities and government agencies, lagged", p. 240
Alcácer & Oxley	2014	Agglomeration economies	Knowledge fit – "citationsi←k is the share of backward citations that patents

(Continued)

Table 16.3 (Cont.)

Author	Year	Construct	Variable
		associated with knowledge flows	in industry I make to industry k, Pklt is the stock of patents generated by firms in industry k in location l at time t, and Plt the total patent stock (across-industries) for location l at time t." p. 1754
Alcácer & Oxley	2014	Concentration of a location's knowledge pool	Herfindahl knowledge index – "Herfindahl index for industry k in location l at year t, is defined as f =1..N b2 fklt, and bfilt is the patent share for firm f of technological classes relevant to industry i in economic area l at year t, and N is the number of firms in a given economic area." p. 1755
Berry	2014	Strength of host country knowledge	"used patent inventor country and main ICL technology class data to calculate the percent of worldwide patents in each technology class that is generated in the host country of the foreign operation in each year. I used patent stocks for both the numerator and denominator for this variable, calculated using a 15 percent depreciation rate" (Hall, Jaffe, & Trajtenberg, 2005) p. 877
Yang et al.	2014	Technological dynamism	"Technological dynamism was controlled for in order to capture the exogenous velocity surrounding a firm's technological endeavors via a multistep approach as follows. We began with the population of all biopharmaceutical patents. For each three-digit patent class we regressed the number of patents over the past five years based on calendar year. We then divided the standard error of the regression coefficient by the average number of patents filed within the specific class during the past five years. This measurement is similarly constructed as environmental dynamism and has been adopted in previous research." (Keats & Hitt, 1988). p. 152
Yayavaram & Chen	2015	Domain complexity	"a weighted measure of the potential for recombination of each of the technological subclasses in which the firm has patents. The weights (gitk) for each subclass are the fraction of patents held by focal firm i in each technological subclass k" (see formula p. 387)

(*Continued*)

Table 16.3 (Cont.)

Author	Year	Construct	Variable
Individual Variables			
Agarwal et al.	2009	Inventor Mobility	"Moving sum of mobility events from the citing to the cited firm over the last five years including the focal year as measured by the application year of the citing firm patent" p. 1360
Carnabuci & Operti	2013	Collaborative integration	"We used copatenting ties between the inventors within each firm to reconstruct the firms' internal collaboration networks over time [...] For each time window, we reconstructed the internal network of each firm by treating patent data as an affiliation, or two-mode, patent-by-inventor network. This network was projected onto a one mode nonvalued, nondirectional, inventor-by-inventor network, where nodes represent a firm's inventors and a tie exists between a pair of inventors if they coauthored at least one patent" p. 1599–1601
Carnabuci & Operti	2013	External ties	"the average number of patent coauthors each of a firm's inventors maintains outside the firm" p. 1601
Carnabuci & Operti	2013	Geographic distribution of inventors	"using a Blau index of diversity [...] Inventors are assigned to locations using the postal addresses that they provided to the USPTO" p. 1601
Carnabuci & Operti	2013	HR engaged in R&D	Number of inventors
Ganco	2013	Co-inventors	"the log of the average number of patent co-inventors at the source firm in a given year for the inventor" p. 678
Ganco	2013	Patenting productivity	"the log of the number of patents the focal inventor applied for at the source firm divided by the tenure at the source firm" p. 677
Ganco	2013	Patenting quality	"the number of citations the focal inventor received within the next five years divided by the number of patents at the source firm" p. 677
Ganco	2013	Proximity to firm core	"calculated as the angular distance [...] between the 'technology' vectors of the focal inventor and all other inventors in the parent firm in the focal year. Each dimension of the vectors is calculated as the proportion of the patenting in a focal main class over the focal year" p. 678

(*Continued*)

Table 16.3 (Cont.)

Author	Year	Construct	Variable
Ganco	2013	Team entrepreneurship	"coded as 1 if the inventor patented together with another inventor within the parent firm and both were listed as start-up cofounders and 0 otherwise" p. 676
Ganco	2013	Team mobility	"coded as 1 if the inventor patented together with the same co-inventor within the parent firm and the recipient firm and 0 otherwise" p. 675
Mindruta	2013	Patenting capabilities (PI)	"Number of patents and patent applications in which the scientist appears as inventor cumulated over a six-year window prior to collaboration and weighted by patent citations (self-cites excluded) as of June 2010. A 10% yearly depreciation rate has been applied." p. 655
Toh & Polidoro	2013	Collaborative invention	Count of patents listing more than one inventor divided by total number of patents
Chatterji & Fabrizio	2014	Physician colaboration	"the count of patents assigned to the firm that are coinvented with a physician in a firm-year observation, where the year is the application year" p. 1436
Stern et al.	2014	Founder patents	"We thus controlled for both founder patents, which equaled the log of the number of patents issued to the founding chief scientist prior to forming the focal alliance" p. 521
Toh	2014	Inventor specialization	"To measure inventor specialization, I compile inventors at each R&D location j in a given year t. For each inventor k, I trace the patent applications the inventor is involved in for year t and their assigned main technology classes. I then calculate a concentration ratio of technology classes for all patents involving inventor k in year t, reflecting how focused this inventor is on particular technological areas. Finally, I take the average of this concentration ratio across all inventors in firm i at R&D location j in year t to create the variable Inventor Specialization ijt." p. 729

(Continued)

Table 16.3 (Cont.)

Author	Year	Construct	Variable
Ganco et al.	2015	Mobility	"binary indicator set to 1 if our matching algorithm identifies the focal inventor on a subsequent patent assigned to a recipient firm other than the focal employer". p. 667
Ganco et al.	2015	Post-mobility patent productivity	"the number of patents the inventor produces at the recipient firm divided by the years the individual is inventively active at that firm." p. 667
Ganco et al.	2015	Post-mobility patent quality	"the average annual number of citations to those patents in a five-year window, divided by the number of patents he or she produced at the firm." p. 667
Ganco et al.	2015	Pre-exit inventor patenting productivity	"tallies the annual number of inventor patents at the firm". p. 667
Ganco et al.	2015	Pre-exit inventor patenting quality	"the average number of citations to those patents in a five-year window". p. 667–668.
Kaplan & Vakili	2015	Average experience	"is measured as the average number of previous patents by the inventors of the focal patent". p. 1446
Kehoe & Tzabbar	2015	Breadth of star's expertise	"expertise is reflected in the breadth and depth of technological field in which a scientist patents". p. 718 (see formula)
Kehoe & Tzabbar	2015	Innovative leadership	"reflects the ability of a firm's (non-star) scientists to initiate and lead research from innovation to patenting." p. 717 (see formula)
Kehoe & Tzabbar	2015	Star collaborative strength	"the average level of co-invention frequency between star and non-star scientists in firm". p. 718 (see formula)
Kehoe & Tzabbar	2015	Star firm	"operationalized the star firm as a dummy variable, where 1 indicates that a firm employs at least one star scientist". p. 717–718.
Steensma et al.	2015	Failureto disclose known relevant prior art	"the extent to which an inventor failed to disclose relevant prior art known to them by counting the inventor's previous granted patents listed as prior art of the focal patent, and added by the patent examiner." p. 1194
Steensma et al.	2015	Inventor patenting experience	"going back to 1975, we counted the total number of patents that had been granted to the inventor before the application year of the sample patent." p. 1194

(Continued)

Table 16.3 (Cont.)

Author	Year	Construct	Variable
Tortoriello	2015	Laboratory leader	"dummy variable to identify laboratory leaders to control for the possibility that, because of their formal role, they might be involved in more patent filings than their colleagues." p. 591
Tortoriello	2015	Number of previous patents	"the number of patents filed by each respondent in the three years before the data collection." p. 591
Tortoriello	2015	Patents	"The number of patents generated by respondents and granted by the USPTO". p. 590

Other Variables

Author	Year	Construct	Variable
Agarwal et al.	2009	Reputation for vigilance in patent enforcement	"Moving sum of patent litigation lawsuits over the last five years including the given year by the cited firm." p. 1360
Agarwal et al.	2009	Total Citations	"Annual number of citations made by the recipient to the source firm's patents." p. 1360
Wang et al.	2009	Firm-specific knowledge resources (self-citations)	"the share of self-citations made, calculated by counting all citations made in a firm's new patents in a certain year that cited the firm's previous patents, then dividing this by the total number of citations made in all of the firm's new patents in that year." p. 1273
Wang et al.	2009	Firm-specific knowledge resources (weighted self-citations)	"Number of prior self – citations made (adjusted by firm size) [times the] extent to which prior self-cited patents are subsequently cited by the focal firm" p. 1273
Clarkson & Toh	2010	Control for Technology Class	"technology class … dummies" p. 1213
Adegbesan & Higgins	2011		Dummy if the firm has a patent at the time of the alliance
Fabrizio & Thomas	2012	Technological expertise	Sum of Ratios of (number patent in tech class j associated with drugs in class)/(number of patents in tech class j associated with drugs) * number patents. This is done at both the firm and the country level
Guler & Nerkar	2012	Unique contributions of patent	"number of claims per patent" p. 542

(*Continued*)

Table 16.3 (Cont.)

Author	Year	Construct	Variable
Kaul	2012	Cites per Patent	"Average citations per patent for the firm (stock); patent citations are adjusted for average citations in that patent class and year (log)" p. 355
Kaul	2012	No patent	"Dummy variable for years in which firm does not apply for a (successful) patent" p. 355
Leone & Reichstein	2012	Technological complexity	"using average number of claims on prior-to-license-agreement patent grants." p. 973
Berrone et al.	2013	Environmental innovation	"we used the total number of citations received by the patents granted each year to a focal firm to measure environmental innovation (Hall et al., 2005). Formally, let C_{ikt} be the number of citations received by any given (environment-related) patent k, granted to firm i (i=1, ... , 326) in period t (t=1997, ... ,2001). Citations are computed over the next years following the granting date (year fixed effects partially control for truncation problems). Our dependent variable is thus equal to $\Sigma_k C_{ikt}$." p. 898
Carnabuci & Operti	2013	Propensity to build on own knowledge	"the share of a firm's patents that reference the firm's own prior patents between t-3 and t-1 (Hall et al., 2001)" p. 1601
Ceccagnoli & Jiang	2013	Codifiability	"the measure is computed as the percentage of science references among all the references made by firm i's patents that were granted in year t and applicable for industry k" p. 415
Ceccagnoli & Jiang	2013	Potential application industries	To identify these application industries for each sample firm, we exploited the concordance developed and maintained by the USPTO. The USPTO concordance links each patent class to one or more of the 56 industries/sectors (hereafter the 'sequence codes') that are expected to produce the product claimed in the patent or to use the new patented processes in the manufacturing of their products p. 410

(*Continued*)

Table 16.3 (Cont.)

Author	Year	Construct	Variable
Ganco	2013	Knowledge complexity	"In keeping with prior work […], I measured knowledge complexity by relying on classification of patents into subclasses … In this research context, the measure of interdependence K is a single-industry measure analogous to the cross-sectional one used in prior studies […]. It is based on the interaction matrix from Kauffman's NK model" (1993) p. 676
Lahiri & Narayanan	2013		Technology class dummies
Berry	2014	Subsequent development of knowledge	"the ratio of forward self-citations to total citations." p. 876
Mudambi & Swift	2014	Citations per patent	"Therefore, citations per patent are estimated by using a modified version of Hall et al.'s (2001) 'fixed-effects' approach. Citations per patent are divided by the average number of citations per patent in the same industry, in the same year." [see formula] p. 133
Mudambi & Swift	2014	Firm knowledge creation	"we adopt Hall et al.'s (2001) 'fixed effects' approach. Each patent's citation count is divided by the average number of citations received for all patents granted in the same industry, during the same year" (see equation on p. 133)
Kaplan & Vakili	2015	# claims	"the number of claims" p. 1446
Kaplan & Vakili	2015	# domestic references	"the total number of patents cited as prior art". p. 1446
Kaplan & Vakili	2015	# family size	"the family is the set of patents that contain identical abstracts and assignees and therefore represent a cluster of patents arounds a single invention". p. 1446–1447.
Kaplan & Vakili	2015	# non-patent references	"the number of non-patent references" p. 1446
Steensma et al.	2015	Examiner diligence	"the percentage of all prior art citations added by the examiner to the sample patent, relative to the total count of prior art citations associated with the patent". p. 1196
Steensma et al.	2015	Examiner technology class-specific experience	"examiner experience in assessing patents of the same class as the focal patent". p. 1195

(Continued)

Table 16.3 (Cont.)

Author	Year	Construct	Variable
Steensma et al.	2015	Examiner-added prior art citations	Count variable
Steensma et al.	2015	Prior art at risk of not being disclosed	"is the total count of prior art associated with the focal patent and known to the inventor. Some prior art may have been disclosed by the inventor and some added by the examiner. The grand total constitutes the risk set for the focal patent." p. 1195
Steensma et al.	2015	Total prior art citations	Count variable
Yayavaram & Chen	2015	Domain size	"the number of the firm's patents that belong to that domain" p. 379
Yayavaram & Chen	2015	Mean technology citation control	"as used by Fleming and Sorenson (2001). For each patent with issue date t, we considered all technology classes to which the patent had been assigned. For each such class, we calculated the average number of citations that patents in that class had received in the five-year window up to t (t-5.5 to t-0.5). We then weighted the term for each technology class to which the patent had been assigned by the proportion of assignments to that class" (see formula p. 388)
Younge et al.	2015	IP Protection	"measure of the mean percentage of product innovations for which patents are an effective mechanism for protecting the underlying knowledge and appropriating the returns." p. 695

Note

1 24 companies in the original sample only received "design" or "reissued" patents in 2000, and information on technology classes and backward citations were unavailable.

References

Adegbesan, J. A., & Higgins, M. J. 2011. The intra-alliance division of value created through collaboration. *Strategic Management Journal*, 32: 187–211.

Agarwal, R., Ganco, M., & Ziedonis, R. H. 2009. Reputations for toughness in patent enforcement: Implications for knowledge spillovers via inventor mobility. *Strategic Management Journal*, 30: 1349–1374.

Aggarwal, V. A., & Hsu, D. H. 2009. Modes of cooperative R&D commercialization by start-ups. *Strategic Management Journal*, 30: 835–864.

Aguinas, H., & Edwards, J. R. 2014. Methodological wishes for the next decade and how to make wishes come true. *Journal of Management Studies*, 51: 143–174.

Ahuja, G., & Katila, R. 2001. Technological acquisitions and the innovation performance of acquiring firms: A longitudinal study. *Strategic Management Journal*, 22: 197–220.

Ahuja, G., & Lampert, C. M. 2001. Entrepreneurship in the large corporation: A longitudinal study of how established firms create breakthrough inventions. *Strategic Management Journal*, 22: 521–543.

Ahuja, G., Polidoro, Jr., F., & Mitchell, W. 2009. Structural homophily or social asymmetry? The formation of alliances by poorly embedded firms. *Strategic Management Journal*, 30: 941–958.

Alcácer, J., & Chung, W. 2014. Location strategies for agglomeration economies. *Strategic Management Journal*, 35: 1749–1761.

Alcácer, J., & Oxley, J. 2014. Learning by supplying. *Strategic Management Journal*, 35: 204–223.

Arend, R. J., Patel, P. C., & Park, H. D. 2014. Explaining post-IPO venture performance through a knowledge-based view typology. *Strategic Management Journal*, 35: 376–397.

Argyres, N. S., & Silverman, B. S. 2004. R&D, organization structure, and the development of corporate technological knowledge. *Strategic Management Journal*, 25(8-9): 929-958.

Arora, A., Belenzon, S., & Rios, L. A. 2014. Make, buy, organize: The interplay between research, external knowledge, and firm structure. *Strategic Management Journal*, 35: 317–337.

Arora, A., & Nandkumar, A. 2012. Insecure advantage? Markets for technology and the value of resources for entrepreneurial ventures. *Strategic Management Journal*, 33: 231–251.

Bacharach, S. B. 1989. Organizational theories: Some criteria for evaluation. *Academy of Management Review*, 14: 496–515.

Bakker, M., & Wicherts, J. 2011. The (mis)reporting of statistical results in psychology journals. *Behavior Research Methods*, 43: 666–678.

Benner, M. J., & Tripsas, M. 2012. The influence of prior industry affiliation on framing in nascent industries: The evolution of digital cameras. *Strategic Management Journal*, 33: 277–302.

Berrone, P., Fosfuri, A., Gelabert, L., & Gomez-Mejia, L. R. 2013. Necessity as the mother of "green" inventions: Institutional pressures and environmental innovations. *Strategic Management Journal*, 34: 891–909.

Berry, H. 2014. Global integration and innovation: Multicountry knowledge generation within MNCs. *Strategic Management Journal*, 35: 869–890.

Boyd, B. K., Bergh, D. D., Ireland, R. D., & Ketchen, D. J., Jr. 2013. Constructs in strategic management. *Organizational Research Methods*, 16: 3–14.

Cameron, G. 1996. *Innovation and economic growth*. CEPDP, 277. London, UK: Centre for Economic Performance, London School of Economics and Political Science.

Carnabuci, G., & Operti, E. 2013. Where do firms' recombinant capabilities come from? Intraorganizational networks, knowledge, and firms' ability to innovate through technological recombination. *Strategic Management Journal*, 34: 1591–1613.

Ceccagnoli, M., & Jiang, L. 2013. The cost of integrating external technologies: Supply and demand drivers of value creation in the markets for technology. *Strategic Management Journal*, 34: 404–425.

Cefis, E., & Marsili, O. 2005. A matter of life and death: Innovation and firm survival. *Industrial and Corporate Change*, 14: 1167–1192.

Chatterji, A. K. 2009. Spawned with a silver spoon? Entrepreneurial performance and innovation in the medical device industry. *Strategic Management Journal*, 30: 185–206.

Chatterji, A. K., & Fabrizio, K. R. 2014. Using users: When does external knowledge enhance corporate product innovation? *Strategic Management Journal*, 35: 1427–1445.

Chung, W., & Yeaple, S. 2008. International knowledge sourcing: Evidence from U.S. firms expanding abroad. *Strategic Management Journal*, 29: 1207–1224.

Clarkson, G., & Toh, P. 2010. "Keep out" signs: The role of deterrence in the competition for resources. *Strategic Management Journal*, 31: 1202–1225.

Conti, R. 2014. Do non-competition agreements lead firms to pursue risky R&D projects? *Strategic Management Journal*, 35: 1230–1248.

Corredoira, R. A., & Rosenkopf, L. 2010. Should auld acquaintance be forgot? The reverse transfer of knowledge through mobility ties. *Strategic Management Journal*, 31: 159–181.

Diestre, L., & Rajagopalan, N. 2012. Are all "sharks" dangerous? New biotechnology ventures and partner selection in R&D alliances. *Strategic Management Journal*, 33: 1115–1134.

Durand, R., Bruyaka, O., & Mangematin, V. 2008. Do science and money go together? The case of the French biotech industry. *Strategic Management Journal*, 29: 1281–1299.

Dushnitsky, G., & Shapira, Z. 2010. Entrepreneurial finance meets organizational reality: Comparing investment practices and performance of corporate and independent venture capitalists. *Strategic Management Journal*, 31: 990–1017.

Edwards, J. R. 2003. Construct validation in organizational behavior research. In Greenberg, J. (Ed.), *Organizational behavior: The state of the science*, 2nd edition: 327–371. Mahwah, NJ: Erlbaum.

Edwards, K., & Smith, E. E. 1996. A disconfirmation bias in the evaluation of arguments. *Journal of Personality and Social Psychology*, 71: 5–24.

Eesley, C. E., Hsu, D. H., & Roberts, E. B. 2014. The contingent effects of top management teams on venture performance: Aligning founding team composition with innovation strategy and commercialization environment. *Strategic Management Journal*, 35: 1798–1817.

Ethiraj, S. K., & Zhu, D. H. 2008. Performance effects of imitative entry. *Strategic Management Journal*, 29: 797–817.

Fabrizio, K. R., & Thomas, L. G. 2012. The impact of local demand on innovation in a global industry. *Strategic Management Journal*, 33: 42–64.

Fanelli, D. 2010. Do pressures to publish increase scientists' bias? An empirical support from US states data. PLoS One, 5: e10271. doi: 10.1371/journal.pone.0010271.

Fernhaber, S. A., & Patel, P. C. 2012. How do young firms manage product portfolio complexity? The role of absorptive capacity and ambidexterity. *Strategic Management Journal*, 33: 1516–1539.

Fugelsang, J. A., Stein, C. B., Green, A. E., & Dunbar, K. N. 2004. Theory and data interactions of the scientific mind: Evidence from the molecular and the cognitive laboratory. *Canadian Journal of Experimental Psychology*, 58: 86–95.

Ganco, M. 2013. Cutting the Gordian knot: The effect of knowledge complexity on employee mobility and entrepreneurship. *Strategic Management Journal*, 34: 666–686.

Ganco, M., Ziedonis, R. H., & Agarwal, R. 2015. More stars stay, but the brightest ones still leave: Job hopping in the shadow of patent enforcement. *Strategic Management Journal*, 36: 659–685.

Grant, R. M. 1996. Toward a knowledge-based theory of the firm. *Strategic Management Journal*, 17: 109–122.

Guler, I., & Nerkar, A. 2012. The impact of global and local cohesion on innovation in the pharmaceutical industry. *Strategic Management Journal*, 33: 535–549.

Hagedoorn, J., & Cloodt, M. 2003. Measuring innovative performance: Is there an advantage in using multiple indicators? *Research Policy*, 32: 1365–1379.

Hall, B. H., Jaffe, A. B., & Trajtenberg, M. 2000. *Market value and patent citations: A first look* (No. w7741). Cambridge, MA: National Bureau of Economic Research.

Hall, B. H., Jaffe, A. B., and Trajtenberg, M. 2001. *The NBER patent citation data file: Lessons, insights and methodological tools* (No. w8498). Cambridge, MA: National Bureau of Economic Research.

Hall, B. H., Jaffe, A., & Trajtenberg, M. 2005. Market value and patent citations. *RAND Journal of Economics*, 36: 16–38.

Hashai, N. 2015. Within-industry diversification and firm performance: An S-shaped hypothesis. *Strategic Management Journal*, 36: 1378–1400.

Heeley, M. B., & Jacobson, R. 2008. The recency of technological inputs and financial performance. *Strategic Management Journal*, 29: 723–744.

Henderson, R., Jaffe, A. B., & Trajtenberg, M. 1998. Universities as a source of commercial technology: a detailed analysis of university patenting, 1965–1988. *Review of Economics and Statistics*, 80(1): 119-127.

Hess, A. M., & Rothaermel, F. T. 2011. When are assets complementary? Star scientists, strategic alliances, and innovation in the pharmaceutical industry. *Strategic Management Journal*, 32: 895–909.

Hoang, H., & Rothaermel, F. T. 2010. Leveraging internal and external experience: Exploration, exploitation, and R&D project performance. *Strategic Management Journal*, 31: 734–758.

Hsu, D. H., & Ziedonis, R. H. 2013. Resources as dual sources of advantage: Implications for valuing entrepreneurial-firm patents. *Strategic Management Journal*, 34: 761–781.

Jaffe, A. B., Trajtenberg, M., & Henderson, R. 1993. Geographic localization of knowledge spillovers as evidenced by patent citations. *Quarterly Journal of Economics*, 108: 577–598.

Jensen, P. H., Thomson, R., & Yong, J. 2011. Estimating the patent premium: Evidence from the Australian Inventor Survey. *Strategic Management Journal*, 32: 1128–1138.

Jiang, L., Tan, J., & Thursby, M. 2011. Incumbent firm invention in emerging fields: Evidence from the semiconductor industry. *Strategic Management Journal*, 32: 55–75.

Joshi, A. M., & Nerkar, A. 2011. When do strategic alliances inhibit innovation by firms? Evidence from patent pools in the global optical disc industry. *Strategic Management Journal*, 32: 1139–1160.

Kalaignanam, K., Shankar, V., & Varadarajan, R. 2007. Asymmetric new product development alliances: Win-win or win-lose partnerships? *Management Science*, 53(3): 357-374.

Kaplan, S., & Vakili, K. 2015. The double-edged sword of recombination in breakthrough innovation. *Strategic Management Journal*, 36: 1435–1457.

Katila, R., & Ahuja, G. 2002. Something old, something new: A longitudinal study of search behavior and new product introduction. *Academy of Management Journal*, 45: 1183–1194.

Kauffman, S. A. 1993. *The origins of order: Self-organization and selection in evolution.* New York City, NY: Oxford University Press.

Kaul, A. 2012. Technology and corporate scope: Firm and rival innovation as antecedents of corporate transactions. *Strategic Management Journal*, 33: 347–367.

Keats, B. W., and Hitt, M. A. 1988. A causal model of linkages among environmental dimensions, macro organizational characteristics, and performance. *Academy of Management Journal*, 31(3): 570–598.

Kehoe, R. R., & Tzabbar, D. 2015. Lighting the way or stealing the shine? An examination of the duality in star scientists' effects on firm innovative performance. *Strategic Management Journal*, 36: 709–727.

Keil, T., Maula, M., Schildt, H., & Zahra, S. A. 2008. The effect of governance modes and relatedness of external business development activities on innovative performance. *Strategic Management Journal*, 29: 895–907.

Ketchen, D. J., Jr., Ireland, R. D., & Baker, L. T. 2013. The use of archival proxies in strategic management studies: Castles made of sand? *Organizational Research Methods*, 16: 32–42.

Kim, S. K., Arthurs, J. D., Sahaym, A., & Cullen, J. B. 2013. Search behavior of the diversified firm: The impact of fit on innovation. *Strategic Management Journal*, 34: 999–1009.

Koellinger, P. 2008. The relationship between technology, innovation, and firm performance – Empirical evidence from e-business in Europe. *Research Policy*, 37: 1317–1328.

Kogut, B., & Zander, U. 1992. Knowledge of the firm, combinative capabilities, and the replication of technology. *Organization Science*, 3: 383–397.

Kotha, R., Zheng, Y., & George, G. 2011. Entry into new niches: The effects of firm age and the expansion of technological capabilities on innovative output and impact. *Strategic Management Journal*, 32: 1011–1024.

Lahiri, N., & Narayanan, S. 2013. Vertical integration, innovation, and alliance portfolio size: Implications for firm performance. *Strategic Management Journal*, 34: 1042–1064.

Leone, M., & Reichstein, T. 2012. Licensing-in fosters rapid invention! The effect of the grant-back clause and technological unfamiliarity. *Strategic Management Journal*, 33: 965–985.

Levitas, E., & McFadyen, M. 2009. Managing liquidity in research-intensive firms: Signaling and cash flow effects of patents and alliance activities. *Strategic Management Journal*, 30: 659–678.

Lichtenthaler, U., & Ernst, H. 2012. Integrated knowledge exploitation: The complementarity of product development and technology licensing. *Strategic Management Journal*, 33: 513–534.

Macher, J. T., & Boerner, C. 2012. Technological development at the boundaries of the firm: A knowledge-based examination in drug development. *Strategic Management Journal*, 33: 1016–1036.

Mahmood, I. P., Zhu, H., & Zajac, E. J. 2011. Where can capabilities come from? Network ties and capability acquisition in business groups. *Strategic Management Journal*, 32: 820–848.

Makri, M., Hitt, M. A., & Lane, P. J. 2010. Complementary technologies, knowledge relatedness, and invention outcomes in high technology mergers and acquisitions. *Strategic Management Journal*, 31: 602–628.

Mindruta, D. 2013. Value creation in university-firm research collaborations: A matching approach. *Strategic Management Journal*, 34: 644–665.

Moore, C. B., Bell, R., Filatotchev, I., & Rasheed, A. A. 2012. Foreign IPO capital market choice: Understanding the institutional fit of corporate governance. *Strategic Management Journal*, 33: 914–937.

Mudambi, R., & Swift, T. 2014. Knowing when to leap: Transitioning between exploitative and explorative R&D. *Strategic Management Journal*, 35: 126–145.

Nadkarni, S., Herrmann, P., & Perez, P. 2011. Domestic mindsets and early international performance: The moderating effect of global industry conditions. *Strategic Management Journal*, 32: 510–531.

Ndofor, H. A., Sirmon, D. G., & He, X. 2011. Firm resources, competitive actions and performance: Investigating a mediated model with evidence from the in-vitro diagnostics industry. *Strategic Management Journal*, 32: 640–657.

Ndofor, H. A., Sirmon, D. G., & He, X. 2015. Utilizing the firm's resources: How TMT heterogeneity and resulting faultlines affect TMT tasks. *Strategic Management Journal*, 36: 1656–1674.

Oriani, R., & Sobrero, M. 2008. Uncertainty and the market valuation of R&D within a real options logic. *Strategic Management Journal*, 29: 343–361.

Ozmel, U., & Guler, I. 2015. Small fish, big fish: The performance effects of the relative standing in partners' affiliate portfolios. *Strategic Management Journal*, 36: 2039–2057.

Park, H., & Steensma, H. 2012. When does corporate venture capital add value for new ventures? *Strategic Management Journal*, 33: 1–22.

Patel, P. C., & Chrisman, J. J. 2014. Risk abatement as a strategy for R&D investments in family firms. *Strategic Management Journal*, 35: 617–627.

Reitzig, M., & Puranam, P. 2009. Value appropriation as an organizational capability: The case of IP protection through patents. *Strategic Management Journal*, 30: 765–789.

Reitzig, M., & Wagner, S. 2010. The hidden costs of outsourcing: Evidence from patent data. *Strategic Management Journal*, 31: 1183–1201.

Rosenkopf, L., & Almeida, P. 2003. Overcoming local search through alliances and mobility. *Management Science*, 49: 751–766.

Rothaermel, F. T., & Boeker, W. 2008. Old technology meets new technology: Complementarities, similarities, and alliance formation. *Strategic Management Journal*, 29: 47–77.

Salomon, R., & Jin, B. 2010. Do leading or lagging firms learn more from exporting? *Strategic Management Journal*, 31: 1088–1113.

Schildt, H., Keil, T., & Maula, M. 2012. The temporal effects of relative and firm-level absorptive capacity on interorganizational learning. *Strategic Management Journal*, 33: 1154–1173.

Schumpeter, J. A. 1950. *Capitalism, socialism and democracy*. London: Routledge.

Schwab, D. P. 1980. Construct validity in organizational behavior. In Cummings, L. L. & Staw, B. M. (eds.), *Research in organizational behavior*, Vol.2, 3-43. Greenwich, CT: JAI Press.

Sears, J., & Hoetker, G. 2014. Technological overlap, technological capabilities, and resource recombination in technological acquisitions. *Strategic Management Journal*, 35: 48–67.

Shane, S. 2001. Technological opportunities and new firm creation. *Management Science*, 47: 205–220.

Soh, P. 2010. Network patterns and competitive advantage before the emergence of a dominant design. *Strategic Management Journal*, 31: 438–461.

Solow, R. 1957. Technical change and the aggregate production function. *Review of Economics and Statistics*, 39: 312–320.

Steensma, H. K., Chari, M., & Heidl, R. 2015. The quest for expansive intellectual property rights and the failure to disclose known relevant prior art. *Strategic Management Journal*, 36: 1186–1204.

Stern, I., Dukerich, J. M., & Zajac, E. 2014. Unmixed signals: How reputation and status affect alliance formation. *Strategic Management Journal*, 35: 512–531.

Theil, H. 1967. *Economics and Information Theory*. Amsterdam, the Netherlands: North-Holland Publishing Company.

Thornhill, S. 2006. Knowledge, innovation and firm performance in high- and low-technology regimes. *Journal of Business Venturing*, 21: 687–703.

Toh, P. K. 2014. Chicken, or the egg, or both? The interrelationship between a firm's inventor specialization and scope of technologies. *Strategic Management Journal*, 35: 723–738.

Toh, P. K., & Polidoro, F. 2013. A competition-based explanation of collaborative invention within the firm. *Strategic Management Journal*, 34: 1186–1208.

Tortoriello, M. 2015. The social underpinnings of absorptive capacity: The moderating effects of structural holes on innovation generation based on external knowledge. *Strategic Management Journal*, 36: 586–597.

Trajtenberg, M. 1990. A penny for your quotes: patent citations and the value of innovations. *The Rand Journal of Economics*, 21(1): 172–187.

Trajtenberg, M., Henderson, R., & Jaffe, A. 1997. University versus corporate patents: A window on the basicness of invention. *Economics of Innovation and New Technology*, 5(1): 19-50.

Valentini, G. 2012. Measuring the effect of M&A on patenting quantity and quality. *Strategic Management Journal*, 33: 336–346.

Van de Vrande, V. 2013. Balancing your technology-sourcing portfolio: How sourcing mode diversity enhances innovative performance. *Strategic Management Journal*, 34: 610–621.

Venkatraman, N., & Grant, J. H. 1986. Construct measurement in organizational strategy research: A critique and proposal. *Academy of Management Review*, 11: 71–87.

Wang, H. C., He, J., & Mahoney, J. T. 2009. Firm-specific knowledge resources and competitive advantage: The roles of economic- and relationship-based employee governance mechanisms. *Strategic Management Journal*, 30: 1265–1285.

Yanadori, Y., & Cui, V. 2013. Creating incentives for innovation? The relationship between pay dispersion in R&D groups and firm innovation performance. *Strategic Management Journal*, 34: 1502–1511.

Yang, H., Lin, Z., & Lin, Y. 2010. A multilevel framework of firm boundaries: Firm characteristics, dyadic differences, and network attributes. *Strategic Management Journal*, 31: 237–261.

Yang, Y., Narayanan, V. K., & De Carolis, D. M. 2014. The relationship between portfolio diversification and firm value: The evidence from corporate venture capital activity. *Strategic Management Journal*, 35: 1993–2011.

Yayavaram, S., & Chen, W. 2015. Changes in firm knowledge couplings and firm innovation performance: The moderating role of technological complexity. *Strategic Management Journal*, 36: 377–396.

Younge, K. A., Tong, T. W., & Fleming, L. 2015. How anticipated employee mobility affects acquisition likelihood: Evidence from a natural experiment. *Strategic Management Journal*, 36: 686–708.

Yu, J., Gilbert, B., & Oviatt, B. M. 2011. Effects of alliances, time, and network cohesion on the initiation of foreign sales by new ventures. *Strategic Management Journal*, 32: 424–446.

17 Strategic renewal in the digital age

The digital marketing core as a starting point

Emile F.J. Lancée

Introduction

The last decade has witnessed an unprecedented momentum of change in the implementation of marketing digitalization (Zwick and Dholakia, 2008; Hirt and Wilmott, 2014; Lamberton and Stephen, 2016). Many physical products like music or news have now become bits and bytes, in the form of services like Spotify, Netflix, or Blendle. In addition, physical retail environments are increasingly distinguished by their digital interactivity. For example, enormous touch display screens in fashion stores, self-scanning services in supermarkets, and not to forget, banking services that have been completely digitalized with the help of automated teller machines as well as internet and mobile banking. As a result even physical money is threatened with extinction thanks to phenomena like this as well as virtual money such as Bitcoins.

In many cases, digitalization has required strategies to be partly or completely reconfigured. Firms have to constantly adjust their strategy, in order to make ultimate use of digital developments and the established digital culture within markets. They realized that both marketing and the nature of the exchange process have radically and irrevocably changed with the arrival and adoption of the internet. This was already documented some years ago by Holbrook and Hulbert (2002) and actively implemented by firms like Netflix that strategically renewed and then intentionally created a new, successful (1) customer-driven (big data) (2) channel with the help of (3) technology and (4) partners. It is for this reason that these four components are the focal point of attention of this study.

Although the internet and digitalization are often mixed-up in marketing literature, in practice, digital marketing stretches beyond internet marketing, meaning that the strategic value of big data, channels, technology, and partners stretches beyond just web-based activities. It also includes the use of non-internet-based technologies, such as mobile (Chaffey and Ellis-Chadwick, 2012), virtual reality, robotization, and the use of digital technology in physical environments to achieve marketing objectives. It was digital technology and not web technology per se, that for example brought: further consumer insight and an immeasurable amount of big data for practitioners (consider as well the upcoming Internet of Things (IoT) and its overwhelming flow of data), network partnerships for digital value creation, an unprecedented growth of channels (omni-channel), and digital technologies that further penetrate our physical world.

It is undeniable then, that marketing (strategy) is on a digitalization journey, as Quinton and Simkin (2016) state, but strategic understanding is still, at best, inconsistent, especially with respect to strategic renewal that increasingly finds its roots in digital possibilities. Forrester research indicates that only 27 percent of operating companies currently have a working digital (marketing) strategy. Therefore, the call for a return to 'Big M' marketing – that is, marketing as a general management responsibility – rather than 'small m' marketing – that is, marketing as an organizational function – has been reinforced by many distinguished scholars (cf., Brown et al., 2005, pp. 1–25; Bolton, 2006) as a means to further benefit from digital opportunities. This is not without good reason, because the level of power that a marketing department can wield has a significant impact on predicting firm performance (Feng, Morgan, and Rego, 2015), meaning that the Digital Marketing Core model proposed in this study should be the starting point for organizational strategic renewal.

But the complexities of digital marketing, as well as the strategic use of digitalization, do require a paradigm shift (Day, 2011; Quinton, 2013) in order to fully enjoy the benefits of the proposed model. The strategic Digital Marketing Core can also be regarded as a research priority and extends beyond the simple use of digital technologies to communicate and interact with a variety of stakeholders (Theodosiou, Kehagias and Katsikea, 2012; Setia, Venkatesh and Joglekar, 2013). The application of the model even implies that businesses embarking upon strategic marketing initiatives should adopt a more flexible approach, even going as far as Mintzberg's emergent strategy (Mintzberg and Waters, 1985) to market in an adaptive style, as a reflection of the digital reality. A dynamic strategic tool such as the model presented in this study can therefore be of significant value, as it provides both the key ingredients and the unceasing process needed for successful strategic renewal in today's dynamic digital reality.

In light of this study, adaptive marketing would include being dynamically responsive to the market, such as making real-time adjustments and regularly reviewing the effect of digitally centric actions around the key components of the model. The contemporary view of organizational design that emerges should therefore be dynamic and interdependent with multiple layers of stakeholders, rather than a static entity with well-defined boundaries. This means that the concepts of processes and routines are forsaken; in their place assumptions are made on continual evolution, localized tensions, and digital action repertoires (Majchrzak, Markus, and Wareham, 2016). The current, often rather passive marketing strategies, employed by many firms, are based on past activity and terms like structure, plans, decisions, iteration, and conditions. They will carry increasingly less weight in the dynamic, digitalized economy (Quinton and Simkin, 2016). Uncertainty and dynamism in the competitive digital environment require regular strategic renewal of organizations (Barrales-Molina, Martínez-Lopez, and Gázquez-Abad, 2014), and this study attempts to explain which elements, relating to digitalization, organizations can adopt to achieve appropriate reconfiguration of the strategy.

Strategic renewal, in this study, includes the process, content, and outcome of refreshment or replacement of attributes in an organization, that have the potential to substantially affect its long-term prospects (Agarwal and Helfat, 2009). In the dynamic digital age, constant strategic renewal is a prerequisite, but it presents both opportunities and challenges for organizations. These opportunities and challenges are discussed within the Digital Marketing Core concept, a tool for strategic renewal. The composition of the core is the result of a review of previous literature in combination with the practical revelation that Netflix, and many more, transformed their strategies with the help of big data, technology, partners, and channels. The remainder of this chapter is therefore organized as follows: first the concept of the Digital Marketing Core will be introduced and deconstructed, followed by an integrative application of the different components of the model, concluding with some managerial takeaways and future research directions.

Deconstructing the Digital Marketing Core

Despite the infiltration of digital technologies and digital marketing into the daily lives of consumers and businesses, many firms are still not creating a digital-centric marketing strategy (Quinton and Simkin, 2016). The decade of digital development has resulted in limited internalization and embedding of the potential offered by the digitalization of marketing. This limited embedding may be partially due to the acknowledged digital-marketing skills gap (Royle and Laing, 2014; Analogbei, Canhoto, Dibb, Quinn, and Simkin, 2015). Zwick and Dholakia (2008) observed that the general response to the digital era has been to produce and deploy multiple tools as tactics to meet specific needs, rather than developing strategic digital concepts and ideas. They suggested that attention should be given to the integration of digital activity into the broader marketing sense and thus aid the formation of a mind-set with a strategic vision.

The inevitable implication arising from this is that marketing strategy needs to incorporate digital marketing deeper into its core. Dynamic marketing capabilities are also needed internally to match the high-velocity and rapidly changing digital marketing environment that necessitates a perpetual evolution of marketing activities as well as reconfiguration of the firm's strategy. As Netflix did, firms should use the Digital Marketing Core, see Figure 17.1, for strategic renewal and comprehend the different elements, as well as the level of strategic entanglement (Kaufman and Horton, 2014) of the different components, in order to successfully reconfigure the firm's offering. But although Michael Porter recognizes that marketing capability is

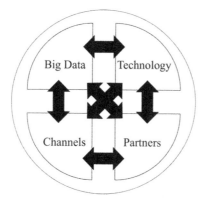

Figure 17.1 Big data

crucial to obtain differentiation (See 8 steps in differentiation, in Porter, 1985, pp. 162–163) the schematic linkage of firms' strategic marketing capability (SMC) to the different dimensions of the Digital Marketing Core is important because although SMC takes a kind of *process enabler* role for creating competitive advantages, it is not able to create competitive advantages itself unless it is effectively and efficiently implemented via the elements of the Digital Marketing Core. As such the focus in this study is more on the dimensions as sources for strategic renewal than the related capabilities a company needs for achieving this.

Big data

Data has been called 'the oil' of the digital economy (Wedel and Kannan, 2016) and is often characterized by the six 'Vs': commonly rendered as volume (terabytes, petabytes, exabytes, or zettabytes), velocity (from one-time snapshots to high-frequency and streaming data) and variety (numeric, network, text, images, and video) (McAfee and Brynjolfsson, 2012) and extended with veracity (reliability and validity), variability, and value (cost) (Gandomi and Haider, 2015). The last 'V' transcends the first four and is vital from a business perspective (Rodríguez-Mazahua et al., 2016; Wedel and Kannan, 2016).

Big data has become one of the four key elements for shrewd strategic renewal in the digital era. It has also intensified its contribution towards organizational performance, which can be defined as 'A firm's competence to change existing business processes, better than competitors do, in terms of coordination/integration, cost reduction, and business intelligence/learning' (Kim, Shin and Kwon, 2012, p. 341). In this regard, big data is linked to the context of organizational intelligence and strategy, as well as to how organizations perceive, assess, and act upon their internal and external environments

(Constantiou and Kallinikos, 2015). Therefore, it is part of the Digital Marketing Core and needs to go beyond one-off initiatives, becoming a dynamic capability within organizations (Braganza, Brooks, Nepelski, Ali, and Moro, 2017). Teece, Pisano, and Shuen (1997) define dynamic capabilities 'as the firm's ability to integrate, build and reconfigure internal and external competences to address rapidly changing environments' (p. 516). Dynamic capabilities, enhanced by insight from big data, ultimately, foster new thinking within organizations resulting in new value (Tellis, Prabhu, and Chandy, 2009; Day, 2014; Kozlenkova, Samaha, and Palmatier, 2014). Netflix, for example, used big data to better understand customer preferences, in the interest of reshaping its content business towards a production company, resulting in in-house series such as House of Cards, Marco Polo, and The Crown.

The concept of 'big data' is generating tremendous attention worldwide, even resulting in the increase of Google searches on the phrases 'big data' and 'analytics' (Agarwal and Dhar, 2014). Firms are increasingly challenged by 'big data', which has emerged as an exciting frontier of productivity and opportunity in the last few years. Big data enables firms to create superior strategic value and gain a sustainable competitive advantage (Davenport, 2006). Thanks to the emergence of big data, for example, sources such as Google Trends, that capture real-time digital consumer searches, it will become progressively more cost effective for marketers to monitor the evolution of consumer tastes (Du, Hu, and Damangir, 2015). This same data can then also be applied for strategic renewal. Imagine, for example, the value for renewal of tracking user-generated content on social media platforms like Facebook, Twitter, Instagram and blogs. This might even result in more detail-rich data about customer beliefs, opinions, and attitudes (Weinberg and Pehlivan, 2011) towards products, services, firms, or brands. It is not a surprise then, that Big Data Analytics Capability (BDAC) is widely considered to be transforming the way in which firms do business (Davenport and Harris, 2007; Barton and Court, 2012) and can be seen as a key component and organizational capability in the digital big data environment (Davenport, 2006).

Recent literature identifies that BDAC has 'the potential to transform management theory and practice' (George, Haas, and Pentland, 2014, p. 325), it is the 'next big thing in innovation' (Gobble, 2013, p. 64); 'the fourth paradigm of science' (Strawn, 2012, p. 34); the next 'management revolution' (McAfee and Brynjolfsson, 2012); and influences firm performance (Akter, Wamba, Gunasekaran, Dubey and Childe, 2016). It can be seen as an interwoven conceptualization of three dimensions (i.e., management, technology, and human). This highlights the importance of the complementary relationship between them, for high level operational efficiency and effectiveness, delivering improved performance, and sustained competitive advantage (Kiron, Prentice and Ferguson, 2014; Akter et al., 2016).

Previous research also highlights the importance of Analytics Capability Business Strategy Alignment (ACBSA) in big data environments, which is defined as the extent to which analytics strategies are aligned with the overall business strategy of the organization (McAfee and Brynjolfsson, 2012; Agarwal and Dhar, 2014) in order to realize strategic improvements and perform better. The rationale behind such statements is that 'big data' is capable of changing competition by 'transforming processes, altering corporate ecosystems, and facilitating innovation' (p. 2) (Brown, Chui, and Manyika, 2011); unlocking organization business value by unleashing new organizational capabilities and value (Davenport, Barth, and Bean, 2012) and facilitating firms to tackle of their business challenges (Gehrke, 2012). Big data, in other words, represents an indispensable dimension for reconfiguring strategies in an on-going digital evolution. One that is, by the way, inevitably related to the second dimension of technology.

Technology

Will the technology superhighway have any pit stops? The rate of digital change and new uses of digital technology for marketing are seen as continuing unabated (Carter, 2009), and it is understood that platforms may change, but the trajectory is ever upward (Wilson and Quinton, 2012). It is also said that the implementation of information technology is critical to success (Bughin, 2008), whilst others declare that it is only tempered by the ability of marketers to actually employ the layers of complex technology that the developers have created (Assael, 2010). Technologists may say that it is simply the marketers' lack of imagination that limits the application of digital technologies, while marketers argue that it is complexity that limits the ease of use.

However, pit stops seem to have been avoided since the introduction of Web 2.0 in 2002. Then there was a smooth migration to Web 3.0 and a relentless move onwards to the Semantic Web from 2007, which has recently morphed into Web 4.0 using more powerful digital interfaces. For almost all industries, technology is considered a major if not the most important strategic asset, especially in the digital era. Technology therefore, is another considerable dimension in the Digital Marketing Core. It has resulted in a veritable explosion of research in marketing, on the impact of the internet and other related digital technologies on firms and the marketplace (Yadav and Pavlou, 2014). In other words, advances in technology impact the way in which marketing is realized.

This means that technology changes the implementation of strategies and tactics in practice (Shugan, 2004; Rust and Espinoza, 2006) and, as a result, also has a significant effect on strategic transition. Therefore, technology is the second element in the Digital Marketing Core and should be taken into account, because it is no longer just an enabler of business processes, but increasingly becoming the core of the firm's business strategy (Srinivasan, Lilien, and Rangaswamy, 2002). In particular, technology has become an essential element of firm effectiveness and a source of sustainable competitive advantage (Lin, 2007). Ultimately, investments in technology and technological capabilities influence the firm's ability to launch 'many and varied competitive actions and that, in turn, these competitive actions are a significant antecedent of firm performance' (Sambamurthy, Bharadwaj, and Grover, 2003, p. 237). Not surprisingly, businesses in the digital age require technology orientation representing a firm's capabilities in recognizing and adapting to emerging technologies (Gatignon and Xuereb, 1997; Zhou, Yim, and Tse, 2005).

In order to successfully use technology, firms should be flexible with regard to strategy, because strategic flexibility enhances the positive relationship between technology, technological capability, and exploration (Zhou and Wu, 2010). Strategic flexibility represents the ability of a firm to reallocate and reconfigure its organizational resources, processes, and strategies to deal with environmental changes (Sanchez, 1995). Sometimes this is also called e-marketing capability (Trainor, Rapp, Skinner Beitelspacher, and Schillewaert, 2011), representing a firm's competence in using the digital environment and other technologies for marketing activities. Netflix renewed its strategy and offering by using technology, to substitute the physical channel with a digital channel (TV, website, mobile) resulting in a new business model that brought the market out of balance.

Increasingly, emerging advances in technology are threatening to disrupt established markets, creating an atmosphere of turmoil and troublesome decision-making for organizations. Recent technologies such as Internet of Things (IoT), augmented reality, virtual reality, 4D printing, autonomous vehicles, nanotube electronics, and power from the air (Gartner, 2016), to name but a few, have provided organizations with alternative strategic avenues for new initiatives over existing technologies. A turbulent technological environment makes current technologies obsolete and requires new ones to be developed (Jansen, Van Den Bosch, and Volberda, 2006) and applied. In a volatile technological environment, a firm tends to acquire greater external technology because such an environment rapidly causes its current technological knowledge and products to become obsolete (Eisenhardt and Martin, 2000; Grant and Baden-Fuller, 2004; Teece, 2007). Firms lacking technological knowledge should acquire new knowledge and swiftly combine it with existing technological knowledge. The benefit of recombining innovation indicates that a wide knowledge base may contain more unique technological areas that provide more combined opportunities (Wu and Shanley, 2009) for renewal.

As a result, many firms became technologically opportunistic, meaning that managers are proactive in responding to new opportunities, in a way that does not violate principles of fairness (Isenberg, 1987; Hutt, Reingen and Ronchetto, 1988). This technological opportunism consists of two different components: technology-sensing capability and technology-response capability. The first is an organization's ability to acquire knowledge and understand new technology developments (Daft and Weick, 1984). The second capability is an organization's willingness and ability to respond to the new technologies it senses in its environment that may affect the organization. This includes the firm's ability to re-engineer its business strategies to exploit opportunities or stave off the threats posed by new technologies.

But in their perpetual search for renewal, firms should also be careful and not become too opportunistic, simply because technological capability has an inverted U-shaped relationship with exploration. A moderate level of technological capability relates to the highest degree of exploration, whereas a high level of technological capability actually inhibits firms' exploration of new alternatives (Zhou and Wu, 2010). In other words, firms with strong technology capabilities may become so entrenched in existing technological trajectories that they might overlook emerging technologies from new territories, and become unwilling or unable to migrate to new technology platforms. Rich experience and expertise in the existing technology base may decrease a firm's intention to explore future opportunities that arise from a new dominant design (Zhou and Wu, 2010). In addition to that, Garrison (2009) found that larger organizations could possibly face greater challenges altering their existing strategy in favour of implementing a new one; not to mention the difficulty in allocating the necessary resources required to supplant, with technology, the existing routines and processes that support the functioning of their core competencies.

But the fact remains, according to Narasimhan, Rajiv, and Dutta (2006), that the acquisition and utilization of technology and related know-how, as a dynamic capability and as absorptive capability, influences the performance of the firm. It is developed over time, accumulated through its past experience and reflects a firm's abilities to employ various technological resources (Afuah, 2002). Firms that try to adapt to the technological changes in their environments tend to become more successful than those who try to maintain the status quo, especially in the case of incumbent firms, which brings about an 'innovator's dilemma': should businesses renew with the help of technology or not (Padgett and Mulvey, 2007, p. 389; See Christensen and Overdorf, 2000 about the 'innovator's dilemma')? A firm 'Yes' should be the conclusion; technology has become an essential component in strategic decision-making.

Partners

> *Coming together is a beginning; keeping together is progress; working together is success*
>
> -Henry Ford

As business activities increasingly shift to the digital environment, the challenge facing corporate management is maintaining competitive advantage, by building strong relations with employees, customers, and upstream/downstream suppliers and partners. And so, the internet has become one of the main drivers behind the growth in the number of partnerships (Man, Stienstra, and Volberda, 2002) and interconnectedness. Therefore, it is an inevitable third dimension of the digital marketing core.

The network nature of the digital environment makes it easier for firms to develop their own unique competencies and bring together or borrow resources as well as expertise from a wide range of partners. Firms without partnerships are becoming rarer; the modern company has multiple ties (Fey and Birkinshaw, 2005; Ettlie and Pavlou, 2006) to increase their adaptability and flexibility to meet the requirements of a more rapidly changing business environment (Lanctot and Swan, 2000) and thus be able to strategically renew. Interfirm integration has become key in the dynamic digital context, and firms should develop partnerships as well as related capabilities to increase performance (Colicev, De Giovanni, and Vinzi, 2016). Partnership dynamic capability refers to the ability of partners to coordinate actions, in pursuit of market opportunities or in response to threats. It reflects the ability of partners to integrate and reconfigure resources to cope with rapidly changing environments (Chang, Chen, and Huang, 2015) and renew strategy accordingly. The partnership dynamic capabilities can be captured by: information exchange, the ability of a firm to share knowledge with its partner in an effective and efficient manner (Wu, Yeniyurt, Kim, and Cavusgil, 2006); relationship-specific knowledge stores, the knowledge stored by an organization regarding an inter-organizational relationship with a specific partner (Menguc and Auh, 2006); and joint actions, the extent to which partners address crucial relational issues when working together toward a common goal (Heide and John, 1990; Subramani and Venkatraman, 2003; Mukherji and Francis, 2008).

Hence, multi-firm structures play an important role, as more of the firm's (e)-supply chain lie outside the company's boundaries. In industries populated by high-technology companies, for example, the speedy development of new offerings is a critical determining factor of success (Faems, De Visser, Andries and Van Looy, 2010). Therefore, strategic technology partnering (STP) has become a common instrument for securing and leveraging technological competencies (Oxley and Sampson, 2004; Kim and Inkpen, 2005; Schulze, Brojerdi, and von Krogh, 2014). The more firms cultivate the cooperation of assets, the more these are relied upon to be valuable in rapidly reacting to favourable new technological chances, in order to renew through various partnerships (Hagedoorn, Roijakkers and van Kranenburg, 2006). Netflix used its technological partners like Amazon, with Amazon RDS, Amazon DynamoDB and Amazon EC2 to name but a few, to transform its business. It is now a streaming digital service instead of a physical video rental company. But it also had to seek cooperative ties with film studios like Warner Bros., DreamWorks, Universal, etc. to be able to renew its strategy and reshape its business offering.

As a result, researchers have proposed an extension of the resource-based view of the firm to take the external network resources and capabilities of partners into account (Lavie, 2006; Wassmer and Dussauge, 2011). In addition to that, Sharif (1995, 1999) stated that strategic partnering in a technological or digital context comprises four assets that firms should leverage to boost performance outcomes (Lavie, Haunschild, and Khanna, 2012): humanware (person-embodied human talents and tacit skills), technoware (object-embodied physical facilities, e.g. equipment and artefacts), infoware (record-embodied codified knowledge, e.g. facts and figures in archives) and orgaware (organization-embodied operational schemes, e.g. methods and practices). This has been extended by Kilubi (2015) with manageware (managerial competencies and leadership skills – without relevant governance and senior management support STP may not have the appropriate attention and focus it requires to be successful) and partnerware (resources and empathy abilities among the B2B-partners, e.g. required to leverage STP benefits) and comes together in their conceptual framework.

Partnerships in the new digitalized economy are created for the same reasons as in the traditional economy, but entering into a collaborative agreement with other firms has become more commonplace and significant in the digital age. Moreover, partnering is more about e-resource management, a way to access needed technological capabilities (Schulze et al., 2014), knowledge (Cummings and Holmberg, 2012), and competitive advantage (Phelps, 2010; van de Vrande, Vanhaverbeke, and Duysters, 2011). The current literature broadly defines partnerships therefore as 'purposive relationships between two or more independent firms that involve the exchange, sharing, or co-development of resources or capabilities to achieve mutually relevant benefits' (Kale and Singh, 2007, p. 46).

Internet-related partnerships in retailing, for example, can be further categorized in terms of: (a) partnerships that deepen product, service, content, and community offerings, (b) give channel access to fulfilment capabilities, (c) give market access to partner's customer bases, (d) diversify revenue sources, and (e) give access to technology and marketing services to improve digital functionality (Chatterjee, 2004). These partnerships represent a diverse array of transaction types, levels of commitment, objectives, performance criteria, creation of specific assets, and integration of operations and can, according to Vitasek and Manrodt (2012) be categorized on the basis of increased shared value versus levels of dependency, in (a) simple transaction providers, (b) approved providers, (c) preferred providers, (d) performance-based relationships, (e) vested relationships, and (f) equitable partners. In general, the performance of a partnership can be measured by its co-created value. Co-created value refers to strategic benefits that cannot be generated by a partner in isolation and can be created only through cooperation between partners (Jap, 1999). In that sense strategic renewal often depends on the input of strategic partners. But these partners should have absorptive capacity, which constitutes a set of organizational routines and processes by which firms acquire, assimilate, transform, and exploit knowledge to achieve and sustain their competitive advantages (Zahra and George, 2002; Malhotra, Gosain, and El Sawy, 2005). Partners with prior, relevant knowledge aptly acquire, assimilate, transform, and exploit new knowledge (Sinkula, 1994), which improves the partnership performance. With that in mind, entering into a collaborative agreement with other firms is considered an indispensable step towards gaining new competitive advantage.

Channels

The digital age is characterized by a multitude of channels; like offline versus online, mobile versus desktop or website versus app or social media platform. As a result, many businesses provide their offerings and manage their customers via different channels. This multiple-channel customer management, which can be formally defined as 'the design, deployment, coordination, and evaluation of channels to enhance customer value through effective customer acquisition, retention, and development' (Neslin et al., 2006, p. 96) is progressively about integration. Many business experts have enthusiastically predicted a seamless world, where people can shop, entertain, and socialize across channels, anywhere and at any time.

Nowadays multi-channel firms are morphing into omni-channel firms. This is an important evolutionary step and will affect how retailers (Verhoef, Kannan and Inman, 2015) and businesses operate in general. It is the final step of the evolution from single channel, to multi-channel, to omni-channel. In the age of single-channel marketing, a company used just a single channel, which was typically a brick-and-mortar store, to market towards consumers. With the advanced digitalization of our society, multi-channel marketing has displaced single-channel marketing and consequently, companies market by using several different channels. This means that in the case of retail, for example, each complete individual purchase process requires just one single channel. But this strategy neglects the increasingly shifting preference of consumers for channels, especially the simultaneous use of channels. Shopping, as well as using services, via multiple channels is a rapidly growing phenomenon, with companies continually adding new channels to their portfolio (Geyskens, Gielens, and Dekimpe, 2002; Ansari, Mela, and Neslin, 2008). And customers are increasingly using various devices like laptops, mobile phones, desktops, and tablets simultaneously, anywhere and at any time (Balasubramanian, Peterson, and Jarvenpaa, 2002; Avery, Steenburgh, Deighton, and Caravella, 2012).

Along with the development of this omni-channel context, many firms are facing new challenges (Zhang, Lee, Wu, and Choy, 2016). On one hand, an increasing number of customers tend to use different channels (Brynjolfsson, Hu, and Rahman, 2013). On the other hand, market competition is also forcing firms and their supply chain partners either to provide novel value-added services or to optimize and renew the existing channel operations, to fulfil the customer requirements (Chan, He, and Wang, 2012). It is no coincidence that channels, therefore, are part of the Digital Marketing Core.

So, omni-channel marketing, sometimes also referred to as cross-channel, should be viewed from a more general perspective, with a specific focus on delivering a superior customer experience (Verhoef et al., 2009). Businesses are implementing omni-channel marketing and solutions, combining and integrating several channels, to meet customers' requirements. Different from multi-channel marketing, omni-channel marketing makes it possible for customers to interact with firms across all available channels when purchasing goods or using services. Verhoef et al. (2015) therefore define omni-channel management as: "the synergetic management of the numerous available channels and customer touch points, in such a way that the customer experience across channels and the performance over channels is optimized", p. 176.

Thereby it is acknowledged that the different channels interact with each other and are used simultaneously. Netflix realized this by offering multiple channels that could be used simultaneously and are seamlessly integrated. Think of someone who is watching a movie via the Netflix app on TV and needs to catch a train to make an appointment. This person can comfortably continue watching the film on a mobile device, via the Netflix app, en route to their appointment. This represents a channel solution that had not been offered by Netflix in their pre-digital business model, showing that channels should really play a significant role in strategic renewal.

The most important strategic implication for strategic renewal that originate from the discussion above are summarized in Table 17.1.

An integrative and practical perspective of the Digital Marketing Core: Some examples

While the development of rigorous frameworks creates deep insights, it can also have a blinding effect that restricts creativity in developing holistic solutions, in this case for strategic renewal. Even though Netflix was used as an example, to demonstrate the individual uses of the Digital Marketing Core elements for strategic renewal, an integrative perspective is still required. This is included in this part, because it stresses the extra value businesses can derive from the digital marketing core, when integrating all or some of the different elements for strategic reconstruction.

Technology and channels

Digital commerce, digital servicing, and retailing, for example, solely rely on information and communication technologies (ICT) (Rao, 2000; Hansen and Tambo, 2011); but the technological infrastructure is expected to ensure mutual effects between electronic and physical channels (Kwon and Lennon, 2009), therefore strengthening the chances of omni-channel success. It is not for nothing that fashion retailer Net-a-Porter has launched a pop-up-window shop and employed image recognition technology, enabling customers to find video content of the clothes and the digital shop.

In addition, the British digital supermarket Ocado has launched a virtual shopping wall at some physical locations: One New Change, Birmingham's Bullring shopping centre, and in Bristol. Customers can shop by using Ocado's 'on the go' app, to scan a product's barcode on the wall. Technology and management of technology as well as ICT (Pantano and

Table 17.1 Key implications of the Digital Marketing Core for strategic renewal*

Digital Marketing Core dimension	Relevant strategic implications
Big data	• Big data has intensified its contribution towards organizational performance. • Organizational intelligence has become key in strategic renewal. • Big data enhances dynamic capabilities resulting in new thinking. • Big Data Analytics Capability is widely considered to be transforming the way in which firms do business. • Analytics Capability Business Strategy Alignment is needed to align analytics strategies with the overall business strategy.
Technology	• Technology has become an essential component in strategic decision-making and reconfiguration. • Lack of imagination limits the strategic application of digital technologies. • Technological capabilities influence the firm's ability to launch many and varied competitive actions, of which strategic renewal is one. • Technological capability has an inverted U-shaped relationship with exploration. • Technology-sensing capability and technology-response capability are relevant for strategic renewal. • Strategic flexibility enhances the positive relationship between technology, technological capability, and exploration.
Partners	• Interfirm integration has become key in the dynamic digital context. • Partnership dynamic capability reflects the ability of partners to integrate and reconfigure resources to cope with rapidly changing environments. • Strategic technology partnering (STP) has become a common instrument for securing and leveraging technological competencies in favour of strategic renovation. • Partnering in a technological or digital context comprises four assets that firms should leverage: humanware, technoware, infoware and orgaware.
Channels	• Use of multiple channels is progressively about integration. • Constant renewal of the existing channel operations is necessary to stay competitive. • New technologies can result in new channels and therefore channel capabilities often originate in technology.

* Strategic implications are presented at the dimension level and do not cover integration of different dimensions.

Timmermans, 2011) play a critical and expanding role in the use of multiple channels. They integrate seamlessly and although they are both a driving force for innovation as well as strategic renewal, they often go hand-in-hand (see Figure 17.2).

The emergence of omni-channel capabilities has affected the need for a practical design of the supply chain network (SCN), with the purpose of

Technology ⟺ Channels

Figure 17.2 Channels, partners, and technology

providing better products and services for customers with partners (Sachan and Datta, 2005). In today's hyper competitive digital market, a firm's individual efforts are insufficient in responding to market changes in a timely and effective manner. A renewed strategic model for designing SCN with multiple distribution channels (MDCSCN) can be an important point of attention for businesses that want to strategically renew in the hyper-dynamic digital era (Zhang et al., 2016). Such a model benefits customers by providing products and services directly from available facilities, instead of the conventional flow of products and services. A well-designed supply chain, that respects the multitude of channels, should be treated as a flexible and scalable system platform, which supports other operations and activities. Renewal often means integrating channel processes in a harmonious and complementary way throughout the organizational and IT chain, and includes external partners in these processes (Fairchild, 2014).

In the day-to-day operations of our digitalized world, businesses are dependent on optimal utilization of partner networks. It is assumed that these networks will have a critical role in non-product innovation, be it technologies as enablers or new channels, as well as processes for differentiation (Tambo, 2014). In 2014, the UK retail chain Argos, which sells electronics and clothing as well as a wide range of sports, health and beauty, and home products, launched its 'Get Set Go Argo' campaign. It was the biggest strategic change in the company's 40-year history. In-store, customers are now able to browse products and place orders on iPads and then go to a collection point to pick up their items. Hence, the integration of channels with the help of technology. But in addition to that, a 'Check & Reserve' service allows consumers to research online whether a product is available in an Argos store and then pick it up at the physical outlet within 60 seconds of arriving there; items purchased on eBay can also be retrieved in this way at Argos stores, which is a perfect example of strategic reconfiguration in terms of which channels, technologies, and partners are being integrated (see Figure 17.3).

With regard to technology, it is known that technological alignment with partners, that is, the extent to which supply chain partners strive to ensure their technology remains compatible with each other to streamline and improve the efficiency of their supply chain activities (Sanders and Premus, 2002; Gunasekaran and Ngai, 2004; Rai, Patnayakuni and Seth, 2006), is necessary to successfully renew strategies. Enhanced interfirm integrations likely aid the supply chain as a whole, in strategically responding to changing

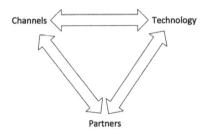

Figure 17.3 Partners and technology

market conditions and environments more successfully (Gunasekaran and Ngai, 2004; Wuyts and Geyskens, 2005; Davis and Golicic, 2010). But it requires both their extensive interfirm coordination and willingness to sacrifice their short-term interests (Wu, Yeniyurt, Kim, and Cavusgil, 2006). The strategic importance of supply chain partners motivates technology alignment, setting the stage for enhanced relationship-enabled responsiveness to the market, and subsequently, customer value creation for the firm (Kim, Cavusgil, and Gavusgil, 2013).

On top of that, strategic technology partnering (STP) has become a common instrument for securing and leveraging technological competencies (Oxley and Sampson, 2004; Kim and Inkpen, 2005; Schulze et al., 2014). Businesses need to remain aware that in the global, competitive digital environment surrounding firms these days, investment in high technology is pivotal to their strategic development and sustainability. It may even be crucial to their survival. One way of garnering this investment is through the formation of technological partnerships (see Figure 17.4). Processor designs from ARM Holdings, for example, have powered mobile phones for many years. In 2005, more than 1 billion ARM cores went into mobile phones. But in 2010, Apple took the big step of using an ARM processor for the iPad. A completely novel idea at that time. The iPad's runaway success has made ARM the default choice for powering other tablets and was the result of close partnering with this supplier. Even Microsoft made the next version of Windows run on ARM chips, breaking the long, exclusive use of Intel's x86 processor design.

The more firms cultivate the cooperation of assets, the more these are relied upon to be valuable, in rapidly reacting to favourable new technological opportunities through various partnerships (Hagedoorn et al., 2006) and thus helping strategic reconfiguration. This does not mean that leveraging external technological competencies can be a substitute for internal technological capabilities. Firms that have already made substantial investments in internal technological accumulation are then, for example, in a better position to interact with technology partners. Also they can look to other organizations that have made technology commitments in the past and seek to learn from their accumulated competences. Such firms can 'learn-by-interacting' (Lundvall, 2010), and are more likely to effectively utilize linkages, to obtain access to supplementary valuable assets and complement their internal capability, creating interactive dynamic capabilities that might help to follow new strategic paths of innovation (Caloghirou, Kastelli, and Tsakanikas, 2004; Cassiman and Veugelers, 2006; Lin, Fang, Fang, and Tsai, 2009; Schmidt, 2010; Lin, Wu, Chang, Wang, and Lee, 2012; Voudouris, Lioukas, Latrelli, and Caloghirou, 2012).

Information exchange has been identified as the most fundamental ability in the supply-chain process (Shore and Venkatachalam, 2003). Such knowledge includes, for example, end-users' information related to needs, preferences, and buying behaviours. Knowledge must be exchanged and created for rapid market-demand responses, and this depends on big data. By accelerating the speed of information exchange, dedicated technological assets can ensure the availability and timeliness of relevant and critical information to related parties (Tippins and Sohi, 2003), showcasing the integration of partners, big data, and technology (see Figure 17.4).

Taken together, for effective communication and coordination between supply chain partners, having a communication system with compatible technology is critical (Richey, Daugherty, and Roath, 2007). Information exchange, as a form of partner knowledge sharing, also improves partnership efficiency in acquiring, interpreting, and storing accurate and necessary knowledge (Madhok and Tallman, 1998; Selnes and Sallis, 2003). This leads to the expectation that information exchange facilitates strategic renewal.

Information technology improvements guarantee the increasing importance and usage of computationally intensive data processing and 'big data.' (Chen and Zhang, 2014). Big data represents both big opportunities and big challenges for CIOs (Chief Information Officers). What they should understand though, is that technology, and more specifically information technology, is front and centre in big data activities. And consumer analytics is at the epicentre of a big data revolution (Erevelles, Fukawa, and Swayne, 2016). Technology helps with capturing rich and plentiful data on different consumer phenomena. And always in real time, which helps the organization in making more accurate strategic decisions. Hence, capabilities that an organization should acquire, to succeed in their big data endeavours, give rise to an effective analytics culture, which is built on the backs of more advanced technologies.

In the context of big data, technological resources include software or a platform that a firm uses to collect, store, or analyse big data. Traditional

Figure 17.4 Big data, partners, and technology

software is simply not capable of analysing big data (Bharadwaj, El Sawy, Pavlou, and Venkatraman, 2013). Thus, firms need to establish a platform that is capable of storing and analysing large amounts (volume) of data, continuously flowing in real-time (velocity) from many different sources (variety) (Davenport et al., 2012). Firms may need to alter organization and business processes to act on the insights from big data (Viaene, 2013). Technology and big data help in transforming consumer activities into a sustainable competitive advantage (Erevelles et al., 2016). Ingram, one of the leading book distribution companies in the world, integrated technology with partners and big data to renew its strategy in the book distribution industry and became a full digital distribution company. Thanks to technology it created a digital platform for retailers and publishers to easily distribute books around the globe. Currently 2,400 distribution partners are linked to the system in addition to more than 3,900 retailers and libraries. Publishers can easily make their book available in print-on-demand or e-book format and sell it to the world. The flow of data that comes from all these parties is being managed by the same system and provides, for example, publishers with real-time sales data from around the word. Ingram, a family-owned business for more than 50 years, has wisely used components of the Digital Marketing Core to renew its strategy and business offering (see Figure 17.5).

Concluding thoughts, managerial takeaways, and future research directions

While the model presented is interesting, it is important to step back and view it in terms of the future of digital marketing strategy practice and research. The fact is that the most relevant digital marketing questions are strategy related (Schibrowsky, Peltier, and Nill, 2007). Interestingly, this study fits with the movement of digital marketing research as it finally shifts away from descriptive types of studies towards research related to improving the

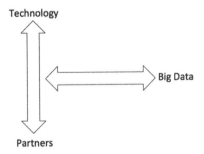

Figure 17.5 Concluding thoughts, managerial takeaways, and future research directions

effectiveness and efficiency (strategy), and from more narrowly defined studies in this emergent field, towards a more holistic understanding.

The study has identified specific digital dimensions and their application within opportunities to realize strategic reconfiguration. This conceptual framework was also utilized by this research, to explain how different digital dimensions combine to realize strategic renovation. The Digital Marketing Core provided a platform for interpreting the emerging literature on big data, technology, channels, and partners. It also acts as the interconnector for these components within digital innovation, underpinning the research in this paper.

The integrating literature review and conceptual findings presented in this study provide a considerable contribution to theoretical development in the field of strategic renewal in a further digitalized economy. It provides insight into specific dimensions that play an important role within strategic value creation, which can be combined in order to strategically renew. Given its fragmented nature, the integrated literature review provided, with the help of the Digital Marketing Core, offers researchers in the digital marketing era a basis for developing more unified thinking. Development of further studies can contribute to the advancement of a theoretical basis for strategic renewal with the help of the Digital Marketing Core. In particular the role of related capabilities, the related integration effects and capabilities that are needed to fully make use of the interaction between the different dimensions, might give further insight. Future research would prove useful, for example, if they explore these interactions, in various business contexts, so that transferable knowledge can be accumulated with respect to their transformation into specific renewal strategies. In addition, then, researchers should also examine how the competitive environment relates to the Digital Marketing Core concept. What are the possible competitive implications of applying such a model?

Also, the role of how the individual (owner, manager, or employee) acts in the dynamic application of this model might be of interest. Although many marketing studies deal with abstract concepts and applications, the role of the individual cannot be underestimated, even in digital environments. And, especially with respect to the big data phenomenon. Given the increasing importance of strategic data and the presumed positive effect of marketing intelligence capabilities on performance (Germann, Lilien, and Rangaswamy, 2012), it is important to know how firms can build these functions, and which employees they should attract to make ultimate use of data for strategic renovation. This is certainly the case when the presented interactions, with the other three components in the model, are taken into account. Although data can often be automatically analysed, humans remain of high importance when linking it strategically to the rest of the model. In addition, researchers should further examine the use of big data in relation to strategic renewal. There seems to be a general lack of digital-analytics–related studies. As the amount and sophistication of digital-related analytics has significantly increased over time, opportunities arise to study both the usefulness of the data, and the impact that it has on the adaptive marketing strategies available for digital-based marketers, which brings us to the practical implications of this study.

'To improve is to change; to be perfect is to change often.' (Winston Churchill). Businesses embarking on strategic marketing should therefore adopt a more flexible approach, even going as far as Mintzberg's emergent strategy (Mintzberg and Waters, 1985) in order to market in an adaptive fashion, as a reflection of the digital environment. Adaptive marketing would include being dynamically responsive to the market, making both significant as well as small, real-time adjustments and regularly reviewing the impact of digitally centric actions.

The current, often rather passive marketing strategies employed by many organizations, based on past activity, will have increasingly less significance in the digitalized economy. Therefore, the Digital Marketing Core was introduced in this study as a tool for managers to find new strategic opportunities. And so, the framework presented has serious implications for marketing managers, within the context of strategic renewal.

It affords marketing managers a better understanding of the integrative power of the different components within the framework for strategic use, in a world that takes giant digital steps. In other words, understanding the integrative power of the framework will be critical in creating new advantages for a company, either in a full digital context or a physical context, in which digital tools and application are being used. Each component of the Digital Marketing Core framework becomes an effective driver of successful strategic renewal through this integration. It is vital that their potential interactions with one another are taken into consideration in choosing new strategic initiatives. This also means that organizations should develop the right capabilities for each component as well as capabilities that facilitate smooth integration of the different components. This often requires further integration of the organization as well, meaning that organizations should no longer follow traditional structures with different departments for different functions. The world is changing so fast, that proactive and flexible strategy processes instead of a linear process are a prerequisite. The holistic rugby style, taking into account all the factors, actors, and the organization's functions at the same time, should be the new standard in digital contexts. One characteristic of this is that the strategic renewal process resembles a rugby team engaging in a scrum; this way all elements are in contact with each other, instead of being a linear process. Hence, the representation of the Digital Marketing Core within the organization.

Critically, marketers need to continually monitor their strategy, to ensure consistency and effectiveness throughout their activities in a world that, with each passing day, becomes more digitalized. An additional relevant implication is that strategic renewal represents a valid concept for assessing the Digital Marketing Core and the management of it. Besides, managers should be aware of the fact that the Digital Marketing Core can deliver real value to customers, stretching beyond revenue generation. With the dimensions of the framework and an integrative perspective, marketers can begin to change their core products or services, or create added value around their core products and services. In turn, this will permit the development of more positive brand associations and loyalty, and offer protection against increasing commoditization (which is also a consequence of further digitalization), for example.

The interactions between the pillars represent the fuel needed to strategically lift businesses to a new level in the digital world. Examples have been given. While the framework is at a formative stage, the Digital Marketing Core appears to be a simple but robust conceptual framework.

References

Afuah, A., 2002. Mapping technological capabilities into product markets and competitive advantage: The case of cholesterol drugs, *Strategic Management Journal*, 23(2), 171–179.

Agarwal, R. & Dhar, V., 2014. Editorial-big data, data science, and analytics: The opportunity and challenge for IS research, *Information Systems Research*, 25, 443–448.

Agarwal, R. & Helfat, C.E., 2009. Strategic renewal of organizations, *Organization Science*, 20(2), 281–293.

Akter, S., Wamba, S.M., Gunasekaran, A., Dubey, R. & Childe, S.J., 2016. How to improve firm performance using big data analytics capability and business strategy alignment? *International Journal of Production Economics*, 182, 113–131.

Analogbei, M., Canhoto, A., Dibb, S., Quinn, L. & Simkin, L., 2015. Is marketing in the digital era losing its magic? Paper presented at the Academy of Marketing Conference, Limerick, July.

Ansari, A., Mela, C.F. & Neslin, S.A., 2008. Customer channel migration, *Journal of Marketing Research*, 45(1), 60–76.

Assael, H., 2010. From silos to synergy: A fifty year review of cross media research, *Journal of Advertising Research*, 51, 43–58.

Avery, J., Steenburgh, T.J., Deighton, J. & Caravella, M., 2012. Adding bricks to clicks: Predicting the patterns of cross-channel elasticities over time, *Journal of Marketing*, 76(3), 96–111.

Balasubramanian, S., Peterson, R.A. & Jarvenpaa, S.L., 2002. Exploring the implications of m-commerce for markets and marketing, *Journal of the Academy of Marketing Science*, 30(4), 348–361.

Barrales-Molina, V., Martínez-Lopez, F.J. & Gázquez-Abad, J.C., 2014. Dynamic marketing capabilities: Toward an integrative framework, *International Journal of Management Reviews*, 16, 397–416.

Barton, D. & Court, D., 2012. Making advanced analytics work for you, *Harvard Business Review*, 90, 78.

Bharadwaj, A., El Sawy, O.A., Pavlou, P.A., & Venkatraman, N., 2013. Digital business strategy: Toward a next generation of insights, *MIS Quarterly*, 37(2), 471–482.

Bolton, R.N., 2006. The implications of "Big M" marketing for modeling service and relationships, *Marketing Science*, 25(6), 584–586.

Braganza, A., Brooks, L., Nepelski, D., Ali, M. & Moro, R. 2017. Resource management in big data initiatives: Processes and dynamic capabilities, *Journal of Business Research*, 70, 328–337.

Brown, B., Chui, M. & Manyika, J. 2011. Are you ready for the era of 'big data', *McKinsey Quarterly*, 4(1), 24–35.

Brown, S.W., Webster, F.E. Jr., Steenkamp, J.-B.E.M., Wilkie, W.L., Sheth, J.N., Sisodia, R.R., Kerin, R.A., MacInnis, D., McAlister, L., Raju, J.S., Bauerly, R.J., Johnson, D.T., Singh, M. & Staelin, R., 2005. Marketing renaissance: Opportunities and imperatives for improving marketing thought, practice and infrastructure, *Journal of Marketing*, 69(4), 1–25.

Brynjolfsson, E., Hu, Y.J. & Rahman, M.S., 2013. Competing in the age of omnichannel retailing, *MIT Sloan Management Review*, 54, 23–29.

Bughin, J., 2008. The rise of enterprise 2.0, *Journal of Direct, Data and Digital Marketing Practice*, 9, 251–259.

Caloghirou, Y., Kastelli, I. & Tsakanikas, A., 2004. Internal capabilities and external knowledge sources: Complements or substitutes for innovative performance? *Technovation*, 24(1), 29–39.

Carter, E.V., 2009. Competency codes; marketing management for the digital future, *Marketing Management Journal*, 19, 16–36.

Cassiman, B. & Veugelers, R., 2006. In search of complementarity in innovation strategy: Internal R&D and external knowledge acquisition, *Management Science*, 52(1), 68–82.

Chaffey, D. & Ellis-Chadwick, F., 2012. *Digital marketing: Strategy, implementation and practice*, Harlow: Pearson.

Chan, H.K., He, H. & Wang, W.Y.C., 2012. Green marketing and its impact on supply chain management in industrial markets, *Industrial Marketing Management*, 41, 557–562.

Chang, K.H., Chen, Y.R. & Huang, H.F., 2015. Information technology and partnership dynamic capabilities in international subcontracting relationships, *International Business Review*, 24, 276–286.

Chatterjee, P., 2004. Interfirm alliances in online retailing, *Journal of Business Research*, 57(7), 714–723.

Chen, C.L.P. & Zhang, C.Y., 2014. Data-intensive applications, challenges, techniques and technologies: A survey on big data, *Information Sciences*, 275, 314–347.

Christensen, C.M. & Overdorf, M., 2000. Meeting the challenge of disruptive change, *Harvard Business Review*, 78(1), 67–76.

Colicev, A., De Giovanni, P & Vinzi, V.E., 2016. An empirical investigation of the antecedents of partnering capability, *International Journal of Production Economics*, 178, 144–153.

Constantiou, I. D. & Kallinikos, J. 2015. New games, new rules: big data and the changing context of strategy. *Journal of Information Technology*, 30(1), 44–57.

Cummings, J.L. & Holmberg, S.R., 2012. Best-fit alliance partners: The use of critical success factors in a comprehensive partner selection process, *Long Range Planning*, 45, 136–159.

Daft, R.L. & Weick, K.E., 1984. Toward a model of organizations as interpretation systems, *Academy of Management Review*, 9(2), 284–295.

Davenport, T.H., 2006. Competing on analytics, *Harvard Business Review*, 84, 98–107.

Davenport, T.H., Barth, P. & Bean, R., 2012. How 'big data' is different, *MIT Sloan Management Review*, 54(1), 22–24.

Davenport, T.H. & Harris, J.G., 2007. *Competing on analytics: The new science of winning*, Brighton, Boston: Harvard Business School Press.

Davis, D.F. & Golicic, S.L., 2010. Gaining comparative advantage in supply chain relationships: The mediating role of market-oriented IT competence, *Journal of the Academy of Marketing Science*, 38(1), 56–70.

Day, G.S., 2011. Closing the marketing capabilities gap, *Journal of Marketing*, 75, 183–195.

Day, G.S., 2014. An outside-in approach to resource-based theories, *Journal of the Academy of Marketing Science*, 42(1), 27–28.

Du, R.Y., Hu, Y. & Damangir, S., 2015. Leveraging trends in online searches for product features in market response modeling, *Journal of Marketing*, 79, 29–43.

Eisenhardt, K.M. & Martin, J.A., 2000. Dynamic capabilities: What are they? *Strategic Management Journal*, 21(10–11), 1105–1121.

Erevelles, S., Fukawa, N. & Swayne, L., 2016. Big data consumer analytics and the transformation of marketing, *Journal of Business Research*, 69(2), 897–904.

Ettlie, J.E. & Pavlou, P.A., 2006. Technology-based new product development partnerships, *Decision Sciences*, 37(2), 117–147.

Faems, D., De Visser, M., Andries, P. & Van Looy, B., 2010. Technology alliance portfolios and financial performance: Value-enhancing and cost-increasing effects of open innovation, *Journal of Product Innovation Management*, 27(6), 785–796.

Fairchild, A.M., 2014. Extending the network: Defining product delivery partnering preferences for omni-channel commerce, *Procedia Technology*, 16, 447–451.

Feng, H., Morgan, N.A. & Rego, L.L., 2015. Marketing department power and firm performance, *Journal of Marketing*, 79(September), 1–20.

Fey, C.F. & Birkinshaw, J., 2005. External sources of knowledge, governance mode, and R&D performance, *Journal of Management*, 31(4), 597–621.

Gandomi, A. & Haider, M., 2015. Beyond the hype: Big data concepts, methods, and analytics, *International Journal of Information Management*, 35(2), 137–144.

Garrison, G., 2009. An assessment of organizational size and sense and response capability on the early adoption of disruptive technology, *Computers in Human Behavior*, 25, 444–449.

Gartner, 2016. Gartner's 2016 hypecycle for emerging technologies, www.gartner.com /newsroom/id/3412017.

Gatignon, H. & Xuereb, J.M., 1997. Strategic orientation of the firm and new product performance, *Journal of Marketing Research*, 34(1), 77–90.

Gehrke, J., 2012. Quo vadis, data privacy? *Annals of the New York Academy of Sciences*, 1260(1), 45–54.

George, G., Haas, M.R. & Pentland, A., 2014. big data and management: From the editors, *Academy of Management Journal*, 57(2), 321–326.

Germann, F., Lilien, G.L. & Rangaswamy, A., 2012. Performance implications of deploying marketing analytics, *International Journal of Research in Marketing*, 30(2), 114–128.

Geyskens, I., Gielens, K. & Dekimpe, M.G., 2002. The market valuation of Internet channel additions, *Journal of Marketing*, 66(2), 102–119.

Gobble, M.M., 2013. big data: The next big thing in innovation, *Research-Technology Management*, 56(1), 64–67.

Grant, R.M. & Baden-Fuller, C., 2004. A knowledge accessing theory of strategic alliances, *Journal of Management Studies*, 41(1), 61–84.

Gunasekaran, A. & Ngai, E.W.T., 2004. Information systems in supply chain integration and management, *European Journal of Operational Research*, 159, 269–295.

Hagedoorn, J., Roijakkers, N. & van Kranenburg, H., 2006. Inter-firm R&D networks: The importance of strategic network capabilities for high-tech partnership formation, *British Journal of Management*, 17(1), 39–53.

Hansen, R. & Tambo, T., 2011. Branding and channel issues in E-commerce from an information systems perspective, Proceedings of the 33th Information Systems Research Seminar, Turkey.

Heide, J.B. & John, G., 1990. Alliances in industrial purchasing: The determinants of joint action in buyer-supplier relationships, *Journal of Marketing Research*, 17, 24–36.

Hirt, M. & Wilmott, P., 2014. Strategic principles for competing in a digital age, *McKinsey Quarterly*, May, 1–13.

Holbrook, M.B. & Hulbert, J.M., 2002. Elegy on the death of marketing – Never send to know why we have come to bury marketing but to ask what you can do for your country churchyard, *European Journal of Marketing*, 36, 706–732.

Hutt, M.D., Reingen, P.H. & Ronchetto J.R. Jr., 1988. Tracing emergent processes in marketing strategy formation, *Journal of Marketing*, 52(January), 4–19.

Isenberg, D.J., 1987. The tactics of strategic opportunism, *Harvard Business Review*, 65 (March/April), 92–97.

Jansen, J.J.P., Van Den Bosch, F.A.J. & Volberda, H.W., 2006. Exploratory innovation, exploitative innovation, and performance: Effects of organizational antecedents and environmental moderators, *Management Science*, 52(11), 1661–1674.

Jap, S.D., 1999. Pie-expansion effects: Collaboration processes in buyer–seller relationships, *Journal of Marketing Research*, 36(4), 461–475.

Kale, P. & Singh, H., 2007. Building firm capabilities through learning: The role of the alliance learning process in alliance capability and firm-level alliance success, *Strategic Management Journal*, 28, 981–1000.

Kaufman, I. & Horton, C., 2014. *Digital marketing: Integrating strategy and tactics with values, a guidebook for executives, managers, and students*, New York, NY: Routledge, p. 49.

Kilubi, I., 2015. Strategic technology partnering: A framework extension, *The Journal of High Technology Management Research*, 26(1), 27–37.

Kim, C.S. & Inkpen, A.C., 2005. Cross-border R&D alliances, absorptive capacity and technology learning, *Journal of International Management*, 11(3), 313–329.

Kim, D., Cavusgil, S.T. & Gavusgil, E., 2013. Does IT alignment between supply chain partners enhance customer value creation? An empirical investigation, *Industrial Marketing Management*, 42(6), 880–889.

Kim, G., Shin, B. & Kwon, O. 2012. Investigating the value of sociomaterialism in conceptualizing IT capability of a firm. *Journal of Management Information Systems*, 29(3), 327–362.

Kiron, D., Prentice, P.K. & Ferguson, R.B., 2014. The analytics mandate, *MIT Sloan Management Review*, 55, 1–25.

Kozlenkova, I.V., Samaha, S.A. & Palmatier, R.W., 2014. Resource-based theory in marketing, Journal of the Academy of Marketing Science, 42(1), 1–21.

Kwon, W.S. & Lennon, S.J., 2009. Reciprocal effects between multichannel retailers' offline and online brand images, *Journal of Retailing*, 85(3), 376–390.

Lamberton, C. & Stephen, A.T., 2016. A thematic exploration of digital, social media, and mobile marketing; research evolution from 2000 to 2015 and an agenda for future inquiry, *Journal of Marketing*, 80(November), 146–172.

Lanctot, A. & Swan, K.S., 2000. Technology acquisition strategy in an internationally competitive environment, *Journal of International Management*, 6(3), 187–215.

Lavie, D., 2006. The competitive advantage of interconnected firms: An extension of the resource-based view, *Academy of Management Review*, 31(3), 638–658.

Lavie, D., Haunschild, P.R. & Khanna, P., 2012. Organizational differences, relational mechanisms, and alliance performance, *Strategic Management Journal*, 33(12), 453–1479.

Lin, B.W., 2007. Information technology capability and value creation: Evidence from the US banking industry, *Technology in Society*, 29(1), 93–106.

Lin, C., Wu, Y.J., Chang, C, Wang, W. & Lee, C.Y., 2012. The alliance innovation performance of R&D alliances – The absorptive capacity perspective, *Technovation*, 32(5), 282–292.

Lin, J.L., Fang, S.C., Fang, S.R. & Tsai, F.S., 2009. Network embeddedness and technology transfer performace in R&D consortia in Taiwan, *Technovation*, 29, 763–774.

Lundvall, B.A., 2010. *National systems of innovation: Towards a theory of innovation and interactive learning*, London, UK: Anthem Press.

Madhok, A. & Tallman, S.B., 1998. Resources, transactions and rents: Managing value through interfirm collaborative relationships, *Organization Science*, 9, 326–339.

Majchrzak, A., Markus, M.L. & Wareham, J., 2016. Designing for digital transformation: Lessons for information systems research from the study of ICT and societal challenges, *MIS Quarterly*, 40(2), 267–277.

Malhotra, A., Gosain, S. & El Sawy, O.A., 2005. Absorptive capacity configurations in supply chains: Gearing for partner-enabled market knowledge creation, *MIS Quarterly*, 29(1), 145–187.

Man, de, A.P., Stienstra, M. & Volberda, H.W., 2002. e-Partnering: Moving bricks and mortar online, *European Management Journal*, 20(4), 329–339.

McAfee, A. & Brynjolfsson, E., 2012. Big data: The management revolution, *Harvard Business Review*, 90, 60–68.

Menguc, B. & Auh, S., 2006. Creating a firm-level dynamic capability through capitalizing on market orientation and innovativeness, *Journal of the Academy of Marketing Science*, 24(1), 63–73.

Mintzberg, H. & Waters, J.A., 1985. Of strategies, deliberate and emergent, *Strategic Management Journal*, 6, 257–272.

Mukherji, A. & Francis, J.D., 2008. Mutual adaptation in buyer-supplier relationships, *Journal of Business Research*, 61(2), 154–161.

Narasimhan, O., Rajiv, S. & Dutta, S., 2006. Absorptive capacity in high-technology markets: The competitive advantage of the haves, *Marketing Science*, 25(5), 510–524.

Neslin, S.A., Grewal, D., Leghorn, R., Shankar, V., Teerling, M.L., Thomas, J.S. & Verhoef, P.C., 2006. Challenges and opportunities in multichannel customer management, *Journal of Service Research*, 9(2), 95–112.

Oxley, E. & Sampson, R.C., 2004. The scope and governance of international R&D alliances, *Strategic Management Journal*, 25(8–9), 723–749.

Padgett, D. & Mulvey, M.S., 2007. Differentiation via technology: Strategic positioning of services following the introduction of disruptive technology, *Journal of Retailing*, 83(4), 375–391.

Pantano, E. & Timmermans, H., (Eds.), 2011. *Advanced technologies management for retailing – Frameworks and cases*, Hershey, PA: IGI Global.

Phelps, C.C., 2010. A longitudinal study of the influence of alliance network structure and composition on firm exploratory innovation, *Academy of Management Journal*, 53(4), 890–913.

Porter, M.E., 1985. *The competitive advantage: Creating and sustaining superior performance*, New York City, NY: Free Press.

Quinton, A. & Simkin, L., 2016. The digital journey: Reflected learnings and emerging challenges, *International Journal of Management Reviews*, 0, 1–18.

Quinton, S., 2013. The community brand paradigm: A response to brand management's dilemma in the digital era, *Journal of Marketing Management*, 29, 912–932.

Rai, A., Patnayakuni, R. & Seth, N., 2006. Firm performance impacts of digitally enabled supply chain integration capabilities, *MIS Quarterly*, 30(2), 225–246.

Rao, B.P., 2000. Improving retail effectiveness through technology: A survey of analytical tools for physical and online retailers, *Technology in Society*, 22, 111–122.

Richey, R.G., Daugherty, P.J. & Roath, A.S., 2007. Firm technological readiness and complementarity: Capabilities impacting logistics service competency and performance, *Journal of Business Logistics*, 28(1), 195–228.

Rodríguez-Mazahua, L., Rodríguez-Enríquez, C. A., Sánchez-Cervantes, J. L., Cervantes, J., García-Alcaraz, J. L. & Alor-Hernández, G. 2016. A general perspective of Big Data: applications, tools, challenges and trends. *The Journal of Supercomputing*, 72(8), 3073–3113.

Royle, J. & Laing, A., 2014. The digital marketing skills gap: Developing a digital marketer model for the communication industries, *International Journal of Information Management*, 34(2), 65–73.

Rust, R.T. & Espinoza, F., 2006. How technology advances influence business research and marketing strategy, *Journal of Business Research*, 59(10–11), 1072–1078.

Sachan, A. & Datta, S., 2005. Review of supply chain management and logistics research, *International Journal of Physical Distribution & Logistics Management*, 35, 664–705.

Sambamurthy, V., Bharadwaj, A. & Grover, V., 2003. Shaping agility through digital options: Reconceptualizing the role of information technology in contemporary firms, *MIS Quarterly*, 27(2), 237–263.

Sanchez, R., 1995. Strategic flexibility in product competition, *Strategic Management Journal*, 16(Summer Special Issue), 135–159.

Sanders, N.R. & Premus, R., 2002. IT applications in supply chain organizations: A link between competitive priorities and organizational benefits, *Journal of Business Logistics*, 23(1), 65–83.

Schibrowsky, J.A., Peltier, J.W. and Nill, A., 2007. The state of internet marketing research: A review of the literature and future research direction, *European Journal of Marketing*, 41(7), 722–733.

Schmidt, T., 2010. Absorptive capacity – One size fits all? A firm-level analysis of absorptive capacity for different kinds of knowledge, *Mangerial and Decision Economics*, 31(1), 1–18.

Schulze, A., Brojerdi, G. & von Krogh, G., 2014. Those who know, do. Those who understand, teach. Disseminative capability and knowledge transfer in the automotive industry, *Journal of Product Innovation Management*, 31(1), 79–97.

Selnes, F. & Sallis, J., 2003. Promoting relationship learning, *Journal of Marketing*, 67, 80–95.

Setia, P., Venkatesh, V. & Joglekar, S., 2013. Leveraging digital technologies: How information quality leads to localized capabilities and customer service performance, *MIS Quarterly*, 37, 565–590.

Sharif, N., 1995. The evolution of technology management studies: Technoeconomics to technometrics, *Technology Management: Strategies and Applications for Practitioners*, 2(3), 113–148.

Sharif, N., 1999. Strategic role of technological self-reliance in development management, *Technological Forecasting and Social Change*, 62(3), 219–238.

Shore, B. & Venkatachalam, A.R., 2003. Evaluating the information sharing capabilities of supply chain partners; a fuzzy logic model, *International Journal of Physical Distribution & Logistics Management*, 33(9), 804–824.

Shugan, S.M., 2004. The impact of advancing technology on marketing and academic research, *Marketing Science*, 23(4), 469–475.

Sinkula, J.M., 1994. Market information processing and organizational learning, *Journal of Marketing*, 58(January), 35–45.

Srinivasan, R., Lilien, G.L. & Rangaswamy, A., 2002. Technological opportunism and radical technology adoption: An application to e-business, *Journal of Marketing*, 66, 47–60.

Strawn, G.O., 2012. Scientific research: How many paradigms? *Educause Review*, May/June, 26–34.

Subramani, M.R., & Venkatraman, N., 2003. Safeguarding investments in asymmetric inter-organizational relationships: Theory and evidence, *Academy of Management Journal*, 46(1), 46–62.

Tambo, T., 2014. Collaboration on technological innovation in Danish fashion chains: A network perspective, *Journal of Retailing and Consumer Services*, 21(5), 827–835.

Teece, D.J., 2007. Explicating dynamic capabilities: The nature and microfoundations of (sustainable) enterprise performance, *Strategic Management Journal*, 28(13), 1319–1350.

Teece, D.J., Pisano, G. & Shuen, A., 1997. Dynamic capabilities and strategic management, *Strategic Management Journal*, 18(7), 509–533.

Tellis, G. J., Prabhu, J. C. & Chandy, R. K. 2009. Radical innovation across nations: The preeminence of corporate culture. *Journal of Marketing*, 73(1), 3–23.

Theodosiou, M., Kehagias, J. & Katsikea, E., 2012. Strategic orientations, marketing capabilities and firm performance: An empirical investigation in the context of frontline managers in service organizations, *Industrial Marketing Management*, 41, 1058–1070.

Tippins, M.J. & Sohi, R.S., 2003. IT competency and firm performance: Is irganizational learning a missing link? *Strategic Management Journal*, 24, 745–761.

Trainor, K.J., Rapp, A., Skinner Beitelspacher, L. & Schillewaert, N., 2011. Integrating information technology and marketing: An examination of the drivers and outcomes of e-marketing capability, *Industrial Marketing Management*, 40(1), 162–174.

van de Vrande, V., Vanhaverbeke, W. & Duysters, G., 2011. Technology in-sourcing and the creation of pioneering technologies, *Journal of Product Innovation Management*, 28(6), 974–987.

Verhoef, P.C., Kannan, P.K. & Inman, J.J., 2015. From multi-channel retailing to omni-channel retailing; introduction to the special issue on multi-channel retailing, *Journal of Retailing*, 91(2), 174–181.

Verhoef, P. C., Lemon, K. N., Parasuraman, A., Roggeveen, A., Tsiros, M., & Schlesinger, L. A. 2009. Customer experience creation: Determinants, dynamics and management strategies. *Journal of Retailing*, *85*(1), 31–41.

Verhoef, P. C., Neslin, S. A. & Vroomen, B. 2007. Multichannel customer management: Understanding the research-shopper phenomenon. *International Journal of Research in Marketing*, 24(2), 129–148.

Viaene, S., 2013. Data scientistst aren't domein experts, *IT Professional*, 15(6), 12–17.

Vitasek, K. & Manrodt, K., 2012. Vested outsourcing: A flexible framework for collaborative outsourcing, *Strategic Outsourcing: An International Journal*, 5(1), 4–14.

Voudouris, I., Lioukas, S., Latrelli, M. & Caloghirou, Y., 2012. Effectiveness of technology investment: Impact of internal technological capability, networking and investment's strategic importance, *Technovation*, 32(6), 400–414.

Wassmer, U. & Dussauge, P., 2011. Value creation in alliance portfolios: The benefits and costs of network resource interdependencies, *European Management Review*, 8(1), 47–64.

Weinberg, B.D. & Pehlivan, E., 2011. Social spending: Managing the social media mix, *Business Horizons*, 54(3), 275–282.

Wilson, D. & Quinton, S., 2012. Let's talk about wine – Does Twitter have value, *International Journal of Wine Business Research*, 24, 35–48.

Wu, F., Yeniyurt, S., Kim, D., & Cavusgil, S.T., 2006. The impact of information technology on supply chain capabilities and firm performance: A resource-based view, *Industrial Marketing Management*, 35, 493–504.

Wu, J. & Shanley, M.T., 2009. Knowledge stock, exploration, and innovation: Research on the United States electromedical device industry, *Journal of Business Research*, 62, 474–483.

Wuyts, S. & Geyskens, I., 2005. The formation of buyer-supplier relationships: Detailed contract drafting and close partner selection, *Journal of Marketing*, 69(4), 103–117.

Yadav, M.S. & Pavlou, P.A., 2014. Marketing in computer-mediated environments: Research synthesis and new directions, *Journal of Marketing*, 78, 20–40.

Zahra, S., & George, G., 2002. Absorptive capability: A review, re-conceptualization, and extension, *Academy of Management Review*, 27(2), 185–203.

Zhang, S., Lee, C.K.M., Wu, K. & Choy, K.L., 2016. Multi-objective optimization for sustainable supply chain network design considering multiple distribution channels, *Expert Systems with Applications*, 65, 87–99.

Zhou, K.Z. & Wu, F., 2010. Technological capability, strategic flexibility, and product innovation, *Strategic Management Journal*, 31, 547–561.

Zhou, K.Z., Yim, C.K. & Tse, D.T., 2005. The effects of strategic orientations on technology- and market-based breakthrough innovations, *Journal of Marketing*, 69(2), 42–60.

Zwick, D. & Dholakia, N., 2008. Infotransformation of markets: Introduction to the special issue on marketing and information technology, *Journal of Macromarketing*, 28, 318–332.

18 Dynamic game plans

Using gamification to entrain strategic renewal with environmental velocity

Kirk Plangger, Ian P. McCarthy, Jan Kietzmann, Karen Robson, and Leyland F. Pitt

Introduction

It is widely recognized that competitive advantages are temporary, especially in innovation-driven industries. Consequently, for organizations to cope with changing industry conditions and to survive over time, they need to appropriately reinvent themselves. This is a process known as strategic renewal. It involves organizations altering their strategic intent and related practices and capabilities so as to ensure alignment with their environment and long-term survival (Agarwal and Helfat, 2009; Lechner and Floyd, 2012; Schmitt et al., 2016). Furthermore, as we highlight in this chapter, the approach to organizational strategic renewal depends on the dynamics of the firm's environment.

Prior research on strategic renewal has focused on why organizations are driven to renew (Crossan and Berdrow, 2003; Salvato, 2009); the different types of strategic renewal that take place (e.g., discontinuous versus incremental) (Agarwal and Helfat, 2009; Floyd and Lane, 2000); and the organizational conditions and processes needed to achieve renewal (Kwee et al., 2011; Simons, 1994; Tippmann et al., 2014). As management control systems are used to formulate and implement new strategic directions (McCarthy and Gordon, 2011; Simons, 1994), they are viewed as a vital method for strategic renewal (Henri, 2006; Marginson, 2002). They provide the "process by which managers assure that resources are obtained and used effectively and efficiently in the accomplishment of the organization's objectives" (Anthony, 1965: 17). Furthermore, management control systems can be used to balance and reconcile two organizational learning behaviors that are fundamental to strategic renewal: exploitation and exploration (McCarthy and Gordon, 2011; Raisch et al., 2009). Exploration includes activities such as searching, risk taking, experimentation, and discovery, whereas exploitation includes activities such as refinement, optimization, and continuous improvement. Effective strategic renewal requires directing and supporting employees to pursue the appropriate combinations of exploration and exploitation necessary to thrive in their organization's industry conditions.

In this chapter we propose gamification as a management control system approach for directing employees and other organizational stakeholders to pursue new strategic directions. Gamification is "the application of game design principles in non-gaming contexts" (Robson et al., 2015: 411). In the context of strategic renewal, it would involve using game-like experiences to motivate and engage participants (e.g., employees and other stakeholders) so as to attain the appropriate focus on exploitation and exploration for renewal suited to an organization's environmental dynamics. To characterize the organization-environment fit we use environmental velocity: the rate and direction of change (Eisenhardt, 1989; Eisenhardt and Bourgeois, 1988; McCarthy et al., 2010). We highlight that environmental velocity involves understanding industry changes in terms of its rate *and* direction of change. Consequently, effective gamified strategic renewal is not only a matter of using gamification to align the pace of organizational strategic change with the pace of environmental change, but also of matching the direction of change. To understand how gamified approaches to strategic renewal would thus vary, we present four types of environmental velocity (laminar, irregular, express, and turbulent) based on combinations of its two defining aspects: rate and direction of change. Then, using gamification design principles – mechanics, dynamics, and emotions – (Robson et al., 2015) we explain how gamified strategic renewal would vary to direct different organizational stakeholder behaviors to align with each type of environmental velocity. We conclude the chapter by discussing the academic and practical implications of our ideas.

Literature review

Strategic renewal and industry velocity

An enduring theme in organizational strategy research is that organizations that tailor their strategies and capabilities to align with the conditions of their external environments will outperform organizations that do not (Miller, 1992; Venkatraman and Camillus, 1984; Zajac, Kraatz and Bresser, 2000). Within this theory of organization-environment fit is the notion that organizational strategic renewal has a dynamic element, in that it should occur at a pace that matches the dynamics of environmental change over time (Ben–Menahem et al., 2013). For example, Hannan and Freeman (1984) argue that organizational survival is achieved by aligning the pattern of organizational change with the pattern of change in key environments (i.e., relative inertia).

The construct of environmental velocity can help with understanding the dynamics of change faced by organizations (Eisenhardt, 1989; Eisenhardt and Bourgeois 1988; McCarthy et al., 2010). This construct entered the strategic-management literature in Bourgeois and Eisenhardt's (1988) study of strategic decision making in the micro-computer industry. They describe this industry as a "high-velocity environment", that is, an environment characterized by "rapid and discontinuous change in demand, competitors, technology and/or regulation, such that information is often inaccurate, unavailable, or obsolete" (Bourgeois & Eisenhardt, 1988: 816). This and subsequent work on environmental velocity suggest that it has significant effects on how managers interpret their environments (Nadkarni and Barr, 2008; Nadkarni and Narayanan, 2007) and that superior performance in high-velocity industries is linked to fast and formal strategic decision making (Bourgeois and Eisenhardt, 1988; Eisenhardt, 1989; Judge and Miller, 1991), rapid organizational adaptation and fast product innovation (Eisenhardt and Tabrizi, 1995), and heuristic reasoning (Oliver and Roos, 2005).

In line with this prior research, we argue that when an organization's strategic renewal dynamic is aligned with its environmental velocity, this will lead to better organizational performance. However, it is important to note that prior research that uses environmental velocity typically focuses only on the rate of environmental change, despite environmental velocity being a vector, defined by the rate *and* direction of change in a number of dimensions (McCarthy et al., 2010). In contrast, for the dimensions of the environment such as demand, competitors, technology, products, and regulations, we treat each as having its own velocity made up of the rate and also the direction of change. The velocities of these dimensions combine to produce patterns of environmental velocity.

Focusing on both parts (rate and direction) of environmental velocity, we present a typology of four environmental velocity types (see Figure 18.1). The rate of environmental change is the relative amount (low to high) of change in the environment over a set period of time in dimensions such as demand, competitors, technology, products, and regulation. The direction of environmental change can be characterized as continuous or discontinuous (McCarthy et al., 2010; Wholey and Brittain 1989). Continuous change is consistent, relatively more predictable, and represents an extension of what has happened in the past (e.g., consistent, increasing demand for a product over time). In contrast, discontinuous change is variable or inconsistent in its course and thus hard to predict. It not more of the same, as the environmental dimensions such as demand and regulations switch between increasing and decreasing over time.

We now explore each type of environmental velocity and explain how these would require different strategic renewal approaches.

Irregular velocity occurs when the direction of environmental change is discontinuous and the rate of environmental change is low. We call this irregular because the direction of the environmental change follows different paths gradually over time. For example, consider the biotechnology industry that can produce radical drug therapies but involves very long product development lead-times i.e., product velocity in this industry is relatively discontinuous and slow (McCarthy et al., 2010). With respect to strategic renewal, the rate and direction of change for this environmental velocity type is suited to slow exploration. Exploration behaviors such as risk taking and experimentation are required to produce strategic changes that align with discontinuous changes in the environment. These behaviors and their outcomes can be rolled out slowly to match the low rate of change with this velocity type.

Turbulent velocity occurs when the direction of environmental change is discontinuous and the rate of environmental change is high, or, in other words,

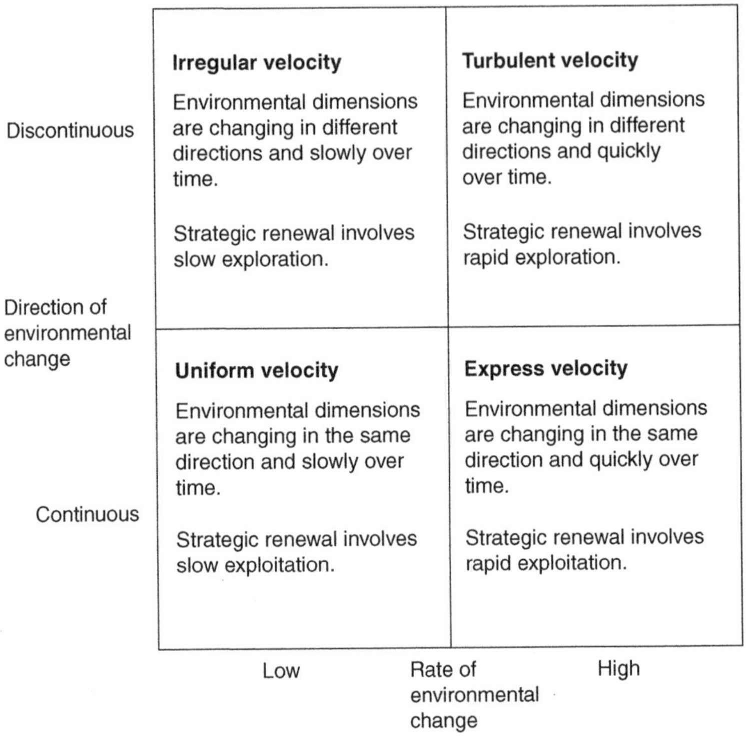

Discontinuous	**Irregular velocity** Environmental dimensions are changing in different directions and slowly over time. Strategic renewal involves slow exploration.	**Turbulent velocity** Environmental dimensions are changing in different directions and quickly over time. Strategic renewal involves rapid exploration.
Continuous	**Uniform velocity** Environmental dimensions are changing in the same direction and slowly over time. Strategic renewal involves slow exploitation.	**Express velocity** Environmental dimensions are changing in the same direction and quickly over time. Strategic renewal involves rapid exploitation.

Direction of environmental change

Low   Rate of   High
             environmental
             change

Figure 18.1 Typology of environmental velocity types

when the direction of environmental change is quickly shifting over time. A historical example of this type of velocity is the computer industry from approximately 1982 to 1995, when the microprocessor and personal computer were invented. During this period, this industry was characterized by fast and unpredictable changes in factors such as technological innovation, competition, consumer demand, and regulation, among others (Bourgeois & Eisenhardt, 1988). Effective strategic renewal in a turbulent velocity type is more likely to occur when organizations actively engage in rapid exploration. In other words, organizations need to quickly pursue and deliver industry changing strategy, as opposed to producing a strategy and value propositions that simply refine and build on a previous strategy.

Laminar velocity is described as such since the direction of environmental change is continuous and the rate of environmental change is low. The environmental velocity dimensions are changing in the same direction at a slow rate over time, producing an industry dynamic that is relatively ordered and streamline. For example, consider the U.K. tableware industry from the mid-1950s to the late 1970s. During this period, this industry faced changes in regulations, demand, product, technology, and competition that were all relatively slow and continuous in nature (e.g., Imrie, 1989). In terms of strategic renewal, laminar velocity types are likely to reward slow exploitation. Existing strategies are gradually refined to ensure that strategic change is entrained with pace and direction of environmental change.

Express velocity occurs when the direction of environmental change is continuous and the rate of environmental change is quick. It is termed "express" as changes in the environmental velocity dimensions are changing in the same direction and at a relatively high rate over time. For example, consider the mainstream fashion apparel industry and companies such as Zara that are known for "fast fashion". This industry has high rates of innovation each year as governed by the different seasons of the year. Yet, the product innovations offered are largely continuous in nature, as companies in this industry reveal innovations with the same core clothing items, only with different colors and cuts. To ensure strategic renewal initiatives are suitably entrained for these velocity conditions, the renewal would involve rapid exploitation. Like "fast fashion" this approach relies on monitoring changes in the industry and being a fast follower, as opposed to a proactive leader.

Gamification as a management control system

Management control is the act of ensuring "that resources are obtained and used effectively and efficiently in the accomplishment of the organization's objectives" (Anthony, 1965: 17). This means that management control systems are the formal and informal mechanisms, technologies, and processes used by organizations for directing, monitoring, and adjusting behaviors and performance to pursue and implement strategies (Chenhall, 2003; Simons, 1994). We suggest that the aims and principles of gamification can be used to deliver highly engaged forms of management control. Gamification is "the application of game design principles in non-gaming contexts", whereby organizations turn "traditional processes into deeper, more engaging game-like experiences for many of their customers and for their employees" (Robson et al., 2015: 411).

Robson et al. (2015, 2016) introduce and define three gamification principles: mechanics, dynamics, and emotions (MDE). Built from the game-design literature (e.g., El–Nasr & Smith, 2006; Hunicke, LeBlanc and Zubek, 2004; Sicart, 2008), these gamification principles form the MDE framework, which is used to describe the underlying aspects of a gamified experience. By combining the so-called designer's journey (the experience of designing a game) and the player's journey (the experience of playing a game) into an overall gamification framework, MDE provides a useful lens for organizational decision makers to understand how to design an engaging, gamified experience that will lead to the intended behavior changes by evoking desired emotions. Thus, we propose that these gamification design principles can be used as a management control system to engage and direct the behaviors of employees and other organizational stakeholders to realize new strategies for renewal.

Gamification mechanics set up the "rules" of how the strategic renewal will be pursued (Robson et al., 2015). This might include different roles and responsibilities for different types of stakeholders in an organization (i.e., for a game, defining how various pieces move in chess), and how success is measured (i.e., for game, how a winner or a stalemate is decided in chess). Everyone should follow the same mechanics in a strategic renewal exercise, much like all players follow the same rules in chess. Also, as strategic renewal typically involves shifting from one strategy to another, then the goals, targets, and rules and associated behaviors to pursue this new strategy would be reflected by the mechanics that seek to control the process of renewal.

There are three categories of gamification mechanics, known as setup mechanics, rule mechanics, and progression mechanics. Setup mechanics dictate where, when, and how the gamified strategic renewal occurs. For example, setup mechanics may dictate that the strategic renewal activities occur in an office during regular operating hours or off-site as part of a work retreat. Rule mechanics dictate what the goals of the gamified strategic renewal are and what actions players (employees) are allowed to take in their pursuit of these goals. For example, rule mechanics may dictate that players are expected or only allowed a certain amount of time to achieve the end goal. For a specific example, consider Google Inc's. 80/20 policy, where many employees are expected to allocate 20% of their working time to creative side projects. Progression mechanics signal to players whether they are moving forward in their pursuit of the designated goal. For example, progression mechanics include points, badges, or rewards, which signal to a player that they are on the right track toward a renewal goal.

Gamification dynamics are the types of player behaviors that emerge as players partake in any gamified strategic renewal experience (Robson et al., 2015). Contrary to mechanics, which are set by the designer, the gamification dynamics are produced by how players follow those chosen mechanics. As a result, the dynamics emerge from player interactions with each other and with the gamified experience; dynamics are the in-game behaviors, strategic actions, and interactions that emerge during play (Camerer, 2003). For example, the mechanics of the multiplayer card game poker include rules for shuffling, card dealing, betting, and winning hands, from which different dynamics like bluffing, playing tight versus loose, and playing passive versus aggressive can emerge. In terms of strategic renewal, dynamics such as experimentation, optimization, and exploration are essential for achieving strategic change.

Gamification emotions are the mental affective states evoked among individual players when they participate in a gamified experience (Robson et al., 2015). For example, emotions that occur during gamified experiences could be happiness, sadness, or surprise. These emotions are a product of how players follow the mechanics and respond to the dynamics that develop. They are derived from the hedonic nature of the gamified experiences and can serve as a strong motivational force (e.g., Higgins, 2006). Emotions exert considerable influence on decision making (Schwarz & Clore, 1996), can deepen the player engagement (i.e., motivate players to continue interacting with the gamified experience), disengage players (Higgins, 2006; Pham & Avnet 2009; Scholer & Higgins 2009; Sweetser & Wyeth, 2005), and affect their decision to continue or abandon an experience (Avnet, Pham and Stephen, 2012; Pham & Avnet, 2009). During strategic renewal, employees will experience emotions such as anticipation, trust, and surprise, as they engage in different types of renewal for the different types of industry velocity faced by their organization.

The MDE framework helps clarify how designers (managers) and players (employees) perceive and follow different strategic renewal processes. On the one hand, gamification designers' foremost focus is on selecting appropriate mechanics in order to retain control over the renewal, followed by dynamics, and lastly by players' emotions. This is to ensure that players are guided by the gamified renewal into outcomes that conform to the organization's goals. In optimized gamified renewal processes, players' emotional responses, and the dynamics that emerge during play, should be understood by the designers, who should tweak the mechanics as necessary. In this way, in optimized gamification experiences, emotions, and dynamics should in fact shape the mechanics that govern play, and vice versa. As a result, understanding gamification mechanics, dynamics, and emotions, and how these principles relate to one another, is key for successfully gamifying an undertaking such as strategic renewal.

Gamifying strategic renewal

Gamification is most successful when tailored to the aims toward which it is intended to be used. For gamified strategic renewal, this means considering the type of environmental velocity an organization faces so as to determine the mechanics of gamified strategic renewal, which, in turn, produce the resulting dynamics and emotions. Thus, in this section, we explore how the different conditions associated with each type of environmental velocity (Figure 18.1) influence the goals and mechanics, dynamics, and emotions of gamified strategic renewal (see Figure 18.2).

To do this we draw on strategy and decision-making research that highlights the link between the dynamics of an organization's environment and how associated organizational rules (i.e., mechanics) should vary both in terms of their number and the extent to which the rules clearly define a specific strategic outcome. Strategy research (see: Davis, Eisenhardt and Bingham, 2009; Eisenhardt and Sull, 2001) suggests that the more simple and inert an organization's environment is, the more the organization can afford to have, and will likely be rewarded for having, complex strategies and

behaviors based on many rules. Conversely, when an organization's environment is characterized as rapidly changing and complex, then organizations
benefit from approaches to strategic renewal based on fewer and simpler
rules. We also rely on research on how leaders should tailor their decision-
making approaches to fit the dynamic complexities of the circumstances they
face (Snowden and Boone, 2007). The mechanics of strategic decision
making requires leaders to diagnose situations and to act in contextually
appropriate ways based on the discontinuity versus predictability of the situation. When the situation is discontinuous, there are no clear cause-and-
effect relationships, and there is no point in having rules based on specifying
the desired outcomes. Thus, decision making in this context should be
a process of acting, sensing, and then responding. Conversely, in contexts
where the change is continuous and more predictable in nature, there are
clear cause-and effect-relationships, and leaders simply need to sense, categor-
ize, and respond. We extend these strategy and decision-making logics to the
mechanics aspect of our gamified strategic framework. The rate of environmental change is positively linked to gamification in terms of number of rules
(low rate = many rules, and high rate = few rules); and the direction of
environmental change is positively linked to the extent mechanics define
outcomes or not (continuous = defined outcomes, and discontinuous =
undefined outcomes).

For an industry with a laminar velocity, the environmental dimensions are
changing in the same direction and slowly over time. As this change is relatively predictable and slow, it is typically important for organizations to build
on their core capabilities and capture more market share. Consequently,
effective strategic renewal involves slow exploitation or a careful pursuit of
more of the same. To attain this goal, managers would use gamification
mechanics that involve many rules with defined outcomes. Having many
rules produces a context for strategic renewal that calls for and allows
employees to investigate and grapple with several strategic options that
govern the strategic future of the organization. The many rules and their
combinations are also linked to known strategic outcomes in terms of specific
improvements in areas such as product cost, service speed, and quality.
Together these mechanics produce a renewal dynamic of "optimization". As
a gamification dynamic is how the players (i.e., the employees) enact the
mechanic (Robson et al., 2015), optimization is a behavior whereby the
organization attempts to produce the best strategy for known competitive
advantage. The associated emotion, or gamified mental state (Robson et al.,
2015), for this approach to gamified strategic renewal is one of "trust" (e.g.,
Plutchik, 1980). This means that people in the organization will tend to favor
a strong confidence and reliability about what needs to happen. They know
and have faith in the outcome of the gamified strategic renewal and how to
produce it. Consider, for example, the consumer banking industry where an
organization changes an offer to its customers, and then competitors react by
either matching or beating that offer within the many rules governing the

industry. The gaming analogy for such mechanics would be the game of trad-itional chess, which has about 100 rules governing the setup and the movement and taking of pieces. In traditional chess, such mechanics combine to produce a slow, repetitive dynamic of strategic optimization of the rules, in pursuit of a clearly defined outcome: a win or draw.

When organizations operate in environments with an express velocity type, the environmental dimensions are changing in the same direction and quickly over time. Thus, fast continuous strategic renewal is needed to deliver rapid exploitation. To ensure gamified strategic renewal is responsive enough, it requires mechanics that are few in number and have defined out-comes. The dynamics of the express velocity environmental type, like the laminar velocity type, are characterized by a clear cause–effect relationship where the required outcome is clearly discernible. Knowing what to do is not the challenge. Achieving the known outcome quickly is. This requires the gamified strategic renewal to have a "responsive" dynamic to ensure it aligns with the rate and continuous changes in technology, regulations, demand, completion, and products. A responsive dynamic underlies the organizational capability of being alert and receptive to rapidly changing and relatively predictable industry conditions (Zaheer and Zaheer, 1997). This in turn would foster the emotion of "vigilance" (Plutchik, 1980), where employees maintain concentrated monitoring of the environmental conditions for prolonged periods of time so as to effectively detect and respond to changes. Consider again the example of Zara and its "fast fash-ion" strategy, which is driven by a renewal process that involves continually and rapidly refining its offering to customers by sensing and responding to changing trends and needs, as opposed to creating those trends and needs. In terms of a game equivalent, consider checkers (or draughts), which like traditional chess has an easy-to-understand outcome, but much fewer rules and a more rapid dynamic. Checkers has just two types of pieces (men and king) and few rules governing the movement of pieces and the taking of opponent pieces. Consequently, checkers is played at a much quicker pace than chess, and players must be able to quickly track and respond to the moves of their opponents.

For an organization undertaking gamified strategic renewal in an irregular velocity type, the environmental dimensions are changing in different direc-tions and slowly over time, which rewards renewal goals of slow exploration. To attain this goal, the mechanics of gamified strategic renewal would be like those for the laminar velocity type, in that there can be many rules that drive a careful and judicious renewal. However, the key difference with this approach to gamified strategic renewal is that a precise outcome of the renewal is not specified by the mechanics – there are many different ways to play and win. The organization seeking to reinvent itself does not know what this reinvention will lead to – it unfolds during the process. This pro-duces a dynamic of "discovery". This is a behavior enacted from the mechan-ics where employees imagine and realize a number of unfamiliar potential strategies, such as producing completely new offerings for existing markets or serving totally new markets with existing offerings. This dynamic in turn produces the emotion of "anticipation" (Plutchik, 1980), where employees are excited or anxious about the pursuit of this undefined strategic renewal outcome. An example of an industry that rewards organizations taking this approach gamified strategic renewal would be a high-technology industry producing consumer products. Here it is common place for organizations to keep closely guarded secrets about their technological innovations, but also to engage in the deliberate leaking of secrets to inform, misdirect, or provoke reactions in the industry (Hannah et al., 2015). The game equivalent for this approach to gamified strategic renewal would be some form of the card game poker. Playing poker has many rules and ways of winning, but players don't know what will win and what they have won with, until they have won. It is a process of constant discovery, where you learn what cards you have and imagine what cards your opponents have based on their betting actions and previously declared starting hands. Players must constantly anticipate and react accordingly to the strengths, weaknesses, tells, and bluffs of other players.

The fourth approach to gamified renewal in our framework is derived when organizations face turbulent velocity types that we suggest reward a fast action approach to renewal. In such conditions, there is no immediately known relationship between cause and effect, thus effective renewal is much more a process of emergence, as opposed to searching for, making sense of, and selecting a best-practice strategy that is new to the organization. Thus, we contend that gamified renewal for this velocity type involves rapidly producing and testing new strategies and then adopting effective ones. To attain this renewal through gamification requires mechanics based on few rules and undefined outcomes. The small number of rules allows the renewal to be fast and evolving in nature, while having undefined outcomes means that strategic renewal can be based on testing novel strategies to see what works, as opposed to searching for and copying existing best practices. The early years of the computer-disk-drive industry, which was described as experiencing "commercial and technological turbulence" (Christensen, 1993: 531) is a good example of the environment that would suit and reward gamified strategic renewal based on fast action The game equivalent for this approach to gamified strategic renewal would typically be some form of unstructured playing activity such as exaggeration circle, where one player starts with a little gesture, the next player takes it over and makes it bigger, and so on. It focuses on acts of improvisation and creativity. This and other unstructured games are defined by few rules and undefined outcomes so as to produce the ABC of play: Agility (responding quickly and easily); Balance (staying steady while responding) and Coordination (using different parts of the body and mind) (Bishop, 2010).

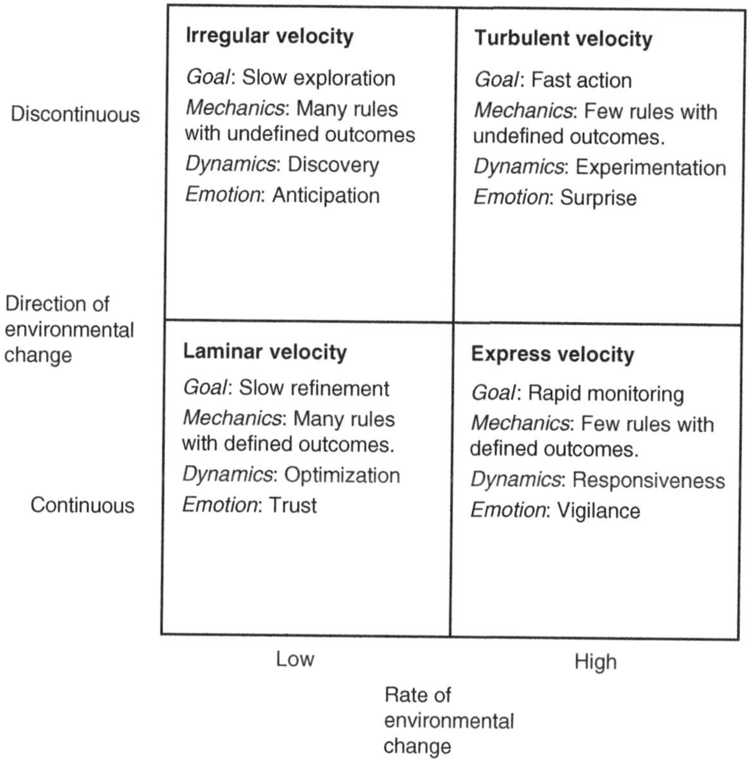

	Irregular velocity	Turbulent velocity
Discontinuous	*Goal*: Slow exploration *Mechanics*: Many rules with undefined outcomes *Dynamics*: Discovery *Emotion*: Anticipation	*Goal*: Fast action *Mechanics*: Few rules with undefined outcomes. *Dynamics*: Experimentation *Emotion*: Surprise
Laminar velocity	**Laminar velocity**	**Express velocity**
Continuous	*Goal*: Slow refinement *Mechanics*: Many rules with defined outcomes. *Dynamics*: Optimization *Emotion*: Trust	*Goal*: Rapid monitoring *Mechanics*: Few rules with defined outcomes. *Dynamics*: Responsiveness *Emotion*: Vigilance

Direction of environmental change

Low   High

Rate of environmental change

Figure 18.2 Gamification approaches for strategic renewal

Discussion and concluding thoughts

In this chapter we presented a framework to explain the interrelations between strategic renewal, environmental velocity, and management control using gamification. This involved introducing a framework of four environmental velocity types (*laminar, irregular, turbulent* and *express*) based on variations in the rate (low or high) and direction (continuous or discontinuous) of change in environmental dimensions such as demand, competitors, technology, products, and regulations (Figure 18.1). We described how each environmental velocity type is suited to different forms of strategic renewal based on the extent and pace to which exploration or exploitation is pursued. From this we then highlighted how different forms of strategic renewal can be attained by using different gamification mechanics to direct and control different organizational dynamics, emotions, and renewal outcomes (Figure 18.2). In sum, these contributions emphasize some of the strategic renewal control challenges that come with different environmental velocity types, as well as the opportunities to use gamification practices to effectively deal with these control challenges. We believe these contributions have a number of implications for scholars and managers and related future research prospects, which we now outline.

Implications and future work

For management practice there are several major takeaways. First, our ideas and framework highlight that decision makers should consider the velocity conditions of their industry when formulating *and* implementing strategic renewal initiatives. Managers should be aware of how variations in the rate (low or high) and direction (continuous or discontinuous) of change in environmental dimensions produce distinct types of velocity conditions that suit specific approaches to strategic renewal. Research and practice focus on the importance of ensuring that an organization's strategy is viable over time. Our argument is that an organization's renewal process also needs to be congruent with the environmental conditions. Rather than focusing just on the how fitting the renewal *output* is, managers must also grapple with and determine how fitting the renewal *process* is.

Second, and relatedly, when "doing" strategic renewal, managers should consider using gamification principles to provide the management control for this process. In doing so, managers should ensure that the gamification approach fits with or is matched to desirable organizational outcomes. Our framework can be used to help guide managers in understanding appropriate gamification mechanics, dynamics, and emotions, which can be used to motivate behavior changes in employees.

Another major takeaway from this chapter is the importance of fit between an organization's environmental velocity and a gamified approach to strategic renewal. The frameworks we present offer descriptions and explanations of this alignment, and provide a basis for future studies to develop and test related predictions for shaping and enhancing understanding of strategic renewal implementation. More specifically, we add to the literature on strategic renewal and co-alignment, which is concerned with organizations maintaining a strategic fit with their environment (Ben–Menahem et al., 2013). This extant research largely focuses on the consequences of organizations having a (mis)fit with their environments, and thus "why" organizations should adopt renewal initiatives (Volberda et al., 2001). The ideas and arguments presented in this chapter add to this literature by providing novel ideas as to "how" organizations might pursue and realize a renewal initiative using gamification principles. Furthermore, by focusing on the environmental velocity conditions that organizations operate in, we complement other studies that have focused on other aspects of the environment, such as scarcity (Schmitt et al., 2016), and level of competitiveness (Kim and Pennings, 2009).

We also join with and add to research that recognizes the relationship between environmental conditions, strategic action, and managerial cognition (i.e., how managers make sense of their worlds). For example, prior research has examined where strategic decision makers focus their attention in terms of what is changing and how this affects the speed with which their organization respond to events (Nadkarni and Barr, 2008). In the same way that this prior research suggests that an organization's environmental conditions significantly influence managerial attention, we suggest that a similar impact exists with management control systems and strategic renewal.

References

Agarwal, R. and Helfat, C.E., 2009. Strategic renewal of organizations. *Organization Science*, 20(2), pp. 281–293.

Anthony, R., 1965. *Planning and Control Systems: A Framework for Analysis*, Harvard: Boston, MA.

Avnet, T., Pham, M.T., and Stephen, A.T. 2012. Consumers' trust in feelings as information. *Journal of Consumer Research*, 39(4), pp. 720–735.

Ben–Menahem, S.M., Kwee, Z., Volberda, H.W., and Van Den Bosch, F.A., 2013. Strategic renewal over time: The enabling role of potential absorptive capacity in aligning internal and external rates of change. *Long Range Planning*, 46(3), pp. 216–235.

Bishop, R., 2010. When *play was play: Why pick–up games matter*. SUNY Press: Albany, NY.

Bourgeois III, L.J. and Eisenhardt, K.M., 1988. Strategic decision processes in high velocity environments: Four cases in the microcomputer industry. *Management Science*, 34(7), pp. 816–835.

Camerer, C.F. 2003. Behavioural studies of strategic thinking in games. *Trends in Cognitive Sciences*, 7(5), pp. 225–231.

Chenhall, R.H. 2003. Management control systems design within its organizational context: findings from contingency–based research and directions for the future. *Accounting, Organizations and Society*, 28(2–3), pp. 127–168.

Christensen, C.M., 1993. The rigid disk drive industry: A history of commercial and technological turbulence. *Business History Review*, 67(4), pp. 531–588.

Crossan, M.M. and Berdrow, I., 2003. Organizational learning and strategic renewal. *Strategic Management Journal*, 24(11), pp. 1087–1105.

Davis, J.P., Eisenhardt, K M. and Bingham, C B. 2009. Optimal structure, market dynamism, and the strategy of simple rules. *Administrative Science Quarterly*, 54(3), pp. 413–452.

Eisenhardt, K.M., 1989. Making fast strategic decisions in high–velocity environments. *Academy of Management Journal*, 32(3), pp. 543–576.

Eisenhardt, K.M. and Bourgeois, L.J. 1988. Politics of strategic decision making in high–velocity environments: Toward a midrange theory. *Academy of Management Journal*, 31(4), pp. 737–770.

Eisenhardt, K.M., and Sull, D.N. 2001. Strategy as simple rules. *Harvard Business Review*, 79(1), pp. 106–119.

Eisenhardt, K.M. and Tabrizi, B.N., 1995. Accelerating adaptive processes: Product innovation in the global computer industry. *Administrative Science Quarterly*, 40(1), pp. 84–110.

El–Nasr, M.S., and Smith, B.K. 2006. Learning through game modding. *Computers in Entertainment (CIE)*, 4(1), p. 7.

Floyd, S.W. and Lane, P.J., 2000. Strategizing throughout the organization: Managing role conflict in strategic renewal. *Academy of Management Review*, 25(1), pp. 154–177.

Hannah, D.R., McCarthy, I.P. and Kietzmann, J., 2015. We're leaking, and everything's fine: How and why companies deliberately leak secrets. *Business Horizons*, 58(6), pp. 659–667.

Hannan, M.T., and Freeman, J. 1984. Structural inertia and organizational change. *American Sociological Review*, 49(2), pp. 149–164.

Henri, J.F., 2006. Management control systems and strategy: A resource–based perspective. *Accounting, Organizations and Society*, 31(6), pp. 529–558.

Higgins, E.T. 2006. Value from hedonic experience and engagement. *Psychological Review*, 113(3), p. 439.

Hunicke, R., LeBlanc, M., and Zubek, R. 2004, July. MDA: A formal approach to game design and game research. In Proceedings of the AAAI Workshop on Challenges in Game AI (Vol. 4, No. 1, p. 1722).

Imrie, R.F. 1989. Industrial restructuring, labour, and locality: The case of the British pottery industry. *Environment and Planning A*, 21(1), pp. 3–26.

Judge, W.Q. and Miller, A., 1991. Antecedents and outcomes of decision speed in different environmental context. *Academy of Management Journal*, 34(2), pp. 449–463.

Kim, H.E., and Pennings, J.M., 2009. Innovation and strategic renewal in mature markets: A study of the tennis racket industry. *Organization Science*, 20(2), pp. 368–383.

Kwee, Z., Van Den Bosch, F.A. and Volberda, H.W., 2011. The influence of top management team's corporate governance orientation on strategic renewal trajectories: A longitudinal analysis of Royal Dutch Shell plc, 1907–2004. *Journal of Management Studies*, 48(5), pp. 984–1014.

Lechner, C. and Floyd, S.W., 2012. Group influence activities and the performance of strategic initiatives. *Strategic Management Journal*, 33(5), pp. 478–495.

Marginson, D.E., 2002. Management control systems and their effects on strategy formation at middle-management levels: Evidence from a UK organization. *Strategic Management Journal*, 23(11), pp. 1019–1031.

McCarthy, I.P. and Gordon, B.R., 2011. Achieving contextual ambidexterity in R&D organizations: A management control system approach. *R&D Management*, 41(3), pp. 240–258.

McCarthy, I.P., Lawrence, T.B., Wixted, B. and Gordon, B.R., 2010. A multidimensional conceptualization of environmental velocity. *Academy of Management Review*, 35(4), pp. 604–626.

Miller, D., 1992. Environmental fit versus internal fit. *Organization Science*, 3(2), pp. 159–178.

Nadkarni, S. and Barr, P.S., 2008. Environmental context, managerial cognition, and strategic action: An integrated view. *Strategic Management Journal*, 29(13), pp. 1395–1427.

Nadkarni, S. and Narayanan, V.K., 2007. The evolution of collective strategy frames in high–and low–velocity industries. *Organization Science*, 18(4), pp. 688–710.

Oliver, D. and Roos, J., 2005. Decision–making in high–velocity environments: The importance of guiding principles. *Organization Studies*, 26(6), pp. 889–913.

Pham, M.T., and Avnet, T. 2009. Contingent reliance on the affect heuristic as a function of regulatory focus. *Organizational Behavior and Human Decision Processes*, 108(2), pp. 267–278.

Plutchik R. 1980. Measurement Implications of a Psychoevolutionary Theory of Emotions. In Blankstein K.R., Pliner P., Polivy J. (Eds.), *Assessment and Modification of Emotional Behavior. Advances in the Study of Communication and Affect*, vol 6. Springer: Boston, MA.

Raisch, S., Birkinshaw, J., Probst, G., and Tushman, M.L. (2009). Organizational ambidexterity: Balancing exploitation and exploration for sustained performance. *Organization Science*, 20(4), pp. 685–695.

Robson, K., Plangger, K., Kietzmann, J.H., McCarthy, I. and Pitt, L., 2015. Is it all a game? Understanding the principles of gamification. *Business Horizons*, 58(4), pp. 411–420.

Robson, K., Plangger, K., Kietzmann, J.H., McCarthy, I. and Pitt, L., 2016. Game on: Engaging customers and employees through gamification. *Business Horizons*, 59(1), pp. 29–36.

Salvato, C., 2009. Capabilities unveiled: The role of ordinary activities in the evolution of product development processes. *Organization Science*, 20(2), pp. 384–409.

Schmitt, A., Barker, V.L., Raisch, S. and Whetten, D., 2016. Strategic renewal in times of environmental scarcity. *Long Range Planning*, 49(3), pp. 361–376.

Scholer, A.A., and Higgins, E.T. 2009. Exploring the complexities of value creation: The role of engagement strength. *Journal of Consumer Psychology*, 19(2), pp. 137–143.

Schwarz, N., and Clore, G.L. 1996. Feelings and phenomenal experiences. In Kruglanski, A.W. and Higgins, E.T. (Eds.), *Social psychology: Handbook of Basic Principles* (pp. 385–407), Guilford Press: New York City, NY.

Sicart, M. 2008. Defining game mechanics. *Game Studies*, 8(2). Online resource, retrieved from: http://www.caseyodonnell.org/files/TC839/Defining_Game_Mechanics.pdf

Simons, R., 1994. How new top managers use control systems as levers of strategic renewal. *Strategic Management Journal*, 15(3), pp. 169–189.

Snowden, D.J. and Boone, M.E., 2007. A leader's framework for decision making. *Harvard Business Review*, 85(11), p. 68.

Sweetser, P., and Wyeth, P. 2005. GameFlow: a model for evaluating player enjoyment in games. *Computers in Entertainment (CIE)*, 3(3), pp. 3–3.

Tippmann, E., Scott, P.S. and Mangematin, V., 2014. Stimulating knowledge search routines and architecture competences: The role of organizational context and middle management. *Long Range Planning*, 47(4), pp. 206–223.

Venkatraman, N. and Camillus, J.C., 1984. Exploring the concept of "fit" in strategic management. *Academy of Management Review*, 9(3), pp. 513–525.

Volberda, H., Baden–Fuller, C. and Van Den Bosch, F.A.J., 2001. Mastering strategic renewal: Mobilising renewal journeys in multi–unit firms. *Long Range Planning*, 34(2), pp. 159–178.

Wholey, D.R. and Brittain, J., 1989. Characterizing environmental variation. *Academy of Management Journal*, 32(4), pp. 867–882.

Zaheer, A. and Zaheer, S., 1997. Catching the wave: Alertness, responsiveness, and market influence in global electronic networks. *Management Science*, 43(11), pp. 1493–1509.

Zajac, E.J., Kraatz, M.S. and Bresser, R.K., 2000. Modeling the dynamics of strategic fit: A normative approach to strategic change. *Strategic Management Journal*, 21(4), pp. 429–453.

Index

Note: 'f' following the page number denotes figures and 't' refers to tables.